Advances in Spatial Science

The Regional Science Series

Series Editors

Manfred M. Fischer, Institute for Economic Geography and GIScience, Vienna University of Economics and Business, Vienna, Austria

Jean-Claude Thill, Department of Geography & Earth Sciences, University of North Carolina at Charlotte, Charlotte, NC, USA

Jouke van Dijk, Faculty of Spatial Sciences, University of Groningen, Groningen, Groningen, The Netherlands

Hans Westlund, Royal Institute of Technology, Stockholm, Sweden

Advisory Editors

Geoffrey J.D. Hewings, University of Illinois, Urbana, IL, USA

Peter Nijkamp, Free University, Amsterdam, The Netherlands

Folke Snickars, Editorial Board, Heidelberg, Baden-Württemberg, Germany

This series contains scientific studies focusing on spatial phenomena, utilising theoretical frameworks, analytical methods, and empirical procedures specifically designed for spatial analysis. Advances in Spatial Science brings together innovative spatial research utilising concepts, perspectives, and methods relevant to both basic science and policy making. The aim is to present advances in spatial science to an informed readership in universities, research organisations, and policy-making institutions throughout the world. The type of material considered for publication in the series includes: Monographs of theoretical and applied research in spatial science; state-of-the-art volumes in areas of basic research; reports of innovative theories and methods in spatial science; tightly edited reports from specially organised research seminars.

The series and the volumes published in it are indexed by Scopus.

For further information on the series and to submit a proposal for consideration, please contact Johannes Glaeser (Senior Editor Economics) Johannes.glaeser@springer.com.

Eduardo A. Haddad · Jaime Bonet ·
Geoffrey J. D. Hewings
Editors

The Colombian Economy and Its Regional Structural Challenges

A Linkages Approach

Editors
Eduardo A. Haddad
Department of Economics
Universidade de São Paulo
São Paulo, Brazil

Geoffrey J. D. Hewings
Regional Economics and Applications Laboratory
University of Illinois Urbana-Champaign
Urbana, IL, USA

Jaime Bonet
Centro de Estudios Económicos Regionales (CEER)
Banco de la República
Cartagena, Colombia

ISSN 1430-9602 ISSN 2197-9375 (electronic)
Advances in Spatial Science
ISBN 978-3-031-22652-6 ISBN 978-3-031-22653-3 (eBook)
https://doi.org/10.1007/978-3-031-22653-3

© The Editor(s) (if applicable) and The Author(s), under exclusive license to Springer Nature Switzerland AG 2023

This work is subject to copyright. All rights are solely and exclusively licensed by the Publisher, whether the whole or part of the material is concerned, specifically the rights of translation, reprinting, reuse of illustrations, recitation, broadcasting, reproduction on microfilms or in any other physical way, and transmission or information storage and retrieval, electronic adaptation, computer software, or by similar or dissimilar methodology now known or hereafter developed.

The use of general descriptive names, registered names, trademarks, service marks, etc. in this publication does not imply, even in the absence of a specific statement, that such names are exempt from the relevant protective laws and regulations and therefore free for general use.

The publisher, the authors, and the editors are safe to assume that the advice and information in this book are believed to be true and accurate at the date of publication. Neither the publisher nor the authors or the editors give a warranty, expressed or implied, with respect to the material contained herein or for any errors or omissions that may have been made. The publisher remains neutral with regard to jurisdictional claims in published maps and institutional affiliations.

This Springer imprint is published by the registered company Springer Nature Switzerland AG
The registered company address is: Gewerbestrasse 11, 6330 Cham, Switzerland

For Werner Baer, 1931–2016

Preface

I have been teaching a Ph.D. course on "Applied General Equilibrium Models" at the University of São Paulo, Department of Economics, since 1999. Over the last editions of the course, the material was built around specific countries or regions, selected to be the object of modeling practices undertaken by the students. This praxis turned out to be very rewarding for the students since they were motivated to apply different techniques to study concrete problems in a common economic system. Throughout this process, they had the opportunity to collaborate among themselves and interact with scholars from the study regions, often generating scholarly publications.

We had already worked with countries such as Brazil, Chile, Greece, and Paraguay, and with different regional contexts, especially within Brazil. Colombia had always been a top candidate to receive our attention. Our previous engagement with colleagues from the Centro de Estudios Económicos Regionales (CEER), a research center specialized in Regional and Urban Economics at the Banco de la República—the Colombian Central Bank—provided a unique opportunity to develop a special edition of the course on the country. During a visit to Cartagena in 2019, Jaime Bonet and I finally agreed to use Colombia as the case study in the forthcoming edition of the course. We designed the Colombian edition in innovative and challenging ways, raising the bar for the expected outcomes, including a workshop to be hosted in Cartagena in 2020[1] and the publication of a volume including the contributions by different authors forming a cohesive unit.

We built the activities upon solid collaboration between the teams at the University of São Paulo Regional and Urban Economics Lab (NEREUS) and at CEER, involving altogether 24 scholars. Researchers from both institutions already had a long-standing record of continued collaboration initiated in 2003 under the guidance of Geoffrey J. D. Hewings from the University of Illinois Regional Economics Applications Lab (REAL). A few years later, we built Colombia's first fully operational

---

[1] The "International Workshop on Interregional Economic Modeling: Applications for the Colombian Economy" was originally scheduled to take place during March 19–21, 2020, in Cartagena. However, due to the COVID-19 pandemic we had to cancel the event one week before the trip.

interregional CGE model.[2] Since then, we developed further our modeling efforts focusing on improving and updating interregional input–output and CGE systems to broaden the scope of applications for the country.

The study of regional development issues has a long tradition in Colombia. Moreover, there is also a tradition in the Regional Science literature on the analysis of economic structures based on intersectoral and interregnal linkages, literature built upon the shoulders of Wassily Leontief and Walter Isard that gained momentum in the policy arena in Latin America after the publication of Albert Hirschman's "The Strategy of Economic Development" in 1958. Interestingly, some of Hirschman's main insights on the relationship between linkages and economic development arose during his intensive experiences in Colombia from 1952 to 1956, when he acted as an official economic advisor for the Colombian government and as a private consultant. As an analytical tool, the linkages have since led an active life devised for a better understanding of the growth patterns of developing countries.

The organization of this volume contributes to disseminating and discussing an increasingly high-quality body of research on Colombian territorial problems and policies, limited in its reach due to the fact that the majority of the studies have been published in Spanish. We decided to publish an English-language book with a coherent, policy-relevant mission. From a disaggregated analysis of multiregional and multisectoral linkages, the book builds up a systematic, integrated account of unaddressed structural challenges that have historically held back Colombia's more equitable regional development. The volume also witnesses the growth and flourishing of Regional Science in Latin America. The region provides a fertile landscape that offers many potential applications for developing countries with strong socioeconomic spatial diversity. The growing presence of the discipline in Latin America is heavily influenced by proximity mechanisms embedded in an evolving scientific network. Moreover, studies that have benefitted most from the development of such a network, such as this book, are primarily focused on applied economic research, maintaining a long-lasting tradition of regional development research in Colombia and other countries in the region.

The nurturing of the volume somehow benefitted from the pandemic. After an initial disappointment with the cancelation of the Cartagena workshop, the authors had enough time to prepare the manuscripts and engage in two rounds of anonymous reviews to improve the final texts. The outcome also benefitted from presentations and discussions of specific chapters in different arenas in Colombia and worldwide, including online seminars and conferences during the pandemic and in-presence discussions after COVID-19-related health indicators improved.

It is fair to say that this book is heavily rooted in the perennial influence of Professor Werner Baer in shaping economics graduate studies in Latin America. The partnership between Werner Baer and Geoffrey J. D. Hewings has been fundamental to maintaining a regular flow of Latin American scholars to the University of Illinois at

---

[2] Haddad, E. A., Bonet, J., Hewings, G. J. D. & Perobelli, F. S. (2009). Spatial Aspects of Trade Liberalization in Colombia: A General Equilibrium Approach. *Papers in Regional Science*, v. 88, p. 699–732.

Urbana-Champaign (UIUC). The constant and increasing flow of Ph.D. students from Brazil, Colombia, and other Latin American countries to UIUC in the late 1980s and early 1990s, together with the creation of REAL in 1989, provided the opportunity for a fruitful partnership between Werner Baer and Geoffrey J. D. Hewings and among members of their respective academic genealogy. In many ways, this book serves as a vivid example that reflects a pattern of evolving collaboration networks in Regional Science in scientifically emerging economies rooted in the initial contributions by Werner Baer, to whom we dedicate this work.

Gonçalves, Minas Gerais, Brazil Eduardo A. Haddad
October 2022

Acknowledgments

As this book goes to press, important milestones are achieved related to two of the institutions deeply involved in the elaboration of this project. In 2022, the University of São Paulo Regional and Urban Economics Lab (NEREUS) celebrated its 20th anniversary and the Centro de Estudios Económicos Regionales (CEER) its 25th anniversary.

The editors are grateful to all authors that accepted the invitation to contribute to this book, embracing the project in order to assure it a high standard. Special thanks also go to Inácio Araújo, Karina Bugarin, and Perlita Esquenazi, who provided assistance during different stages of the process.

Eduardo A. Haddad acknowledges financial support from CNPq (Grant 302861/2018-1), FAPESP (Grant 2018/08337-8), and the National Institute of Science and Technology for Climate Change Phase 2 under CNPq (Grant 465501/2014-1) and FAPESP (Grant 2014/50848-9). He is grateful for his family's constant support and unconditional love, especially for his wife, Maria Amélia, and his daughters, Helena and Sophia.

Jaime Bonet is grateful to Juan Esteban Carranza, from Banco de la República, for his continuous support of the project. He extends his heartfelt gratitude to his wife, Male, and his children, Mariana and Juanca.

Geoffrey J. D. Hewings acknowledges the invitation from the Cartagena branch of the Banco de la República to attend a conference in the city that began many years of collaboration with students and scholars. He also thanks his co-editors for the invitation to join them in editing this important initiative.

Some of the chapters are based on material previously circulated as working papers in the Banco de la República series. Chapter 12 is based on a revised version of the paper "Regional Differences in the Economic Impact of Lockdown Measures to Prevent the Spread of COVID-19: A Case Study for Colombia" published in the Colombian journal *Cuadernos de Economía*, Vol. 40, núm. 85 (2021), pp. 977–998. https://doi.org/10.15446/cuad.econ.v40n85.90803. We thank the editor, Gonzalo Cómbita Mora, the editorial board, and the Universidad Nacional de Colombia for authorizing its publication in the current volume.

Contents

1 **Introduction and Overview** 1
  Eduardo A. Haddad, Jaime Bonet, and Geoffrey J. D. Hewings

Part I Regional Setting

2 **Is There a Case for Regional Policies in Colombia?** 19
  Jaime Bonet, Karina Acosta, Gerson Javier Pérez-Valbuena, and Jhorland Ayala-García

3 **Income Inequalities in Colombia** 37
  Leonardo Bonilla, Luis Armando Galvis-Aponte, Andrea Otero-Cortés, and Diana Ricciulli

4 **Regional Convergence in Colombia in the Twenty-First Century** 77
  Karina Acosta and Jaime Bonet

Part II Modelling Framework

5 **The Interregional Input–Output System for Colombia** 113
  Eduardo A. Haddad, Luis Armando Galvis-Aponte, and Inácio F. Araújo

6 **The Interregional Computable General Equilibrium Model for Colombia** 161
  Eduardo A. Haddad and Inácio F. Araújo

Part III Structural Analysis

7 **Revisiting the Structural Interdependence Among Colombian Departments** 185
  Fernando S. Perobelli and Geoffrey J. D. Hewings

8	Economic Base and Regional Specialization in Colombia: A Note on Input–Output Linkages 205
	Inácio F. Araújo, Alexandre L. Gomes, Diana Ricciulli, and Eduardo A. Haddad
9	Trade in Value-Added: Does MFN Status Matter for Colombian Regions? 239
	Rodrigo Pacheco, Raphael P. Fernandes, Inácio F. Araújo, and Eduardo A. Haddad
10	Chaining Juan Valdez: Linkages in the Colombian Coffee Production 273
	Márcia Istake, Karina S. Sass, Andrea Otero-Cortés, and Pedro Levy Sayon
11	Urban Travelers Go to the Beach: Regional Effects of Domestic Tourism in Colombia 297
	Eduardo Sanguinet, Luis Armando Galvis-Aponte, Inácio F. Araújo, and Eduardo A. Haddad
12	Regional Differences in the Economic Impact of Lockdown Measures to Prevent the Spread of COVID-19: A Case Study for Colombia 327
	Jaime Bonet, Diana Ricciulli, Gerson Javier Pérez-Valbuena, Eduardo A. Haddad, Inácio F. Araújo, and Fernando S. Perobelli

Part IV Structural Development Issues

13	Boiling Hot! Economy-Wide Impacts of Climate Change on Colombian Coffee Yields 361
	Pedro Levy Sayon, Andrea Otero-Cortés, Federico Ceballos-Sierra, and Eduardo A. Haddad
14	The Geography of Manufacturing Productivity Shocks in Colombia 383
	Gerson Javier Pérez-Valbuena, Carlos Eduardo Campos, Ademir Rocha, and Eduardo A. Haddad
15	The Interplay of Services Productivity and the Competitiveness of Colombian Exports 401
	Inácio F. Araújo, Eduardo A. Haddad, Maria Aparecida S. Oliveira, and Diana Ricciulli

16 **Impact Assessment of Interregional Transfers Scenarios in the Colombian Economy** 425
Luis Armando Galvis-Aponte, Inácio F. Araújo, Vinícius A. Vale, and Eduardo A. Haddad

17 **Royalties and Regional Disparities** 455
Jaime Bonet, Gerson Javier Pérez-Valbuena, and Eduardo A. Haddad

Editors and Contributors

About the Editors

Eduardo A. Haddad is a full professor at the Department of Economics at the University of São Paulo, Brazil, where he directs the Regional and Urban Economics Lab (NEREUS). He is an affiliate professor at the Faculty of Governance, Economic and Social Sciences of the Mohammed VI University and Senior Fellow at the Policy Center for the New South, Rabat, Morocco. He was the president of the Regional Science Association International, RSAI (2021–2022).

Jaime Bonet is an economist from the Universidad de Los Andes in Bogotá with a master's degree in economics and a Ph.D. in regional planning from the University of Illinois at Urbana-Champaign. His research areas include regional and urban economics, local public finance, local economic development, and regional development history in Colombia.

Geoffrey J. D. Hewings is an emeritus director, Regional Economics Applications Laboratory (REAL). He is an emeritus professor of Geography and Regional Science, Economics, and Urban and Regional Planning. He was the president of the Regional Science Association International, RSAI (2001–2002).

Contributors

Karina Acosta Banco de la República, Cartagena, Colombia

Inácio F. Araújo University of São Paulo, São Paulo, Brazil

Jhorland Ayala-García Banco de la República, Cartagena, Colombia

Jaime Bonet Banco de la República, Cartagena, Colombia

Leonardo Bonilla Banco de la República, Medellín, Colombia

Carlos Eduardo Campos Federal University of São Carlos, São Carlos, Brazil

Federico Ceballos-Sierra International Center for Tropical Agriculture, Cali, Colombia

Raphael P. Fernandes University of São Paulo, São Paulo, Brazil

Luis Armando Galvis-Aponte Banco de la República, Cartagena, Colombia

Alexandre L. Gomes Federal University of São Carlos, São Carlos, Brazil

Eduardo A. Haddad University of São Paulo, São Paulo, Brazil

Geoffrey J. D. Hewings University of Illinois at Urbana-Champaign, Champaign, USA

Márcia Istake University of Maringá, Maringá, Brazil

Maria Aparecida S. Oliveira Federal University of São Carlos, São Carlos, Brazil

Andrea Otero-Cortés Banco de la República, Cartagena, Colombia

Rodrigo Pacheco University of São Paulo, São Paulo, Brazil

Fernando S. Perobelli Federal University of Juiz de Fora, Juiz de Fora, Brazil

Gerson Javier Pérez-Valbuena Banco de la República, Cartagena, Colombia

Diana Ricciulli Banco de la República, Cartagena, Colombia;
Center for Regional Economic Studies, Central Bank of Colombia, Cartagena, Colombia

Ademir Rocha University of São Paulo, São Paulo, Brazil

Eduardo Sanguinet Instituto de Economía Agraria, Universidad Austral de Chile, Valdivia, Los Ríos, Chile

Karina S. Sass University of São Paulo, São Paulo, Brazil

Pedro Levy Sayon University of São Paulo, São Paulo, Brazil

Vinícius A. Vale Federal University of Paraná, Curitiba, Brazil

Chapter 1
Introduction and Overview

Eduardo A. Haddad, Jaime Bonet, and Geoffrey J. D. Hewings

1.1 Background

Colombia possesses an economy of enormous potential that has rapidly risen in regional and global importance after decades of political violence. One of the economic sectors showing that positive trend in Colombia is tourism. According to the World Tourism Organization (UNWTO), international tourist arrivals increased from 2.0 million in 2011 to 3.9 million in 2018. In 2018, tourism exports were USD 6.6 billion, around 13% of Colombian exports.

One of the outstanding characteristics of Colombia is the presence of several regions differentiated from each other in cultural, geographical, economic, and historical aspects. The heterogeneous geography of the country, one of the most fragmented in the world, has played a definitive role in this. For all these reasons, it is striking that studies on the role and development of integrated regional economic structures are at an incipient stage in the country. Perhaps this situation is partly explained by the growing centralism in the economic activity of the country since the 1950s when Bogotá D.C evolved to become the epicenter of the economy, society, and national political life (Gouëset, 1998).

However, despite periods of regional convergence in the first half of the last century, when the country developed its road network (Bonet & Meisel, 1999), in later decades, episodes of political unrest and retrenchment always seem to intervene, generating economic and political centralization and frustrating the full realization of a continuing process of polarization reversal (Hahn & Meisel, 2020). This

E. A. Haddad (✉)
University of São Paulo, São Paulo, Brazil
e-mail: ehaddad@usp.br

J. Bonet
Banco de la República, Cartagena, Colombia

G. J. D. Hewings
University of Illinois at Urbana-Champaign, Champaign, USA

long-established pattern that reinforced Bogotá D.C's primacy in the country can be illustrated by the fact that the capital city's share in GDP is now greater than 25%. Bogotá D.C's primacy has provided one of the more stable patterns in Colombia's recent history; in contrast, redressing regional disparities has proven to be a slow process in the country, given structural inertia.

This book considers some of the regional structural challenges that need to be overcome if Colombia is to break free from the past and finally embark on a path of sustained social cohesion and regionally inclusive growth. The challenges to be examined broadly fall into three areas: (i) those centering on competitiveness and the supply side, (ii) those arising from critical business cycle demand side issues, and (iii) those connected with environmental sustainability, employment, and social inclusion. This volume examines each of these domains, approaching selected topics through quantitative simulations based on a unified general equilibrium framework. It highlights vital topics such as Colombia's competitive insertion in global markets, competitiveness, human capital profiles, and public and private mechanisms of inter-regional income transfers. Challenges around high-profile long-term issues such as productivity gains and climate change are also analyzed. The book argues that policy-makers often neglected such issues even when windows of opportunity were created during periods of progress and expansion. The same criticism could be applied to Colombia's chronic failure to tackle regional disparities during macroeconomic instability.

This book sets Colombia's experience in an international comparative context. It argues that many of the challenges faced by Colombia are shared by other developing economies, drawing on evidence from different countries. In this sense, the policy lessons, which emanate from this volume, have broader international relevance, especially for Latin American countries that face similar institutional frameworks and similar regional challenges.

As its core message, this book argues that critical structural obstacles will need to be tackled if the Colombian economy is to realize its potential and reduce its regional inequality entirely.

1.2 Statement of Aims

The main themes and objectives of the book are:

- To gain a better and more holistic understanding of the contemporary regional development of one of Latin America's largest economies.
- To analyze why the Colombian economy has remained so prone to persistent high regional inequality. It involves highlighting the main regional structural challenges that will need to be overcome if Colombia's regional inequality is to be reduced and its economy can engage in a path of sustained social cohesion and regionally inclusive growth. The structural challenges center on the critical issues of competitiveness, position in global value chains, and the role of

active regional policies by the central government. Other policy challenges include climate change and the relevance of regional specialization. The non-exhaustive list of bottlenecks addressed in the volume takes a linkage/connectivity look at the Colombian economy in tandem with the structural multisectoral modeling approaches selected as the methodological anchors.
- To analyze these challenges and structural features—where appropriate and feasible—in an international, comparative context. In particular, this involves assessing how Colombia's experiences in critical areas compare or contrast with those of other developing economies in Latin America, Asia, and Africa. The idea here is to show the extent to which Colombia and its counterparts elsewhere confront a common series of challenges. These challenges are being encountered as Colombia attempts to build on the development achievements of recent years and to address the myriad issues associated with the "urban primacy" of Bogotá D.C. The comparative aspect of this analysis draws upon the experience the editors have gained in leading different research projects on modeling integrated regional systems across several developing countries.
- To introduce readers to some of the commonly used tool kits in regional science that help understand and interpret the complexity of the spatial linkages structure of integrated sub-national economies.

1.3 What Does This Book Do Differently?

Compared with recent books about the Colombian economy, this book offers a fresh approach in the following senses:
- It has a coherent, policy-relevant mission. From a disaggregated analysis of multiregional and multisectoral linkages, the book builds up a systematic, integrated account of the unaddressed structural challenges that have historically held back Colombia's more equitable regional development. Other volumes effectively shed light on particular macroeconomic, sectoral, or structural features of the Colombian economy from a historical perspective (e.g., Luzardo-Luna, 2019; Robinson & Urrutia, 2007), but they do not directly share the objectives of this book. For this reason, they do not offer or claim to offer the systematic sub-national evaluation or diagnosis that this volume does.
- This volume places Colombia in a global comparative context. Most recent volumes analyzing Colombia's economy tend to do so based on an isolated evaluation, examining performance concerning past periods, but much more rarely in relation to valid international comparators. This volume aims to break this mold by engaging, wherever appropriate, in a more systematic, internationally comparative evaluation. Part of the idea here is to show that Colombia shares many similar challenges to its developing countries' counterparts elsewhere. Thus, the book has a relevance that stretches beyond the case of Colombia itself. When many consider that developing economies may collectively face regional divides that enhance further discontentment, this is a timely attribute.

- Methodological relevance. By making available the replication files for every simulation exercise, based on the general equilibrium modeling framework that serves as the unifying methodological anchor, this book adds serious value for researchers and practitioners in the field of regional science. It will be able to take on board the often-needed hands-on experience. This book is in a unique position to offer an interface between applied theory and practice, bringing important insights from integrated interregional systems in the developing world.

1.4 What Does This Book Leave Aside and Why?

The chapters intentionally share a common multisectoral and multiregional general equilibrium approach, namely input–output and Computable General Equilibrium (CGE) modeling, which has been part of the traditional toolbox of regional scientists for decades. On the one hand, it provides a way to wrap up the discussion of the linkages structure of the Colombian economy within a methodological anchor. It also provides the opportunity to discuss some of the recent developments associated with these tools. On the other hand, our option constrains the range of facets of Colombia's regional economies that can be effectively discussed in the book.

Issues involving the linkages structure of integrated interregional systems are complex. It serves no good purpose to pretend that they are not. Compared to input–output and CGE models, other existing, commonly used policy tools do not come anywhere close to capturing some of the most important channels through which exogenous and policy shocks are transmitted across regions through a country's linkages structure. Models are usually issue(s)-specific. Trying to "force" a model to answer questions that it is not designed to address hampers our ability to address relevant policy questions. Thus, the aspects of regional economies that are broached across the various chapters of the book follow a relatively conventional depiction of an economy. However, the models developed in the book, calibrated with Colombian data, can tell a coherent story about the Colombian economy and some of its regional structural challenges. It would be desirable for a volume on regional issues in Colombia to also include dimensions that stand out as influential in discussing the state and trajectory of Colombia's economy, such as land tenure, ethnic minorities, social disparities and inclusion, innovation, human capital, and regional governance. These appear to be some additional bottlenecks of contemporary regional economies in different parts of the world. Nevertheless, they do not feature in the book since they go beyond its proposed scope.

Finally, specific historical and social issues in Colombia attract the attention of many readers. Discussions of the legacy of the decades of active engagement with non-state agents left deep scars in the country. However, other publications have discussed the economic healing process more broadly (e.g., Luzardo-Luna, 2019; Robinson & Urrutia, 2007).

1.5 Structure of the Book

The chapters are grouped into four parts, Regional Setting, Modeling Framework, Structural Analysis, and Structural Development Issues. Part I describes the evolution of regional disparities in the country, setting the scene for the forthcoming material in the book. Part II highlights the analytical framework to be deployed. It centers on the specification and implementation of an interregional input–output system and an interregional computable general equilibrium model for Colombia, providing a unified methodological anchor to be used in Parts III and IV. As stated in Aroca and Hewings (2006, p 0.5), macroeconomic analysis tends to ignore what goes on inside an economy; however, most economies are characterized by significant core–periphery dichotomies, often exacerbated by a strong primacy city. For many Latin American countries, the disparities in levels of regional welfare have been large and persistent, notwithstanding long-standing government intervention. The case of Colombia is no different; Colombia's regional structure is characterized by strong polarization from the capital city, Bogotá D.C, whose location may, at first, present a puzzle. Bogotá D.C is located at the geographic center of Colombia, on a high plateau in the Andes Mountains, with difficult access to the main seaports and with poor connections to other regions and countries by land (Pachón & Ramírez, 2006). The very location of Bogotá D.C presents a challenge to Colombian global integration as market/supply access from/to the economic core of the country is hindered by high internal transportation costs.

In a broader territorial context, the presence of other relevant, relatively more integrated economic spaces outside the manufacturing "golden triangle" (Bogotá-Cundinamarca-Medellín-Cali) reveals a contiguous economic core of the Colombian economy comprising nine out of the 33 regions, namely Atlántico, Bolívar, Antioquia, Caldas, Risaralda, Valle, Cundinamarca, Bogotá D. C. and Santander, which, together, are responsible for 75% of the national GDP. Given the ostrich-shaped-like cartographical representation of this cluster's territorial limits (see Fig. 1.1), this set of regions is referred to as the "Colombian ostrich". This area concentrates economic activity and presents more favorable socioeconomic indicators in different dimensions. Using a constructed database, we present a detailed "picture" of the existing economic structure of Colombia as a result of a series of historical events.

Part I: Regional Setting

The key component of Chap. 2, animated by a conceptual discussion, focuses on the relevance of structural constraints as factors underpinning Colombia's uneven spatial development performance. This aspect of the chapter draws on concepts derived from the regional economics literature, especially concerning the rationale behind the existence of (or the need for) regional policies in general. Cases in which excessive concentration or inequality hinders national economic growth are natural candidates for regional policies. If concentration and inequality favor national growth and competitiveness, regional interventions call for different sorts of arguments, such as national unity or cohesion. Any regional policy has sectoral and national consequences, and any sectoral or national policy has regional consequences. Should public

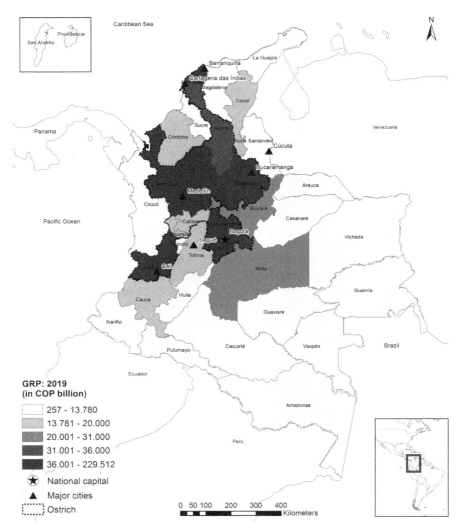

Fig. 1.1 Regional Distribution of GDP in Colombia, 2019

authorities engage in explicit regional policies (place-based) or sectoral or social policies (people-based) with desirable regional implications? Finally, if regional policies are implemented, how do we evaluate them?

Chapter 3 studies the determinants of changes in labor and non-labor income inequality from a microeconomic perspective to help design and formulate public policies that improve the situation of income inequalities in Colombia. The study is carried out for the nation as a whole and the 23 major cities and their metropolitan areas. The authors use a micro-decomposition methodology following Bourguignon and Ferreira (2005), which allows comparisons of income distribution changes over time. The results show that income inequality in Colombia dropped during the 2010s. Labor income accounted for most of this change. Returns to education and the stock of human capital were the main drivers of the reduction in inequalities in labor income, while non-labor income inequality also fell during this period, driven mainly by rental income. A crucial part of the results points to the importance of education as a factor that helps reduce inequalities. Therefore, policies that improve educational attainment and quality are of vital importance. Low-income families also benefit from owning a house, as it provides them with an additional source of income. Therefore, housing ownership programs for low-income households also contributes to reducing inequality.

The studies aiming to answer whether wealthier areas in Colombia are growing slower than poorer areas have yielded mixed results. Chapter 4 updates such estimates of *unconditional beta convergence* of the GDP per capita for the first years of the twenty-first century, when substantial structural changes occurred. Furthermore, it decomposes the *beta* by sectoral changes throughout the period while estimating it with a moving starting year. This assessment is supplemented by a convergence analysis of additional social and economic indicators. The results suggest an increasing, yet non-significant, *beta*, indicating that Colombia is moving from a subtle convergence to a more frequent period of divergence. Moreover, the authors find that the prime convergence sectoral forces from most of the period are mines and quarrying, along with the public sector. In contrast, there is strong evidence of tax revenues per capita convergence and an apparent faster reduction of multidimensional poverty in wealthier areas in the last intercensal period.

Part II: Modeling Framework

The first objective of Chap. 5 is to present a detailed description of the procedures used to construct the interregional input–output system for Colombia with 2015 data. This tool facilitates analyzing the interrelationships among departments of the country concerning trade flows. It makes available the details of the methodological procedures adopted to generate the interregional system and the database itself to be used by other researchers and practitioners. Different applications are discussed in Part III of this volume, identifying structural features of Colombia's regional economies. In this chapter, the authors also present illustrative analyses using different indicators from the estimated database, revealing some of the main structural features of the Colombian economy.

In our unified modeling treatment, the database described in Chap. 5 is used to calibrate an interregional computable general equilibrium (ICGE) model for Colombia, the CEER model. Chapter 6 is a technical chapter intended for readers interested in modeling issues, where the authors describe the structure of the CEER model, a fully operational ICGE model for Colombia. The model uses an approach similar to Peter et al. (1996), Haddad (1999), and Haddad and Hewings (2005) to incorporate the interregional economic structure. It uses the absorption matrix as the basis to calibrate the structural coefficients of the ICGE model, together with a set of elasticities either properly estimated or borrowed from the econometric literature applied for Colombia. This database captures economy-wide effects through an intricate plot of input–output relations. The current version of the CEER model identifies the economies of the 32 Colombian Departments and the capital city, Bogotá D.C. Results are based on a bottom-up approach—i.e., national results are obtained from aggregating regional results.

The model differentiates 54 production/investment sectors in each region, producing 54 commodities, one representative household in each region, regional governments and one Central government, and a single foreign area that trades with each domestic region. Two local primary factors are used in the production process, according to regional endowments (capital and labor). Particular groups of equations define macroeconomic and regional aggregates, accumulation relations, and regional labor markets. The CEER model qualifies as a Johansen-type model in that the solutions are obtained by solving the system of linearized equations of the model, following the Australian tradition. A typical result shows the percentage change in the set of endogenous variables after a policy is carried out, compared to their values in the absence of such policy, in a given environment. Interregional linkages play an essential role in the functioning mechanisms of the model. These linkages are driven by trade relations (commodity flows) and factor mobility (capital and labor migration). In the first case, interregional trade flows are incorporated; interregional input–output relations are required to calibrate the model, and interregional trade elasticities play an important role (Haddad, 2009). The CEER model is used in the simulation exercises of Part IV of the book.

Part III: Structural Analysis
The work by Perobelli et al. (2010) is revisited ten years later. Chapter 7 analyzes structural interdependence among Colombian departments from a linkages perspective, using the 2015 database. The results show that Bogotá D.C still has a considerable influence on the other regional economies through the power of its purchases. Additionally, a center-periphery pattern is still present in the spatial concentration of the effects of the hypothetical extraction of any territory. From a policy point of view, the main findings reaffirm the role played by Bogotá D.C in the continuing polarization process observed in the regional economies in Colombia in 2002. Any policy action oriented to reduce these regional disparities should consider that, given the structural interdependence among Colombian departments, the effects of new investments in the lagged regions would flow through Bogotá D.C and the major regional economies, namely Antioquia and Valle del Cauca. The chapter concludes that, despite recent government efforts to reduce regional inequality, there is strong inertia embedded in the linkage structure of the Colombian economy that may act as a spatial trap that drains resources to the core regions through production and income linkages. To overcome this structural challenge it is necessary to implement policies that are more focused and appropriately reflect the endogenous characteristics of the regions—essentially, an implementation of policy that is more sensitive to decentralizing characteristics.

Chapter 8 aims to bring insights into the design of Colombia's regional development policies based on regional specialization strategies and focuses on the discussion of input–output linkages. It combines economic base theory and the concept of Miyazawa multipliers, the latter allowing the formulation of interregional income multipliers and alternative procedures for decomposing an economic system to reveal the specific contributions of output change to different regions. The issues addressed in the chapter consider the extent of the economic base (E.B.) backward and forward linkages. The chapter also looks at the relationship between E.B. and local labor markets in different departments and the implications for regional competitiveness. At the end of the chapter, a typology of departments based on their output and employment linkages emerges.

In summary, trade linkages, besides local capabilities, are crucial to understanding differences in regional performance. While Colombian departments that highly depend on a few sectors focused on trade outside the region had the lowest economic growth between 2015 and 2020, regions specializing in industries with a supply chain more integrated with the rest of the local economy presented a better economic performance. Thus, regions specialized in highly integrated sectors into the local production network have a stronger potential for economic growth. Based on the intersectoral and interregional linkages framework, the results in this chapter reinforce the importance of regional specialization strategies for regional development policies.

Which other department is each Colombian department's main trading partner? Chapter 9 reports on the results of another application with the interregional input–output matrix for Colombia. For each flow originating in one of the Colombian departments, the authors estimate measures of the trade in value-added. The measures of trade in value-added reveal different hierarchies of interregional and international trade integration, with implications for regional inequality in the country. The parsimonious approach proposed in Los et al. (2016), based on "hypothetical extraction", serves as the methodological anchor for the study. The export base theory provides the foundations for different regional development models at the sub-national level. The role of interregional trade in the Colombian departments should not be relegated to a secondary place. The chapter argues that policymakers should consider interregional interactions for a better understanding of how the regional economies are affected, both in the international and in the domestic markets, since for the smaller economies, the performance of the more developed regions may play a crucial role. For some Colombian departments, the future is tied to their ability to compete in the international export market and their position and participation with other domestic markets. Interesting patterns appear from the analysis. Colombia's golden manufacturing triangle (Bogotá D.C, Antioquia, and Valle del Cauca departments) is a hub of the local production chain supplying manufactured products and services to all departments. Meanwhile, producers of natural resource-intensive commodities (Arauca, Casanare, Cesar, Meta, and La Guajira departments) are mainly connected to the global supply chain. The distinctions in foreign-demand-based economies versus local demand-driven economies may suggest that economic changes in Bogotá D.C, for instance, are more important than external shocks for most Colombian departments. Bogotá D.C, Antioquia, and Valle del Cauca play a dominant role in Colombian interregional trade flows. Changes in the supply chain from these regions can propagate effects through intersectoral and interregional trade linkages and significantly affect other regions' economies. Moreover, international trading partners are distinct across Colombian regions. For example, the United States (USA) and Panama are essential for more industrialized places (i.e., Antioquia and Bogotá D.C). At the same time, China and Spain play a relevant role for regions that export natural resource-intensive commodities (i.e., Cesar, Meta, and Casanare). In this context, although trade with certain countries is important for Colombia, it is necessary to know which regions benefit from this trade since trade liberalization policies may benefit some places to the detriment of others. From a policy perspective, trade flows might generate the propagation of feedback effects determined by the hierarchical structure of the Colombian interregional system. Domestic or foreign trade changes that affect a specific place can spread across the economy through the local supply chain impacting employment and income in several regions. Therefore, knowing the domestic and international production networks can help to qualify trade policy and regional planning strategies.

Colombian coffee is renowned worldwide for its quality and delicious taste. It is one of the country's major crops and the world's third-largest producer. Although coffee growing is not relevant in terms of GDP (less than 1%), it plays an important role in employment, with over half a million families benefiting directly from it and many more indirectly. What if the coffee-growing and coffee-producing sectors did not exist? How much value-added is in coffee exports, and how does it compare to direct coffee exports? What are the main regions contributing to value-added in the coffee exports' local value chains? Chapter 10 addresses these questions by exploring the linkages structure of the coffee industry in Colombia. It bases its empirical strategy on the "hypothetical extraction" method to isolate the systemic economic effects of the coffee industry's value chain in a typical year of operations, looking at the impact on regional output and employment profiles by formalization and skills. By exploring the structure of the linkages of the coffee industry in Colombia, the chapter confirms that the regions where coffee-growing and coffee-processing activities have a higher share of total production are those most affected by the extraction of these sectors from the economy. The analysis also shows the effects of a total extraction of coffee-related sectors from the Colombian economy on the national and regional total output, value-added, and employment by type of contract and educational level, revealing the direct and indirect importance of coffee goods to local value chains. The results suggest that policies to increase the value-added of coffee products and the content of services in coffee exports can increase income and employment, especially in regions more dependent on coffee production.

The question addressed in Chap. 11 focuses on the role played by domestic tourism as a mechanism of interregional transfers of income. Domestic tourism can be considered an efficient mechanism of interregional transfers, as consumer decisions to travel may be seen as entirely based on an optimality problem in which preferences and price signals play a crucial role without imposing further market distortions. In Colombia, domestic tourism flows follow a pattern of origin in the central regions and destination in the periphery. In this sense, this chapter aims to analyze the regional impacts of the consumption patterns of expenditures by Colombian tourists, focusing on the Caribe region, using the interregional input–output model described in Chap. 5, together with data from the Internal Tourism Expenditure Survey (EGIT) 2014–2015. The exercises developed in this chapter capture the contribution of domestic tourism to inclusive economic growth in terms of socioeconomic characteristics of jobs and income generation, both directly and indirectly. By addressing the systemic effects of interregional tourism flows across the regions, the authors generate evidence on the multiplier effects of urban travelers on the Caribbean coast—national travelers' leading tourism destination. They captured the positive contribution to inclusive economic growth by recognizing the potential for generating employment and income throughout the tourism production chain. It is important to provide insights for the formulation of tourism-related regional policies. The results suggest that domestic tourism can be considered an important channel to produce a more efficient allocation of resources and reduce inequality among regions in Colombia. Promoting the development of tourist activity at the local level positively impacts both the local destination and the economy through the distributive effects regarding origin–destinations expenditures and investments in the tourism industry, which is particularly relevant to promoting a cycle of sustainable growth in the Colombian Caribbean. This study also highlights the role of tourism in potentially reducing regional inequalities. The results show that policies to promote tourism—expanding local capillarity in terms of pro-tourism structure or through incentives that promote interregional travel—promote efficient redistributive effects. In addition, regional attributes require investments in improving infrastructure to generate incentives to increase demand for sub-national destinations.

Chapter 12 analyzes the regional economic differences in the impact of lockdown measures ordered by Colombia's national government to prevent the spread of COVID-19. Using the input–output model, the authors estimate the regional economic losses of extracting a group of formal and informal workers from different sectors of the economy. Results show regional differences in the impact of lockdown measures on labor markets, local economies, and their productive sectors. The peripheral regions (Amazonía, Caribe, Pacific, Eastern plains, and Orinoquía) account for a higher proportion of informal workers in isolation than the inner regions (Coffee area and Antioquia, and Central), indicating that workers in the former are more vulnerable to lockdown measures. Regarding the economic impact, regional losses range between 5.4% of GDP (Amazonía) and 6.3% (Coffee Area and Antioquia). Sectoral impacts in the Coffee area and Antioquia, Central, Caribe, and Pacific regions are concentrated in service activities, while in Amazonía, Eastern plains, and Orinoquía, the most affected sectors belong to agriculture and mining. Identifying the degree to which the different regions and their sectors are potentially affected by lockdown measures helped better inform policy decisions and minimize the economic impact generated by these preventive measures.

Part IV: Structural Development Issues

Climate change has sparked the discussion about how to overcome the coming hindrances imposed by new weather conditions. Using the forecasts by Ceballos & Dall'Erba (2021), Chap. 13 tries to quantify said hardships within the ICGE framework. Although macro results tend to be relatively small—consistent with Ceballos and Dall'Erba (2021), they are very heterogeneous among sectors and regions. Coffee-related industries (growing and processing) were most affected by the climate shock, which is expected given the commodity's production structure. Even though the climate shock initially affects areas where coffee is grown, the most positively affected sector in the new equilibrium is coffee processing due to its interindustry chaining in the Colombian economy examined in Chap. 10. Elevation plays a significant role in this simulation: Lower regions may become unsuitable for coffee, whereas Andean regions will potentially experience a sharp increase in productivity for this crop. Thus, despite the common expectation that climate change affects the economy negatively, in the case of Colombian coffee, this industry may benefit from an overall increase in temperature, given the country's unique topology. The chapter concludes with a discussion of the implications of these results for current producing regions, especially in terms of their labor force. Custom-designed regional policies should attempt to accommodate the resulting migrations and mitigate the adverse effects of such economic forces in harmed departments/municipalities.

Chapter 14 evaluates the impacts of changes in total factor productivity (TFP) in the manufacturing sectors, classified according to technological intensities, in each Colombian department to understand how productivity shocks propagate across the country. The geography of the Colombian manufacturing sector is concentrated in the "golden triangle" composed of the regions of Bogotá D.C and Cundinamarca, Antioquia, and Valle del Cauca. Mapping regional TFP elasticities brings additional insights into the role played in the Colombian economy by regional-specific policies related to manufacturing activities. From the simulation results, it is possible to identify potential trade-offs between regional equity and efficiency. While some manufacturing sectors promote GDP growth and reduce inequality, others only foster economic growth at the expense of increasing inequality. It is also possible to analyze the existing patterns of regional competition and complementarity. The analysis reveals different dimensions of Colombia's economic concentration and technological intensity in manufacturing sectors: Bogotá D.C, as the country's capital, plays a prominent role, followed by the regions of Antioquia and Valle del Cauca. It poses further structural challenges for pursuing a higher-quality insertion on global value chains with less spatially concentrated benefits. Simulation results show that the change in the Colombian manufacturing sector's TFP (1%) could generate, in the long run, a 0.078% increase in GDP, mainly driven by the export component. The low-technological-intensity manufacturing sector can potentially increase the GDP and reduce inequality between Colombian regions. This pattern is not seen for productivity-enhancing policies to foster medium–high technology intensity sectors. Furthermore, productivity increases in manufacturing sectors in one region may result in potential reductions in the output of other regions (competitive aspect). This chapter brings several analyses around productivity in the manufacturing sector and its regional economic impacts. Insights driven by the results presented here can help guide Colombian incentive policies for investment in more efficient technologies and changes in institutional aspects.

Services are increasingly important worldwide, as their share in global GDP reached 65.0% in 2018, and in Colombia, 57.8%. In Chap. 15, the authors focus on services value-added in exports in Colombia, a country that reveals a historical dependence on natural resource-intensive exports. They place their analysis in the context of the collapse of the boom or "super-cycle" of commodity prices that has generated significant macroeconomic challenges in recent years. They initially apply interregional input–output analysis to measure value-added services in Colombia's exports. The main results show that the internal geography of services value-added in exports vis-à-vis the location patterns of natural resources in Colombia may add another tension to current trade negotiations. The chapter adds another layer of analytical material by simulating TFP changes in Knowledge-Intensive Business Services (KIBS) and assessing their wider impacts. Overall, the competitiveness of firms in open economies is increasingly determined by access to low-cost and high-quality produced services. However, KIBS' low vertical integration with tradable sectors in the Colombian economy weakens the propagation of productivity shocks in the KIBS on the supply chain. The chapter concludes by showing that "servicification" has potential asymmetric locational impacts, benefiting primal cities/regions in the country. Thus, the ability of an industry to become more competitive depends not only on productivity gains in the industry itself but also on shocks that affect its supply chain. The results show that KIBS productivity shocks propagate through the input–output trade relationships and are a channel for technical changes in the economic system.

The final two chapters analyze existing interregional government transfer mechanisms in Colombia. Chapter 16 analyzes the spatial interactions induced by fiscal decentralization policies and their respective impacts on regional growth. It assesses the economic effects of alternative scenarios of regional allocation of Colombia's current interregional transfers scheme through simulations with the CEER model. Highlighting potential trade-offs between regional equity and efficiency, the simulations contribute to analyzing the growth impact related to some of the broad objectives central governments pursue when allocating sub-national transfers to local governments. Changes in the distribution of central national government transfers in an environment that allows for labor mobility between regions can drive migration from less productive regions to more productive regions, affecting regional production and growth.

The results show that when the distribution is based on regional population shares, there are potential gains in national growth and an increase in regional disparities. However, using other redistributive criteria, such as the number of people impoverished or the horizontal equity gaps, there is a potential improvement in regional inequality despite adverse effects on national growth. The chapter concludes by reaffirming that Colombia will have to face such trade-offs as one of the structural challenges, which will need to be overcome if the country decides to embark on a path of sustained social cohesion, and regionally inclusive growth. Tax equalization policies have been used to redistribute tax revenues from areas with the greater financial capacity to more impoverished regions, allowing for a more equitable distribution of public resources. These transfers are based on a criterion of equality, but productivity gains must be considered so that efficiency is not affected and national income is reduced.

The extraction of non-renewable natural resources has the potential to generate income to finance government activities. Rent capturing through taxation may enhance the public sector's ability to harness the potential of natural resources to sustain a broad-based development. Colombia, an important oil and coal producer and exporter in Latin America, is pursuing success in this endeavor. The country's strategy, associated with the General Participation System (SGR), is grounded on asset formation through domestic investment, focusing on the long-term intergenerational transfer of wealth and upfront expenditures to generate short-run growth effects, with a strong focus on social and regional equity. Because royalties are generally payable irrespective of a project's profitability, they tend to be used as a preferable fiscal tool to secure income from natural resources operations. In this context, the Colombian royalties scheme is assessed in this chapter. Alternative uses of the royalty revenue to fund development projects are simulated. Whether there is a fair regional distribution of the rents from mining activities in Colombia remains a disputable debate in the country. For this appraisal, Chap. 17 relies on simulations with the ICGE model for the Colombian economy. Despite the prolonged presence of royalties in the Colombian economy, their general equilibrium effects are still unknown. Taxing mining output may raise government revenue with a low excess burden, at least in the short term. There is also a significant potential for economic growth, welfare increases, and regional inequality reduction from the increased use of royalties. A more effective and efficient regional and sectoral allocation of resources has always been sought after. In that sense, this final chapter sheds light on how the social and economic circumstances would change in Colombia, considering greater and better use of royalties in the economy.

1.6 The Road Ahead

In scientifically emerging economies with large territorial extensions, such as Colombia, it is expected that an expansion of domestic collaboration networks from nodes located in centers of national excellence will take place, parallel to an increase in international scientific collaboration. In the case of Colombia, the *Banco de la República* branch in Cartagena has placed itself, in the last 25 years since the creation of the *Centro de Estudios Económicos Regionales* (CEER), as a focal point for creating and disseminating modeling capacity in Colombia. CEER has established itself as a benchmark in regional and urban studies of Colombia at the national and international levels. This book represents an example of a collaborative endeavor, aggregating researchers and modelers from different countries under the leadership of a group of scholars involved, to different degrees, with the activities of CEER. It reflects a pattern of evolving collaboration networks in regional science in scientifically emerging economies. The future expansion of such a scientific collaboration network in Colombia emerges as a relevant mechanism for both a qualitative leap in national scientific production in regional and urban studies and for disseminating knowledge in peripheral regions of the country. It is expected that, in the next 25 years, it will help develop regional science in the country still further, triggering the second cycle of development of the field in Colombia.

References

Aroca, P., & Hewings, G. J. D. (2006). *Structure and structural change in the Chilean economy*. Palgrave Macmillan.
Bonet, J. & Meisel, A. (1999). La convergencia regional en Colombia: una visión de largo plazo, 1926–1995. In *Documentos de Trabajo sobre Economía Regional*, (p. 8). Banco de la República. Retrieved from https://repositorio.banrep.gov.co/handle/20.500.12134/394
Bourguignon, F., & Ferreira, F. (2005). Decomposing changes in the distribution of household incomes: Methodological aspects. In F. Bourguignon, F. Ferreira, & N. Lustig (Eds.), *The microeconomics of income distribution dynamics in East Asia and Latin America* (pp. 17–46). World Bank and Oxford University Press.
Ceballos-Sierra, F., & Dall'Erba, S. (2021). The effect of climate variability on Colombian coffee productivity: A dynamic panel approach. *Agricultural Systems, 190*, 103–126.
Gouëset, V. (1998). *Bogotá: Nacimiento de una metropoli*. Tercer Mundo Editores, Bogotá.
Haddad, E. A. (1999). *Regional inequality and structural changes: Lessons from the Brazilian experience*. Ashgate.
Haddad, E. A., & Hewings, G. J. D. (2005). Market imperfections in a spatial economy: Some experimental results. *The Quarterly Review of Economics and Finance, 45*(2–3), 476–496.
Haddad, E. A. (2009). Interregional computable general equilibrium models. In M. Sonis, & G. J. D. Hewings (Eds.), *Tool kits in regional science* (pp. 119–154). Berlin: Springer, Heidelberg.
Hahn, L., & Meisel, A. (2020). Regional economic inequality in Colombia, 1926–2018. In D. Tirado-Fabregat, M. Badia-Miró, & H. Willebald (Eds.), *Time and space Latin American regional development in historical perspective. Palgrave studies in economic history*. Palgrave Macmillan. https://doi.org/10.1007/978-3-030-47553-6
Los, B., Timmer, M., & de Vries, G. (2016). Tracing value-added and double counting in gross exports: Comment. *American Economic Review, 106*(4), 1958–1966.
Luzardo-Luna, I. (2019). Colombia's slow economic growth from the nineteenth to the twenty-first century. In *Palgrave studies in economic history*. Palgrave Macmillan. https://doi.org/10.1007/978-3-030-25755-2
Pachón, Á., Ramírez, M. T. (2006). La infraestructura de transporte en Colombia durante el siglo XX. In *Fondo de Cultura Económica*. Banco de la República, Bogotá.
Perobelli, F., Haddad, E. A., Bonet, J., & Hewings, G. J. D. (2010). Structural interdependence among Colombian departments. *Economic Systems Research, 33*(3), 279–300.
Peter, M. W., Horridge, M., Meagher, G. A., Naqvi, F., & Parmenter, B. R. (1996). The theoretical structure of MONASH-MRF. In *Preliminary Working Paper* (n. OP-85). IMPACT Project, Monash University, Clayton.
Robinson, J. & Urrutia, M. (2007). *Economía colombiana del siglo XX. Un análisis cuantitativo*. Bogotá: Fondo de Cultura.

Eduardo A. Haddad, Full Professor at the Department of Economics at the University of São Paulo, Brazil, where he directs the Regional and Urban Economics Lab (NEREUS). Affiliate Professor at the Faculty of Governance, Economic and Social Sciences of the Mohammed VI University and Senior Fellow at the Policy Center for the New South, Rabat, Morocco. President of the Regional Science Association International, RSAI (2021–2022).

Jaime Bonet is an economist from the Universidad de Los Andes in Bogotá with a master's degree in economics and a Ph. D. in regional planning from the University of Illinois at Urbana-Champaign. His research areas include regional and urban economics, local public finance, local economic development, and regional development history in Colombia.

Geoffrey J. D. Hewings, Emeritus Director, Regional Economics Applications Laboratory (REAL). Emeritus Professor of Geography and Regional Science, Economics, and Urban and Regional Planning. President of the Regional Science Association International, RSAI (2001–2002).

Part I
Regional Setting

Chapter 2
Is There a Case for Regional Policies in Colombia?

Jaime Bonet, Karina Acosta, Gerson Javier Pérez-Valbuena, and Jhorland Ayala-García

2.1 Introduction

The emergence of regional-oriented policies has been driven by the profound territorial disparities within countries worldwide. These differences are not restricted to economic concerns, but to a broader view that affects the standard of living and the population's well-being, such as the provision of health, education, sanitation, and many other amenities-related provisions (Meisel & Pérez, 2013; Pérez & Rowland, 2004). However the presence of disparities is a necessary condition in support of the rationale behind the need for regional policies, the persistence of such imbalances is the main reason countries implement measures to improve the population's living standard in the lagging regions. Although many countries have recognized the presence of regional disparities and, consequently, have decided to implement policies to reduce them, some of the most extensively researched cases are those of Italy, Brazil, and Spain, for individual countries, and the European Union (Pérez & Rowland, 2004).

In the case of Colombia, regional disparities have been discussed and analyzed for many years. The first evidence on record dates to the early twentieth century with a movement called *Liga Costeña*, a political and entrepreneurial association of the Caribbean coast, focused on promoting the reduction of disparities with the rest of the country (Meisel, 2020). Since the 1960s, some social movements in the Pacific region have sought to make their precarious socioeconomic situation, lack of opportunities, and abandonment by state institutions visible to the national authorities looking for social vindication (Bonet et al., 2018).

At the end of the twentieth century, according to Cárdenas et al. (1993), a period where regional disparities were formally evaluated began, focusing on per capita income convergence. Using yearly departmental data between 1950 and 1983, the

---

J. Bonet (✉) · K. Acosta · G. J. Pérez-Valbuena · J. Ayala-García
Banco de la República, Cartagena, Colombia
e-mail: jbonetmo@banrep.gov.co

authors found evidence supporting the reduction of regional disparities, with the poorest regions growing faster than the richer ones. On the one hand, these results are consistent with Gómez (2006), Royuela and García (2015), and León and Benavides (2015). On the other hand, there is a growing literature showing that even though there are improvements in reducing regional disparities in Colombia, they are still persistent so that no or weak indication of convergence is evident (Bonet & Meisel, 1999; Franco & Raymond, 2009; Galvis & Hahn, 2015; Galvis & Meisel, 2001, 2010; Galvis et al., 2017; Martínez, 2006)[1] The prior research highlights the need to design and implement regional policies that contribute to a better distribution of resources and opportunities among the territories.

Within the most recent literature studying the performance of inequalities in Colombia, we find Galvis et al. (2017)[2], who analyzed this phenomenon along several dimensions over the last two decades. Results show a slight reduction in the labor revenue's Gini coefficient between 2010 (0.57) and 2019 (0.53), together with a 12% increase in real labor income. Simultaneously, poverty and extreme poverty were reduced by half during the same period. Notwithstanding the positive results, after carefully decomposing the Gini coefficient, the authors found that the reduction of total inequality is mainly explained by the within cities/regions' component rather than the between cities/regions inequality, supporting previous evidence of persistent regional imbalances.

Under the existing circumstances, and considering the most recent research, if Colombia's purpose is to achieve a society with a better balance of opportunities among the different territories, differentiated public policies are required to help those lagging regions. Over the last two decades, there has been a growing interest in disclosing the sources and origins of regional inequalities in Colombia and several initiatives to alleviate them. One of the first was Moncayo (2002), who described the transition between regional policies led by the central government (between the 1950s and the 1970s), to another, under a decentralized scheme, where regions themselves, through their local governments, are responsible for advancing measures to enhance their development[3].

Barón et al. (2004) go deeper in recognizing the persistence of regional inequalities across many different socioeconomic variables and argue that the presence of such imbalances can have adverse effects on national policy objectives. The authors also offer a review of proven international instruments, which include macro and micro-policies, where the first set is concerned with stimulating changes in the general regional income and expenditures (different policies in different regions). In contrast, the second set focuses on allocating and relocating capital and labor between regions.

---

[1] See Chap. 3.

[2] The main findings are discussed in Chap. 4.

[3] In particular, the first stage's policies are related to national stimulus, such as fiscal incentives, central government's investments in lagged regions as well as deterrents for firms to invest in already industrious and developed regions. The second stage is related to the first steps of the decentralization processes in their various dimensions, administrative, political, and fiscal, where more autonomy, responsibilities, and resources were given to local governments to drive the catching up with the more able regions.

The authors include a detailed set of policies, with their strengths and weaknesses, that have been implemented in different countries worldwide.

Similarly, Fernández et al., (2007) and Galvis (2017) offer a rich set of measures to reduce the deep gap between developed and less developed regions in Colombia. Although providing nationwide policies and recommendations, Fernández et al., (2007) focus on how the Caribbean region could take a big step to reduce its socioeconomic distance from the more developed regions. The concerns are human capital transformation, culture and institutions, demographic transition, corruption, rural poverty, tourism, and port activities. On the other hand, and with the same purpose, Galvis (2017), after offering abundant evidence on the precarious and disadvantaged situation of the Pacific region and showing how persistent these disparities have been, provides a series of actions in terms of overcoming the large socioeconomic gap between this region and the rest of the country. The problems facing the Pacific region for which the authors make proposals center on morbidity, social mobility, the persistence of poverty, labor informality and job quality, and nutrition.

In short, the evidence shows that the various authorities in Colombia have taken significant steps over the years to improve the population's socioeconomic condition. However, it is also clear that, despite all these efforts, lagging regions remain distant from the most prosperous ones, or even worse, the gap has been increasing over time. These facts show that public policies should be regionally differentiated and multidimensional. This approach is consistent with the proposal of an asymmetric decentralization, meaning a particular fiscal arrangement for every local government/region in recognition of their distinct endowments, resource, development paths, and capabilities (OECD, 2019). This proposal mainly targets the reduction of regional disparities, which highly depend on how decentralized policies are designed and implemented.

The objective of this chapter is to discuss whether there is still room for regional policies in Colombia. Starting from the existing literature on regional development policies, Sect. 2.2 will review the main existing restrictions for enhancing development in lagging regions. In addition, Sect. 2.3 will present the main regional or local development strategies implemented in Colombia in the last decades. Finally, based on the evidence found, Sect. 2.4 will reflect on the importance of adopting development policies that consider the existing regional differences in the country. Any regional policy has sectoral and national consequences, and any sectoral or national policy has regional consequences. Should public authorities engage in explicit regional policies (place-based) or sectoral or social policies (people-based) with desirable regional implications? Finally, if regional policies are implemented, how to evaluate them?

2.2 Literature Review

Much of the literature on regional policies in Colombia is concentrated on analyzing the decentralization process initiated in the 1980s and strengthened with the Constitution of 1991. Following this trend, this section reviews the main studies that have analyzed decentralization in Colombia in the last 30 years. According to Schneider (2003), despite variability in the definition of decentralization, it can be described mainly as the transfer of power and funds from national governments to local governments and can be classified into three areas: political, fiscal, and administrative. The former refers to the political representativeness and functions at different non-central scales. Fiscal decentralization denotes the degree of fiscal control conveyed from central governments to local governments. Finally, administrative decentralization can be understood as how much freedom to make decisions that the territorial entities have when compared to the national government.

Multiple studies have tried to identify the benefits and pitfalls of such regional autonomy allowed by the relatively recent territorial policies. The scholarly work encountered in Colombia concurs with a pro-decentralization scheme, subject to certain conditions. In this section, we gather the central literature on regional policy balances, which also risked to present proposals. We summarize and group the main advice on decentralization by the key areas suggested by Schneider (2003). They are primarily fiscal and administrative. Though much has been said about regional policies and the effects of political decentralization on multiple outcomes in Colombia, we concentrate on propositional studies.

2.2.1 Fiscal Decentralization

Among the first studies on fiscal policies in Colombia are Acosta and Bird (2005) and Chaparro et al. (2005), compiled by Bird et al. (2005). They resulted from the Mission on Public Income created in late 2001 by the central government. Indeed, fiscal decentralization is one of the critical matters of regional policies, as the flexibility of economic decisions and their impact depend on it.

Acosta and Bird (2005) conclude that decentralization in Colombia has been a feeble process. However, it will not be improved by more centralized policies but rather by better-decentralized policies. These authors differentiate regional policies for departments and municipalities[4]. They consider departments a problematic and perhaps superfluous division, the elimination of which is not feasible due to political reasons. Although constitutionally the main roles of departments are the promotion of local development and planning, in practice, it has been largely limited to the administration of inflexible expenses of national programs on health and education. Acosta and Bird (2005) suggest two strategies to overcome these flaws: (1) develop an efficient conditional transfer system, which can be achieved by incentivizing the maximization of local revenues collection and avoiding penalization of those who are trying but whose potential is limited and (2) differentiate departments by their capacity and needs to match financial realities and obligations.

---

[4] Colombia is a unitary country made up of three levels of government: national, departments, and municipalities. There are also districts that are municipalities with a higher category, which allows them to have greater powers and resources.

Moreover, Acosta and Bird (2005) proposed a more precise definition of responsibilities in the departments. This issue is not a characteristic of municipalities, which have a clearer delineation of their functions; they also have more financial autonomy. However, it is suggested that municipalities´ performance can improve following strategies (1) and (2) noted above and be complemented with public recognition of outstanding performance. In a nutshell, those authors focus on the balance between power and resources of municipalities and departments to generate a more effective fiscal decentralization.

After a revision of the evolution of municipalities regimes in Colombia, Chaparro et al. (2005) propose (1) the generation of information on local revenue capacity, a source of information that was not consistently available by the time of the mission of Public Income; (2) estimation of the local capacity and revenues; (3) equalization of municipal transfers based on (2); and (4) adjustment of transfers according to fiscal needs. Absent these initiatives, the authors suggest that the designed fiscal distribution would yield undesirable inequalities. They conclude that to achieve regional social expenditures equity and well-being, it is necessary to make fiscal policies clearer and simpler while balancing the needs and capacity of local territories.

Bonet (2006) reviewed the relationship between regional income disparities and decentralization for the period 1990–2000. Using an inter-departmental panel data set, this author finds evidence supporting the thesis that the fiscal decentralization process increased regional income disparities during the period analyzed. This behavior seems to be explained by a set of factors: the allocation of a major portion of the new local resources to current spending (e.g., wages and salaries), instead of capital or infrastructure investments, the lack of a redistributive component in the national transfers, the absence of adequate incentives from the national to the subnational levels to promote an efficient use of them, and the lack of institutional capacity at the subnational governments.

Iregui et al. (2001) review the fiscal scheme of Colombia, and a reform suggested by the draft of a legislative act presented around 2001 to the National Congress. Their analysis suggests that if the national aim is to have long-term territorial equity, transfers subjected to the fluctuating current incomes could favor inter-territorial disequilibria. Moreover, these authors suggest the need for a more straightforward transfer criterion that reflects equity and efficiency; this could be accompanied by updated information, local effort rewards, and greater territorial spending and tax creation.

Bonet (2007) also recognizes the imbalance produced by the fiscal decentralization system operating in Colombia. This author offers three fiscal strategies: (i) the inclusion of a redistributive system of transfers, aiming for additional aid for lagging regions; (ii) strengthening of taxation across territories; and (iii) incentivizing efficiency of local expenses. Additionally, he suggests the creation of an organism responsible for coordinating the public institutions related to decentralization, along with the systematic generation of information. Complementarily, Fernández (2007) proposes promoting austerity and stimulating efforts to increase local revenues, particularly property, industry, and commerce taxes, with an efficient, simple, transparent, and flexible tax system. Cortés and Vargas (2012) further emphasize the need to build rural tax capacity through a cadastral actualization. These authors also put forward the reallocation of the transfer system (SGP[5]) based on social indicator improvements. Furthermore, in contrast to most of the literature, Cortés and Vargas (2012) imply the centralization of royalties from non-renewable natural resources, which should be redistributed to regions after collection.

In the same vein as the previous literature on fiscal decentralization, OECD (2019) advocates for asymmetric decentralization. This document proposes ten comprehensive strategies aiming at a redistribution of powers and revenues of regions in Colombia: (1) reform of the SGP, moving toward territorial equality through its simplification, flexibility, and adaptability to local needs; (2) enhancing of the tax system to stimulate local capacity for collection of revenues, starting with the actualization of cadastral registries; (3) enhancement of human capital of public employees in subnational positions and incentivizing the work of high-quality professionals in remote areas; (4) incentivizing economies of scale, allowing network development between municipalities with the help of already institutionalized laws such as Organic Law Governing the Territorial Organization (LOOT); (5) a coordinated regrouping of municipalities and departments and a reconsideration of the variables considered to define such classifications; (6) conducting experiments, increasing autonomy of municipalities in spending and revenues; (7) supporting areas governed by indigenous with policies that strengthen the outcomes of their autonomy; (8) reinforcing and simplifying the publication of information for monitoring purposes; (9) redefining and clarification of territorial levels functions, avoiding overlaps; and (10) intensifying *Contratos Plan*[6], projects coordinated by the three levels of governance (municipalities–departments–nation), developed to bolster public policy impacts in specific locations. It is also highlighted that of all these suggestions (1) and (2) are crucial.

Figure 2.1 condenses the most common words in the recommendations of the texts of the summarized documentation and other authors including Zapata (2010), Sánchez and Gutiérrez (1994), García (2004), Bonet et al. (2016), and Bonet and Perez (2020). They agree that fiscal decentralization is and has been necessary but imprecise in its formulation in the case of Colombia. The fiscal reforms have failed to meet their primary goal, generating a precarious effect on the equitable distribution of provisions of public services and resources across the Colombian territories. According to this literature, a new direction to territorial fiscal policies should accurately transform the transfer system, local tax system, and local incentives. All these

---

[5] SGP is the main transfer system from the national to the subnational governments in Colombia. See Bonet, Pérez and Ayala (2016) for more details about SGP. –also Chapter 16 talks about this.

[6] *Contratos Plan* legally began with the Laws 1450 of 2011 and the decree 819 of 2012. In the same vein, *Contratos Paz* were created during the government of President Juan Manuel Santos to contribute to adaptation of areas that are more exposed to post conflict. During the government of Iván Duque, *Contratos Plan'* structure was also adapted under the name of *Pactos Territoriales*. Altogether, these initiatives represent three phases toward the regionalization of development and indicate new stages of decentralization (de la Torre, 2020).

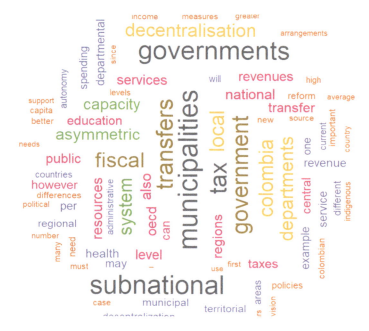

Fig. 2.1 Common words in fiscal policies literature in Colombia

should be informed and adjusted by transparent data, developed in a simple fashion, promote autonomy, be subject to capacity, and be powered up by better education[7].

2.2.2 Administrative Decentralization

2.2.2.1 Health and Education

Funding for health, education, safe drinking water, and basic sanitation have been the primary responsibilities and destinations of the transfers from the national government to departments, municipalities, or districts in Colombia since 1991 (Bonet et al., 2016). This review of the regional administrative policies suggested by the literature in Colombia aligns with these topics. Moreover, most recommendations are directed predominantly to education, as shown in Fig. 2.2.

After a thorough diagnosis of the regional status of education, Sánchez and Otero (2014) conclude that, despite significant improvements in education coverage, its quality is still lagged and unevenly spatially distributed across Colombia. Based on the compilation of studies on education by Sánchez and Otero (2014), Meisel (2014) concludes that education policies in Colombia are generally vague. Meisel

---

[7] Figure 2.1 for key words.

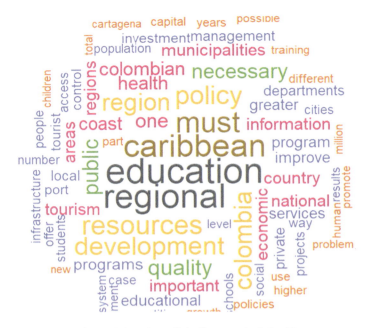

Fig. 2.2 Common words in administrative policies literature in Colombia

also presents four key regional policies targeting the reduction of regional disparities in education. Although suggested for the Caribbean region, it can also be applied to other areas. They are the development of a local focalized program to eliminate illiteracy in the periphery, reduce inequality through the equalization of schooling hours per day, even out and increase the education of teachers in the regions, and make possible education achievement convergence of minorities groups versus others. This vision is shared by Viloria (2007).

Likewise, OECD (2019) concludes that educational decentralization has unleashed response to local needs in a segmented set of municipalities and departments. OECD (2019) proposes that proper education decentralization requires cooperation and coherent strategies toward a common goal to achieve desired goals. Specifically, it highlighted that the fragmentation of autonomy between different entities can produce unsmooth and uneven protection of education from the early stages to advanced stages. A collaboration is suggested to enhance the human and financial capacity of Certified Territorial Entities (CTE)[8], an asymmetric treatment of municipalities, assistance of local offices of the Secretary of Public Education, and development of a shared long-term vision.

---

[8] According to legislation, the territorial entities must follow a certification process to manage the funds for the different sectors. CTE are those who get that certification for the respective ministry. For health, this certification should be approved by the Ministry of Health, for education is the Ministry of Education, and for water and sewage systems is the Ministry of Housing.

In short, most proposals on education regional policy support the relevance of a decentralized structure. By contrast, Cortés and Vargas (2012) provide the only study that implies that decentralization of educational investment might represent a sacrifice of efficiency. These authors propose additional funds for lagged areas, conditional on performance. They were directed explicitly to well-being topics such as education and health. Nevertheless, they propose that it should be accompanied by a national entity monitoring local targets.

Concerning the proposals on regional health policies, Bonet and Guzmán (2017) summarize the consensus on this topic. Drawing on the findings of multiple studies on the topic of health, these authors claim that, as in the case of education, administrative and fiscal decentralization has been important in the process of increasing health system coverage across space. Still, there is not equal quality and availability in all the territories. These authors recommend an asymmetric distribution of public health responsibilities between municipalities in this context. Specifically, they suggest that more intervention from the national government is needed in areas with small populations with low services supply. Also, they suggest planned coordination within an interdepartmental health services network.

2.2.2.2 Miscellaneous Administrative Policies

In a comprehensive assessment of the appropriateness of regional policies aiming to close internal disparities in Colombia, Fernandez et al. (2007) compile the foremost challenges for a regional policy in Colombia from multiple angles. The studies supply explicit regional policies on multiple topics, including demographic, institutional, touristic, port, education, and fiscal policies. The major recommendations offered in this compilation, besides the topics of fiscal and education decentralization already described, follow.

Romero and Meisel (2007) stress four critical elements for a balanced territorial development: (i) a long-term commitment to regional policies, which are sensitive to political instability, integrating them into state policy; (ii) local policies that ought to be shaped by territorial peculiarities, fostering initiatives for equitable opportunities regardless of the place of birth; (iii) homogenize the income per person available for territorial governments through a regional compensation fund; and (iv) to match educational resources across space, standardizing quality, and expenses per student.

In a detailed examination of municipalities, Fenández (2007) reports that these entities suffer from various forms of local administration issues. It is worth clarifying that municipalities represent a crucial instrument for implementing policies at a local scale in Colombia. They have more scope for action compared to departments. Some of Fernandez's recommendations for a better municipality administration are (i) to enhance the provision of public services, targeting not only quantity but also quality; (ii) social housing: make efforts at the local level in partnership with the national government to co-fund housing programs; (iii) security: development of municipal strategic plans, which reduces the rotation of policy directors, prioritization of prevention expenditure, and generation of adequate information systems; (iv) poor and vulnerable population: complement national policies with local initiatives; and (v) planning: the creation of territories associations such as Administrative Regions for Planning (RAP)[9], which would allow the coordination of efforts for a common interest, without the need for creation of other official entities, which would add bureaucracy.

On the tourism front, Aguilera et al. (2007) summarize all the tourism-oriented public policies in Colombia. They conclude that there is a need for a Regional Tourism Agency that would serve as a coordinator between touristic entities from municipalities, districts, and departments to enhance this sector's impact. On the demographic front, Pérez (2007) recommends the promotion and launching of massive municipal programs related to the control of fertility, mainly centered on the most vulnerable populations.

In a different publication, Cortés and Vargas (2012) present five sets of recommendations: state organization, institutions, infrastructure, education, and fiscal policies. On the first three points, they propose the creation of an administrative department devoted to coordinating decentralization, goal tracking, and managing royalties-related projects. In other words, the constitution of a monitoring and control regional organization can be assisted by a departments' classification. It was also recommended that a political reform should be advanced, geared toward the elimination of local preferential votes. Finally, the third set is related to enhancing transportation and other forms of connectivity for dispersed areas.

Regardless of the initiatives designed to equalize opportunities and social conditions across regions, Guerra et al. (2007) claim that it will depend on the efficiency and legitimation of local institutions.

2.2.3 Political Decentralization

Colombia has had a fixed hierarchical political structure since 1991. The political powers are from the top-down: nation, departments, and municipalities. They are governed by the president, governors, and mayors, respectively, all of whom are elected by popular vote. Although the national president has been elected by popular vote since the Republic was constituted, the popular election of mayors was introduced only in 1988 and the governors in 1991. Some initiatives have proposed the institution of regional governors, a new form of power that constitutes regions and is designed to cluster similar departments (FND, 2020a, 06; FND, 2020b, 07). It would aim for the autonomy of regions.

Nevertheless, this vision has not found consensus in the literature. Fernández (2007) and, implicitly, Acosta and Bird (2005) assert that forming an additional level of power in the territorial political administration would produce unnecessary

---

[9] RAP is an alliance between departments to achieve common goals: exploit shared natural resources, develop projects in specific areas, or other initiative based on common infrastructure (FNS, nd).

bureaucracy and inefficiencies. Moreover, according to Álvarez (2020), despite the possibility of creating the idea of regions implicit in the National Constitution (NC) 1991, its formation is not feasible as legally autonomous areas. Some of the ideas on this front suggest the constitution of regions resembling the Spanish model of autonomous provinces. According to Álvarez (2020), it is not viable because the NC defines Colombia as a unitary state, and thus it does not allow federal legislation, as suggested by the Spanish political structure.

Even though decentralization aimed to produce autonomy and local revenue generation to fund social investments and debt service payments and balance opportunities and powers in Colombia, the gains in coverage and quality of public services were not as expected. As shown, there is virtual unanimity in the scholars' opinion regarding the need for fiscal and administrative decentralization. However, local policies ought to be reformed to produce the desired results. In contrast, there is no evidence of general agreement on the changes in the current hierarchical political powers.

2.3 Change in Regional Policy

The Constitution of 1991 represents a breakthrough in the history of decentralization in Colombia. However, other relevant decisions have changed the regional public policy, namely the constitutional reform of 1968, the official establishment of the General Participation System (SGP) in 2001, the Territorial Land Use Law (LOOT) in 2011, and the most recent Regions Law in 2019. They also have been accompanied by small reformations. They have imperfectly paved the way to more autonomous territories and regional asymmetric policy designs.

The first traces of official public policies with regional orientation in Colombia are found in 1968 with the constitutional reform that provided territories some administrative and fiscal freedom and created the *Situado Fiscal*, a transfer from national to subnational governments. During the period pre-1991, very few initiatives with regional designs were implemented in Colombia. Although the importance of spatial differentiation of needs and financial capacities was recognized in the different presidential development plans, limited effective initiatives took place (Moncayo, 2019).

The long-term national plan for a more decentralized country was firmly consolidated with the 1991 national constitution anchor, the allocation of territorial governors' responsibilities with Law 60 in 1993, and the election of local mayors in 1986. Jointly, they constitute a triple decentralization in Colombia: political, fiscal, and administrative. Since 1991, most regulations have been designed to provide more fiscal regional sovereignties, local planning design flexibility, and territorial cooperation and formation (Fig. 2.3). They are thought to be aiming for more equity across space.

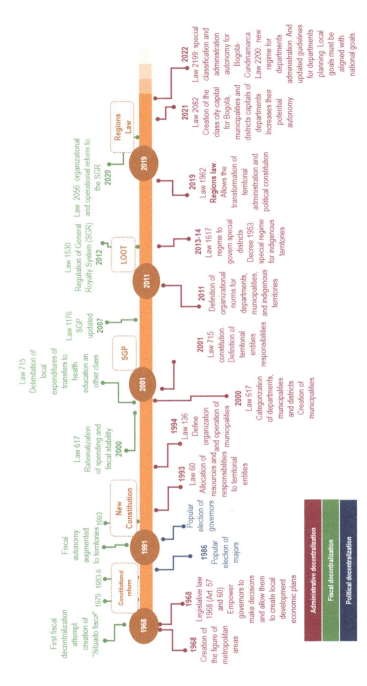

Fig. 2.3 Timeline of fiscal, administrative, and political decentralization initiatives in Colombia (*Source* Based mainly on Garnica (2022) and complemented with Falleti (2010), Moncayo (2019), and Chaparro et al. (2005))

From a summary of the major political decisions in the country, we can conclude that most of the decentralization process has taken place primarily in the administrative arena. A key recent move toward more territorial control and policy independence has been the so-called Regions Law created in 2019. It strengthened the existing regional instruments: the Administrative and Planning Region (RAP) and the Territorial Entity Region (RET). The former represents a temporal association between territories for a common purpose. In other words, departments can partner to manage a specific project of interest to their parts. For instance, development of a project to streamline and monitor the use of a natural park belonging to different administrative territories, such as an association between the departments Caldas, Risaralda, and Quindío to protect Nevado del Ruiz (ejecafeterorap, n.d.).

On the other hand, the RET represents a formal administrative-territorial formation. Another recent national creation like RET and RAP has been the Territorial Covenant (Pactos Territoriales, PT). They were constituted in the national development plan of 2018–2022 and consist of territorial alliances of different levels to develop a financial plan and local policies to foster a high-impact project. For example, the *Golfo de Morrosquillo* PT integrates multiple municipalities from the departments of Córdoba and Sucre, intending to consolidate it as a prime touristic destination in Colombia (DNP, 2020).

Another relevant entity in the process of administrative decentralization in Colombia is the set of government agencies. They represent a kind of diversification of the functions of ministries. During the governments of Uribe I and II, and particularly of Santos I and II, the creation of government agencies was promoted prior to the dismantling of central activities of the ministries or the liquidation of national institutes responsible for essential public policies of the nation, under an apparent new modality of national public management, which was deemed to be more efficient and effective (Moreno, 2020). In contrast to the ministries, national agencies are characterized by their technicality and autonomy (Garrido, 2017). Some examples of these agencies are the National Infrastructure Agency (ANI) and the National Mining Agency (ANM), among others. Other related organizations within the Colombian public policies are the Regional Autonomous Corporations (CAR). They operate as planners and policy managers in environmental and natural resources projects.

Conversely, the most recent decisions, such as Law 2200 from 2022, have limited the administrative decentralization and have required compliance of local decisions/policies to a national plan. It has been suggested by most of the propositional authors on the regional policy in Colombia described. López-Murcia (2021) also underscores that Colombia is under a re-centralization process. This author claims that some recent reforms have restricted the control of transfer expenditures such as for water and sewage systems.

Some evidence of such a re-centralization process may be found in the laws of fiscal responsibility, the reforms of the royalty system, and the creation of organisms like ADRES (Managing Entity of the Resources of the General System of Social Security in Health). ADRES is a specific example of such re-centralization for the case of health. It was created with the Law 1753 of 2015, is attached to the Ministry of Health and Social Protection, and operates autonomously. It centralized the control of funds directed to health, including those of the SGP transferred to departments and municipalities for this sector.

In contrast to administrative decisions, fiscal territorial regulation has been more generous with the national control than subnational entities. According to López-Murcia (2021) and Bonet et al. (2016), the transfers to local governments as a percentage of GDP have decreased within the last decades, evidence of a growing concentration of fiscal power. López-Murcia (2021) hypothesized that it was further enhanced by the SGP rule change in 2001.

It can be concluded from Fig. 2.3 that most of the reforms directed to policies designed to transfer more autonomy to the regions have been administrative. Nonetheless, a series of fiscal reforms has contrasted with the augmented administrative autonomies in recent years.

2.4 Final Considerations

Despite the efforts toward reducing the regional disparities in Colombia, there are persistent regional differences in development and the well-being of the population. The Constitution of 1991 increased decentralization and gave municipalities and departments more autonomy and resources to provide public goods and services. However, it was done without considering the preexisting regional imbalances in tax capacity and fiscal needs. After several decades, the transfer system does not yet fully account for the persistent regional disparities. As a result, for example, the increase in coverage of basic services such as education and health care contrasts with the territorial gap in the quality of those services.

The persistent regional disparities in living standards in Colombia create a demand for public policies that increase convergence in the provision of basic public goods and services. It will require reform to the fiscal transfers system, which currently does not consider the tax revenue capacity resulting from the spatial distribution of economic activity across the country and the differences in fiscal needs, often with strong historical origins. Regional policies should focus on strengthening the capacity of lagging regions to increase fiscal revenue. That would allow them to finance local policies and be involved in joint projects with the central government. On the other hand, some regions face structural constraints in providing the same amount of goods and services due to historical reasons or higher provision costs. It means that the transfer system should consider the expenditure needs and create equalization transfers that do not punish territories with low tax capacity.

To reduce regional disparities, more significant investments should be made in places with lower coverage or quality, and the interventions should be evaluated to measure their impact. The policies should focus on the convergence in living standards and access to publicly provided goods and services across the country, especially in education, health care, drinking water, and sanitation. It can be achieved with local effort complemented by national resources. However, the current decentralization policies in the country are not effective at incentivizing more local tax efforts, which favors wealthier regions where most of the national economic activity is concentrated. Boosting local administrative capacity is difficult but increasing public institutions' human capital in places with low fiscal and administrative performance can produce the desired results.

References

Acosta, O., & Bird, R. (2005). The dilemma of decentralization in Colombia. In R. Bird, J. Poterba, & J. Slemrod (Eds.), *Fiscal reform in Colombia: Problems and prospects* (pp. 247–286). The MIT Press.
Aguilera, M., Bernal, C., & Quintero, P. (2007). Turismo y desarrollo en el Caribe colombiano. In M. Fernández, W. Guerra, & A. Meisel (Eds.), *Políticas para reducir las desigualdades regionales en Colombia* (pp. 320–369). Bogotá D. C., Colombia: Banco de la República de Colombia.
Álvarez, O. (2020). El estado regional y su aplicablidad en Colombia. *Verba Luris, 43*, 249–266.
Barón, J., Pérez, G., & Rowland, P. (2004). A regional economic policy for Colombia. *Revista De Economía Del Rosario, 7*(2), 49–87.
Bird, R., Poterba, J., & Slemrod, J. (2005). *Fiscal reform in Colombia: Problems and prospects*. The MPI Press.
Bonet, J. & Meisel, A. (1999). La convergencia regional en Colombia: una visión de largo plazo, 1926–1995. In *Documentos de Trabajo sobre Economía Regional* (Vol. 8). Banco de la República. Retrieved from https://repositorio.banrep.gov.co/handle/20.500.12134/394
Bonet, J. (2006). Fiscal decentralization and regional income disparities: evidence from the Colombian experience. *The Annals of Regional Science, 40*(3), 661–676.
Bonet, J. (2007). Desequilibrios regional en la política de descentralización en Colombia. In Fernández, Guerra and Meisel (Eds.), *Políticas para reducir las desigualdades regionales en Colombia*. Bogotá: Banco de la República. Retrieved from https://www.banrep.gov.co/sites/default/files/publicaciones/archivos/lbr_desigualdades_regionales.pdf
Bonet, J., Pérez, G. & Ayala, J. (2016). Contexto histórico y evolución del SGP en Colombia. In J. Bonet, & L. A. Galvis (Eds.), *Sistemas de Transferencias Subnacionales: Lecciones para una reforma en Colombia*. Banco de la República-Colección Economía Regional, Cartagena.
Bonet, J., & Guzmán, K. (2017). Un análisis regional de la salud en Colombia. In L. Hahn, J. Bonet, & K. Guzmán (Eds.), *La salud en Colombia: una perspectiva regional* (pp. XI–XXXVI). Bogotá D. C., Colombia: Banco de la República de Colombia.
Bonet, J., Reina, Y. & Ricciulli, D. (2018). Movimientos sociales y desarrollo económico en Chocó y Buenaventura. In *Documentos de Trabajo sobre Economía Regional* (Vol. 270). Banco de la República. Retrieved from https://doi.org/10.32468/dtseru.270
Bonet, J. & Perez, G. (2020). 20 años de estudios sobre el Caribe colombiano. In *Colección de Economía Regional*. Bogotá: Banco de la República de Colombia. Retrieved from https://doi.org/10.32468/Ebook.664-409-9
Cárdenas, M., Pontón, A. & Trujillo, J. (1993). Convergencia y migraciones interdepartamentales en Colombia: 1950–1983. *Coyuntura Económica, 23*(1), 111–137. Retrieved from https://www.repository.fedesarrollo.org.co/handle/11445/2270
Chaparro, J., Smart, M., & Zapata, J. (2005). Intergovernmental transfers and municipal finance in Colombia. In R. Bird, J. Poterba, & J. Slemrod (Eds.), *Fiscal reform in Colombia: Problems and prospects* (pp. 287–318). The MIT Press.
Cortés, D., & Vargas, J. (2012). Inequidad regional en Colombia. *Documentos CEDE, 34*, 1–71.
DNP. (2020). *Pacto Territorial Golfo de Morrosquillo INFORME SEMESTRAL II*.
Ejecafeterorap. (n.d.). *RAP Eje cafetero*. Retrieved from https://ejecafeterorap.gov.co/quienes-somos/

Falleti, T. (2010). *Decentralization and subnational politics in Latin America*. Cambridge University Press.
Fernández, M. (2007). Ciudades bien administradas. In Fernández, Guerra, & Meisel (Eds.), *Políticas para reducir las desigualdades regionales en Colombia*. Bogotá: Banco de la República. Retrieved from https://www.banrep.gov.co/sites/default/files/publicaciones/archivos/lbr_desigualdades_regionales.pdf
Fernández, M., Guerra W. & Meisel, A. (Eds.). (2007). *Políticas para reducir las desigualdades regionales en Colombia*. Bogotá: Banco de la República. Retrieved from https://www.banrep.gov.co/sites/default/files/publicaciones/archivos/lbr_desigualdades_regionales.pdf
FND. (2020a, 06). *Ley de Regiones, la apuesta por la descentralización y autonomía de los departamentos*. Retrieved from Federación Nacional de Departamentos: https://www.fnd.org.co/sala-de-prensa/sala-de-prensa/4698-aniversario-de-la-ley-de-regiones-mensaje-del-presidente-de-la-rep%C3%BAblica-iv%C3%A1n-duque-m%C3%A1rquez.html
FND. (2020b, 07). *Entre descentralización y federalismo*. Retrieved from Federación Nacional de Departamentos: https://www.fnd.org.co/sala-de-prensa/nuestro-director/4751-entre-descentralizaci%C3%B3n-y-federalismo.html
Franco, L. & Raymond, J. (2009). Convergencia económica regional: el caso de los Departamentos colombianos. *Ecos de Economía, 13*(28), 167–197. Retrieved from https://www.redalyc.org/pdf/3290/329027278005.pdf
Galvis, L. & Meisel, A. (2001). El crecimiento económico de las ciudades colombianas y sus determinantes, 1973–1998. *Coyuntura Económica, 31*(1), 69–90. Retrieved from http://hdl.handle.net/11445/2097
Galvis, L. & Meisel, A. (2010). Persistencia de las desigualdades regionales en Colombia: un análisis especial. In *Documentos de Trabajo sobre Economía Regional y Urbana* (Vol. 120). Banco de la República de Colombia, Cartagena.
Galvis, L. & Hahn, L. (2015). Crecimiento municipal en Colombia: el papel de las externalidades espaciales, el capital humano y el capital físico. In *Documentos de Trabajo Sobre Economía Regional y Urbana (DTSERU)* (Vol. 264). Banco de la República – Centro de Estudios Económicos Regionales (CEER), Cartagena de Indias, Colombia. Retrieved from https://doi.org/10.32468/dtseru.216
Galvis, L. (Ed.). (2017). *Estudios sociales del Pacífico colombiano*. Bogotá: Banco de la República.
Galvis, L., Galvis, W. & Hahn, L. (2017). Una revisión de los estudios de convergencia regional en Colombia. In *Documentos de Trabajo Sobre Economía Regional y Urbana (DTSERU)* (Vol. 264). Banco de la República – Centro de Estudios Económicos Regionales (CEER), Cartagena de Indias, Colombia. Retrieved from https://doi.org/10.32468/dtseru.264
García, J. (2004). ¿Por qué la descentralización fiscal? Mecanismos para hacerla efectiva. In *Documentos de Trabajo Sobre Economía Regional* (Vol. 41).
Garnica, L. (2022). *Misión de Descentralización: Construyendo desde las regiones*. [PowerPoint slides] Departamento Nacional de Planeación.
Garrido, M. (2017). Las agencias estatales de naturaleza especial en Colombia- II. *Revista Digital De Derecho Administrativo, 18*, 117–152.
Gómez, C. (2006). Convergencia regional en Colombia: un enfoque en los Agregados Monetarios y en el Sector Exportador. In *Ensayos sobre economía regional* (Vol. 45). Banco de la República. Retrieved from https://doi.org/10.32460/eser.45
Guerra, W., Navarro, J., & Albis, N. (2007). Cultura, instituciones y desarrollo en el Caribe colombiano: Elementos para un debate abierto. In M. Fernández, W. Guerra, & A. Meisel (Eds.), *Políticas para reducir las desigualdades regionales en Colombia* (pp. 118–161). Bogotá D. C., Colombia: Banco de la República de Colombia.
Iregui, A., Ramos, J., & Saavedra, L. (2001). Análisis de la descentralización fiscal en Colombia. *Borradores de Economía*, 1–35.
León, G., & Benavides, H. (2015). Inversión pública en Colombia y sus efectos sobre el crecimiento y la convergencia departamentales. *Dimensión Empresarial, 13*(1), 57–72. https://doi.org/10.15665/rde.v13i1.338

López-Murcia, J. (2021). *Recentralisation in Colombia*. Palgrave Macmillan.

Martínez, C. (2006). Determinantes del PIB per cápita de los departamentos colombianos 1975–2003. In *Archivos de Economía*, núm. 318. Retrieved from https://colaboracion.dnp.gov.co/CDT/Estudios%20Econmicos/318.pdf

Meisel, A. & Pérez, G. (2013). *Las ciudades colombianas y sus atractivos*. Bogotá: Departamento nacional de Planeación (DNP) – Misión del Sistema de Ciudades. Retrieved from https://publicaciones.uexternado.edu.co/media/pageflip/acceso-abierto/pdf/seguimiento-y-analisis-de-politicas-publicas-en-colombia-uext.pdf

Meisel, A. (2014). El sueño de los radicales y las desigualdades regionales en Colombia: la educación de calidad para todos como política de desarrollo regional. In A. Sánchez, & A. Otero (Eds.), *Educación y desarrollo regional en Colombia*. Bogotá D. C., Colombia: Banco de la República de Colombia.

Meisel, A. (2020). Casandra del desarrollo regional La Liga Costeña de 1919. In Universidad del Norte (Ed.), *Colección Roble Amarillo*, Tomo 19. Barranquilla. Retrieved from https://manglar.uninorte.edu.co/bitstream/handle/10584/8852/9789587891980%20eCasandra%20La%20liga%20coste%C3%B1a.pdf?sequence=3

Moncayo, E. (2002). Nuevos enfoques teóricos, evolución de las políticas regionales e impacto territorial de la globalización. In *Serie gestión pública* (Vol. 27). Instituto Latinoamericano y del Caribe de Planificación Económica y Social (ILPES) – CEPAL, Santiago de Chile, Chile. Retrieved from http://hdl.handle.net/11362/7277

Moncayo, E. (2019). Las políticas regionales y la planeación en Colombia: una visión panorámica. Periodo 1958–2018. In C. Soto (ed.), *Seguimiento y análisis de políticas públicas en Colombia* (pp. 135–153). Bogotá D.C.: Universidad Externado de Colombia. Retrieved from https://publicaciones.uexternado.edu.co/media/pageflip/acceso-abierto/pdf/seguimiento-y-analisis-de-politicas-publicas-en-colombia-uext.pdf

Moreno, J. (2020). El estado-agencia en Colombia. *Vademecúm De La Administración Pública*, 2(1), 167–202.

OECD. (2019). Asymmetric decentralization: Policy implications in Colombia. In *OECD Multi-level governance studies*. Retrieved from https://www.oecd.org/colombia/Asymmetric_decentralisation_Colombia.pdf

Pérez, G. (2007). Dinámica demográfica y desarrollo regional en Colombia. In M. Fernández, W. Guerra, & A. Meisel (Eds.), *Políticas para reducir las desigualdades regionales en Colombia* (pp. 163–211). Bogotá D. C., Colombia: Banco de la República de Colombia.

Pérez, G. & Rowland, P. (2004). A regional economic policy for Colombia. In *Borradores de economía* (Vol. 301). Banco de la República, Bogotá, D.C., Colombia. Retrieved from https://repositorio.banrep.gov.co/bitstream/handle/20.500.12134/5319/be_301.pdf

Romero, J., & Meisel, A. (2007). Igualdad de oportunidades para todas las regiones. In M. Fernández, W. Guerra, & A. Meisel (Eds.), *Políticas para reducir las desigualdades regionales en Colombia* (pp. 14–43). Bogotá D. C., Colombia: Banco de la República de Colombia.

Royuela, V., & García, G. (2015). Economic and social convergence in Colombia. *Regional Studies*, 49(2), 219–239. https://doi.org/10.1080/00343404.2012.762086

Sánchez, F., & Gutierrez, C. (1994). La descentralización fiscal en Colombia: problemas y perspectivas. In *Informe fedesarrollo*.

Sánchez, A., & Otero, A. (2014). *Educación y desarrollo regional en Colombia*. Bogotá D. C., Colombia: Banco de la República de Colombia.

Schneider, A. (2003). Decentralization: Conceptualization and measurement. *Studies in Comparative International Development*, 38, 32–56.

Viloria, J. (2007). Políticas para transformar el capital humano en el Caribe colombiano. In M. Fernández, W. Guerra-Curvelo, & A. Meisel-Roca (Eds.), *Políticas para reducir las desigualdades regionales en Colombia* (pp. 82–116). Bogotá D. C., Colombia: Banco de la República de Colombia.

Zapata, J. (2010). Las finanzas territoriales en Colombia. In *Documento de Trabajo*. Bogotá: Fedesarrollo.

Jaime Bonet is an economist from the Universidad de Los Andes in Bogotá with a master's degree in economics and a Ph.D. in regional planning from the University of Illinois at Urbana-Champaign. His research areas include regional and urban economics, local public finance, local economic development, and regional development history in Colombia. He is the Director of the Center for Regional Economics Studies (CEER) at the Banco de la República, Colombia.

Karina Acosta Ph.D. in Regional Science, Cornell University. Junior researcher at the Center for Regional Economic Studies (CEER) at the Banco de la República, Colombia. Her research interest lies at the intersection of development, spatial statistics, and demography. She has published book chapters and academic journal articles on development and regional economics, and demographic transition.

Gerson Javier Pérez-Valbuena Ph.D. in economics, University of Essex (United Kingdom). Senior Researcher at the Center for Regional Economic Studies (CEER) at the Banco de la República, Colombia. He has published several articles and book chapters on topics related to regional and urban economics and subnational public finances.

Jhorland Ayala-García economist from the Universidad Tecnológica de Bolívar, MA in Economics from the Universidad de los Andes, and Ph.D. in Applied Economics from the University of Illinois at Urbana-Champaign. Junior researcher at the Center for Regional Economic Studies (CEER) at the Banco de la República, Colombia. His research area includes regional economics, public economics, local public finances, local government quality, and environmental economics.

Chapter 3
Income Inequalities in Colombia

Leonardo Bonilla, Luis Armando Galvis-Aponte, Andrea Otero-Cortés, and Diana Ricciulli

3.1 Introduction

The living conditions currently enjoyed by humanity are better than those of our ancestors (Kenny, 2012). Today, most people, on average, enjoy greater longevity and complete more years of education (Becker et al., 2005; Deaton, 2015). Significant progress has also been made regarding political, economic, and human rights freedoms (Deaton, 2015). In most countries, life expectancy continues to increase at a rate that has not changed significantly in the last 200 years; people are spending more time living and less time suffering from chronic diseases (Ridley, 2010). However, because of wide inequalities, not all individuals similarly enjoy these benefits and comforts.

Latin America is listed as one of the most unequal regions in the world (Kliksberg, 2005), a condition that has persisted over time (López-Calva & Lustig, 2010). In the 2000s, however, improvements in this area were observed in several countries of the continent (Lustig, 2020; Messina & Silva, 2018); Colombia was no stranger to that trend. As measured using the Gini coefficient, inequality in total income fell in the country from 0.57 in 2002 to 0.53 in 2019.

This chapter studies the determinants of changes in labor and non-labor income inequality from a microeconomic perspective to answer the question: what are the determinants of the change in income inequality in the 2010s? To do this, a microdecomposition methodology is used following Bourguignon and Ferreira (2005),

---

Parts of this document are reproduced from previous work published in the journal Ensayos Sobre Política Económica #101, Banco de la República. Special thanks to Roberto Gómez for his assistance during the preparation of this manuscript.

L. A. Galvis-Aponte (✉) · A. Otero-Cortés · D. Ricciulli
Banco de la República, Cartagena, Colombia
e-mail: lgalviap@banrep.gov.co

L. Bonilla
Banco de la República, Medellín, Colombia

© The Author(s), under exclusive license to Springer Nature Switzerland AG 2023
E. A. Haddad et al. (eds.), *The Colombian Economy and Its Regional Structural Challenges*, Advances in Spatial Science, https://doi.org/10.1007/978-3-031-22653-3_3

comparing changes in income distribution over time. We use the microdata from the Integrated Household Survey (GEIH).

The results show that reductions in inequality are mainly associated with labor-related components. This reduction is primarily due to changes in returns to education and the stock of human capital. In the non-labor income component, there is an important share of rents, which in most cases acts as an equalizing factor.

The chapter is divided into four additional sections. Section 3.1 characterizes inequalities in Colombia. Section 3.2 summarizes the methodological approach used to break down changes in inequalities. Section 3.3 shows the decomposition results for the national total and by cities, identifying what factors explain the fall in inequalities in total income between 2010 and 2019. Finally, Sect. 3.4 concludes and discusses the implications of economic policy.

3.2 Stylized Facts of the Inequalities in Colombia

Colombia, for several decades, has been known to experience the persistent problem of inequalities (Galvis & Meisel, 2010). Figure 3.1 reconstructs the Gini coefficient series to document these considerations with data from major cities. It is observed that until 2010, inequality had been increasing, reaching record figures in that period, but in the last decade, this trend changed.

The behavior of inequality shown in the graph is part of the motivation to investigate what factors contributed to this reduction. Notice, however, that income inequality has not been reduced at the same rate or by the same magnitude throughout the national territory. In other words, between 2010 and 2019, although there was

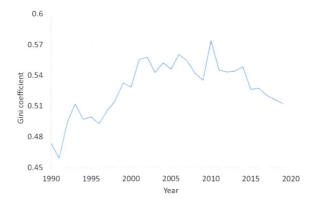

Fig. 3.1 Gini coefficient of labor income. Average for seven cities, 1990–2019 (*Note* The graph shows figures only for the seven major cities because data for the 23 cities are not available for the entire period represented. The Gini coefficient (G) measures how far a distribution moves away from the equidistribution measure, $G = 0$, or total concentration, $G = 1$) (*Source* Authors' elaboration based on DNP and DANE)

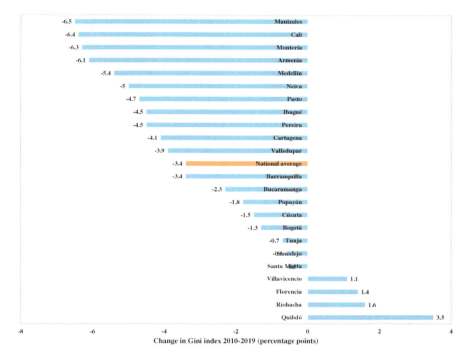

Fig. 3.2 Change in the Gini index of total income by city, 2010–2019 (*Source* Authors' elaboration based on DANE (GEIH))

a significant drop in national inequality and in most of the capital cities, within the main cities, this was heterogeneous in magnitude. For example, in Florencia, Quibdó, Riohacha, and Villavicencio, there were increases in inequality. In five capital cities (Cali, Armenia, Montería, Manizales, and Medellín), inequality fell by more than 5 pp, significantly greater than the 3.4 pp drop we observed for the national total (Fig. 3.2).

Along these lines, it is important to understand what factors contributed to decreasing or increasing inequality in each city studied to improve public policy targeting. In addition, the factors associated with this decrease in inequalities are not the same throughout the country since there are disparities in access to highly ranked universities according to the department of origin (Laajaj et al., 2018) or the socioeconomic stratum of the individual (Londoño-Vélez et al., 2017); regional gender gaps in wage distribution (Galvis, 2010); regional differences in the likelihood of employment in informal jobs (Arango et al., 2020); as well as divergence in regional unemployment rates (Díaz, 2016). That is why the study is carried out for the national total and the 23 main cities and their metropolitan areas (Appendix Fig. 3.16).

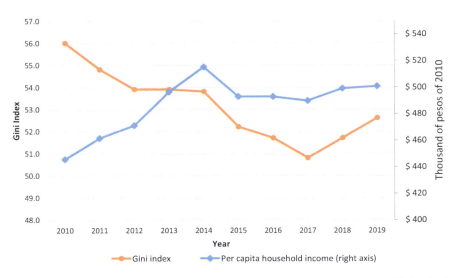

Fig. 3.3 Gini index versus per capita income for the national total (thousands of pesos 2010 values) (*Source* Authors' elaboration based on DANE (GEIH))

3.2.1 Changes in Inequalities in the 2010s

Colombia began the twenty-first century experiencing a decline in income inequalities, which deepened during the 2010s. Specifically, the Gini coefficient went from 0.56 to 0.51 between 2010 and 2017. This indicator increased slightly at the end of the decade, with a figure of 0.53 in 2019. On the other hand, an increase in households' real per capita income was also observed in 2010–2019, growing at an average annual rate of over 1% (Fig. 3.3).

At the same time, the percentage of people living in monetary poverty in Colombia declined from 49.7% in 2002 to 27.0% in 2018, and extreme poverty fell from 17.7 to 7.2% during this same period. In other words, real per capita household income increased between 2010 and 2014 and, despite lower dynamics up to 2019, did not experience reductions compared to the figures for the early 2010s (Fig. 3.3). That is, inequalities were reduced in that decade, and on average, income increased.[1]

---

[1] When studying the relationship between inequalities and poverty in the national total, it is also found that falls in the Gini index are accompanied by reductions in monetary poverty. In the regional detail, it is found that some cities do present increases in monetary poverty in the 2010s. Such is the case of Bucaramanga, Cúcuta and Riohacha, and, marginally, of Valledupar.

3.2.2 Factors Associated with Changes in Inequalities

Several factors have been highlighted in the literature as determinants of lower-income inequality in Latin American countries, from labor, demographic, and educational variables to tax policies and monetary transfers to households (Lustig, 2020; Messina & Silva, 2018). From a series of descriptive statistics, the subsections below present the behavior of some of these factors for the Colombian case, providing some intuition about their impact on the fall in inequality. The analysis is disaggregated by income quintiles to deepen our understanding of the possible heterogeneity in these changes.

3.2.2.1 Labor Income

Figure 3.4 presents the average salary of Colombians by income quintiles for 2010 and 2019 and the percentage change between these two years. As can be seen, while the two lowest quintiles experienced an increase in their salaries of 15.7 and 16.9%, in the highest quintile, the variation was close to 0% (−0.4%; Fig. 3.4).

This reduction in wage gaps is partly explained by a fall in wage premiums by educational level. While the wages of people with primary school or less increased by 2.6% between 2010 and 2019, for those with technical or technological education and with a university or postgraduate degree, wages fell by − 10.1 and − 8.8%, respectively (Fig. 3.5). The smallest variation was observed in the salaries of those with secondary education, which experienced an increase of 0.8%.

Parallel to this change in salaries by educational level, or what is known in the literature as educational premiums, Colombians have managed in recent decades to increase school attainment considerably. According to data from the GEIH, between

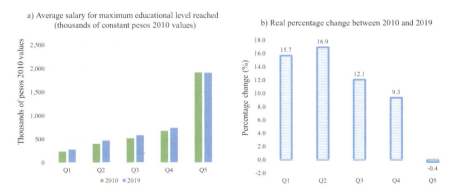

Fig. 3.4 Average monthly salary by income quintiles, 2010 and 2019 (*Note* This graph takes the total income to calculate the distribution by quintiles and, from those figures that mark the separation between quintiles, the average salary is calculated in thousands of pesos in 2010) (*Source* Authors' elaboration based on DANE (GEIH))

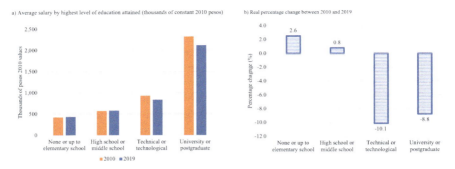

Fig. 3.5 Average monthly salary by educational level, 2010 and 2019 (*Note* The average wage is calculated by including labor income by educational level and is deflated at 2010 prices using the consumer price index (CPI)) (*Source* Authors' elaboration based on DANE (GEIH))

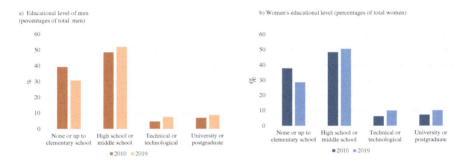

Fig. 3.6 Changes in educational level, 2010 and 2019 (*Source* Authors' elaboration based on DANE (GEIH))

2010 and 2019, there was a fall in the percentage of people without education or with only primary school, while the percentage who managed to finish secondary, or obtain some higher education degree, increased (Fig. 3.6). In the case of men, there is a reduction of 8.4 percentage points (pp) in the group without education or with only primary school, and an increase in those with secondary education, technical, and with a university or postgraduate degree of 3.6, 2.9 and 1.9 pp, respectively. In the case of women, the fall is like that of men in the group with less education (−9.1), but greater increases are observed for the case of higher education, with an increase of 3.8 pp in those with a technical or technological degree and 3 pp in the group with university or postgraduate education. This phenomenon has resulted in an abundance of workers with a higher education degree, which could contribute to the fall in wages observed for this population group between 2010 and 2019. The fall in wages may also be the result of more people entering these ranks but at entry-level wages, thereby depressing median wage levels.

Behind these trends are decades of public policies focused on strengthening access to education in Colombia. According to Delgado (2014), in the early years of the twenty-first century, there was a significant increase in spending on education as a proportion of gross domestic product (GDP) in Colombia, reaching figures higher than those observed in countries such as Argentina, Brazil, Mexico, Chile, the USA, and even some European countries (OECD, 2013). In the case of basic and secondary education, transfers from the General Participation System (GPS) became its primary source of financing, with stable growth and independent of the economic and fiscal conditions of the country. In addition, the decision to allocate these resources based on the population served, and to be served, contributed to the accelerated increase in coverage at these levels (Delgado, 2014).

In the case of tertiary education, in the last decade, the educational credit programs offered by the Colombian Institute of Educational Credit and Technical Studies Abroad (Icetex) have been strengthened, which facilitates access to higher education institutions and improves the financial conditions of the loans offered to students (Melo et al., 2017). In addition, the National Learning Service (SENA) has prioritized access to technical and technological education. In particular, according to Melo et al. (2017), between 2000 and 2014, the number of students enrolled in technical and technological education went from 152,324 to 713,500, where SENA offered 60% of the places in this last year.

The increasing access to secondary and tertiary education also coincides with fertility rates fall. Figure 3.7 reveals that while the percentage of households without children increased by 6.1 pp between 2010 and 2019, the percentage of households with three or more children fell by 6.4 pp. The World Bank (2011) relates this phenomenon in Latin America to changes in income distribution and finds that this fall in fertility rates has been particularly concentrated in lower-income households, which reduces indicators of economic dependence and, in general, improves the economic and labor situation of these households.

Finally, the reduction in the wage gap observed in Fig. 3.4 could also be associated with a greater number of the employed population, better employability conditions, or changes in the number of hours worked. For example, the wage increase in the lowest quintile of the distribution would be associated with a greater number of hours

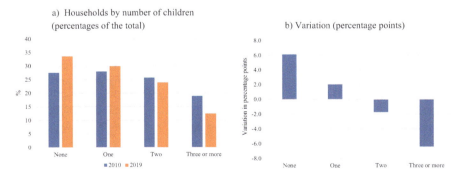

Fig. 3.7 Number of children in the household, 2010 and 2019 (*Source* Authors' elaboration based on DANE (GEIH))

Fig. 3.8 Average hours worked per week by income quintile, 2010 and 2019 (*Source* Authors' elaboration based on DANE (GEIH))

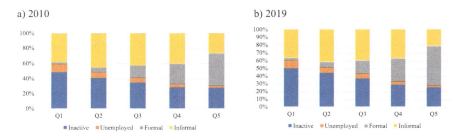

Fig. 3.9 Composition of the working-age population, 2010 and 2019 (Note The classification of informality is made following the institutionalist definition, according to which informal workers are those who do not make contributions to the social security system, specifically to pensions) (*Source* Authors' elaboration based on DANE (GEIH))

worked. To assess the changes in these dimensions, we explore the hours worked on a weekly average (Fig. 3.8) and the composition of the working-age population for 2010 and 2019 (Fig. 3.9). In the first case, there are no significant changes in the average number of hours worked between 2010 and 2019. While in quintile 1 of income, the average hours worked per week remains around 40, quintile 5 remains at around 47 h. Overall, despite a slight reduction between 2010 and 2019, this drop is common for all income quintiles, indicating that the reduction in the wage gap or the observed increase in labor income for the lowest quintile is not explained by a differential change in the number of hours worked across the distribution.

Similarly, the composition of the working-age population between 2010 and 2019 does not show significant transformations. In both years, a higher percentage of the inactive or unemployed population is observed in the lowest income quintile (about

60%), compared to about 30% in the highest quintile. It is also observed that there is an increase in the formal population, with a respective decrease in informality. This move to formality, likely contributing to the reduction of inequalities starting in 2010, took place partly because of policy decisions on payroll taxes.[2]

3.2.2.2 Non-Labor Income

Non-labor income is also an important share of the budget of Colombian households. It comprises rental income, pensions, and transfers from other households in Colombia and abroad (remittances), and institutional transfers. Figure 3.10 presents the average income received for each component, which has a private origin, according to income quintiles for 2010 and 2019. As can be seen, in all cases, the average income in these areas increased for the lowest quintiles, while in the highest, the average falls.

In the case of rental income, in the lowest quintile, the average received increased by 26.1%, while in the highest quintile, it decreased by 16.3%. The data from GEIH also shows that in 2019 there was a relative increase in the number of people renting a room or part of a house. This is particularly noticeable in households that are in quintiles 1 and 2 of the income distribution. This phenomenon has been documented in studies such as that of Camargo (2020), who finds that one of the most common practices in low-income neighborhoods is the conception of housing as an asset that generates additional resources through the rental or installation of businesses, that is, a house offers complementary income. Parias-Durán (2020), in a survey applied to informal neighborhoods in Bogotá D.C, finds that 36% of renters pay for a small bedroom or part of a house. This represents a source of additional income in addition to labor income, whose rental fee is close to a third of the minimum wage. Therefore, these factors are expected to have improved incomes, especially at the bottom of the distribution, and will contribute to reducing inequality.

Regarding pension income, in the lower part of the distribution, the average increased by 5.5%, and in the upper part, it fell by 8.7%. Finally, in the income corresponding to transfers from other households in Colombia and remittances, in quintile 1, the average increased by 10.7%, and in quintile 5, it fell by 26.5%.

Within non-labor income, the item with the greatest probability of reducing income inequalities in Latin America is conditional cash transfers to households (Cecchini & Atuesta, 2017). In particular, Lustig (2020) points out two benefits of these programs: first, to increase in the short term the incomes of the most vulnerable

---

[2] On the increase in formality from the policies of incentives via payroll taxes, the literature indicates that the reduction by 13.5 pp of employers' social security contributions in favor of their employees, proposed by the Tax Reform of 2012, had a positive effect on formal employment (Bernal et al., 2017; Fernández & Villar, 2017; Morales & Medina, 2017). On the other hand, Samaniego de la Parra, Otero and Morales (2021) also find positive effects on formality derived from the promulgation of Decree 2616 of 2013. With this decree, the formal hiring of part-time workers was made more flexible, which allowed social security contributions to be made for weeks without requiring low-income workers to migrate from the subsidized health system to the contributory regime.

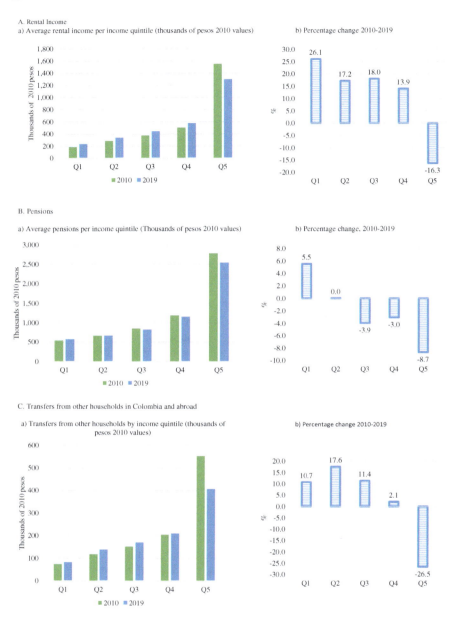

Fig. 3.10 Non-labor income by income quintiles, 2010 and 2019 (*Source* Authors' elaboration based on DANE (GEIH))

households and mitigate their impact in the face of unexpected economic shocks; and second, through their conditioning to the use of certain social services, they have a positive impact on health and education and, as a consequence, on the accumulation of human capital in the long term.

As in Latin America, in Colombia, conditional transfer programs have played a leading role in social policy in recent decades (Urrutia & Robles-Báez, 2021). The introduction of this type of program, after the economic fall of the late 1990s, made it possible to compensate for the loss of income that households had suffered during the crisis and, in turn, to guarantee the development of the human capital of children (Llano, 2014). These first appeared in 2001 through the programs known as conditional cash transfers and training for unemployed youth, which later became "Más Familias en Acción" (MFEA) and "Jóvenes en Acción" (JEA).

In the case of MFEA, this program consists of monetary transfers to households, conditional on children's attendance in schools and regular medical check-ups (Llano, 2014). The program JEA focuses on young people between 16 and 24 years old in conditions of poverty, and its primary purpose is for this population group to continue its educational formation process. One of the latter conditions is to be enrolled in a higher education institution or the SENA (Núñez et al., 2020). Finally, another important cash transfer program of the last decade is "Colombia Mayor" (CM), which is designed for older adults who do not have access to a pension or income and who are classified as vulnerable according to the information provided by the Identification System for Potential Beneficiaries of Social Programs (SISBEN) (Núñez et al., 2020). SISBEN is a poverty targeting system.

To provide an approach to the current situation of these programs and their evolution in the 2010s, Fig. 3.11 presents the percentage of households that received income from transfers of public or private institutions in 2010 and 2019. As can be seen, the most significant increases occurred in households at the bottom of the income distribution. In the case of the first quintile, the percentage of households receiving transfers from institutions went from 20.6% in 2010 to 34.9% in 2019. In contrast, households receiving such transfers in quintile 5 were 1.4% and 1.7% in 2010 and 2019.

The GEIH data for 2010 does not allow disaggregating the transfers received by households between public and private or according to the different programs that make up the group of public transfers. However, for the year 2019, it is possible to carry out this separation. Figure 3.11 shows the percentage of households receiving public and private transfers in 2019 and the percentage receiving transfers through each of the major government programs mentioned. Panel A reveals that the percentage of households receiving public transfers significantly exceeds those receiving private transfers in all income quintiles. For example, in the case of income quintile 1, the proportion of households that received public transfers was 31.1% in 2019, and in the case of households receiving private transfers, it was only 0.2%. This would indicate that public transfer programs have led to the observed changes in coverage between 2010 and 2019.

Regarding public transfer programs (Fig. 3.12, panel B), MFEA takes the largest share, with coverage of 15.1 and 16.3% in households in quintiles 1 and 2. This is

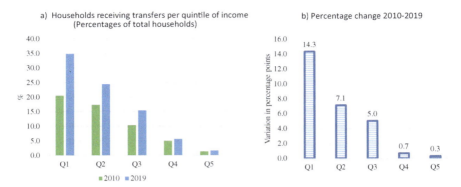

Fig. 3.11 Percentage of households receiving transfers from public and private institutions, 2010 and 2019 (*Source* Authors' elaboration based on DANE (GEIH))

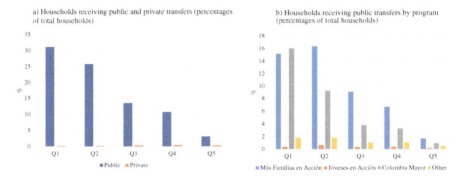

Fig. 3.12 Percentage of households receiving transfers by a source of resources, 2019 (*Source* Authors' elaboration based on DANE (GEIH))

followed by CM, with 16.0 and 9.4% of households in these same quintiles, and JEA, with a coverage of 0.3% and 0.6% of households in these income groups.

The descriptive statistics presented in this section point to several relevant factors when explaining Colombia's fall in inequality between 2010 and 2019. Wages appear to play a crucial role through an increase in the educational level of the population and the reduction of educational bonuses. On the other hand, within non-labor income, public transfer programs appear as the central axis of social policy in the last decade, with a progressive effect on income distribution. Similarly, the income from leases, pensions, and transfers from other households, points in the same direction, with greater progressivity over the past decade.

On pensions, specifically, they are expected to have contributed to reducing inequalities, as an effect of the change in composition shown in Fig. 3.10 (panel B). This variation in pensions may be due to institutional factors such as readjustments in the minimum wage, which guide the changes in minimum pensions, compared to the variation in inflation, a rate from which readjustments in pensions of greater value are

Fig. 3.13 Inflation rate and minimum wage change, 2010–2019 (*Note* Inflation is calculated as the annual growth rate of the CPI as of December of each year) (*Source* Authors' elaboration based on DANE)

defined. Specifically, changes in the minimum wage have outpaced inflation adjustments (Fig. 3.13), so this may have been a contributing factor to the progressivity in pension income. For the rest of the individuals who are active in the labor market, increases in the minimum wage could reduce inequality to the extent that they bring a large portion of the population that earns it, on average, closer to the incomes of those at the top of the distribution.

The effects of the minimum wage on inequality are, however, questions that require more detailed research. The academic literature has shown that there are indeed nonnegligible effects. In particular, the introduction of the minimum wage in Germany in 2015 accounts for about 50% of the reduction in subsequent wage inequalities (Bossler & Schank, 2020). In Colombia, the increased hiring in the formal sector of the economy, with wages equal to or above the minimum, has contributed to the reduction of regional wage gaps (Herrera-Idárraga et al., 2021). The effects of increases in the minimum wage on inequality have also been documented in countries as inequitable as Brazil (Sotomayor, 2021).

3.3 Data and Methodology

To evaluate the relevance of the different factors mentioned in the change in inequality between 2010 and 2019, the micro-decomposition methodology proposed by Bourguignon and Ferreira (2005) is followed. In previous studies for Colombia, this methodology was used to identify differences in the determinants of income distribution comparing the major cities to Bogotá D.C (Bonilla, 2009), as well as to explore the factors explaining the changes in income inequality in Colombia between 1978 and 1995 (Velez et al., 2005).

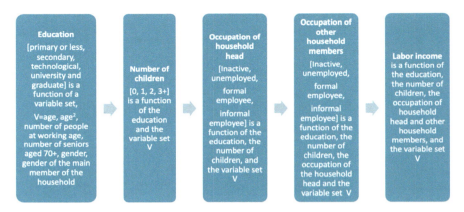

Fig. 3.14 Flow diagram of the estimation of labor income

In the first stage, individuals' labor income $\left(Y_{it}^L\right)$ is estimated as a function of several observable features (X_{it}) and parameters (β_t) for the years 2010 and 2019. In the second stage, simulations of wages are performed by exchanging the characteristics and parameters of t (2010) with the characteristics and parameters of t' (2019). In particular, following the patterns observed in the descriptive statistics of the previous section, simulations are carried out based on the methodology of Bourguignon and Ferreira (2005) through multinomial variables regarding educational level, the number of children, the occupation of the head of the household and other members of the household, and, finally, the income derived from the occupation based on the previous decisions.

At each stage, the level reached by the modeled variable is predicted and included as an explanatory factor in the following equation to be estimated, along with the other covariates described in Fig. 3.14.

In each category, the following random utilities associated with each alternative are considered, always taking alternative 1 as the base category and exchanging the parameters of t (2010) with those of t' (2019):

$$\begin{Bmatrix} U_{1,i} = 0 \\ U_{2,i} = X_{2,i}\beta_2 + \varepsilon_{2,i} \\ U_{3,i} = X_{3,i}\beta_3 + \varepsilon_{3i} \\ U_{4,i} = X_{4,i}\beta_4 + \varepsilon_{4i} \end{Bmatrix} \tag{3.1}$$

In each case, the individual will choose the alternative that generates the greatest utility. However, to know the value of each utility, it is necessary to calculate the errors associated with each one. To do this, we start by estimating the multinomial logit model for the base year t and calculate the linear predictions $\left(X_k\hat{\beta}_k\right)$ and probabilities of each alternative $\left(P_{k,i}\right)$. Based on these calculations, the steps proposed by Train and Wilson (2008) are followed to simulate errors.

We start from the function of distribution of the errors type extreme value, conditioned in the choice of the alternative k:

$$F(\varepsilon_k | D_i = k) = \exp\left(-\frac{1}{P_{k,i}}\exp(\varepsilon_k)\right) \qquad (3.2)$$

By calculating the inverse of this distribution, the estimated errors of the selected alternative are obtained:

$$\widehat{\varepsilon_k} = \ln\left(\frac{1}{P_{k,i}}\right) - \ln(-\ln(\mu)) \qquad (3.3)$$

where μ represents a random probability obtained from a uniform distribution. The errors of the rest of the alternatives j can be estimated from the error of the alternative k as follows:

$$\widehat{\varepsilon_k} = -\ln\left(-\ln\left(m\left(\widehat{\varepsilon_k}\right)\mu\right)\right) \qquad (3.4)$$

With $m\left(\widehat{\varepsilon_k}\right) = \exp\left(-\exp\left(-\left(V_{kj} + \varepsilon_k\right)\right)\right)$
with $V_{kj} = X_k\widehat{\beta_k} - X_j\widehat{\beta_j} V_{kj} = X_k\widehat{\beta_k} - X_j\widehat{\beta_j}$

For more details on error simulation, refer to the appendix by Train and Wilson (2008).

Estimates are made separately for men and women and include the following variables in the vector of observable characteristics (X_{it}): the maximum level of education attained, age, age squared, whether the person is head of the household, whether the individual has an informal occupation, and the number of children in the household.

$$Y_{it}^L = F(X_{it}, \beta_t, \varepsilon_{it}) \qquad (3.5)$$

The main challenge in estimating Eq. (3.5) is what is known as the selection bias problem, which is associated with the non-random absence of observations in the sample (in this case, of observations corresponding to individuals who do not receive a salary). This selectivity in the sample generates a bias in the coefficients and is equivalent to omitting relevant variables from the analysis. The equations are estimated using a two-stage Heckman regression model to address this problem. In the first one, the probability of receiving a salary is estimated, and the inverse of the Mills ratio, λ_i, is calculated as follows: $\lambda_i = \phi(Z_i)/(1 - \Phi(Z_i))$, where ϕ and Φ are the probability density functions and the cumulative density, respectively. In the second stage, the equation of the logarithm of wages is estimated by ordinary least squares, including as an additional regressor the term of correction of bias is selected, λ_i.

A first simulation consists of calculating the counterfactual of the 2010 income as if the characteristics of 2019 held. To do this, we predict the values of the equations estimated in 2010, using the coefficients that were obtained for 2019:

$$Y_{it}^L(\boldsymbol{\beta}_{t'}) = F(X_{it}, \boldsymbol{\beta}_{t'}, \varepsilon_{it}) \qquad (3.6)$$

The scenario in which the distribution of the endowments of the year 2019, $X_{it'}$, is used is also considered to simulate the income that would have been generated if this distribution had been observed in 2010:

$$Y_{it}^L(\boldsymbol{X}_{it'}) = F(\boldsymbol{X}_{it'}, \beta_{t'}, \varepsilon_{it}) \qquad (3.7)$$

Finally, all these aggregate changes are simulated to assess the joint effect of the change in household labor income between 2010 and 2019 (Eq. (3.8)).

$$Y_{it}^L(\boldsymbol{X}_{it'}, \boldsymbol{\beta}_{t'}) = F(\boldsymbol{X}_{it'}, \boldsymbol{\beta}_{t'}, \varepsilon_{it}) \qquad (3.8)$$

To simulate the changes in the decisions of educational level and the number of children within the vector $X_{it'}$, the sequential estimate proposed by Bourguignon and Ferreira (2005) is followed, where individuals initially decide their educational level (none or even primary; up to secondary or middle; technical or technological; university or postgraduate); then, the number of children (none; one; two; three or more), and finally, they make their occupation decisions (inactive; unemployed; formally employed; informally occupied). As illustrated in Fig. 3.14, at each stage, the result of the decisions of the previous stages and a vector of variables are included as independent variables V_{it}, which includes demographic variables, such as age, gender, number of people of working age, and the number of adults over the age of 70. These simulations are performed using multinomial logit regression models. In the last stage, we model the logarithm of wages according to their determinants, which in the literature is known as Mincer's equation.

On the other hand, and following the same methodology used for the wages, estimates and simulations of aggregate non-labor income, Y_{ht}^K, and its most important items are made, i.e., rental income, pensions, transfers from public and private institutions, and transfers from other households.

$$Y_{ht}^K = F(X_{ht}, \beta_t, \varepsilon_{ht}) \qquad (3.9)$$

In this case, Y_{ht}^K refers to the per capita income of the household in item K of non-labor income. In addition, the estimation of this component involves an additional step, in which the probability of receiving each item of non-labor income is predicted (Fig. 3.15). Using this prediction, the simulations are carried out, starting with the households that are most likely to receive the non-labor income until reaching the percentage of households in the entire 2019 sample that effectively receives income for this category.

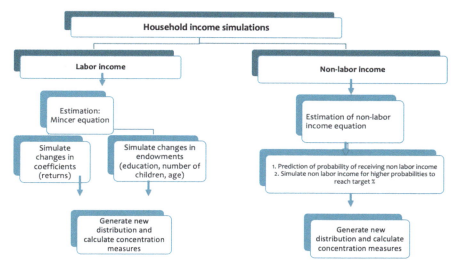

Fig. 3.15 Household income simulations

Finally, the new per capita income of the household (Eq. (3.10)) and the counterfactual distributions that allow knowing the change in inequality explained by each of the factors analyzed are calculated. In general, the final purpose is to know the sign and magnitude in which each factor mentioned affects income distribution, measured with the Gini coefficient.

$$Y_{ht} = \left[\frac{1}{N}\sum_{i=1}^{N} Y_{it}^{L}\right] + \sum_{k=1}^{K} Y_{ht}^{k} \tag{3.10}$$

Alternative methods of decomposition of change in inequalities are widely used in the literature. One of them is that of Pyatt (1976), which allows for calculating the decomposition by groups of individuals. For their part, Lerman and Yitzhaki (1985) propose a methodology to measure how sources of income affect inequality. Likewise, the approach of Azevedo et al., (2013) also follows the line of decomposition disaggregated by components, in which the possible variations of inequality between two years can be explained by changes in different elements, such as labor income, pensions, transfers, capital income, among others. An advantage of the proposal of Bourguignon and Ferreira (2005) is that the factors that drive changes in these sources of income are considered not to be exogenous and therefore include explicit modeling of their behavior.

To apply the above methodology, data from household surveys are used, specifically from DANE's survey GEIH. The main limitation of measuring inequality with this source is the deficient way this database captures income at the upper end of the distribution, mainly income from capital, which represents a significant proportion of the income of the wealthiest population (Lustig, 2020). In general, the literature on the subject indicates that inequality is higher than that estimated by household surveys when incorporating information from other administrative sources and national accounts (Lustig, 2020). Given these limitations, it is important to clarify that the analysis presented below refers to labor and non-labor income inequality, disregarding a critical part of the latter item corresponding to capital income.

Another source of inaccuracies in calculations arises when some individuals reject the question about labor income, as some information that may affect calculations of inequalities may be censored. In the information used in the calculations, it was found that in 2010 0.4% of the employed did not report labor income. In 2019, that figure was 0.5%. It is assumed, in this case, that these omitted data do not have any deterministic pattern as to their distribution among the income quintiles.

Similarly, it should be borne in mind that the analysis is relevant to urban inequalities, presumably greater than those in rural areas. However, in rural areas, the problem of land concentration involves additional elements to consider in modeling that may well be deepened in future work.

It is important to clarify that the methodology adopted may have some limitations for the analysis. In the first instance, the analysis aims not to identify causal effects. The estimates correspond to a reduced form and not a general equilibrium model. In addition, it is assumed that individuals make decisions starting from the most exogenous variables following the semi-endogenous ones without considering any recursive patterns (for instance, higher wages would not change the decisions around fertility). Additionally, the heterogeneities observed in disposable income are not captured in the analysis because we work with labor and non-labor income, not net income after taxes and subsidies.

The following section breaks down the changes in distribution for the national aggregate between 2010 and 2019. Then, emphasis is placed on the particularities of these changes by cities.

3.4 Decomposition of Changes in Income Distribution

Following the previously discussed micro-decomposition methodology, this section disaggregates the observed reduction in income inequality through its different components: labor and non-labor. The first group studies the role of changes in educational level, returns from education, and demographic variables such as age and number of children. On the other hand, within non-labor income, the impact of monetary transfers to households, both public and private, and other essential items, such as rental income and pensions, is studied.

3.4.1 Components Associated with the National Variation in Inequalities, 2010–2019

As mentioned in the methodology, the empirical strategy starts from estimating the equations of the determinants of labor participation, which corresponds to the first stage of Heckman's model, where the probability that individuals belong to the labor force is predicted. Subsequently, the determinants of wages, using Mincer-style equations, for the years 2010 and 2019 are modeled, using the Heckman correction for selection bias. Specifically, in Table 3.1, we present the results of the second stage of the Heckman model, where the logarithm of wages is modeled according to the variables mentioned in Fig. 3.15 and correcting for selection bias. As can be seen, the main variables have the expected signs. Age has positive but decreasing effects on wages, while education wage premiums are positive and increase with the degree attained, and informal work has a negative effect on wages.

As for the results over time, there is a significant drop in educational premiums for both men and women. In 2010, men with a technical or technological education degree had a salary that was 60% higher than those without any educational level or with only primary school. On the other hand, women observed a return that was 55% higher than those who reached the maximum primary level. In 2019, this percentage fell to 45% for women and 42% for men.

Additionally, some differential patterns between men and women stand out. In the first instance, for 2019, having one or more children represented a fall in women's salary ranging between − 4 and − 10%, while for men, there is no negative impact. On the other hand, being informal in 2019 meant a fall in women's salaries by 95% compared to their formal peers, while in the case of men, this same percentage was 55%. This phenomenon has been supported by previous literature in Colombia. For example, it has been shown that in the country, women of reproductive age are less likely to get formal employment than men (Abadía & De La Rica, 2011; Bustamante-Ramírez et al., 2015), which refers to a disadvantage, since informal jobs have on average lower salaries and with high variability, depending on the region where the individual works (Herrera-Idárraga et al., 2015).

As for labor income, in the estimation of non-labor income, we also employ a model that corrects for sample selection bias, following the Heckman two-step method[3]. Subsequently, counterfactual scenarios are simulated. For example, what would have been the results in 2010 if we had observed the endowments or returns of 2019. For this, the estimated coefficients of the returns on education obtained in 2019 are replaced in the equation estimated in 2010.

---

[3] For the purpose of simplifying the presentation of results, the estimates for each of the types of non-labor income studied are omitted, and the results of the simulations of counterfactual scenarios are presented directly.

Table 3.1 Estimates of the logarithm equation of labor income

Variables	Women		Men	
	2010	2019	2010	2019
Age	0.022***	0.034***	0.023***	0.018***
	(0.001)	(0.001)	(0.000)	(0.000)
Age^2	− 0.278***	− 0.421***	− 0.222***	− 0.196***
	(0.010)	(0.009)	(0.003)	(0.003)
Household head	0.080***	0.099***	0.132***	0.104***
	(0.003)	(0.002)	(0.001)	(0.001)
Secondary education	0.273***	0.267***	0.321***	0.241***
	(0.001)	(0.001)	(0.001)	(0.001)
Technological	0.547***	0.453***	0.600***	0.420***
	(0.004)	(0.003)	(0.001)	(0.001)
University / graduate	1.207***	1.094***	1.310***	1.103***
	(0.004)	(0.003)	(0.001)	(0.001)
One child	− 0.026***	− 0.041***	0.068***	0.032***
	(0.001)	(0.001)	(0.001)	(0.001)
Two children	− 0.030***	− 0.065***	0.053***	0.045***
	(0.001)	(0.001)	(0.001)	(0.001)
Three children or more	− 0.082***	− 0.103***	0.026***	− 0.000
	(0.002)	(0.001)	(0.001)	(0.001)
Informal worker	− 0.831***	− 0.955***	− 0.502***	− 0.555***
	(0.001)	(0.001)	(0.001)	(0.000)
Constant	12.859***	12.623***	12.728***	12.970***
	(0.024)	(0.021)	(0.007)	(0.006)
Observations	16,062,463	18,227,258	15,485,042	17,461,834

Note Robust standards in parentheses. *** $p < 0.01$; ** $p < 0.05$; * $p < 0.1$. The equations are estimated using a Heckman regression model in two stages simultaneously to obtain the correct standard errors. The age square is divided by 1000 to rescale the resulting coefficient.
Source Authors' elaboration based on DANE (GEIH)

Table 3.2 shows the results indicating the changes in inequality that result in each of the simulations performed. In the first instance, it is observed that the proposed model manages to simulate about 3 pp of the fall in inequality between 2010 and 2019, compared to a fall of 3.4 pp in the observed data. In accordance with the descriptive statistics reported before, an important part of the changes (−1.80 pp) is explained by variations in the distribution of wages. In particular, in the labor and demographic component, the decrease in educational premiums played an important role, which explains a reduction in inequality of 1.97 pp, as well as changes in educational

Table 3.2 Household income simulations

	Direction of the change in determinants	Change in Gini index (percentage points)
Observed		− 3.40
Simulated		− 2.96
Labor market and demographic components		− 1.80
Education premium	↘	− 1.97
Schooling level	↗	− 0.98
Number of children	↘	0.18
Age	↗	0.52
Non-labor components		− 1.27
Rental income	↗	− 0.22
Pensions	↘	− 0.16
Transfers from other households	↗	− 0.11
Transfers from institutions	↗	− 0.49

Note The figures indicate changes in percentage points in the Gini index. The arrows indicate whether the average values of each variable increase or decrease. A reduction, for example, in the variable *number of children* means that households decreased family size on average. It can have positive or negative effects on inequalities, depending on the household segment that has had the most significant reductions. For the simulations, in the case of educational premiums, and non-labor components, we substitute the coefficients. For the simulation of age variations, we substitute the characteristics so that the age distribution in 2010 resembled that observed in 2019. In the rest of the rows, coefficients and characteristics of individuals and households are substituted.
Source Authors' elaboration based on DANE (GEIH)

level, which resulted in a fall of 0.97 pp.[4] Concerning educational premiums, in Fig. 3.5, we had shown that wages were reduced at all levels. However, the reduction was particularly pronounced for higher educational levels. It implies that wage gaps narrowed in the 2010s; however, there are still appreciable differentials between wages at the highest levels relative to those reaching primary school levels only.

The changes in inequality attributable to the number of children have a positive sign (0.18 pp), which is surprising since, between 2010 and 2019, the average number of children decreased. However, when these variations between income quintiles are investigated, it is found that there were more significant reductions, in percentage terms, in the higher quintiles than in the lower-income quintiles. It suggests that the

---

[4] We should bear in mind that when the result is analyzed by components, the contribution of change of each variable is not equal to the total change, because in the regressions there are other variables, which are considered within the determinants of the distribution of income and the probability of receiving them, of which a counterfactual scenario is not constructed. On the other hand, the analysis includes rents, transfers, and pensions that account for 70% of non-labor income, but there is a remnant. Hence, there will be a residual component that is not being explained by the individual change in each variable analyzed.

effect of the demographic transition was more pronounced for high-income households, which can achieve much greater labor participation and contributions to the economy than that achieved by low-income households, increasing inequalities.

Variations in age between 2010 and 2019, on the other hand, show a greater concentration toward older age groups. It is also consistent with a process of demographic transition that moves toward higher medians of the age of the population, which has already been documented in previous demographic analyses (Romero, 2015). This demographic transition would be accompanied by greater labor participation since there would be a greater proportion of the working-age population. However, this component also appears to be benefiting, to a greater degree, the groups at the top of the distribution, who have significantly reduced more the number of children and pushed the average age upwards.

On the other hand, within the non-labor income, rental income stands out with a contribution to the reduction in inequality of -0.22 pp, pensions with -0.16 pp, and income from transfers from public and private institutions with -0.49 pp. This last component of transfers includes the effects derived from government programs that, in Colombia, compared to other countries in the region, have a moderate effect on the reduction of inequalities once disposable income, net of transfers and taxes, is considered.

It is worth noting that leases, transfers, and pensions comprise around 70% of non-labor income, with leases being the most important. That is why it is not surprising that having income from this last item is an equalizing mechanism that, as indicated in Fig. 3.10, grew more in the lowest income quintiles.

Finally, transfers from other households in Colombia and remittances contributed to a lesser extent to the decrease in inequality, with only -0.11 pp. These patterns coincide with what was observed in Fig. 3.10, where the average income from these items decreased in the highest quintile of the distribution. At the same time, it increased in households with lower incomes.

3.4.2 Changes in Regional Income Inequalities in the 2010s

To better understand the regional behavior of income inequalities, we study the changes and determinants in the reduction of total income inequality within cities, considering the economic structure (Haddad et al., 2016) and labor, goods, and services markets vary at the city level (Cárdenas-Hurtado et al., 2014). Thus, studying the role of labor and non-labor income in reducing inequality within local markets is relevant.

This section includes regional analysis of the changes in inequality between 2010 and 2019 for the 23 main capital cities of Colombia and their metropolitan areas, following the same methodology proposed in the previous section. The results of this section are crucial to understanding the existing heterogeneity of income inequality within cities.

3.4.2.1 Changes in Regional Income Inequality

When reviewing the changes in the Gini index decomposition between the two sources of variation included in the decomposition model (labor income and non-labor income), we find some significant differences between cities (Table 3.3). These results are suggestive; however, we should appreciate that the model fails to capture all the determinants of the change in inequality due to technical aspects such as the number of variables included in the model and the number of observations.[5] In general, labor income was the main factor contributing to reducing inequality in the cities analyzed. It happens in some cases because the distribution of labor income became more compact compared to the distribution in 2010.

It is also important to add that in Quibdó, Riohacha, and Florencia, according to the model results, labor income contributed to increasing inequality. This increase is associated with the age structure in the three cities. Florencia's case is also due to the educational premiums associated with having a higher schooling level than primary education, as we will explain in the following subsection.

Non-labor income increased inequality in 18 out of the 23 cities included in the study, while labor income had an equalizing effect. On the net, the drop in inequality due to labor income was greater than the increase in inequality that could be generated through non-labor income. In Cúcuta, on the other hand, this did not happen; non-labor income increased inequality by 0.67 pp, and labor income reduced inequality by − 0.08, which means that the latter did not compensate for the increase in the former.

Regarding labor income, the additional gain or premium of each schooling level concerning primary education is the most important factor associated with changes in inequality, followed by the stock of years of education (Table 3.4). These changes in the premiums associated with each additional level of education are determined in the labor market and depend both on individual characteristics (quality, quantity and relevance of education, ability, and effort, among others), as well as on structural factors of the cities (industrial composition, demographics, and local labor market).

In this regard, education returns contributed significantly to reducing inequality in the 23 cities studied, except in Florencia (Table 3.5) where the features of this city caused the returns associated with secondary and higher education concerning primary education to have increased over time instead of decreasing as occurred in the rest of the country's departmental capital cities.

It is also important to note that there are significant differences in additional earnings by gender. Indeed, the change in premiums at different educational levels between 2010 and 2019 for women positively correlates with the change in inequality. For men, on the other hand, this is valid only in the case of higher education since there is no correlation between the changes in premiums for secondary and technical education concerning primary education and changes in inequality. It implies that women's schooling positively impacted reducing wage inequality.

---

[5] It is important to mention that the prediction power of the model is reduced when working with data at the city level due to the reduction in the number of observations compared to the national level estimate. As a result, potential measurement errors and outliers in the income reported by respondents become more relevant.

Table 3.3 Decomposition of the change in the Gini index (percentage points), 2010–2019

	Change in simulated Gini index	Contribution	
		Labor income	Non-labor income
Pacific Region			
Cali	− 3.49	− 3.14	− 0.22
Pasto	− 1.91	− 2.37	0.76
Popayán	− 0.34	− 1.70	1.27
Quibdó	1.33	1.97	− 0.66
Central Region			
Armenia	− 2.32	− 3.23	0.92
Bogotá	− 0.44	− 1.27	0.75
Bucaramanga	− 1.65	− 1.69	0.22
Cúcuta	0.65	− 0.08	0.67
Florencia	0.42	0.51	0.09
Ibagué	− 1.43	− 2.58	1.10
Manizales	− 2.48	− 3.26	0.71
Medellín	− 2.57	− 2.47	− 0.15
Neiva	− 2.15	− 1.74	− 0.44
Pereira	0.35	− 2.12	2.31
Tunja	0.58	− 1.05	1.56
Villavicencio	− 0.61	− 1.11	0.60
Caribbean Region			
Barranquilla	− 0.69	− 0.58	− 0.13
Cartagena	− 0.90	− 1.01	0.16
Montería	− 3.09	− 3.05	− 0.03
Riohacha	2.95	1.87	1.14
Santa Marta	0.05	− 1.18	1.19
Sincelejo	− 0.83	− 1.72	0.82
Valledupar	− 0.05	− 1.61	1.52

Source Authors' elaboration based on DANE (GEIH)

Finally, the number of children does not seem to be a determining factor in the change in inequality in any city, but age is associated with an increase in inequality, especially in Cartagena, Florencia, and Villavicencio (Table 3.5). For the aggregate results, this may be the case due to a demographic transition process that has benefited chiefly groups in the upper part of the income distribution. Changes in the average age of the population have produced an inverted population pyramid.

Regarding non-labor income, pensions tend to increase inequality in most cities (16 out of 23). The results of the estimated model for Valledupar and Pereira reveal that pensions have the largest effect on the increase in inequality. The direction of

Table 3.4 Decomposition of the change in the Gini index in percentage points due to labor income determinants, 2010–2019

	Contribution of the determinants of labor income			
	Education premium	Schooling level	Number of children	Age
Pacific Region				
Cali	− 2.34	− 0.44	0.02	0.63
Pasto	− 2.35	0.12	0.07	0.43
Popayán	− 1.34	− 0.87	0.13	0.69
Quibdó	− 1.26	− 0.35	0.05	1.09
Central and Eastern Region				
Armenia	− 3.05	− 1.04	0.08	0.41
Bogotá D.C	− 1.65	− 0.33	0.01	0.60
Bucaramanga	− 2.69	− 0.67	0.05	0.56
Cúcuta	− 1.17	− 0.33	0.02	0.70
Florencia	0.47	− 0.22	0.04	1.66
Ibagué	− 3.16	− 0.78	0.08	0.30
Manizales	− 2.60	− 0.67	0.01	1.16
Medellín	− 1.74	− 0.61	0.05	0.35
Neiva	− 2.57	− 0.64	0.02	0.20
Pereira	− 2.85	− 0.87	0.04	0.77
Tunja	− 2.23	− 1.12	0.09	0.49
Villavicencio	− 2.11	− 0.69	0.04	1.35
Caribbean Region				
Barranquilla	− 0.77	0.08	0.09	0.52
Cartagena	− 1.42	− 0.59	0.09	1.41
Montería	− 3.33	− 0.96	0.01	0.36
Riohacha	− 1.04	− 0.28	0.17	0.20
Santa Marta	− 0.68	− 1.04	− 0.01	0.60
Sincelejo	− 3.86	− 0.88	0.10	0.49
Valledupar	− 1.67	− 0.51	− 0.03	− 0.04

Source Authors' elaboration based on DANE (GEIH)

the effect of pensions indicates that between 2010 and 2019, the average pension decreased, which may be the result of a composition effect: now, there is a larger number of individuals retiring with the minimum pension. Rental income, for its part, reduces inequality in 12 of the 23 cities studied, while in the remaining 11, it increases or does not alter inequality (Table 3.6).

Transfers by the government reduced inequality in most cities, but its effect is small in magnitude. It may happen because the amounts of the transfers are small with respect to the total income distribution of each city.

Table 3.5 Changes in returns to schooling levels concerning primary education, 2010–2019

City	Women			Men		
	High-school	Technical	University	High-school	Technical	University
Medellín	− 0.044	− 0.069	− 0.127	− 0.014	− 0.065	− 0.167
Barranquilla	0.028	− 0.113	− 0.226	− 0.042	− 0.165	− 0.101
Bogotá D.C	− 0.053	− 0.159	− 0.197	− 0.082	− 0.117	− 0.163
Cartagena	− 0.031	− 0.21	− 0.148	− 0.068	− 0.181	− 0.198
Tunja	− 0.1049	− 0.163	− 0.125	− 0.07	− 0.061	− 0.156
Manizales	0.012	− 0.045	− 0.069	− 0.015	− 0.164	− 0.284
Florencia	0.002	0.019	0.114	− 0.077	− 0.196	− 0.045
Popayán	− 0.021	0.056	0.058	− 0.136	− 0.208	− 0.273
Valledupar	− 0.022	− 0.212	− 0.099	− 0.1652	− 0.335	− 0.297
Montería	− 0.001	− 0.312	− 0.22	− 0.061	− 0.201	− 0.24
Quibdó	0.198	0.18	0.208	− 0.169	− 0.214	− 0.425
Neiva	− 0.115	− 0.315	− 0.371	− 0.053	− 0.133	− 0.185
Riohacha	0.005	− 0.031	− 0.054	0.019	0.039	− 0.015
Santa Marta	0.1507	0.3867	0.313	− 0.004	− 0.052	− 0.134
Villavicencio	− 0.095	− 0.113	− 0.226	− 0.105	− 0.334	− 0.177
Pasto	− 0.132	− 0.434	− 0.416	− 0.125	− 0.122	− 0.297
Cúcuta	0.095	0.002	− 0.009	− 0.094	− 0.212	− 0.22
Armenia	− 0.096	− 0.409	− 0.394	− 0.071	− 0.146	− 0.213
Pereira	− 0.0586	− 0.2834	− 0.336	− 0.1365	− 0.234	− 0.256
Bucaramanga	− 0.1639	− 0.403	− 0.526	− 0.059	− 0.18	− 0.215
Sincelejo	− 0.01	− 0.246	− 0.258	− 0.079	− 0.256	− 0.243
Ibagué	− 0.0828	− 0.3094	− 0.437	− 0.158	− 0.207	− 0.311
Cali	− 0.007	− 0.25	− 0.188	− 0.085	− 0.157	− 0.354

Source Authors' elaboration based on DANE (GEIH)

3.4.2.2 Distribution of Total Income and Non-Labor Income by Cities

Since there are differences in how non-labor income affects inequality, it is important to analyze the source of this heterogeneity to design policy recommendations that consider each city's context. In this exercise, we calculate the percentage of people in each quartile of the income distribution that receives each source of non-labor income: rental income, pensions, and transfers.[6]

Table 3.7 shows the distribution of total income for individuals who reported having a positive total income in 2010 and 2019 for each city included in the study.

---

[6] The analysis of this section is done using quartiles and quintiles as is standard in the literature, because there is not enough variation to allow calculating quintiles in several of the cities and variables studied.

Table 3.6 Decomposition of the change in Gini index due to non-labor income, 2010–2019

	Rental income	Pensions	Transfers
Pacific Region			
Cali	− 0.43	− 0.45	0.01
Pasto	− 0.08	0.55	− 0.17
Popayán	0.44	0.41	− 0.03
Quibdó	− 0.05	− 0.75	− 0.32
Central Region			
Armenia	0.11	0.24	0.26
Bogotá D.C	− 0.27	0.82	0.00
Bucaramanga	− 0.22	0.10	0.06
Cúcuta	0.17	0.00	− 0.03
Florencia	− 0.79	0.24	0.17
Ibagué	0.19	0.37	0.06
Manizales	0.01	0.36	− 0.03
Medellín	− 0.07	− 0.42	0.04
Neiva	0.09	− 0.81	0.15
Pereira	0.33	1.63	− 0.10
Tunja	0.50	0.96	− 0.01
Villavicencio	− 0.18	0.06	− 0.14
Caribbean Region			
Barranquilla	− 0.10	− 0.45	− 0.08
Cartagena	− 0.12	− 0.42	− 0.01
Montería	− 0.19	0.01	− 0.09
Riohacha	0.34	0.37	− 0.15
Santa Marta	0.77	0.03	− 0.04
Sincelejo	0.06	0.81	− 0.21
Valledupar	− 0.28	1.55	− 0.07

Source Authors' elaboration based on DANE (GEIH)

We find significant differences within and between cities in income distribution by quartiles. Regarding intra-city comparisons, the income in the highest quartile is almost 20 times greater than in the lowest quartile. When making between-cities comparisons, Bogotá D.C is the city with the highest average bottom quartile income, the average of said quartile being COP$ 264,623. While in Quibdó, the average income in the same quartile is, on average, COP$ 89,430. In the top quartile, where people with higher incomes are located, there is also considerable heterogeneity; the average total income in quartile 4 for Bogotá D.C is COP$ 3,936,165, while this value for Sincelejo is COP$ 1,517,167.

When analyzing non-labor income, there are also considerable differences between and within cities (Tables 3.8 and 3.9). In 2010, Manizales was the city where

Table 3.7 Total income distribution (constant pesos of 2010)

City	Q1		Q2		Q3		Q4	
	2010	2019	2010	2019	2010	2019	2010	2019
Pacific Region								
Cali	108,193	163,705	430,544	566,261	671,252	798,543	2,165,048	2,192,433
Pasto	117,276	149,834	312,841	464,79	542,073	693,356	1,700,706	2,025,133
Popayán	135,746	149,518	390,014	464,117	612,982	683,281	1,860,682	1,906,492
Quibdó	89,43	111,739	296,991	387,647	552,127	733,939	1,715,173	2,171,396
Central and Eastern Region								
Armenia	116,087	151,027	422,83	528,42	656,447	730,008	2,063,041	1,951,849
Bogotá D.C	264,623	251,395	561,486	604,431	892,091	875,288	3,936,165	3,148,750
Bucaramanga	191,084	208,362	546,026	556,758	829,393	758,335	2,397,575	1,897,506
Cúcuta	93,066	124,298	383,296	390,327	595,571	612,767	1,574,768	1,404,600
Florencia	128,222	148,728	401,239	470,422	586,055	705,138	1,604,480	1,973,449
Ibagué	125,092	176,389	442,719	544,879	717,551	753,883	2,282,487	2,039,184
Manizales	203,931	256,313	503,342	577,652	698,744	767,946	2,150,623	2,016,592
Medellín	134,901	194,822	489,152	589,546	756,655	828,397	2,747,889	2,525,214
Neiva	151,473	160,485	462,831	519,968	750,931	754,727	2,396,578	2,048,445
Pereira	179,168	222,789	478,748	573,449	660,187	709,574	1,702,387	1,749,928
Tunja	254,982	235,718	545,907	580,159	913,865	902,575	2,345,148	2,526,440
Villavicencio	184,251	196,81	516,977	586,206	752,065	855,065	2,002,279	2,589,193
Caribbean Region								
Barranquilla	131,402	135,774	404,174	476,823	576,975	690,785	2,732,925	1,920,951
Cartagena	166,946	197,242	451,867	524,982	656,479	718,912	1,784,273	1,712,148
Montería	123,249	140,615	394,438	448,313	609,766	633,922	2,161,540	1,725,321
Riohacha	108,666	107,147	378,853	385,789	639,686	671,468	1,813,178	2,002,051
Santa Marta	174,168	156,217	455,611	469,627	657,207	669,533	1,882,047	1,806,431
Sincelejo	136,871	111,17	361,863	377,287	545,333	615,228	1,517,167	1,734,690
Valledupar	131,026	154,435	394,454	466,054	622,318	658,012	2,005,682	1,709,416

Source Authors' elaboration based on DANE (GEIH)

a higher percentage of the population reported receiving income from pensions (15%) and, in general, in the cities of the country's central region, between 9 and 12% of people reported having pension income. On the other hand, in Sincelejo, only 4.3% of people receive income from pensions. We also find that the largest share of individuals receiving pension income is in the top quartile of the income distribution, which can explain why this kind of income might increase inequality.

Regarding rental income, it is concentrated in the top quartile, although in several cities, there is an interesting phenomenon where a higher proportion of individuals

Table 3.8 Share of the population that reports receiving non-labor income by quartiles, 2010 (in percentage terms)

	Pensions					Rental income					Transfers				
	Q1	Q2	Q3	Q4	Total	Q1	Q2	Q3	Q4	Total	Q1	Q2	Q3	Q4	Total
Pacific Region															
Cali	1.0	10.0	8.4	20.2	9.9	6.3	7.0	7.9	15.9	9.3	9.7	1.8	1.3	0.3	3.3
Pasto	0.5	0.6	11.2	24.7	9.1	4.7	5.6	4.7	13.4	7.0	4.2	2.7	0.8	0.1	2.0
Popayán	0.5	2.8	17.3	23.7	10.7	3.6	4.7	4.8	9.9	5.7	20.7	5.5	2.1	0.7	7.4
Quibdó	2.0	0.1	7.2	19.8	7.2	1.4	1.1	2.1	6.6	2.8	11.1	10.1	5.1	1.1	6.9
Central and Eastern Region															
Armenia	0.3	9.1	9.3	25.8	10.7	3.5	3.5	5.4	13.6	6.1	20.2	5.0	3.0	0.4	7.5
Bogotá D.C	1.9	9.9	10.5	18.8	9.9	7.8	3.9	12.1	18.6	10.6	7.7	1.5	0.7	0.5	2.8
Bucaramanga	0.5	8.8	7.3	20.0	9.0	7.6	6.2	9.9	18.7	10.6	9.9	3.0	2.2	0.8	4.1
Cúcuta	0.3	4.1	6.0	13.3	5.9	4.0	5.8	3.7	9.6	5.8	28.9	9.2	4.5	1.9	11.3
Florencia	0.1	0.7	5.6	12.4	4.4	3.4	4.4	3.3	6.9	4.6	37.0	15.7	10.8	4.2	17.4
Ibagué	0.4	7.5	11.0	29.9	12.1	5.2	6.0	8.8	16.6	9.1	13.1	4.9	3.2	0.5	5.4
Manizales	0.5	20.3	15.0	26.5	15.1	6.6	2.3	10.4	15.8	8.8	7.0	0.6	1.0	0.2	2.4
Medellín	1.1	12.8	12.1	20.5	11.5	4.4	2.9	6.4	15.4	7.2	10.4	2.0	0.8	0.7	3.5
Neiva	0.5	6.7	8.3	19.4	8.6	5.8	5.3	7.6	12.6	7.8	23.0	7.3	3.2	0.8	8.7
Pereira	0.7	13.0	8.9	22.1	11.1	5.1	3.3	7.1	15.3	7.6	7.6	1.0	1.0	0.4	2.6
Tunja	0.4	9.4	15.3	21.1	11.5	6.8	3.3	10.2	12.7	8.2	4.3	0.5	0.2	–	1.2
Villavicencio	0.8	3.7	6.0	15.2	6.3	10.0	5.2	8.0	14.7	9.3	3.4	0.6	1.0	0.4	1.3

(continued)

Table 3.8 (continued)

	Pensions					Rental income					Transfers				
	Q1	Q2	Q3	Q4	Total	Q1	Q2	Q3	Q4	Total	Q1	Q2	Q3	Q4	Total
Caribbean Region															
Barranquilla	0.5	1.8	9.6	17.0	7.1	2.7	2.6	1.2	4.5	2.7	12.9	2.1	0.8	0.3	4.0
Cartagena	0.3	4.7	5.8	22.9	7.8	2.6	2.8	3.5	10.2	4.6	15.9	3.4	1.5	0.3	5.7
Montería	0.1	0.4	6.6	19.7	6.1	4.5	3.7	4.7	11.7	6.0	10.7	2.8	1.2	0.1	3.9
Riohacha	0.1	0.4	3.2	7.8	2.8	2.7	2.9	3.8	12.1	5.3	16.5	4.3	2.7	1.2	6.3
Santa Marta	0.9	7.3	5.2	23.1	8.7	3.6	2.5	4.0	8.4	4.5	9.3	1.9	1.5	0.4	3.6
Sincelejo	0.1	0.3	4.6	12.7	4.3	1.9	2.4	1.6	5.5	2.9	16.3	6.6	4.3	1.1	7.3
Valledupar	0.5	1.2	4.1	12.1	4.2	5.4	5.0	4.2	10.4	6.1	13.3	4.2	2.5	1.2	5.6

Source Authors' elaboration based on DANE (GEIH)

Table 3.9 Share of the population that reports receiving non-labor income by quartiles, 2019 (in percentage terms)

	Pensions					Rental income					Transfers				
	Q1	Q2	Q3	Q4	Total	Q1	Q2	Q3	Q4	Total	Q1	Q2	Q3	Q4	Total
Pacific Region															
Cali	0.8	14.2	11.2	19.9	11.5	6.6	4.1	8.1	14.4	8.3	16.6	1.6	1.0	0.1	4.8
Pasto	0.3	4.5	11.5	24.4	10.1	3.9	5.2	4.5	13.2	6.7	23.8	7.9	3.2	0.6	9.1
Popayán	1.0	8.7	14.0	23.2	11.5	2.5	3.8	2.3	9.6	4.5	23.1	5.2	1.7	0.5	8.1
Quibdó	0.1	1.9	13.6	24.6	9.9	0.5	1.9	1.8	6.4	2.6	26.5	13.5	3.9	1.0	11.6
Central and Eastern Region															
Armenia	1.0	14.2	9.6	28.1	13.4	4.3	3.1	4.5	11.9	5.9	19.7	1.8	1.1	0.5	5.8
Bogotá D.C	8.1	9.0	10.1	18.8	11.5	8.2	3.8	11.6	18.5	10.5	11.5	0.8	0.8	0.2	3.3
Bucaramanga	0.7	13.8	7.1	20.5	10.5	5.3	2.7	6.7	14.1	7.1	13.3	1.9	1.5	0.6	4.5
Cúcuta	0.1	1.0	11.0	14.8	6.7	2.7	4.9	1.9	8.4	4.5	32.9	7.1	2.9	1.4	11.2
Florencia	0.2	1.7	7.9	17.6	6.7	3.3	4.8	3.9	8.8	5.1	41.0	12.1	5.1	1.5	15.8
Ibagué	0.6	9.2	13.2	28.3	12.7	4.8	4.8	6.7	14.3	7.6	21.3	3.7	1.9	0.5	6.9
Manizales	2.3	21.7	14.9	28.8	16.9	6.5	1.4	8.9	16.2	8.1	15.2	0.7	1.2	0.3	4.4
Medellín	1.7	20.7	10.3	20.5	13.2	4.6	1.8	5.7	14.6	6.7	14.9	1.7	1.5	0.6	4.7
Neiva	0.3	8.0	12.7	27.0	11.9	3.9	3.6	4.4	10.5	5.5	27.9	4.4	2.1	0.4	8.7
Pereira	0.7	17.5	7.5	24.3	12.1	5.1	2.0	4.5	12.7	5.9	14.7	1.4	1.4	1.0	4.7
Tunja	1.0	10.5	15.3	26.6	13.0	5.9	3.0	7.3	12.1	7.0	7.6	1.0	0.4	0.4	2.5
Villavicencio	0.5	6.7	7.9	21.4	8.8	7.0	5.0	7.0	17.9	8.9	20.1	3.1	2.4	0.7	6.6

(continued)

Table 3.9 (continued)

	Pensions					Rental income					Transfers				
	Q1	Q2	Q3	Q4	Total	Q1	Q2	Q3	Q4	Total	Q1	Q2	Q3	Q4	Total
Caribbean Region															
Barranquilla	0.2	5.8	6.6	16.8	7.0	1.8	2.3	1.5	6.9	3.0	16.3	2.7	1.3	0.7	5.4
Cartagena	0.2	6.0	5.5	22.2	7.9	2.8	2.5	3.5	7.1	3.8	18.4	2.0	1.2	0.2	5.7
Montería	0.2	0.7	8.0	19.9	7.0	3.0	4.1	1.7	7.0	4.0	29.8	7.4	3.7	1.6	11.5
Riohacha	0.1	0.6	4.4	12.1	4.2	1.5	3.8	3.0	10.2	4.5	23.3	8.0	3.4	1.4	9.1
Santa Marta	0.7	9.5	4.9	21.7	9.1	2.1	3.7	2.5	7.4	3.9	17.4	4.0	2.0	0.5	6.1
Sincelejo	0.1	0.1	5.1	14.6	4.6	0.7	2.3	1.4	4.7	2.2	29.1	9.4	3.6	1.9	11.2
Valledupar	1.3	2.8	5.9	16.7	6.6	3.9	5.2	2.8	10.1	5.5	23.9	4.4	2.6	0.8	8.1

Source Authors' elaboration based on DANE (GEIH)

in quartile 1 report rental income compared to people in quartile 2 of the income distribution.

Regarding transfers, which are the institutional tool designed to reduce extreme poverty, we find that they are indeed given to individuals in the bottom quartile of the income distribution for all cities. In particular, in cities with a high incidence of moderate and extreme monetary poverty, such as Florencia and Cúcuta, around 30% of individuals in the bottom quartile of the income distribution receive transfers.

It is noteworthy that in cities with historically high poverty rates, such as Quibdó (Robledo-Caicedo, 2019) or Riohacha (Ricciulli et al., 2018), the percentage of people in quartile 1 who received transfers in 2010 was not exceptionally high (11.1 and 16.5%, respectively), while in cities with a lower incidence of poverty, such as Armenia, Neiva, and Popayán, more than 20% of people located in the same quartile reported receiving transfers (Table 3.9). This result per se cannot be taken as a sign of poor targeting of transfers in 2010, since in all cities, the people located in the lowest quartile of the income distribution are the ones who receive the most transfers.[7] However, it can signal that transfers coverage was low among the potential beneficiaries.

Moving in time to 2019, we find that there is a slight increase in the percentage of people who received income from pensions in the 23 main cities of the country, except in Barranquilla, where there was virtually no change. Neiva was the city where this percentage increased the most, going from 8.6% in 2010 to 11.9% in 2019. On the other hand, the percentage of people who receive rental income fell in all cities, but in Bucaramanga, this drop was particularly marked, going from 10.6% in 2010 to 7.1% in 2019.

Finally, the most significant change occurs in the percentage of people who receive government transfers. On average, in the 23 main cities, recipients of transfers increased by 2 pp between 2010 and 2019. In fact, in the bottom quartile of the income distribution, the percentage of people who receive transfers increased by 7.6 pp, while in quartiles 3 and 4, there was a fall in the percentage of people who get transfers, which would show that the increase in transfer coverage has been correctly focused on the lower-income population group.

The cities in which there is a higher proportion of low-income people who received transfers in 2019 are Florencia (41%), Cúcuta (32.9%), Montería (29.8%), and Sincelejo (29.1%), although there are five other cities in which more than 20% of the people in the bottom quartile of the income distribution received transfers. In contrast, Tunja is the city with the lowest percentage of people in the bottom quartile who received transfers, with 7.6% of individuals in said quartile receiving them (Table 3.9).

---

[7] It is worth clarifying that in 2010 transfers by government institutions or by institutions outside the country (remittances) cannot be discriminated against. However, for 2019, the year in which the GEIH allows a breakdown of transfers by the government and by private institutions, transfers by the government represent close to 95% of the total amount transferred for transfers to households in the three lowest quartiles of the income distribution.

3.5 Conclusions and Discussion

We study the determinants of the reduction of income inequality between 2010 and 2019 for Colombia and its main cities, using a micro-decomposition methodology based on Bourguignon and Ferreira (2005). The decomposition allows us to differentiate changes in income inequality that are due to labor income from changes that are due to non-labor income. In terms of labor income, we included educational level, returns to education, and demographic variables such as age and number of children as determinants. While for non-labor income, we include monetary transfers to households, rental income, and pensions.

Our results show that the decrease in income inequality during the 2010s decade resulted from several factors. First, there is evidence of an increase in labor income, especially between 2010–2014, when the country experienced real economic growth of 5.0%. In the subsequent years, the growth rate dropped to an annual 2.4%, and household wage income stopped increasing. It suggests that economic growth is essential for reducing income inequality as workers benefit via the labor market.

Within the labor market, there is a reduction in the wage spread due to greater access to education, which reduces wage premiums for secondary and higher education concerning primary education. It is also accompanied by better enforcement of the labor laws that protect low-earning workers from receiving wages below the minimum wage. For non-wage income, the greater progressivity observed in rental income and transfers stands out, but pensions are still regressive.

In general, we find a positive association between improving education access and conditional cash transfers and reductions in inequality, highlighting the potential that public policies can have in reducing inequality in developing countries. It supports the findings of Lustig (2020) for the case of Latin America; she argues that the reduction of inequality in the region has been linked to two critical components of social policy: 1) the increase in education spending that positively impacted the schooling of the population, and 2) the expansion of cash transfer programs targeted at the most vulnerable population. However, as mentioned before, there is still ample space for improvement to continue reducing inequality.

The analysis of inequality at the regional level reveals considerable differences within the main 23 cities of the country, which are hidden behind the result of the national aggregate. It is important to highlight that in 19 of the 23 main cities, there was a reduction in total income inequality, measured through the Gini coefficient, and in five of these cities, the drop in inequality was more than 5 pp. However, inequality increased in peripheral cities like Florencia, Quibdó, Riohacha, and Villavicencio.

On the one hand, for labor income, the reduction in the spread in the returns to education is the main factor contributing to the decrease in inequality. This applies to those cities that saw a decrease in inequality. On the other hand, non-labor income is not an equalizing factor in most cities. It happens partly due to pensions, as most people in the top quartile of the income distribution have access to a pension income. However, the non-labor income also includes government transfers, and we find that these are associated with reductions in inequality and are well-targeted to individuals in the bottom quartile of the income distribution.

The drop in inequality and poverty indicators in Colombia during the 2010 decade was accompanied by important social advances in other dimensions. In education, access at all levels improved markedly. According to administrative records from the Ministry of Education (2020), the most significant increases occurred in secondary education, in which net enrollment rates increased 20 pp between 2002 and 2019. Similarly, in higher education, the coverage rate went from 34.1 to 52.8% between 2008 and 2018, with increases in enrollment in both university and technical and technological programs. It has resulted from policies aimed at increasing higher education coverage, which has also allowed low-income youth to have increased access to tertiary education (Carranza & Ferreyra, 2019).

Parallel to the advances in education, an ambitious conditional cash transfer program was put in place targeting the poor, MFEA. The idea behind the program was to improve households' income in the short term and provide them with incentives to give better nutrition and enroll their children into the education system, to have long-lasting effects on the labor market performance and economic conditions of the household (Llano, 2014). According to Urrutia and Robles-Báez (2021), MFEA, the conditional transfer program in Colombia with the largest budget, has managed to benefit more than 1,600,000 families annually from 2001 to 2017, which is equivalent to about 10,000,000 individuals or 20% of the current population of the country.

Regarding rental income, we would like to call attention to the housing policy that has allowed low-income people to buy low-cost subsidized housing (called VIS) and generate income from renting parts of it. Housing is the main asset of most households in Colombia and many other developing countries. Thus, the policies focused on helping households to buy houses, especially VIS, help to solve the housing deficit but can also result in additional income for the beneficiaries (families do not have to pay for rent, and they can also derive profit from it by leasing parts of the house). In this context, housing policies that allow low-income individuals to generate additional income via rentals help to reduce inequality.

Even though there have been significant social advances, they have been insufficient (Caballero & Machado, 2020). Latin America continues to be the region with the largest income inequality in the world, and Colombia is one of the most unequal countries in the region (Lustig, 2020).

Appendix

Cities included in the sample (Fig. 3.16).

Fig. 3.16 Sample of cities included in the study

References

Abadía-Alvarado, L. K., & De la Rica, S. (2011). Changes in the gender wage gap and the role of education and other job characteristics Colombia: 1994–2010. In *Vniversitas Económicas* (Vol. 010088). Bogotá: Universidad Javeriana.

Arango-Thomas, L. E., Flórez, L. A., & Guerrero, L. D. (2020). Minimum wage effects on informality across demographic groups in Colombia. In *Borradores de Economía* (Vol. 1104). Banco de la República de Colombia.

Azevedo, J. P., Inchauste, G., & Sanfelice, V. (2013). Decomposing the recent inequality decline in Latin America. In *Policy research working paper series* (Vol. 6715). Washington, D. C.: World Bank. Retrieved from https://openknowledge.worldbank.org/handle/10986/16931

Becker, G. S., Philipson, T. J., & Soares, R. R. (2005). The quantity and quality of life and the evolution of world inequality. *The American Economic Review, 95*(1), 277–291.

Bernal, R., Eslava, M., Meléndez, M., & Pinzón, Á. (2017). Switching from payroll taxes to corporate income taxes: Firms' employment and wages after the 2012 Colombian tax reform. *Economía, 18*, 41–74.

Bonilla-Mejía, L. (2009). Causas de las diferencias regionales en la distribución del ingreso en Colombia, un ejercicio de microdescomposición. In *Documentos de Trabajo Sobre Economía Regional y Urbana* (Vol. 111). Cartagena: Banco de la República de Colombia.

Bossler, M., & Schank, T. (2020). Wage inequality in Germany after the minimum wage introduction. In *IZA discussion papers* (Vol. 13003). Bonn: Institute of Labor Economics (IZA).

Bourguignon, F., & Ferreira, F. (2005). Decomposing changes in the distribution of household incomes: methodological aspects. In F. Bourguignon, F. Ferreira, & N. Lustig (Eds.), *The microeconomics of income distribution dynamics in East Asia and Latin America* (pp. 17–46). World Bank and Oxford University Press.

Bustamante-Ramírez, N., Tribín-Uribe, A. M., & Vargas-Riaño, C. O. (2015). Maternity and labor markets: impact of legislation in Colombia. In *Borradores de Economía* (Vol. 870). Banco de la República de Colombia.

Caballero, C., & Machado, G. (2020). De la crisis de 'fin de siglo' a la del 'coronavirus'. La economía colombiana en el siglo XXI. *Coyuntura Económica: Investigación Económica y Social, 50*, 15–74. Bogotá, D. C.: Fedesarrollo.

Camargo-Sierra, A. (2020). Prácticas residenciales de propietarios en barrios de origen informal consolidados en Bogotá: Movilización de recursos para la construcción de la vivienda. In D. Niño-Muñoz, & D. Osorio Gómez (Eds.), *Políticas urbanas y dinámicas socioespaciales. vivienda, renovación urbana y patrimonio* (pp. 137–156). Bogotá: Universidad Sergio Arboleda.

Cárdenas-Hurtado, C. A., Hernández-Montes, M. A., & Torres-Gorron, J. E. (2014). An exploratory analysis of heterogeneity on regional labour markets and unemployment rates in Colombia: An MFACT approach. In *Borradores de Economía* (Vol. 802). Banco de la República de Colombia.

Carranza, J. E., & Ferreyra, M. M. (2019). Increasing higher education coverage: Supply expansion and student sorting in Colombia. *Journal of Human Capital, 13*(1), 95–136.

Cecchini, S., & Atuesta, B. (2017). Programa de transferencias condicionadas en América Latina y el Caribe: Tendencias de cobertura e inversion. In *Serie de Políticas Sociales* (Vol. 224). Santiago, Chile: CEPAL.

Deaton, A. (2015). *El gran escape. Salud, riqueza y los orígenes de la desigualdad*. México: Fondo de Cultura Económica.

Delgado, M. (2014). La educación básica y media en Colombia: Retos en equidad y calidad. In *Reportes de investigación*. Bogotá, Colombia: Fedesarrollo.

Díaz, A. M. (2016). Spatial unemployment differentials in Colombia. *Revista Desarrollo y Sociedad, 76*, 123–163.

Fernández, C., & Villar, L. (2017). The impact of lowering the payroll tax on informality in Colombia. *Economía, 18*(1), 125–155.

Galvis-Aponte, L. A. (2010). Diferenciales salariales por género y región en Colombia: Una aproximación con regresión por cuantiles. *Revista de Economía del Rosario, 13*(2), 235–277. Retrieved from https://revistas.urosario.edu.co/index.php/economia/article/view/2193

Galvis-Aponte, L. A., & Meisel, A. (2010). Persistencia de las desigualdades regionales en Colombia: Un análisis especial. In *Documentos de Trabajo sobre Economía Regional y Urbana* (Vol. 120). Cartagena: Banco de la República de Colombia.

Haddad, E. A., Rodrigues-Faria, W., Galvis-Aponte, L. A., & Hahn-de-Castro, L. W. (2016). Matriz insumo-producto interregional para Colombia, 2012. In *Documentos de Trabajo Sobre Economía Regional y Urbana* (Vol. 247). Cartagena: Banco de la República de Colombia.

Herrera-Idárraga, P., López-Bazo, E., & Motellón, E. (2015). Regional wage gaps, education, and informality in an emerging country. The case of Colombia. In *AQR working papers* (Vol. 201507). University of Barcelona, Regional Quantitative Analysis Group.

Herrera-Idárraga, P., Garlati-Bertoldi, P. A., & Torres, J. D. (2021). Urban wage gaps in colombia and the impact of a national payroll tax policy. *Regional Studies*. https://doi.org/10.1080/003 43404.2021.1908535

Kenny, C. (2012). *Getting better: Why global development is succeeding-and how we can improve the world even more*. Basic Books.

Kliksberg, B. (2005). América Latina: La región más desigual de todas. *Revista de Ciencias Sociales*, 11(3), 411–421. Retrieved from http://ve.scielo.org/scielo.php?script=sci_arttext&pid=S13159 5182005000300002&lng=es&tlng=es

Laajaj, R., Moya, A., & Sánchez, F. (2018). Equality of opportunity and human capital accumulation: Motivational effect of a nationwide scholarship in Colombia. In *Serie Documentos Cede* (Vol. 016352). Colombia: Centro de Estudios sobre Desarrollo Económico, Universidad de los Andes.

Lerman, R. I., & Yitzhaki, S. (1985). Income inequality effects by income source: A new approach and application to the United States. *The Review of Economics and Statistics, 67*(1), 151–156.

Llano, J. (2014). Familias en Acción: La historia a la luz de sus impactos. *Coyuntura Económica, 44*(1), 77–120.

Londoño-Vélez, J., Rodríguez, C., & Sánchez, F. (2017). The intended and unintended impacts of a merit-based financial aid program for the poor: The case of ser pilo paga. In *Serie Documentos Cede* (Vol. 015466). Colombia: Universidad de los Andes.

López-Calva, L. F., & Lustig, N. (Eds.). (2010). *Declining inequality in Latin America: A decade of progress?* Washington, D. C.: Brookings Institution Press. Retrieved from https://www.jstor.org/stable/https://doi.org/10.7864/j.ctt6wpdkq

Lustig, N. (2020). Desigualdad y política social en América Latina. In *CEQ working paper* (Vol. 94). Tulane University, Commitment to Equity Institute.

Melo-Becerra, L., Ramos-Forero, J., & Hernández-Santamaría, P. (2017). La educación superior en Colombia: Situación actual y análisis de eficiencia. *Desarrollo y Sociedad, 78*, 59–111. Colombia: Universidad de los Andes.

Messina, J., & Silva, J. (2018). Wage inequality in Latin America. In *The world bank* (Vol. 28682). Washington, D. C.: World Bank Publications.

Ministerio de Educación. (2020). *Información y estadísticas sectorials*. Retrieved from https://www.mineducacion.gov.co/1759/w3-propertyname-3377.html

Morales, L., & Medina, C. (2017). Assessing the effect of payroll taxes on formal employment: The case of the 2013 tax reform in Colombia. *Economía, 18*(1), 75–124.

Núñez, J., Olivieri, S., Parra, J. & Pico, J. (2020). The distributive impact of taxes and expenditures in Colombia. In *Policy research working paper* (Vol. 9171). Washington, D. C.: World Bank Group.

OCDE. (2013). *OECD economic surveys*. París: Colombia Economic Assessment.

Parias-Durán, A. (2020). La política de vivienda dirigida al mercado en Colombia y configuración urbana: 1990–2017. El caso de Bogotá. In D. Niño-Muñoz & D. Osorio-Gómez (Eds.), *Políticas urbanas y dinámicas socioespaciales: Vivienda, renovación urbana y patrimonio* (pp. 61–94). Fondo de publicaciones Universidad Sergio Arboleda.

Pyatt, G. (1976). On the interpretation and disaggregation of Gini coefficients. *The Economic Journal, 86*, 243–255.

Ricciulli-Marín, D., Arismendi, C., & Romero, E. (2018). La pobreza en Riohacha: diagnóstico, análisis y propuestas. In *Documentos de Trabajo sobre Economía Regional y Urbana* (Vol. 275). Cartagena: Banco de la República de Colombia.

Ridley, M. (2010). *The rational optimist: How prosperity evolves*. Harper.

Robledo-Caicedo, J. (2019). La pobreza en Quibdó: Norte de carencias. In *Documentos de Trabajo sobre Economía Regional y Urbana* (Vol. 277). Cartagena: Banco de la República de Colombia.

Romero, J. E. (2015). Población y desarrollo en el Pacífico colombiano. In *Documentos de Trabajo sobre Economía Regional* (Vol. 232). Banco de la República de Colombia.

Samaniego de la Parra, B., Otero-Cortés, A., & Morales, L. F. (2021). The labor market effects of part-time contributions to social security: Evidence from Colombia. In *Documentos de Trabajo sobre Economía Regional* (Vol. 302). Cartagena: Banco de la República.

Sotomayor, O. J. (2021) Can the minimum wage reduce poverty and inequality in the developing world? Evidence from Brazil. In *World Development* (Vol. 138). Retrieved from https://doi.org/10.1016/j.worlddev.2020.105182

Train, K., & Wilson, W. (2008). Estimation on stated-preference experiments constructed from revealed-preference choices. *Transportation Research Part B: Methodological, 42*(3), 191–203.

Urrutia-Montoya, M., & Robles-Báez, C. (2021). *Política social para la equidad en Colombia: Historia y experiencias.* Bogotá, Colombia: Ediciones Uniandes

Vélez, C. E., Leibovich, J., Kugler, A., Bouillón, C., & Núñez, J. (2005). The reversal of inequality trends in Colombia, 1978–1995: A combination of persistent and fluctuating forces. In F. Bourguignon, F. Ferreira, & N. Lustig (Eds.), *The microeconomics of income distribution dynamics in East Asia and Latin America* (pp. 17–46). World Bank and Oxford University Press.

World Bank. (2011). A break with history: Fifteen years of inequality reduction in Latin America. In *LCSPP poverty and labor brief* (Vol. 2). Retrieved from https://openknowledge.worldbank.org/handle/10986/2747

Leonardo Bonilla Ph.D. (Econ.), University of Illinois. Researcher at Banco de la República, Colombia. Research fields: labor, education, environment, and political economy.

Luis Armando Galvis-Aponte Ph.D. (Geog.), University of Illinois. Senior researcher, Center for Regional Economic Studies, Banco de la República, Colombia. Research fields: econometric methods, economic development, and regional economics.

Andrea Otero-Cortés Ph.D. (Econ), University of North Carolina at Chapel Hill. Researcher, Center for Regional Economic Studies, Banco de la República, Colombia. Research fields: labor economics, development, and regional economics.

Diana Ricciulli Ph.D. Student (Econ.), University of British Columbia. Professional researcher, Center for Regional Economic Studies, Banco de la República, Colombia. Research fields: political economy, economic history, and economic development.

Chapter 4
Regional Convergence in Colombia in the Twenty-First Century

Karina Acosta and Jaime Bonet

4.1 Introduction

A vast wave of literature has been concerned with whether countries or subnational areas are embarking on the global trends of economic growth at a progressive pace. That is, poorer areas growing more rapidly than richer areas, converging to the same equilibria. The main driver of such concern is the need to answer if, eventually, there would exist geographical economic equality. Much of the international literature on these topics is summarized by Islam (2003) and Johnson and Papageorgiou (2020). They have shown that the prevailing discourse on convergence is led by the neoclassical growth theory introduced by Solow (1956) and formally tested by Barro and Sala-i-Martin (1992).

There has been a branch of convergence studies in Colombia at a local level, which has completed around 30 years of international research, starting with Cárdenas et al. (1993). This literature has used different scales of geography (regions, departments, and municipalities) and various conclusive periods about the economy's persistent and unequal spatial distribution. Ambiguous conclusions can be obtained on convergence in Colombia, resembling international findings. However, there is evidence that such spatial heterogeneity of economic growth across space has resulted in a lack of historical convergence of the GDP per capita among regions (Galvis-Aponte, 2002; Meisel-Roca & Hahn, 2020). Some authors show mixed results. For instance, Bonet and Meisel (1999) claim convergence between 1926 and 1960 and divergence between 1960 and 1995. Meisel-Roca and Hahn (2020), using a more extended period (1926–2018), distinctly illustrate that, in the long run, convergence between Colombian regions has been absent. Those results contrast with studies focused on

---

K. Acosta (✉) · J. Bonet
Banco de la República, Cartagena, Colombia
e-mail: kacostor@banrep.gov.co

J. Bonet
e-mail: jbonetmo@banrep.gov.co

© The Author(s), under exclusive license to Springer Nature Switzerland AG 2023
E. A. Haddad et al. (eds.), *The Colombian Economy and Its Regional Structural Challenges*, Advances in Spatial Science, https://doi.org/10.1007/978-3-031-22653-3_4

more recent periods and using departments as units of analysis, showing a modest economic convergence.

This chapter aims to study the concept of unconditional convergence during the first 20 years of the twenty-first century in Colombia. Notable changes were experienced during this time. The twenty-first century began with the recovery from a crisis called the "End of the Century Crisis." It was characterized by a substantial drop in economic growth in 1999 and a massive loss of housing ownership due to a partially pervasive unregulated financial sector in Colombia (Caballero & Machado, 2020; Perez-Reyna, 2017). Whereas Colombia expected economic growth of 2%, the actual growth was −4.1% in 1998. Although most authors conclude that external factors primarily drove it, internal characteristics aggravated it, such as internal financial frictions (Perez-Reyna, 2017). The first two decades of the century conclude with the landing of COVID-19 in the country in 2020, where the economic growth fell to −6.8%, the worst drop since it has been measured. Also, 2020 was accompanied by a significant unbalanced fiscal impact, partly explained by an increase in transitory expenses valued at around 2.7% of the total GDP (Caballero & Machado, 2020).

Therefore, the targeted period of the analysis is assembled between two significant crises. Furthermore, it is signalized by the transition of the Colombian economy from a coffee dependency to an oil dependency, along with the international ripple effect of the global financial crisis in 2008. For almost one hundred years, the coffee sector was one of the prime drivers of Colombian capital accumulation and take-off (De Corso, 2018). However, according to the historical analysis of De Corso (2018), this change accompanied other structural transformations. The mining and energy sectors have gained significant relative weight, increasing production and investment, primarily during the first decade of the twenty-first century. Simultaneously, the relative weight of coffee exports has shrunk rapidly since the early 1980s. In fact, according to the most recent data on the economic reactivation of the Colombian economy in 2021, it will not be primarily explained by consumption expansion but rather by the hydrocarbon sector (Editorial La República, 2021). Along with these economic changes, the Colombian government signed the peace agreement with the guerrilla group FARC in 2016, ending one of the world's longest-lasting internal conflicts.

In this setting, we intend to understand if there is a pattern of convergence and its changes over the targeted years and whether such changes can be explained by the economic architecture and its adjustment in individual departments during a period with very peculiar characteristics in the economic history of Colombia. Additionally, this chapter explores the role of spatial dependence on the existence or not of convergence. Finally, this analysis contrasts the findings of economic convergence with the convergence of other development indicators.

This chapter is organized as follows. The following section describes the overall trends of the Colombian economy. Section 4.3 summarizes the international and national literature on convergence. Sections 4.4 and 4.5 describe the methodology and data used, respectively. Section 4.6 introduces the main results, and Sect. 4.7 concludes with a discussion of the key findings.

4.2 The Colombian Economy During the 21st Century

The Colombian economic growth during the twenty-first century can be classified into three phases: (1) recovery (from 2000 to 2007), (2) financial Crisis (from 2008 to 2011), and (3) oil price volatility (from 2012 to 2020) (Fig. 4.1). The first period illustrates an upward slope that can be explained by a recovery from the crises at the end of the twentieth century, accompanied by the stimulation of the enhanced world trade and a positive effect on the price of exporting goods, a pattern common in the rest of Latin America (Cervo, 2016).

The second phase depicts a deep U-shape, reflecting the fast contraction and recovery of the economic growth from the Global Financial Crisis. Figure 4.1 shows that the Colombian reduction of its economic growth was not as precipitous as observed in an average Latin American economy. Finally, after the speedy recovery from this crisis, it follows a gradual decline until the precipitous 2020 drop. These changes are primarily driven by variations in the crude oil prices and conclude with the sizable decrease in 2020 because of the pandemic. Overall, it could be concluded that the economic growth of Colombia somewhat matches the behavior of its counterpart economies in the region, providing evidence of its strong integration and dependency on other economies. Nonetheless, there is a slightly better performance than the regional trends, continuously evident in the third phase.

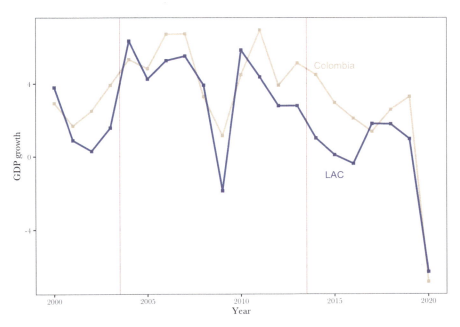

Fig. 4.1 Economic growth of Colombia and Latin American countries. *Source* World Bank Data (2021)

Internally, the structure of the Colombian economy has not considerably changed in the last 20 years. Figure 4.2 displays the participation of individual sector value-added between 2005 and 2020. Even though there are no dramatic changes in the sectoral composition, three observations have been reshaping the economy in the last years. In the first place, there is an apparent switch between manufacturing and the public sector. While manufacturing has continually declined, the public sector participation steadily rose over the same period. Despite the decrease in the relative participation of manufacturing, this sector has steady growth during the first 16 years of the twenty-first century. Overall, the loss of the comparative participation of the industrial sectors can be primarily traced to a deceleration of the demand for industrial goods as well as its vertical disintegration, which is aligned with a global trend (Carranza-Romero et al., 2018).

Figure 4.2 also highlights the rapid change in the last years of multiple sectors' contributions, including the public sector, which became the dominant contributor to the value-added of the Colombian economy in 2020. The increasing participation of the public sector is supported by the findings of Marín-Llanes et al. (2018), who indicate that there was a critical change after 2008 in the investments of the National General Budget (NGB), which was primarily intended for social inclusion and driven by the hydrocarbons royalties bonanza between 2008 and 2016. Additionally, the steady upward trend of the participation of the financial sector is noticeable, while mining and construction experienced a decline in their relative importance during this last phase.

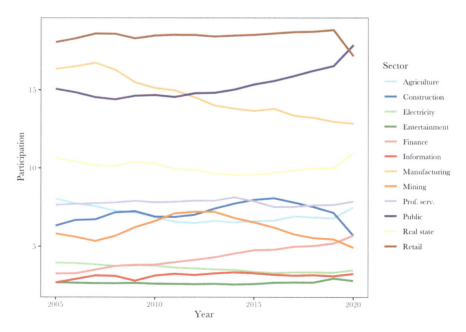

Fig. 4.2 Dynamics of the economic composition. *Source* DANE, National accounts

Geographically, the contributions of different administrative areas to the total GDP of Colombia have remained virtually invariant. The primary adjustment between 2000 and 2020 was a sizeable increase in the participation of the Meta department in the total real GDP between 2011 and 2013, coinciding with a positive shock to oil prices providing the explanation of this change given the dependency of this department on mining and quarrying. Indeed, Meta's mine participation in its GDP has increased from around 10% in the early 2000s to around 30% in the last years. Moreover, Meta has increased its participation in the total value-added of mines and quarrying from 9% during the first years of the century to 35% in the last years, according to the sectorial data of the National Administrative Department of Statistics (DANE).

To gain insights into the minor changes in the decomposition of the GDP by departments, a comparison between contributions in 2000 and 2020 was performed (Fig. 4.3).The top two departments with the most significant positive change were Meta and Bogotá D.C, increasing 1.5 p.p. and 1.4 p.p, respectively. On the other hand, the bottom two changes are new departments[1] and Tolima. The top three contributors to the national GDP have remained unchanged, namely Bogotá D.C, Antioquia, and Valle del Cauca. In 2000, these departments[2] contributed 49%, and in 2020, there was a slight increase to 51.1%.

The seemingly stable composition of departments' contributions to the national GDP might be masking internal dynamics across space—particularly the convergence of GDP per capita within the country. Figure 4.4 shows the time-variation relationship between initial income per capita and the economic growth between 2000 and 2019. Two perceptible observations motivate this study. In the first place, as the initial year moves forward, the relationship between GDP per capita and economic growth by departments in Colombia starts to change. Moving from the top-left to the bottom-right plots in Fig. 4.4, it can be concluded that the slope of such a relationship has a counterclockwise movement, indicating that the country is slowly moving from a sluggish convergent scenario to a divergent paradigm.

Additionally, two departments started lagging behind the rest of the departments when Amazonía departments were excluded. The two red points, which correspond to La Guajira and Chocó, fall apart from the patterns observed in the rest of the country. In the early 2000s, these two departments had growth rates similar to the rest of the country, but since the second half of the period, they started to persistently have near zero and negative growth rates, locating them in the bottom left quadrant. Besides, Fig. 4.4 is conclusive that the largest GDP per capita is consistently concentrated in the largest departments, based on population size.

---

[1] New departments are San Andrés and Providencia Islands, Caquetá, Putumayo, Amazonas, Guainía, Guaviare, and Vaupés. Except for San Andrés, they belong to the Amazon region. They receive this name because they were created by the Political Constitution of 1991.

[2] Colombia is a unitary country made up of three levels of governments: nation, 33 departments, and 1100 municipalities. There are also some districts which are territories with mixed characteristics of departments and municipalities.

Fig. 4.3 Departments' participation in the National Real GDP 2000 and 2020. *Source* DANE, National accounts

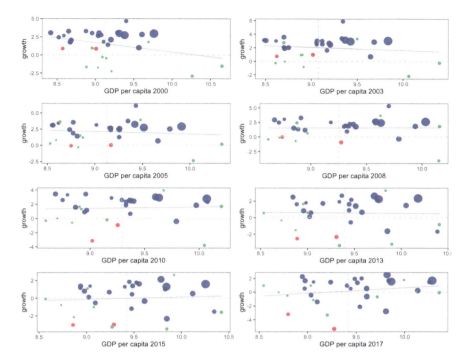

Fig. 4.4 Economic growth (2019/variant year) versus initial GDP per capita. *Note* The green bubbles represent the Amazonía departments and San Andrés and Providencia islands. The red points identify La Guajira and Chocó, and the blue dots represent the remaining 22 departments. The sizes of the bubbles show the relative population size of each department. The dotted vertical line represents the median GDP per capita each year, and the straight gray line is the linear fitted line for all values

4.3 International and National Literature

The papers of Barro and Sala-i-Martin (1992) and Mankiw et al. (1992) initiated a significant new wave of interest in the process of convergence/divergence between and within national economies. Despite the numerous critiques of their test specifications, and the sensitivity to the period explored, among others, the hypothesis test proposed by Barro and Sala-i-Martin (1992) remains the predominant empirical paradigm to measure convergence in different aspects. Although a cumbersome task, Islam (2003) and Johnson and Papageorgiou (2020) synthesized the surveyed literature on convergence. These revisions conclude that even though there is not a straightforward path to understanding and estimating convergence because it can be assessed in multiple forms, "[...] understanding convergence would get us closer to understanding the process of economic growth—a truly humbling endeavor" (Johnson & Papageorgiou, 2020). Furthermore, according to Islam (2003), a closer look at the results discloses some similarities in a deceptive bundle of different conclusions and methodologies.

Johnson and Papageorgiou (2020) grouped the approaches to measure convergence into three collections: (1) linear models that follow the classical approach—here, we find some contributions from the Regional Science literature, which proposes the inclusion of spatial dependence to avoid bias (Le Gallo et al., 2003; Rey & Le Gallo, 2009); (2) non-linear models that attempt to explore the possibility of group divergence or club convergence; this group also includes the Quah' methodology and other distributional non-parametric models; (3) time series models, a group that has increased its visibility in recent research; and (4) cross-individual distribution income that has focused on individual income rather than aggregated values by country.

Convergence is theoretical concept, and thus, Johnson and Papageorgiou (2020) conclude that the peculiarities and development stages of countries will partially define the convergence status of individual countries. Likewise, these authors propose that the centrality of the discussion ought to take a deviation from seeking evidence on convergence or divergence and instead focus on the mechanisms that underlies growth dynamics. We add to such a conclusion that it is about understanding the dynamics of economic growth per capita and for all areas in a sustainable and inclusive fashion.

The Colombian literature has made substantial contributions to finding evidence of convergence or divergence since 1993. This literature is summarized by Galvis-Aponte et al. (2017). As disclosed by these authors and Table 4.1, there is no consensus even within Colombia on the estimation of convergence. Nonetheless, results are sensitive to the chosen period analyzed, as shown in this chapter. Although this research is important, empirical tests are not sufficient to conclude if Colombian administrative units will eventually converge in the long run. Provided the existence of a theoretical equilibrium, the lack of agreement of conclusions even using the same methodology is evidence of the unstable relationship between GDP per capita growth and initial economic conditions. The results, especially those coming from beta and Quah's methods, help us answer the question suggested by their specification: given a period of analysis, is there evidence of less prosperous economies growing at a faster pace or not? We also argue that finding patterns behind convergence estimations, and their architecture provides elements to target the best mechanisms to promote lagging areas, as Johnson and Papageorgiou (2020) suggested.

Additionally, the evidence on convergence has also motivated the discussions on the recent discourses about sustainable economic growth, which attempt to answer if the arrangements for economic growth are translated to human development indicators. The literature in Colombia shows a more apparent consensus on the convergence patterns of development indicators (Table 4.1). Using life expectancy, Human Development Index (HDI), school enrollment, and others as a proxy of social development, most of the literatures indicate that lagging areas are advancing faster in reducing gaps in those indicators.

The review of Colombian literature also shows that for most of the studies, the sample was restricted to 24 departments, and new departments were treated as one administrative area due to data limitations. Furthermore, in the literature encountered,

Table 4.1 Summary of convergence literature in Colombia

Study	Period	Number of states	Type of convergence	Conclusion
Cardenas et al. (1993)	1950–1989	25	Beta	Convergence
			Sigma	Historical reduction trend
Birchenall and Murcia (1997)	1960–1990	25	Quah	Divergence
Rocha and Vivas (1998)	1980–1994	20	Canova-Marcet	Neutral
			Quah-type	Divergence
Soto (1998)	1960–1995	25	Beta	Divergence
Bonet and Meisel (1999)	1926–1995	25	Beta and sigma	Convergence 1926–1960
				Divergence 1960–1995
Ardila-Rueda (2004)	1985–1996	25	Quah	Divergence
Barón and Meisel (2003)	1990–2000	24	Beta and sigma	Neutral
Acevedo (2003)	1980–2000	24	Beta	Convergence 1980–1990
				Divergence 1990–2000
			Sigma	Convergence during recessions and divergence during expansions
Bonet and Meisel (2007)	1975–2000	25	Quah	Convergence (without Bogota)
			Sgma	Convergence (unconditional)
Franco and Raymond (2009)	1975–2005	24	Beta and sigma	Divergence and club convergence
Galvis and Meisel (2012)	1990–2011	33	Beta	Convergence 2001–2011
			Sigma	Historical reduction trend
Royuela and Garcia Cruz (2015)	1975–2005	28	Beta	Convergence
			Sigma	Divergence

(continued)

Table 4.1 (continued)

Study	Period	Number of states	Type of convergence	Conclusion	
Galvis-Aponte and Hanh (2016)	1993–2012	Municipalities	Beta	Neutral	
Galvis-Aponte et al. (2017)	1995–2015	33	Beta, sigma and Quah	Divergence	
Hanh and Meisel (2018)	1926–2018	Regions	Beta	Convergence	
			Sigma	Inconclusive with a positive trend in the last 50 years	
			Tme series	Inconclusive	
Social indicators					
				Indicator	Conclusion
Aguirre (2005)	1985–1990		Beta and quah	Life expectancy	Convergence
				Illiterate	Divergence
				Infant mortality	Convergence
Branisa and Cardoso (2009)	1973–2005		Beta	literacy	Convergence
			Quah-type	infant survival and life expectancy	Neutral
León and Rios (2013)	1990–2010			HDI	Convergence
				Life expectancy	
				School enrollment	
				Income	
Santos-Marquez and Mendez (2021)	2010–2018		Beta	homicides and personal injuries	Convergence
			Sigma		Convergence
Murillo and Gaviria (2008)	1993–2005		Beta	Human capital	Convergence
Royuela and Garcia Cruz (2015)	1975–2005		Beta, sigma and stochastic kernel	Health, education and crime	Primarily Convergence

we did not find evidence of the decomposition of the beta convergence to understand its dynamics. In this scenario, we aim to contribute to the discussion on the drivers of convergence and divergence in Colombian areas in the last 20 years. We hope that such inquiry will equip the Colombian economy with additional instruments to promote more equitable economic growth across space. Also, the complementary analysis with social indicator convergence will add an important understanding of the dynamics of human development, in contrast with other economic indicators.

4.4 Convergence Estimation and Its Decomposition

We employ standard absolute beta convergence and sigma approaches. We follow such a procedure for comparison with the existing literature because it is recognized as the most broadly accepted method in the convergence literature and an appropriate starting point in the analysis of convergence. Moreover, in its simplest form, it helps us answer our primary question: Whether Colombian poorest areas' per capita product grows faster than the richest one for various periods.

The basic convergence concept inspired by Solow (1956), renowned as beta convergence, is defined by a log-linear form of the most straightforward neoclassical growth model, given by:

$$\frac{1}{T-s} \ln\left(\frac{y_{(i,T)}}{y_{(i,T-s)}}\right) = \alpha + \beta \ln\left(y_{(i,T-t)}\right) + \varepsilon \quad (4.1)$$

where $y_{(i,T)}$ and $y_{(i,T-t)}$ define a vector of income in a given area i and year T and the lagged income in year $T-t$, for any $t > 0$. β represents the parameter of interest, which indicates convergence if its statistical test leads to the conclusion that it is larger than zero and divergence if smaller than 0. ε is an error term. The explicit test described by Barro and Sala-i-Martin (1992) is defined as follows:

$$\frac{1}{T-t} \ln\left(\frac{y_{(i,T)}}{y_{(i,T-s)}}\right) = \alpha - \left(\frac{1-e^{-B(T-t)}}{T-t}\right) \ln\left(y_{(i,T-t)}\right) + \varepsilon \quad (4.2)$$

The difference between B and β is that the first one estimates the speed of convergence. The results described in the following section present the results of β because the interpretation is more clearly read and facilitates interpretation of the decomposition analysis that further complements this analysis. Notice that the results are sensitive to the selection of the initial and last year compared. Patel et al. (2021) have pointed out the dependency of convergence analysis on the variation of the year of analysis in a cross-country comparison. Their analysis is conclusive about the dependence of convergence to the time period chosen, but also that there can exist different trends of the β coefficient depending on the starting point in time that is chosen. Our analysis selected 2019 as the endpoint and employed different initial years varying from 2000 to 2018.

4.4.1 Decomposition

In addition, this research decomposes the beta (β) estimated for different starting points according to the contributions of different sectors. The decomposition follows the initial proposal of Maddison (1952), which has been applied in the decomposition of convergence in different scenarios such as Wong (2006), McMillan et al. (2014), Rodrik et al. (2019), and recently by Dieppe and Matsuoka (2021). In contrast to this study, the literature has been concentrated on the decomposition of one type of productivity convergence, primarily defined as the rate between GDP and the working force. We use a modified version of the proposal by Maddison (1952) that posits that convergence can be partitioned into three components:

$$\frac{\Delta y}{y} = \sum_{s=1}^{S} \frac{Y_s^0}{Y_0} \Delta y_s + \sum_{s=1}^{S} \frac{y_s^0}{y_0} \Delta p_s + \sum_{s=1}^{S} \frac{y_s^0}{y_0} \Delta y_s \Delta p_s \qquad (4.3)$$

The right-hand side in Eq. 4.3 defines, respectively, the total growth effect within sectors (changes for each sector, with fixed the economic structure), total shift effect (the effect of convergence due to variation in the structure), and the interaction effect (the combined effect of changing growth and the economic structure). Δy_s is the changes of each sectorial real product s, Δp_s denotes the changes in sectorial participation,[3] Y_0 is the aggregated GDP at time 0, Y_s^0 the aggregated output of sector s at time 0, y_s^0 is the per capita GDP of each sector s, and y_0 is the total per capita GDP.

In order to estimate the beta decomposition corresponding to each component, a further step is required. This task is completed by regressing each component for a given sector on each starting year GDP per capita (ln (y_s)). In our case, as the starting point changes, this analysis was done for each separate year. Each component can be defined as the aggregation of all sector estimates. Once each of the three components is estimated, their aggregation should resemble the beta obtained from regressing the classical beta defined above.

4.4.2 Spatial Dependence

Recent literature on economic convergence has advocated for the inclusion and importance of spatial dependence in this process. It is indeed likely that the lack of

---

[3] In the standard literature that decomposes productivity understood as the rate GDP/workers, the first component describes changes in labor productivity, and the second component is represented by changes in labor participation. Due to the absence of labor sectorial participation over time/department, we use this alternative approach, which can also approximate the total GDP per capita change. The aggregation of the estimated components of the decomposition closely recovers the aggregated beta estimates in our case.

inclusion of spatial dependence generates issues associated with the model's misspecification due to the spillover effect related to proximity (LeSage & Pace, 2009; Rey & Le Gallo, 2009). The potential importance of spatial dependence has been acknowledged in recent literature on convergence (Andreano et al., 2017; Cartone et al., 2021; Postiglione et al., 2013). The most well-known model used in this context is the spatial autoregressive model (SAR), which has the following specification:

$$\frac{1}{T-s} \ln\left(\frac{y_{(i,T)}}{y_{(i,T-s)}}\right) = \alpha + \rho W \frac{1}{T-s} \ln\left(\frac{y_{(i,T)}}{y_{(i,T-s)}}\right) + \beta \ln\left(y_{(i,T-t)}\right) + \varepsilon \quad (4.4)$$

The key difference between Eqs. 4.1 and 4.4 is the spatial dependence component described by the second term of the right-hand side of Eq. 4.4, which describes the associated spatial effect ρ and the neighbors' dependence W. The neighbors' matrix applied in this application uses a queen-type contiguity matrix.

To be precise and select the most appropriate model, either lag or spatial error alternative, we run tests that would suggest the correct selection. The recommended steps for selecting the most appropriate spatial model advocate the following (Anselin, 2005): run the pertinent OLS regression, estimate the Lagrange multiplier (LM) diagnostic, error, and lag. If none of them is significant, then it suggests that spatial dependence is irrelevant. If one of them is significant, it would indicate the models of the corresponding type. If both are significant, we claim the theoretical framework, which indicates that the SAR model is the most appropriate in this context. The results ultimately specified the final selection using only SAR models, given that for the year where we find evidence of spatial dependence, the LM error, and lag, and their robust forms are significant, in which case we follow the standard form used in the literature as described by Eq. 4.4. It is important to note that San Andrés and Providencia were excluded from the sample for the estimation of spatial models due to their status as an island.

4.5 Data and Methodology

The primary source of data used in the convergence analysis is the real GDP with the reference year 2015, the real GDP by sectors, and the population of Colombia. The data are provided by DANE and are freely available. The data are disaggregated at the department level from the entire analysis period (2000–2020). Nevertheless, out of the 33 departments that comprise Colombia, the so-called new departments (9) do not have complete information between 2000 and 2004 using the latest base (2015). To complete this information, we estimate the participation of each missing department from the new department's total, which is observed in the data available at current prices for the year 2005 and applied such proportions to the GDP reported for new departments between 2000 and 2004 at the aggregated level.

The sectorial information is available at two different aggregated levels. The dataset used is compounded of eight sectorial activities: (I) agriculture: agriculture, livestock, forestry, and fishing, (II) mines: mines and quarries exploitations, (III) manufacturing industries, (IV) construction, (V) electricity, gas, and water, (VI) retail: retail, transport, repairing, and accommodation, (VII) finance: financial activities, real estate, business, and communication, (VIII) public: public administration, education, health; artistic activities and entertainment; individual households activities. Due to the lack of information from 2000 to 2004 for the new departments, we backward forecast the trends of each of these sectors, given that they present a smooth pattern in the observed data.

Additionally, as a complementary exercise, we estimate beta convergence for other indicators to validate the results using other economic indicators and explore if different patterns are found in those indicators. The additional indicators used are (1) the income per capita reported by the Integrated Household Survey (GEIH), which has information for 24 departments (excludes new departments) between 2011 and 2020, (2) the income tax revenue as a proxy of the performance of independent income for all departments, available at TerriData by the National Planning Department (DNP), (3) the multidimensional poverty index (MPI) also obtained from TerriData, which is available for the last two Census periods at the department level (2005 and 2018), and (4) the human development index (HDI) available on the Global Data Lab (Institute for Management Research, n.d.).

The tax revenue and household income used are their real value with a 2015 base. To translate their nominal value to a real value, we estimated the GDP deflator of each department-year using the indirect deflator obtained from the reported GDP series produced by DANE with 2015 base: nominal Y_i/real Y_i, where Y_i is the GDP of each department.

Figure 4.5 summarizes the evolution of our main variable, the GDP per capita of all departments of Colombia between 2000 and 2019. Colombia has experienced some structural changes in the GDP per capita in recent years. If Casanare and Arauca, the departments with the most significant variations, are excluded from the equation, the remaining departments display an upward trend in their GDP per capita. Nevertheless, it is noteworthy that the GDP per capita at the beginning of the period was more similar accross departments than toward the end. This implies that, as sigma converges (Appendix), the differences between departments in Colombia are increasing, where some departments are growing at a steady and faster pace than others. Bogotá D.C and Risaralda, which are among the wealthier areas, were the only ones with a non-negative yearly increase during the whole period; further, Santander only experienced a slight decrease between 2002 and 2001.

In addition to the expansion of the dispersion observed in the data, there has been some changes in rank. In 2000, the departments with the largest GDP per capita, in its order, were Casanare, Arauca, Bogotá D.C, Santander, Cundinamarca, Meta, Antioquia, Valle del Cauca, Boyacá, and Atlántico. The order from bottom-up was Vichada, Nariño, Sucre, Chocó, Caquetá, Amazonas, Cauca, Guainía, Córdoba, and Magdalena. In 2019, the order of the wealthier department per capita was Casanare, Bogotá D.C, Meta, Santander, San Andrés, Antioquia, Valle del Cauca, Boyacá, Cundinamarca, and Arauca. From bottom-up, the order was Vichada, Vaupés, Chocó, Guainía, Sucre, Nariño, Córdoba, Magdalena, Guaviare, and Amazonas. Although

4 Regional Convergence in Colombia in the Twenty-First Century

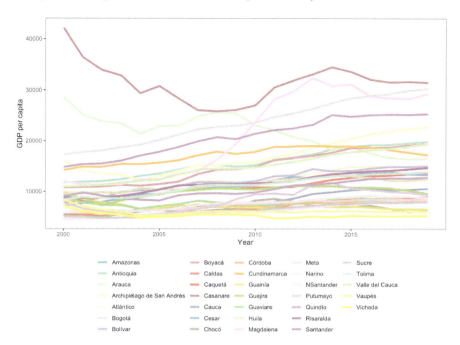

Fig. 4.5 Evolution of the GDP per capita per department. *Source* Own estimations based on national accounts

some changes are perceived, the rank is conclusive about the fact the areas with lower-income per capita in both years are predominantly located in the peripheral regions: Amazonas, Pacific, and Caribbean coast. Moreover, one of the largest advances within the period was San Andrés y Providencia.

The summary of additional data sources used in this study is compiled in Table 4.2. It is noticeable that all the variables considered have positive changes. The average real GDP per capita, tax revenues per capita, income per capita, and HDI have increased over the observed years. The most significant gains are concentrated in the tax revenues per capita, which virtually quadruple in 2019, compared to its average in 2000. Likewise, there have been important gains in multidimensional poverty reduction, which decreased from an average of 60–37%.

Table 4.2 Descriptive statistics of the main variables

Variable	2000 Mean	2000 St. dev.	2019 Mean	2019 St. dev.	2005 Mean	2005 St. dev.	2011 Mean	2011 St. dev.	2018 Mean	2018 St. dev.
Population	1,186,063.0	1,413,083.7	1,496,838.7	1,745,353.5						
Real GDP pc	10,644.9	7,328.8	13,990.6	7,250.8						
Tax revenues pc	101,089.5	71,406.6	454,470.3	202,419.3						
MPI					60.3	16.3			37.2	18.3
HDI	0.662		0.744	0.037						
HH income pc			429,407.7	163,925.5			416,959.0	140,915.4		

Note Real GDP pc in Colombian pesos 2015 (thousands), real GDP pc, tax revenues pc, and HH income pc in Colombian pesos

4.6 Results

4.6.1 Beta Convergence Timing

Figure 4.5 presents the unconditional β and its corresponding confidence interval. As noted earlier, this parameter was estimated using a sequence of starting years from 2000 to 2019 and using two last years of reference (2019 and 2020). Most of our analysis will be concentrated on the results associated with the year 2019 because of the critical changes produced by the COVID-19 pandemic in 2020. This year's results were also estimated to measure the effect of this crisis on the convergence trends.

The test of convergence, which compares the hypothesis of a $\beta = 0$ versus $\beta \neq 0$, , is conclusive that in the case of Colombia, except for the first starting point (2000), there is no statistically significant evidence to claim that there is convergence or divergence. As shown in Fig. 4.5, the 95% confidence interval covers the horizontal zero line as the year varies. Moreover, since beta shows a positive value of 2000, there is statistical evidence of convergence this year. Nonetheless, Fig. 4.6 is also persuasive about two other facts. While fixing the year 2019 as our endpoint, there is a positive trend in the estimated beta as the starting year gets closer to 2019. Thus, indicating that Colombia has some evidence of moving from a slow convergence scenario to a divergence if the upward trend remains. For instance, although insignificant, in 2009, 2010, and 2014 onwards, the β estimates move from a positive sign to a negative.

When the last years of reference change from 2019 to 2020, there is a slight downwards movement of the ascendant beta trends, showing that the 2020 crisis might have a pro-convergence effect in Colombia. This result is consistent with the evidence encountered by Acevedo (2003) who shows evidence of convergence (or similar behavior of economic growth) during recessions and the opposite during expansions in Colombia.

Until recently, most of the convergence studies in Colombia were limited to 24 departments because of the constraint of data availability disaggregated for new departments; most of those studies have suggested the existence of beta convergence. In order to compare those results, we replicate the exercise displayed in Fig. 4.6 for 24 departments (excludes new departments) and for 22 departments (excluding La Guajira, Chocó, and new departments) in Fig. 4.7. The final sample with 22 and 24 departments gathers a large proportion of the Colombian population. According to the projections of the DANE, the 22 and 24 departments account for 93.9% and 96.9% of the total population in 2020, respectively.

The results presented in Fig. 4.6 show that, although statistically insignificant over the period analyzed, the beta trend indicates different patterns than Fig. 4.7. The restricted 24 departments displayed a slow divergence until 2010. However, as suggested in the initial exploratory analysis from Fig. 4.4, La Guajira and Chocó have substantial differences compared to the rest of the 22 departments. This is reflected in the descendant movement of the convergence line, whereas Chocó and La Guajira are excluded. The results indicate a continual reduction of beta until 2011, and its

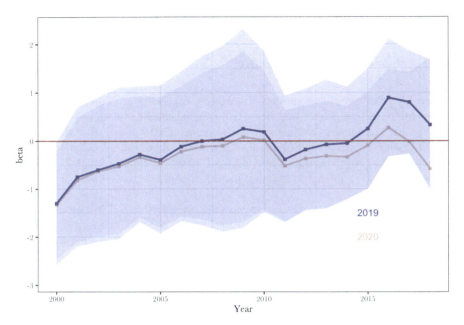

Fig. 4.6 Beta convergence from 2000 to 2018 (reference years: 2019 and 2020). *Note* own estimations based on GDP per capita. The bands correspond to the 95% confidence interval resulting from robust standard errors

value remains negative over most of the period analyzed. Moreover, notice an upward trend toward divergence after 2010 regardless of the inclusion or exclusion of Chocó and La Guajira.

4.6.2 Beta Convergence Decomposition

Growth convergence matters, but also its nature. Even in the absence of statistically significant convergence, the understanding of the decomposition provides additional tools that can contribute to redirecting policies aiming to have a more equal income per capita distribution across space.

Figure 4.8 presents the beta decomposition for different starting years and by its components. It is conclusive that the significant convergence effect until 2009 in Colombia was the total growth effect (TE), also known as the within sectorial effect. The growth within sectors was one of the main motors of the weak convergence observed during that period. However, the last years (2015 and onwards) show that the total effect has become the primary driver of divergence. A reading of these results should be cautious because shorter periods of growth are highly susceptible to temporal shocks.

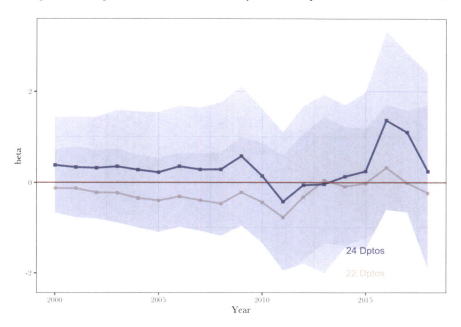

Fig. 4.7 Beta convergence from 2000 to 2018 (Reference year: 2019) for 24 departments (excludes new departments) and 22 departments (excludes Chocó, La Guajira, and new departments). *Note* own estimations based on GDP per capita. The bands correspond to the 95% confidence interval resulting from robust standard errors

Further exploration of the TE decomposition provides additional insights into the contribution by sectors (Fig. 4.9). There is a distinct change of patterns in the relative importance of each sector to the beta coefficient. Moreover, based on these results, the analysis period could be split into two periods, before and after 2010. Before 2010, the convergence was primarily driven by mining, the public sector, and construction. This scenario had a significant adjustment in the last years when mining became a major divergence force. It is also evident that the public sector's role in convergence has been stable and important. Conversely, throughout the twenty-first century, it has also been observed that financial services/real estate and commerce/transportation have increased their contribution to divergence in Colombia. Overall, we can claim that the convergence effect in Colombia has been highly dependent on the public and mining sectors in recent years, and such dependency could be detrimental to a stable path of convergence in Colombia in the long run, given the high reliance on mining to the international market and prices.

The data show that mine production has become highly concentrated in primarily seven departments (Meta, Casanare, Cesar, Antioquia, Santander, Arauca, and Boyacá), which accounted for around 83% of the total production of this sector in 2020. The concentration was even more evident among the departments of Meta, Casanare, and Cesar, who account for around 62% of the national mining gross

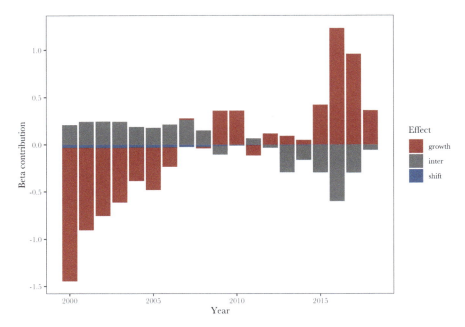

Fig. 4.8 Sectorial decomposition: total growth effect, inter effect, and shift effect. *Note* [1] te: total sectorial growth effect, [2] shift: sectorial shift effect, and [3] inter: intersectoral effect

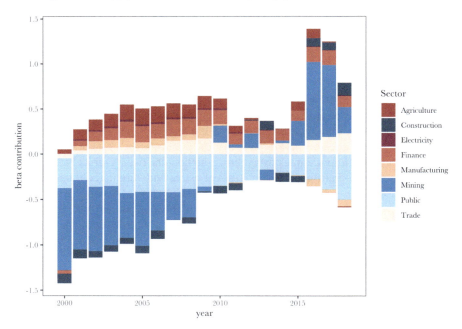

Fig. 4.9 Sectorial decomposition of total growth effect (TE)

product. This scenario is entirely different from that observed at the beginning of the twenty-first century, when the primary departments were Casanare, Arauca, and La Guajira. A closer inspection of the data indicates that some of the lagging areas that used to have a relatively important rank in Colombia's mining production, namely Chocó and La Guajira, are progressively declining their participation. It has been doing so markedly in Chocó since 2010 when its contribution dropped from 4.6% in 2010 to 1.2% in 2020. In addition, in La Guajira, the decline started in 2007 and its participation dropped from 11.4% in 2007 to 3.5% in 2020.

This section's major results state that Colombia would be primarily diverging for most of the century in the absence of mining and the public sector. Provided that such dependency on mining has changed in the last years, this is a call to action to rethink or reboot the economies of departments that are lagging and are highly dependent on the instability of commodities and public expenses.

4.6.3 Spatial Dependence

Even though there is strong argumentation and evidence in favor of spatial interaction to understand convergence (Lesage & Fischer, 2008), the results we encountered from Colombia in the period targeted suggest that such dependence has lost importance in the economic growth of Colombian departments. According to our results, where we test the spatial dependence hypothesis varying the starting year, such spatial dependence is only applicable between 2000 and 2003. When the initial year to test unconditional convergence changes from 2003 to 2004, the spatial dependence tests stay insignificant for the remaining period (Fig. 4.10).

The simple economic growth model from Eq. 4.1 and the spatial dependence model from Eq. 4.4 were estimated for the entire period. As the tests show, it is evident that physical neighbors do not significantly affect the beta after 2003. Moreover, it is also clear from Fig. 4.9 that the absence of spatial dependence overestimates the convergence rate between 2000 and 2003. In other words, the spatial dependence effects contribute to divergence, especially during that period.

We hypothesize that two potential factors might be explaining these results. First, although Colombian connectivity (measured through transportation) is still relatively limited compared to other countries, the road network has shown important advances in the last two decades. According to Ramirez-Giraldo et al. (2021), a steep increase in the road network per capita started around 2005. These authors claim that the pressing demand for faster freight transportation at low cost, which was not met by the river and rail transportation in the early twentieth century, generated substantial reallocation of transportation investments toward road investments. As this infrastructure expansion progressed, we argue that it released spatial constraints so that departments could expand their economic networks to further markets, consequently limiting the spatial dependence of growth on physical neighbors. Others might argue that increased spatial connectivity (lower transportation costs) would increase dependence as firms could exploit scale economies and thus explore larger markets.

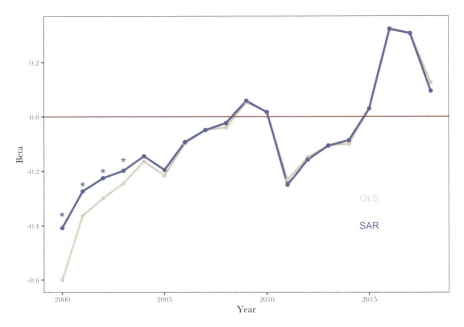

Fig. 4.10 Beta estimations based on SAR versus non-spatial. *Note* The stars indicate significant LM tests for spatial relevance

Secondly, we argue that the mining sector's production, which is the main activity driving convergence during the period and is aimed at sales abroad, could have been affecting these results. In the same vein as the argument related to the road network, internal production is more sensitive to international market accessibility and less to physical neighbors. One evidence of increasing dependence on international economies is the acceleration of exports and imports since 2004 due to the oil and coal export boom. Although exports decreased between 2014 and 2015, they have not reached levels like those observed at the beginning of the twenty-first century (Fig. 4.11). It is noticeable that exports and imports in 2014, when a summit was reached, accounted for almost six times the values observed between 2000 and 2003. Such a rate has remained high even in more recent periods. This observation indicates the significant change in Colombian markets' integration with international markets, leading to a smaller dependence on local economies.

4.6.4 Convergence on Other Indicators

To supplement the analysis of beta convergence in GDP per capita, we estimate the convergence of four other indicators: tax revenue, MPI, HDI, and income per capita reported by households. The latter is only available for 24 departments between 2011

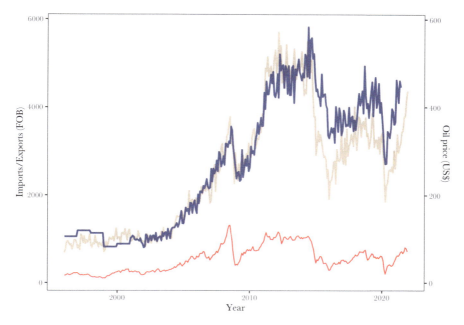

Fig. 4.11 Exports and imports Colombia 2000–2021. *Source* Central Bank of Colombia

and 2020. This exercise sheds light on whether the performance of macroeconomic indicators is also observed and potentially translated to other indicators.

Paradoxically, although GDP per capita does not show a beta convergence trend in the last 20 years, the opposite has happened with the revenue tax per capita collected by individual administrative units (Fig. 4.12). Conversely, the tax revenue per capita beta has been negative compared to the encountered patterns. As the starting year varies throughout the analysis, it has remained significant until 2017, and with a decreasing trend, evidence of an increase in the convergence pattern. These are positive observations, given that local governments are the primary force to redistribute income in society. Moreover, this finding is aligned with the beta decomposition we observed, where the public sector has a positive pressing effect on convergence through the twenty-first century.

Contrariwise, the comparison of the two observed points of MPI (2005 and 2018) indicates that progress on the social front does not have the same outcome. There is, in fact, a positive and significant beta, signifying that the departments that have had the most significant gains in poverty reduction between 2005 and 2018 were also those with relatively low poverty rates in 2005. Moreover, the HDI, which has a longer period of data availability, indicates a significant convergence until 2008. After 2008, the HDI beta has positive values, indicating divergence. Notice, there is an increasing trend over the years. Therefore, it is relevant to ask about the quality of public expenditures. One explanation of these conflicting results is that some regional investments are concentrated on long-term programs with the expectation

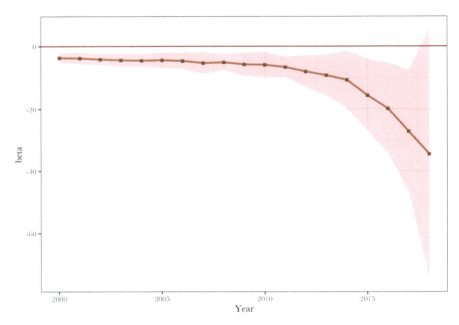

Fig. 4.12 Per capita tax revenue beta convergence

that the gains/benefits will be achieved in the longer term. According to the NGB 2019, indeed the poorest regions benefited most from increases in budget allocation, with many programs focusing on social inclusion such as Primera Infancia (early childcare), Jóvenes en Acción (Youth in action), Obras para la prosperidad (Work for prosperity), among others (DNP, 2020).

Even though allocations to social inclusion are a critical piece to bridging economic growth performance, local government income, and social indicators, it is also possible that inefficient and inadequate quality of expenses transforms that relationship or even leads to the opposite effect if the resources are concentrated in the incorrect share of the population. This will require further research on the quality of regional expenses and the potential impediment that can overshadow the pipeline between macroeconomic indicators and social well-being. In an analysis of the public expenditures in Colombia, Espitia et al. (2019) succinctly summarize this issue, claiming that: "Contrary to conventional short-term analyzes, to achieve the aforementioned purposes, greater public spending is required, which is allocated and executed in an efficient and equitable manner that avoids corrupt practices." Given the patterns we perceive in the data, the divergence of MPI, the convergence of tax revenues (which hold when we restrict the data to the period of the MPI), and the beginning of divergence in recent years of HDI, we can claim that there might be an imbalance between expenses and needs, which is worth exploring (Fig. 4.13).

Finally, the income per capita convergence patterns appear to follow the GDP per capita path, as shown in Fig. 4.14. However, the beta associated with the income per

4 Regional Convergence in Colombia in the Twenty-First Century

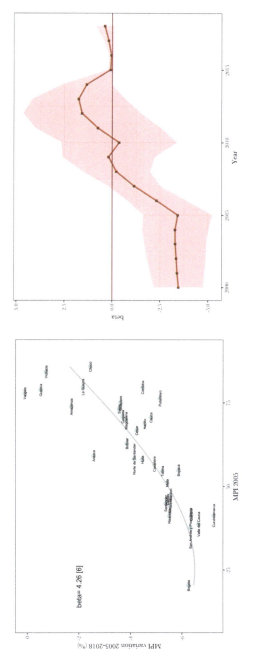

Fig. 4.13 MPI (left) and HDI (right) Beta convergence

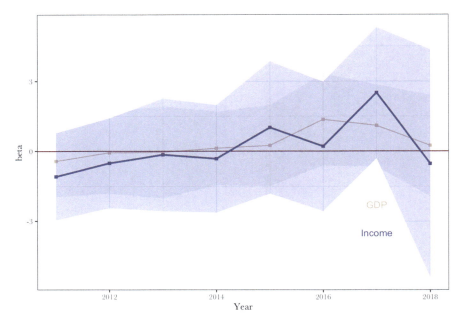

Fig. 4.14 Beta convergence for 24 departments GDP per capita versus household income per capita

capita reported by the households was smaller than the one observed in the GDP until 2014, when higher variants started to appear between them, and a divergent (insignificant) pattern emerged. We can conclude that the households' income is slightly associated with the macroeconomic performance of the economy, as expected. Nonetheless, this relationship is not stable and less evident in the short term. Furthermore, the convergence of household income is more sensitive to change over time than the GDP per capita.

4.7 Final Considerations

The first 20 years of the twenty-first century of the Colombian economy are placed between two significant crises: the crisis of the end of the century in 1999 and the coronavirus crisis in 2020. These are the most significant economic downturn since the 1960s. In the former, the economic growth was −4.2, and in the latter −6.8, which was also accompanied by the less detrimental (to Colombia) international crisis in 2008. During this period, and perhaps due to these critical changes, the economy has experienced significant fluctuations: manufacturing and mining and quarrying have lost participation, while the public sector, finance, and retail have acquired a larger contribution to GDP. Another meaningful change was increasing construction participation, declining in 2015.

Against this backdrop, the exploration of the overall trends of the unconditional beta convergence between 2000 and 2020 reveals mixed results. Even though the static depictions of the beta converge would conclude that there has been a slight convergence between 2000 and 2007 (compared to 2019), when seen as a whole, the beta trends, although insignificant, show an upward trend as the initial year varies, indicating that there is a trend toward divergence in Colombia. Such results are compatible with the sigma trend of GDP per capita. The trends also warn about increasing potential divergence in Colombia that can further deteriorate the already dissimilarities of wealth distribution.

These findings suggest that having a coherent and exhaustive understanding of beta convergence is relevant to monitoring its evolution over time. We advise that beta analysis should not be static because such views might ignore essential changes throughout the time that might affect such estimates. Indeed, some of the most recent studies related to convergence are moving from a static to a dynamic beta (Kremer et al., 2021; Patel et al., 2021). When the beta is further decomposed by sectors, the results indicate that, until recently, mining and the public sectors were the leading drivers of convergence in Colombia. In other words, if these sectors are removed from the GDP, Colombian regional economies would be primarily diverging. The message is then to promote efficiency in the sectors of lower-income departments and/or boost productive sectors in lagging areas, for which economic growth is highly dependent on public transfers.

Our estimates, including spatial analysis, suggest that spatial dependence has lost its relevance. Even though Colombia is a country of departments, it seems that economic growth dependence has lost predominance in the internal market. A department's economic growth is less dependent on their neighbors' performance in more recent years; this is more evident since 2003. We hypothesize that an increasingly open economy and advances in internal transportation connectivity could explain these results. Furthermore, given that some of the least developed areas are highly dependent on enclave economies based on mining and oil commodities, and therefore on exports, their dependence on local neighbors diminishes in importance. In our view, this can be an opportunity and a thread for poorer areas. If more efforts are concentrated on those areas with poorer performance, they can take advantage of the openness of the Colombian economy and higher interconnectivity. Otherwise, their economies can become island economies, as they might not be able to take advantage of their neighbors' prosperity due to the increasingly dwindling dependence.

In addition, our results concentrated on other indicators that reflect some inconsistencies in the trends. While the tax revenues per capita are increasing and converging, which are objectively the primary source of social investments, social indicators are not doing so. Between the two years for which there is information on the multidimensional poverty index by departments, the more significant gains occurred in poorer departments. Moreover, the HDI initially shows a converging pattern but less so in recent years.

The findings of this research provide insights into the relevance of time and the need to go beyond the more narrowly focused concept of convergence and move toward characteristics that can explain it, as well as a deeper study of those areas that are not contribution directly to the engine of economic growth. Notably, we highlight the relevance of understanding growth from its multidimensional nature and its composition's architecture while considering the structure and dependency of individual economies.

Appendix

See Fig. 4.15, Tables 4.3 and 4.4.

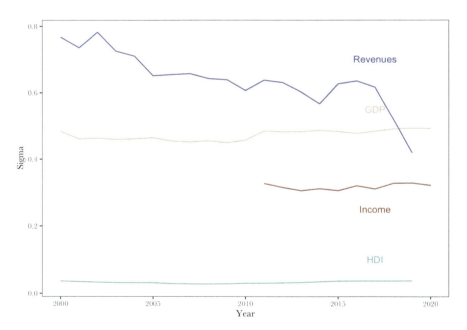

Fig. 4.15 Sigma-convergence: standard-deviation by indicator

Table 4.3 GDP per capita beta estimates (all departments)

Year	Beta	Robust Std. err	p-val
2000	−1.305	0.625	0.045
2001	−0.751	0.713	0.3
2002	−0.604	0.738	0.419
2003	−0.471	0.772	0.546
2004	−0.281	0.694	0.689
2005	−0.393	0.757	0.607
2006	−0.120	0.763	0.877
2007	−0.004	0.862	0.996
2008	0.031	0.947	0.974
2009	0.252	1.013	0.805
2010	0.184	0.821	0.824
2011	−0.383	0.647	0.558
2012	−0.181	0.621	0.773
2013	−0.074	0.656	0.91
2014	−0.051	0.573	0.93
2015	0.253	0.615	0.684
2016	0.891	0.598	0.146
2017	0.800	0.524	0.137
2018	0.332	0.659	0.618

Table 4.4 Beta decomposition by sectors

Year	Agricultura	Mineoa	Manuf.	Construe.	Electr.	Retail	Finance	Public	Rest	Shift	Inter	Beta
2000	0.046	−0.902*	0.005	−0.108***	0.002	−0.045	−0.037	−0.331***	−0.044	−0.031**	0.207	−1.238
2001	0.114	−0.765**	0.046	−0.096***	0.011	0.042	0.060	−0.287***	0.002	−0.032**	0.244	−0.660
2002	0.121	−0.708**	0.081	−0.069**	0.016	0.060	0.107	−0.361***	0.031	−0.033**	0.245	−0.510
2003	0.143**	−0.652	0.083	−0.069	0.020	0.071	0.132	−0.352***	0.044	−0.033**	0.243	−0.369
2004	0.167*	−0.492	0.099	−0.066	0.022**	0.077	0.185	−0.429***	0.082	−0.030**	0.188	−0.198
2005	0.177**	−0.594	0.064	−0.080	0.019	0.066	0.182	−0.416***	0.133	−0.032**	0.177	−0.305
2006	0.178*	−0.427	0.078	−0.091	0.018	0.096	0.162	−0.416***	0.196**	−0.029**	0.211	−0.025
2007	0.158**	−0.304	0.049	−0.002	0.019	0.147	0.190	−0.421***	0.180	−0.026**	0.261	0.252
2008	0.137	−0.314	0.062	−0.067	0.019	0.156	0.175	−0.384***	0.198	−0.023**	0.150	0.110
2009	0.133	−0.054	0.141	−0.012	0.018	0.173	0.178	−0.359***	0.141	−0.015	−0.092	0.252
2010	0.105	0.191	0.015	−0.082	0.022	0.125	0.157	−0.351***	0.179	−0.008	−0.003	0.349
2011	0.074	0.036	−0.011	−0.077	0.013	0.070	0.120	−0.311***	−0.028	−0.004	0.064	−0.054
2012	0.019	0.161	0.004	0.005	0.006	0.068	0.138	−0.291***	0.005	−0.006	−0.028	0.082
2013	−0.003	−0.115	0.015	0.101	0.007	0.101	0.144	−0.170	0.011	−0.009*	−0.287	−0.204
2014	0.007	0.027	0.000	−0.101	0.001	0.121	0.127	−0.207*	0.073	−0.009***	−0.155	−0.116
2015	0.097	0.277	−0.008	−0.067	0.000	0.093	0.115	−0.234*	0.149***	−0.006*	−0.291	0.123
2016	0.105	0.867	−0.079	0.091	0.006	0.155	0.165**	−0.277***	0.197***	−0.004*	−0.596	0.631
2017	0.012	0.798	−0.037	0.081	0.004	0.190**	0.164**	−0.390***	0.136***	−0.002***	−0.297	0.659
2018	−0.012	0.292	−0.072	0.142	0.007	0.231*	0.117*	−0.502***	0.158***	−0.001	−0.057*	0.303

Note *, **, and *** corresponds to 10, 5 and 1% significance level, and match their robust standard errors

References

Acevedo, S. (2003). Convergencia y crecimiento económico en Colombia 1980–2000. *Ecos de Economía: A Latin American Journal of Applied Economics, 7*(17), 51–78.

Aguirre, K. (2005). Convergencia en indicadores sociales en Colombia. Una aproximación desde los enfoques tradicional y no paramétrico. *Revista Desarrollo y Sociedad, 56*, 147–176.

Andreano, M. S., Benedetti, R., & Postiglione, P. (2017). Spatial regimes in regional European growth: An iterated spatially weighted regression approach. *Quality & Quantity: International Journal of Methodology, 51*(6), 2665–2684.

Anselin, L. (2005). *Exploring spatial data with GeoDa: A workbook. spatial analysis laboratory.* Department of Geography, University of Illinois. http://www.csiss.org/clearinghouse/GeoDa/geodaworkbook.pdf

Ardila-Rueda, L. (2004). Gasto público y convergencia regional en Colombia. *Revista Ensayos Sobre Política Económica, 22*(45), 222–268. https://doi.org/10.32468/Espe.4506

Barón, J. D., & Meisel, A. (2003, Septiembre). La descentralización y las disparidades económicas regionales en Colombia en la década de 1990. *Coyuntura Económica*, 105–141.

Barro, R. J., & Sala-i-Martin, X. (1992). Convergence. *Journal of Political Economy, 100*(2), 223–251.

Birchenall, J., & Murcia, G. (1997). Convergencia regional: Una revisiÃ³n del caso colombiano. *Revista Desarrollo y Sociedad, 40*, 273–308.

Bonet, J., & Meisel, A. (1999). La convergencia regional en Colombia: Una visión de largo plazo 1926–1995. *Coyuntura Económica, 29*(1), 69–106.

Bonet, J., & Meisel, A. (2007). Polarización del ingreso per cápita departamental en Colombia, 1975–2000. *Ensayos Sobre Política Económica, 25*(54), 12–43.

Branisa, B., & Cardozo, A. (2009). *Regional growth convergence in Colombia using social indicators*. Discussion Papers 195, Goettingen, Germany, Ibero America Institute for Econ. Research (Ibero-America Institute for Economic Research. https://ideas.repec.org/p/got/iaidps/195.html

Caballero, C., & Machado, G. (2020). De la crisis de "fin de siglo" a la del "coronavirus". La economía colombiana en el siglo XXI. *Coyuntura Económica: Investigación Económica y Social, 50*, 15–74.

Cárdenas, M., Pontón, A., & Trujillo, J. P. (1993). Convergencia y migraciones interdepartamentales en Colombia: 1950–1983. *Coyuntura Económica, 23*(1), 111–137.

Carranza-Romero, J. E., Arias-Rodríguez, F., Bejarano-Rojas, J. A., Casas, C., González-Ramírez, A., Moreno-Burbano, S. A., & Vélez-Velásquez, J. S. (2018). La industria colombiana en el siglo XXI. *Ensayos Sobre Politica Economica, 87*, 1–69.

Cartone, A., Postiglione, P., & Hewings, G. (2021). Does economic convergence hold? A spatial quantile analysis on European regions. *Economic Modelling, 95*(C), 408–417.

Cervo, A. (2016). Latin America's slow pace in the 21st century. *AUSTRAL: Brazilian Journal of Strategy & International Relations, 5*(9), 11–31.

Dane, D. T. de M. y P. E.–D. (n.d.). *Cuentas Nacionales.* www.dane.gov.co

De Corso, G. (2018). Crecimiento económico colombiano de 1888 a 2013: Una nueva serie del producto interno bruto. *Revista De Economía Institucional., 21*(40), 259–289.

Dieppe, A., & Matsuoka, H. (2021). *Sectoral decomposition of convergence in labor productivity: A re-examination from a new dataset.* The World Bank.

DNP. (n.d.). *TerriData: DNP.* Retrieved November 16, 2021, from https://terridata.dnp.gov.co/

DNP. (2020). *Regionalización del presupuesto general de la Nación 2020.* DNP.

Editorial La República, E. L. R. (2021). *El petróleo será lo que reactivará la economía.* Diario La República. https://www.larepublica.co/opinion/editorial/el-petroleo-sera-lo-que-reactivara-la-economia-3137855

Espitia, J., Ferrari, C., González, J. I., Hernández, I., Reyes, L. C., Romero, A., Tassara, C., Varela, D., Villabona, J., & Zafra, G. (2019). El gasto público en Colombia. Reflexiones y propuestas. *Revista De Economía Institucional, 21*(40), 291–326.

Franco, L., & Raymond, J.-L. (2009). Convergencia económica regional: El caso de los Departamentos colombianos. *Ecos de Economía, 28*, 168–197.

Galvis-Aponte, L. A. (2002). Determinantes de la migración interdepartamental en Colombia: 1988–1993. *Revista de Economia del Rosario, 5*(1), 93–118. https://doi.org/10.32468/dtseru.29

Galvis-Aponte, L. A., & Meisel, A. (2012). *Convergencia y trampas espaciales de pobreza en Colombia: Evidencia reciente*. Documentos de trabajo sobre Economía Regional y Urbana, 177, Cartagena, Banco de la República de Colombia.

Galvis-Aponte, L. A., & Hahn, L. (2016). Crecimiento municipal en Colombia: El papel de las externalidades espaciales, el capital humano y el capital físico. *Sociedad y Economía, 31*, 149–174.

Galvis-Aponte, L. A., Hahn, L., & Galvis-Larios, W. (2017). *Una revisión de los estudios de convergencia regional en Colombia. Documentos de Trabajo Sobre Economía Regional y Urbana 264*. Banco de la Republica de Colombia.

Hahn, L., & Meisel, A. (2018). La desigualdad económica entre las regiones de Colombia, 1926–2016. *Cuadernos de Historia Económica*, No. 47.

Institute for Management Research. (n.d.). *Global data lab—Innovative instruments for turning data into knowledge*. Retrieved November 16, 2021, from https://globaldatalab.org/

Islam, N. (2003). What have We Learnt from the Convergence Debate? *Journal of Economic Surveys, 17*(3), 309–362. https://doi.org/10.1111/1467-6419.00197

Johnson, P., & Papageorgiou, C. (2020). What remains of cross-country convergence? *Journal of Economic Literature, 58*(1), 129–175. https://doi.org/10.1257/jel.20181207

Kremer, M., Willis, J., & You, Y. (2021). *Converging to convergence*. Working Paper, *29484*, 49. Cambridge, MA, USA. National Bureau of Economic Research.

Le Gallo, J., Ertur, C., & Baumont, C. (2003). A spatial econometric analysis of convergence across European regions, 1980–1995. In B. Fingleton (Eds.), European regional growth. Advances in Spatial Science. Heidelberg. https://doi.org/10.1007/978-3-662-07136-6_4

León, D., & Ríos, H. (2013). Convergencia regional en el índice de desarrollo humano en Colombia. *Equidad y Desarrollo, 1*(20), 105–141.

Lesage, J. P., & Fischer, M. M. (2008). Spatial growth regressions: Model specification, estimation and interpretation. *Spatial Economic Analysis, 3*(3), 275–304.

LeSage, J. P., & Pace, R. K. (2009). *Introduction to spatial econometrics*. https://www.routledge.com/Introduction-to-Spatial-Econometrics/LeSage-Pace/p/book/9781420064247

Maddison, A. (1952). Productivity in an expanding economy. *The Economic Journal, 62*(247), 584–594.

Mankiw, N. G., Romer, D., & Weil, D. N. (1992). A contribution to the empirics of economic growth. *The Quarterly Journal of Economics, 107*(2), 407–437.

Marín-Llanes, L., Bonet-Morón, J., & Pérez-Valbuena, G. J. (2018). *"¿Cuál es la dimensión y en que se gastó la reciente bonanza en Colombia?" Documentos de trabajo sobre Economía Regional y Urbana, 273*. Banco de la República de Colombia.

McMillan, M., Rodrik, D., & Verduzco-Gallo, Í. (2014). Globalization, structural change, and productivity growth, with an update on Africa. *World Development, 63*, 11–32.

Meisel-Roca, A. E., & Hahn, L. (2020). Regional economic inequality in Colombia, 1926–2018. In D.A. Tirado-Fabregat, M. Badia-Miró, H. Willebald (Eds.), *Time and space Latin American regional development in historical perspective*. Palgrave Studies in Economic History. Palgrave Macmillan. https://doi.org/10.1007/978-3-030-47553-6_8

Murillo, M., & Gaviria, M. A. (2008). Convergencia en Capital Humano en Colombia: Un Análisis para el Período 1993–2005. *Revista Gestión y Región, 6*, 91–126.

Patel, D., Sandefur, J., & Subramanian, A. (2021). The new era of unconditional convergence. *Journal of Development Economics, 152*(102687), 1–18.

Perez-Reyna, D. (2017). Historia del Banco de la República: Crisis de 1999 (pp. 437–463), Banco de la Republica de Colombia

Postiglione, P., Andreano, M. S., & Benedetti, R. (2013). Using constrained optimization for the identification of convergence clubs. *Computational Economics, 42*(2), 151–174.

Ramirez-Giraldo, M., Collazos-Gaitán, M. M., García-García, J., De-Castro, L. W. H.-, Melo-Becerra, L. A., Montenegro-Trujillo, A., Montes-Uribe, E., Lancheros-Ramírez, P., Toro-Córdoba, J., & Zárate-Solano, H. M. (2021). La inversión en infraestructura de transporte y la economía colombiana. *Ensayos Sobre Política Económica, 99*, 1–134

Rey, S. J., & Le Gallo, J. (2009). Spatial analysis of economic convergence. In T. Mills, & K. Patterson (Eds.), *Palgrave Handbook of Econometrics: Volume 2: Applied Econometrics* (pp. 1251–1290). Palgrave Macmillan.

Rocha, R. R., & Vivas, A. V. (1998). Crecimiento regional en Colombia: ¿Persiste la desigualdad? *Revista de Economía del Rosario, 1*(1), 67–108.

Rodrik, D., Diao, X., & McMillan, M. (2019). *The Palgrave Handbook of development economics.* Palgrave Macmillan.

Royuela, V., & García Cruz, G. (2015). Economic and social convergence in Colombia. *Regional Studies, 49*, 219–239.

Santos-Marquez, F., & Mendez, C. (2021). Regional convergence, spatial scale, and spatial dependence: Evidence from homicides and personal injuries in Colombia 2010–2018. *Regional Science Policy & Practice, 13*(4), 1162–1184.

Solow, R. M. (1956). A contribution to the theory of economic growth. *The Quarterly Journal of Economics, 70*(1), 65–94.

Soto, J. (1998). *Crecimiento y convergencia departamental. Una aproximación de panel al caso colombiano 1960–1995,* 5 (tesis de maestría). Universidad de los Andes, Bogotá, Colombia.

The World Bank Data. (2021). GDP growth (annual %). World Bank national accounts data, and OECD National Accounts data files. Retrieved from http://data.worldbank.org/indicator/NY.GDP.MKTP.KD.ZG.

Wong, W.-K. (2006). OECD convergence: A sectoral decomposition exercise. *Economics Letters, 93*(2), 210–214.

Karina Acosta Ph.D. (Regional Science), Cornell University. Junior researcher at the Center for Regional Economic Studies (CEER) at the Banco de la República, Colombia. Her research interest lies at the intersection of development, spatial statistics, and demography. She has published book chapters and academic journal articles on development and regional economics, and demography.

Jaime Bonet is an economist from the Universidad de Los Andes in Bogotá with a master's degree in economics and a Ph.D. in regional planning from the University of Illinois at Urbana-Champaign. His research areas include regional and urban economics, local public finance, local economic development, and regional development history in Colombia.

Part II
Modelling Framework

Chapter 5
The Interregional Input–Output System for Colombia

Eduardo A. Haddad, Luis Armando Galvis-Aponte, and Inácio F. Araújo

5.1 Introduction

Despite its old-fashioned approach to economic growth theory, Harold Innis' staple theory (Watkins, 1963), together with Douglass North's economic base theory (North, 1955) and Albert Hirschman's approach to describing the mechanisms of growth transmission in an interregional system (Hirschman, 1958), provides a way of looking at integrated economic systems and describing them around the concept of trade linkages. The Innis–North–Hirschman (INH) linkages framework is a descriptive model of how a country or a region develops from natural-resource intensive exports.

A brief account of these authors' narratives sets the scene to understand the static picture of integrated interregional systems. Despite their interests in growth processes, we can borrow from them the hierarchical structure of linkages as a fundamental concept that unifies their works (Altman, 2003). According to Hirschman (1984), the linkage concept was devised to understand the industrialization process better. Fairly soon, however, the concept caught on even more in the analysis of the growth patterns of developing countries during the phase when their main engine of growth was the export of primary products.

Insights from the Staple Theory of Growth—the idea that a small range of products (agricultural or resource base) generate export demand, further generating a domestic multiplier or ripple effect—served as a primary starting point for reshaping the views on regional economic growth (North, 1955). If this process worked at the national

---

E. A. Haddad (✉) · I. F. Araújo
University of São Paulo, São Paulo, Brazil
e-mail: ehaddad@usp.br

I. F. Araújo
e-mail: inacio.araujo@usp.br

L. A. Galvis-Aponte
Banco de la República, Cartagena, Colombia
e-mail: lgalviap@banrep.gov.co

level, could we not apply the same principles to explain the growth of regions? Accordingly, the success of the export base would be the determining factor in the rate of growth of regions. Therefore, to understand this growth, we must examine the locational factors that have enabled the staples to develop, generating a growth pole. We should devote attention to the importance of international and interregional trade in staple exports.

Bringing location principles into this debate explicitly introduces the spatial dimension (seen as a network), reinforcing the role of infrastructure connectivity on the strength of the economic base spread's effects. A growth pole connects to other areas through linkages between industries and firms, and its positive performance induces growth in other connected firms and regions (Perroux, 1950). Hirschman (1958) identified additional possible connectors (purchase of goods, hiring labor, competition, and trade barriers), which may result in positive or negative trickle-down effects in other regions given the growth of the pole.

The introduction of the concept of economic linkages related to input–output analysis pioneered by Wassily Leontief (1936) resulted in a more affluent and analytically more rigorous framework associated with the staple/economic base theories (Altman, 2003). Measurement of an existing linkage structure can be achieved through input–output tables. The idea that a net increase in the rate of foreign exports (and other autonomous injections) propagates in the entire system generating higher-order effects is even more appealing in multi-sectoral and multi-regional contexts.

Isard (1951) further developed the notion of a foreign trade multiplier in the context of regions within a single country. As this notion worked for countries linked by trade flows, this could be applied to domestic trading regions. Thus, changes in regional income would result from (and as a multiple of) a change in regional investment, exports, or both. The critical point is that, in complex economic structures, neither sectors nor regions are isolated entities. By employing a multi-sectoral interregional framework, we may learn something about the cyclical sensitivities of other regions and how their cycles may spread through the region. This type of study leads to a more precise formulation of multiplier effects and the mechanisms by which cycles are spatially transmitted within the system of regions (Haddad et al., 2020a, 2020b, 2020c).

In Colombia, as in many other countries, there are no official data about trade flows between subnational regions. Then, the estimation of interregional input–output systems under conditions of limited information has been the subject of research efforts since the pioneering work by Walter Isard and collaborators in the 1950s. Interregional input–output systems are powerful tools that help public managers allocate scarce resources to promote regional development (Isard et al., 1998). Much has advanced since the first incursions of Isard (1951) and Leontief et al. (1953) in regional and interregional extensions of input–output models.

The DANE regularly publishes the national input–output matrices for Colombia. However, since it treats the whole country as a single region, the national matrix cannot capture the interdependence relations among the Colombian regions, especially concerning trade flows. The scarcity of information and the high cost of obtaining them through surveys, especially interregional trade flows, have been the main obstacles in estimating interregional input–output systems, setting the scene for the development of different non-survey estimation methods (Round, 1983).[1]

Bonet (2005) pioneered using the interregional input–output tables in Colombia, analyzing data for three years (1987, 1992, and 1997). He concluded that (a) key sectors have shifted from primary and secondary to tertiary activities in the period considered; and (b) there was relative self-sufficiency of the sectors in most regions, which supported the idea of a country with relatively weak interregional dependence.[2] However, his work presented a limitation to the aggregation of the Colombian territorial entities into seven macro-regions. Such a high level of aggregation could be hiding higher levels of trade among departments within each region considered in the study. In this way, the conclusion leading to a low level of spatial integration in Colombia could be biased by the aggregation adopted.

In order to overcome this possible limitation, subsequent studies undertaken by researchers associated with the University of São Paulo, and the Center for Regional Economic Studies (CEER) at the Central Bank of Colombia further examined the Colombian structure in more disaggregated regional settings for the year 2004 (Perobelli et al., 2010) and 2012 (Haddad et al., 2018). However, the high level of sectoral aggregation remained a limitation for a more comprehensive approach to structural features of the Colombian economy.

In this context, the first objective of this chapter is to present a detailed description of the procedures used for the construction of the interregional input–output system for Colombia with 2015 data, including not only its 33 regions (departments) but also a relatively highly disaggregated sectoral scheme. This tool allows the analysis of the interrelationships among the country's departments concerning trade flows. We make available the details of the methodological procedures adopted to generate the interregional system and the database itself to be used by other researchers and practitioners. Different applications are discussed in Part III of this volume, identifying additional structural features of Colombia's regional economies. This chapter also presents initial illustrative analyses using different indicators from the estimated database, revealing some of the main structural features of Colombia's economy.

This chapter is organized as follows. The following section describes in detail the methodological procedure used in the construction of the interregional system for Colombia based on the IIOAS method. Section 5.3 presents the procedure for estimating trade matrices between Colombian departments. Section 5.4 reveals some of the main structural features of Colombia's economy using indicators derived from the estimated databases. Section 5.5 concludes the chapter.

---

[1] For surveys on recent approaches to non-survey estimation of inter-regional trade systems, refer to Gabela (2020) and Hewings & Oosterhaven (2021).

[2] Acosta and Bonet in Chap. 4 of this book found limited interregional spillover effects in the economic growth of Colombian departments derived from a spatial econometric estimation.

5.2 Interregional Input–Output Matrix for Colombia

5.2.1 Initial Data Treatment

The estimation of the Interregional Input–Output Matrix for Colombia (IIOM-COL) is based on the Interregional Input–Output Adjustment System (IIOAS) method.[3] The IIOAS method was developed to estimate interregional input–output systems under conditions of limited information. In the case of Colombia, we have anchored our estimation in data from national and regional accounts provided by DANE for the year 2015. The data consist mainly of the Supply and Use Tables (SUT) at the national level, regional data on sectoral Gross Regional Product (GRP), and macro-regional aggregates (DANE, 2020).

Step 1 The first step in data treatment is to build the national input–output matrix for Colombia from the SUT. We have organized the information available at DANE, according to Figs. 5.1 and 5.2. The structure of the Supply Table is then used to transform the new Use Table from a commodity by sector into a sector-by-sector system of information. The auxiliary matrix generated by the structure of the Make Table is often called the market share matrix. Finally, the national structure of 60 sectors was aggregated into 54 sectors to match the auxiliary data available at the regional level.

Step 2 The next step is to disaggregate the national data into the 33 departments of Colombia. The details of such a procedure are described in Sects. 5.2.1 and 5.2.2.

We use shares from specific variables to estimate the departmental value for investment demand, household consumption, non-profit institutions serving households (NPISH) demand, government consumption, and foreign exports. For each component, the variables used to calculate the shares were the following:

1. Investment demand: employment of the construction sector estimated from DANE's national survey GEIH.
2. Household consumption: labor income (*"ingreso laboral"*) estimated using national survey GEIH.
3. NPISH demand: total employment estimated from DANE's national survey GEIH.
4. Government consumption: value-added of the public administration sector obtained from the regional accounts published by DANE.
5. Foreign exports were obtained from the DANE's database Estadísticas de Exportaciones.

---

[3] This approach has been applied for distinct interregional systems: interisland model for the Azores (Haddad et al., 2015), interregional models for Brazil (Haddad et al., 2017), Colombia (Haddad et al., 2018), Egypt (Haddad et al., 2016a, 2016b), Greece (Haddad et al., 2020a), Lebanon (Haddad, 2014), Mexico (Haddad et al., 2020b), Morocco (Haddad et al., 2020c), and Paraguay (Haddad et al., 2021).

5 The Interregional Input–Output System for Colombia

	Size	Absorption Matrix					
		1	2	3	4	5	6
		Producers	Investors	Household	Export	Government	NPISH
	Size	J x Q	J x Q	Q	1	Q	Q
Basic Flows	I x S	BAS1	BAS2	BAS3	BAS4	BAS5	BAS6
Margins	I x S x R	MAR1	MAR2	MAR3	MAR4	MAR5	MAR6
Taxes	I x S	TAX1	TAX2	TAX3	TAX4	TAX5	TAX6
Labor	1	LABR					
Capital	1	CPTL					
Other costs	1	OCTS					

Make	I
Q	MAKE

Fig. 5.1 Schematic structure of the IIOM-COL. *Note* J sectors; Q regions; I products; S sources (domestic and import); R margins

	Size	Absorption Matrix					
		1	2	3	4	5	6
		Producers	Investors	Household	Export	Government	NPISH
	Size	J x Q	J x Q	Q	1	Q	Q
Basic Flows	I x S	635,966	176,446	455,951	118,647	118,005	3,164
Margins	I x S x R	42,273	9,481	56,553	350	871	0
Taxes	I x S	32,160	5,378	30,862	263	312	6
Labor	1	274,307					
Capital	1	434,752					
Other costs	1	21,484					

Make	I
Q	1,440,942

Fig. 5.2 Structure of the national input–output system for Colombia: summary results, 2015 (in COP billions)

Region	Department	Investment Demand	Household Demand	NPISH Demand	Government Demand	Foreing Exports
R1	Antioquia	0.1477	0.1487	0.1244	0.1118	0.1343
R2	Atlántico	0.0497	0.0382	0.0519	0.0457	0.0549
R3	Bogotá D.C.	0.1676	0.2822	0.1891	0.2616	0.1109
R4	Bolívar	0.0502	0.0270	0.0414	0.0421	0.0237
R5	Boyacá	0.0380	0.0235	0.0303	0.0243	0.0040
R6	Caldas	0.0135	0.0194	0.0200	0.0174	0.0182
R7	Caquetá	0.0084	0.0087	0.0102	0.0085	0.0007
R8	Cauca	0.0222	0.0169	0.0273	0.0242	0.0113
R9	Cesar	0.0149	0.0159	0.0198	0.0206	0.0603
R10	Córdoba	0.0216	0.0200	0.0313	0.0309	0.0039
R11	Cundinamarca	0.0649	0.0488	0.0517	0.0462	0.0412
R12	Chocó	0.0031	0.0053	0.0095	0.0096	0.0007
R13	Huila	0.0367	0.0177	0.0225	0.0204	0.0105
R14	La Guajira	0.0080	0.0141	0.0184	0.0146	0.0440
R15	Magdalena	0.0172	0.0164	0.0223	0.0244	0.0129
R16	Meta	0.0337	0.0207	0.0191	0.0195	0.1543
R17	Nariño	0.0204	0.0247	0.0399	0.0278	0.0032
R18	Norte de Santander	0.0229	0.0222	0.0287	0.0246	0.0091
R19	Quindío	0.0116	0.0129	0.0156	0.0097	0.0032
R20	Risaralda	0.0164	0.0215	0.0226	0.0176	0.0204
R21	Santander	0.1076	0.0558	0.0520	0.0428	0.0779
R22	Sucre	0.0117	0.0120	0.0163	0.0177	0.0020
R23	Tolima	0.0243	0.0260	0.0308	0.0249	0.0060
R24	Valle del Cauca	0.0571	0.0906	0.0960	0.0839	0.0670
R25	Arauca	0.0080	0.0017	0.0013	0.0055	0.0239
R26	Casanare	0.0138	0.0044	0.0029	0.0082	0.0898
R27	Putumayo	0.0037	0.0008	0.0007	0.0068	0.0090
R28	San Andrés	0.0006	0.0016	0.0016	0.0016	0.0017
R29	Amazonas	0.0005	0.0004	0.0005	0.0016	0.0004
R30	Guainía	0.0009	0.0003	0.0002	0.0010	0.0005
R31	Guaviare	0.0016	0.0010	0.0009	0.0021	0.0001
R32	Vaupés	0.0005	0.0004	0.0002	0.0009	0.0001
R33	Vichada	0.0009	0.0003	0.0003	0.0016	0.0001
	TOTAL	1.0000	1.0000	1.0000	1.0000	1.0000

Fig. 5.3 Shares used to estimate the components of the GRP of Colombia, 2015

Figure 5.3 presents the regional shares for investment demand, household consumption, NPISH demand, government consumption, and foreign exports. A general result is the spatial concentration of aggregate demand, influenced by the distribution of economic activity and population across the departments. Bogotá D.C, together with Antioquia and Valle del Cauca, concentrates almost half of the national household consumption, 45.8% of the government demand, and nearly 37.3% of the investment demand. On the other hand, Meta and Casanare present meaningful participation in the total exports, mainly influenced by crude and refined oil sales.

5.2.2 Estimation of the Interregional Trade Matrices

Step 3 In order to estimate the interregional system, it is necessary to estimate the trade matrices among the 33 departments of Colombia. This procedure is done by calculating three components: (i) the regional demand for domestic products; (ii) the regional demand for imported products; and (iii) the total supply of each region to the domestic and foreign markets by sector.

Step 4 We assume that regional demands for domestic and imported products follow the national pattern for all users. In other words, economic agents share the same technology and preferences everywhere. However, it is essential to note different trade matrices are estimated for each sector, which allows us to have different regional sourcing for intermediate inputs and final products.

Step 5 The regional demand for domestic products is calculated, for each user (intermediate consumption and domestic absorption components), using the information provided in the matrix of demand-generating coefficients (DOMGEN). These coefficients are defined as the ratio of each element of the national use matrix to its respective column total.

For intermediate consumption, we define the ratio as follows:

$$\text{cic}_{ij}^{\text{dom}} = \frac{z_{ij}^{\text{dom}}}{x_j}, \quad \forall i, j = 1, \ldots, 54 \tag{5.1}$$

where $\text{cic}_{ij}^{\text{dom}}$ is the national coefficient of intermediate consumption of domestic inputs, z_{ij}^{dom} is the intermediate consumption of domestic inputs by sector, and x_j is the total sectoral output. From Eq. 5.1, we get a matrix of size 54×54 (sector $\times$ sector), cic^{dom}, with all the intermediate consumption ratios ($\text{cic}_{ij}^{\text{dom}}$).

Regarding the domestic absorption components (investment, household consumption, and government expenditure),[4] we use the ratio of each i-element to its respective column sum:

$$\text{cinv}_i^{\text{dom}} = \frac{\text{inv}_i^{\text{dom}}}{\text{inv}t}, \quad \forall i = 1, \ldots, 54 \tag{5.2}$$

$$\text{chou}_i^{\text{dom}} = \frac{\text{hou}_i^{\text{dom}}}{\text{hou}t}, \quad \forall i = 1, \ldots, 54 \tag{5.3}$$

$$\text{cgov}_i^{\text{dom}} = \frac{\text{gov}_i^{\text{dom}}}{\text{gov}t}, \quad \forall i = 1, \ldots, 54 \tag{5.4}$$

---

[4] In the following presentation, we abstract from the NPISH component of final demand, whose treatment follows the same procedure as those presented for the other components of domestic absorption.

where $\text{inv}_i^{\text{dom}}$, hou_i^{dom}, and $\text{gov}_i^{\text{dom}}$ are the investment demand, household consumption, and government expenditure of each i-element in the national use matrix, respectively, and invt, hout and govt are the respective column sums, including tax. Thus, from Eqs. 5.2–5.4, we generate vectors of size 54×1, cinv^{dom}, chou^{dom}, and cgov^{dom}, with all the investment demand, household consumption, and government expenditure ratios, respectively.

Step 6 The gross regional demand for domestic products is obtained by multiplying these coefficients—Eqs. 5.1–5.4—by (i) a matrix with the total sectoral output of each region in the main diagonal and zero elsewhere, X^r; (ii) the total investment demand in each region, invt^r; (iii) the total household consumption in each region, hout^r; and (iv) the total government expenditure in each region, govt^r:

$$\text{IC}^{r,\,\text{dom}} = \text{CIC}^{\text{dom}} * X^r, \quad \forall r = 1, \ldots, 33 \tag{5.5}$$

$$\text{inv}^{r,\,\text{dom}} = \text{cinv}^{\text{dom}} * \text{invt}^r, \quad \forall r = 1, \ldots, 33 \tag{5.6}$$

$$\text{hou}^{r,\,\text{dom}} = \text{chou}^{\text{dom}} * hout^r, \quad \forall r = 1, \ldots, 33 \tag{5.7}$$

$$\text{gov}^{r,\text{dom}} = \text{cgov}^{\text{dom}} * \text{govt}^r, \quad \forall r = 1, \ldots, 33 \tag{5.8}$$

where $\text{IC}^{r,\text{dom}}$ is a matrix of intermediate consumption of domestic products; $\text{inv}^{r,\text{dom}}$ is the consumption vector of capital goods produced domestically $\text{hou}^{r,\text{dom}}$ is the household consumption vector of domestic products; and $\text{gov}^{r,\text{dom}}$ is the vector of government expenditure on domestic products, all for each region r.

Therefore, the (gross) total demand for domestic products in each region is given by

$$\text{demdom}^r = \sum_{j=1}^{54} \text{IC}^{r,\text{dom}} + \text{inv}^{r,\text{dom}} + \text{hou}^{r,\text{dom}} + \text{gov}^{r,\text{dom}} \quad for\ all\ r = 1, \ldots, 33 \tag{5.9}$$

where demdom^r is the total demand vector for domestic products of size 54×1 for each region r.

Step 7 The procedure to estimate the demand for imported products is similar. Analogously, we create a matrix of demand-generating coefficients for imported products (IMPGEN), defined as the ratio of each element of the national matrix of imports over the respective column sum in the use matrix.

For intermediate consumption, the coefficient represents the share of imports in terms of national production as follows:

5 The Interregional Input–Output System for Colombia

$$\text{cic}_{ij}^{\text{imp}} = \frac{z_{ij}^{\text{imp}}}{x_j}, \quad \forall i, j = 1, \ldots, 54 \quad (5.10)$$

where $\text{cic}_{ij}^{\text{imp}}$ is the intermediate consumption coefficient of imported inputs; z_{ij}^{imp} is the intermediate consumption of imported inputs; and x_j is the total sectoral output.

Analogously to domestic ratios, from Eq. 5.10, we get a matrix of size 54 × 54 (sector × sector), CIC^{imp}, with all the intermediate consumption ratios related to imported inputs.

Further, the coefficients for the final demand elements are given by

$$\text{cinv}_i^{\text{imp}} = \frac{\text{inv}_i^{\text{imp}}}{\text{inv}t}, \quad \forall r = 1, \ldots, 33 \quad (5.11)$$

$$\text{chou}_i^{\text{imp}} = \frac{\text{hou}_i^{\text{imp}}}{\text{hou}t}, \quad \forall r = 1, \ldots, 33 \quad (5.12)$$

$$\text{cgov}_i^{\text{imp}} = \frac{\text{gov}_i^{\text{imp}}}{\text{gov}t}, \quad \forall r = 1, \ldots, 33 \quad (5.13)$$

where $\text{inv}_i^{\text{imp}}$, $\text{hou}_i^{\text{imp}}$, and $\text{gov}_i^{\text{imp}}$ are the investment demand, household consumption, and government expenditure of each i-element in the national imported matrix, respectively. Thus, $\text{cinv}_i^{\text{imp}}$, $\text{chou}_i^{\text{imp}}$, and $\text{cgov}_i^{\text{imp}}$ are demand shares of imported products related to investment demand, household consumption, and government expenditure, respectively. From Eqs. 5.11–5.13, we get cinv^{imp}, chou^{imp}, and cgov^{imp}, which are vectors of size 54 × 1 and correspond to the investment demand, household consumption, and government expenditure ratios, respectively.

Therefore, the demands for imported products, by region, are defined as

$$\text{IC}^{r,\,\text{imp}} = \text{CIC}^{\text{imp}} * X^r, \quad \forall r = 1, \ldots, 33 \quad (5.14)$$

$$\text{inv}^{r,\,\text{imp}} = \text{cinv}^{\text{imp}} * invt^r, \quad \forall r = 1, \ldots, 33 \quad (5.15)$$

$$\text{hou}^{r,\,\text{imp}} = \text{chou}^{\text{imp}} * hout^r, \quad \forall r = 1, \ldots, 33 \quad (5.16)$$

$$\text{gov}^{r,\,\text{imp}} = \text{cgov}^{\text{imp}} * govt^r, \quad \forall r = 1, \ldots, 33 \quad (5.17)$$

where $\text{IC}^{r,\text{imp}}$ is a matrix with imports of intermediate inputs; $\text{inv}^{r,\text{imp}}$ is the imports vector of capital goods; $\text{hou}^{r,\text{imp}}$ is the vector of imports by household; and $\text{gov}^{r,\text{imp}}$ is the vector of government expenditure on imports, all for each region r.

The total demand for imported products by region is given by

$$\text{demimp}^r = \sum_{j=1}^{54} \text{IC}^{r,\text{imp}} + \text{inv}^{r,\text{imp}} + \text{hou}^{r,\text{imp}} + \text{gov}^{r,\text{imp}}, \ \forall r = 1, \ldots, 33 \quad (5.18)$$

In order to generate a matrix of regional demands for domestic products, we place all demand vectors for domestic products (demdom^r, $\forall\ r = 1,\ldots,33$) side by side, which allow us to have a matrix of size 54×33 (sector × region)—DEMDOM, where each row represents the domestic demand for sector i by region r. Similarly, we reproduce the same procedure with the demand vectors for imported products (demimp^r, $\forall\ r = 1,\ldots,33$), which creates a matrix of 54×33 (sector × region)—DEMIMP, where each row represents the sectoral imports by each region r.

Step 8 The next step is to estimate the sectoral domestic supply (supdom^r) in each region, which is done by taking the difference between the sectoral total output (x^r) and the sectoral exports (exp^r) in each region.

$$\text{supdom}^r = x^r - \text{exp}^r, \ \forall r = 1, \ldots, 33 \quad (5.19)$$

Similarly, placing all regional vectors side by side, a 54×33 (sector × region) matrix is created—SUPDOM, where each row represents the total regional domestic supply of sector i.

Thus, having the sectoral domestic demand and supply by region (DEMDOM and SUPDOM), equilibrium between them in aggregate terms is required. Consequently, we adjust the aggregate value of (gross) total domestic demand for each sector to have total domestic demand equivalent to total domestic supply.

Step 9 The next step is to construct, for each sector, matrices with regional trade shares (SHIN^i). In other words, matrices for each sector represent the regional share of the total domestic trade. Considering s origin regions and d destination regions, we estimate 54 matrices (one for each sector) of 33×33 (origin × destination).

These shares are estimated using Eq. 5.20 and Eq. 5.21, based on previous work done by Dixon and Rimmer (2004). Hence, Eq. 5.20 is used to calculate the initial ratio of the intraregional trade (main diagonal of the trade matrix), while Eq. 5.21 is used to estimate the interregional trade flows.

Thus, the intraregional trade share is given by

$$\text{shin}^i_{s,d} = \text{Min}\left\{ \frac{\text{supdom}^i_s}{\text{demdom}^i_s}, 1 \right\} * f, \ \forall i = 1, \ldots, 54;$$
$$\text{where } s, d = 1, \ldots, 33; \ s = d \quad (5.20)$$

where shin$^i_{s,d}$ is the share of sector i in the national trade within each region. The intraregional trade flow is defined to be the ratio of supply to demand of sector i within the region. If supply is greater than demand, we assume that all demand is met internally. However, based on Haddad et al., (2016a, 2016b), we multiply the result

5 The Interregional Input–Output System for Colombia

by a factor (f), which gives us the extent of tradability of a given commodity. For non-tradable sectors, usually services, we assume that the local economy typically provides them. Thus, we use initial f values close to unity (0.9) for non-tradable sectors and 0.5 for tradable sectors.

Moreover, the interregional trade is given by

$$\text{shin}_{s,d}^i = \left\{ \frac{1}{\text{imped}_{s,d}^\beta} * \frac{\text{supdom}_s^i}{\sum_{k=1}^{32} \text{supdom}_k^i} \right\} * \left\{ \frac{1 - \text{shin}_{s,s}^i}{\sum_{s=1, s \neq d}^{32} \left[\frac{1}{\text{imped}_{s,d}^\beta} * \frac{\text{supdom}_s^i}{\sum_{k=1}^{32} \text{supdom}_k^i} \right]} \right\},$$

$$\forall i = 1, \ldots, 54; \quad s, d = 1, \ldots, 33; \quad k = s; \text{ and } s \neq d \quad (5.21)$$

where $\text{shin}_{s,d}^i$ is the share of trade flows of sector i with origin in region s and destination in region d, and $\text{imped}_{s,d}$ is given by the average travel time between two trading regions.

Step 10 We truncate the travel time matrix using information from the 2013 origin–destination (OD) matrices, published by the Ministry of Transportation, and information on interregional cargo flows by air. We assume nonzero values in the estimated sectoral trade matrices whenever we observe a positive flow in tons in the transportation database. We use an extremely high travel time to generate a zero trade flow for a specific origin–destination pair to make this operational.[5] (Appendix 4).

Step 11 We estimate the impedance parameters, β, combining the information on trade flows in tons from the OD matrices with the travel time estimates in the context of gravity equations.[6] Equation 5.22 presents the general specification adopted, while Table 5.1 presents the Poisson pseudo maximum likelihood (PPML) estimator results. For presentation purposes, we present the results for specific groups of sectors, namely total (0), manufactured agricultural products (1), manufacturing (2), mining (3), and agriculture (4).

$$T_{ij} = \alpha_0 Y_i^{\alpha_1} Y_j^{\alpha_2} D_{ij}^\beta e^{\theta_i d_i + \theta_j d_j} \quad (5.22)$$

where T_{ij} denotes the trade flow from department i to department j. Y_i is the GRP of the origin department i. Y_j is the GRP of the destination department j. D_{ij} is the travel time (in minutes) between i and j. $\alpha_0, \alpha_1, \alpha_2, \beta, \theta_i$ and θ_i are unknown parameters. d_i and d_j are dummies for the origin and destination department. We estimate Eq. 5.22 separately for each sector.

---

[5] The OD matrix provides information for the following sectors: S1-S3, S5-S6, S10-S13, S15-S32, and S44. For the remaining sectors, we used the most similar sector available.

[6] Cai (2022) discusses a calibration procedure for estimating bilateral trade between the regions of a country.

Table 5.1 Estimates of the impedance factor using the OD-2013 database, selected groups of sectors

Dependent variable: trade flow from department i to department j					
Variables	(0)	(1)	(2)	(3)	(4)
	Total	Manufacture agricultural products	Manufacturing	Mining	Agriculture
GRP—origin ($\ln Y_i$)	0.984***	1.268***	0.965***	0.641***	1.040***
	(0.088)	(0.205)	(0.126)	(0.096)	(0.155)
GRP—destination ($\ln Y_j$)	1.090***	0.948***	1.076***	0.940***	1.146***
	(0.091)	(0.141)	(0.120)	(0.210)	(0.176)
Travel time in minutes ($\ln D_{ij}$)	−0.561***	−0.723***	−0.652***	−0.790***	−0.640***
	(0.083)	(0.097)	(0.076)	(0.199)	(0.070)
Constant	−5.420***	−7.972***	−4.826**	−2.955	−7.746***
	(1.634)	(2.905)	(2.098)	(3.135)	(2.717)
Observations	812	784	812	812	812
R-squared	0.719	0.690	0.763	0.750	0.801
Origin department FE	Yes	Yes	Yes	Yes	Yes
Destination department FE	Yes	Yes	Yes	Yes	Yes

Robust standard errors in parentheses. *** $p < 0.01$, ** $p < 0.05$, * $p < 0.1$

Step 12 From Eqs. 5.20 and 5.21, we generate matrices of size 33 × 33 (region × region) for each sector—SHIN^i, where the intraregional trade shares are placed on the main diagonal and the interregional trade shares off diagonal. Note that the column values add to one.

Step 13 Using the SHIN^i matrices, we estimate initial values for the trade matrices by multiplying each SHIN^i by its respective reference value in DEMDOM:

$$\text{TRADE}^i = \text{SHIN}^i * \text{DEMDOM}^{*i}, \quad i = 1, \ldots, 54 \quad (5.23)$$

where TRADE^i is the trade matrix for sector i with origin in region s and destination in region d, and DEMDOM^{*i} is a diagonal matrix where values related to sector i from DEMDOM have been placed on the main diagonal and zero elsewhere.

This procedure ensures that the column sums of each TRADE^i matrix is equivalent to the demand of the respective region d for the products of region s (for each sector i). However, the row sum is not necessarily equivalent to the supply of each sector i from region s to region d. Thus, we have used a RAS procedure[7] to ensure that

---

[7] For more details, see Miller and Blair (2009).

supply and demand balance out. Figure 5.4 illustrates the estimated trade flows for selected sectors and groups of sectors, identifying supplying and demanding regions, as well as the main trade flows.

Step 14 After the RAS procedure, we have included in each $\text{TRADE}^i_{s,d}$ matrix the respective row from DEMIMP. In other words, we added the Rest of the World as one of the origins. Thus, now s is equal to 34 since it represents the 33 Colombian Departments plus the Rest of the World.

5.3 Regionalization Procedure

Step 15 The 54 trade matrices estimated are consistent with each sector's national supply and demand. The trade matrices, after the inclusion of the import row, TRADE^{i*}, consider the sales of each Colombian region to the other Colombian regions and their purchases from domestic and foreign supply regions. However, from these matrices, we cannot know if the sales were purchased by industries (intermediate consumption) or by final users in the other regions.

In order to deal with this issue, we use a regionalization strategy proposed originally by Chenery (1956) and Moses (1955). We apply the same regional proportion in acquiring inputs for all sectors and final products by all final users within a given region. In other words, we use the same trade coefficients for all sectors or final users in the destination. The idea behind this procedure is that users in a specific region face the supply of a *pool good* composed of fixed shares of related goods from the different sourcing regions.

The following steps describe the regionalization procedure. The first step is given by the calculation of a new matrix for each sector with the trade shares, SHIN_N^i. This matrix is estimated based on the TRADE^{i*} matrices as follows:

$$\text{SHIN\_}N^i = \text{TRADE}^{i*} * \left[\text{TRADE}^{*i*}\right]^{-1}, \quad i = 1, ..., 54 \quad (5.24)$$

where TRADE^{i*} is a matrix diagonal whose ($\sum_{s=1}^{33} \text{Trade}^i_{s,d}$) are placed on the main diagonal and zero elsewhere, being $\text{Trade}^i_{s,d}$ each element of TRADE^{i*} matrix; s represents the 34 origin regions (33 regions of Colombia plus the Rest of the World), and d represents the 33 destination regions (Colombia).

Subsequently, we employ elements from the national use matrix to estimate the national coefficients (domestic plus imports) of intermediate consumption, investment demand, household consumption, and government expenditure.

For intermediate consumption, the matrix of coefficients is given by

$$\text{CIC}^N = Z^{\text{DOM+IMP}} * \left(\text{ICT}^{N*}\right)^{-1} \quad (5.25)$$

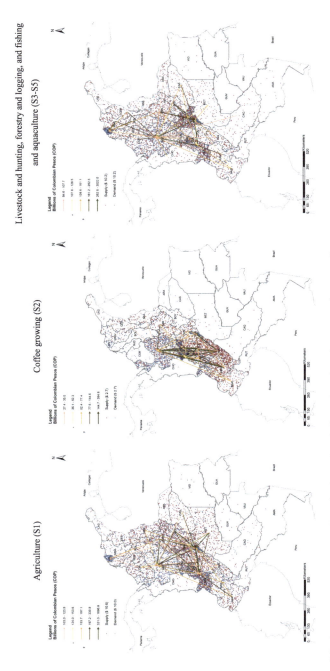

Fig. 5.4 Cartographical representation of estimated trade flows, by selected sectors and groups of sectors

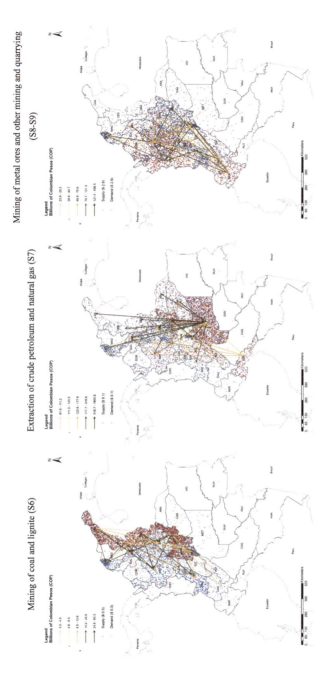

Fig. 5.4 (continued)

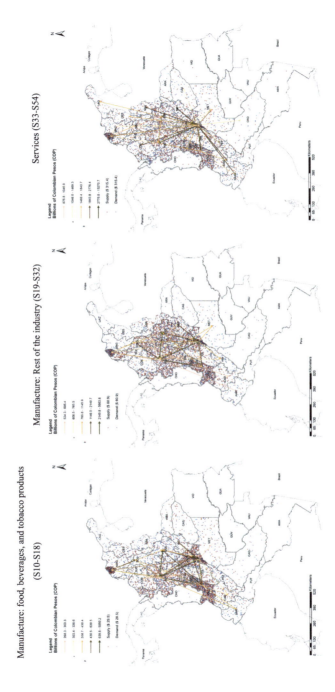

Fig. 5.4 (continued)

where $Z^{DOM+IMP}$ is the intermediate consumption matrix (domestic + imported), and ICT^{N*} is a diagonal matrix with the values from the vector of total intermediate consumption for each sector of destination j (ICT^N) in the main diagonal. This vector, ICT^N, is defined as

$$ICT^N = x^N - va^N \tag{5.26}$$

where x^N is the vector with all national total sectoral output, and va^N is the vector with all national sectoral value-added.

We take each vector element over its respective total (including indirect taxes). Thus, the investment demand, household consumption, and government expenditure coefficients are defined as follows:

$$cinv_i^N = \frac{inv_i^{DOM+IMP}}{invt^N}, \quad \forall i = 1, \ldots, 54 \tag{5.27}$$

$$chou_i^N = \frac{hou_i^{DOM+IMP}}{hout^N}, \quad \forall i = 1, \ldots, 54 \tag{5.28}$$

$$cgov_i^N = \frac{gov_i^{DOM+IMP}}{govt^N}, \quad \forall i = 1, \ldots, 54 \tag{5.29}$$

where $inv_i^{DOM+IMP}$, $hou_i^{DOM+IMP}$, and $gov_i^{DOM+IMP}$ represent each element in the investment demand, household consumption, and government expenditure vectors, respectively (including domestic and imported sources); $invt^N$, $hout^N$, and $govt^N$ are the respective column sum, including also indirect taxes.

From Eqs. 5.27–5.29, we generate vectors with coefficients of investment demand ($cinv^N$), household consumption ($chou^N$), and government expenditure ($cgov^N$).

The next step is to estimate the regional coefficients. In order to obtain the intermediate consumption shares, RICC, we transform the 54 SHIN_N matrices into 34 SHIN$_s$ matrices of size 54 × 33, which represent, for each origin, foreign region inclusive, the consumption share of each sector in each destination region. Thus, each SHIN_S matrix represents one origin trade region, where rows show the sectors and columns the destination regions.

Therefore, using Antioquia (the first region) as an example, the SHIN_S for this region is composed of all the first rows of each 54 SHIN_N. For the second region, Atlántico, the SHIN_S includes all the second rows of each of the 54 SHIN_N, and so on. Further, to estimate RICC, each column of each SHIN_S matrix is diagonalized and multiplied by CIC^N:

$$RICC^{sd} = SHIN\_S^* * CIC^N \tag{5.30}$$

where SHIN_S* is a diagonal matrix whose nonzero elements come from the SHIN_S; s represents the 34 origin regions, and d represents the 33 destination regions.

From Eq. 5.30, we estimate 33 destination matrices of size 54 × 54 (sector × sector) for each origin region. These matrices contain the shares of each sector in the intermediate consumption in each destination region.

Similarly, for each of the final demand components, we estimate, for each origin region, 34 vectors of size 54 × 1, SHIN_S, which represents the shares of each destination region d in the acquisition of the output from each of the 54 sectors.

The final demand for capital goods (investment demand) for each region is given by.

$$\text{rcinv}^{sd} = \text{SHIN\_S}^{**} * \text{cinv}^N, \forall s = 1, \ldots, 34; \text{ and } d = 1, \ldots, 33 \quad (5.31)$$

where SHIN_S^{**} is a diagonal matrix of the vector SHIN_S.

For household consumption:

$$\text{rchou}^{sd} = \text{SHIN\_ }S^{**} * \text{chou}^N, \forall s = 1, \ldots, 34; \text{ and } d = 1, \ldots, 33 \quad (5.32)$$

and for government expenditure:

$$\text{rcgov}^{sa} = \text{SHIN\_S}^{**} * \text{cgov}^N, \forall s = 1, \ldots, 34; \text{ and } d = 1, \ldots, 33 \quad (5.33)$$

In order to obtain the regional share for the indirect tax paid by each user, we calculate some coefficients from the national tax matrix. These coefficients are calculated for intermediate consumption, investment, household consumption, and government expenditure as follows:

The matrix with the national indirect tax coefficients related to intermediate consumption (TCIC^N) is given by

$$\text{TCIC}^N = \text{TIC}^N * (\text{ICT}^N)^{-1} \quad (5.34)$$

where TIC^N is a matrix of size 54 × 54 (sector × sector) with the indirect taxes related to intermediate consumption in the national tax matrix, and ICT^N is a diagonal matrix with the sectoral total intermediate consumption.

The vector with national indirect tax coefficients relatsed to investment (tcinv^N) is

$$\text{tcinv}^N = \text{tinv}^N * \left(\text{invt}^N\right)^{-1} \quad (5.35)$$

where tinv^N is the vector with tax related to investment, and $invt^N$ is the total demand for investment from the national use matrix.

The vector with national tax coefficients related to household consumption (tchou^N) is given by

$$\text{tchou}^N = \text{thou}^N * \left(\text{hout}^N\right)^{-1} \quad (5.36)$$

5 The Interregional Input–Output System for Colombia

where $thou^N$ is the vector with tax related to household consumption, and $hout^N$ is the total demand for households from the national use matrix.

Finally, the vector with national tax related to government expenditure ($tcgov^N$) is

$$tcgov^N = tgov^N * (govt^N)^{-1} \qquad (5.37)$$

where $tgov^N$ is the vector with tax related to government consumption, and $govt^N$ is the total demand for the government from the national use matrix.

The regional coefficients are obtained by multiplying each column of SHIN_ S by the national tax coefficient. Thus, the regional coefficient for indirect tax related to intermediate consumption is given by

$$RTCIC^{sd} = SHIN\_S^* * TCIC^N, \forall s = 1, ..., 34; \text{ and } d = 1, ..., 33 \qquad (5.38)$$

which generates 1122 matrices of size 54×54 (sector × sector). These matrices represent the regional indirect tax coefficients for each pair of regions $s \times d$ (origin × destination).

For investment demand:

$$rtcinv^{sd} = SHIN\_S^* * tcinv^N, \forall s = 1, ..., 34; \text{ and } d = 1, ..., 33 \qquad (5.39)$$

which gives us 1122 vectors of size 54×1 representing the proportion paid in tax related to the acquisition of products for investment in each pair of regions $s \times d$.

Similarly, we have the regional coefficient for household consumption:

$$rtchou^{sd} = SHIN\_S^* * tchou^N, \forall s = 1, ..., 34; \text{ and } d = 1, ..., 33 \qquad (5.40)$$

and for government expenditure:

$$rtcgov^{sd} = SHIN\_S^* * tcgov^N, \forall s = 1, ..., 34; \text{ and } d = 1, ..., 33 \qquad (5.41)$$

In order to have all regional coefficients in monetary flows, we multiply the coefficients defined above by the regional values presented in Sect. 5.2.2.

Intermediate consumption:

$$RIC^{sd} = RICC^{sd} * RICT^d, \forall s = 1, ..., 34; \text{ and } d = 1, ..., 33 \qquad (5.42)$$

where RIC^{sd} is the regional intermediate consumption matrix for each pair of regions $(s \times d)$, and $RICT^d$ is a matrix with the total regional intermediate consumption in the main diagonal and zero elsewhere.

Investment demand:

$$rinv^{sd} = rcinv^{sd} * rinvt^d, \forall s = 1, ..., 34; \text{ and } d = 1, ..., 33 \qquad (5.43)$$

where rinv^{sd} is the vector of demand for regional investment for each pair of regions ($s \times d$), and rinvt^d is the total regional for investment.

Household consumption:

$$\text{rhou}^{sd} = \text{rchou}^{sd} * \text{rhout}^d, \forall s = 1, \ldots, 34; \text{ and } d = 1, \ldots, 33 \quad (5.44)$$

where rhou^{sd} is the vector of regional household consumption for each pair of regions ($s \times d$), and $rhout^d$ is the total regional household consumption.

Government expenditure:

$$\text{rgov}^{sd} = \text{rcgov}^{sd} * \text{rgovt}^d, \forall s = 1, \ldots, 34; \text{ and } d = 1, \ldots, 33 \quad (5.45)$$

where rgov^{sd} iss the vector of regional government expenditures for each pair of regions ($s \times d$), and rgovt^d is the total regional government expenditures.

Given the estimates of sectoral foreign exports by region (exp^r), the values are allocated directly in the relevant column of the interregional system. Through the DANE, we had access to foreign exports of manufacturing sectors by region. For those sectors for which regionally disaggregated foreign exports were not available, we assume the same ratio of sectoral foreign exports to sectoral gross output to allocate foreign exports across regions.

A similar procedure is used to transform indirect tax coefficients in monetary flows as follows:

For tax related to intermediate consumption:

$$\text{RTIC}^{sd} = \text{RTCIC}^{sd} * \text{RICT}^d, \forall s = 1, \ldots, 34; \text{ and } d = 1, \ldots, 33 \quad (5.46)$$

Investment:

$$\text{rtinv}^{sd} = \text{rtcinv}^{sd} * \text{rinvt}^d, \forall s = 1, \ldots, 34; \text{ and } d = 1, \ldots, 33 \quad (5.47)$$

Household consumption:

$$\text{rthou}^{sd} = \text{rtchou}^{sd} * \text{rhout}^d, \forall s = 1, \ldots, 34; \text{ and } d = 1, \ldots, 33 \quad (5.48)$$

and government expenditure:

$$\text{rtgov}^{sd} = \text{rtcgov}^{sd} * \text{rgovt}^d, \forall s = 1, \ldots, 34; \text{ and } d = 1, \ldots, 33 \quad (5.49)$$

In order to have a complete interregional system, we need the regional value-added components (VA^R). In the interregional input–output system, the total regional output (x^R) should be equivalent to the total demand of each region (DT^R). This balance checking can be done using the following identities.

Total regional output:

5 The Interregional Input–Output System for Colombia

$$x^R = \sum_{i=1}^{54} \text{RIC}^{sd} + \sum_{i=1}^{54} \text{RTIC}^{sd} + \text{rva}^{sd} \qquad (5.50)$$

where x^R is the vector of sectoral regional total output; RIC^{sd} is the regional intermediate consumption matrix; RTIC^{sd} is the indirect tax matrix related to intermediate consumption; and rva^{sd} is the vector of regional value-added.

Total demand:

$$dt^R = \sum_{j=1}^{37} \text{RIC}^{sd} + \text{rinv}^{sd} + \text{rhou}^{sd} + \text{expr}^{sd} + \text{rgov}^{sd} \qquad (5.51)$$

where dt^R is the total demand vector; rinv^{sd} is the investment demand; rhou^{sd} is the household consumption; expr^{sd} is the export vector; and rgov^{sd} is the government expenditure.

Finally, an adjustment in Stocks (stock^R) needs to be done to complete the interregional system (Fig. 5.5):

$$\text{stock}^R = x^{R'} - dt^R \qquad (5.52)$$

z_{ij}^{rs}, with $i, j = 1, \ldots, n$ and $r, s = 1, \ldots, r$, represents interindustry sales from industry i in region r to industry j in region s.

m_i^s and t_i^s with $i = 1, \ldots, n, c, i, g, e$ represent, respectively, imports and indirect taxes payments in region s.

l_i^s and L_i^s with $i = 1, \ldots, n$ and $s = 1, \ldots, r$ represent, respectively, payments by sectors for labor services and the total number of workers in region s.

n_j^s, with $j = 1, \ldots, n$ and $s = 1, \ldots, r$, represents payments by sectors for all other value-added items in region s.

$c_i^{r\bullet}, i_i^{r\bullet}, g_i^{r\bullet}$, and $e_i^{r\bullet}$ with $i = 1, \ldots, n$ and $r = 1, \ldots, r$ represent the regional components of final demand, $f_i^{r\bullet}$, respectively, household purchases, investment purchases, government purchases, and exports from region r.

x_i^r, with $i = 1, \ldots, n$ and $r = 1, \ldots, r$, is the total sectoral output in region r.

5.4 Structural Analysis

In this section, some of the main structural features of Colombia's economy are revealed using indicators derived from the IIOM-COL.

		\multicolumn{4}{c	}{Processing sectors}	\multicolumn{4}{c	}{Final demand}	Total output
		11	...	rn	r1 ... rm					

		Processing sectors					Final demand			Total output
		11	...	rn	r1 ... rm					
Processing sectors	11	z_{11}^{11}	...	z_{1n}^{11}	z_{11}^{1r} ... z_{1n}^{1r}	c_1^{1*}	i_1^{1*}	g_1^{1*}	e_1^{1*}	x_1^1
	...	...	⋱	...	... ⋱ ...	...	...	...	...	...
	1n	z_{n1}^{11}	...	z_{nn}^{11}	z_{n1}^{1r} ... z_{nn}^{1r}	c_n^{1*}	i_n^{1*}	g_n^{1*}	e_n^{1*}	x_n^1
	r1	z_{11}^{r1}	...	z_{1n}^{r1}	z_{11}^{rr} ... z_{1n}^{rr}	c_1^{r*}	i_1^{r*}	g_1^{r*}	e_1^{r*}	x_1^r
	...	...	⋱	...	... ⋱ ...	...	...	...	...	...
	rm	z_{n1}^{r1}	...	z_{nn}^{r1}	z_{n1}^{rr} ... z_{nn}^{rr}	c_n^{r*}	i_n^{r*}	g_n^{r*}	e_n^{r*}	x_n^r
Imports		m_1^1	...	m_n^1	m_1^r ... m_n^r	m_c^*	m_i^*	m_g^*	m_e^*	m
Indirect taxes		t_1^1	...	t_n^1	t_1^r ... t_n^r	t_c^*	t_i^*	t_g^*	t_e^*	t
Labor payments		l_1^1	...	l_n^1	l_1^r ... l_n^r					
Other payments		n_1^1	...	n_n^1	n_1^r ... n_n^r					n
Outlays		x_1^1	...	x_n^1	x_1^r ... x_n^r	c	i	g	e	
Employment		L_1^1	...	L_n^1	L_1^r ... L_n^r					

Fig. 5.5 Structure of the interregional flows database

5.4.1 Output Composition

Figure 5.6 presents the regional output shares for the departments in Colombia. Bogotá D.C, Antioquia, and Valle del Cauca dominate the national production, with shares of 23.9%, 14.9%, and 9.7% in total output, respectively.

The regional output shares by sectors in Colombia reveal some evidence of spatial concentration of specific activities: agriculture in Cundinamarca, Antioquia, Valle del Cauca, and Santander (44.7% of total output); mining of coal in Cesar and La Guajira

Region	Department	S1	S2	S3-S5	S6	S7	S8-S9	S10-S18	S19-S32	S33-S54	TOTAL
R1	Antioquia	0.1269	0.1399	0.1275	0.0015	0.0224	0.2848	0.1826	0.2068	0.1429	0.1490
R2	Atlántico	0.0033	0.0000	0.0163	0.0000	0.0000	0.0182	0.0729	0.0547	0.0499	0.0472
R3	Bogotá D.C.	0.0003	0.0000	0.0004	0.0000	0.0000	0.0609	0.1677	0.2149	0.2914	0.2390
R4	Bolívar	0.0240	0.0006	0.0341	0.0000	0.0116	0.0508	0.0066	0.0795	0.0366	0.0391
R5	Boyacá	0.0575	0.0049	0.0367	0.0285	0.0492	0.0435	0.0178	0.0281	0.0270	0.0285
R6	Caldas	0.0211	0.0790	0.0172	0.0000	0.0000	0.0240	0.0382	0.0111	0.0162	0.0167
R7	Caquetá	0.0050	0.0030	0.0200	0.0000	0.0000	0.0031	0.0024	0.0004	0.0052	0.0043
R8	Cauca	0.0213	0.1193	0.0280	0.0001	0.0011	0.0597	0.0269	0.0206	0.0167	0.0184
R9	Cesar	0.0241	0.0185	0.0339	0.5284	0.0091	0.0035	0.0149	0.0021	0.0139	0.0171
R10	Córdoba	0.0344	0.0000	0.0398	0.0000	0.0000	0.0333	0.0281	0.0076	0.0191	0.0178
R11	Cundinamarca	0.1416	0.0428	0.1493	0.0346	0.0005	0.0316	0.1218	0.0701	0.0513	0.0610
R12	Chocó	0.0074	0.0002	0.0183	0.0000	0.0000	0.1507	0.0006	0.0002	0.0038	0.0041
R13	Huila	0.0290	0.1738	0.0251	0.0000	0.0289	0.0115	0.0112	0.0031	0.0192	0.0177
R14	La Guajira	0.0048	0.0042	0.0112	0.3784	0.0087	0.0016	0.0011	0.0001	0.0087	0.0100
R15	Magdalena	0.0313	0.0167	0.0416	0.0000	0.0004	0.0047	0.0122	0.0023	0.0153	0.0133
R16	Meta	0.0687	0.0026	0.0314	0.0000	0.4965	0.0090	0.0165	0.0032	0.0203	0.0391
R17	Nariño	0.0369	0.0407	0.0326	0.0000	0.0003	0.0794	0.0048	0.0029	0.0171	0.0146
R18	Norte de Santander	0.0335	0.0169	0.0127	0.0263	0.0041	0.0054	0.0060	0.0126	0.0180	0.0160
R19	Quindío	0.0159	0.0308	0.0217	0.0000	0.0000	0.0050	0.0071	0.0023	0.0090	0.0079
R20	Risaralda	0.0103	0.0497	0.0184	0.0000	0.0000	0.0082	0.0350	0.0137	0.0169	0.0168
R21	Santander	0.0856	0.0579	0.0760	0.0019	0.0628	0.0516	0.0201	0.1176	0.0553	0.0634
R22	Sucre	0.0108	0.0000	0.0193	0.0000	0.0010	0.0020	0.0041	0.0058	0.0096	0.0083
R23	Tolima	0.0597	0.1296	0.0272	0.0000	0.0194	0.0146	0.0230	0.0164	0.0209	0.0219
R24	Valle del Cauca	0.0929	0.0680	0.0897	0.0003	0.0000	0.0289	0.1648	0.1222	0.0927	0.0968
R25	Arauca	0.0140	0.0000	0.0239	0.0000	0.0513	0.0015	0.0045	0.0003	0.0038	0.0060
R26	Casanare	0.0282	0.0005	0.0305	0.0000	0.1913	0.0053	0.0079	0.0008	0.0101	0.0171
R27	Putumayo	0.0036	0.0002	0.0051	0.0000	0.0412	0.0005	0.0005	0.0002	0.0034	0.0043
R28	San Andrés	0.0000	0.0000	0.0008	0.0000	0.0000	0.0002	0.0003	0.0000	0.0023	0.0016
R29	Amazonas	0.0001	0.0000	0.0050	0.0000	0.0000	0.0002	0.0001	0.0001	0.0009	0.0007
R30	Guainía	0.0002	0.0000	0.0010	0.0000	0.0000	0.0055	0.0001	0.0000	0.0005	0.0004
R31	Guaviare	0.0039	0.0000	0.0012	0.0000	0.0000	0.0006	0.0001	0.0001	0.0010	0.0008
R32	Vaupés	0.0004	0.0000	0.0002	0.0000	0.0000	0.0002	0.0000	0.0000	0.0004	0.0003
R33	Vichada	0.0033	0.0000	0.0039	0.0000	0.0000	0.0004	0.0001	0.0000	0.0007	0.0006
	TOTAL	1.0000	1.0000	1.0000	1.0000	1.0000	1.0000	1.0000	1.0000	1.0000	1.0000

Fig. 5.6 Regional structure of sectoral output: Colombia, 2015

(90.7%); manufacturing of food and beverage in Antioquia, Bogotá D.C, Cundinamarca, Valle del Cauca (63.7%); and other manufacturing in Antioquia, Bogotá D.C, Santander, Valle del Cauca (66.2%). Services, in general, are concentrated in Bogotá D.C, Antioquia, and Valle del Cauca (52.7%).

Figure 5.7 shows the sectoral shares in regional output. It reveals the critical role of some activities in relatively specialized regions: the dominant role of extraction of crude petroleum and natural gas in Meta (54.5% of total regional output) and Casanare (48.1%); the relevance of the services sector in San Andrés and Providencia (97.2%) and Bogotá D.C (81.4%).

Region	Department	S1	S2	S3-S5	S6	S7	S8-S9	S10-S18	S19-S32	S33-S54	TOTAL
R1	Antioquia	0.0227	0.0054	0.0184	0.0001	0.0065	0.0123	0.0850	0.2100	0.6397	1.0000
R2	Atlántico	0.0019	0.0000	0.0074	0.0000	0.0000	0.0025	0.1072	0.1756	0.7055	1.0000
R3	Bogotá D.C.	0.0000	0.0000	0.0000	0.0000	0.0000	0.0016	0.0487	0.1361	0.8135	1.0000
R4	Bolívar	0.0164	0.0001	0.0188	0.0000	0.0128	0.0083	0.0117	0.3073	0.6247	1.0000
R5	Boyacá	0.0538	0.0010	0.0277	0.0088	0.0741	0.0098	0.0434	0.1492	0.6322	1.0000
R6	Caldas	0.0337	0.0271	0.0222	0.0000	0.0000	0.0092	0.1588	0.1011	0.6479	1.0000
R7	Caquetá	0.0312	0.0040	0.1008	0.0000	0.0000	0.0046	0.0387	0.0133	0.8072	1.0000
R8	Cauca	0.0308	0.0371	0.0327	0.0001	0.0026	0.0208	0.1013	0.1695	0.6052	1.0000
R9	Cesar	0.0375	0.0062	0.0426	0.2710	0.0227	0.0013	0.0602	0.0186	0.5398	1.0000
R10	Córdoba	0.0515	0.0000	0.0482	0.0000	0.0000	0.0120	0.1093	0.0648	0.7142	1.0000
R11	Cundinamarca	0.0619	0.0040	0.0527	0.0050	0.0003	0.0033	0.1385	0.1739	0.5603	1.0000
R12	Chocó	0.0478	0.0002	0.0949	0.0000	0.0000	0.2330	0.0096	0.0082	0.6063	1.0000
R13	Huila	0.0437	0.0561	0.0305	0.0000	0.0700	0.0042	0.0437	0.0263	0.7254	1.0000
R14	La Guajira	0.0128	0.0024	0.0242	0.3322	0.0375	0.0010	0.0078	0.0015	0.5806	1.0000
R15	Magdalena	0.0629	0.0072	0.0675	0.0000	0.0013	0.0023	0.0640	0.0259	0.7689	1.0000
R16	Meta	0.0469	0.0004	0.0173	0.0000	0.5450	0.0015	0.0293	0.0125	0.3472	1.0000
R17	Nariño	0.0673	0.0159	0.0479	0.0000	0.0010	0.0347	0.0225	0.0304	0.7803	1.0000
R18	Norte de Santander	0.0557	0.0060	0.0171	0.0144	0.0109	0.0021	0.0260	0.1187	0.7490	1.0000
R19	Quindío	0.0534	0.0222	0.0589	0.0000	0.0000	0.0040	0.0621	0.0439	0.7555	1.0000
R20	Risaralda	0.0163	0.0169	0.0236	0.0000	0.0000	0.0031	0.1448	0.1239	0.6714	1.0000
R21	Santander	0.0360	0.0052	0.0258	0.0003	0.0425	0.0052	0.0220	0.2807	0.5823	1.0000
R22	Sucre	0.0345	0.0000	0.0499	0.0000	0.0049	0.0016	0.0339	0.1052	0.7700	1.0000
R23	Tolima	0.0728	0.0339	0.0267	0.0000	0.0381	0.0043	0.0731	0.1132	0.6380	1.0000
R24	Valle del Cauca	0.0256	0.0040	0.0200	0.0000	0.0000	0.0019	0.1181	0.1912	0.6392	1.0000
R25	Arauca	0.0623	0.0000	0.0860	0.0000	0.3679	0.0016	0.0527	0.0082	0.4214	1.0000
R26	Casanare	0.0440	0.0002	0.0384	0.0000	0.4809	0.0020	0.0320	0.0067	0.3958	1.0000
R27	Putumayo	0.0221	0.0003	0.0252	0.0000	0.4074	0.0007	0.0086	0.0070	0.5287	1.0000
R28	San Andrés	0.0000	0.0000	0.0115	0.0000	0.0000	0.0009	0.0114	0.0045	0.9718	1.0000
R29	Amazonas	0.0039	0.0000	0.1480	0.0000	0.0000	0.0017	0.0086	0.0196	0.8183	1.0000
R30	Guainía	0.0141	0.0000	0.0557	0.0000	0.0000	0.0895	0.0198	0.0185	0.8024	1.0000
R31	Guaviare	0.1252	0.0000	0.0311	0.0000	0.0000	0.0045	0.0120	0.0166	0.8106	1.0000
R32	Vaupés	0.0391	0.0000	0.0159	0.0000	0.0000	0.0042	0.0025	0.0000	0.9384	1.0000
R33	Vichada	0.1423	0.0000	0.1357	0.0000	0.0000	0.0039	0.0136	0.0029	0.7016	1.0000
	TOTAL	0.0267	0.0057	0.0215	0.0088	0.0429	0.0064	0.0694	0.1513	0.6672	1.0000

Fig. 5.7 Sectoral structure of regional output: Colombia, 2015

5.4.2 Multiplier Analysis

We computed the column multipliers derived from the Leontief inverse matrix, B (Miller & Blair, 2022). An output multiplier is defined for each sector j, in each region r, as the total value of production in all sectors and in all regions of the economy necessary to satisfy a unit's worth of final demand for sector j's output.

Further, the multiplier effect can be decomposed into intraregional (internal multiplier) and interregional (external multiplier) effects. The former represents the impacts on the outputs of sectors within the region where the final demand change was generated. The latter shows the impacts on the other regions of the system (interregional spillover effects).

Table 5.2 shows the intraregional and interregional shares for the average total output multipliers of the 33 departments of Colombia. It also shows the equivalent shares for the direct and indirect effects of a unit change in final demand in each sector for each region net of the initial injection (the total output multiplier effect net of the initial change). The entries are shown in percentage terms, providing insights into the degree of dependence of each region on the other regions.

Valle del Cauca, Antioquia, Atlántico, Bogotá D.C, and Bolívar are the most self-sufficient departments; the average flow-on effects from a unit change in sectoral final demand are among the highest. The average net effect exceeds 46% for those regions. For some regions, such as Chocó, Caquetá, La Guajira, Vaupés, Guaviare, and Arauca, the degree of regional self-sufficiency is lower, and the net intraregional flow-on effects, on average, are below 25% of the total interregional effects.

5.4.3 Interregional Linkages

In this section, a brief comparative analysis of regional economic structures is carried out to illustrate some of the system's features. We considered production linkages between sectors by analyzing the intermediate inputs of the interregional input–output database. Both the direct and indirect production linkage effects of the economy are captured by adopting different methods based on the evaluation of the Leontief inverse matrix.

The conventional input–output model is given by

$$x = Ax + f \qquad (5.53)$$

and

$$x = (I - A)^{-1} f = Bf \qquad (5.54)$$

where x and f are, respectively, the vectors of gross output and final demand; A is a matrix with the input–output coefficients a_{ij} defined as the amount of product i

Table 5.2 Regional percentage distribution of the average total and net output multipliers: Colombia, 2015

Region	Department	Simple decomposition		Net decomposition	
		Intraregional	Interregional	Intraregional	Interregional
R1	Antioquia	0.8030	0.1970	0.5270	0.4730
R2	Atlántico	0.7911	0.2089	0.4756	0.5244
R3	Bogotá D.C	0.7857	0.2143	0.4674	0.5326
R4	Bolívar	0.7847	0.2153	0.4608	0.5392
R5	Boyacá	0.7584	0.2416	0.3976	0.6024
R6	Caldas	0.7639	0.2361	0.4080	0.5920
R7	Caquetá	0.6799	0.3201	0.2035	0.7965
R8	Cauca	0.7355	0.2645	0.3657	0.6343
R9	Cesar	0.7272	0.2728	0.3373	0.6627
R10	Córdoba	0.7573	0.2427	0.3959	0.6041
R11	Cundinamarca	0.7344	0.2656	0.3473	0.6527
R12	Chocó	0.6805	0.3195	0.1842	0.8158
R13	Huila	0.7256	0.2744	0.3381	0.6619
R14	La Guajira	0.6908	0.3092	0.2085	0.7915
R15	Magdalena	0.7087	0.2913	0.2969	0.7031
R16	Meta	0.7229	0.2771	0.3090	0.6910
R17	Nariño	0.7088	0.2912	0.2915	0.7085
R18	Norte de Santander	0.7352	0.2648	0.3374	0.6626
R19	Quindío	0.7213	0.2787	0.3120	0.6880
R20	Risaralda	0.7492	0.2508	0.3780	0.6220
R21	Santander	0.7531	0.2469	0.4150	0.5850
R22	Sucre	0.7027	0.2973	0.2757	0.7243
R23	Tolima	0.7419	0.2581	0.3782	0.6218
R24	Valle del Cauca	0.8053	0.1947	0.5338	0.4662
R25	Arauca	0.7431	0.2569	0.2497	0.7503
R26	Casanare	0.7630	0.2370	0.3348	0.6652
R27	Putumayo	0.7383	0.2617	0.2764	0.7236
R28	San Andrés	0.8625	0.1375	0.3942	0.6058
R29	Amazonas	0.7771	0.2229	0.3341	0.6659
R30	Guainía	0.7732	0.2268	0.2527	0.7473
R31	Guaviare	0.7176	0.2824	0.2196	0.7804
R32	Vaupés	0.8453	0.1547	0.2146	0.7854
R33	Vichada	0.7750	0.2250	0.2682	0.7318

5 The Interregional Input–Output System for Colombia

required per unit of product j (in monetary terms)—$i, j = 1, \ldots, n$; and B is known as the Leontief inverse.

Let us consider Eq. 5.53 and Eq. 5.54 in an interregional context, with r different regions, so that

$$x = \begin{bmatrix} x^1 \\ \vdots \\ x^R \end{bmatrix}; \ A = \begin{bmatrix} A^{11} & \cdots & A^{1R} \\ \vdots & \ddots & \vdots \\ A^{R1} & \cdots & A^{RR} \end{bmatrix}; \ f = \begin{bmatrix} f^1 \\ \vdots \\ f^R \end{bmatrix}; \text{ and } B = \begin{bmatrix} B^{11} & \cdots & B^{1R} \\ \vdots & \ddots & \vdots \\ B^{R1} & \cdots & B^{RR} \end{bmatrix} \quad (5.55)$$

and

$$\begin{aligned} x^1 &= B^{11} f^1 + \ldots + B^{1R} f^R \\ &\vdots \\ x^R &= B^{R1} f^1 + \ldots + B^{RR} f^R \end{aligned} \quad (5.56)$$

Furthermore, we consider different components of f, which include demands originating in the specific regions, V, and abroad, e. We obtain information on final demand from origin s in the IIOM-COL, allowing us to treat V as a matrix, which provides the monetary values of final demand expenditures from the domestic regions in Colombia and the foreign region.

$$V = \begin{bmatrix} V^{11} & \cdots & V^{1R} \\ \vdots & \ddots & \vdots \\ V^{R1} & \cdots & V^{RR} \end{bmatrix}; \text{ and } e = \begin{bmatrix} e^1 \\ \vdots \\ e^R \end{bmatrix} \quad (5.57)$$

Thus, we can rewrite Eq. 5.57 as

$$\begin{aligned} x^1 &= B^{11}(V^{11} + \ldots + V^{R1} + e^1) + \ldots + B^{1R}(V^{1R} + \ldots + V^{RR} + e^R) \\ &\vdots \\ x^R &= B^{R1}(V^{11} + \ldots + V^{R1} + e^1) + \ldots + B^{RR}(V^{1R} + \ldots + V^{RR} + e^R) \end{aligned} \quad (5.58)$$

From Eq. 5.58, we can compute the contribution of final demand from different origins on regional output. It is clear from Eq. 5.58 that regional output depends on demand originating in the region and on the degree of interregional integration, as well as on demand from outside the region.

In what follows, interdependence among sectors in different regions is considered by analyzing the complete intermediate input portion of the interregional input–output table. Based on Eq. 5.56, the Leontief inverse matrix will be considered, and some summary interpretations of the structure of the economy derived from it will be provided. To illustrate the nature of interregional linkages in Colombia, we examine the structure of the Colombian economy derived from the Leontief inverse (multipliers) matrix, focusing on the database for 2015.

5.4.3.1 Output Decomposition

In order to complement the multiplier analysis, the regional output decomposition is carried out in this section. We consider the multiplier structure and final demand structure for the 33 domestic and foreign regions.

Following Eq. 5.58, regional output (for each region) was decomposed, and the contributions of the components of final demand from different areas were calculated. The results are presented in Table 3.6. As expected, the main contributions to a region's final demand are given by themselves, so the highest values in the table are on the diagonal. In addition, the importance of Antioquia (R1), Bogotá D.C (R3), Santander (R21), and Valle del Cauca (R24) for the Colombian economy is verified, with the final demand originating in these regions generating the most significant contribution to the output of the other regions.

The final demand for Bogotá D.C (R3) contributes to 21.6% of the Colombian output, and, at the regional level, it contributes mainly to the departments Cundinamarca (R11), San Andrés (R28), and Vichada (R33). Final demand originating in Antioquia (R1) contributes 12.2% of total national output, and final demand originating in Valle del Cauca (R24) contributes 7.0%. It is worth noting the importance of the Rest of the World's demand for Colombian production, with a contribution of 14.5%.[8]

A more systematic approach to visualize the influence of final demand from different regions is to map the columns' original estimates generated in Fig. 5.8. The results, illustrated in Fig. 5.9, provide an attempt to reveal the spatial patterns of income dependence upon specific sources of final demand. The 33 departments are grouped into six different categories on each map so that darker colors represent higher values.

5.5 Final Considerations

The calibration of the ICGE model, which will be described in Chap. 6, requires the assignment of values to the relevant parameters and coefficients of the model, which produce an initial solution. Such a procedure is heavily based on the data described in this chapter. By working with percentage changes rather than absolute changes, we will see that the model's coefficients are interpretable in terms of cost and sales shares, and they can be derived from input–output tables. Together with values of substitution elasticities and supplementary data on capital stocks, depreciation rates,

---

[8] The contribution of external demand for regional output varies considerably by Department (see Chap. 9 of this book).

5 The Interregional Input–Output System for Colombia 141

Fig. 5.8 Components of decomposition of regional output based on the sources of final demand: Colombia, 2015 (in %)

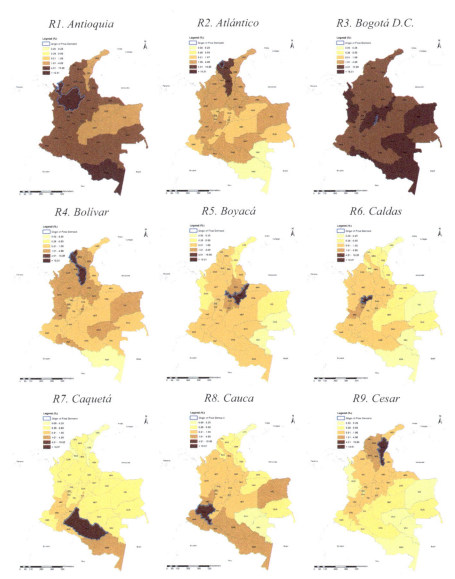

Fig. 5.9 Identification of regions relatively more affected by a specific regional demand, by origin of final demand

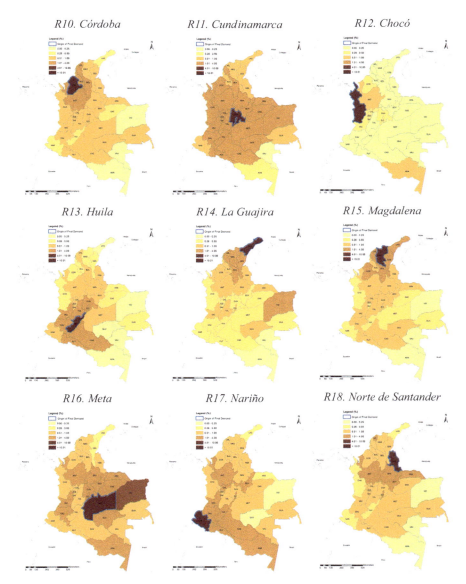

Fig. 5.9 (continued)

demographic variables, and some other variables, an initial equilibrium solution for the model can be computed.

This chapter has described the interregional input–output system necessary to calibrate the model. The data provide a detailed picture of the Colombian economic structure used as the benchmark for the analyses in this book, which is an essential

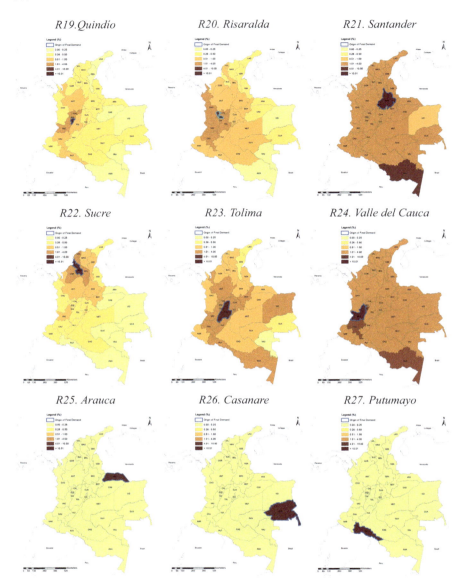

Fig. 5.9 (continued)

requirement for counterfactual exercises. In particular, in this chapter we examine the interdependence among sectors in different regions through the interregional input–output table. This analysis illustrates the nature of interregional linkages in Colombia and provides some interpretations of the structure of their economy. Acosta and Bonet, in the previous chapter, showed a limited interregional dependence in the

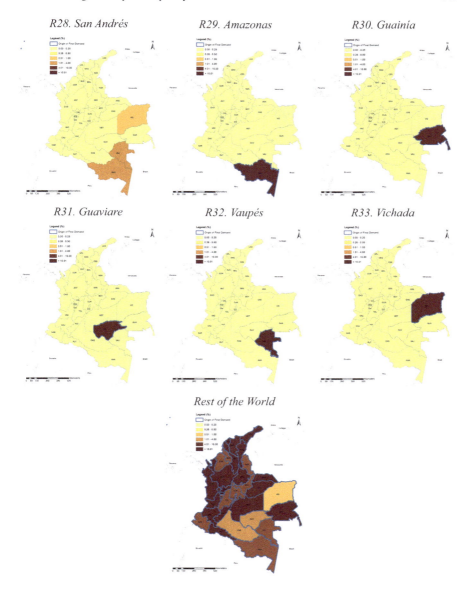

Fig. 5.9 (continued)

economic growth of Colombian departments derived from a spatial econometric estimation. These characteristics of the Colombian economy raise a number of research topics that are explored in the remaining chapters of this book.

In the following technical chapter, intended for readers interested in modeling issues, we will describe the structure of the CEER model, a fully operational ICGE model for Colombia.

Appendix 1: List of Regions

DANE Code	Region	Department
5	R1	Antioquia
8	R2	Atlántico
11	R3	Bogotá D.C
13	R4	Bolívar
15	R5	Boyacá
17	R6	Caldas
18	R7	Caquetá
19	R8	Cauca
20	R9	Cesar
23	R10	Córdoba
25	R11	Cundinamarca
27	R12	Chocó
41	R13	Huila
44	R14	La Guajira
47	R15	Magdalena
50	R16	Meta
52	R17	Nariño
54	R18	Norte de Santander
63	R19	Quindío
66	R20	Risaralda
68	R21	Santander
70	R22	Sucre
73	R23	Tolima
76	R24	Valle del Cauca
81	R25	Arauca
85	R26	Casanare
86	R27	Putumayo
88	R28	San Andrés
91	R29	Amazonas
94	R30	Guainía

(continued)

(continued)

DANE Code	Region	Department
95	R31	Guaviare
97	R32	Vaupés
99	R33	Vichada

Appendix 2: List of sectors

Id	Sector	CIIU Rev. 4 AC
S1	Agriculture	A0101
S2	Coffee growing	003
S3	Livestock and hunting	A0102
S4	Forestry and logging	A02
S5	Fishing and aquaculture	A03
S6	Mining of coal and lignite	017
S7	Extraction of crude petroleum and natural gas	018 021 022
S8	Mining of metal ores	019
S9	Other mining and quarrying	020
S10	Processing and preserving of meat and preserving of fish, crustaceans, and mollusks	023 024 025
S11	Processing of vegetable and animal oils and fats	026
S12	Processing of dairy products	027
S13	Processing of grain mill products, starches, and starch products	028 032 035
S14	Processing of coffee products	029
S15	Processing of sugar	030 031
S16	Processing of cocoa, chocolate, and sugar confectionery	033
S17	Processing and preserving of fruit and vegetables	034
S18	Manufacture of beverages; manufacture of tobacco products	036
S19	Manufacture of textiles; manufacture of wearing apparel	037 038
S20	Manufacture of leather and related products	039
S21	Manufacture of wood and products of wood and cork, except furniture; manufacture of articles of straw and plaiting materials	040
S22	Manufacture of paper and paper products; printing and reproduction of recorded media	041 042
S23	Manufacture of coke and refined petroleum products	043 044
S24	Manufacture of chemicals and chemical products; manufacture of pharmaceuticals, medicinal chemical, and botanical products	045 046 047

(continued)

(continued)

Id	Sector	CIIU Rev. 4 AC
S25	Manufacture of rubber and plastics products	048
S26	Manufacture of other non-metallic mineral products	049
S27	Manufacture of basic metals; manufacture of fabricated metal products, except machinery and equipment	050 051
S28	Manufacture of electrical equipment; manufacture of computer, electronic and optical products	052
S29	Manufacture of machinery and equipment NEC; repair and installation of machinery and equipment	053 057
S30	Manufacture of motor vehicles, trailers, and semi-trailers; Manufacture of other transport equipment	054
S31	Manufacture of furniture	055
S32	Other manufacturing	056
S33	Electricity	058 059 060
S34	Gas, steam and air conditioning supply	061
S35	Water collection, treatment and supply	062
S36	Sewerage; waste collection, treatment and disposal activities; materials recovery	063 064 065 066
S37	Construction	067 068 069
S38	Wholesale and retail trade	070
S39	Repair of motor vehicles and motorcycles	071
S40	Land transport and transport via pipelines	072 074
S41	Water transport	073
S42	Air transport	075
S43	Warehousing and support activities for transportation	076
S44	Postal and courier activities	077
S45	Accommodation and food service activities	I (078–080)
S46	Information and communication	J (081–084)
S47	Financial and insurance activities	K (085–088)
S48	Real estate activities	089
S49	Professional, scientific and technical activities; administrative and support service activities	M + N (090–097)
S50	Public administration and defense; compulsory social security	O (098–099)
S51	Education	100 101
S52	Human health and social work activities	Q (102–103)
S53	Arts, entertainment, and recreation; other service activities	R + S (104–108)
S54	Activities of households as employers	109

Appendix 3: Sectoral GRP Data

DANE publishes sectoral GRP information for 12 activity sectors in the 33 regions of Colombia for 2015. To obtain a more disaggregated sectoral structure, we disaggregated the sectoral structure using regional shares from other databases. This disaggregation procedure considered the consistency with the sectoral information available at the SUT at the national level. Table 5.3 shows the sectoral structure after the disaggregation of the sectors. This table also exhibits the variables used to calculate regional shares.

After calculating the regional shares for each SUT sector, the respective sectoral value-added estimates at the national level (from the national IO table) were distributed across the 33 Colombian regions. Next, the consistency of the regionalized data with GRP estimates was ensured using the bi-proportional adjustment method, RAS.

DANE publishes information about international trade statistics for 97 products and 33 departments. After calculating the regional shares for each IIOM-COL sector, the respective sectoral exports estimate at the national level (from the national IO table) were distributed across the 33 Colombian regions (Table 5.4).

Appendix 4: Average Travel Time (in Minutes)

See Fig. 5.10.

Appendix 5A: Interregional Trade in Colombia, 2015 (in COP Billions)

See Fig. 5.11.

Appendix 5B: Interregional Trade in Colombia: Purchases Shares, 2015

See Fig. 5.12.

Appendix 5C: Interregional Trade in Colombia: Sales Shares, 2015

See Fig. 5.13.

Table 5.3 Data sources used to calculate regional shares of sectoral output

IIOM-COL	Cuentas Nacionales Departamentales (Base 2015)—Producto Interno Bruto por actividades economicas—12 agrupaciones—Secciones CIIU Rev. 4 A.C.		Cuentas Departamentales (Ano Base 2005)—Producto Interno Bruto	
Sector	Sector	Description	Sector	Description
S1	1	Agricultura, ganaderia, caza, silvicultura y pesca	1	Cultivo de otros productos agricolas
S2			2	Cultivo de cafe
S3			3	Production pecuaria y caza incluyendo las actividades veterinarias
S4			4	Silvicultura, extraccion de madera y actividades conexas
S5			5	Pesca, produccion de peces en criaderos y granjas piscicolas
S6	2	Explotacion de minas y canteras	6	Extraccion de carbon, carbon lignitico y turba
S7			7	Extraccion de petroleo crudo y de gas natural
S8			8	Extraccion de minerales metaliferos
S9			9	Extraccion de minerales no metalicos
S10–S18	3	Industrias manufactureras	10	Alimentos, bebidas y tabaco
S19–S32			11	Resto de la Industria
S33	4	Suministro de electricidad, gas, vapor y aire acondicionado; distribucion de agua; evacuacion y tratamiento de aguas residuales, gestion de desechos y actividades de saneamiento ambiental	12	Generacion, captacion y distribucion de energia electrica
S34			13	Fabricacion de gas; distribucion de combustibles gaseosos por tuberias; suministro de vapor y agua caliente
S35			14	Captacion, depuracion y distribucion de agua

(continued)

Table 5.3 (continued)

IIOM-COL	Cuentas Nacionales Departamentales (Base 2015)—Producto Interno Bruto por actividades economicas—12 agrupaciones—Secciones CIIU Rev. 4 A.C.		Cuentas Departamentales (Ano Base 2005)—Producto Interno Bruto	
Sector	Sector	Description	Sector	Description
S36			15	Eliminacion de desperdicios y aguas residuales, saneamiento y actividades similares
S37	5	Construccion	16	Construccion de edificaciones completas y de partes de edificaciones; acondicionamiento de edificaciones
			17	Construccion de obras de ingenieria civil
S38	6	Comercio al por mayor y al por menor; reparacion de vehiculos automotores y motocicletas; transporte y almacenamiento; alojamiento y servicios de comida	18	Comercio
S39			19	Mantenimiento y reparacion de vehiculos automotores; reparacion de efectos personales y enseres domesticos
S40			21	Transporte por via terrestre
S41			22	Transporte por via acuatica
S42			23	Transporte por via aerea
S43			24	Actividades complementarias y auxiliares al transporte; actividades de agencias de viajes
S44			25	Correo y telecomunicaciones
S45			20	Hoteles, restaurantes, bares y similares
S46	7	Informacion y comunicaciones	28	Actividades de servicios a las empresas except servicios financieros e inmobiliarios
S47	8	Actividades financieras y de seguros	6	Intermediacion financiera

(continued)

Table 5.3 (continued)

IIOM-COL	Cuentas Nacionales Departamentales (Base 2015)—Producto Interno Bruto por actividades economicas—12 agrupaciones—Secciones CIIU Rev. 4 A.C.		Cuentas Departamentales (Ano Base 2005)—Producto Interno Bruto	
Sector	Sector	Description	Sector	Description
S48	9	Actividades inmobiliarias	7	Actividades inmobiliarias y alquiler de vivienda
S49	10	Actividades profesionales, científicas y tecnicas; actividades de servicios administrativos y de apoyo		
S50	11	Administracion publica y defensa; planes de seguridad social de afiliacion obligatoria; educacion; actividades de atencion de la salud humana y de servicios sociales	29	Administracion publica y defensa; seguridad social de afiliacion obligatoria
S51			30 + 31	Educacion de mercado / Educacion de no mercado
S52			32	Servicios sociales y de salud de mercado
S53	12	Actividades artisticas, de entretenimiento y recreacion y otras actividades de servicios; actividades de los hogares individuales en calidad de empleadores	33 + 34	Actividades de asociaciones n.c.p.; actividades de esparcimiento y actividades culturales y deportivas; otras actividades de servicios de mercado
S54			35	Hogares privados con servicio domestico

5 The Interregional Input–Output System for Colombia 153

Table 5.4 Data sources used to calculate regional shares of sectoral output (manufacturing)

IIOM-COL	Cuentas Departamentales (Ano Base2005)—Producto Interno Bruto		Fuerza de trabajo—Gran Encuesta Integrada de Hogares—GEIH—2015	
Sector	Sector	Description	Sector	Description
S10	10	Alimentos, bebidas y tabaco	10	Carnes y pescados
S11			11	Aceites y grasas animales y vegetales
S12			12	Productos lacteos
S13			13	Productos de molineria, almidones y sus productos
S14			14	Productos de cafe y trilla
S15			15	Azucar y panela
S16			16	Cacao, chocolate y productos de confiteria
S17			17	Productos alimenticios n.c.p
S18			18 + 19	Bebidas / productos de tabaco
S19	11	Resto de la Industria	20 + 21 + 22	Fibras textiles / articulos textiles
S20			23	Curtido y preparado de cueros, productos de cuero y calzado
S21			24	Productos de madera, corcho, paja y materiales
				Trenzables
S22			25 + 26	Productos de papel / edicion, impression
S23			27	Productos de la refinacion del petroleo;
				combustible nuclear
S24			28	Sustancias y productos quimicos
S25			29	Productos de caucho y de plastico
S26			30	Productos minerales no metalicos
S27			31	Productos metalurgicos basicos (excepto maquinaria y equipo)
S28			33	Otra maquinaria y suministro electrico
S29			32	Maquinaria y equipo
S30			34	Equipo de transporte
S31			35	Muebles
S32			36	Otros bienes manufacturados N.C.P.

	R1	R2	R3	R4	R5	R6	R7	R8	R9	R10	R11	R12	R13	R14	R15	R16	R17	R18	R19	R20	R21	R22	R23	R24	R25	R26	R27	R28	R29	R30	R31	R32	R33
R1	0	813	464	801	547	306	786	644	724	478	494	417	539	898	801	881	971	737	390	331	438	599	412	515	1142	801	912	NaN	NaN	NaN	1154	NaN	1734
R2	851	0	949	123	886	971	1271	1362	290	401	979	1262	1024	273	131	1310	1689	722	1082	1038	587	291	898	1233	1043	1140	1397	NaN	NaN	NaN	1584	NaN	2163
R3	483	956	0	1062	141	429	556	684	827	935	30	791	310	1001	904	449	1011	714	388	422	512	953	210	559	742	402	682	NaN	NaN	NaN	722	NaN	1302
R4	800	125	1054	0	990	1076	1375	1428	395	331	1084	1185	1129	389	248	1414	1754	827	1162	1103	691	216	1002	1299	1147	1245	1502	NaN	NaN	NaN	1688	NaN	2268
R5	552	892	141	998	0	530	684	791	763	938	171	918	438	937	840	437	1117	597	516	597	384	883	339	688	625	285	811	NaN	NaN	NaN	711	NaN	1291
R6	293	967	420	1037	529	0	694	402	838	811	450	453	447	1011	915	836	729	850	137	78	552	888	291	273	1130	789	807	NaN	NaN	NaN	1110	NaN	1689
R7	793	1266	554	1372	686	695	0	416	1137	1245	584	1008	255	1310	1214	993	624	1150	607	645	851	1257	429	567	1287	946	319	NaN	NaN	NaN	1267	NaN	1847
R8	639	1348	682	1436	814	397	415	0	1218	1158	712	656	371	1393	1296	1121	333	1232	300	328	933	1235	482	160	1404	1074	413	NaN	NaN	NaN	1384	NaN	1975
R9	723	293	822	399	758	843	1143	1234	0	433	852	1133	896	192	241	1182	1561	594	954	909	459	323	769	1105	915	1013	1269	NaN	NaN	NaN	1455	NaN	2035
R10	532	399	935	335	911	807	1257	1150	434	0	965	868	1010	624	498	1336	1477	830	885	825	695	134	883	1021	1152	1166	1383	NaN	NaN	NaN	1609	NaN	2189
R11	513	986	30	1092	171	459	586	714	857	965	0	821	340	1031	934	479	1041	744	418	452	542	983	240	589	772	432	712	NaN	NaN	NaN	752	NaN	1332
R12	407	1259	784	1189	916	451	1003	659	1128	868	814	0	757	1301	1205	1224	985	1140	425	382	842	994	584	530	1517	1177	1063	NaN	NaN	NaN	1497	NaN	2077
R13	551	1024	312	1130	444	453	259	365	895	1003	342	766	0	1069	972	751	692	908	365	403	609	1015	187	471	1045	704	385	NaN	NaN	NaN	1025	NaN	1605
R14	894	276	992	388	929	1014	1314	1405	194	622	1022	1304	1067	0	171	1353	1732	765	1125	1081	630	512	941	1276	826	1183	1440	NaN	NaN	NaN	1627	NaN	2206
R15	802	131	900	243	836	922	1221	1313	240	502	930	1211	975	173	0	1260	1640	673	1033	988	537	391	848	1184	993	1091	1348	NaN	NaN	NaN	1534	NaN	2114
R16	897	1321	453	1427	442	842	997	1103	1192	1349	483	1230	750	1365	1269	0	1429	963	828	867	813	1311	651	1000	615	275	1123	NaN	NaN	NaN	278	NaN	940
R17	936	1644	977	1733	1109	703	624	313	1515	1454	1007	962	678	1689	1592	1416	0	1538	606	634	1239	1532	788	466	1710	1369	320	NaN	NaN	NaN	1690	NaN	2269
R18	732	739	723	845	604	852	1151	1243	610	845	753	1142	905	784	687	966	1570	0	963	918	298	735	778	1114	329	766	1278	NaN	NaN	NaN	1239	NaN	1819
R19	369	1075	389	1166	521	136	608	309	945	887	419	430	361	1119	1022	829	636	958	0	67	659	965	189	180	1122	782	714	NaN	NaN	NaN	1102	NaN	1682
R20	308	1026	429	1105	588	75	648	333	897	826	459	384	402	1070	974	895	660	910	70	0	611	903	229	204	1189	848	738	NaN	NaN	NaN	1169	NaN	1722
R21	439	593	498	699	370	559	859	951	464	694	528	849	612	638	541	795	1277	307	671	626	0	584	486	822	792	625	985	NaN	NaN	NaN	1069	NaN	1648
R22	600	291	949	217	885	886	1271	1228	326	132	979	992	1025	515	389	1309	1555	722	963	904	586	0	897	1099	1042	1139	1397	NaN	NaN	NaN	1583	NaN	2162
R23	425	898	218	1004	351	296	437	499	769	877	248	601	191	943	846	658	826	782	199	237	483	889	0	370	952	611	564	NaN	NaN	NaN	932	NaN	1511
R24	515	1222	556	1312	688	273	571	164	1095	1034	589	531	473	1269	1172	995	491	1106	174	204	807	1111	356	0	1289	948	569	NaN	NaN	NaN	1269	NaN	1849
R25	1143	1058	746	1164	627	1135	1289	1396	928	1159	776	1523	1043	827	995	611	1722	332	1121	1160	774	1048	944	1293	0	338	1416	NaN	NaN	NaN	885	NaN	1464
R26	805	1146	408	1252	289	797	951	1058	1016	1191	438	1215	705	1190	1094	273	1384	763	783	864	637	1136	606	955	341	0	1078	NaN	NaN	NaN	547	NaN	1126
R27	913	1386	674	1492	806	801	318	413	1257	1365	704	1060	375	1431	1334	1113	320	1270	704	732	971	1377	549	564	1407	1066	0	NaN	NaN	NaN	1387	NaN	1967
R28	NaN	NaN	NaN	NaN	NaN	NaN	NaN	NaN	NaN	NaN	NaN	NaN	NaN	NaN	NaN	NaN	NaN	NaN	NaN	NaN	NaN	NaN	NaN	NaN	NaN	NaN	NaN	0	NaN	NaN	NaN	NaN	NaN
R29	NaN	NaN	NaN	NaN	NaN	NaN	NaN	NaN	NaN	NaN	NaN	NaN	NaN	NaN	NaN	NaN	NaN	NaN	NaN	NaN	NaN	NaN	NaN	NaN	NaN	NaN	NaN	NaN	0	NaN	NaN	NaN	NaN
R30	NaN	NaN	NaN	NaN	NaN	NaN	NaN	NaN	NaN	NaN	NaN	NaN	NaN	NaN	NaN	NaN	NaN	NaN	NaN	NaN	NaN	NaN	NaN	NaN	NaN	NaN	NaN	NaN	NaN	0	NaN	NaN	NaN
R31	1170	1374	726	1480	715	1116	1270	1376	1245	1352	756	1504	1023	1419	1322	277	1703	1236	1102	1140	1086	1369	924	1273	889	548	1396	NaN	NaN	NaN	0	NaN	1198
R32	NaN	NaN	NaN	NaN	NaN	NaN	NaN	NaN	NaN	NaN	NaN	NaN	NaN	NaN	NaN	NaN	NaN	NaN	NaN	NaN	NaN	NaN	NaN	NaN	NaN	NaN	NaN	NaN	NaN	NaN	NaN	0	NaN
R33	1752	2037	1308	2143	1297	1697	1852	1958	1908	2016	1338	2085	1605	2082	1985	937	2284	1818	1683	1722	1668	2033	1506	1855	1470	1130	1978	NaN	NaN	NaN	1196	NaN	0

Fig. 5.10 Average travel time (in minutes) matrix

5 The Interregional Input–Output System for Colombia

Fig. 5.11 Interregional trade in Colombia, 2015 (in COP billions)

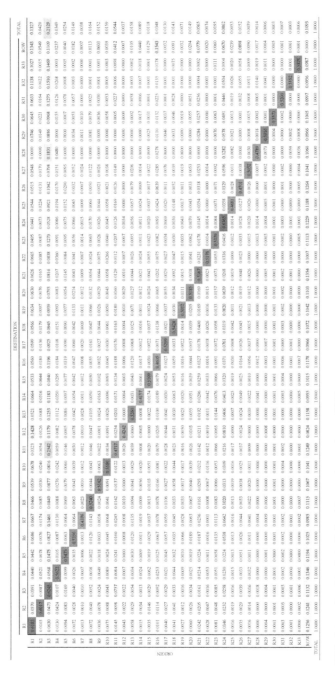

Fig. 5.12 Interregional trade in Colombia: purchases shares, 2015

5 The Interregional Input–Output System for Colombia

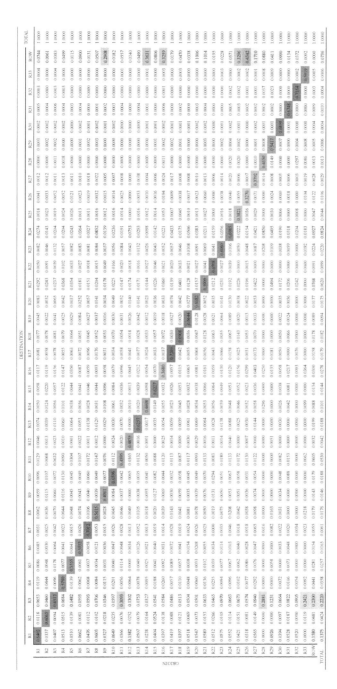

Fig. 5.13 Interregional trade in Colombia: sales shares, 2015

References

Altman, M. (2003). Staple theory and export-led growth: constructing differential growth. *Australian Economic History Review, 43*(3), 230–255.
Bonet, J. (2005). *Regional structural changes in Columbia: An input output approach, Borradores de Economia, 341*. Banco de la República de Colombia.
Chenery, H. B. (1956). Interregional and international input-output analysis. In T. Barna (Ed.), *The structure interdependence of the economy* (pp. 341–356). Wiley.
Cai, M. (2022). A calibrated gravity model of interregional trade. *Spatial Economic Analysis*, 1–19.
Dixon, P. B. & Rimmer, M. T. (2004). *Disaggregation of results from a detailed general equilibrium model of de US to the State level*. General Working Paper n. 145. Centre of Policy Studies.
Gabela, J. G. F. (2020). On the accuracy of gravity-RAS approaches used for inter-regional trade estimation: evidence using the 2005 inter-regional input-output table of Japan. *Economic Systems Research, 32*(4), 521–539.
Haddad, E. A., Araújo, I. F., Ibarrarán, M. E., Boyd, R., Elizondo, A., & Belausteguigoitia, J. C. (2020b). Interstate input-output model for Mexico, 2013. *Análisis Económico, 35*(90), 7–43. http://www.analisiseconomico.azc.uam.mx/index.php/rae/article/view/527/380
Haddad, E. A., Cotarelli, N., Simonato, T. C., Vale, V. A., & Visentin, J. C. (2020b). The grand tour: Keynes and Goodwin go to Greece. *Economic Structures, 9*(31), 1–21.
Haddad, E. A., Farajalla, N., Camargo, M., Lopes, R. L., & Vieira, F. V. (2014). Climate change in Lebanon: Higher-order regional impacts from agriculture. *The Region, 1*(1), 9–24.
Haddad, E. A., Gonçalves, C. A., & Nascimento, T. (2017). Matriz Interestadual de Insumo-Produto para o Brasil: Uma Aplicação do Método IIOAS. *Revista Brasileira De Estudos Regionais e Urbanos, 11*(4), 424–446.
Haddad, E. A., Mengoub, F. E., & Vale, V. A. (2020c). Water content in trade: A regional analysis for Morocco. *Economic Systems Research, 32*(4), 565–584.
Haddad, E. A., Silva, V., Porsse, A. A., & Dentinho, T. P. (2015). Multipliers in an Island economy: The case of the Azores. In A. A. Batabyal & P. Nijkamp (Eds.), *The region and trade: New analytical directions* (pp. 205–226). World Scientific.
Haddad, E., Faria, W., Galvis, L. A., & Hahn, L. W. (2018). Matriz Insumo-Producto Interregional para Colombia. *Revista De Economía Del Caribe, 21*, 1–24.
Haddad, E., Faria, W., Galvis, L. A., & Hahn, L. W. (2016a). *Interregional input-output matrix for Colombia, Borradores de Economia, 923*. Banco de la República.
Haddad, E. A., Lahr, M., Elshahawany, D., & Vassallo, M. (2016b). Regional analysis of domestic integration in Egypt: An interregional CGE approach. *Economic Structures, 5*(25), 1–33.
Haddad, E.A., Perobelli, F. S., Castro, G. Araújo, I. Ramirez-Alvarez, P. E., & Fernandes, R. (2021). *Tool kits in multi-regional and multi-sectoral general equilibrium modeling for paraguay*. TD NEREUS 1–2021, Núcleo de Economia Regional e Urbana da Universidade de São Paulo (NEREUS).
Hewings, G. J., & Oosterhaven, J. (2021). Interregional trade: Models and analyses. In M. M. Fischer & P. Nijkamp (Eds.), *Handbook of regional science* (pp. 373–395). Springer.
Hirschman, A. O. (1958). *The strategy of economic development*. New Haven, Conn: Yale University Press.
Hirschman, A. O. (1984). A dissenter's confession: 'The strategy of economic development' revisited. In G. M. Meier & D. Seers (Eds.,. *Pioneers in development* (pp. 85–111). The World Bank and Oxford University Press.
Isard, W. (1951). Interregional input-output analysis: A model of a space economy. *Review of Economics and Statistics, 33*, 318–328.
Isard W., Azis I. J., Drennan M. P., Miller R. E., Saltzman S., & Thorbecke E. (1998). *Methods of interregional and regional analysis*. Ashgate.
Leontief, W. (1936). Quantitative input-output relations in the economic systems of the United States. *Review of Economics and Statistics, 18*, 105–125.

Leontief, W., Hollis, B., Chenery, P., Clark, P., Duesenberry, J., Ferguson, A., Grosse, R., et al. (1953). *Studies in the structure of the American economy*. White Plains, NY: International Arts and Science Press.

Miller, R. E., & Blair, P. D. (2022). *Input-output analysis: Foundations and eExtensions* (3rd ed.). Cambridge University Press.

Moses, L. N. (1955). The stability of interregional trading patterns and input-output analysis. *American Economic Review, 45*(5), 803–832.

North, D. C. (1955). Location theory and regional economic growth. *Journal of Political Economy, 63*(3), 243–258.

Perobelli, F. S., Haddad, E. A., Moron, J. B., & Hewings, G. J. (2010). Structural interdependence among Colombian departments. *Economic Systems Research, 22*(3), 279–300.

Perroux, F. (1950). Economic space: Theory and applications. *The Quarterly Journal of Economics, 64*(1), 89–104.

Round, J. I. (1983). Nonsurvey techniques: A critical review of the theory and the evidence. *International Regional Science Review. 8*(3), 189–2.

Watkins, M. H. (1963). A staple theory of economic growth. *Canadian Journal of Economics and Political Science, 29*(2), 141–158.

Eduardo A. Haddad Full Professor at the Department of Economics at the University of São Paulo, Brazil, where he directs the Regional and Urban Economics Lab (NEREUS). Affiliate Professor at the Faculty of Governance, Economic and Social Sciences of the Mohammed VI University and Senior Fellow at the Policy Center for the New South, Rabat, Morocco. President of the Regional Science Association International, RSAI (2021-2022).

Luis Armando Galvis-Aponte Ph.D. (Geog.), University of Illinois. Senior researcher, Center for Regional Economic Studies, Banco de la República, Colombia. Research fields: econometric methods, economic development, and regional economics.

Inácio F. Araújo Doctor in Economics, Federal University of Juiz de Fora. Pos-doctoral researcher, University of São Paulo, Brazil. Research fields: regional economics, input-output methods, and international trade.

Chapter 6
The Interregional Computable General Equilibrium Model for Colombia

Eduardo A. Haddad and Inácio F. Araújo

6.1 Introduction

More than 65 years have passed since Milton Friedman first drew attention to the so-called Cournot problem. In his review of William Jaffé's translation of Léon Walras' *Elements of Pure Economics*, Friedman (1955) highlighted the task Cournot (1838) had outlined in his *Researches* as the proper way of dealing with the interrelationships in an economic system. In this author's opinion, the development of economic analysis of concrete problems should pursue a *general equilibrium* framework, as "in reality, the economic system is a whole of which all the parts are connected and react on each other" (op. cit. p. 127). *Partial equilibrium* analysis, even though more tractable from an analytical perspective, would not provide a complete and rigorous solution for the problems relative to some parts of the economic system, as it does not accomplish considering the whole system. However, Cournot recognized that the existing mathematical, statistical, and computational benchmarks, at the time of his writings, were far from sufficient for approaching the problem in a general equilibrium context:

> It seems, therefore, as if, for a complete and rigorous solution of the problems relative to some parts of the economic system, it were indispensable to take the entire system into consideration. But this would surpass the powers of mathematical analysis and of our practical methods of calculation, even if the values of all the constants could be assigned to them numerically. (op. cit., p. 127)

The quest for solving Cournot's problem may be evoked considering five principal lines of contributors: (i) the predecessors that provided the intellectual background which influenced the work by Léon Walras, including pioneering efforts of

---

E. A. Haddad (✉) · I. F. Araújo
University of São Paulo, São Paulo, Brazil
e-mail: ehaddad@usp.br

I. F. Araújo
e-mail: inacio.araujo@usp.br

the eighteenth century economists Richard Cantillon and François Quesnay toward the provision of a methodological foundation for the circular flow of income, as well as the often neglected influence by Achylle-Nicolas Isnard (Schumpeter, 1954); (ii) the critical role played by Léon Walras himself, whose central "achievement was to having constructed a mathematical system displaying in considerable detail precisely the interrelationships emphasized by Cournot" (Friedman, 1955, p. 904); (iii) a line of economists, led by Kenneth J. Arrow and Gérard Debreu, whose successful accomplishments in the realm of pure theory reinforced Walras' initial strategy of emptying Cournot's problem of its empirical content and producing a complete and rigorous solution *in principle*, making no pretense that it could be used directly in numerical calculations[1]; (iv) the seminal works by Wassily Leontief, Leif Johansen, Sir Richard Stone and Herbert Scarf, in the realm of applied theory, whose contributions represent milestones in the development of the leading schools of computable general equilibrium (CGE) modeling; finally, (v) in the realm of actual practice, the development of CGE models, which offer an adequate framework for policy analysis, by quantifying linkages between different parts of the economy and providing valuable insights into the likely effects of disturbances in one part of the economy on activities in other parts (Dixon & Parmenter, 1996).

The general equilibrium approach treats the economy as a system of many interrelated markets in which the equilibrium of all variables must be determined simultaneously. Any perturbation of the economic environment can be evaluated by recomputing the new set of endogenous variables in the economy. This methodological feature of general equilibrium analysis attracted many researchers to develop its applied dimension, as it seemed to be a natural way to deal with Cournot's problem.

The desire to convert general equilibrium theory into a practical tool for evaluating economic policy motivated the construction of algorithms for computing solutions to numerically specified general equilibrium models. Johansen's (1960) work is regarded as a benchmark in the literature of CGE modeling. His model for Norway is considered the first CGE model developed based on the premises of general equilibrium theory (Dixon & Parmenter, 1996). Departing from Johansen's algorithm, the Australian economist Peter Dixon took general equilibrium from the realm of pure theory and applied theory into practice. He also combined his sound theoretical background with skillful academic entrepreneurship, becoming the founder of the Australian tradition in CGE modeling. The ORANI model he developed with his associates represents a milestone in the field (Dixon et al., 1982). The model developed for Colombia, used in different applications throughout this volume, follows this tradition adopting the Johansen approach.

The recognition of the spatial element in the formation of a general equilibrium in a complex space economy already dates back to the early work of Lösch, Isard, and Samuelson (Van den Bergh et al., 1996). In the realm of pure theory, Walter Isard's

---

[1] Friedman called this strategy a solution for the problem of form, not of content: of displaying an idealized picture of the economic system, not of constructing an engine for analyzing concrete problems (Friedman, 1955, p. 904).

initial efforts provided an attempt to incorporate space explicitly in the general equilibrium theory (Isard, 1969). Later on, he recognized that the future would be characterized by computerized, multiregional, complex simulation models that would endeavor to unravel the complex tapestry of interregional interconnectedness (Isard et al., 1998).

This chapter presents the analytical, functional, and numerical structures[2] of the general equilibrium model for Colombia—the CEER model—that explicitly considers a complex system of interregional linkages based on some of its structural characteristics depending on the regions' responses to the policies analyzed. Interregional linkages play an essential role in the functioning of the CEER model, and these linkages are driven by trade relations (commodity flows) and factor mobility (capital and labor migration). In the first case, interregional trade flows are incorporated into the model. The interregional input–output database described in Chap. 5 is used to calibrate the model. In the specification and implementation of the CEER model, we attempt to place interregional trade in its proper place by considering a fully specified interregional system of accounts specially developed to calibrate the model.

In the CGE context, when explicitly modeled, interregional feedback has proven to provide more refined results. The scale of feedback effects is also relevant (Dixon et al., 2010; Ghaith et al., 2021; Horridge et al., 2005; McGregor et al., 1996; Watanuki, 1996; Wing & Anderson, 2007). When disaggregated results are considered, CGE models provide more insights into the impacts on regional economies. For some regions, interregional trade can generate the potential for propagating feedback effects, which could be quantitatively more important than international trade. Nonetheless, the impact of feedback effects will partly be determined by the hierarchical structure of the economy's regional system (Haddad & Hewings, 1999). A more in-depth analysis of trade flows between sub-national spaces regarding the type of trade involved may help better understand the implications of other structural differences in the coordination and implementation of development policies (Giesecke & Madden, 2012; Haddad, 2009; Haddad et al., 2002; Partridge & Rickman, 2010; Munroe et al., 2007; Wittwer, 2017).

Moreover, regional trade elasticities also play an essential role in the CEER model. The degree of interregional interaction of markets may also be quantified through specifications that encompass elasticities of substitution between similar commodities produced in different regions. A common assumption widely used in interregional CGE models, the Armington assumption, considers similar commodities produced in different regions as close substitutes but unique goods (Armington, 1969). It allows for the incorporation of estimates of elasticities of substitution between domestically produced products and similar imported products, and between regionally produced

---

[2] "An empirical economic model (...) embodies three types of information: analytical, functional and numerical. The analytical structure is the background theoretical material which identifies the variables of interest and posits their causal relations. The functional structure is the mathematical representation of the analytical material and consists of the algebraic equations which make up the actual model. The numerical structure consists of the signs and magnitudes of the coefficients in the equations which form the functional structure" (McKitrick, 1998, p. 545).

products and similar products from other regions, suggesting nested multiple-stage demand functions, such as those specified in the CEER model.[3]

Finally, factor mobility also plays a vital role in the CEER model to treat interregional linkages. Factors might be allowed to move across sectors and regions. Short-run and long-run closures vary in the treatment given to the mobility of capital and labor. Capital is commonly assumed immobile in short-run simulations. Capital movements are conventionally stimulated by rate of return differentials across sectors, regions, and productivity differentials in the long run. The primary stimulator of labor migration in the CEER model is regional unemployment rates.

6.2 The Johansen Approach[4]

The CEER model falls into a class of CGE models known as Johansen-type CGE models in the sense that the solutions are obtained by solving the system of linearized equations of the model.[5] A typical result shows the percentage change in the set of endogenous variables after a policy is carried out, compared to their values in the absence of such policy in a given environment. In Johansen-type CGE models, the system of equations of the model[6] can be written as:

$$F(V) = 0 \tag{6.1}$$

where V is an equilibrium vector of length n (number of variables) and F is a vector function of length m (number of equations), which is assumed to be differentiable. Regarding the dimensions, n and m, it is assumed that the total number of variables is greater than the total number of equations in the system $(n > m)$. Thus, $(n-m)$ variables must be set exogenously. For calibration of the system, it is fundamental to assume that $\exists V = V^*$ s.t. $F(V^*) = 0$ and the initial solution, V^*, is known.

The Johansen approach consists of using a differential or log differential version of Eq. 6.1, which may be represented as:

$$A(V)v = 0 \tag{6.2}$$

---

[3] Spencer (1988) points out that this assumption is extraordinarily convenient for (interregional) CGE work, since it admits the presence of cross hauling in a standard neoclassical model and reduces concern about small changes having big effects on the pattern of trade and production (ruling out specialization in consumption).

[4] We have followed closely the notation and exposition of the Johansen approach presented in Dixon et al. (1992).

[5] More details can be found in Dixon et al., (1982, 1992), and Dixon & Parmenter (1996).

[6] A CGE model is simply the formalization of this general representation, along with the equilibrium constraints defined by the Walrasian paradigm. CGE models differ in how they define their analytical, functional and numerical structures.

where $A(V)$ is a $(m \times n)$ matrix containing partial derivatives or elasticities and v is appropriately calculated as changes, log-changes, or percentage changes in vector V.

The procedure to obtain approximate estimates of (percentage) changes in endogenous variables is to evaluate $A(.)$ on a known initial equilibrium vector V^I and then solve Eq. 6.2. It is helpful to partition matrix A and vector v into two parts each, separating the endogenous and exogenous variables. The endogenous and exogenous parts of the system are indexed α and β, respectively:

$$A(V^I)v = A_\alpha(V^I)v_\alpha + A_\beta(V^I)v_\beta = 0 \tag{6.3}$$

$$v_\alpha = -A_\alpha(V^I)^{-1} A_\beta(V^I) v_\beta \tag{6.4}$$

$$v_\alpha = B(V^I) v_\beta \tag{6.5}$$

where A_α is $(m \times n)$, v_α is $(m \times 1)$, A_β is $(m \times n\text{-}m)$, v_β is $(n\text{-}m \times 1)$, and $B(V^I)$ is defined as $A_\alpha(V^I)^{-1} A_\beta(V^I)$.

6.3 Specification of the CEER Model

We present the specification of the linearized form of the CEER model, $A(V)v = 0$, based on different groups of equations. The notational convention uses uppercase letters to represent the levels of the variables and lowercase for their percentage change representation. Superscripts (u), $u = 0, 1j, 2j, 3, 4, 5, 6$ refer, respectively, to output (0) and the six different regional-specific users of the products identified in the model[7]: producers in sector j (1j), investors in sector j (2j), households (3), purchasers of exports (4), regional governments (5), and central government (6); the second superscript (r) identifies the domestic region where the user is located. Two subscripts identify inputs: the first (i) takes the values $1, ..., g$, for commodities and $g + 1$ for primary factors; the second subscript identifies the source of the input, being it from domestic region b (1b) or imported (2) or coming from labor (1) or capital (2), the two primary factors in the model. The symbol ($\bullet$) is employed to indicate a sum over an index.

We define the following sets: $G = \{1, ..., g\}$, where g is the number of composite goods; $G^* = \{1, ..., g, g + 1\}$, where $g + 1$ is the number of composite goods and primary factors, with $G^* \supset G$; $H = \{1, ..., h\}$, where h is the number of industries; $U = \{(3), (4b), (5), (6), (kj)\}$ for $k = (1), (2)$ and $j \in H$, is the set of all users in the model; $U^* = \{(3), (5), (6), (kj)\}$ for $k = (1), (2)$ and $j \in H$, with $U \supset U^*$, is the subset of domestic users; $S = \{1, ..., r, r + 1\}$, where $r + 1$ is the number of

---

[7] We have specified a seventh residual user, (7), to deal with statistical discrepancies in the balancing of the model's absorption matrix based on the Colombian interregional input–output system (IIOS).

all regions (including foreign); $S^* = \{1, \ldots, r\}$, with $S \supset S^*$, is the subset with the r domestic regions; and $F = \{1, \ldots, f\}$ is the set of primary factors. In the CEER model, $g = h = 54$, $r = 33$, and $f = 2$.

We model the sourcing of composite goods based on multilevel structures, enabling a significant number of substitution possibilities. We employ nested sourcing functions to create composite goods available for consumption in the regions of the model. We assume that domestic users such as firms, investors, households, and government use combinations of composite goods specified within two-level Constant Elasticity of Substitution (CES) nests. At the bottom level, bundles of domestically produced goods are formed as combinations of goods from different regional sources. At the top level, substitution is possible between domestically produced and imported goods. Equations 6.6 and 6.7 describe the regional sourcing of domestic goods and the substitution between domestic and imported products.

$$x_{(i(1b))}^{(u)r} = x_{(i(1\bullet))}^{(u)r} - \sigma 1_{(i)}^{(u)r} \left(p_{(i(1b))}^{(u)r} - \sum_{l \in S^*} \left(\frac{V(i, 1l, (u), r)}{V(i, 1\bullet, (u), r)} \right) \left(p_{(i(1l))}^{(u)r} \right) \right)$$

$$i \in G; \ b \in S^*; \ (u) \in U^*; \ r \in S^* \tag{6.6}$$

where $x_{(i(1b))}^{(u)r}$ is the demand by the user (u) in region r for good i in the domestic region $(1b)$; $p_{(i(1b))}^{(u)r}$ is the price paid by user (u) in region r for good i in the domestic region $(1b)$; $\sigma 1_{(i)}^{(u)r}$ is a parameter measuring the user-specific elasticity of substitution between alternative domestic sources of commodity i, known as the regional trade Armington elasticity; and $V(i, 1l, (u), r)$ is an input–output flow coefficient that measures purchasers' value of good i from domestic source l used by the user (u) in region r.

$$x_{(is)}^{(u)r} = x_{(i\bullet)}^{(u)r} - \sigma 2_{(i)}^{(u)r} \left(p_{(is)}^{(u)r} - \sum_{l=1\bullet, 2} \left(\frac{V(i, l, (u), r)}{V(i, \bullet, (u), r)} \right) \left(p_{(il)}^{(u)r} \right) \right)$$

$$i \in G; \ s = 1\bullet, 2; \ (u) \in U^*; \ r \in S^* \tag{6.7}$$

where $x_{(is)}^{(u)r}$ is the demand by the user (u) in region r for either the domestic composite or the foreign good i; $p_{(is)}^{(u)r}$ is the price paid by user (u) in region r for either the domestic composite or the foreign good i; $\sigma 2_{(i)}^{(u)r}$ is a parameter measuring the user-specific elasticity of substitution between the domestic bundle and imports of good i, known as the international trade Armington elasticity; and $V(i, l, (u), r)$ is an input–output flow coefficient that measures purchasers' value of good i from either the aggregate domestic source or the foreign source l used by the user (u) in region r.

In addition to goods used as intermediate inputs, firms in the model also demand primary factors of production. The equations that describe the industry j's demands inputs are derived under the assumption of Leontief technology with Armington nests (imperfect substitution between inputs of the same type from different sources). In our specification of the nested production functions, we assume firms use combinations of composite intermediate inputs, formed according to Eqs. 6.6 and 6.7, and primary factor composites. In the case of the primary factor bundle, substitution is possible among different types of primary factors. Equation 6.8 specifies the model's substitution between labor and capital. It is derived under the assumption that industries choose their primary factor inputs to minimize costs subject to obtaining sufficient primary factor inputs to satisfy their technological requirements (nested Leontief/CES specification). We have included technical change variables to allow for factor-specific productivity shocks. We model the combination of intermediate inputs and the value-added (primary factors) aggregate in fixed proportions at the top of the nested production function, assuming no substitution between primary factors and other inputs. The Leontief specification is presented in Eq. 6.9. Due to data availability constraints, more flexible functional forms have rarely been introduced in multiregional models. In addition to a technical coefficient in the relation between the sectoral demand for the primary factor composite and the total output, we have also included a scale parameter. This modeling procedure is based on previous studies made by Haddad and Hewings (2005), which allows for the introduction of Marshallian agglomeration (external) economies by exploring the local properties of the CES function.

$$x_{(g+1,s)}^{(1j)r} - a_{(g+1,s)}^{(1j)r} = \alpha_{(g+1,s)}^{(1j)r} x_{(g+1,\cdot)}^{(1j)r}$$
$$- \sigma 3_{(g+1)}^{(1j)r} \left(\begin{array}{c} p_{(g+1,s)}^{(1j)r} + a_{(g+1,s)}^{(1j)r} \\ - \sum_{l \in F} \left(\dfrac{V(g+1, l, (1j), r)}{V(g+1, \cdot, (1j), r)} \right) \left(p_{(g+1,l)}^{(1j)r} + a_{(g+1,l)}^{(1j)r} \right) \end{array} \right)$$
$$j \in H; \ s \in F; \ r \in S^* \qquad (6.8)$$

where $x_{(g+1,s)}^{(1j)r}$ is the demand by sector j in region r for each primary factor; $a_{(g+1,s)}^{(1j)r}$ is the exogenous sector-specific variable of (saving) technical change for primary factor s in region r; $p_{(g+1,s)}^{(1j)r}$ is the price paid by sector j in region r for primary factor s; $\sigma 3_{(g+1)}^{(1j)r}$ is a parameter measuring the sector-specific elasticity of substitution among different primary factors; and $V(g+1, l, (1j), r)$ is an input–output flow coefficient that measures purchasers' value of factor l used by sector j in region r.

$$x_{(i\bullet)}^{(1j)r} = \mu_{(g+1,\bullet)}^{(1j)r} z^{(1j)r} + a_{(i)}^{(1j)r}$$
$$j \in H; \ i \in G^*; \ r \in S^* \qquad (6.9)$$

where $x_{(i\bullet)}^{(1j)r}$ is the demand by sector j in region r for the bundles of composite intermediate inputs and primary factors i; $z^{(1j)r}$ is the total output of sector j in region r; $a_{(i)}^{(1j)r}$ is the exogenous sector-specific variable of technical change for composite intermediate inputs and primary factors in region r; and $\mu_{(i\bullet)}^{(1j)r}$ is a scale parameter measuring the sector-specific returns to the composite of primary factors in each region.

Units of capital stock are created for industry j at minimum cost. Commodities are combined via a Leontief function, as specified in Eq. 6.10. In Eqs. 6.6 and 6.7, regional and domestic-imported commodities are combined, respectively, via a CES specification (Armington assumption). No primary factors are used in capital creation. The use of these inputs is recognized through the capital goods-producing sectors in the model, mainly machinery and equipment industries, construction, and support services.

$$x_{(i\bullet)}^{(2j)r} = z^{(2j)r} + a_{(i)}^{(2j)r}$$
$$j \in H;\ i \in G;\ r \in S^* \tag{6.10}$$

where $x_{(i\bullet)}^{(2j)r}$ is the demand by sector j in region r for the bundles of composite capital goods i; $z^{(2j)r}$ is the total investment of sector j in region r; $a_{(i)}^{(2j)r}$ is the exogenous sector-specific variable of technical change for changing the composition of the sectoral unit of capital in region r.

In deriving the household demands for composite commodities, we assume that households in each region behave as a single, budget-constrained, utility-maximizing entity. The utility function is of the Stone-Geary or Klein-Rubin form. Equation 6.11 determines the optimal composition of household demand in each region. Total regional household consumption is determined as a function of real household income. The demands for the commodity bundles in the nesting structure of household demand follow the CES pattern established in Eqs. 6.6 and 6.7, in which an activity variable and a price-substitution term play significant roles. In Eq. 6.11, consumption of each commodity i depends on two components: first, for the subsistence component, which is defined as the minimum expenditure requirement for each commodity, changes in demand are generated by changes in the number of households and tastes; second, for the luxury or supernumerary part of the expenditures in each good, demand moves with changes in the regional supernumerary expenditures, changes in tastes, and changes in the price of the composite commodity. The two components of household expenditures on the composite commodities are weighted by their respective shares in the total consumption of the composite commodity.

$$V(i, \bullet, (3), r)\left(p_{(i\bullet)}^{(3)r} + x_{(i\bullet)}^{(3)r} - a_{(i\bullet)}^{(3)r}\right)$$
$$= \gamma_{(i)}^r P_{(i\bullet)}^{(3)r} Q^r \left(p_{(i\bullet)}^{(3)r} + x_{(i\bullet)}^{(3)r} - a_{(i\bullet)}^{(3)r}\right)$$
$$+ \beta_{(i)}^r \left(C^r - \sum_{j \in G} \gamma_{(j)}^r P_{(j\bullet)}^{(3)r} Q^r \left(p_{(j\bullet)}^{(3)r} + x_{(j\bullet)}^{(3)r} - a_{(j\bullet)}^{(3)r}\right)\right)$$
$$i \in G;\ r \in S^* \tag{6.11}$$

where $p_{(i\bullet)}^{(3)r}$ is the price paid by household in region r for the composite good i; $x_{(i\bullet)}^{(3)r}$ is the household demand in region r for the composite good i; $a_{(i\bullet)}^{(3)r}$ is the commodity-specific variable of regional taste change; Q^r is the number of households in region r; C^r is the total expenditure by household in region r, which is proportional to regional labor income; $\gamma_{(i)}^r$ is the subsistence parameter in the linear expenditure system for commodity i in region r; $\beta_{(i)}^r$ is the parameter defined for commodity i in region r measuring the marginal budget shares in the linear expenditure system; and $V(i, \bullet, (3), r)$ is an input–output flow coefficient that measures purchasers' value of good i consumed by households in region r.

As noted by Peter et al. (1996), a feature of the Stone-Geary utility function is that only the above-subsistence, or luxury, component of real household consumption, $utility^{(r)}$, affects the per-household utility, as described in Eq. 6.12.

$$utility^{(r)} = \left(C^r - \sum_{j \in G} \gamma_{(j)}^r P_{(j\bullet)}^{(3)r} Q^r \left(p_{(j\bullet)}^{(3)r} + x_{(j\bullet)}^{(3)r} - a_{(i\bullet)}^{(3)r} \right) \right)$$
$$- q^r - \sum_{i \in G} \beta_{(i)}^r p_{(i\bullet)}^{(3)r}$$
$$r \in S^* \tag{6.12}$$

where q^r is the percentage change in the number of households in each region.

In Eq. 6.13, foreign demands (exports) for domestic good i depend on the percentage changes in a price and three-shift variables which allow for vertical and horizontal movements in the demand curves. The price variable that influences export demands is the purchaser's price in foreign countries, including the relevant taxes and margins. The parameter $\eta_{(is)}^r$ controls the sensitivity of export demand to price changes.

$$\left(x_{(is)}^{(4)r} - fq_{(is)}^{(4)r} \right) = \eta_{(is)}^r \left(p_{(is)}^{(4)r} - phi - fp_{(is)}^{(4)r} \right)$$
$$i \in G; \ r, s \in S^* \tag{6.13}$$

where $x_{(is)}^{(4)r}$ is foreign demand for domestic good i produced in region s and sold from region r (in the model, there are no re-exports, so that $r = s$); $p_{(is)}^{(4)r}$ is the purchasers' price in the domestic currency of exported good i demand in region r; phi is the nominal exchange rate; $fq_{(is)}^{(4)r}$ and $fp_{(is)}^{(4)r}$ are, respectively, quantity and price shift variables in foreign demand curves for regional exports.

Governments consume mainly public goods provided by the public administration sectors. Equations 6.14 and 6.15 show the movement of government consumption concerning movements in real tax revenue for regional governments and the central government, respectively.

$$x_{(is)}^{(5)r} = taxrev^r + f_{(is)}^{(5)r} + f^{(5)r} + f^{(5)}$$

$$i \in G; \ s = 1b, 2; \ r, b \in S^* \tag{6.14}$$

$$x_{(is)}^{(6)r}; = \text{nattaxrev} + f_{(is)}^{(6)r} + f^{(6)r} + f^{(6)}$$
$$i \in G; \ s = 1b, 2; \ r, b \in S^* \tag{6.15}$$

where $x_{(is)}^{(5)r}$ and $x_{(is)}^{(6)r}$ are regional (6.5) and central (6.6) governments demand in region r for good i from region s; $f_{(is)}^{(5)r}$, $f^{(5)r}$ and $f^{(5)}$ are, respectively, commodity and source-specific shift terms for regional government expenditures in region r, shift term for regional governments expenditures in region r, and an overall shift term for regional governments expenditures. Similar shift terms ($f_{(is)}^{(6)r}$, $f^{(6)r}$ and $f^{(6)}$) appear in Eq. 6.15 related to central government expenditures. Finally, taxrev^r is the percentage change in real revenue from indirect taxes in region r, and nattaxrev refers to the percentage change in aggregate real revenue from indirect taxes, so that government demand moves with endogenous changes in regional and national tax bases.

Equation 6.16 specifies the sales tax rates for different users. They allow for variations in tax rates across commodities, their sources, and destinations. Tax changes are expressed as percentage-point changes in the ad valorem tax rates.

$$t_{(is)}^{(u)r} = f_i + f_i^{(u)} + f_i^{(u)r}$$
$$i \in G; \ s = 1b, 2; \ b, \ r \in S^*; \ u \in U \tag{6.16}$$

where $t_{(is)}^{(u)r}$ is the power of the tax on sales of the commodity (is) to the user (u) in region r; and f_i, $f_i^{(u)}$, and $f_i^{(u)r}$ are different shift terms allowing percentage changes in the power of taxation.

Equations 6.17 and 6.18 impose the equilibrium conditions in the market's domestic and imported commodities. Notice that there is no margin commodity in the model. Moreover, there is no secondary production in the model. In Eq. 6.17, demand equals supply for regional domestic commodities.

$$\sum_{j \in H} Y(l, j, r) x_{(l1)}^{(0j)r} = \sum_{(u) \in U} B(l, 1b, (u), r) x_{(l1)}^{(u)r}$$
$$l \in G, b, \ r \in S^* \tag{6.17}$$

where $x_{(l1)}^{(0j)r}$ is the output of domestic good l by industry j in region r; $x_{(l1)}^{(u)r}$ is the demand of the domestic good l by the user (u) in region r; $Y(l, j, r)$ is the input–output flow measuring the basic value of the output of domestic good l by industry j in region r; and $B(l, 1, (u), r)$ is the input–output flow measuring the basic value of domestic good l used by (u) in region r.

Equation 6.18 imposes zero pure profits in importing, where $p_{(i(2))}^{(0)}$ is the basic price in the domestic currency of good i from a foreign source; $p_{(i(2))}^{(w)}$ is the world

6 The Interregional Computable General Equilibrium Model for Colombia

Cost, Insurance and Freight (CIF) price of imported commodity i; phi is the nominal exchange rate; and $t^{(0)}_{(i(2))}$ is the power of the tariff, i.e., one plus the tariff rate, on imports of i. Equation 6.18, thus, defines the basic price of a unit of imported commodity i—the revenue earned per unit by the importer—as the international CIF price converted to domestic currency, including import tariffs.

$$p^{(0)}_{(i(2))} = p^{(w)}_{(i(2))} - phi + t^{(0)}_{(i(2))}$$
$$i \in G \tag{6.18}$$

Together with Eqs. 6.18–6.20 constitute the model's pricing system. The price received for any activity equals the costs per unit of output. As can be noticed, the assumption of constant returns to scale adopted here precludes any activity variable from influencing basic prices, i.e., unit costs are independent of the scale at which activities are conducted. Thus, Eq. 6.19 defines the percentage change in the price received by producers in regional industry j per unit of output as equal to the percentage change in j's costs, which are affected by changes in technology and input prices.

$$\sum_{l \in G} Y(l, j, r) \left(p^{(0)r}_{(l1)} + a^{(0)r}_{(l1)} \right) = \sum_{l \in G^*, F} \sum_{s \in S} V(l, s, (1j), r) p^{(1j)r}_{(ls)}$$
$$j \in H; \quad r \in S^* \tag{6.19}$$

where $p^{(0)r}_{(l1)}$ is the basic price of domestic good i in region r; $a^{(0)r}_{(l1)}$ refers to technological changes, measured as a weighted average of the different types of technical changes with influence on j's unit costs; $p^{(1j)r}_{(ls)}$ is the unit cost of sector j in region r; $Y(l, j, r)$ is the input–output flow measuring the basic value of the output of domestic good l by industry j in region r; and $V(l, s, (1j), r)$ are input–output flows measuring purchasers' value of good or factor l from source s used by sector j in region r.

Equation 6.20 imposes zero pure profits in the distribution of commodities to different users. Prices paid for commodity i from region s in industry j in region r by each user equate to the sum of its basic value and the costs of the relevant taxes.

$$V(i, s, (u), r) p^{(u)r}_{(is)} = (B(i, s, (u), r) + T(i, s, (u), r)) \left(p^{(0)}_{(is)} + t^{(u)r}_{(is)} \right)$$
$$i \in G; \quad s = 1b, 2; \quad b, \ r \in S^*; \quad u \in U \tag{6.20}$$

where $p^{(u)r}_{(is)}$ is the price paid by user (u) in region r for good (is); $p^{(0)}_{(is)}$ is the basic price of domestic good (is); $t^{(u)r}_{(is)}$ is the power of the tax on sales of the commodity (is) to the user (u) in region r; $V(i, s, (u), r)$ are input–output flows measuring purchasers' value of good i from source s used by the user (u) in region r; $B(i, s, (u), r)$ is the input–output flow measuring the basic value of the good (is) used by (u) in region r; and $T(i, s, (u), r)$ is the input–output flow associated with tax revenue of the sales of (is) to (u) in region r.

The theory of investment allocation across industries is represented in Eqs. 6.21–6.24. The comparative-static nature of the model restricts its use to short-run and long-run policy analyses. There is no fixed relationship between capital and investment when running the model in the comparative-static mode. The user decides the required relationship based on the specific simulation requirements. Equation 6.21 defines the percentage change in the current rate of return on fixed capital in regional sectors. Under static expectations, rates of return are defined as the ratio between the rental values and the cost of a unit of capital in each industry—defined in Eq. 6.22—minus the depreciation rate.

$$r_{(j)}^r = \psi_{(j)}^r \left(p_{(g+1,2)}^{(1j)r} - p_{(k)}^{(1j)r} \right)$$
$$j \in H; \ r \in S^* \tag{6.21}$$

where $r_{(j)}^r$ is the regional-industry-specific rate of return; $p_{(g+1,2)}^{(1j)r}$ is the rental value of capital in sector j in region r; $p_{(k)}^{(1j)r}$ is the cost of constructing units of capital for regional industries; and $\psi_{(j)}^r$ is a regional-industry-specific parameter referring to the ratio of the gross to the net rate of return.

Equation 6.21 defines $p_{(k)}^{(1j)r}$ as:

$$V(\bullet, \bullet, (2j), r)\left(p_{(k)}^{(1j)r} - a_{(k)}^{(1j)r}\right) = \sum_{i \in G} \sum_{s \in S} V(i, s, (2j), r)$$
$$\left(p_{(is)}^{(2j)r} - a_{(is)}^{(2j)r}\right)$$
$$j \in H; \ r \in S^* \tag{6.22}$$

where $p_{(is)}^{(2j)r}$ is the price paid by user $(2j)$ in region r for good (is); $a_{(k)}^{(1j)r}$ and $a_{(is)}^{(2j)r}$ are technical terms; and $V(i, s, (2j), r)$ represents input–output flows measuring purchasers' value of good i from source s used by the user $(2j)$ in region r.

Equation 6.23 says that if the percentage change in the rate of return in a regional industry grows faster than the national average, capital stocks in that industry will increase at a higher rate than the average national stock. For industries with a lower-than-average increase in their rates of return to fixed capital, capital stocks increase at a lower-than-average rate, i.e., capital is attracted to higher return industries. The shift variable, $f_{(k)}^{(1j)r}$—exogenous in long-run simulation—allows shifts in the industry's rates of return.

$$r_{(j)}^r - \omega = \varepsilon_{(j)}^r \left(x_{(g+1,2)}^{(1j)r} - x_{(g+1,2)}^{()r} \right) + f_{(k)}^{(1j)r}$$
$$j \in H; \ r \in S^* \tag{6.23}$$

where $r_{(j)}^r$ is the regional-industry-specific rate of return; ω is the overall rate of return on capital; $x_{(g+1,2)}^{(1j)r}$ is the capital stock in industry j in region r; $f_{(k)}^{(1j)r}$ is the

6 The Interregional Computable General Equilibrium Model for Colombia

capital shift term in sector j in region r; and $\varepsilon^r_{(j)}$ measures the sensitivity of capital growth to rates of return of industry j in region r.

Equation 6.24 implies that the percentage change in an industry's capital stock, $x^{(1j)r}_{(g+1,2)}$, is equal to the percentage change in the industry's investments in the period, $z^{(2j)r}$.

$$z^{(2j)r} = x^{(1j)r}_{(g+1,2)} + f^{(2j)r}_{(k)}$$
$$j \in H; r \in S^* \qquad (6.24)$$

where $f^{(2j)r}_{(k)}$ allows for exogenous shifts in sectoral investments in region r.

Equation 6.25 defines the regional aggregation of labor prices (wages) across industries in the specification of the labor market. Equation 6.26 shows movements in regional wage differentials, wage_diff$^{(r)}$, defined as the difference between the movement in the aggregate regional real wage received by workers and the national real wage.

$$V(g+1, 1, \bullet, r)\left(p^{(\bullet)r}_{(g+1,1)} - a^{(\bullet)r}_{(g+1,1)}\right) = \sum_{j \in H} V(g+1, 1, (1j), r)$$
$$\left(p^{(1j)r}_{(g+1,1)} - a^{(1j)r}_{(g+1,1)}\right)$$
$$r \in S^* \qquad (6.25)$$

where $p^{(1j)r}_{(g+1,1)}$ is the wage in sector j in region r, $a^{(1j)r}_{(g+1,1)}$ is a technical term, and $V(g+1, 1, (1j), r)$ represents input–output flows measuring sectoral labor payments in region r.

$$\text{wage\_diff}^{(r)} = p^{(\bullet)r}_{(g+1,1)} - \text{cpi} - \text{natrealwage}$$
$$r \in S^* \qquad (6.26)$$

where cpi is the national consumer price index, computed as the weighted average of $p^{(3)r}_{(is)}$ across regions r and consumption goods (is); and *natrealwage* is the national consumer real wage.

The regional population is defined by interacting demographic variables, including interregional migration. Links between regional population and regional labor supply are provided. Demographic variables are usually defined exogenously, and together with the specification of some of the labor market settings, labor supply can be determined together with interregional wage differentials or regional unemployment rates. In summary, labor supply and wage differentials determine unemployment rates, or labor supply and unemployment rates determine wage differentials.

Equation 6.27 defines the percentage-point change in regional unemployment rates in terms of percentage changes in labor supply and employed workers.

$$\text{LABSUP}(r)\text{del\_unr}^{(r)} = \text{EMPLOY}(r)\left(\text{labsup}^{(r)} - x^{(r)}_{(g+1,1)}\right)$$
$$r \in S^* \quad (6.27)$$

where del_ unr$^{(r)}$ measures percentage-point changes in the regional unemployment rate; labsup$^{(r)}$ is the variable for regional labor supply; and the coefficients LABSUP(r) and EMPLOY(r) are the benchmark values for regional labor supply and regional employment, respectively. The variable labsup$^{(r)}$ moves with regional workforce participation rate, proportional to the regional population, and population of working age. Equation 6.28 defines regional population changes in the model as ordinary changes in the flows of net regional migration ($d\_\text{rm}^{(r)}$), net foreign migration ($d\_\text{fm}^{(r)}$), and natural population growth ($d\_g^{(r)}$).

$$\text{POP}(r)\text{pop}^{(r)} = d\_\text{rm}^{(r)} + d\_\text{fm}^{(r)} + d\_g^{(r)}$$
$$r \in S^* \quad (6.28)$$

where POP(r) is a coefficient measuring regional population in the benchmark year.

Equation 6.29 shows movements in per-household utility differentials, util_diff$^{(r)}$, defined as the difference between the movement in regional utility and the overall national utility (agg_util), including a shift variable, futil$^{(r)}$.

$$\text{util\_diff}^{(r)} = \text{utility}^{(r)} - \text{agg\_util} + \text{futil}^{(r)}$$
$$r \in S^* \quad (6.29)$$

Finally, we can define changes in regional output as weighted averages of changes in regional aggregates, according to Eq. 6.30 below:

$$\begin{aligned}\text{GRP}^r \text{grp}^r &= C^r x^{(3)r}_{\bullet\bullet} + \text{INV}^r z^{(2\bullet)r} \\ &+ \text{GOV}^{(5)r} x^{(5)r}_{(\bullet\bullet)} + \text{GOV}^{(6)r} x^{(6)r}_{(\bullet\bullet)} \\ &+ \left(\text{FEXP}^r x^{(4)r}_{(\bullet\bullet)} - \text{FIMP}^r x^{(\bullet)r}_{(\bullet 2)}\right) \\ &+ \left(\text{DEXP}^r x^{(\bullet)s}_{(\bullet(1r))} - \text{DIMP}^r x^{(\bullet)r}_{(\bullet(1s))}\right) \\ & r \in S^*; \ s \in S^* \text{ for } s \neq r \end{aligned} \quad (6.30)$$

where grp^r is the percentage change in real Gross Regional Product (GRP) in region r; and the coefficients GRP^r, INV^r, GOV$^{(5)r}$, GOV$^{(6)r}$, FEXP^r, FIMP^r, DEXP^r, DIMP^r represent, respectively, the following regional aggregates: investment, regional government spending, central government spending, foreign exports, foreign imports, domestic exports, and domestic imports. National output, GDP, is, thus, the sum of GRP^r across all regions r. Notice that regional domestic trade balances cancel out.

To close the model, we set the following variables exogenously, which are usually exogenous both in short-run and long-run simulations: $a^{(1j)r}_{(g+1,s)}$, $a^{(1j)r}_{(i)}$, $a^{(2j)r}_{(i)}$, $a^{(3)r}_{(i)}$,

$fq_{(is)}^{(4)r}$, $fp_{(is)}^{(4)r}$, $f_{(is)}^{(5)r}$, $f^{(5)r}$, $f^{(5)}$, $f_{(is)}^{(6)r}$, $f^{(6)r}$, $f^{(6)}$, f_i, $f_i^{(u)}$, $f_i^{(u)r}$, $p_{(i(2))}^{(w)}$, $t_{(i(2))}^{(0)}$, $a_{(l1)}^{(0)r}$, $a_{(k)}^{(1j)r}$, $a_{(is)}^{(2j)r}$, $a_{(g+1,1)}^{(\bullet)r}$, ω, $f_{(k)}^{(2j)r}$, $d\_fm^{(r)}$, $d\_g^{(r)}$, and $futil^{(r)}$. To complete the short-run environment, we also set unchanged current stocks of capital ($x_{(g+1,2)}^{(1j)r}$), the national real wage (*natrealwage*), regional wage differentials, (wage_diff$^{(r)}$), and regional population, by keeping regional migration unchanged ($d\_rm^{(r)}$).[8]

Other definitions of variables are computed using outcomes from simulations based on Eqs. 6.6–6.30. Of particular interest to our discussion is the definition of regional/national GDP and its components.

6.4 Calibration

The calibration of the CEER model requires two subsets of data to define its numerical structure to implement the model empirically. First, we need information from an absorption matrix derived from interregional input–output sources (see Chap. 5 to calculate the coefficients of the model based on the following input–output flows (Table 6.1):

- $B(i, 1b, (u), r)$, with $i \in G^*$, $(u) \in U$, $b, r \in S^*$
- $M(i, s, (u), r)$, with $i \in G^*$, $s \in S$, $(u) \in U$, $r \in S^* M(i, s, (u), r) B(i, 1b, (u), r)$
- $T(i, s, (u), r)$, with $i \in G^*$, $s \in S$, $(u) \in U$, $r \in S^*$
- $V(i, s, (u), r)$, with $i \in G^*$, $s \in S$, $F, (u) \in U$, $r \in S^*$
- $Y(i, j, r)$, with $i \in G^*$, $j \in H$, $r \in S^*$

We complete this information with supplementary demographic data from the DANE to calibrate the coefficients LABSUP(r), EMPLOY(r), and POP(r), with $r \in S^*$. Because these estimates are based on snapshot observations for a single year revealing the economic structure of the economic system, this subset of data is denoted "structural coefficients" (Haddad et al., 2002).

The second piece of information necessary to calibrate the model is represented by the subset of data defining various parameters, mainly elasticities; these are referred to as "behavioral parameters."

In the CEER model, the trade elasticities in the Armington demand structure determine the substitution possibilities between goods from different sources (foreign and domestic). Smaller trade elasticities imply weaker substitution among geographical sources in the model, reducing the potential strength of the linkage structure in post-shock adjustments. Table 6.2 gives the default values for regional trade elasticities ($\sigma 1_{(i)}^{(u)r}$) in Eq. 6.6, and international trade elasticities ($\sigma 2_{(i)}^{(u)r}$) in Eq. 6.7 in the

---

[8] In a long run closure, the assumptions on interregional mobility of capital and labor are relaxed by swapping variables $x_{(g+1,2)}^{(1j)r}$, natrealwage, wage_diff$^{(r)}$ and $d\_rm^{(r)}$, for $f_{(k)}^{(1j)r}$, del_unr$^{(r)}$ and util_diff$^{(r)}$.

Table 6.1 Aggregate flows in the absorption matrix: Colombia, 2015 (Haddad et al., 2019)

Labels	User (1j)ʳ	User (2j)ʳ	User (3)ʳ	User (4)	User (5)ʳ	User (6)ʳ	User (7)	Total
i ∈ G, s ∈ S*	B(i,1b,(1j),r)	B(i,1b,(2j),r)	B(i,1b,(3),r)	B(i,1b,(4))	B(i,1b,(5),r)	B(i,1b,(6),r)	B(i,1b,(7))	B(i,1b,(•),•)
i ∈ G, s ∈ S-S*	B(i,2,(1j),r)	B(i,2,(2j),r)	B(i,2,(3),r)	B(i,2,(4))	B(i,2,(5),r)	B(i,2,(6),r)	B(i,2,(7))	B(i,2,(•),•)
i ∈ G, s ∈ S	T(i,s,(1j),r)	T(i,s,(2j),r)	T(i,s,(3),r)	T(i,s,(4))	T(i,s,(5),r)	T(i,s,(6),r)	–	T(i,s,(•),•)
s ∈ F	V(g+1,s,(1j),r)	–	–	–	–	–	–	V(g+1,s,(•),•)
Total	Y(•,•,r)	V(•,•(2j),r)	V(•,•,(3),r)	V(•,•,(4))	V(•,•,(5),r)	V(•,•,(6),r)	V(•,•,(7))	V(•,•(•),•)
2015								
i ∈ G, s ∈ S*	584,016	157,554	460,601	118,997	69,872	49,902	0	1,440,942
i ∈ G, s ∈ S-S*	94,223	28,373	51,902	1	1,330	936	0	176,766
i ∈ G, s ∈ S	32,160	5,378	30,863	263	185	132	–	68,981
s ∈ F	730,543	–	–	–	–	–	–	730,543
Total	1,440,942	191,305	543,367	119,261	71,387	50,970	0	2,417,232

aggregation used in this version of the model. The foreign-domestic substitution elasticities (Armington elasticities) reflect how imports respond to changes in the relative prices between imported and domestic goods (Dixon & Rimmer, 2013). Elasticities of substitution between domestic and imported goods ($\sigma 2_{(i)}^{(u)r}$) in the CEER model are obtained from the Global Trade Analysis Project (GTAP) model (GTAP 9 Data Base). The GTAP model lists values for the Armington elasticities for 57 products estimated by Hertel et al. (2007). From these estimates, we computed sector-based elasticities for the 54 Colombian sectors considering the structure of the national make table. The values specified for the regional trade elasticities ($\sigma 1_{(i)}^{(u)r}$) are twice as large as those for the international trade elasticities. The arbitrary choice of the values is based on the international literature that addresses this type of elasticity estimation, but it also carries some personal judgment. It is implicitly assumed that substitution between goods from different regions inside the country is stronger than substitution between domestic and imported commodities (Haddad, 1999).

We have estimated the export-demand elasticities, $\eta_{(is)}^r$ in Eq. 6.13. Such price elasticities of export demand for Colombian products specify a relationship between the export price and the quantity exported of a specific commodity. For simplicity, the world is assumed to consist of one exporting country (Colombia) and one importer (the Rest of the World). The estimated equation takes the following form:

$$\ln X_{it} = \alpha + \beta \ln P_{it} + D_t + v_i + u_{it} \qquad (6.31)$$

where, X_{it} is the export demand for a Colombian commodity i in time t; P_{it} is the price of the commodity; D_t is a time effect term; v_i is a fixed effect that captures the influence of unobserved variables (such as exchange rates, transportation costs, policy, and other prices); u_{it} is the error term; α and β are coefficients to be estimated. The number of commodities defines the observations i in the classification system at a basic 10-digit level ($i = 12{,}780$ commodities) over time t ($t = 2011\text{--}2015$). The dependent variable (X_{it}) is the Free on Board Price (FOB) value of exports in USD. We calculate the commodity price (P_{it}) as the value of exports divided by their weight.

We use the exports microdata from the Department of Methodology and Statistical Production (DIMPE) and the DANE. We harmonized the commodities specified in the microdata using the correspondence dictionary created by DANE that associates the 12,780 commodities (POSAR classification[9]) with the 499 activity codes of the "International Standard Industrial Classification" (Clases CIIU Rev. 4 AC). Then, we grouped the CIIU activities under 392 products (Clases CPC Vers. 2 AC) and 67 products (Divisiones CPC 2.0 A.C.) of the "System of National Accounts" specified in the Supply and Use Tables (SUT) for Colombia.

We estimated Eq. 6.31 at the basic 10-digit level (POSAR classification) in separate equations for each of the 392 products (Clases) and 67 products (Divisiones). We were interested in the price elasticity of export demand at the level of 392 products

---

[9] POSAR is the import and export classification system used in the DIMPE at a basic 10-digit level. It is used to identify products/commodities.

Table 6.2 Behavioral parameters used in the CEER model

Sector	Regional trade elasticities (Equation 6.6)	International trade elasticities (Equation 6.7)	Export demand elasticities (Equation 6.13)
S1	2.016	1.008	−0.407
S2	2.016	0.000	0.000
S3	1.227	0.614	−0.526
S4	1.185	0.593	−0.425
S5	0.664	0.332	−1.793
S6	3.022	1.511	−0.420
S7	4.277	2.139	−0.478
S8	0.111	0.056	−0.040
S9	0.913	0.457	−1.658
S10	3.872	1.936	−0.678
S11	3.239	1.620	−0.864
S12	2.995	1.497	−2.076
S13	2.155	1.077	−0.989
S14	3.088	1.544	−0.721
S15	2.328	1.164	−0.634
S16	2.025	1.012	−0.880
S17	2.513	1.256	−0.880
S18	1.233	0.617	−1.433
S19	3.489	1.744	−0.662
S20	3.779	1.890	−1.116
S21	3.358	1.679	−1.288
S22	2.771	1.386	−0.883
S23	0.656	0.328	−0.353
S24	3.021	1.511	−0.675
S25	3.218	1.609	−0.768
S26	2.831	1.416	−1.518
S27	2.909	1.455	−1.046
S28	3.818	1.909	−0.630
S29	1.282	0.641	−0.273
S30	1.955	0.978	−0.499
S31	3.651	1.826	−0.600
S32	3.673	1.836	−0.523
S33	2.135	1.067	−0.663
S34	2.794	1.397	−0.694
S35	2.724	1.362	−0.678

(continued)

Table 6.2 (continued)

Sector	Regional trade elasticities (Equation 6.6)	International trade elasticities (Equation 6.7)	Export demand elasticities (Equation 6.13)
S36	1.436	0.718	−0.369
S37	0.472	0.236	−0.170
S38	1.865	0.933	−0.682
S39	1.900	0.950	−0.694
S40	1.900	0.950	−0.694
S41	0.391	0.196	−0.143
S42	1.900	0.950	−0.694
S43	1.047	0.523	−0.383
S44	1.900	0.950	−0.694
S45	1.908	0.954	−0.698
S46	1.864	0.932	−0.671
S47	1.884	0.942	−0.646
S48	0.312	0.156	−0.114
S49	1.699	0.849	−0.623
S50	1.863	0.931	−0.023
S51	1.081	0.540	−0.393
S52	1.695	0.847	−0.620
S53	1.753	0.877	−0.575
S54	0.000	0.000	−0.694

(Clases); however, when the estimated coefficients for this aggregation level were not statistically significant, we used the estimated coefficient at the level of aggregation of 67 products (Divisiones). DIMPE/DANE export microdata specify only agricultural, mineral, and manufactured commodities, which comprise 140 products (Clases) and 37 products (Divisiones). The price elasticity of export demand for the services products equals the coefficient estimated in Eq. 6.31 in a single regression for the 12,780 commodities (POSAR). Finally, we transformed the export-demand elasticity coefficients for 392 products into 54 sectors of the CEER model using the market share matrix (generated by the Make Table).

The price elasticity of export demand reflects the change in foreign demand caused by a foreign currency FOB price variation. The export-demand elasticity is negative, i.e., in Eq. 6.13, exports are a negative function of their foreign currency prices on world markets. Dixon and Rimmer (2010) discuss the sensitivity of CGE models' results to the export-demand elasticities. The sensibility analysis or results from historical simulations are used to assess the parameters estimated in the econometric models (Dixon & Rimmer, 2013).

Empirical estimates for some of the parameters of the model are not available in the literature. We have thus relied on "best guesstimates" based on typical values employed in similar models. Substitution elasticity between primary factors, $\sigma 3_{(g+1)}^{(1j)r}$ in Eq. 6.8 was set to 0.5. The current version of the model runs under constant returns to scale so that we set to 1.0 the values of $\mu_{(g+1,)}^{(1j)r}$ in Eq. 6.9. The marginal budget shares in regional household consumption, $\beta_{(i)}^r$ in Eq. 6.6, were calibrated from the input–output data and expenditure elasticities from Cortés and Pérez (2010), adjusting the average budget shares with the estimates for different groups of goods and services,[10] and the subsistence parameter $\gamma_{(i)}^r$, also in Eq. 6.11, associated with a Frisch parameter equal to -1.6578. The ratio of gross to the net rate of return, $\psi_{(j)}^r$ in Eq. 6.21, was set to 1.20. Finally, we set to 3.0184 the parameter for the sensitivity of capital growth to rates of return, $\varepsilon_{(j)}^r$ in Eq. 6.23.

6.5 Final Considerations

The model described in this chapter will be used in the fourth part of the book to examine selected topics through quantitative simulations based on a unified general equilibrium framework. The simulations will focus on Colombia's competitive insertion in global markets, competitiveness profiles, and mechanisms of interregional transfers of income. Challenges around high-profile long-term issues such as climate change, productivity gains, and intergovernmental transfers will be analyzed.

References

Cortés, D., & Pérez, J. E. (2010). El Consumo de los Hogares Colombianos, 2006–2007: Estimación de Sistemas de Demanda. *Desarrollo y Sociedad, 66*, 7–44.
Cournot, A. A. (1838). *Recherches sur les Principes Mathématiques de la Théorie des Richesses*. France, Nabu Press.
Dixon, P. B., & Parmenter, B. R. (1996). Computable general equilibrium modelling for policy analysis and forecasting. In H. M. Amman, D. A. Kendrick, & J. Rust (Eds.), *Handbook of computational economics: Agent-based computational economics*. Elsevier.
Dixon, P. B., & Rimmer, M. T. (2010). Optimal tariffs: Should Australia cut automotive tariffs unilaterally? *Economic Record, 86*(273), 143–161.
Dixon, P. B., & Rimmer, M. T. (2013). Validation in computable general qquilibrium modeling. In P. B. Dixon & D. Jorgenson (Eds.), *Handbook of computable general equilibrium modeling* (Vol. 1, pp. 1271–1330). North-Holland.
Dixon, P. B., Madden, J. R., & Rimmer, M. T. (2010). Linking national and multi-regional computable general equilibrium (CGE) models: The effects of an increase in award wage rates in Australia. *Regional Studies, 44*(10), 1369–1385.
Dixon, P. B., Parmenter, B. R., Powell, A. A., & Wilcoxen, P. J. (1992). *Notes and problems in applied general equilibrium economics. Advanced Textbooks in Economics*. North-Holland.

---

[10] Expenditure elasticities used in the calibration: food (0.786), health (0.973), clothing (1.025), housing (1.043), personal services and other goods (1.131), transportation (1.115), culture and education (1.186).

Dixon, P. B., Parmenter, B. R., Sutton, J., & Vincent, D. P. (1982). *ORANI: A multisectoral model of the Australian economy*. North-Holland.
Friedman, M. (1955). Leon Walras and his economic system. *The American Economic Review, 54*(5), 900–909.
Ghaith, Z., Kulshreshtha, S., Natcher, D., & Cameron, B. (2021). Regional computable general equilibrium models: a review. *Journal of Policy Modeling, 43*(3), 710–724.
Giesecke, J. A., & Madden, J.R. (2012). Regional computable general equilibrium modeling. In B. P. Dixon & D. Jorgenson (Eds.), *Handbook of CGE modeling* (Vols. 1A and 1B, pp. 379–476). North Holland.
Haddad, E. A. (1999). *Regional inequality and structural changes: Lessons from the Brazilian experience*. Ashgate.
Haddad, E. A. (2009). Interregional computable general equilibrium models. In M. Sonis & G.J.D. Hewings (Eds.), *Tool kits in regional science* (pp. 119–154). Springer.
Haddad, E. A., & Hewings, G. J. D. (1999). The short-run regional effects of new investments and technological upgrade in the Brazilian automobile industry: An interregional computable general equilibrium analysis. *Oxford Development Studies, 27*(3), 359–383.
Haddad, E. A., & Hewings, G. J. D. (2005). Market imperfections in a spatial economy: Some experimental results. *The Quarterly Review of Economics and Finance, 45*(2–3), 476–496.
Haddad, E. A., Araújo, I., & Galvis-Aponte, L. (2019). Matriz Insumo-Producto Interregional de Colombia, 2015 *Texto para Discussão*, n. 10–2019. Núcleo de Economia Regional e Urbana da Universidade de São Paulo (NEREUS).
Haddad, E. A., Domingues, E. P., & Perobelli, F. S. (2002). Regional effects of economic integration: The case of Brazil. *Journal of Policy Modeling, 24*(5), 453–482.
Hertel, T., Hummels, D., Ivanic, M., & Keeney, R. (2007). How confident can we be of CGE-based assessments of free trade agreements? *Economic Modelling, 24*(4), 611–635.
Horridge, M., Madden, J., & Wittwer, G. (2005). The impact of the 2002–2003 drought on Australia. *Journal of Policy Modeling, 27*(3), 285–308.
Isard, W. (1969). *General theory: Social, political, economic, and regional with particular reference to decision-making analysis*. MIT Press.
Isard, W., Azis, I., Drennan, M. P., Miller, R. E., Saltzman, S., & Thorbecke, E. (1998). *Methods of interregional and regional analysis*. Ashgate.
Johansen, L. (1960). *A multi-sectoral study of economic growth*. North-Holland.
McGregor, P. G., J. Swales, K. & Yin., Y. P. (1996, May). *AMOS-RUK: An interregional computable general equilibrium model of Scotland and rest of the UK*. Paper presented at the 5th World Congress of the Regional Science Association, Tokyo
McKitrick, R. R. (1998). The econometric critique of computable general equilibrium modeling: The role of functional forms. *Economic Modelling, 15*(4), 543–573.
Munroe, D.K., Hewings G.J.D., & Guo, D. (2007). The role of intraindustry trade in interregional trade in the Midwest of the US. In R. J. Cooper, K. P. Donaghy, J. D. G. Geoffrey Hewings (Eds.), *Globalization and regional economic modeling*. Springer-Verlag.
Partridge, M. D., & Rickman, D. S. (2010). Computable general equilibrium (CGE) modelling for regional economic development analysis. *Regional Studies, 44*(10), 1311–1328.
Peter, M. W., Horridge, M., Meagher, G. A., Naqvi, F. & Parmenter, B. R. (1996, April). *The theoretical structure of MONASH-MRF*. Preliminary Working Paper, n. OP-85, IMPACT Project, Monash University, Clayton
Schumpeter, J. A. (1954). *History of economic analysis*. Oxford University Press.
Spencer, J. E. (1988). Computable general equilibrium, trade, factor mobility, and the regions. In F. Harrigan & P. G. McGregor (Eds.). *Recent advances in regional economic modelling*. Pion, London Papers in Regional Science.
Van den Bergh, J. C. J. M., Nijkamp, P., & Rietveld, P. (Eds.). (1996). *Recent advances in spatial equilibrium modelling*. Springer-Verlag.

Watanuki, M. (1996). *Regional development policy analysis of Indonesia: Interregional CGE modeling approach.* Paper presented at the 43rd North American Meeting of the Regional Science Association International, Washington, DC

Wing, I. S., & Anderson, W. (2007). Modeling small area economic change in conjunction with a multiregional CGE model. In R. Cooper, K. P. Donaghy, & G. J. D. Hewings (Eds.), *2007* (pp. 87–105). Springer-Verlag, Berlin, Heidelberg.

Wittwer, G. (Ed.). (2017). *Multiregional dynamic general equilibrium modelling of the US economy: USAGE-TERM development and applications. Advances in Applied General Equilibrium Modeling.* Springer.

Eduardo A. Haddad Full Professor at the Department of Economics at the University of São Paulo, Brazil, where he directs the Regional and Urban Economics Lab (NEREUS). Affiliate Professor at the Faculty of Governance, Economic and Social Sciences of the Mohammed VI University and Senior Fellow at the Policy Center for the New South, Rabat, Morocco. President of the Regional Science Association International, RSAI (2021-2022).

Inácio F. Araújo Doctor in Economics, Federal University of Juiz de Fora. Post-doctoral researcher, University of São Paulo, Brazil. Research fields: regional economics, input-output methods, and international trade.

Part III
Structural Analysis

Chapter 7
Revisiting the Structural Interdependence Among Colombian Departments

Fernando S. Perobelli and Geoffrey J. D. Hewings

7.1 Introduction

Different indicators can be used to measure regional interdependence. This chapter will address this issue by analyzing the interdependence from an intersectoral linkages perspective. The focus will be on the intermediate consumption part of the Colombian interregional input–output database; since data are now available for 2004 and 2015, it is possible to explore the nature of the structural changes over these 12 years. The analysis of the structure of regional interdependence plays an essential role in contributing to a better design of regional policies. According to Williamson (1965), regional inequality is inextricably related to economic development. Accordingly, inequalities are generated at the early stages of development; as an economy matures accompanied by growth in real per capita income, Williamson's expectation was that there would be regional convergence or a decrease in regional inequality.

Colombia comprises heterogeneous departments in terms of industrial composition, population density, and per capita income. Observing regional data from Colombia, we verify that the Central and Andean Regions are the ones in which the largest proportion of population concentrates within the major cities. These regions are characterized by the concentration of manufacturing industry and commerce in the cities with coffee plantations and other large-scale agricultural production surrounding the urban areas. Bogotá D.C and the departments of Cundinamarca, Antioquia, and Valle del Cauca account for 46.16% of total employment and for 53.47% of total GDP. It is important to highlight that Bogotá D.C has the highest share in total GDP (24.13%).

F. S. Perobelli (✉)
Federal University of Juiz de Fora, Juiz de Fora, Brazil
e-mail: fernandosalgueiro.perobelli@gmail.com

G. J. D. Hewings
University of Illinois at Urbana-Champaign, Champaign, USA

The GDP of the departments in the Caribbean Region is based upon mining, small-scale agriculture, and cattle farming. La Guajira and Cesar are the two largest coal producers, while Córdoba is the largest nickel producer. Relative to the Colombian average, the Pacific Region comprises three poor departments and one wealthy one (Valle del Cauca). Chocó, the poorest department in the country, is predominantly rural and sparsely populated, with extensive tropical rain forests and humid areas. It is the rainiest area in the country (and even one of the rainiest worldwide) and is geographically isolated from the rest of the country due to a chain of mountains to the east and the ocean to the west (Bonet, 2007). In contrast to Chocó, Valle del Cauca is the country's third-largest departmental economy after Bogotá D.C and Antioquia. This department has some of the most productive agricultural areas and a high level of participation in the manufacturing sector.

According to Roca and Hahn (2020), in contrast to Williamson's (1965) expectations, the degree of disparities will not spontaneously disappear only through market forces. His findings are based on observing several Colombian characteristics like geographical conditions of the country, the agglomeration processes around the largest cities, and the disparities in infrastructure, especially transportation.

The regional disparities among Colombian departments have generated debates from different perspectives. There is a group of papers that deal with the idea of convergence (Galvis-Aponte, et al. 2017; León & Benavides, 2015; Royuela & García, 2015; León & Ríos, 2013; González, 2011; Galvis, 2010; Branisa & Cardozo, 2009a, 2009b; Franco & Raymond, 2009; Aguirre, 2005; Ardila, 2004; Acevedo, 2003; Bonet & Meisel, 1999; Birchenall & Murcia, 1997). These papers dealt with different convergence measures, like β and σ, and calculated the convergence for different periods. The variables used in the studies include both economic (i.e., GDP, per capita GDP) and social indicators (i.e., Gini and Theil index). The results are mixed, but the studies that focus on estimating the regional distribution of wealth and its evolution over time affirm that Colombia is not a case of regional convergence, especially in economic terms. Many of the authors suggest that as the current differences in the per capita production are so high, it is unlikely that the poorest Colombian regions can achieve similar results to the prosperous regions in the short run. The variety of methods available to study regional convergence has influenced the academic debate and sometimes the political debate in Colombia over the last two decades. From the urban perspective, Galvis (2015) evaluated the economic and population growth from 1985 to 2012. The author observed a high degree of concentration in the major Colombian cities leading to a regional polarization. Bonet and Meisel (1999) evaluated the regional economic growth from 1980 to 1996 using a shift-share analysis and found that the local factors determine regional growth in Colombia (see also in this Chapter). In other words, the specific factors that determine the local competitiveness explain the variations in regional dynamics. For example, the higher relative growth of La Guajira is explained by the existence of mineral resources, while for Bogotá D.C and Cundinamarca is explained by the processes of agglomeration around the Capital District.

Perobelli et al. (2010) analyzed structural interdependence among Colombian departments using an input–output matrix for 2004. The results revealed that Bogotá

D.C had a considerable influence on the other regional economies through the power of its purchases. Additionally, a center-periphery pattern emerges in the spatial concentration of the effects on any territory's hypothetical extraction. From a policy point of view, the main findings reaffirmed the role played by Bogotá D.C in the recent polarization process observed in the regional economies in Colombia. Thus, the objective of the present chapter is to revisit Perobelli et al. (2010) using an interregional input–output matrix for 2015 to explore whether the degree of interdependence among the Colombian departments has changed and in what ways.

The remainder of the chapter is divided into four additional sections. Section 7.2 presents the Colombian regional and international trade structure, while Sect. 7.3 introduces the dataset and methods. Section 7.4 presents and discusses the results, and the chapter concludes with some further reflections on the findings.

7.2 The Structure of Colombian Regional and International Trade

This section will analyze the Colombian department's regional and international trade structure, observing some structural components. We will use data from the interregional input–output matrix for 2015 and present some indicators that will help us better understand each Colombian department's intra-regional, interregional, and international trade performance. To assist in this goal, we use trade indicators such as the degree of openness, coverage index, and intra-regional trade share; these indicators will provide some baseline descriptive statistics for investigating trade in the Colombian departments. After that, we will focus on capturing the interdependence among the departments based on a systemic analysis that considers all the linkages of the economy and then simulates the impact upon the GRP due to an interruption of the trade from the purchase side.

As trade is highly correlated with GDP, we present, in Fig. 7.1, the spatial distribution of GDP. Note the high degree of spatial concentration; the departments of Bogotá D.C, Antioquia, Valle Del Calca, Santander, and Cundinamarca are responsible for 60.93% of the total Colombian GDP. It is important to highlight that those departments also contain 49.24% of the Colombian population and 51.35% of Colombian employment. Not only is there a high degree of spatial concentration among the Colombian departments, but these departments are also located near to Bogotá D.C.

In Fig. 7.2, we present the intra-regional trade shares. Bogotá D.C, Antioquia, and Valle del Cauca are the regions that have the highest values for the indicator (around 82%). The national average is around 62%, and 22 departments present an indicator above the average, meaning that intra-regional trade is a dominant characteristic for the Colombian departments. Thus, as observed in Fig. 7.2, the departments with an indicator higher than the average are spread around the country and feature both large and small departments in terms of the GDP share. Comparing 2015 data with 2004, it is possible to affirm that the pattern of intra-regional trade shares has changed. The

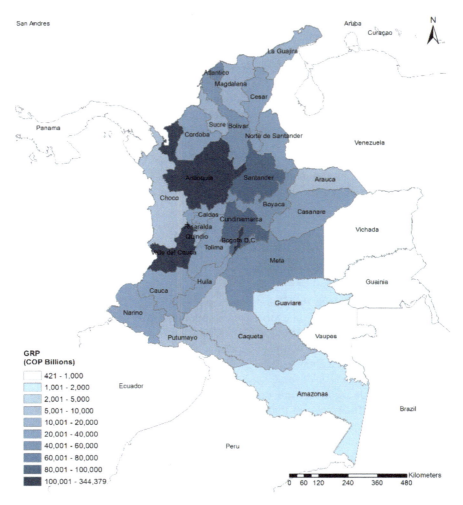

Fig. 7.1 Spatial distribution of GDP. *Source* Elaborated by the authors based on the interregional input–output table for Colombia, 2015

intra-regional trade shares for Bogotá D.C, Antioquia, and Valle del Cauca increased over this period, while only eight departments decreased their intra-regional trade share.

The spatial distribution of the interregional openness to trade and the international openness to trade are presented in Fig. 7.3. We use those two indicators to capture the importance of interregional and international trade in the economy; the weight of trade relations measures this (in our case, the exchange of goods and services inside the country and with the outside world) for 2015.[1] Several factors can influence the

---

[1] See Chap. 9 for a complementary analysis.

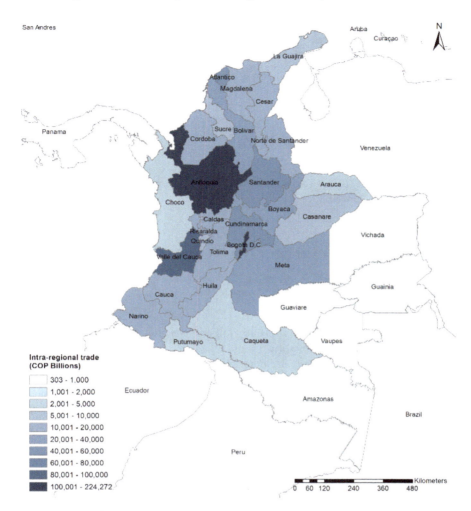

Fig. 7.2 Intra-regional trade share. *Source* Elaborated by the authors based on the interregional input–output table for Colombia, 2015

value of this indicator. For example, both interregional and international trade tend to be more critical (higher indicator) for small regions (in terms of geographic size or population) than for large regions (relatively more self-sufficient). To complete the analysis, we present in Fig. 7.4 and Fig. 7.5 the decomposition of the openness to trade indicator into the export intensity and import penetration. We observe that for Chocó and Caquetá, the export intensity is greater than import penetration and for San Andrés is the other way around (Fig. 7.4). In Fig. 7.5, we present the same indicators but for international trade. Casanare, La Guajira, and Arauca are regions with a higher degree of openness; for these three regions, the export intensity contributes more to

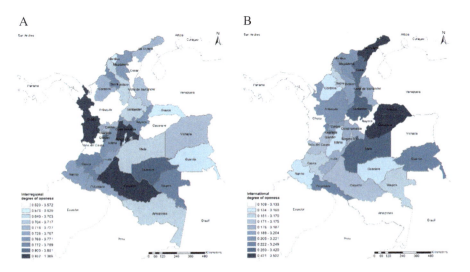

Fig. 7.3 Interregional and international openness to trade. *Source* Elaborated by the authors based on the interregional input–output table for Colombia, 2015

the result of the indicator. This is partially linked to the characteristic of the regions (primarily, exporters of commodities).

Figures 7.6 and 7.7 present the interregional and international coverage index results. This is a simple indicator that shows the percentage of imports covered by exports. A coverage rate greater than 1 (or 100%, if expressed as a percentage) means that the region has a strong commercial position (commercial competitiveness), while a rate less than 1 indicates a weak position or trade dependency (negative trade balance). For the interregional coverage index, note the relative importance of Bogotá D.C, Cundinamarca, Antioquia, and Valle del Cauca. The results can be explained by two factors: the share of intra-regional trade and the size of those economies. These two factors lead to more significant interregional exports but smaller interregional imports.

For the international coverage index, the six departments that present results above one are as follows: Casanare (4.9)—petroleum, Arauca (3.4)—coffee, Meta (3.4)—petroleum, La Guajira (3.3)—petroleum, Cesar (2.8)—coal, and Putumayo (2.2)—petroleum. We observe that the main exported goods are the ones that compose the main products dominating Colombia's exports. Thus, the strong position of those regions is linked to the external trade and the exports of commodities.

Summarizing the interregional and international trade analysis presented in this section enables us to affirm that Colombian departments have a hierarchical structure in terms of their importance in trade relations. From the internal side, we observe the relative strength of the departments located near Bogotá D.C that have the highest share of GDP, employment, and population. From the international trade side, we observe that the relative importance is primarily based on commodities exports.

7 Revisiting the Structural Interdependence Among Colombian Departments   191

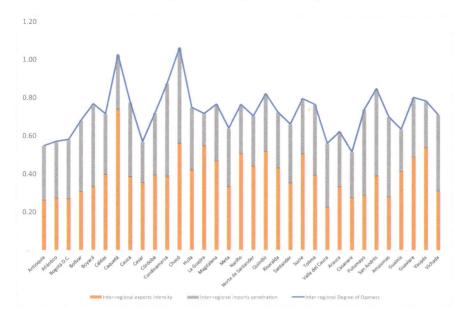

Fig. 7.4 Decomposition of the interregional degree of openness

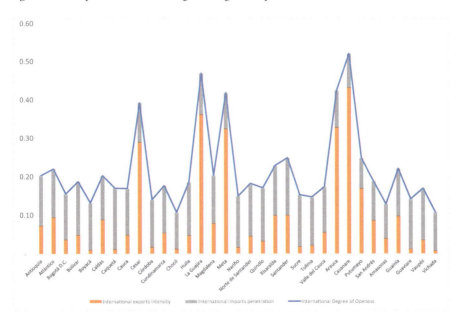

Fig. 7.5 Decomposition of the international degree of openness

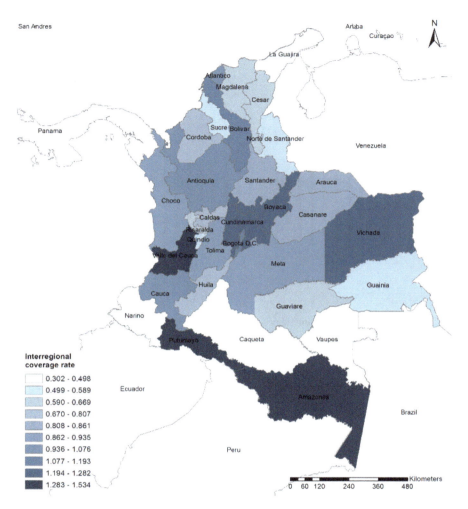

Fig. 7.6 Interregional coverage rate. *Source* Elaborated by the authors based on the interregional input–output table for Colombia, 2015

In essence, the economy presents a degree of heterogeneity in terms of the nature and strength of its dependencies. Regarding the contribution to the GDP, the main departments have an essential role in the domestic economy while the departments specialized in the exported commodities have a weak integration with the rest of the country. Hence, it will be essential to explore the central question of this chapter: to what degree structural interdependence among Colombian departments exist? In other words, how can the systemic analysis of dependence contribute to understanding the weakness or strength of Colombian regional integration?

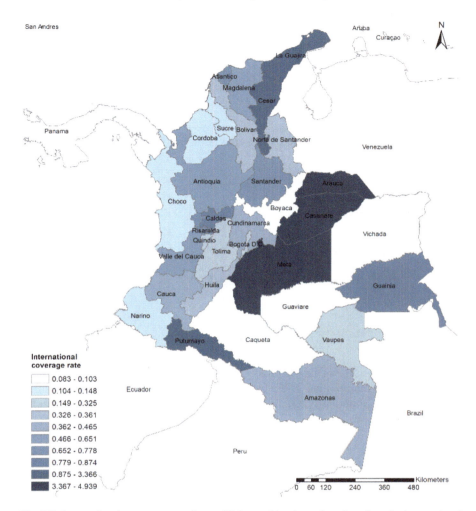

Fig. 7.7 International coverage rate. *Source* Elaborated by the authors based on the interregional input–output table for Colombia, 2015

7.3 Data and Methodology

7.3.1 Data

The data to analyze the structure of internal interdependence among Colombian departments are derived from Haddad et al. (2019). The construction of the tables follows a common conceptual framework (see Chap. 5) based on officially published input–output tables in conjunction with regional accounts from the country's official

Table 7.1 Interregional input–output database

Region (R)	33
Industry (N)	54
Dimension (NR x NR)	1782 × 1782
Year	2015
Currency	COP billions

statistical institute. Table 7.1 summarizes the information from the database we use in our analysis.

7.3.2 Methodology

The traditional input–output model is defined by:

$$\mathbf{x} = \mathbf{A}\mathbf{x} + \mathbf{f} \tag{7.1}$$

and

$$\mathbf{x} = (\mathbf{I} - \mathbf{A})^{-1}\mathbf{f} = \mathbf{B}\mathbf{f} \tag{7.2}$$

where $\mathbf{x}$ and $\mathbf{f}$ are the vectors of gross output and final demand, respectively, $\mathbf{A}$ is the matrix with technological coefficients, $[a_{ij}]$, defined as the quantity of product i required per unit of output j (in monetary terms)–$i, j = 1, ..., n$, and $\mathbf{B}$ is the Leontief inverse matrix.

Modifying Eq. (7.1) and Eq. (7.2) to an interregional context, with r different regions, generates:

$$\mathbf{x} = \begin{bmatrix} \mathbf{x}^1 \\ \vdots \\ \mathbf{x}^R \end{bmatrix}; \mathbf{A} = \begin{bmatrix} \mathbf{A}^{11} & \cdots & \mathbf{A}^{1R} \\ \vdots & \ddots & \vdots \\ \mathbf{A}^{R1} & \cdots & \mathbf{A}^{RR} \end{bmatrix}; \mathbf{f} = \begin{bmatrix} \mathbf{f}^1 \\ \vdots \\ \mathbf{f}^R \end{bmatrix}; \mathbf{B} = \begin{bmatrix} \mathbf{B}^{11} & \cdots & \mathbf{B}^{1R} \\ \vdots & \ddots & \vdots \\ \mathbf{B}^{R1} & \cdots & \mathbf{B}^{RR} \end{bmatrix} \tag{7.3}$$

and

$$\mathbf{x}^1 = \mathbf{B}^{11}\mathbf{f}^1 + \ldots + \mathbf{B}^{1R}\mathbf{f}^R$$
$$\vdots$$
$$\mathbf{x}^R = \mathbf{B}^{R1}\mathbf{f}^1 + \ldots + \mathbf{B}^{RR}\mathbf{f}^R$$

We use Eq. (7.3) to implement the hypothetical regional extraction to better understand and analyze the interdependence from the intermediate inputs side.

The extraction method, described in Dietzenbacher et al. (1993), consists of the hypothetical extraction of a sector in the input–output matrix. The purpose is to

7 Revisiting the Structural Interdependence Among Colombian Departments

determine how much the total output of an economy with n sectors could change (or decrease) if a particular sector was removed from the economy. This technique identifies the importance of a sector in an economic structure, given the extraction and the consequent reduction in the level of economic activity, the greater the degree of interdependence of a sector with the others, the bigger the impact. We can apply the same rationale to the extraction of all sectors in a region.

Using Eq. (7.2) to represent the general model with all regions, the reduced model or the model with the hypothetical regional extraction can be represented by:

$$\bar{\mathbf{x}} = (\mathbf{I} - \bar{\mathbf{A}})^{-1} \bar{\mathbf{f}} \qquad (7.4)$$

where $\bar{\bar{A}}$. is the technical coefficient matrix after the extraction of a specific region, $\bar{f}$. is the final demand vector after the extraction of a specific region, and $\bar{x}$ is the final output vector after the extraction of a specific region.

Comparing the two models, Eq. (7.2) and Eq. (7.4), we obtain:

$$\mathbf{T} = \mathbf{i}'\mathbf{x} - \mathbf{i}'\bar{\mathbf{x}} \qquad (7.5)$$

where **T** is the aggregate measure of the annual loss in the economy (reduction in total output without production associated with a specific region); thus, Eq. (7.5) presents a measure of the relative importance of the activities carried out by a specific region or the total linkages to which such a region is associated.

The indicators above show the global impact and total interdependence, but the methodology is flexible and can separate the backward and forward effects of a hypothetical extraction.[2] Thus, to represent the hypothetical backward regional extraction, we assume that all sectors j located in the region r buy no intermediate inputs from any production sector, which means that all sector j's backward linkages are removed in region r. This exercise is done for all regions, one at a time. This is done by replacing all columns j in A of region r with zeros. Denote this new matrix $A_{(cj)}$. The earlier representation of $\bar{\bar{A}}$ denotes a structure in which row and column j of a region r were deleted. To represent the backward impact, we put a "c" to indicate that it is all column j at region r that was extracted. Then, the reduced model to represent the hypothetical extraction of all buying sector j located at the region r is represented by:

$$x_{(cj)} = (I - A_{(cj)})^{-1} f \qquad (7.6)$$

and the aggregated measure of backward linkage for all sector j located at region r is as follows:

$$T_j = \mathbf{i}'\mathbf{x} - \mathbf{i}' x_{(cj)} \qquad (7.7)$$

---

[2] At this chapter, we will show the results of the buying extraction (i.e., backward linkages) to compare with the results from Perobelli et al. (2010).

7.4 Results

In Figs. 7.8, 7.9 and 7.10, we present the spatial distribution of the hypothetical extraction impacts of the buying sector upon the Colombian economy. Light blue colors represent the lowest impact, and dark blue colors represent the highest impacts. Figure 7.7 provides a map that exemplifies the hypothetical extraction of the buying sectors of Bogotá D.C. The departments that face the highest reductions in GDP are Bogotá D.C, Antioquia, and Cundinamarca. These departments have Bogotá D.C as an important market for their products. This evidences that the more prominent regional economies mainly trade among themselves. The results for Cundinamarca reinforce the high degree of dependence of those two regions due to their spatial proximity.

On the other hand, the departments that face the smallest reductions in GDP are Guainía, Guaviare, and Vaupés, all located in the Amazonian portion of the country. From Fig. 7.8, we can observe two spatial patterns. Most of the departments located on the east side of Bogotá D.C have a small interaction with it. The interdependence of Bogotá D.C with the departments located in the Caribbean and the axis from Medellín–Bogotá D.C (west side of Bogotá D.C) is more intense.

The spatial distribution of the variation in GDP when the buying sector of Antioquia is hypothetically extracted can be observed in Fig. 7.9. The most significant impact is upon Antioquia (internal effect), followed by the impacts upon Atlántico and Bogotá D.C. The spatial pattern is similar to the one presented for the Bogotá D.C case. The highest impact can be found in the Pacific portion of the country, and the smallest impact is located in the Amazonian portion of the country.

The relative importance of the buying sector located in Valle del Cauca is also highly spatially concentrated. The major impacts upon GDP are internal, especially upon Bogotá D.C and Antioquia. The spatial dimension of the impacts is well defined: the Caribbean portion of the country presents the highest impact while the Amazonian part the smallest.

From these figures, we can affirm that the three departments with the highest internal impact have more interdependence, mainly with the other departments located in the Caribbean portion of the country. Furthermore, the major impacts are predominantly along the Bogotá–Medellín axis and a secondary role played by other departments within the "*Colombian Ostrich.*" It is also important to highlight the central role played by Bogotá D.C for those departments. In contrast, we observe a lack of integration among the departments located in the Pacific region with the ones located in the Amazonian region of the country. We observe that those departments have weaker linkages with the extracted departments in all examples.

Perobelli et al. (2010) concluded that all departments have a net dependence upon Bogotá D.C. Their results reinforced the central role of Bogotá D.C's purchases upon the other regional economies. The global picture shows a spatial concentration of any territory's hypothetical buying extraction effects on the capital district, Bogotá D.C. The results for Antioquia and Valle del Cauca follow the spatial dimension of

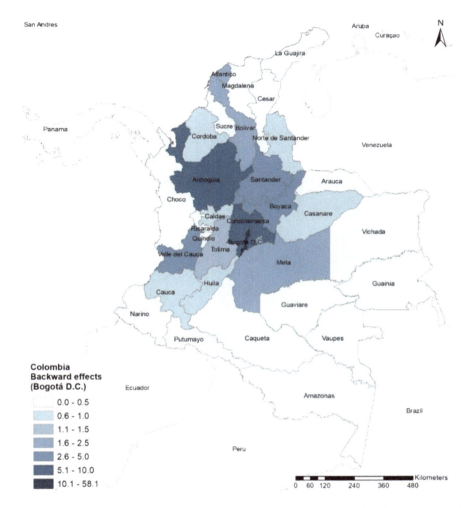

Fig. 7.8 Backward effects: percentile map (Bogotá D.C). *Source* Elaborated by the authors based on the hypothetical extraction

the results for Bogotá D.C. Hence, the authors identified a clear center-periphery pattern.

Perobelli et al. (2010) also presented three summary indicators to capture the degree of interdependence between Colombian departments: *BL*—which represents the hypothetically isolated department's backward dependence on the rest of the Colombian economy, *IFb*—which represents the backward dependence of the rest of Colombia on the hypothetically isolated department, and *NBL*—which measures the net backward dependency between Colombian departments. Table 7.2 compares the results of the three indicators for the period of analysis (2004 and 2015).

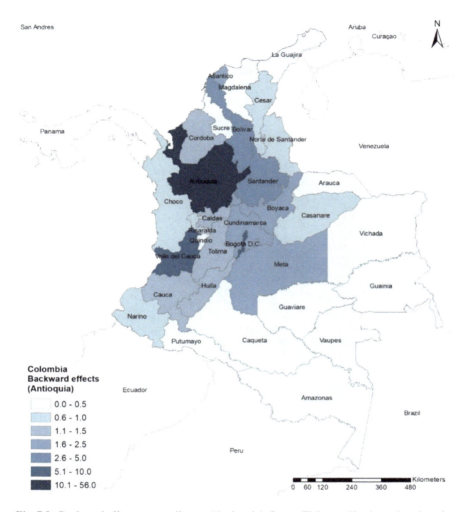

Fig. 7.9 Backward effects: percentile map (Antioquia). *Source* Elaborated by the authors based on the hypothetical extraction

We have a slight change in the five departments with the highest indicator for the backward dependence of the hypothetically isolated department on the rest of the Colombian economy (BL). In 2015, Atlántico and Córdoba were among those with a small backward dependence on the rest of the Colombian economy. There is a difference of three departments for the five departments most dependent on the rest of the Colombian economy. In 2015, Chocó, Caquetá, and Arauca formed the group together with Guaviare and Vaupés. The last two are also in the group of the five smallest interdependence indicators in 2004.

7 Revisiting the Structural Interdependence Among Colombian Departments

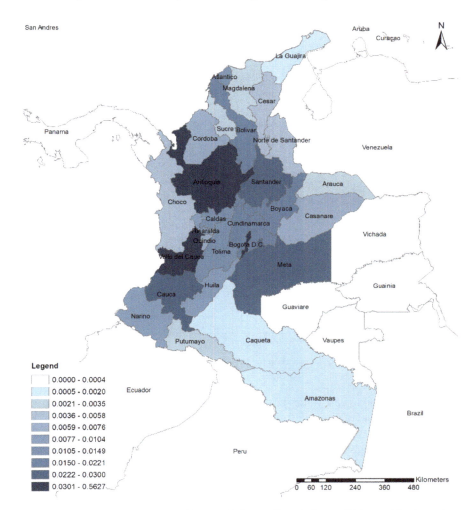

Fig. 7.10 Backward effects: percentile map (Valle Del Cauca). *Source* Elaborated by the authors based on the hypothetical extraction

Regarding the *IFb* indicator, the backward dependence of the rest of Colombia on the hypothetically isolated department, there is also a small change for the departments with a higher value for the indicator. For the year 2015, the departments of Santander and Cundinamarca are on the list. The departments that present the lowest value for the indicator, i.e., the departments with which the rest of Colombia has a small dependence, have no modification over the period.

As for the net dependency indicator, in 2015, the departments of Boyacá and Bolívar were included in the group with the highest value for the indicator, and in

Table 7.2 Interdependence indicators: 2004 and 2015

Ranking	BL		IFb		NFL	
	2004	2015	2004	2015	2004	2015
5 highest						
	Bogotá D.C	Bogotá D.C	Bogotá D.C	Bogotá D.C	Bogotá D.C	Boyacá
	Antioquia	Valle del Cauca	Atlantico	Antioquia	Antioquia	Bolívar
	Valle del Cauca	Antioquia	Valle del Cauca	Valle del Cauca	Valle del Cauca	Valle del Cauca
	Santander	Atlántico	Antioquia	Santander	Santander	Antioquia
	Cundinamarca	Córdoba	Bolívar	Cundinamarca	Cundinamarca	Bogotá D.C
5 smallest						
	Guaviare	Guaviare	Guaviare	Amazonas	San Andrés	San Andrés
	Vichada	Vaupés	Vichada	Guaviare	Vichada	Vaupés
	Amazonas	Chocó	Amazonas	Vichada	Amazonas	La Guajira
	Vaupés	Caquetá	Vaupés	Guainía	Guainía	Caquetá
	Guainía	Arauca	Guainía	Vaupés	Vaupés	Guainía

Source Elaborated by the authors based on the hypothetical extraction

the group with the lowest value for the indicator, there was also the inclusion of the departments of La Guajira and Caquetá.

The comparison presented in Table 7.2 raised some significant findings regarding the central role Bogotá D.C played. We observe that the departments that present the highest results for all the indicators also reveal some changes, but the changes do not represent a spatial dispersion of the results. The results strengthen the dependence on Bogotá D.C and surrounding departments. In other words, the hierarchy of the systemic interdependence among Colombian departments moves from Bogotá D.C. On the other hand, the changes for the departments with the smallest results for the three indicators reveal some differences in its composition between the years analyzed, but non-significant changes occurred in terms of the spatial dimension.

We calculated the weighted Williamson coefficient using GDP and population data from the simulation exercise results of each department's hypothetical extraction. The objective is to compare the indicator as to the complete system (i.e., all departments)—orange line in Fig. 7.11, with the system when implementing the simulation exercise, consisting of the hypothetical extraction of each department—the blue line in Fig. 7.11.

An examination of Fig. 7.11 reveals an increase in the inequality indicator using GDP when the departments of Bogotá D.C, Atlántico, Santander, and Boyacá are hypothetically extracted from the system. On the other hand, there is a reduction in

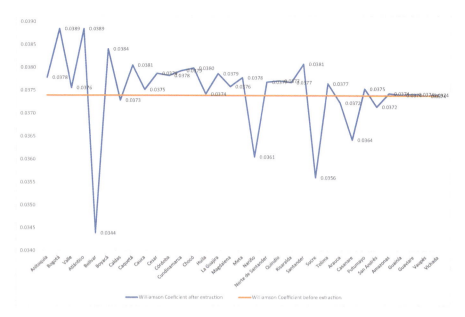

Fig. 7.11 Williamson coefficient. *Source* Elaborated by the authors based on the hypothetical extraction

the indicator when the departments of Bolívar, Sucre, and Nariño are hypothetically extracted from the system.

7.5 Final Considerations

This chapter analyzed the regional interdependence among Colombian departments from a systemic perspective. To measure this issue, we implemented a simulation exercise in which we hypothetically extracted the buying sector of the three most important regions of the country (i.e., Bogotá D.C, Antioquia, and Valle del Cauca). This simulation is based on two premises. First, to verify the degree of the spatial dispersion of the results and the Colombian integration departing from the main regions in terms of the share on total GDP, employment, and population. Secondly, to make a comparison with Perobelli et al. (2010) study to verify whether and to what degree the structure of the interdependence changed along the period analyzed.

For the first objective, the results show that the interdependence among the Colombian departments analyzed from the purchase side of the largest regions in terms of its contribution to national GDP shows a similar spatial pattern among the three simulations implemented.[3] The global picture strengthens the notion of the *Colombian Ostrich,* leading to a concentration of the most impacted regions along the Bogotá–Medellín axis.

For the second objective, we do not observe a significant change in terms of the spatial dispersion of the impacts. The global picture does not change from the period 2004 to 2015. Thus, the picture of a country composed of relatively isolated regions noted in Perobelli et al. (2010) for 2004 is still present. While there are several explanations for these results, there is no doubt that the topographical conditions of the country generate significant difficulties in connecting the regions by surface transportation systems leading to a high cost of transportation. These problems are exacerbated by the absence of an efficient transport network that leads to isolation and inaccessibility of some regions.

It is not our aim to evaluate the efficiency of the regional policy in Colombia for the recent period, but the results from our exercise could generate some hypotheses about the initiatives that have been proposed for the country. There is a consensus in the literature that efficient transport infrastructure is essential to boost economic growth and to offer any possibility to reduce interregional disparities. Countries with low transport costs can better allocate resources, take advantage of economies of scale, and fully exploit their comparative advantages in international trade. In Colombia, as in other Latin American countries, roads constitute the most critical component of the transport infrastructure network and thus represent an essential piece in their development puzzle. However, the transport network remains relatively undeveloped.

According to Nupia (2014), from 2000 to 2012, the central government implemented various Productive Development Policies (PDPs). However, there is an impression in the regions that the central government designed the PDPs without considering the needs or potentialities of specific regions. If so, the investment of many of the resources in the regions could end up being underutilized and therefore having a low impact in terms of the impact on regional growth. Among the PDP initiatives, the investments in transport infrastructure have not significantly contributed to enhancing connectivity. Nieto-Parra et al. (2013) analyzed the transport infrastructure policy from 2002 to 2010, and Melo-Becerra (2020) described investment in transport infrastructure presenting data from the past and the investments forecasts by departments and municipalities in the country. Both authors show that beyond increasing investment in transport infrastructure, the challenge in Colombia is to invest more effectively.

Putting together our results, showing the persistence of the spatial pattern of interdependence, leading to the reinforcement of the *Colombian Ostrich,* and the discussion about transport infrastructure investments, we could affirm that to overcome this structural challenge is necessary to implement policies that are not only more focused, but appropriately reflect the endogenous characteristics of the regions—essentially an implementation of policy that is more sensitive to decentralizing characteristics.

From a policy point of view, our findings reaffirm the role played by Bogotá D.C in the polarization process observed in the regional economies in Colombia in the recent

---

[3] The hypothetical extraction of Bogotá D.C, Antioquia, and Valle del Cauca.

period. Any policy to reduce these regional disparities should consider that, given the structural interdependence among Colombian departments, new investment in the lagged regions would potentially flow through Bogotá D.C and the surrounding regional economies.

References

Acevedo, S. (2003). Convergencia y crecimiento económico en Colombia 1980–2000. *Ecos De Economía, 7*(17), 51–78.
Aguirre, K. (2005). Convergencia en indicadores sociales en Colombia. Una aproximación desde los enfoques tradicional y no paramétrico. *Revista Desarrollo y Sociedad, 56*, 147–176.
Ardila, L. (2004). Gasto público y convergencia regional en Colombia. *Revista ESPE, 45*, 222–268.
Birchenall, J., & Murcia, G. (1997). Convergencia regional: Una revisión del caso colombiano. *Revista Desarrollo y Sociedad, 40*, 273–308.
Bonet, J., & Meisel, A. (1999). La convergencia regional en Colombia: Una visión de largo plazo, 1926–1995. *Documentos de Trabajo sobre Economía Regional*, 8, Cartagena das Indias, Banco de la República.
Bonet, J. (2007). La terciarización de las estructuras económicas regionales en Colombia. *Revista de economía del Rosario, 10*(1), 1–19.
Branisa, B., & Cardozo, A. (2009a). Regional growth convergence in Colombia using social indicators. *Discussion papers*, 195. Georg-August-Universität, Ibero-America Institute for Economic Research.
Branisa, B., & Cardozo, A. (2009b). Revisiting the regional growth convergence debate in Colombia using income indicators. *Discussion Papers*, 194. Georg-August-Universität, Ibero-America Institute for Economic Research.
Dietzenbacher, E., Linden J. A. V. A, & Steenge A. E. (1993). The regional extraction method: EC input–output comparisons. *Economic Systems Research, 5*(2), 185–206.
Franco Vásquez, L., & Raymond Bara, J. (2009). Convergencia económica regional: El caso de los Departamentos colombianos. *Ecos De Economía, 13*(28), 167–197.
Galvis, L. (2010). Comportamiento de los salarios reales en Colombia: Un análisis de convergencia condicional, 1984–2009. In *Documentos de Trabajo sobre Economía Regional*, 27, Cartagena das Indias, Banco de la República.
Galvis-Aponte, L. A. (2015). La eficiencia del gasto público en educación en Colombia.
Galvis-Aponte, L., Galvis-Larios, W., & De-Castro, L. W. H. (2017). Una revisión de los estudios de convergencia regional en Colombia.
Gómez, C. (2006). Convergencia regional en Colombia: Un enfoque en los Agregados Monetarios y en el Sector Exportador. *Ensayos sobre Economía Regional*, 45.
González, N. (2011). ¿Otra vez? Una sencilla visión de la convergencia económica en los departamentos de Colombia: 1975–2005. Universidad Nacional de Colombia.
Haddad, E. A., Araújo, I. F., & Galvis, L.A. (2019). Matriz Insumo-producto Interregional de Colombia, 2015 (Nota Técnica). In *Texto para Discussão, 10 NEREUS*. Universidade de São Paulo.
Haddad, E. A., Bonet, J., Hewings, G. J. D., & Perobelli, F. S. (2009). Spatial aspects of trade liberalization in Colombia: A general equilibrium approach. *Papers in Regional Science, 88*(4), 699–732.
León, D., & Ríos, H. (2013). Convergencia regional en el índice de desarrollo humano en Colombia. *Equidad y Desarrollo, 20*, 105–141.
León, G., & Benavides, H. (2015). Inversión pública en Colombia y sus efectos sobre el crecimiento y la convergencia departamentales. *Dimensión Empresarial, 13*(1), 57–72.

Nupia, O. (2014). DistribuciÃ³n Regional de las PolÃticas de Desarrollo Productivo en Colombia y Brechas Regionales en Productividad y Empleo. No. 012059. Universidad de los Andes-CEDE.

Nieto-Parra, S., Olivera, M., & Tibocha, A. (2013). The politics of transport infrastructure policies in Colombia.

Perobelli, F., Haddad, E. A., Bonet, J., & Hewings, G. J. D. (2010). Structural interdependence among Colombian departments. *Economic Systems Research, 33*(3), 279–300.

Roca, A. M., & Hahn, L. (2020). Regional economic inequality in Colombia, 1926–2018. *Time and Space* (pp. 183–210). Palgrave Macmillan.

Royuela, V., & García, G. (2015). Economic and social convergence in Colombia. *Regional Studies, 49*(2), 219–239.

Williamson, J. (1965). Regional inequality and the process of national development: A description of the patterns. *Economic Development and Cultural Change, 13*, 1–84.

Fernando S. Perobelli Doctor in Economics, University of Sao Paulo, Full Professor at Department of Economics at the Federal University of Juiz de Fora. He has published several articles in academic journals on topics such as energy, environment, regional economics, and sectorial analysis.

Geoffrey J. D. Hewings Emeritus Director, Regional Economics Applications Laboratory (REAL). Emeritus Professor of Geography and Regional Science, Economics, and Urban and Regional Planning. President of the Regional Science Association International, RSAI (2001–2002).

Chapter 8
Economic Base and Regional Specialization in Colombia: A Note on Input–Output Linkages

Inácio F. Araújo, Alexandre L. Gomes, Diana Ricciulli, and Eduardo A. Haddad

8.1 Introduction

This chapter aims to bring insights into the design of Colombia's regional development policies based on regional specialization strategies and focuses on the discussion of input–output linkages. It combines economic base theory and the concept of Miyazawa multipliers. We decompose the Colombian economic interregional system into three groups of analysis: (i) sectors of the economic base (EB) within the region; (ii) non-economic-base sectors within the region; and (iii) the rest of the country.

The chapter looks at the relationship between the EB and local labor markets. We analyze the capacity of the EB to create additional jobs in the local economy and the composition of jobs associated with the EB. We also evaluate the integration of the regional economic base with the rest of the economy and their implications for regional competitiveness. To do so, we decompose the economic-base output multiplier and estimate the effect of trade linkages on regional performance.

The chapter has five other sections besides this introductory section. The following section discusses the conceptual framework that support our analysis. Section 8.3

I. F. Araújo (✉) · E. A. Haddad
University of São Paulo, São Paulo, Brazil
e-mail: inacio.araujo@usp.br

E. A. Haddad
e-mail: ehaddad@usp.br

A. L. Gomes
Federal University of São Carlos, São Carlos, Brazil
e-mail: algomes@ufscar.br

D. Ricciulli
Center for Regional Economic Studies, Central Bank of Colombia, Cartagena, Colombia
e-mail: driccima@banrep.gov.co

presents the data, and the methodology applied. Section 8.4 describes the departmental productive specialization in Colombia in the context of the local economic base. Section 8.5 presents and discusses the results, and, finally, the last section draws the main conclusions.

8.2 Economic Base and Regional Specialization

The success of a region and the difference in regional performance can be related to the economic base (North, 1955),[1] and the nature of intersectoral linkages and regional interdependence (Hirchman, 1958; 1984). More recently, local productive specialization and production linkages became the basis for the so-called smart specialization strategies (Foray et al., 2009; McCann & Argilés, 2015).

Smart specialization strategies reinforce the need for correspondence between investment in knowledge, human capital, and the regions' industrial and technological competencies (Foray, 2015; Foray et al., 2009). Thus, regions should specialize based on their existing place-based capabilities (Camagni & Capello, 2017). These are the central ideas promoted by the smart specialization strategies to formulate regional development policies. The place-based capabilities associated with trading linkages can provide the basis for the development of new economic activities and the upgrading of existing activities in regions (Boschma & Iammarino, 2009). Previous analyzes on smart specializations strategies have primarily focused on the role of local capabilities, but few studies have assessed the importance of intraregional and interregional linkages (Boschma, 2017; Balland & Boschman, 2021).

Trade linkages can help regions develop industrial diversification through activities that complement local specialization (Boschma & Iammarino, 2009; Balland & Boschman, 2021). The local and non-local flows and linkages that make up interconnections in the different production networks are crucial drivers of diversification and explain regional growth (Yeung, 2021). Hence, trade linkages can be a way for regions to make better use of their economic base and encourage the emergence of activities related to local specialization.

---

[1] Tiebout (1956, p. 164), in a comment about the role of the export base in regional development made by North (1955), highlights that "as an explanatory factor in regional growth, the idea of the export base should not subsume the key role of residentiary activities (…). Since a region must optimize the use of factors as between exports and residentiary outputs, a decline in export activity may even be accompanied by rising regional income".

8.3 Data and Methodology

8.3.1 Economic-Base Output Multiplier

To compute the economic-base output multiplier of each Colombian department, we use the Interregional Input–Output Matrix for Colombia (IIOM-COL) for the year 2015. These data describe the structure of the national economy in the context of its 33 departments and 54 sectors.[2] The input–output model is given by:

$$\mathbf{x} = \mathbf{Bf} \tag{8.1}$$

where $\mathbf{x}$ and $\mathbf{f}$ are the vectors of gross output and final demand, and $\mathbf{B}$ is the Leontief inverse. Focusing on the elements directly related to the economic base, we consider new final demand vectors-$\mathbf{f}^*$—in which only the cells in the row representing economic base sectors have their actual values, and all other final demand is set to 0. The choice for a specific final demand $\mathbf{f}^*$ determines which economic base is considered. Thus, we can rewrite Eq. (8.1) in a context with R different regions, as:

$$\begin{aligned} \mathbf{x}^1 &= \mathbf{B}^{11}\mathbf{f}^{*1} + \ldots + \mathbf{B}^{1R}\mathbf{f}^{*R} \\ &\vdots \\ \mathbf{x}^R &= \mathbf{B}^{R1}\mathbf{f}^{*1} + \ldots + \mathbf{B}^{RR}\mathbf{f}^{*R} \end{aligned} \tag{8.2}$$

From Eq. (8.2), we can then compute the contribution of the economic base to the regional output. In this interregional system, the economic-base output multiplier for each department is the ratio of the total effects generated in the Colombian economy by the departmental economic base to the economic base itself.

To analyze production-related employment, represented by the matrix $\mathbf{U}^R$, we define employ-intensity coefficients $\mathbf{v}^R$ as the amount of employment per unit of output, and we multiply this by the corresponding output. Then, Eq. (8.2) becomes:

$$\mathbf{U}^R = \mathbf{v}^R \mathbf{B}^{RR} \mathbf{F}^{*R} \tag{8.3}$$

The $\mathbf{U}^R$ matrix contains production-related employment for each departmental economic base.

---

[2] See Chap. 5 of this book.

8.3.2 Partition Analysis of Indirect Production Generation by the Economic Base[3]

Interactions between a set of economic base sectors (EB) and a set of rest of the sectors (Non-EB) are analyzed using a form of decomposition analysis proposed by Miyazawa (1966, 1968 and 1971) and subsequently modified by Sonis and Hewings (1993) and Fritz et al. (1998).

We start from the IIOM-COL to build an input–output table for each Colombian department. Then, the department's economy is divided into the economic base sectors (EB) and the rest of the sectors (Non-EB). The system may be represented by the block matrix, $\mathbf{A}$, of direct inputs:

$$\mathbf{A} = \begin{pmatrix} \mathbf{A}_{bb} & \mathbf{A}_{bn} \\ \mathbf{A}_{nb} & \mathbf{A}_{nn} \end{pmatrix} \tag{8.4}$$

where $\mathbf{A}_{bb}$ and $\mathbf{A}_{nn}$ are square matrices accounting for the internal input flows among the EB and Non-EB sectors, respectively, and $\mathbf{A}_{nb}$ and $\mathbf{A}_{bn}$ are rectangular matrices representing input flows between EB and Non-EB sectors. The Leontief inverses of the EB and Non-EB sectors are referred to as the internal matrix multipliers (Miyazawa, 1966) and are defined as follows:

$$\mathbf{B}_b = (\mathbf{I} - \mathbf{A}_{bb})^{-1} \tag{8.4a}$$

$$\mathbf{B}_n = (\mathbf{I} - \mathbf{A}_{nn})^{-1} \tag{8.4b}$$

Based on Sonis and Hewings (1993), the following definitions of the external multipliers are used:

$$\Delta_b = (\mathbf{I} - \mathbf{A}_{bb} - \mathbf{A}_{bn}\mathbf{B}_n\mathbf{A}_{nb})^{-1} \tag{8.5a}$$

$$\Delta_n = (\mathbf{I} - \mathbf{A}_{nn} - \mathbf{A}_{nb}\mathbf{B}_b\mathbf{A}_{bn})^{-1} \tag{8.5b}$$

Thus, the Leontief inverse for the Non-EB sectors includes the internal direct and indirect demand for Non-EB commodities and the demand induced by inputs from the EB sectors. The following decomposition of the matrix in Eq. (8.4) may be obtained (Sonis & Hewings, 1993):

$$(\mathbf{I} - \mathbf{A})^{-1} = \begin{pmatrix} \Delta_b & \mathbf{B}_b\mathbf{A}_{bn}\Delta_n \\ \Delta_n\mathbf{A}_{nb}\mathbf{B}_b & \Delta_n \end{pmatrix} \tag{8.6}$$

---

[3] This section is based on Fritz et al. (1998), following their mathematical notation most of the time.

This interpretation of the Leontief inverse will be used to analyze the transactions between the EB and Non-EB sectors. Since the focus of this study is on EB sectors, the influence that the Non-EB sectors exert on the EB sectors will be ignored when irrelevant to the EB multiplier.

Furthermore, the Miyazawa external multipliers for the EB and Non-EB, respectively, are introduced:

$$\Delta_{bb} = (\mathbf{I} - \mathbf{B}_b \mathbf{A}_{bn} \mathbf{B}_n \mathbf{A}_{nb})^{-1} \tag{8.7a}$$

$$\Delta_{nn} = (\mathbf{I} - \mathbf{B}_n \mathbf{A}_{nb} \mathbf{B}_b \mathbf{A}_{bn})^{-1} \tag{8.7b}$$

Δ_{nn} includes the direct, indirect, and induced effects of the Non-EB sectors' input demand from the EB sector on the Non-EB sectors' production. The multipliers in Eq. (8.5a) and Eq. (8.5b) can then be written as:

$$\Delta_b = \Delta_{bb} \mathbf{B}_b \tag{8.8a}$$

$$\Delta_n = \Delta_{nn} \mathbf{B}_n \tag{8.8b}$$

The matrix multiplier of interest in the decomposed Leontief inverse of Eq. 8.6, $\mathbf{M}_b = \Delta_n \mathbf{A}_{nb} \mathbf{B}_b$, reveals the EB sectors' internal propagation influence on the other sectors' output levels. $\mathbf{M}_b$ is the output multipliers whose elements, $m_{i_n j_b}$, represent the increase in output generated by the Non-EB sector, i_n, as a result of a unit increase in final demand in the EB sector, i_b. To evaluate the total amount of output generated by a unit increase in an economic base industry's output level, the appropriate column multipliers are calculated:

$$\overline{m}_{jb} = \sum_{i_n} m_{i_n j_b} \tag{8.9}$$

where $\overline{m}_{jb}$ is the sector j_b's column multiplier. We analyze the interaction of three multiplier matrices, Δ_{nn}, $\mathbf{B}_n$, $\mathbf{B}_b$ and the matrix $\mathbf{A}_{nb}$ to evaluate the EB sectors' impact to drive the local economy. The sources of effect induced by the EB sectors' production activities can be unveiled by looking at the column sums of these matrices concerning other sectors:

$\mathbf{A}_{nb}$: product generated by direct input requirements of the EB sectors.

$\mathbf{A}_{nb} \mathbf{B}_b$: product generated by direct and indirect input requirements of the EB sectors.

$\mathbf{B}_n \mathbf{A}_{nb} \mathbf{B}_b$: product generated by internal propagation of EB sectors and the induced direct and indirect production of the Non-EB sectors.

$\Delta_{nn} \mathbf{B}_n \mathbf{A}_{nb} \mathbf{B}_b$: total output multiplier of the EB sector caused by the internal propagation of EB sectors and the induced internal and external propagation of the Non-EB sectors.

Industry j_b's column sums concerning these matrices are denoted as m_{jb}^1, m_{jb}^2, m_{jb}^3, m_{jb}, respectively. The following definitions will be employed in the empirical analysis:

m_{jb}^1/m_{jb}: share of direct input requirements in the total multiplier;

$m_{jb}^2 - m_{jb}^1/m_{jb}$: share of indirect input requirements in the total multiplier;

$m_{jb}^3 - m_{jb}^2/m_{jb}$: share of internal propagation of the Non-EB sectors in the total multiplier;

$m_{jb} - m_{jb}^3/m_{jb}$: share of external propagation of the Non-EB sectors in the total multiplier.

8.3.3 Econometric Model

We estimate an econometric model to assess the relationship between intersectoral and interregional linkages and the short-term growth of Colombian departments. The estimated equation takes the following form:

$$y_i = \mathbf{X}_i \beta + \mathbf{Z}_i \gamma + u_i. \tag{8.10}$$

The dependent variable, y_i, is the gross regional product (GRP) growth in department i between 2015 and 2020.[4] We seek to explain this as a function of the economic-base output multiplier and Miyazawa multipliers, $\mathbf{X}_i$. Equation (8.10) further includes a control matrix of additional regional characteristics, $\mathbf{Z}_i$ (including a constant term), and the error term, u_i.

The GRP at constant prices from the National Account database provided by the DANE (2021) is used to calculate the GRP growth by department between 2015 and 2020.

The explanatory variables, $\mathbf{X}_i$, include the economic-base output multiplier and their decomposition into intraregional and interregional effects (Sect. 8.3.1). The variables set also consists of the Miyazawa multipliers (Sect. 8.3.2), i.e., direct, indirect, internal, and external multipliers. All these variables are derived from the IIOM-COL for the year 2015.

The intraregional component of the economic-base output multiplier reflects the regional absorption capacity of the demand generated by the economic base. The intraregional (Non-EB) component of the economic-base output multiplier and the effects induced by the internal and external propagation of the economic base on the Non-EB sectors measure the integration of the economic base with the rest of the local economy. These variables are indicators of sectoral diversity and productive complementarity. Industrial diversification occurs in regions with highly complementary sectors and can drive higher regional growth rates (Yeung, 2021).

---

[4] Additionally, to examine the relationship between long-run growth volatility and the economic-base output multiplier and Miyazawa multipliers, we estimate a set of models using the coefficient of variation of the annual GRP growth rate in 2005–2020 as the dependent variable.

The matrix Z_i comprises a set of variables that have been identified as determinants of the GRP growth and that are important to incorporate as additional controls. First, we control for a measure of the share of the mining of coal and the extraction of crude petroleum in GRP. Colombian exports have a natural resource-intensive pattern, concentrated in mineral commodities. The export concentration on a few commodities generated externally-induced vulnerability of the Colombian economy during the 2010s because of the strong oscillation in World commodity prices (Melo-Becerra et al., 2020). The coal sector concentrates 39.9% of the value-added in La Guajira. This department lost about a quarter of its GRP between 2015 and 2020–COP 8.665 billion in 2015 to COP 6.471 billion in 2020 (DANE, 2021). Meanwhile, the crude petroleum sector concentrated 40.5% of the value-added in Putumayo, which lost about a fifth of its GRP between 2015 and 2020–COP 3.481 billion in 2015 to COP 2.821 billion in 2020 (DANE, 2021). The share of the coal and extraction of crude petroleum sectors in value-added is derived from the IIOM-COP for 2015.

Additionally, we experiment with specifications that include the economic-base share in regional value-added. We also verify whether interregional transfers from Colombia's Central National Government (CNG) are positively associated with local growth. The subnational transfers from CNG are used to reduce regional disparities in the context of fiscal decentralization (Bonet et al., 2016).[5] The interregional transfers database comes from the Budget Execution Reports of the National Planning Department (DNP) of Colombia for 2012. Thus, we use a dummy variable for the interregional transfer's share in value added greater than the national average that includes the departments of Caquetá, Cauca, Córdoba, Chocó, Nariño, Sucre, Amazonas, Guainía, Guaviare, Vaupés, and Vichada.

Table 8.1 shows the statistical summary of the econometric model variables. Table 8.2 presents the simple partial correlation between the variables. Growth in GRP in 2015–2020 is negatively correlated with the economic base share. The components of the economic-base output multiplier and Miyazawa multiplier are not correlated with the share of the economic base in regional value-added.

8.4 Economic Base of the Colombian Departments

We use the IIOM-COL to classify the 54 industries into economic base sectors (EB) and non-economic base sectors (Non-EB) in each Colombian department. The regional specialization, called the economic base, comprises sectors that simultaneously meet three criteria:

i. Sectors that are relatively more concentrated regionally (location quotient greater than one);
ii. Sectors with a production share greater than the value expected if all 54 industries had the same size in each department (share in the sectorial production greater than 1.85%, i.e., 1/54);

---
[5] Chapter 16 of this book assesses the impact of interregional transfers in the Colombian economy.

Table 8.1 Summary statistics

Variable	Obs	Mean	Std. Dev	Min	Max
GRP growth between 2015 and 2020	33	0.989	0.072	0.747	1.062
Economic-base output multiplier	33	1.701	0.139	1.470	2.047
Output multiplier: intraregional (EB)	33	0.164	0.081	0.046	0.358
Output multiplier: intraregional (Non-EB)	33	0.183	0.054	0.101	0.367
Output multiplier: interregional	33	0.652	0.113	0.275	0.819
Miyazawa multiplier: direct effect	33	0.757	0.056	0.663	0.876
Miyazawa multiplier: indirect effect	33	0.079	0.033	0.027	0.149
Miyazawa multiplier: internal effect	33	0.158	0.034	0.086	0.213
Miyazawa multiplier: external effect	33	0.005	0.004	0.001	0.020
Mining of coal (% in value-added)	33	0.023	0.089	0.000	0.400
Extraction of crude petroleum (% in value added)	33	0.066	0.151	0.000	0.553
Economic-base share in value-added	33	0.419	0.150	0.216	0.692
Interregional transfers share in value-added	33	0.333	0.479	0.000	1.000

iii. Export-oriented sectors—measure the importance of the inter-regional and foreign exports: (a) tradable sectors (agriculture, mining, and manufacturing) with over 50% of sales from outside the region; (b) non-tradable sectors (services) with over 25% of sales for outside the region. The shares for tradable and non-tradable sectors are defined from the F Factors used to estimate the sectoral trade matrices of the IIOAS method (see the SHIN Tables estimation procedures in Chap. 5 of this book), in which the non-tradable sectors are essentially aimed at local consumption.

Colombia has six natural regions: Amazonía, Andina, Caribe, Insular, La Orinoquía, and Pacífico. The departments of the Amazonía and La Orinoquía regions have fewer sectors associated with the economic base when compared to the other areas, emphasizing the departments of Meta and Vaupés (Table 8.3). These regions have less sectoral diversification and a production specialization mainly associated with natural resource-intensive commodities. Amazonía and La Orinoquía are also relatively isolated geographically compared to other Colombian regions. The economic base comprises more sectors in departments with better infrastructure and sectorial diversity, such as Atlántico, Córdoba, Cauca, and Valle del Cauca.

The Caribe region is strategic geographically because the main ports in Colombia are found therein. This region has eight departments: Atlántico, Bolívar, Cesar, Córdoba, La Guajira, Magdalena, and Sucre. The economic base of this region, with great sectoral diversity, is mainly associated with agriculture, livestock, the food industry, and the manufacture of other non-metallic mineral products and services. In the Bolívar department, similar to San Andres in the Insular region, services related to tourism are also highlighted, such as land and air transport, accommodation, and food service activities.

Table 8.2 Correlations matrix

		(1)	(2)	(3)	(4)	(5)	(6)	(7)	(8)	(9)	(10)	(11)	(12)	(13)
(1)	GRP growth between 2015 and 2020	1												
(2)	Economic-base output multipliers	0.363	1											
(3)	Output multipliers: intraregional (EB)	0.334	0.041	1										
(4)	Output multipliers: intraregional (Non-EB)	0.339	−0.090	0.382	1									
(5)	Output multipliers: interregional	−0.401	0.014	−0.897	−0.751	1								
(6)	Miyazawa multiplier: direct effect	−0.249	−0.425	−0.746	−0.371	0.710	1							
(7)	Miyazawa multiplier: indirect effect	0.057	0.128	0.751	0.127	−0.597	−0.802	1						
(8)	Miyazawa multiplier: internal effect	0.310	0.566	0.438	0.403	−0.505	−0.813	0.309	1					
(9)	Miyazawa multiplier: external effect	0.389	0.139	0.558	0.709	−0.738	−0.548	0.384	0.410	1				
(10)	Mining of coal (% in value-added)	−0.530	−0.321	−0.230	−0.049	0.188	0.007	0.164	−0.153	−0.151	1			
(11)	Extraction of crude petroleum (% in value added)	−0.430	−0.063	−0.182	−0.216	0.233	0.137	−0.134	−0.068	−0.230	−0.067	1		
(12)	Economic-base share in value-added	−0.558	−0.609	−0.136	−0.174	0.180	0.325	−0.136	−0.378	−0.237	0.157	0.490	1	
(13)	Interregional transfers share in value-added	0.151	−0.354	−0.106	−0.240	0.190	0.519	−0.326	−0.504	−0.335	−0.189	−0.309	0.121	1

Table 8.3 Sectors of the economic base, by Colombian department

Natural regions	Department	Sectors of the economic base
Andina	Antioquia	S10; S13; S19; S24; S26; S27; S33; S49
Caribe	Atlántico	S10, S11; S18; S23; S24; S26; S33; S40; S45; S52
Andina	Bogotá D.C	S24; S38; S46; S47; S48; S53
Caribe	Bolívar	S23; S26; S40; S45; S52
Andina	Boyacá	S1; S3; S7; S26; S27; S32; S33; S40
Andina	Caldas	S1; S2; S10; S14; S26; S33; S45
Amazonía	Caquetá	S1; S3; S45; S50
Pacífica	Cauca	S1; S2; S3; S15; S24; S26; S45; S49; S51; S52
Caribe	Cesar	S1; S3; S6; S45; S52
Caribe	Córdoba	S1; S3; S10; S12; S13; S33; S45; S51; S52
Andina	Cundinamarca	S1; S3; S10; S18; S19; S26; S33
Pacífica	Chocó	S1; S3; S4; S8; S45; S51
Andina	Huila	S1; S2; S3; S7; S33; S40
Caribe	La Guajira	S3; S6; S33; S45
Caribe	Magdalena	S1; S3; S11; S45; S51; S52
La Orinoquía	Meta	S1; S7
Pacífica	Nariño	S1; S3; S8; S45
Andina	Norte de Santander	S1; S23; S40; S45; S53
Andina	Quindío	S1; S2; S3; S14; S45
Andina	Risaralda	S10; S13; S18; S29; S45; S49
Andina	Santander	S1; S3; S19; S23; S26; S27; S40
Caribe	Sucre	S1; S3; S26; S43; S45; S52
Andina	Tolima	S1; S2; S3; S10; S13; S26; S45
Pacífica	Valle del Cauca	S10; S13; S15; S22; S24; S27; S40; S48; S49
La Orinoquía	Arauca	S1; S3; S7; S10; S45; S50
La Orinoquía	Casanare	S1; S3; S7; S42
Amazonía	Putumayo	S7; S45; S51; S52
Insular	San Andrés	S38; S42; S45; S50
Amazonía	Amazonas	S4; S5; S38; S42; S45; S51
Amazonía	Guainía	S5; S8; S45; S51; S52
Amazonía	Guaviare	S1; S3; S45; S50
Amazonía	Vaupés	S42; S45; S51
La Orinoquía	Vichada	S1; S3; S4; S45; S51; S52

Note Description of sectors in Chap. 5 of this book

Arauca, Casanare, Meta, and Vichada, located in La Orinoquía, have an economic base formed mainly by natural-intensive resource activities, such as agriculture, livestock, forestry, logging, and the extraction of crude petroleum. The Amazonía region, formed by Caquetá, Putumayo, Amazonas, Guainía, Guaviare, and Vaupés, is located in the southeast of the Colombian territory. The region's economic base is mainly related to agriculture, livestock, forestry, logging, and fishing. Some service sectors, such as accommodation and food service activities, education, health, and social work activities, also constitute the economic base of this region.

The Colombian capital, in the Andina region, Bogotá D.C, concentrated 25.7% of the GDP in 2015 (DANE, 2021). Bogotá D.C has an economic base formed by service sectors characteristic of large urban centers, such as commerce, communication services, financial activities, real estate activities, and entertainment activities, besides the chemical industry. The Department of Antioquia, the second largest in Colombia's GDP share (14.3%), has eight sectors classified as an economic base (preservation of meat and fish, processing of grain mill products, manufacture of textile, chemicals, non-metallic mineral, and metal products, electricity, and business services).

Valle del Cauca, where the municipality of Cali is located, contributes 9.7% of the GDP and stands out for its sectorial diversity. The department has nine sectors classified as part of its economic base. These sectors are associated with processing grain mill products and sugar, paper products, chemicals, and metals, besides the service sectors.

Santander contributes 6.5% of the GDP and has in its economic base sectors associated with agriculture, livestock, textiles, refined petroleum products, metal products, and land transport. At Cundinamarca, which accounts for 6.0% of the GDP, the economic base includes manufacturing sectors such as meat processing, beverages, textiles, non-metallic minerals, and electric power generation.

Figure 8.1 shows the share of the economic base in gross output by department. The economic base in the departments of San Andrés, Arauca, Putumayo, Amazonas, Meta, Casanare, Chocó, and La Guajira contributes with more than half of the departmental production.

The relative importance of the economic base within each department suggests a measure of the regional dependence on these sectors. This aspect of the productive structure motivates us to investigate whether these sectors can contribute to more significant local growth. From this perspective, the following section assesses the productive regional specialization, called the economic base, through intersectoral and inter-regional linkages.

8.5 Results

Table 8.4 presents the employment created by EB inside the region (in EB and Non-EB sectors) and outside the region. San Andrés (55.7%) and Amazonas (52.1%) have most of the local employment focused on activities of the economic base. Casanare

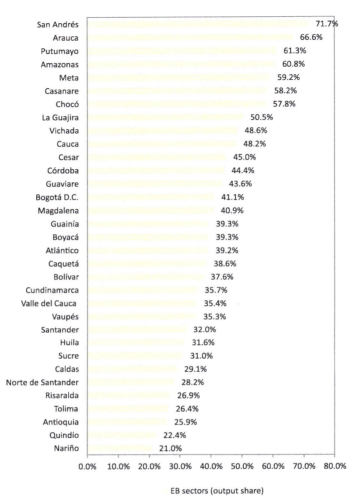

Fig. 8.1 Economic base share in the gross output, by Colombia department

(2.5%), Arauca (13.3%), Meta (15.3%), and Putumayo (17.8%) generate fewer jobs concentrated locally; that is, the economic base of these departments has a low capacity to generate additional employment inside the region.

Table 8.5 shows the composition of jobs associated with the EB compared to the overall labor composition in the region. Employment is classified by skill, income, social security, and gender. Arauca, Casanare, and Putumayo-the weaker generators of local employment-have an economic base composed of jobs in non-labor intensity and non-high-income sectors. However, these departments have jobs with composition mainly based on median-high-skill, formal employment, and male-biased.

Table 8.4 Impact of the economic base on employment generation

Department	Employment	Impact of the economic base			EB sectors (inside the region)/Total employment
		Inside the region		Outside the region	Total	
		EB sectors	Non-EB sectors			
Antioquia	2,762,614	221,423	92,395	213,489	527,307	11.4%
Atlántico	1,153,283	251,242	68,101	134,118	453,461	27.7%
Bogotá D.C	4,199,281	846,310	210,686	111,758	1,168,754	25.2%
Bolívar	918,757	162,234	34,397	41,078	237,709	21.4%
Boyacá	673,203	92,321	9909	17,467	119,698	15.2%
Caldas	443,516	71,128	15,750	116,542	203,421	19.6%
Caquetá	227,544	50,909	8721	12,390	72,020	26.2%
Cauca	606,765	190,204	17,426	45,215	252,846	34.2%
Cesar	439,133	100,534	28,856	40,754	170,143	29.5%
Córdoba	695,086	219,183	36,882	52,731	308,796	36.8%
Cundinamarca	1,148,159	173,444	36,611	148,736	358,790	18.3%
Chocó	211,834	55,849	6303	9854	72,005	29.3%
Huila	499,509	55,141	8451	12,556	76,148	12.7%
La Guajira	409,451	47,708	28,903	35,159	111,771	18.7%
Magdalena	494,311	151,660	26,183	36,700	214,543	36.0%
Meta	424,726	25,026	32,898	105,240	163,164	13.6%
Nariño	885,960	172,706	15,724	16,788	205,218	21.3%
Norte de Santander	637,970	111,281	20,134	21,851	153,265	20.6%
Quindío	346,300	64,580	6876	20,688	92,144	20.6%
Risaralda	502,487	63,524	39,472	125,285	228,281	20.5%
Santander	1,155,374	132,674	19,035	54,415	206,124	13.1%
Sucre	362,360	91,311	10,292	14,493	116,096	28.0%
Tolima	683,732	133,111	15,976	37,321	186,408	21.8%
Valle del Cauca	2,132,169	179,258	86,085	164,854	430,197	12.4%
Arauca	29,031	5120	4081	29,301	38,502	31.7%
Casanare	64,048	1536	7357	52,117	61,010	13.9%
Putumayo	14,708	3207	1629	13,178	18,014	32.9%
San Andrés	28,584	12,611	3318	7338	23,267	55.7%
Amazonas	11,535	5245	765	2424	8434	52.1%
Guainía	4616	929	328	1107	2365	27.2%
Guaviare	20,771	4931	1492	2382	8805	30.9%
Vaupés	5209	903	229	734	1866	21.7%
Vichada	5842	1423	362	1080	2866	30.6%

(continued)

Table 8.4 (continued)

Department	Employment	Impact of the economic base				EB sectors (inside the region)/Total employment
		Inside the region		Outside the region	Total	
		EB sectors	Non-EB sectors			
Colombia	22,197,869	3,698,665	895,626	1,699,143	6,293,434	–

8.5.1 Interregional Multiplier Effects of the Economic Base

This section presents the economic-base output multiplier derived from the IIOM-COL. We first look at the output multipliers in the Colombian departments (Fig. 8.2). The output multiplier for each department is the ratio of the total effects generated in the Colombian economy by the departmental economic base to the economic base itself. We decompose this multiplier between the intraregional effects-for the sectors of the economic base (EB) and the other sectors of the local economy (Non-EB)-and the interregional effect. Figure 8.3 shows the geographic distribution of the output multiplier.

The composition of the economic base, and consequently the trade linkages of the sectors included in the economic base, determines the value of the output multiplier of each department. For instance, Bogotá D.C, specializing in service sectors that, on average, have a smaller output multiplier in the Colombian input–output system, has a smaller economic-base output multiplier. On the other hand, Risaralda and Caldas, specializing in the agriculture and manufacturing sectors, have larger economic-base output multipliers (Figs. 8.2 and 8.3).

The departmental economic base generates trade flows within or outside their origin region through the supply chain. Thus, we decompose the output multiplier which reveals the structural interdependence in the supply chain related to the economic base (Fig. 8.4). The intraregional component measures the integration of the EB sector into the rest of the local economy. Meanwhile, the economic-base output multiplier's interregional component measures the production leaks outside the region.

The results in Fig. 8.4 allow us to assess productive leakages from the economic base, i.e., the inability of local economies to internalize the multiplier effects of their respective economic bases. The intraregional (Non-EB) component of the economic-base output multipliers reflects the capacity of the economic base to domestically integrate its productive structure with the rest of the local economy. For instance, the economic base of Bogotá D.C (36.7%) and Valle del Cauca (30.6%) are the most integrated with the other local sectors. Although Risaralda and Caldas have the biggest multipliers, most of their economic effects, 74.7% and 70.9%, respectively, are absorbed by other departments (Fig. 8.4). Thereby, the supply chain of the

Table 8.5 Relative employment-use intensity of economic base from Colombian departments

Department	Employment				
	Total	Skill	Income	Social security	Gender
Antioquia		Median-high-skill		Formal	Male-biased
Atlántico	Labor intensive	Median-high-skill	High-income		Male-biased
Bogotá D.C		Median-high-skill		Formal	
Bolívar	Labor intensive	Median-high-skill	High-income		
Boyacá	Labor intensive		High-income		
Caldas	Labor intensive				Male-biased
Caquetá	Labor intensive				Male-biased
Cauca	Labor intensive				
Cesar		Median-high-skill			
Córdoba	Labor intensive		High-income		Male-biased
Cundinamarca				Formal	
Chocó	Labor intensive		High-income		
Huila	Labor intensive				Male-biased
La Guajira			High-income		Male-biased
Magdalena	Labor intensive	Median-high-skill			Male-biased
Meta		Median-high-skill		Formal	
Nariño	Labor intensive		High-income		Male-biased
Norte de Santander	Labor intensive		High-income		
Quindío	Labor intensive		High-income		Male-biased
Risaralda	Labor intensive				Male-biased
Santander			High-income		Male-biased
Sucre	Labor intensive				Male-biased

(continued)

Table 8.5 (continued)

Department	Employment				
	Total	Skill	Income	Social security	Gender
Tolima	Labor intensive		High-income		Male-biased
Valle del Cauca		Median-high-skill		Formal	
Arauca		Median-high-skill		Formal	Male-biased
Casanare		Median-high-skill		Formal	Male-biased
Putumayo		Median-high-skill		Formal	Male-biased
San Andrés		Median-high-skill		Formal	Male-biased
Amazonas		Median-high-skill	High-income	Formal	Male-biased
Guainía		Median-high-skill		Formal	
Guaviare	Labor intensive	Median-high-skill		Formal	
Vaupés		Median-high-skill		Formal	Male-biased
Vichada		Median-high-skill		Formal	Male-biased

economic base of these departments is located outside the region, implying productive leakages to other regions of Colombia.[6]

We establish a regional typology to account for geographical differences among the Colombian departments. Thus, we classify the regions above or below the average value of the economic-base output multiplier (1.68) and the Non-EB intraregional component of the output multiplier (19.9%). Figures 8.5 and 8.6 show the departments classified into four groups: (1) small economic base multipliers, but highly connected with Non-EB in the region, (2) large economic base multipliers and highly connected with Non-EB in the region, (3) large economic base multipliers, but weakly connected with Non-EB in the region, (4) small economic base multipliers and weakly connected with Non-EB in the region.

In summary, the departments in the natural regions of Amazonía and La Orinoquía are relatively isolated geographically, specialized in natural-intensive resources activities, and target production for interregional and foreign exports. On the other hand, departments with less dependence on the economic base, such as Bogotá D.C, Córdoba, Antioquia, Valle del Cauca, Bolívar, and Atlántico, showed greater sectoral diversity and greater capacity to integrate the economic base with the rest of the local economy.

We can draw some remarks about sectoral and regional interdependence in Colombia's departments: (i) Sectoral composition of the economic base is related to the regional ability to internalize the economic base multiplier effects; (ii) departments with less sectoral diversification and larger economic base share in gross output

---

[6] Chapter 9 of this book deepens the discussion on the characteristics of the Colombian interregional system through intersectoral and interregional linkages.

Department	Intraregional (EB)	Intraregional (Non-EB)	Interregional	Total
Bogotá D.C.	1.17	0.17	0.13	1.47
Vichada	1.11	0.09	0.31	1.51
Cesar	1.05	0.12	0.34	1.51
La Guajira	1.04	0.07	0.42	1.54
Chocó	1.04	0.05	0.44	1.54
Guainía	1.08	0.09	0.41	1.59
Vaupés	1.03	0.08	0.48	1.60
Magdalena	1.12	0.13	0.37	1.61
Valle del Cauca	1.11	0.19	0.31	1.61
Guaviare	1.03	0.11	0.48	1.62
Amazonas	1.13	0.10	0.40	1.63
Cauca	1.17	0.10	0.39	1.65
Nariño	1.05	0.13	0.47	1.66
Putumayo	1.09	0.10	0.47	1.66
Meta	1.10	0.10	0.47	1.67
Casanare	1.05	0.13	0.49	1.67
Caquetá	1.03	0.13	0.52	1.68
Boyacá	1.19	0.11	0.38	1.68
Huila	1.18	0.10	0.41	1.69
San Andrés	1.08	0.15	0.47	1.70
Arauca	1.07	0.08	0.55	1.70
Sucre	1.19	0.11	0.42	1.72
Tolima	1.11	0.15	0.48	1.74
Norte de Santander	1.12	0.13	0.50	1.74
Córdoba	1.22	0.16	0.38	1.75
Cundinamarca	1.12	0.14	0.51	1.77
Quindío	1.10	0.14	0.55	1.79
Bolívar	1.22	0.17	0.46	1.85
Atlántico	1.21	0.19	0.48	1.88
Santander	1.16	0.11	0.62	1.89
Antioquia	1.20	0.26	0.48	1.94
Risaralda	1.07	0.18	0.76	2.01
Caldas	1.15	0.15	0.74	2.05

Economic-Base Output Multipliers

Intraregional (EB) Intraregional (Non-EB) Interregional

Fig. 8.2 Economic-base output multipliers in the Colombian departments

have production specialization in activities that are less integrated with other sectors inside the region; (iii) departments with a highly connected economic base with Non-EB are less dependent on inputs from other regions and capable of domestically internalizing the supply chain required by the economic base. This pattern may suggest a better production integration between the sectors of these departments and greater sectoral diversity and complementarity. Our findings on the structural interdependence of the economic base are related to the discussion of the spatial pattern of interdependence among Colombian departments in Chaps. 7 and 9 of this book.

Typology 4 concentrates most of the departments, only 16.1% of the population and 15.1% of the Colombian GDP (Table 8.6). The departments classified in this typology, in general, also have the highest economic base share in the regional

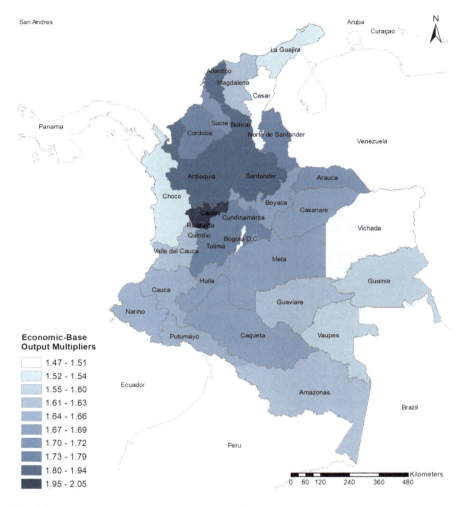

Fig. 8.3 Economic-base output multiplier in the Colombian departments

gross output. An issue closely related to these regional typologies is how to design regional development strategies considering regional production specialization and the patterns of intersectoral and interregional linkages.

Miyazawa's analysis in the next section explores the connection between the economic base sectors and the other sectors inside the region. In this way, we hope to understand better the role of the regional production specialization and trade linkages through the intra-regional (Non-EB) component of the economic base output multiplier.

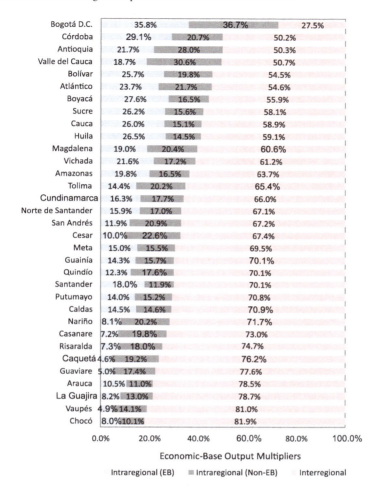

Fig. 8.4 Decomposition of the output multiplier of the Colombian departmental economic bases

8.5.2 Miyazawa's Analysis

Miyazawa's analysis measures the interdependency between the economic base sectors and the other sectors in the local economy. The usual Leontief inverse reveals only the ultimate total effects but not the separate partial multiplier effects (Miyazawa, 1978). After we identify the coefficients of the induced effect on production, we can break down the original Leontief inverse in terms of the combined effects of internal and external multipliers and their induced multipliers. The share of internal propagation reveals the induced effects on output or input activities between Non-EB and EB sectors and is called the production-generating process in succession. The aspects of the interaction process in the induced effects naturally lead to another intersectoral

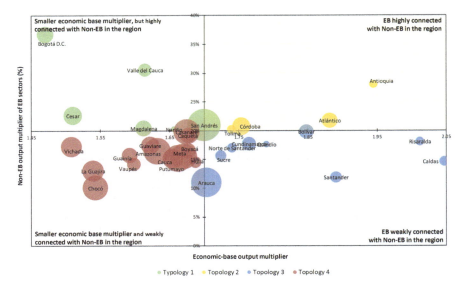

Fig. 8.5 Regional typology based on intersectoral linkages. *Note*: The department circle is proportional to the economic base share in the regional gross output (see Fig. 8.1)

multiplier that we could call the external multipliers of the Non-EB and EB sectors. These induced effects elucidate some inherent properties of the interaction between the Non-EB and EB sectors.

Figures 8.7 and 8.8 summarize the Miyazawa multipliers indicating the interaction between EB and Non-EB sectors. The results show the share of direct and indirect requirements in the total multiplier, besides the shares of internal and external propagation of Non-EB sectors in EB sectors' output multipliers.

We are especially emphasizing the internal propagation in EB sectors in our discussion. By examining Fig. 8.7, we can see which department's EB-producing sector generates more Non-EB activity. Among the results, the values for Bolívar, Atlántico, Tolima, Antioquia, Caldas, Santander, and Córdoba are distinctly high-it ranges about 19.0% ~ 21.3%. Thus, the capacity of the EB sectors to induce Non-EB sectors is most significant in these departments. The effects of internal propagation on the Non-EB sectors show the share of multiplier starting from Non-EB-input used in the Non-EB activities induced by final demand in EB sectors.

Such internal propagation in the Non-EB sectors leads to external (or circular) repercussions on the Non-EB sectors themselves through the EB-producing activities that start with the consumption of EB in the Non-EB sectors. Among the round-about external effects, the departments of Valle del Cauca, Bogotá D.C, Antioquia, and Atlántico have the highest values for all Colombian regions-it ranges about 1.1% ~ 2.0%. Thus, the internal propagation patterns and the external repercussion patterns depict the characteristic of intersectoral propagation in the Non-EB sectors. In a smart specialization strategy, as highlighted by Boschma (2017), Yeung (2021) and

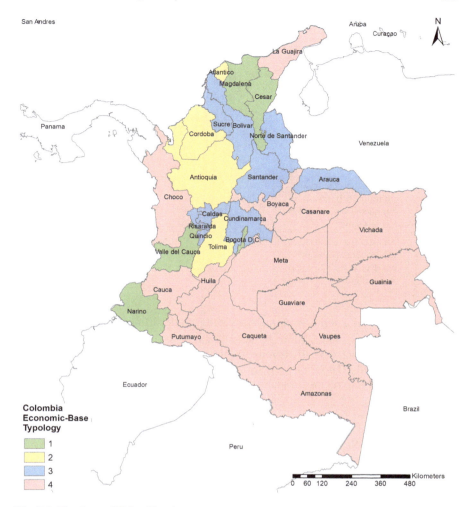

Fig. 8.6 Typology of Colombian departments

Balland and Boschma (2021), the EB and Non-EB linkages can be crucial drivers of diversification and regional growth.

The Miyazawa decomposition offers the possibility to view each of the components of the interdependency between EB and Non-EB sectors in turn and to build a more valuable and accurate picture of the economic interactions. Variations in the shares of direct and indirect inputs requirements, and internal and external propagation in the Non-EB sectors play an important role in determining the economic-base output multiplier. These findings would not have been revealed through a more classical approach of identification of the economic base.

Table 8.6 Characteristics of the regional typologies

Typology		Number of departments	Population (%)	GRP (%)
1	Small economic base multipliers, but highly connected with Non-EB in the region	6	34.5	40.0
2	Large economic base multipliers and highly connected with Non-EB in the region	4	25.0	22.7
3	Large economic base multipliers, but weakly connected with Non-EB in the region	9	24.4	22.2
4	Small economic base multipliers and weakly connected with Non-EB in the region	14	16.1	15.1

The internal and external multipliers reflect each department's sectoral diversity and complementarity. Thus, higher induced effects indicate a denser local production chain and greater capacity of regions to internalize the economic base multiplier effects domestically. The following section investigates the potential effects of the intersectoral and interregional linkages on local growth.

8.5.3 Results of the Econometric Model

Table 8.7 shows the association between intersectoral and interregional linkages and short-term local growth in Colombian departments. The economic-base output multiplier positively affects local growth, but only its intraregional component. The positive and statistically significant coefficient for the intraregional (Non–EB) component of the output multiplier suggests that the departments that manage to integrate the regional economic base (EB) with the rest of the local economy have more significant economic growth in the period (column 3). On the other hand, the interregional component of the output multiplier (column 4) and the direct input requirements (column 5) have a negative and statistically significant effect on local growth. The positive and statistically significant effect of the intersectoral propagation in the Non-EB sectors is identified through the internal propagation (column 7) and external repercussion (column 8) of the Miyazawa multipliers. Additionally, we include the shares of the coal sector and the extraction of the crude petroleum sector in value-added as control variables. The negative effect of mineral commodities on local growth is evident in all estimated models (columns 1–8). It is worth noting that the

8 Economic Base and Regional Specialization in Colombia: A Note …   227

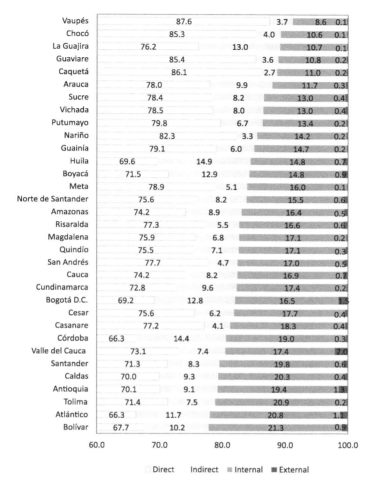

Fig. 8.7 Shares of direct, indirect, internal and external effects in the economic-base output multipliers (in %)

impact of these sectors comes much more indirectly from receipts of foreign currency rather than interindustry effects. Chaps. 4 and 17 have highlighted the enclave nature of these sectors.

In Table 8.8, we repeat the exercise from Table 8.7 using our second set of control variables. This alternative specification reassuringly corroborates our earlier findings on how trade linkages influence local growth outcomes. The economic-base share in value-added is negative and significantly different from zero at the 1% level except in one specification (column 1). We consistently find a positive and significant effect of interregional transfers on local growth. The remaining coefficients are consistent with the results from Table 8.7, although with a change in the level of statistical

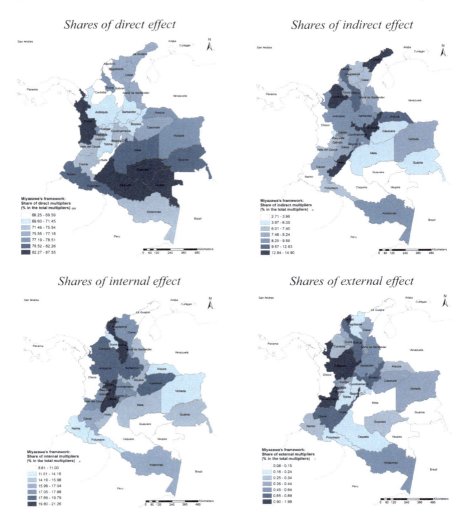

Fig. 8.8 Spatial patterns of the direct, indirect, internal and external effects in the economic-base output multipliers

significance of the economic-base output multipliers, intraregional (EB) component, and internal effect (columns 1, 2, 7).

Finally, Table 8.9 shows the association between intersectoral and interregional linkages, and long-term growth volatility in Colombian departments. This analysis indicates that the stronger and highly connected local activities tend to smooth growth volatility, working as a buffer for external shocks. We find a negative correlation between the EB and Non-EB intraregional components of the EB output multipliers with the GRP growth volatility in 2005–2025. Moreover, we identify the benefits of

Table 8.7 Results of regression I

	Dependent variable: GRP growth between 2015 and 2020							
	(1)	(2)	(3)	(4)	(5)	(6)	(7)	(8)
Economic–base output multipliers	0.089*							
	(0.050)							
Output multipliers: intraregional (EB)		0.118						
		(0.083)						
Output multipliers: intraregional (Non–EB)			0.295**					
			(0.138)					
Output multipliers: interregional				−0.131**				
				(0.061)				
Miyazawa multiplier: direct effect					−0.237*			
					(0.120)			
Miyazawa multiplier: indirect effect						0.197		
						(0.286)		
Miyazawa multiplier: internal effect							0.424*	
							(0.242)	
Miyazawa multiplier: external effect								3.554***
								(1.162)
Mining of coal (% in value added)	−0.409**	−0.429**	−0.443***	−0.421**	−0.452**	−0.466**	−0.429***	−0.426**
	(0.182)	(0.175)	(0.147)	(0.163)	(0.172)	(0.187)	(0.148)	(0.165)
Extraction of crude petroleum (% in value added)	−0.216***	−0.210***	−0.199**	−0.198**	−0.211***	−0.217***	−0.215***	−0.198**
	(0.073)	(0.075)	(0.074)	(0.075)	(0.071)	(0.075)	(0.072)	(0.072)

(continued)

Table 8.7 (continued)

	Dependent variable: GRP growth between 2015 and 2020							
	(1)	(2)	(3)	(4)	(5)	(6)	(7)	(8)
Constant	0.860***	0.993***	0.958***	1.097***	1.192***	0.998***	0.946***	0.993***
	(0.091)	(0.020)	(0.029)	(0.036)	(0.087)	(0.027)	(0.041)	(0.013)
Observations	33	33	33	33	33	33	33	33
R–squared	0.525	0.514	0.545	0.537	0.532	0.506	0.536	0.541

Note Robust standard errors in parentheses. *** $p < 0.01$, ** $p < 0.05$, * $p < 0.1$

Table 8.8 Results of regression II

	Dependent variable: GRP growth between 2015 and 2020							
	(1)	(2)	(3)	(4)	(5)	(6)	(7)	(8)
Economic–base output multipliers	0.080							
	(0.120)							
Output multipliers: intraregional (EB)		0.256**						
		(0.105)						
Output multipliers: intraregional (Non–EB)			0.423**					
			(0.181)					
Output multipliers: interregional				−0.230**				
				(0.085)				
Miyazawa multiplier: direct effect					−0.349**			
					(0.147)			
Miyazawa multiplier: indirect effect						0.136		
						(0.392)		
Miyazawa multiplier: internal effect							0.679	
							(0.484)	
Miyazawa multiplier: external effect								6.411***
								(2.122)
Economic–base share in value added	−0.244**	−0.269***	−0.265***	−0.259***	−0.254***	−0.284***	−0.239***	−0.251***
	(0.092)	(0.073)	(0.076)	(0.073)	(0.070)	(0.081)	(0.062)	(0.069)
Interregional transfers share in value added	0.043	0.040*	0.047*	0.046**	0.056**	0.040**	0.058*	0.054**
	(0.026)	(0.020)	(0.024)	(0.022)	(0.025)	(0.018)	(0.033)	(0.023)

(continued)

Table 8.8 (continued)

	Dependent variable: GRP growth between 2015 and 2020							
	(1)	(2)	(3)	(4)	(5)	(6)	(7)	(8)
Constant	0.940***	1.046***	1.006***	1.232***	1.340***	1.083***	0.962***	1.043***
	(0.239)	(0.026)	(0.032)	(0.064)	(0.111)	(0.049)	(0.087)	(0.027)
Observations	33	33	33	33	33	33	33	33
R-squared	0.383	0.450	0.463	0.492	0.419	0.373	0.435	0.497

Note Robust standard errors in parentheses. *** $p < 0.01$, ** $p < 0.05$, * $p < 0.1$

a locally, relatively more integrated economic base by showing negative and statistically significant coefficients for the internal propagation (column 7) and external repercussion (column 8) of the Miyazawa multipliers.

Tables 8.7, 8.8 and 8.9 suggest that the regional specialization, measured through the economic base sectors, can contribute to smoother, higher local growth, especially if these sectors are integrated with other industries inside the region. Thereby, assessing trade linkages, besides local capabilities, is critical to understanding regional performance differences. Our results reinforce previous evidence (e.g., Frenken et al., 2007; Yeung, 2021) that show that sectoral diversification, in our case measured by intersectoral linkages, is an essential factor to explain regional growth.

These results may prompt important questions. For instance, policymakers in regions such as Risaralda and Caldas-with the largest economic-base output multipliers, but most of their economic effects absorbed by other departments-may be interested in knowing how to internalize the supply chain of its economic base inside the region. However, some productive leakages are not likely to be internalized in the local production structure. The region's potential to integrate the economic base (EB) with the local production chain is related to the specificities of each industry and regional economic potential. The departments require an absorptive capacity to exploit and benefit from external knowledge and create local production capacities (Boschma & Iammarino, 2009). In order to increase local growth, policymakers should look at local productive capacities and assess the potential for integrating sectors with the rest of the economy. Thereby, when choosing sectors to be prioritized, it is perhaps more relevant for policymakers to know which industries are more integrated into the local productive structure (or likely to be integrated domestically). However, it is worth highlighting that the local and non-local trade linkages also are drivers of diversification and can encourage the emergence of activities related to local specialization (Yeung, 2021). Therefore, in the context of smart specialization strategy, if a region is generating significant spillovers, policymakers must take into account the trade-off between domestically internalizing the supply chain of the economic base, in a regional import substitution strategy, and promoting the interregional linkages.

In summary, the regional development strategies encouraging productive specializations can contribute to local growth if the economic activities are integrated with the production structure inside the region. The policy targets should be the sectors with greater capacity to create a dense supply chain within the region. Our results, therefore, show that evaluating the structure of intersectoral linkages is essential for understanding the location of economic activity in space.

Table 8.9 Results of regression III

	Dependent variable: Long-term growth volatility (GRP growth between 2005 and 2020)							
	(1)	(2)	(3)	(4)	(5)	(6)	(7)	(8)
Economic–base output multipliers	−0.178**							
	(0.068)							
Output multipliers: intraregional (EB)		−0.320***						
		(0.116)						
Output multipliers: intraregional (Non–EB)			−0.522***					
			(0.173)					
Output multipliers: interregional				0.283***				
				(0.084)				
Miyazawa multiplier: direct effect					0.499**			
					(0.222)			
Miyazawa multiplier: indirect effect						−0.601		
						(0.402)		
Miyazawa multiplier: internal effect							−0.686*	
							(0.340)	
Miyazawa multiplier: external effect								−7.604***
								(2.584)
Constant	0.498***	0.248***	0.291***	0.011	−0.183	0.243***	0.304***	0.234***
	(0.125)	(0.029)	(0.041)	(0.047)	(0.160)	(0.039)	(0.061)	(0.024)
Observations	33	33	33	33	33	33	33	33
R-squared	0.096	0.104	0.125	0.160	0.122	0.061	0.083	0.171

Note Robust standard errors in parentheses. *** $p < 0.01$, ** $p < 0.05$, * $p < 0.1$

8.6 Final Considerations

Regions that are specialized in sectors that are highly integrated into the local production network have a stronger potential for economic growth. Based on the intersectoral and interregional linkages framework, our results reinforce the importance of specialization strategies for regional development policies.

The main findings of this chapter can be summarized as follows. The study has identified the sectors that make up the economic base for each Colombian department. Then, we have shown the relationship between the economic base and the local labor markets. We also propose a regional typology based on intersectoral linkages using the decomposition of the economic-base output multiplier. We calculate the internal and external multipliers of the Miyazawa analysis to evaluate the interdependency among the economic base sectors and the other sectors in the local economy.

We also use the multipliers of the interregional input–output model in an econometric model. We find a positive relationship between trade linkages and GRP growth, specifically, the intraregional (Non-EB) component of the economic-base output multiplier and the internal and external propagation. Meanwhile, the economic-base output multiplier's interregional component is negatively associated with regional performance. This result suggests that the regional specialization, measured through the economic base sectors, can contribute to local growth, especially if these sectors are integrated with the rest of the local economy.

A final point refers to the role of industrial concentration. Our results reaffirm the tension in regional development policy between promoting a region's comparative advantage or diversifying the region's economy. In the former case, the region may be subject to cyclical demand, generating more significant EB multiplier effects and greater disruption whenever the EB industries expand or decline in importance. Nonetheless, in the latter case, the region may become more recession-proof so that expansion/recession periods generate less aggregate impact but gains in terms of stability.

References

Balland, P. A., & Boschma, R. (2021). Complementary interregional linkages and smart specialisation: An empirical study on European regions. *Regional Studies, 55*(6), 1059–1070.

Bonet, J., Pérez, G. J., & Ayala-García, J. (2016). Contexto Histórico y Evolución del SGP en Colombia. In: J. Bonet & L. A. Galvis-Aponte (Eds.), *Sistemas de Transferencias Subnacionales: Lecciones para una Reforma en Colombia.* Banco de la República.

Boschma, R. (2017). Relatedness as driver of regional diversification: A research agenda. *Regional Studies, 51*(3), 351–364.

Boschma, R., & Iammarino, S. (2009). Related variety, trade linkages, and regional growth in Italy. *Economic Geography, 85*(3), 289–311.

Camagni, R., & Capello, R. (2017). Regional innovation patterns and the EU regional policy reform: Towards smart innovation policies. In Seminal studies in regional and urban economics (pp. 313–343). Springer, Cham.

DANE. (2021). *Cuentas nacionales departamentales*. Producto Interno Bruto—PIB a precios constantes. Cuadro 2: Producto Interno Bruto por departamento, series encadenadas de volumen con año de referencia 2015, 2005–2020pr. Departamento Administrativo Nacional de Estadística. Actualizado el 25 de junio de 2021.

Foray, D. (2015). *Smart specialisation: Opportunities and challenges for regional innovation policy*. Routledge/Regional Studies Association.

Foray, D., David, P., & Hall, B. (2009). Smart specialisation: The concept. *Knowledge Economists Policy Brief, 9*, 1–5.

Frenken, K., Van Oort, F., & Verburg, T. (2007). Related variety, unrelated variety and regional economic growth. *Regional Studies, 41*(5), 685–697.

Fritz, O. M., Sonis, M., & Hewings, G. J. (1998). A Miyazawa analysis of interactions between polluting and non-polluting sectors. *Structural Change and Economic Dynamics, 9*(3), 289–305.

Haddad, E., Silva, V., Porsse, A., & Dentinho, T. (2015). Multipliers in an Island economy: The case of the Azores. In Batabyal, A., & Nijkamp, P. (Eds.), *The region and trade: New analytical directions*. World Scientific Publishing Company.

Hirschman, A. O. (1958). *The strategy of economic development*. Yale University Press.

Hirschman, A. O. (1984). A dissenter's confession: The strategy of economic development revisited. In G. M. Meier & D. Seers (Eds.), *Pioneers in development* (pp. 85–111). Published for The World Bank and Oxford University Press.

Mccann, P., & Argilés, R. O. (2015). Smart specialization, regional growth and applications to European union cohesion policy. *Regional Studies, 49*(8), 1291–1302.

Melo-Becerra, L. A., Parrado-Galvis, L. M., Ramos-Forero, J., & Zarate-Solano, H. M. (2020). Effects of booms and oil crisis on Colombian economy: A time-varying vector autoregressive approach. *Revista de Economía del Rosario, 23*(1), 31–63.

Miyazawa, K. (1966). Internal and external matrix multipliers in the input–output model. *Hitotsubashi Journal of Economics, 7*(1), 38–55.

Miyazawa, K. (1968). Input–output analysis and interrelational income multiplier is a matrix. *Hitotsubashi Journal of Economics, 8*(2), 39–58.

Miyazawa, K. (1971). An analysis of the interdependence between service and goods-producing sectors. *Hitotsubashi Journal of Economics, 12*(1), 10–21.

North, D. C. (1955). Location theory and regional economic growth. *Journal of Political Economy, 63*(3), 243–258.

Sonis, M., & Hewings, G. J. (1993). Hierarchies of Regional sub-structures and their multipliers within input–output systems: Miyazawa revisited. *Hitotsubashi Journal of Economics*, 33–44.

Tiebout, C. M. (1956). Exports and regional economic growth. *Journal of Political Economy, 64*(2), 160–164.

Yeung, H. W. C. (2021). Regional worlds: From related variety in regional diversification to strategic coupling in global production networks. *Regional Studies, 55*(6), 989–1010.

Inácio F. Araújo Doctor in Economics, Federal University of Juiz de Fora. Post-doctoral researcher, University of São Paulo, Brazil. Research fields: regional economics and input-output methods.

Alexandre L. Gomes Ph.D. (Econ.), Department of Economics, Federal University of São Carlos, Brazil. His research interests focus on applied economics, with an emphasis on computable general equilibrium and input-output models. His most recent work includes industrial interdependence, regional economics, and environmental economics.

Diana Ricciulli Ph.D. Student (Econ.), University of British Columbia. Professional researcher, Center for Regional Economic Studies, Banco de la República, Colombia. Research fields: political economy, economic history, and economic development.

Eduardo A. Haddad Full Professor at the Department of Economics at the University of São Paulo, Brazil, where he directs the Regional and Urban Economics Lab (NEREUS). Affiliate Professor at the Faculty of Governance, Economic and Social Sciences of the Mohammed VI University and Senior Fellow at the Policy Center for the New South, Rabat, Morocco. President of the Regional Science Association International, RSAI (2021–2022).

Chapter 9
Trade in Value-Added: Does MFN Status Matter for Colombian Regions?

Rodrigo Pacheco, Raphael P. Fernandes, Inácio F. Araújo, and Eduardo A. Haddad

9.1 Introduction

The role of interregional trade for the Colombian departments should not be relegated to a secondary place in the formulation of spatial development policies. For example, the research literature combining insights from economic geography and trade theory shows how trade may create spatial structures that are highly uneven (Venables, 2019). The domestic trade flows among regions of a country are a significant economic force and impact economic growth (Munroe et al., 2007). Interregional trade can boost income transfers through production linkages that benefit core regions. Analyzing the structural interdependence among Colombian departments, Perobelli et al. (2010)[1] show a center-periphery pattern in the spatial concentration that emerges from the influence of Bogotá D.C on the other regional economies due to the power of its purchases. Previous evidence has highlighted economic challenges resulting from this spatial concentration pattern (e.g., Galvis & Meisel, 2013).

The focus of this chapter is the dual pattern of trade in the Colombian economy (Haddad & Araújo, 2020). Colombia's golden manufacturing triangle (Bogotá-Medellín-Cali) is a hub of the local production chain supplying manufactured products and services to all departments. Meanwhile, producers of natural resource-intensive commodities (Arauca, Casanare, Cesar, Meta, and La Guajira departments) are mainly connected to the global supply chain. Economic impacts of domestic trade related to the 'golden triangle' are expected to differ from those of the export-oriented departments with natural resource-intensive products. Economic activity

---
[1] The analysis developed by Perobelli et al. (2010) is revisited in Chap. 5 of this book.

R. Pacheco · R. P. Fernandes · I. F. Araújo (✉) · E. A. Haddad
University of São Paulo, São Paulo, Brazil
e-mail: inacio.araujo@usp.br

E. A. Haddad
e-mail: ehaddad@usp.br

in Colombia is unevenly distributed across space, and this spatial distribution is shaped, among other factors, by trade. This dual pattern in foreign and domestic trade allows us to assess distinct spatial regimes associated with the geography of economic activity in Colombia. In this context, this chapter analyzes the extent of spatial interactions through intersectoral and interregional linkages to understand the implications of these interactions for the spatial distribution of economic activity across Colombian departments. This analysis follows the discussion about sectoral and spatial interdependence elaborate in Chaps. 7 and 8 of this book.

In this chapter, we examine the value-added embodied in domestic and foreign exports and, in doing so, measure the role of trade in generating value-added in the Colombian regions. To accomplish this task, we estimate measures of value-added trade for each flow between each origin–destination pair. The analysis provides evidence to answer two major issues: Who are the main trading partners for each Colombian department? What are the differences in international and interregional trade patterns between regions?

To estimate the trade in value-added, we employed a parsimonious approach proposed in Los et al. (2016) and adapted to an interregional context by Haddad et al., (2020, 2021), based on "hypothetical extraction" that serves as the study's methodological anchor. We used the Interregional Input–Output Table for Colombia in 2015 (see Chap. 3). The advantage of using an input–output model is the possibility of performing a systematic analysis of all linkages in the production chains. Furthermore, this analysis provides insights into properties associated with spatial interaction related to feedback effects and hierarchy (Sonis et al., 2002). Thus, our analysis contributes to a literature in which the relationship between geography and trade remains in an area where progress is needed to develop robust decision-making tools (Venables, 2019).

This chapter is organized as follows. Section 9.2 presents different dimensions of regional disparities in Colombia, given the country's export spatial patterns. Section 9.3 details the method and data used to measure international and interregional trade in value-added in Colombia. Section 9.4 presents our results, and a conclusion is provided in Sect. 9.5.

9.2 International and Domestic Trade in Colombia

9.2.1 Colombian Participation in International Trade

The United States accounts for 26% of Colombian exports, followed by Panama (7%), China (6.7%), and Spain (5%). Together, these countries represent nearly half of the country's export volume (Table 9.1). Figure 9.1 maps the relative importance of the countries in Colombian exports.

The Americas provide the primary destination for Colombian exports, especially the United States, Panama, Brazil, Mexico, Peru, Venezuela, and Ecuador. Asia has

Table 9.1 Colombian export destination: 2015

Country	Exports (COP billions)	Share (%)
United States	30,888	26.0
Panama	8332	7.0
China	7926	6.7
Spain	5368	4.5
Rest of the world	66,483	55.9
Total	118,997	100.0

Source Author elaboration using data from Interregional Input–Output Table (IIOT) for Colombia (2015). We disaggregated the foreign export vector to 209 destination countries in the IIOT using DIMPE (2019)

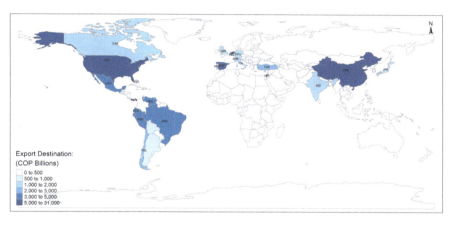

Fig. 9.1 Colombian export destination mapping: 2015. *Source* Author elaboration using data from interregional input–output table (IIOT) for Colombia (2015). We disaggregated the foreign export vector to 209 destination countries in the IIOT using DIMPE (2019)

become an important destination since the 2000s due to China's increased petroleum demand (Fig. 9.2). Colombian exports have a natural resource-intensive pattern, concentrated in mineral commodities (bituminous coal, petroleum, gold, coal, and coke) and agriculture commodities (coffee, cut flowers, and bananas). The relative importance of coal, petroleum, and gold has increased over time (Fig. 9.3).

The top 20 relations of commodity-destination represent nearly 50% of Colombian exports (Table 9.2). The concentration on few destinations and commodities may cause external vulnerability to the domestic economy because of the strong oscillations in commodity prices i.e., shocks to the Colombian economy during the 2010s caused by the oil prices and production (Melo-Becerra et al., 2020).

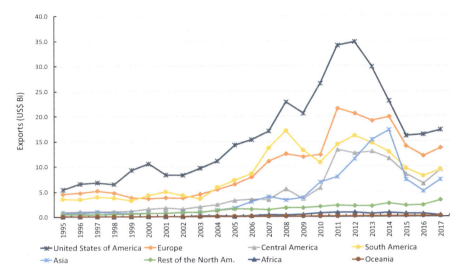

Fig. 9.2 Evolution of colombian exports by destination: 1995–2017. *Note* Exports (US$ billions) at 2017 prices. Constant price estimates using the "Producer price index by commodity" data of the bureau of labor statistics, United States of America. *Source* Author elaboration using data from BACI (2019)

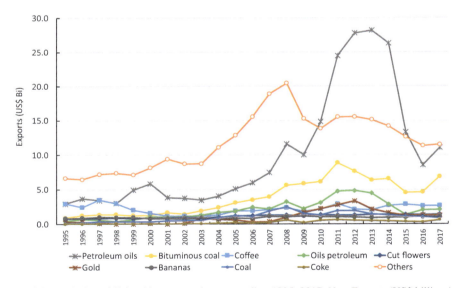

Fig. 9.3 Evolution of Colombian exports by commodity: 1995–2017. *Note* Exports (US$ billions) at 2017 prices. Constant price estimates using the "Producer price index by commodity" data of the bureau of labor statistics, United States of America. *Source* Author elaboration using data from BACI (2019)

Table 9.2 Top 20 Colombian commodity by export destination: 2017

	Export destination	Commodity	Percentage
1	United States of America	Petroleum oils, oils from bituminous minerals, crude	11.6
2	Panama	Petroleum oils, oils from bituminous minerals, crude	5.5
3	China	Petroleum oils, oils from bituminous minerals, crude	4.1
4	Turkey	Bituminous coal, not agglomerated	3.3
5	United States of America	Coffee, not roasted, not decaffeinated	2.8
6	United States of America	Cut flowers and flower buds for bouquets, etc., fresh	2.8
7	Netherlands	Bituminous coal, not agglomerated	2.6
8	United States of America	Oils petroleum, bituminous, distillates, except crude	2.5
9	United States of America	Gold in unwrought forms non-monetary	2.2
10	Bahamas	Petroleum oils, oils from bituminous minerals, crude	2.0
11	Saint Lucia	Petroleum oils, oils from bituminous minerals, crude	1.5
12	Mexico	Bituminous coal, not agglomerated	1.4
13	Chile	Bituminous coal, not agglomerated	1.3
14	United States of America	Bituminous coal, not agglomerated	1.1
15	Spain	Bituminous coal, not agglomerated	1.0
16	Portugal	Bituminous coal, not agglomerated	1.0
17	Brazil	Bituminous coal, not agglomerated	0.9
18	Netherlands	Coal except anthracite or bituminous, not agglomerate	0.9
19	Belgium	Bananas, including plantains, fresh or dried	0.7
20	Switzerland	Gold in unwrought forms non-monetary	0.7
	Total		49.9

Source Author elaboration using data from BACI (2019)

9.2.2 International and Interregional Trade in Colombia by Department

This section examines Colombian trade from a regional perspective. This approach is important to understand the profile of the domestic and global value chains addressed in Sect. 9.4. Table 9.3 reveals a spatially uneven regional distribution of interregional trade. Bogotá D.C (23.0%), Antioquia (13.2%), Valle del Cauca (10.0%), and Cundinamarca (9.2%) dominate interregional exports, representing 55.4% of total domestic trade flows. The Colombian economy is concentrated, mainly in the Bogotá-Medellín axis, while the departments within the "Colombian Ostrich"[2] economic core play a secondary role (Fig. 9.4). Meta (15.4%), Antioquia (13.4%), Bogotá D.C (11.1%), and Casanare (9.0%) concentrate 48.9% of total foreign exports (Fig. 9.5). The availability of natural resources heavily influences the export's geographical behavior (Haddad & Araujo, 2020). Meta and Casanare are responsible for 76% of Colombia's oil and gas exports and represent, together, 25% of the Colombian foreign export volume.

Table 9.3 presents the interregional and international export coefficients for the 33 Colombian departments. This table reveals the relative importance of domestic and foreign trade per Colombian department. Cundinamarca, San Andrés, Chocó, Boyacá, and Bolívar are the departments with the largest participation of domestic exports in the GRP. In contrast, some regions are more dependent on foreign exports: Casanare's foreign exports represent 83.1% of the GRP, followed by Arauca (64.2%), La Guajira (62.6%), Meta (61.9%), and Cesar (51.0%).

Table 9.3 also reveals other characteristics of the Colombian interregional system. The regions with the lowest exposure to foreign trade are Boyacá, Chocó, and Vichada. International export coefficients are higher than interregional coefficients in Cesar, La Guajira, Meta, Arauca, and Casanare. These estimates reveal the importance of domestic trade for regional economies. Haddad et al. (2002) identify a pattern of commercial integration for the Brazilian economy similar to the Colombian case. Munroe et al. (2007) also show that the volume of trade among states exceeds the volume of foreign trade originating from those states by several orders of magnitude in the US Midwest.

9.3 Data and Methodology

9.3.1 Data

The data to analyze the value-added embodied in trade comes from the IIOT for Colombia in 2015. These data describe the structure of the national economy in the context of its 33 departments and 54 sectors (see Chap. 3 of this book for further detail). The IIOT has only one vector of foreign exports. We have disaggregated the vector of foreign exports by 209 destinations abroad, specifying all countries in the world, using microdata from the DIMPE and the DANE. The microdata identifies the commodities exported by "*subpartida arancelaria*"[3] at FOB US$ per country of destination. The geographic unit of the data is the Colombian department of commodity origin (DIMPE, 2019).

We harmonize the commodities specified in the microdata using the correspondence dictionary created by DANE that associates the 12,780 commodities (POSAR

---

[2] On the "Colombian Ostrich", please see Haddad et al. (2009).

[3] The "*subpartida arancelaria*" is the import and export classification system used in the DIMPE at a basic 10-digit level. It is used to identify products/commodities.

Table 9.3 Domestic and foreign exports in Colombia, 2015

Department	Interregional exports (COP bi)	Foreign exports (COP bi)	GRP	Interregional exports/GRP (A)	Foreign exports/GRP (B)	A/B
Antioquia	61,300	15,978	104,903	0.584	0.152	3.837
Atlántico	20,212	6532	32,207	0.628	0.203	3.094
Bogotá D.C	106,909	13,197	184,882	0.578	0.071	8.101
Bolívar	20,977	2814	24,968	0.840	0.113	7.453
Boyacá	17,775	471	20,647	0.861	0.023	37.736
Caldas	7610	2165	11,522	0.660	0.188	3.516
Caquetá	1761	81	3185	0.553	0.025	21.736
Cauca	10,291	1344	13,340	0.771	0.101	7.655
Cesar	5258	7173	14,057	0.374	0.510	0.733
Córdoba	8267	467	12,827	0.644	0.036	17.689
Cundinamarca	42,628	4903	43,112	0.989	0.114	8.695
Chocó	2993	84	3472	0.862	0.024	35.834
Huila	8297	1250	13,065	0.635	0.096	6.638
La Guajira	2408	5232	8361	0.288	0.626	0.460
Magdalena	5667	1540	9972	0.568	0.154	3.680
Meta	17,253	18,363	29,666	0.582	0.619	0.940
Nariño	5387	377	11,613	0.464	0.033	14.271
Norte de Santander	6053	1085	11,804	0.513	0.092	5.581
Quindío	3450	386	6016	0.573	0.064	8.927
Risaralda	7042	2433	11,550	0.610	0.211	2.894
Santander	28,120	9266	42,583	0.660	0.218	3.035
Sucre	3478	234	6202	0.561	0.038	14.880
Tolima	11,703	717	16,160	0.724	0.044	16.315
Valle del Cauca	46,620	7968	70,363	0.663	0.113	5.851
Arauca	2487	2844	4428	0.562	0.642	0.875
Casanare	5879	10,685	12,858	0.457	0.831	0.550
Putumayo	2817	1071	3368	0.836	0.318	2.631
San Andrés	1028	198	1154	0.891	0.172	5.190
Amazonas	438	43	565	0.776	0.076	10.140
Guainía	124	56	297	0.418	0.188	2.223
Guaviare	377	16	654	0.577	0.025	23.341
Vaupés	103	16	226	0.455	0.069	6.573
Vichada	357	8	514	0.694	0.016	43.476
Colombia	465,068	118,997	730,543	0.637	0.163	3.908

Source Author elaboration using data from interregional input–output table for Colombia (2015)

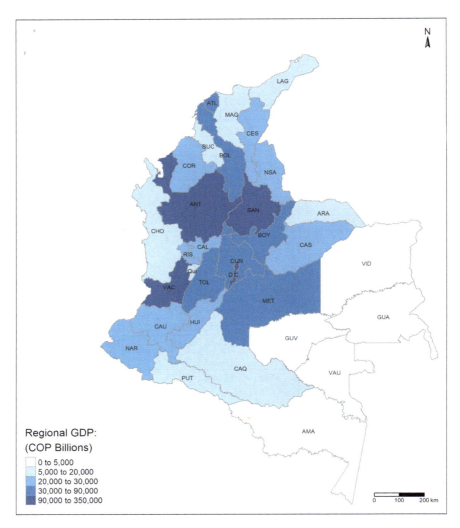

Fig. 9.4 Gross regional product: 2015. *Source* Author elaboration using data from interregional input–output system for Colombia (2015)

classification—"Arancelaria") with the 499 economic activity codes of the CIIU Rev. 4AC. Then, we group the CIIU activities under 392 commodities (Clases CPC Vers. 2 AC) of the "System of National Accounts" specified in the SUT for Colombia.[4]

To complete the data harmonization steps, we aggregate the 392 commodities into 54 sectors of the Interregional Input-Output Table with the market share matrix (generated by the Make Table). We then obtain an Export Matrix with specifications

---

[4] *Nomenclatura das classificações DANE* in: https://www.dane.gov.co/index.php/sistema-estadi stico-nacional-sen/normas-y-estandares/nomenclaturas-y-clasificaciones.

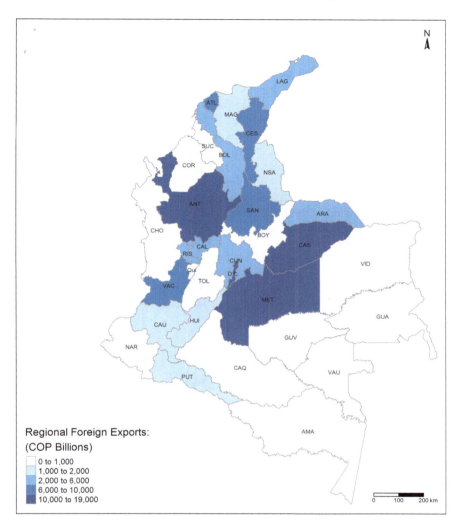

Fig. 9.5 Foreign exports: 2015. *Source* Author elaboration using data from interregional input–output system for Colombia (2015)

for 54 sectors and 209 destination countries for each of the 33 Colombian departments. The shares built from this Export Matrix are used to open the foreign export vector of the Interregional Input-Output Table for Colombia. This strategy ensures the consistency of the SUT data with the export statistics from DIMPE (2019).

9.3.2 Hierarchy of Spatial Production and Feedback Analysis

Economic geography and trade theory supports the hypothesis that geography influences trade volume between places. Consequently, trade influences the economic activity to the extent that it is usually unevenly distributed across space within countries (Venables, 2019). This finding motivates us to analyze the geography of trade in Colombia through the value-added embodied in domestic and foreign trade. Figure 9.6 shows the mapping of production chain through intraregional, interregional, and international trade. This figure draws attention to *vertical specialization* in the production chain; in this case, good is produced in multiple sequential stages, and the input crosses a domestic or foreign border at more than one stage (Johnson & Noguera, 2012). Analyzes based on the gross exports neglect the value-added contributions from the origin of the trade flows. Thus, it is indispensable to measure the value-added embodied in domestic and foreign exports to understand the importance of trade to the regions.

Input–output analysis, in the context of vertical specialization, provides insights into properties of spatial interaction related to feedback effects and hierarchy (Sonis et al., 2002). Haddad et al. (2002) show that, on one hand, interregional trade might generate the potential for the propagation of feedback effects that, in quantitative

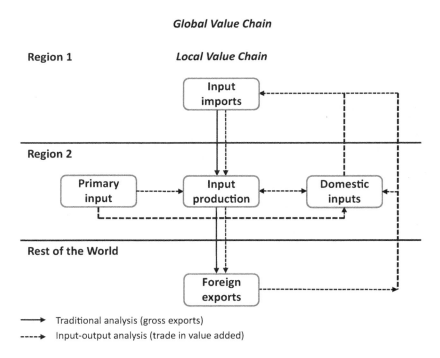

Fig. 9.6 Vertical trade in local and global value chains

terms, could be larger than the effects generated by international trade. On the other hand, the impact of feedback effects is partially determined by the hierarchical structure of the given interregional system.

The analysis of the spatial geographic structure of the trade flows lends itself readily to the identification of the feedback effects and hierarchy of interregional and international trade integration (Sonis et al., 2002). This spatial analysis can be obtained from the value-added flow embodied in trade, providing additional insights into the nature and strengths of interregional connectivity. The next section of this chapter addresses the method for analyzing this issue through the spatial structure of trade.

9.4 Measurement of Regional Value-Added in Interregional and International Trade Flows

We measure regional value-added in interregional and international trade flows using a parsimonious approach, based on the hypothetical extraction procedure proposed by Los et al. (2016) and adapted to an interregional context by Haddad et al., (2020, 2021). This approach measures how much domestic value-added is included in a region's exports. This is done by computing value-added in a modified economy in which some trade flows are set to zero. Essentially, some trade linkages between regions are extracted in this hypothetical economy. We then define domestic value-added in regional exports as the region's value-added associated with the extracted linkages.

Let us consider an interregional input–output table with n domestic regions ($r = 1, 2, \ldots, n$), and k different sectors, which exports to m different countries ($c = 1, 2, \ldots, m$). We can partition the input coefficients matrix, **A**, in the following way:

$$A = \begin{bmatrix} A_{11} & \cdots & A_{1n} \\ \vdots & \ddots & \vdots \\ A_{n1} & \cdots & A_{nn} \end{bmatrix} \quad (9.1)$$

where the element $\boldsymbol{A}_{rr}$ is a $k \times k$ matrix where the element a_{lk} is the input coefficients, the value units of intermediate goods from industry i required to produce one value unit of gross output in industry j. We partition the final demand matrix, **Y**, in the following way:

$$Y = \begin{bmatrix} y_{11} & \cdots & y_{1n} & e_{11} & \cdots & e_{1m} \\ \vdots & \ddots & \vdots & \vdots & \ddots & \vdots \\ y_{n1} & \cdots & y_{nn} & e_{n1} & \cdots & e_{nm} \end{bmatrix} \quad (9.2)$$

where the element y_{rs} is the final demand of region s that comes from region r, and the element e_{rc} is the foreign exports to country c by region r.

Let $\mathbf{v}$ be a row vector containing value-added to gross output ratios in industries for all regions. Using the same partition, we can write: $v = [v_1, v_2, \ldots, v_n]$. Define $\tilde{v}_1$ as the value-added ratios for industries in the first region (v_1) and zeros elsewhere: $\tilde{v}_1 = [v_1, 0, \ldots, 0]$. The value-added in region one, VA_1, is given by:

$$\text{VA}_1 = \tilde{v}_1 \cdot (I - A)^{-1} \cdot Y \cdot i \qquad (9.3)$$

where I is the identity matrix of appropriate dimensions, $\mathbf{i}$ is a column vector where all elements are unity, and $(I - A)^{-1}$ is the Leontief inverse.

We now estimate the amount of domestic value-added attributed to exports from region s. To measure this, we create a hypothetical situation in which region s does not export anything to region r, leaving the rest of the economic structure unaffected. That is, blocks A_{rs} and y_{rs} are set to zero.

$$A^* = \begin{bmatrix} A_{11} & \cdots & A_{1n-1} & 0 \\ A_{21} & \cdots & A_{2n-1} & A_{2n} \\ \vdots & \ddots & \vdots & \vdots \\ A_{n1} & \cdots & A_{nn-1} & A_{nn} \end{bmatrix} \qquad (9.4)$$

$$Y^* = \begin{bmatrix} y_{11} & \cdots & y_{1n-1} & 0 & e_{11} & \cdots & e_{1m} \\ y_{21} & \cdots & y_{2n-1} & y_{2n} & e_{21} & \cdots & e_{2m} \\ \vdots & \ddots & \vdots & \vdots & \vdots & \ddots & \vdots \\ y_{n1} & \cdots & y_{nn-1} & y_{nn} & e_{n1} & \cdots & e_{nm} \end{bmatrix} \qquad (9.5)$$

The domestic value-added in region one generated by trades with region r, VA_{1r}, is given by:

$$\text{VA}_{1r} = \text{VA}_1 - \tilde{v}_1 \cdot (I - A^*)^{-1} \cdot Y^* \cdot i \qquad (9.6)$$

We can use the same strategy to measure the domestic value-added induced by foreign exports to each country c in each domestic region. To estimate the value-added induced by exports to country c in region one, (VA_{1c}), the hypothetical final demand (Y^{**}) is specified as if there is no demand for final products in e_{1c}:

$$Y^{**} = \begin{bmatrix} y_{11} & \cdots & e_{1c-1} & 0 & e_{1c+1} & \cdots & e_{1m} \\ y_{21} & \cdots & e_{2c-1} & e_{2c} & e_{2c+1} & \cdots & e_{2m} \\ \vdots & \ddots & \vdots & \vdots & \vdots & \ddots & \vdots \\ y_{n1} & \cdots & e_{nc-1} & e_{nc} & e_{nc+1} & \cdots & e_{nm} \end{bmatrix} \qquad (9.7)$$

To calculate VA_{1c} one should only extract a part of the final demand matrix, preserving the original intermediate input coefficients matrix:

$$VA_{1c} = VA_1 - \tilde{v}_1 \cdot (I - A)^{-1} \cdot Y^{**} \cdot i \qquad (9.8)$$

VA_{1c} is the domestic value-added induced by foreign exports. This term is large for regions mainly operating in upstream parts of production networks, such as natural resource exporters.

9.5 Results

Interregional trade accounts for 81% of the value-added embodied in total Colombian exports. The remaining 19% are generated by international trade. The four countries with the highest contributions to value-added are the United States, China, Panama, and Spain (Table 9.4). Although the gross export volume to Panama is higher than to China, as shown in Table 9.1, China has a modestly more contribution to the Colombian economy than Panama. Exports record gross flows of goods and services every time they cross borders, which can lead to multiple counting of trade flows, while the value-added measures flows related to the value that is enhanced (labor compensation, other taxes on production and operating surplus, or profits) by a region in the production of any good or service exported, as in OECD (2013).

Figure 9.7 shows the relative importance of foreign and domestic trade for every Colombian department in terms of their respective value-added contribution. Transactions with foreign partners generate 71% of La Guajira's value-added. On the other hand, 98% of Vichada's value-added is generated by interregional trade.

Figure 9.8 shows the top 200 value-added flows for foreign exports. USA, China, Spain, Panama, Mexico, Venezuela, and Germany concentrate most destinations. The largest flows are from Antioquia, Bogotá D.C, Meta, and Casanare, the departments with the highest participation in gross exports. Figure 9.9 shows the top 100

Table 9.4 Value-added embodied in Colombian exports

Source	Value-added (COP billions)	Share (%)
Interregional trade	300,088	81.1
Exports	70,160	18.9
United States	18,659	5.0
China	4860	1.3
Panama	4790	1.3
Spain	3490	0.9
Rest of the world	38,367	10.4
Total	370,247	100.0

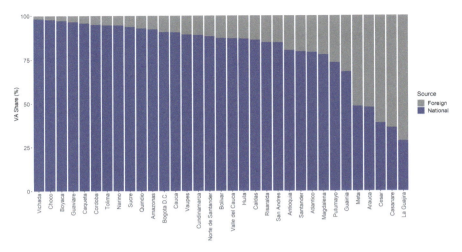

Fig. 9.7 Value-added embodied in exports, by type of trade: Colombian departments

interregional value-added flows among the origin-destination pairs in the Colombian departments. Central and north areas in the country concentrated the highest value-added flows.

Table 9.5 presents the five largest interregional and foreign value-added flows. Bogotá D.C, Antioquia, Cundinamarca, and Santander have the highest value-added flows embodied in domestic exports inside Colombia. These five flows can also be visualized in Figure 9.9: CUN → DC, DC → CUN, DC → ANT, ANT → DC, and DC → SAN, respectively. Trade links to the United States from Antioquia, Meta, Casanare, and Bogotá D.C and to China from Meta have the largest added-value contents incorporated into foreign exports.

Figure 9.10 shows every Colombian department's value-added share for every national partner and the four most important foreign partners (the United States, Panama, China, and Spain). ROW accounts for the contribution of the rest of the world. The intersection of row DC with column ANT represents the contribution of Antioquia to value-added generated in Bogotá D.C, for example, Bogotá D.C and Antioquia departments concentrated the highest shares (the darker blue cells). La Guajira (71.3%), Casanare (63.8%), Cesar (61.0%), Arauca (52.3%), and Meta (51.5%) are more dependent on foreign trade.

Table 9.6 presents the five most important national and foreign partners.[5] On one hand, the major trading partners of Antioquia, Bogotá D.C, and Cundinamarca are domestic destinations. On the other hand, Casanare and Meta have foreign partners as their major trading partners. The United States is the most important foreign partner to every one of these five departments. Considering the 33 departments, the United States is the most important foreign partner for 31 of them. The exceptions are Cesar and Norte de Santander, for which Spain and Panama are the most important partners,

---

[5] Appendix 1 presents Table 7.6 for the 33 Colombian departments.

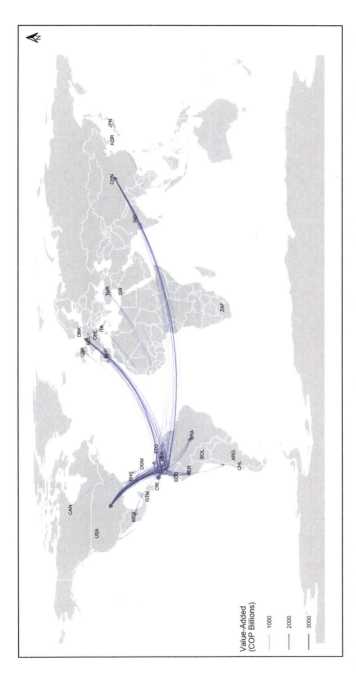

Fig. 9.8 Value-added embodied in foreign exports from Colombian departments. *Note* Curved arrow in the figure represents one trade link between a department and a country. The curved arrow's opacity is proportional to the value-added embodied in foreign exports

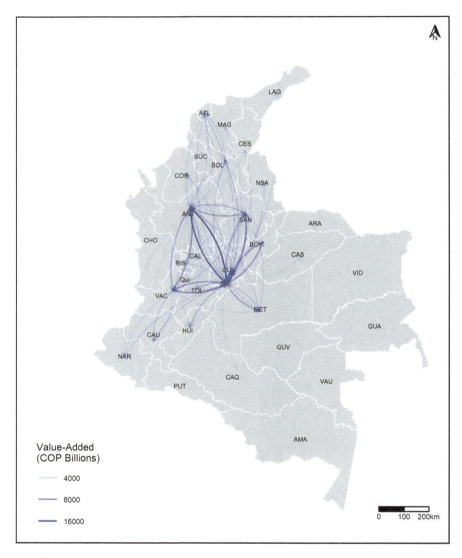

Fig. 9.9 Value-added embodied in domestic exports from Colombian departments. *Note* Curved arrow in the Figure represents a regional value-added flow between the Colombian departments. The curved arrow's opacity is proportional to the value-added embodied in domestic exports

respectively. Bogotá D.C is the most critical partner for 25 departments, considering only national partners. A national department is the most important partner for 28 of 33 departments. The remaining five are Casanare, Arauca, Meta, La Guajira, and Cesar, which are more dependent on trade with a foreign region than any other Colombian department.

Table 9.5 Main trade flows based on value-added embodied in domestic and foreign exports from Colombian departments

Domestic exports			Foreign exports		
Location	Partner	Value-added (COP billions)	Location	Partner	Value-added (COP billions)
Cundinamarca	Bogotá D.C	16,476	Antioquia	United States	3958
Bogotá D.C	Cundinamarca	15,369	Meta	United States	3485
Bogotá D.C	Antioquia	9593	Casanare	United States	1964
Antioquia	Bogotá D.C	8515	Bogotá D.C	United States	1647
Bogotá D.C	Santander	5755	Meta	China	1431

Our results show a distinction between abroad demand-based economies versus local demand-driven economies. Bogotá D.C is the leading trading partner for most domestic regions, while the main partners for Casanare, Arauca, Meta, La Guajira, and Cesar are abroad countries (Table 9.3 and Figure 9.11). Thus, for instance, economic changes in Bogotá D.C are more important than external shocks for most Colombian departments. Our findings also show that the Colombian departments' main commercial partners abroad are distinct (Table 9.7). For example, the United States and Panama are important trading partners for more industrialized places (i.e., Antioquia and Bogotá D.C). At the same time, China and Spain are essential for natural resource-intensive commodity-exporting regions (i.e., Cesar, Meta, and Casanare).

The other countries in Latin America have a pattern of participation in international trade similar to the Colombian one. For example, China is an important trading partner for Brazil and Chile. However, this trading partner is relevant for specific regions of each country. Trade with China is essential for the States of Mato Grosso, Pará, and Minas Gerais (Brazil) or Antofagasta Region (Chile)—grain or mineral producing regions. However, trade with China may be less attractive for the State of São Paulo (Brazil) and Santiago Metropolitan Region (Chile), which specialize in manufacturing and services. In this context, although trade with certain countries is essential for Colombia, it is necessary to know which regions benefit from this trade since trade liberalization policies may benefit some places to the detriment of others. Therefore, knowing the domestic and international production network can help to qualify trade policy and regional planning strategies.

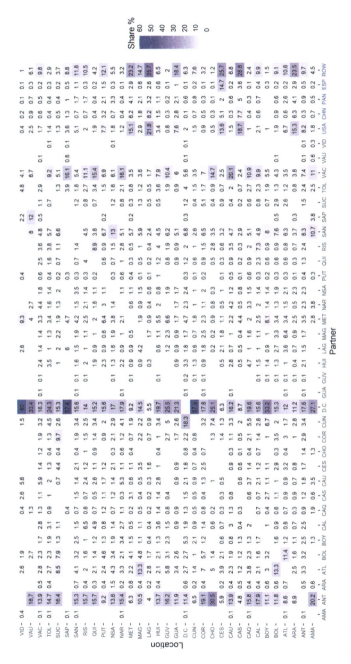

Fig. 9.10 Regional total traded value-added in trade flows: Colombia, 2015. *Note* List of regions in Appendix 2

9 Trade in Value-Added: Does MFN Status Matter for Colombian Regions?

Table 9.6 Most important trade partners, by value-added contribution

Location	Domestic exports			Foreign exports		
	Partner	Value-added	Share (%)	Partner	Value-added	Share (%)
Antioquia	Bogotá D.C	8515	17.6	United States	3958	8.2
	Santander	3996	8.3	Ecuador	575	1.2
	Valle del Cauca	3600	7.4	Germany	564	1.2
	Meta	1689	3.5	Peru	537	1.1
	Cundinamarca	1655	3.4	Netherlands	443	0.9
Bogotá D.C	Cundinamarca	15,369	18.3	United States	1647	2.0
	Antioquia	9593	11.4	Ecuador	1160	1.4
	Santander	5755	6.8	Peru	689	0.8
	Valle del Cauca	4710	5.6	Venezuela	678	0.8
	Boyacá	4437	5.3	Panama	523	0.6
Casanare	Bogotá D.C	914	8.7	United States	1964	18.7
	Antioquia	502	4.8	China	805	7.7
	Meta	463	4.4	Panama	529	5.0
	Santander	308	2.9	Spain	376	3.6
	Valle del Cauca	254	2.4	Netherlands	305	2.9
Cundinamarca	Bogotá D.C	16,476	57.3	United States	419	1.5
	Antioquia	1883	6.5	Panama	237	0.8
	Valle del Cauca	1001	3.5	China	214	0.7
	Santander	755	2.6	Ecuador	174	0.6
	Boyacá	592	2.1	Venezuela	167	0.6
Mta	Bogotá D.C	2111	9.2	United States	3485	15.1
	Antioquia	1448	6.3	China	1431	6.2
	Santander	1302	5.7	Panama	939	4.1
	Bolívar	942	4.1	Spain	669	2.9
	Valle del Cauca	815	3.5	Netherlands	540	2.3

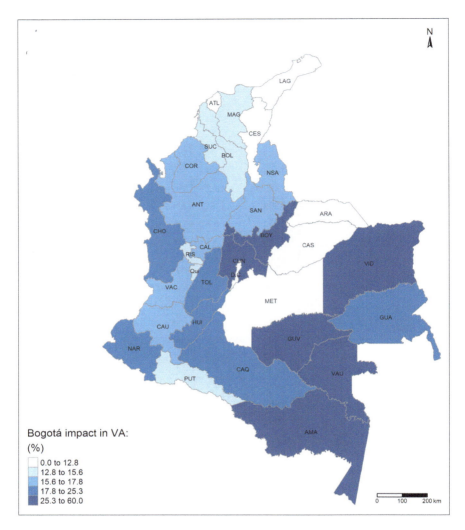

Fig. 9.11 Bogotá D.C shares of VA

9.5.1 Concentration and Structural Interdependence Among Colombian Departments

In this section, we discuss spatial interdependence and concentration of value-added flows in the Colombian departments. Table 9.8 shows the five largest traded value-added shares in interregional trade. This table reveals that Vichada, Cundinamarca, San Andrés, Boyacá and Vaupés heavily depend on trade with Bogotá D.C.

Table 9.7 Value-added embodied in Colombian foreign exports by department, 2015 (%)

Department	USA (%)	CHN (%)	PAN (%)	ESP (%)	ROW (%)
Antioquia	21.2	3.4	9.0	6.4	12.2
Atlántico	5.7	2.0	8.4	1.0	4.4
Bogotá D.C	8.8	2.3	10.9	1.4	13.9
Bolívar	1.2	2.2	1.7	0.7	2.9
Boyacá	0.6	0.0	0.0	1.1	0.5
Caldas	0.6	0.6	0.8	0.7	1.4
Caquetá	0.1	0.1	0.1	0.0	0.1
Cauca	0.6	0.5	0.9	0.3	1.3
Cesar	6.4	9.1	3.6	36.8	5.9
Córdoba	0.3	0.6	0.3	0.2	0.5
Cundinamarca	2.2	4.4	5.0	2.0	5.7
Chocó	0.1	0.1	0.1	0.0	0.1
Huila	1.1	1.9	1.4	1.1	1.1
La Guajira	6.2	8.9	3.5	3.9	4.9
Magdalena	0.7	1.7	2.0	0.8	1.7
Meta	18.7	29.4	19.6	19.2	13.9
Nariño	0.3	0.3	0.3	0.1	0.3
Norte de Santander	0.4	0.6	3.0	0.3	0.6
Quindío	0.2	0.2	0.2	0.1	0.3
Risaralda	0.5	0.8	1.8	0.4	1.4
Santander	5.6	3.0	7.4	6.2	6.3
Sucre	0.2	0.3	0.2	0.1	0.2
Tolima	0.6	0.7	0.6	0.7	0.6
Valle del Cauca	3.2	4.2	4.0	1.7	8.9
Arauca	2.6	4.2	2.8	2.7	2.0
Casanare	10.5	16.6	11.1	10.8	7.9
Putumayo	1.0	1.6	1.1	1.0	0.8
San Andrés	0.1	0.2	0.2	0.1	0.2
Amazonas	0.0	0.0	0.0	0.0	0.0
Guainía	0.0	0.1	0.1	0.0	0.1
Guaviare	0.0	0.0	0.0	0.0	0.0
Vaupés	0.0	0.0	0.0	0.0	0.0
Vichada	0.0	0.0	0.0	0.0	0.0
Total	100.0	100.0	100.0	100.0	100.0

Table 9.8 Largest value-added shares in interregional trade to Bogotá D.C

Location	Partner	Value-added (COP billions)	Share (%)
Vichada	Bogotá D.C	162	60.2
Cundinamarca	Bogotá D.C	16,476	57.3
San Andrés	Bogotá D.C	391	52.3
Boyacá	Bogotá D.C	3901	33.2
Vaupés	Bogotá D.C	24.5	32.8

From Table 9.8, it is possible to see that Bogotá D.C plays a critical role in value-added embodied in interregional trade flows. Figure 9.11 shows the importance of Bogotá D.C to every Colombian department in terms of its contribution to value-added, i.e., a larger fraction of their value-added originates from trading with Bogotá D.C. The externalities associated with the agglomeration effect can explain this concentration in Bogatá D.C.[6] Figure 9.12 brings the same analysis but now considers the USA trade importance to every department.

Figure 9.13 presents the balance of traded value-added by Colombian regions. The only regions with positive net transfers of value-added in interregional trade (surplus with other domestic regions) are in the immediate area of influence of the country's larger urban agglomerations, namely, the departments of Bogotá D.C, Valle del Cauca, Antioquia, Cundinamarca, and Atlántico—except for the departments of Boyacá and Putumayo.

Perobelli et al. (2010), in an analysis of the structural interdependence among Colombian departments, show that all departments have a net dependence on Bogotá D.C. This result suggests the influence of the city capital on the other departments with potential effects on regional concentration in the country. Our analysis supports the previously stated evidence (Perobelli et al., 2010—revisited in Chap. 7 of this book). Additionally, our methodological approach allowed us to measure the net balance value-added in interregional and international trade. In this way, we show that besides Bogotá D.C, other regions can considerably influence the other regional economies through the supply chain, such as Valle del Cauca, Antioquia, Cundinamarca, Boyacá, Atlántico, and Putumayo (Fig. 9.13).

Intersectoral and interregional trade linkages specific to a region, or a region and sector, have the potential to amplify and propagate productivity changes to the rest of the economy (Caliendo et al., 2018). Thus, productivity changes (Chap. 12 of this book) or improvements in roads and connectivity[7] (Duranton, 2015) that affect large urban areas such as Bogotá D.C, Medellín (Antioquia), or Cali (Valle del Cauca) can propagate significant effects along the supply chain to the other regions through interregional and inter-industry linkages.

---

[6] Duranton (2016) explores agglomeration benefits in Colombian cities.

[7] Duranton (2015) provides insight into how transport infrastructure affects trade and the organization of economic activity. The author shows that road distance between cities is a significant impediment to domestic trade in Colombia.

9 Trade in Value-Added: Does MFN Status Matter for Colombian Regions?

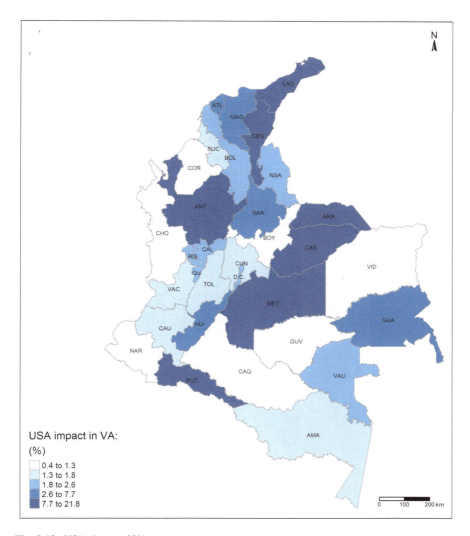

Fig. 9.12 USA shares of VA

9.6 Final Considerations

This study presents a detailed analysis of the trade among the Colombian departments that allows for a better understanding of the interregional economic system of the country. Trade measures in value-added reveal different interregional and international trade integration hierarchies, with implications for regional inequality. This understanding of the composition and the structural differences associated with

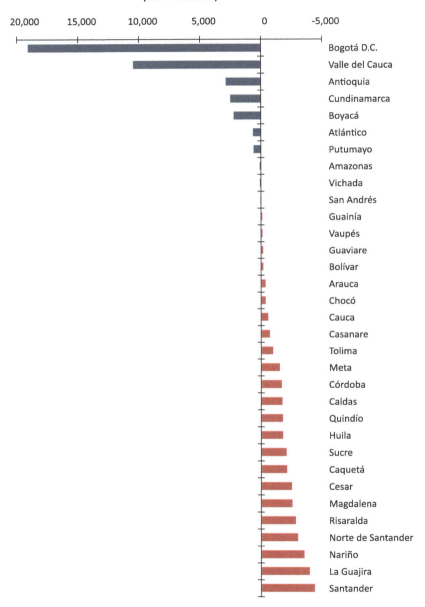

Fig. 9.13 Net value-added trade balance in interregional trade (in COP billions)

trade for each department is essential for implementing and articulating development policies.

The role of interregional trade in the Colombian departments should not be relegated to a second plane. Policymakers should consider interregional interactions to understand better how the regional economies are affected in international and domestic markets; in smaller economies, the performance of more developed regions may play a crucial role *inter alia* in their development (Haddad et al., 2002). For some departments (i.e., Casanare, Arauca, Meta, La Guajira, and Cesar), the economic growth is tied to their ability to compete in the international export market and its articulation with other domestic markets.

McCann (2007) suggests that, from the perspective of trade, the falling spatial transaction costs may be a path allowing geographically peripheral economies more efficient access to domestic and international markets, both in terms of production and consumption—and consequently acting on regional inequalities. However, although the economy can benefit from such falls, the relative distribution of such benefits does not favor peripheral regions unless these regions can themselves generate significant economies of scale (see Haddad & Hewings, 2005, 2009 who show for Brazil that the greater access may benefit the more developed regions since they enjoy greater scale economies). From this perspective, Haddad et al. (2002) show that there is room for government intervention to attenuate the effects of regional inequality caused by domestic production linkages. Thereby, the focus of policymakers may consider aiming at the efficient use of the peripheral regional potential and the creation and consolidation of dynamic comparative advantages in the regions.

The following steps in analyzing the Colombian departments' economic and commercial integration are further aspects that were not addressed in this study. Would the Colombian departments that are poorly linked to foreign markets be fated to an archaic structure of trade, based on the export of less sophisticated products (in terms of value-added) directed to specific domestic markets? How does the Colombian economy adjust to a commodity boom? How do regions absorb oil price shocks? Can we use the CEER ICGE (Chap. 6 of this book) model to look at the long-run effects of Colombia's further integration into foreign markets? Does domestic trade act as a shock absorber for some regions?

Appendix 1

See Table 9.9.

Appendix 2

See Table 9.10.

Table 9.9 Largest value-added flows by department

Location	National			Foreign		
	Partner	Value-added (COP billions)	Share (%)	Partner	Value-added (COP billions)	Share (%)
Amazonas	Bogotá D.C	86	27.1	United States	6	1.8
	Antioquia	64	20.2	China	2	0.7
	Valle del Cauca	35	11.0	Panama	2	0.5
	Santander	34	10.7	Netherlands	1	0.3
	San Andrés	12	3.8	Ecuador	1	0.3
Antioquia	Bogotá D.C	8515	17.6	United States	3958	8.2
	Santander	3996	8.3	Ecuador	575	1.2
	Valle del Cauca	3600	7.4	Germany	564	1.2
	Meta	1689	3.5	Peru	537	1.1
	Cundinamarca	1655	3.4	Netherlands	443	0.9
Arauca	Bogotá D.C	362	11.2	United States	494	15.3
	Antioquia	224	6.9	China	203	6.3
	Valle del Cauca	122	3.8	Panama	133	4.1
	Santander	118	3.7	Spain	95	2.9
	Cundinamarca	91	2.8	Netherlands	77	2.4
Atlántico	Bogotá D.C	1887	12.0	United States	1062	6.7
	Bolívar	1795	11.4	Panama	405	2.6
	Antioquia	1356	8.6	Ecuador	234	1.5
	Magdalena	1011	6.4	Venezuela	202	1.3
	Santander	985	6.3	Aruba	143	0.9
Bogotá D.C	Cundinamarca	15,369	18.3	United States	1647	2.0
	Antioquia	9593	11.4	Ecuador	1160	1.4
	Santander	5755	6.8	Peru	689	0.8
	Valle del Cauca	4710	5.6	Venezuela	678	0.8
	Boyacá	4437	5.3	Panama	523	0.6
Bolívar	Bogotá D.C	1883	15.3	United States	229	1.9
	Atlántico	1639	13.3	China	108	0.9
	Antioquia	1452	11.8	Netherlands	85	0.7
	Santander	937	7.6	Panama	79	0.6
	Valle del Cauca	534	4.3	Ecuador	69	0.6

(continued)

Table 9.9 (continued)

Location	National			Foreign		
	Partner	Value-added (COP billions)	Share (%)	Partner	Value-added (COP billions)	Share (%)
Boyacá	Bogotá D.C	3901	33.2	United States	117	1.0
	Antioquia	1307	11.1	Spain	38	0.3
	Meta	946	8.1	Belgium	35	0.3
	Santander	936	8.0	Costa Rica	31	0.3
	Cundinamarca	782	6.7	Peru	15	0.1
Caldas	Antioquia	992	17.9	United States	117	2.1
	Bogotá D.C	868	15.6	Germany	57	1.0
	Valle del Cauca	551	9.9	Ecuador	54	1.0
	Risaralda	405	7.3	Venezuela	47	0.8
	Santander	270	4.9	Japan	43	0.8
Caquetá	Bogotá D.C	217	19.6	United States	11	1.0
	Antioquia	175	15.8	China	4	0.4
	Valle del Cauca	121	10.9	Panama	3	0.3
	Cundinamarca	61	5.5	Netherlands	2	0.2
	Santander	56	5.1	Ecuador	2	0.2
Casanare	Bogotá D.C	914	8.7	United States	1964	18.7
	Antioquia	502	4.8	China	805	7.7
	Meta	463	4.4	Panama	529	5.0
	Santander	308	2.9	Spain	376	3.6
	Valle del Cauca	254	2.4	Netherlands	305	2.9
Cauca	Valle del Cauca	1447	20.1	United States	107	1.5
	Bogotá D.C	1165	16.2	Peru	48	0.7
	Antioquia	1004	13.9	Panama	42	0.6
	Santander	338	4.7	Chile	40	0.6
	Nariño	303	4.2	Netherlands	31	0.4
Cesar	Bogotá D.C	552	6.3	Spain	1285	14.7
	Antioquia	515	5.9	United States	1191	13.6
	Atlántico	344	3.9	China	444	5.1
	Santander	283	3.2	Portugal	280	3.2

(continued)

Table 9.9 (continued)

Location	National			Foreign		
	Partner	Value-added (COP billions)	Share (%)	Partner	Value-added (COP billions)	Share (%)
	Valle del Cauca	221	2.5	Chile	205	2.3
Chocó	Antioquia	631	30.5	United States	10	0.5
	Bogotá D.C	520	25.1	China	5	0.3
	Valle del Cauca	305	14.7	Panama	3	0.1
	Cundinamarca	154	7.4	Netherlands	2	0.1
	Atlántico	104	5.0	Ecuador	2	0.1
Córdoba	Antioquia	1068	19.1	United States	50	0.9
	Bogotá D.C	995	17.8	China	27	0.5
	Atlántico	391	7.0	Panama	16	0.3
	Valle del Cauca	390	7.0	Netherlands	14	0.3
	Santander	363	6.5	Venezuela	13	0.2
Cundinamarca	Bogotá D.C	16,476	57.3	United States	419	1.5
	Antioquia	1883	6.5	Panama	237	0.8
	Valle del Cauca	1001	3.5	China	214	0.7
	Santander	755	2.6	Ecuador	174	0.6
	Boyacá	592	2.1	Venezuela	167	0.6
Guainía	Bogotá D.C	25	21.3	United States	9	7.6
	Antioquia	14	11.9	China	3	2.8
	Valle del Cauca	7	6.0	Panama	2	2.1
	Santander	6	5.1	Ecuador	2	1.4
	Atlántico	4	3.4	Netherlands	2	1.4
Guaviare	Bogotá D.C	66	25.5	United States	2	0.8
	Antioquia	42	16.2	China	1	0.3
	Valle del Cauca	27	10.4	Panama	1	0.2
	Meta	17	6.6	Netherlands	0	0.2
	Santander	16	6.2	Ecuador	0	0.2
Huila	Bogotá D.C	1235	19.7	United States	214	3.4
	Antioquia	855	13.7	China	92	1.5

(continued)

Table 9.9 (continued)

Location	National			Foreign		
	Partner	Value-added (COP billions)	Share (%)	Partner	Value-added (COP billions)	Share (%)
	Valle del Cauca	493	7.9	Panama	69	1.1
	Meta	347	5.5	Spain	40	0.6
	Santander	281	4.5	Netherlands	36	0.6
La Guajira	Bogotá D.C	290	5.5	United States	1152	21.8
	Antioquia	211	4.0	China	431	8.2
	Atlántico	148	2.8	Portugal	269	5.1
	Santander	128	2.4	Netherlands	185	3.5
	Valle del Cauca	91	1.7	Brazil	170	3.2
Magdalena	Bogotá D.C	658	14.5	United States	131	2.9
	Atlántico	607	13.3	Panama	94	2.1
	Antioquia	476	10.5	China	81	1.8
	Santander	268	5.9	Ecuador	57	1.3
	Bolívar	220	4.8	Venezuela	43	0.9
Meta	Bogotá D.C	2111	9.2	United States	3485	15.1
	Antioquia	1448	6.3	China	1431	6.2
	Santander	1302	5.7	Panama	939	4.1
	Bolívar	942	4.1	Spain	669	2.9
	Valle del Cauca	815	3.5	Netherlands	540	2.3
Nariño	Bogotá D.C	700	17.9	United States	47	1.2
	Valle del Cauca	629	16.1	China	17	0.4
	Antioquia	602	15.4	Panama	16	0.4
	Cauca	209	5.3	Brazil	9	0.2
	Santander	199	5.1	Netherlands	8	0.2
Norte de Santander	Bogotá D.C	729	17.0	Panama	142	3.3
	Antioquia	582	13.6	United States	77	1.8
	Santander	559	13.0	China	29	0.7
	Valle del Cauca	260	6.1	Netherlands	17	0.4
	Atlántico	186	4.3	Ecuador	15	0.4
Putumayo	Bogotá D.C	386	15.6	United States	191	7.7

(continued)

Table 9.9 (continued)

Location	National			Foreign		
	Partner	Value-added (COP billions)	Share (%)	Partner	Value-added (COP billions)	Share (%)
	Antioquia	227	9.2	China	78	3.2
	Valle del Cauca	171	6.9	Panama	51	2.1
	Santander	166	6.7	Spain	36	1.5
	Meta	157	6.4	Netherlands	30	1.2
Quindío	Antioquia	380	15.7	United States	45	1.9
	Valle del Cauca	373	15.4	Panama	10	0.4
	Bogotá D.C	368	15.2	Japan	10	0.4
	Risaralda	216	8.9	Germany	10	0.4
	Caldas	118	4.9	China	9	0.4
Risaralda	Antioquia	810	15.7	United States	102	2.0
	Bogotá D.C	724	14.0	Panama	86	1.7
	Valle del Cauca	570	11.1	Brazil	49	1.0
	Caldas	336	6.5	China	37	0.7
	Santander	231	4.5	Aruba	36	0.7
San Andrés	Bogotá D.C	391	52.4	United States	27	3.6
	Valle del Cauca	120	16.1	China	10	1.3
	La Guajira	45	6.0	Panama	8	1.0
	Meta	35	4.7	Ecuador	5	0.7
	Tolima	29	3.9	Netherlands	5	0.7
Santander	Bogotá D.C	3213	15.6	United States	1046	5.1
	Antioquia	3144	15.3	Panama	355	1.7
	Valle del Cauca	1115	5.4	Spain	217	1.1
	Meta	873	4.2	Netherlands	205	1.0
	Atlántico	847	4.1	Aruba	205	1.0
Sucre	Antioquia	378	16.4	United States	31	1.3
	Bogotá D.C	352	15.3	China	12	0.5
	Córdoba	224	9.7	Panama	10	0.4
	Atlántico	196	8.5	Netherlands	6	0.3
	Bolívar	182	7.9	Ecuador	5	0.2

(continued)

Table 9.9 (continued)

Location	National			Foreign		
	Partner	Value-added (COP billions)	Share (%)	Partner	Value-added (COP billions)	Share (%)
Tolima	Bogotá D.C	1939	24.3	United States	109	1.4
	Antioquia	1177	14.7	China	35	0.4
	Valle del Cauca	738	9.2	Panama	30	0.4
	Santander	459	5.7	Spain	24	0.3
	Cundinamarca	359	4.5	Netherlands	16	0.2
Valle del Cauca	Bogotá D.C	5723	16.3	United States	606	1.7
	Antioquia	4888	13.9	Venezuela	294	0.8
	Cauca	2067	5.9	Peru	226	0.6
	Santander	1688	4.8	Netherlands	215	0.6
	Nariño	1558	4.4	Ecuador	214	0.6
Vaupés	Bogotá D.C	25	33.4	United States	2	2.5
	Antioquia	14	18.7	China	1	0.9
	San Andrés	9	12.0	Panama	1	0.7
	Santander	6	8.0	Netherlands	0	0.5
	Valle del Cauca	5	6.7	Ecuador	0	0.5
Vichada	Bogotá D.C	162	60.0	United States	1	0.4
	Meta	25	9.3	China	0	0.2
	Cauca	15	5.6	Panama	0	0.1
	Tolima	13	4.8	Netherlands	0	0.1
	Valle del Cauca	11	4.1	Ecuador	0	0.1

Table 9.10 List of regions

Region	Code	Description	Region	Code	Description
R1	ANT	Antioquia	R20	RIS	Risaralda
R2	ATL	Atlántico	R21	SAN	Santander
R3	DC	Bogotá D.C	R22	SUC	Sucre
R4	BOL	Bolívar	R23	TOL	Tolima
R5	BOY	Boyacá	R24	VAC	Valle del Cauca
R6	CAL	Caldas	R25	ARA	Arauca
R7	CAQ	Caquetá	R26	CAS	Casanare
R8	CAU	Cauca	R27	PUT	Putumayo
R9	CES	Cesar	R28	SAP	San Andrés

(continued)

Table 9.10 (continued)

Region	Code	Description	Region	Code	Description
R10	COR	Córdoba	R29	AMA	Amazonas
R11	CUN	Cundinamarca	R30	GUA	Guainía
R12	CHO	Chocó	R31	GUV	Guaviare
R13	HUI	Huila	R32	VAU	Vaupés
R14	LAG	La Guajira	R33	VID	Vichada
R15	MAG	Magdalena		USA	United States
R16	MET	Meta		CHN	China
R17	NAR	Nariño		PAN	Panama
R18	NSA	Norte de Santander		ESP	Spain
R19	QUI	Quindío		ROW	Rest of the World

References

BACI. (2019). *International trade database at the product-level.* CEPII. Homepage: http://www.cepii.fr/CEPII/en/bdd_modele/presentation.asp?id=37

Caliendo, L., Parro, F., Rossi-Hansberg, E., & Sarte, P. D. (2018). The impact of regional and sectoral productivity changes on the US economy. *The Review of Economic Studies, 85*(4), 2042–2096.

DIMPE. (2019). Dirección de Metodología y Producción Estadística. *Colombia, Estadísticas de Exportaciones–EXPO–2011–2019.* Departamento Administrativo Nacional de Estadística (DANE). Archivo Nacional de Datos (ANDA). Homepage: http://microdatos.dane.gov.co/index.php/catalog/472/get_microdata

Duranton, G. (2015). Roads and trade in Colombia. *Economics of Transportation, 4*(1), 16–36.

Duranton, G. (2016). Agglomeration effects in Colombia. *Journal of Regional Science, 56*(2), 210–238.

Galvis, L. A., & Meisel, A. (2013). Regional inequalities and regional policies in Colombia: The experience of the last two decades. In J. R. Cuadrado-Roura & P. Aroca (Eds.), *Regional problems and policies in Latin America.* Springer.

Haddad, E. A., Bonet, J., Hewings, G. J., & Perobelli, F. S. (2009). Spatial aspects of trade liberalization in Colombia: A general equilibrium approach. *Papers in Regional Science, 88*(4), 699–732.

Haddad, E. A., Domingues, E. P., & Perobelli, F. S. (2002). Regional effects of economic integration: The case of Brazil. *Journal of Policy Modeling, 24*(5), 453–482.

Haddad, E. A., Mengoub, F. E., & Vale, V. A. (2020). Water content in trade: A regional analysis for Morocco. *Economic Systems Research, 32*(4), 565–584.

Haddad, E. A., Perobelli, F. S., Araújo, I. F., & Dentinho, T. P. (2021). Uneven integration: The case of Angola. *Revista Portuguesa de Estudos Regionais*, 1–32.

Haddad, E. A., & Araujo, I. F. (2020). The internal geography of services value-added in exports: A Latin America perspective. *Papers in Regional Science*, 1–32.

Haddad, E. A., & Hewings, G. J. D. (2005). Market imperfections in a spatial economy: Some experimental results. *The Quarterly Review of Economics and Finance, 45*, 476–496.

Haddad, E. A., & Hewings, G. J. D. (2009). Handling market imperfections in a spatial economy: Some experimental results II. *Ensayos Sobre Política Económica, 27*, 140–193.

Johnson, R. C., & Noguera, G. (2012). Accounting for intermediates: Production sharing and trade in value added. *Journal of International Economics, 86*(2), 224–236.

Los, B., Timmer, M., & de Vries, G. (2016). Tracing value-added and double counting in gross exports: Comment. *American Economic Review, 106*(4), 1958–1966.

McCann, P. (2007). Technology, information and the geography of global and regional trade. In R. Cooper, K. Donaghy, & G. Hewings (Eds.), *Globalization and regional economic modeling* (pp. 15–34). Springer.

Melo-Becerra, L. A., Galvis, L. M. P., Ramos, J., & Solano, H. M. Z. (2020). Effects of booms and oil crisis on Colombian economy: A time-varying vector autoregressive approach. *Revista De Economía Del Rosario, 23*(1), 31–63.

Munroe, D. K., Hewings, G. J., & Guo, D. (2007). The role of intraindustry trade in interregional trade in the midwest of the US. In R. Cooper, K. Donaghy, & G. Hewings (Eds.), *Globalization and regional economic modeling* (pp. 87–105). Springer.

OECD. Organization for economic co-operation and development. *Trade in value added*. OECD statistics on trade in value added (database). Homepage: https://doi.org/10.1787/data-00648-en

Perobelli, F. S., Haddad, E. A., Moron, J. B., & Hewings, G. J. D. (2010). Structural Interdependence among Colombian departments. *Economic Systems Research, 22*(3), 279–300.

Sonis, M., Hewings, G. J., & Okuyama, Y. (2002). Vertical specialization and interregional trade: Hierarchy of spatial production cycles and feedback loop analysis in the midwest economy. In G. J. Hewings, M. Sonis, & D. Boyce (Eds.), *Trade, networks and hierarchies: Modeling regional and interregional economies* (pp. 347–364). Springer.

Venables, A. J. (2019). Economic geography and trade. *Oxford Research Encyclopedia of Economics and Finance*, 1–19.

Rodrigo Pacheco M.Sc. in Economics from the University of São Paulo (USP). Ph.D. Student (Econ.), University of Columbia, USA.

Raphael P. Fernandes M.Sc. in Economics from the University of São Paulo (USP). His research fields/interests are macroeconomics, regional economics, and applied economics. He currently works as a consultant for the World Bank Group, in the Macroeconomics/Fiscal, Trade, and Investment (MTI) area in the Brazilian Country Office, responsible for Macroeconomic Monitoring and Analysis for Brazil.

Inácio F. Araújo Doctor in Economics, Federal University of Juiz de Fora. Post-doctoral researcher, University of São Paulo, Brazil. Research fields: regional economics and input–output methods.

Eduardo A. Haddad Full Professor at the Department of Economics at the University of São Paulo, Brazil, where he directs the Regional and Urban Economics Lab (NEREUS). Affiliate Professor at the Faculty of Governance, Economic and Social Sciences of the Mohammed VI University and Senior Fellow at the Policy Center for the New South, Rabat, Morocco. President of the Regional Science Association International, RSAI (2021–2022).

Chapter 10
Chaining Juan Valdez: Linkages in the Colombian Coffee Production

Márcia Istake, Karina S. Sass, Andrea Otero-Cortés, and Pedro Levy Sayon

10.1 Introduction

A character with a fictitious name created in 1959, Juan Valdez represents the typical Colombian coffee grower with his poncho on his shoulder, straw hat, and his mule Conchita. In advertisements by The National Federation of Coffee Growers of Colombia (FNC), it promotes Colombian coffee globally, presenting it as distinct from other coffees. Juan Valdez shows that Colombian coffee has different benefits, arising from cultivation related to the specificities of the soil, altitude, varieties, and manual harvesting, where only the mature coffee beans are removed from the plant.

Juan Valdez also represents the noble tradition of coffee production in Colombia. In the twentieth century, coffee products helped shape the local market, generating income and employment. They integrated the regions of the country economically by stimulating the construction of roads and railroads (Machado, 2001). Nowadays, coffee growing and coffee processing do not significantly contribute to the total value added of the country. In 2015, according with the data from the Interregional Input-Product Matrix for Colombia, these activities together corresponded to only 0.83% of the total value added. Despite this, coffee products are essential to Colombian foreign exports and the labor market in the coffee-growing regions. The coffee exports allowed the entry of foreign exchange for 6.725 billion COP, ranking as the fifth

---

M. Istake (✉)
University of Maringá, Maringá, Brazil
e-mail: mistake@uem.br

K. S. Sass · P. L. Sayon
University of São Paulo, São Paulo, Brazil
e-mail: pedro.sayon@alumni.usp.br

A. Otero-Cortés
Center for Regional Economic Studies (CEER), Banco de la República, Cartagena, Colombia

largest exported commodity. Regarding the labor market, in cultivation alone, there are over 500,000 growers; most of the workers employed are less educated and are in informal working situations.

What if the coffee-growing and coffee-producing sectors did not exist? What would be the national and regional economic effects as well as the effects on the labor market and the external sector? Answering these questions can provide a closer look at the importance of coffee-related sectors to Colombia as well as contribute policy agenda that seeks to stimulate employment and the surplus in external accounts in Colombia.

This chapter aims to measure and analyze the importance of the coffee production and processing sectors for the Colombian economy and their integration into local value chains. We focus on the two coffee-related sectors present in the Colombian Interregional Input–Output model presented in Chap. 5: coffee growing (S2) and coffee processing (S14). We employed the hypothetical extraction approach to Colombian input–output systems to reach this goal. The initial hypothesis of this study is that the regions that concentrate the production of S2 and S14 are also the ones that most generate value added in local value chains, and if these sectors disappear from the economy, the most significant effects would be felt on them in terms of the loss of value added, employment, and the indirect effects generated by the expenditures from income earned by employees in these two sectors.

This chapter has four more sections. Section 10.2 addresses issues related to coffee production in Colombia, with an emphasis on the labor market and the external sector. Section 10.3 describes the data source and the method used. We presented and discussed the results in Sect. 10.4. Finally, we present the conclusions of the study.

10.2 Coffee Production in Colombia

This section will provide some data about the coffee-related sectors in Colombia. We divided the analysis into three parts. The first shows the spatial characteristics of the production of coffee in Colombia. The second elaborates on the productive structures of the coffee-growing and coffee-processing sectors. The third section examines the place of Colombian coffee in the international market.

10.2.1 Spatial Characteristics of the Coffee Production in Colombia

Coffee production contributed to the economic development of some Latin American countries in the nineteenth and twentieth centuries, including Colombia. Because of its geographical location, Colombia has the ideal climate and soil conditions for coffee growing, making it stand out in the region. The Colombian coffee production

Table 10.1 Classification of coffee producers, percentage share of the number of producers in Colombia, and average area (total area/number of producers)

Property classification	Area size (ha)	Producers (%)	Average area (ha)
Small	≤ 5	95.8	1.3
Medium	$5,1 \leq 10$	3.1	6.6
Large	$10,1 \leq$	1.1	24.8
Total		100.0	1.7

Source Author's elaboration based on FNC (2021)

system was dominated by small properties (Palacios, 1979), and there has been a lack of a clear, defined, and stable policy in respect to coffee, leaving profitability in hands of the global market (Ocampo, 2015). As a result, when the returns on coffee were low, larger properties had a more difficult time paying wages, making small family properties the most likely to survive (Ocampo, 2015). This characteristic is still present in the Colombian coffee-growing sector. Table 10.1 shows a classification of the coffee producers based on the area of the property. As can be seen, 95.8% of coffee producers in Colombia are on small properties, probably linked to family farming. The average area of their property in this classification is 1.3 ha. Producers classified as medium-sized represent 3.1% of the total coffee growers, with an average area of the property of 6.6 ha. Properties with over 10.1 hectares in Colombia account for 1.1% of total producers, with properties of approximately 24.8 ha.

The production of coffee in Colombia increased from 11 million 60 kg bags in 2000 to 14 million 60 kg bags in 2020 (FNC, 2021). Diseases and climatic effects reduced the production in the period from 2009 to 2012, in which the production varied between 8 and 9 million 60 kg bags. To face these problems, producers are changing the traditional coffee plantations to the more resistant and productive "technified" coffee plantations (FNC, 2021). The area cultivated with this type of plantation increased by 46.9% from 2007 to 2019 (FNC, 2021). As a result, while the cultivated area increased only 3% in this period, the production increased 15.4%, suggesting productivity gains due to the substitution of the traditional by the "techinified" plantations.

In Colombia, 22 out of 33 departments and approximately 590 out of 1122 municipalities produce coffee (FNC, 2021). It grows in areas in the western half of the country, specifically in the three Andean Mountains ranges: the Cordillera Occidental, Cordillera Central, and Cordillera Oriental (Fig. 10.1). In these areas, the altitude, air humidity, time of exposure to the sun, rain, and volcanic soils contribute to the production of differentiated Colombian coffee.

The regional share of sectors S2 (coffee growing) and S14 (coffee processing) in total production value is shown in Fig. 10.2. For S2, the main producer regions are Huila, Antioquia, Tolima, and Cauca. Together these four regions account for almost 60% of the coffee produced in Colombia. Regarding S14, its activities are more regionally concentrated. Antioquia alone handles 29% of the total production and, together with Risaralda (20%) and Caldas (20%), account for almost 70% of the total production. The regional share of international exports is identical to the production of S14, as only this sector exports its products.

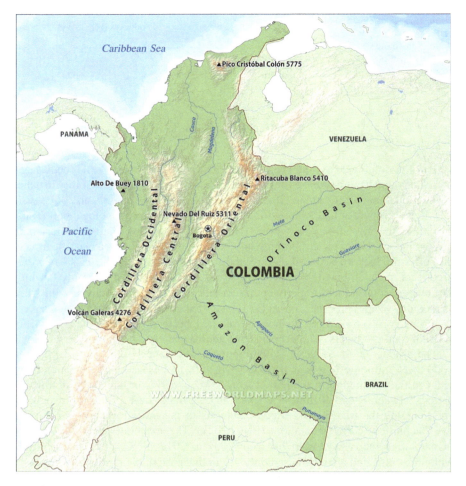

Fig. 10.1 Mountain ranges in Colombia (Free World Map, 2022)

10.2.2 *Coffee Productive Structure in Colombia*

The processing that coffee undergoes after the harvest involves the removal of the outer layers of the beans, selection, and drying. There are different methods to remove the outer layer of coffee beans after harvesting (to separate the pulp from the bean): wet process (most used in Colombia) and drying. Each of the processes can influence the flavor of the coffee produced. After these steps, one achieves what is referred to as parchment coffee. This is the coffee that growers sell together with cooperatives. Once sold, the coffee passes by a peeling process, where the parchment is removed. Then comes the green coffee, which is destined for export. In 2015, 98.1% of all Colombian coffee exported was at this stage (Comtrade, 2021).

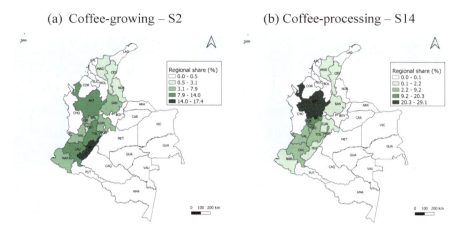

Fig. 10.2 Regional share of sectors S2 and S14. *Source* Interregional Input-Product Matrix for Colombia, 2015

All these steps are related to S2 or S14 activities and demand goods and services from different sectors of the Colombian economy. Figure 10.3 shows the productive chain of S2. The main suppliers are the chemical industry (35.3%), agriculture (28.4%), electrical equipment (13.3%), land transportation (7.8%), and financial activities (4.5%). We can also see that the primary sources of intermediate inputs are domestic. Adding up all imported raw materials used to produce coffee, these represent 22.6% of the total expenditure on inputs.

In Fig. 10.4, the intermediate inputs of S14 are shown. The coffee-growing sector (S2) is the major supplier of inputs (81.6%), followed by the consumption of inputs

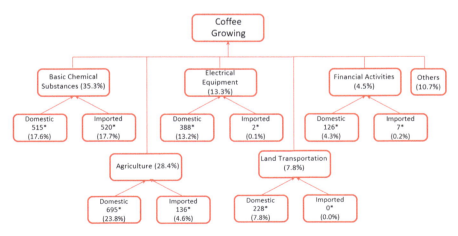

Fig. 10.3 Coffee growing (S2) (COP billions)—intermediate inputs demand. *Source* Interregional Input-Product Matrix for Colombia, 2015

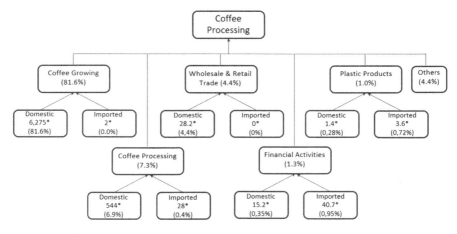

Fig. 10.4 Coffee processing (S14) (COP billions)—intermediate inputs demand. *Source* Interregional Input-Product Matrix for Colombia, 2015. *Note* *billion COP

from the sector itself (7.3%) and by wholesale and retail (4.4%). Only, 2% of the inputs used in the production process come from other countries, with emphasis on inputs used in the sectors related to the financial activity (0.95%) and plastic products (0.72%). This means that the coffee processed and exported is dependent almost entirely on local inputs.

Figure 10.5 shows the total (direct and indirect) interactions between all sectors in the Colombian economy. We can observe that while the sectors covered in this study (S2 and S14) have the strongest interaction within the Colombian economy, the indirect effects reach large number of other sectors.

Another way to see the relationships between the sectors in an economy is through the backward and forward linkages, as presented in Fig. 10.6. The forward linkage index of S2 is greater than one (quadrant III), showing that it depends on inter-industry demand. By turn, the coffee processing sector (S14) is an important demander of inputs, as its backward linkage index is greater than one (quadrant II).

Let us focus now on the use of primary factors. Figures 10.7 and 10.8 bring the share of spending on primary factors by sectors S2 and S14, respectively. We can see that coffee growing is more dependent on primary factors (64.6% of total spending), divided between labor (31.3%) and capital (33.3%).

Production costs associated with coffee processing (S14) are more concentrated in the acquisition of inputs (92.3%) than in the payment for production factors (7.7%), as can be seen in Fig. 10.8. Notably, the largest portion of the payment to production factors goes to remuneration of capital (7.0%), while a small portion goes to remuneration of labor (0.7%).

Together, sectors S2 and S14 accounted for 2.8% of total jobs in Colombia in 2015. The workforce employed in S2 has 621,000 workers, representing 99.2% of the workers employed in the growing and processing of coffee. Coffee processing

10 Chaining Juan Valdez: Linkages in the Colombian Coffee Production

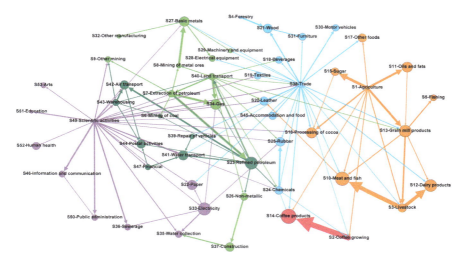

Fig. 10.5 Input–output network in Colombia. *Source* Interregional Input-Product Matrix for Colombia, 2015

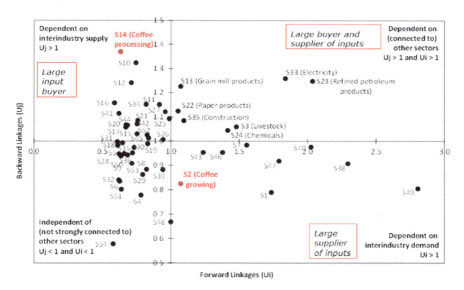

Fig. 10.6 Rasmussen-Hirschman (R-H) backward and forward linkages. *Source* Interregional Input-Product Matrix for Colombia, 2015

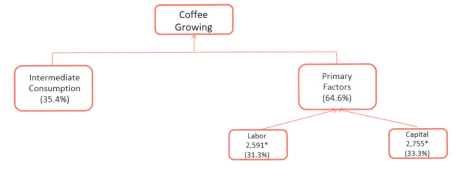

Fig. 10.7 Coffee growing (S2) (COP billions)—primary factors demand. *Source* Interregional Input-Product Matrix for Colombia, 2015. *Note* *Billions of COP

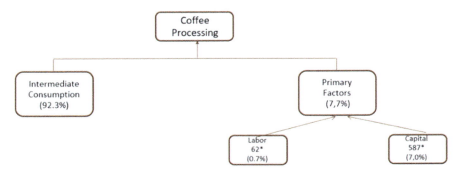

Fig. 10.8 Coffee processing (S14) (COP billions)—primary factors demand. *Source* Interregional Input-Product Matrix for Colombia, 2015

(S14) has 5,000 workers, representing 0.02% of the total employees in Colombia and 0.8% of those involved in coffee.

Figure 10.9 illustrates the proportion of workers by educational level[1] in the sectors S2, S14, the agriculture, and the total of Colombia. On one hand, we can see that most of the people working in coffee growing have a low educational level (73%), a share that is much higher than the average of all sectors (30%). On the other hand, in coffee processing, the workforce is more qualified; 38% have a medium qualification, and 37% have a high qualification.

The labor market in coffee growing is almost all informal. As Fig. 10.10 shows, 97.5% employed in this sector do not have a formal working relationship, while over 80% of coffee-processing employees are in a formal relationship, higher than the country's average (35.5%).

---

[1] A worker who has a maximum of 5 years of study is classified as low skilled. The work considered as medium qualification is the one that has between 6 and 9 years of study and the one that has completed university as high.

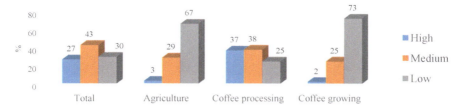

Fig. 10.9 Percentage share by qualification of workers in 2015—total in Colombia, agriculture, coffee processing, and coffee growing. *Source* Interregional Input-Product Matrix for Colombia, 2015

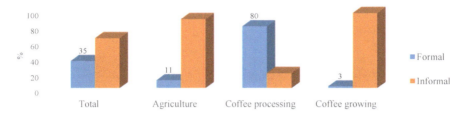

Fig. 10.10 Percentage share of formal and informal work in 2015—total employment, agriculture, coffee processing, and coffee growing in Colombia. *Source* Interregional Input-Product Matrix for Colombia, 2015

Turning now to the worker's income in the coffee-related sectors, we analyze it in terms of minimum wages, which in 2015 was 644,000 COP. Workers who earn less than one minimum wage account for 82% and 57% in sectors S2 and S14, respectively. This proportion is higher than the average of all sectors (23%) and agriculture (42%), as can be seen in Fig. 10.11. Two facts can explain this pattern. First, as mentioned before, the activity of coffee growing in Colombia is developed on small properties, and in all, probably, the workers are relatives. Secondly, the workers can move from one farm to another after the harvest, so the salaries are low, and there are no incentives to formalize the relationship between the farmers and the workers.

In summary, over 500,000 producers work primarily on small properties, and many use family labor and temporary employment in the coffee-growing sector. The workers have low qualifications; 11% of them did not attend school, and 73% have a maximum of 5 years of study. Income is not well distributed, as 81% of workers do not even receive one minimum wage, and 14% receive over 10. The data of the coffee-processing sector are a little better, as there are more formal jobs and higher qualifications and income. However, 57% of workers still earn less than the minimum wage. These patterns is similar in all the regions in Colombia.

The coffee produced in Colombia has two main destinations: intermediate consumption and exportation. In Fig. 10.12 we can see that almost all the production from S2 goes to sector S14; export activity is concentrated in the latter sector;

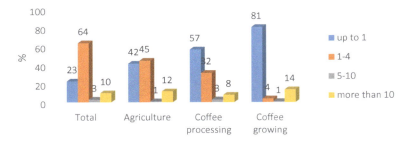

Fig. 10.11 Percentage share of worker income in Colombia in 2015, agriculture and coffee production and processing sectors. *Source* Interregional Input-Product Matrix for Colombia, 2015

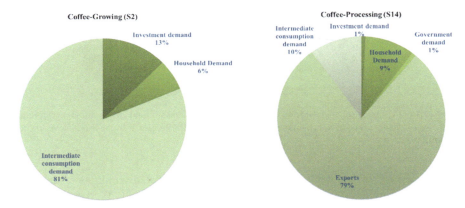

Fig. 10.12 Destination of production—share on total production (%), S2 and S14, 2015. *Source* Interregional Input-Product Matrix for Colombia, 2015

with 80% of its production exported, 10% goes for further intermediate consumption demand, and the household sector consumes the remaining 10%.

10.3 Data and Methodology: The Hypothetical Extraction Method and Data Source

The extraction method, initially proposed by Dietzenbacher et al. (1993), comprises the hypothetical extraction of a sector/region in the input–output matrix. The purpose is to quantify how much the total output of an economy with n sectors and R regions could change (or reduce) if a particular sector/region was removed from this economy. This technique allows the analysis of the importance of a sector/region in an economic structure given its extraction and consequent reduction in the level of activity in the economy. It should be emphasized that the greater the level of interdependence of

10 Chaining Juan Valdez: Linkages in the Colombian Coffee Production

this sector/region concerning the others, the greater the impact systemically. The description of the extraction method that follows is based on Dietzenbacher et al. (1993) and Miller and Blair (2022).

Consider a complete model, with n sectors and R regions, the output of the economy is given by

$$\mathbf{x} = (\mathbf{I} - \mathbf{A})^{-1}\mathbf{f} \tag{10.1}$$

where

$\mathbf{x}$ = the nR element column output vector.

$\mathbf{A}$ = the $nRxnR$ matrix of technical coefficient.

$\mathbf{f}$ = the nR element column vector of final demand.

$(\mathbf{I} - \mathbf{A})^{-1}$ = the Leontief inverse.

Assume that sector j is deleted from all the regions. The extraction of this sector will initially affect the matrix of technical production coefficient $\mathbf{A}$, which now has r rows and r columns less. The extraction also affects the rows corresponding to sector j in the vector of final demand $\mathbf{f}$.

Using $\overline{\mathbf{A}}_{(j)}$ for the matrix of dimensions $(n-1)R \times (n-1)R$ without the sector j, and $\overline{\mathbf{f}}_{(j)}$ the vector with dimension $(n-1)R$ for the reduced final demand vector (i.e., without sector j), the production in the reduced economy (i.e., without sector j) will be given by:

$$\overline{\mathbf{x}}_{(j)} = \left(\mathbf{I} - \overline{\mathbf{A}}_{(j)}\right)^{-1}\overline{\mathbf{f}}_{(j)} \tag{10.2}$$

Thus, we can write:

$$T_j = i'\mathbf{x} - i'\overline{\mathbf{x}}_{(j)} \tag{10.3}$$

where T_j is the aggregate measure of loss in the economy—decrease in total output if the sector j "disappears." In other words, it is a measure of the relative importance of sector j as a result of the removal of the total linkages of sector j. We can also calculate $\overline{\mathbf{x}}_{(j)}$ and T_j for a specific region. In this case, we will have the regional relative importance of sector j.

From Eq. 10.3, we can analyze a situation where the production of sector j, $\mathbf{x}_j$ is not included in $i'\mathbf{x}$. In this way, we have:

$$T_j = (i'\mathbf{x} - \mathbf{x}_j) - \overline{\mathbf{x}}_{(j)} \tag{10.4}$$

as a measure of the importance of sector j for other sectors in the economy.

In both cases, dividing T_j by $i'x$ and multiplying by 100 gives an estimation of the decrease of the economic activity in percentage chances:

$$\overline{T}_j = 100 \frac{(i'\mathbf{x} - \overline{\mathbf{x}}_{(j)})}{i'\mathbf{x}} \tag{10.5}$$

As usual in input–output models, we can observe the sectorial gross output outcomes in other variable's outcomes, like value added and employment. In this case, we can multiply the vectors $\mathbf{x}$ or $\overline{\mathbf{x}}$ by a diagonal matrix $\hat{\mathbf{v}}$, whose main diagonal contains the variable's coefficient. These coefficients are the ratios of the variable's values by respective gross output.

Our interest here is to evaluate the importance of coffee production for Colombia. Thus, we extracted the coffee-growing (S2) and the coffee-processing (S14) sectors integrally from the Interregional Input–Output model for Colombia. As both sectors have a small share in the GDP, we verified the combined effect of their extraction. We explore the results in gross production, value added, and employment.

The idea behind the extraction method is that it can evaluate a sector's value added in a region r. This idea that Los et al. (2016) proposed summarizes as follows.

The value added in region r ($\mathbf{VA}_r$) can be given by:

$$\mathbf{VA}_r = \mathbf{v}_r(\mathbf{I} - \mathbf{A})^{-1}\mathbf{f}i \tag{10.6}$$

where $\mathbf{v}_r$ is a row vector with ratios of value added to gross output in industries in region r as the first element and zeros elsewhere, and i is a column vector in which all elements are unity.

To evaluate the domestic value added in exports from region r to region n, we consider a hypothetical world where the first does not export anything to the last. In this case, the new $\mathbf{VA}$ or hypothetical $\mathbf{VA}$ is represented by:

$$\mathbf{VA}_{r,n}^* = \mathbf{v}_r\left(\mathbf{I} - \mathbf{A}_{r,n}^*\right)^{-1}\mathbf{f}_{r,n}^* i \tag{10.7}$$

where $\mathbf{A}_{r,n}^*$ and $\mathbf{f}_{r,n}^*$ are the hypothetical matrix of input coefficient and final demand, respectively.

From Eqs. (10.7) and (10.6), the domestic value added in exports (**DVA**) from region r to region n is given by:

$$\mathbf{DVA}_{r,n} = \mathbf{VA}_r - \mathbf{VA}_{r,n}^* \tag{10.8}$$

We can calculate the **DVA** for all other regions of the model and from each to the n-regions, excluding itself. This study calculates the domestic value added in the sector S14 exports. The results allow us to highlight this sector's direct and indirect importance to local value chain.

10.4 Results

In this section, we present the results of the two strategies of analysis described in the last section: the extraction of the coffee-related sectors and the measures of their local value added.

10.4.1 What if the Coffee-Growing and Coffee-Processing Sectors Did not Exist?

Table 10.2 shows the effects on the gross value of production per region and sector of the exclusion of the sectors S2 and S14 from the Colombian economy. The total value of production would decline 1.4% if Colombia stopped the cultivation and the processing of coffee. The most affected sectors would be S1 (Agriculture), S24 (Manufacturing of chemical and chemical products), S38 (Wholesale and retail trade), and S40 (Land transport and transport via pipelines). All of them are directly related to the cultivation or processing of coffee, as shown in the productive structure in Sect. 10.2. The most affected regions would be Caldas (-10.5%), Risaralda (-9.5%), and Huila (-6.7%). In Sect. 10.2, we showed that the production of both S2 and S14 is concentrated in these regions; hence, these results are to be expected.

In terms of impact on value added (Table 10.3), the total value added in Colombia will be reduced by 1%. We also observe that the most affected sectors have the highest impact on gross production (agriculture, manufacture of chemicals and chemical products, and wholesale and retail trade). Regarding the impact on the value added of the regions, there are some differences when comparing with the ones from the gross production values. The regions that would lose are Huila (-7.9%), Caldas (-5.7%), and Cauca (-5.4%).

The results of the effects on the labor market are provided in Table 10.4. Together, sectors S2 and S14 employ 717,000 workers who would have to search for other occupations if these sectors stop production. Regarding the other sectors, the most affected are agriculture (-1.81%), manufacturing of chemical and chemical products (-1.48%), and wholesale and retail trade (-0.71%). Again, they have the highest impact on gross production and value added.

The jobs losses would occur in all the regions, including Bogotá D.C, which does not have any production of coffee. The regions that would have more job losses are Huila (-18.07%), Caldas (-15.18%), and Risaralda (-13.01%). These are some of the most important regions for both production and processing of coffee.

We also analyzed the effects on the labor market in S2 and S14 in terms of the working relationship (formal and informal) and the education level of the workers. These results are also in Table 10.4. We can see that the most affected workers are those in informal working relationships (-4.71%) and with low (-7.84%) and medium (-4.02%) qualifications. Regionally, losing jobs would be the worst in the primary producer regions. In Caldas (-38.05%), Huila (-35.95%), and Risaralda

Table 10.2 Hypothetical extraction: percentage change in gross output for Colombia (%), 2015

	R1	R3	R6	R8	R11	R13	R15	R17	R19	R20	R21	R23	R24	–	Colombia
	Antioquia	Bogotá D.C	Caldas	Cauca	Cundina-marca	Huila	Magda-lena	Nariño	Quindío	Risaralda	Santander	Tolima	Valle del Cauca	Others	
Agriculture	−0.7	−1.1	−4.3	−4.5	−0.7	−6.7	−0.4	−2.9	−3.3	−3.4	−2.0	−3.4	−1.9	−1.5	−1.8
Coffee growing	−100.0	0.0	−100.0	−100.0	−100.0	−100.0	−100.0	−100.0	−100.0	−100.0	−100.0	−100.0	−100.0	−100.0	−100.0
Livestock and hunting	−0.4	0.0	−0.8	−1.0	−0.1	−1.4	−0.2	−0.6	−0.7	−0.8	−0.4	−0.8	−0.4	−0.2	−0.3
Processing of coffee products	−100.0	−100.0	−100.0	−100.0	−100.0	−100.0	−100.0	−100.0	−100.0	−100.0	−100.0	−100.0	−100.0	−100.0	−100.0
Manufacture of textiles, and wearing apparel	−0.2	−0.1	−0.6	−0.5	−0.1	−0.7	−0.2	−0.2	−0.3	−0.4	−0.1	−0.3	−0.2	−0.1	−0.1
Manufacture of paper and paper products	−0.5	−0.3	−2.4	−0.6	−0.2	−0.8	−0.6	−0.4	−1.0	−2.0	−0.3	−0.6	−0.4	−0.2	−0.4
Manufacture of coke and refined petroleum products	−0.1	−0.1	0.0	0.0	0.0	−0.3	−0.1	0.0	0.0	0.0	0.0	−0.2	−0.1	−0.1	−0.1
Manufacture of chemicals and chemical products	−1.6	−1.4	−3.0	−2.8	−1.0	−9.6	−1.2	−3.4	−4.0	−3.7	−1.7	−5.2	−1.6	−0.4	−1.5
Manufacture of rubber and plastics products	−0.3	−0.2	−1.6	−0.6	−0.1	−0.5	−0.4	−0.4	−0.8	−1.5	−0.2	−0.5	−0.3	−0.1	−0.3

(continued)

Table 10.2 (continued)

	R1	R3	R6	R8	R11	R13	R15	R17	R19	R20	R21	R23	R24	–	Colombia
	Antioquia	Bogotá D.C	Caldas	Cauca	Cundina-marca	Huila	Magda-lena	Nariño	Quindío	Risaralda	Santander	Tolima	Valle del Cauca	Others	
Wholesale and retail trade	−1.0	−0.5	−4.2	−2.7	−0.4	−3.0	−0.8	−1.0	−2.0	−3.6	−0.5	−2.1	−0.8	−0.2	−0.7
Repair of motor vehicles and motorcycles	−0.3	−0.1	−1.3	−1.4	−0.2	−1.2	−0.3	−0.6	−0.7	−0.9	−0.2	−1.2	−0.3	−0.1	−0.3
Land transport and transport via pipelines	−0.7	−0.1	−3.3	−2.8	−0.3	−2.0	−0.7	−1.1	−1.8	−2.6	−0.4	−2.1	−0.6	−0.2	−0.6
Information and communication	−0.2	0.0	−0.8	−0.2	0.0	−0.2	−0.1	−0.1	−0.3	−0.7	0.0	−0.2	−0.1	0.0	−0.1
Financial and insurance activities	−0.5	−0.2	−2.4	−1.7	−0.2	−1.8	−0.5	−0.6	−1.1	−2.0	−0.3	−1.2	−0.4	−0.1	−0.4
Administrative and support service activities	−0.1	0.0	−0.4	−0.1	0.0	−0.1	−0.1	0.0	−0.2	−0.4	0.0	−0.1	0.0	0.0	0.0
Other sectors	0.0	0.0	−0.2	−0.1	0.0	0.0	0.0	0.0	−0.1	−0.1	0.0	0.0	0.0	0.0	0.0
	−1.9	−0.2	−10.5	−5.3	−0.6	−6.7	−1.8	−2.4	−5.1	−9.5	−0.9	−4.7	−1.2	−0.2	−1.4

Table 10.3 Hypothetical extraction: percentage change in value added for Colombia (%), 2015

		R1	R3	R6	R8	R11	R13	R15	R17	R19	R20	R21	R23	R24	-	Colombia
		Antioquia	Bogotá D.C	Caldas	Cauca	Cundina-marca	Huila	Magda-lena	Nariño	Quindío	Risaralda	Santander	Tolima	Valle del Cauca	Others	
S1	Agriculture	−0.7	−1.1	−4.3	−4.5	−0.7	−6.7	−0.4	−2.9	−3.3	−3.4	−2.0	−3.4	−1.9	−1.5	−1.8
S2	Coffee growing	−100.0	0.0	−100.0	−100.0	−100.0	−100.0	−100.0	−100.0	−100.0	−100.0	−100.0	−100.0	−100.0	−100.0	−100.0
S3	Livestock and hunting	−0.4	0.0	−0.8	−1.0	−0.1	−1.4	−0.2	−0.6	−0.7	−0.8	−0.4	−0.8	−0.4	−0.2	−0.3
S14	Processing of coffee products	−100.0	−100.0	−100.0	−100.0	−100.0	−100.0	−100.0	−100.0	−100.0	−100.0	−100.0	−100.0	−100.0	−100.0	−100.0
S19	Manufacture of textiles, and wearing apparel	−0.2	−0.1	−0.6	−0.5	−0.1	−0.7	−0.2	−0.2	−0.3	−0.4	−0.1	−0.3	−0.2	−0.1	−0.1
S22	Manufacture of paper and paper products	−0.5	−0.3	−2.4	−0.6	−0.2	−0.8	−0.6	−0.4	−1.0	−2.0	−0.3	−0.6	−0.4	−0.2	−0.4
S23	Manufacture of coke and refined petroleum products	−0.1	−0.1	0.0	0.0	0.0	−0.3	−0.1	0.0	0.0	0.0	0.0	−0.2	−0.1	−0.1	−0.1
S24	Manufacture of chemicals and chemical products	−1.6	−1.4	−3.0	−2.8	−1.0	−9.6	−1.2	−3.4	−4.0	−3.7	−1.7	−5.2	−1.6	−0.4	−1.5
S25	Manufacture of rubber and plastics products	−0.3	−0.2	−1.6	−0.6	−0.1	−0.5	−0.4	−0.4	−0.8	−1.5	−0.2	−0.5	−0.3	−0.1	−0.3

(continued)

Table 10.3 (continued)

	R1	R3	R6	R8	R11	R13	R15	R17	R19	R20	R21	R23	R24	-	Colombia
	Antioquia	Bogotá D.C	Caldas	Cauca	Cundina-marca	Huila	Magda-lena	Nariño	Quindío	Risaralda	Santander	Tolima	Valle del Cauca	Others	
S38 Wholesale and retail trade	−1.0	−0.5	−4.2	−2.7	−0.4	−3.0	−0.8	−1.0	−2.0	−3.6	−0.5	−2.1	−0.8	−0.2	−0.7
S39 Repair of motor vehicles and motorcycles	−0.3	−0.1	−1.3	−1.4	−0.2	−1.2	−0.3	−0.6	−0.7	−0.9	−0.2	−1.2	−0.3	−0.1	−0.3
S40 Land transport and transport via pipelines	−0.7	−0.1	−3.3	−2.8	−0.3	−2.0	−0.7	−1.1	−1.8	−2.6	−0.4	−2.1	−0.6	−0.2	−0.6
S46 Information and communication	−0.2	0.0	−0.8	−0.2	0.0	−0.2	−0.1	−0.1	−0.3	−0.7	0.0	−0.2	−0.1	0.0	−0.1
S47 Financial and insurance activities	−0.5	−0.2	−2.4	−1.7	−0.2	−1.8	−0.5	−0.6	−1.1	−2.0	−0.3	−1.2	−0.4	−0.1	−0.4
S49 Administrative and support service activities	−0.1	0.0	−0.4	−0.1	0.0	−0.1	−0.1	0.0	−0.2	−0.4	0.0	−0.1	0.0	0.0	0.0
– Other sectors	0.0	0.0	−0.2	−0.1	0.0	0.0	0.0	0.0	0.0	−0.1	0.0	0.0	0.0	0.0	0.0
Total	−1.2	−0.1	−5.7	−5.4	−0.7	−7.9	−1.2	−2.3	−3.7	−4.2	−1.0	−5.1	−0.9	−0.3	−1.0

Table 10.4 Hypothetical extraction: percentage change in employment for Colombia (%), 2015

		R1	R3	R6	R8	R11	R13	R15	R17	R19	R20	R21	R23	R24	–	Colombia
		Antioquia	Bogotá D.C	Caldas	Cauca	Cundina-marca	Huila	Magda-lena	Nariño	Quindío	Risaralda	Santander	Tolima	Valle del Cauca	Others	
S1	Agriculture	−0.69	−1.08	−4.26	−4.49	−0.75	−6.69	−0.43	−2.88	−3.28	−3.37	−1.98	−3.43	−1.95	−1.46	−1.81
S2	Coffee growing	−100.00	0.00	−100.00	−100.00	−100.00	−100.00	−100.00	−100.00	−100.00	−100.00	−100.00	−100.00	−100.00	−100.00	−100.00
S3	Livestock and hunting	−0.36	−0.03	−0.76	−1.03	−0.13	−1.41	−0.24	−0.62	−0.65	−0.82	−0.37	−0.77	−0.43	−0.22	−0.35
S14	Processing of coffee products	−100.00	−100.00	−100.00	−100.00	−100.00	−100.00	−100.00	−100.00	−100.00	−100.00	−100.00	−100.00	−100.00	−100.00	−100.00
S19	Manufacture of textiles, and wearing apparel	−0.15	−0.09	−0.62	−0.49	−0.10	−0.67	−0.17	−0.22	−0.34	−0.44	−0.13	−0.34	−0.15	−0.06	−0.14
S22	Manufacture of paper and paper products	−0.48	−0.32	−2.39	−0.59	−0.19	−0.77	−0.57	−0.39	−1.01	−1.99	−0.34	−0.62	−0.38	−0.18	−0.40
S23	Manufacture of coke and refined petroleum products	−0.09	−0.07	0.00	0.00	0.00	−0.31	−0.08	0.00	0.00	0.00	−0.04	−0.21	−0.10	−0.05	−0.06
S24	Manufacture of chemicals and chemical products	−1.59	−1.35	−2.96	−2.82	−1.03	−9.58	−1.20	−3.36	−4.04	−3.71	−1.69	−5.16	−1.64	−0.40	−1.48
S25	Manufacture of rubber and plastics products	−0.35	−0.22	−1.62	−0.59	−0.13	−0.52	−0.43	−0.35	−0.79	−1.49	−0.24	−0.52	−0.31	−0.12	−0.30

(continued)

Table 10.4 (continued)

		R1 Antioquia	R3 Bogotá D.C	R6 Caldas	R8 Cauca	R11 Cundina-marca	R13 Huila	R15 Magda-lena	R17 Nariño	R19 Quindío	R20 Risaralda	R21 Santander	R23 Tolima	R24 Valle del Cauca	– Others	Colombia
S38	Wholesale and retail trade	−1.00	−0.48	−4.22	−2.66	−0.42	−3.04	−0.79	−0.99	−1.97	−3.60	−0.53	−2.07	−0.82	−0.22	−0.71
S39	Repair of motor vehicles and motorcycles	−0.32	−0.14	−1.29	−1.41	−0.21	−1.23	−0.31	−0.55	−0.73	−0.86	−0.20	−1.18	−0.32	−0.08	−0.29
S40	Land transport and transport via pipelines	−0.67	−0.10	−3.25	−2.79	−0.30	−2.00	−0.72	−1.09	−1.77	−2.59	−0.40	−2.11	−0.58	−0.16	−0.55
S46	Information and communication	−0.15	−0.04	−0.78	−0.25	−0.03	−0.18	−0.11	−0.08	−0.26	−0.72	−0.05	−0.15	−0.09	−0.02	−0.09
S47	Financial and insurance activities	−0.51	−0.23	−2.41	−1.67	−0.21	−1.83	−0.47	−0.58	−1.10	−2.02	−0.30	−1.20	−0.41	−0.10	−0.37
S49	Administrative and support service activities	−0.07	−0.01	−0.42	−0.12	−0.02	−0.12	−0.06	−0.05	−0.16	−0.38	−0.02	−0.09	−0.05	−0.01	−0.05
–	Other sectors	−0.04	−0.01	−0.18	−0.06	−0.02	−0.03	−0.02	−0.01	−0.05	−0.14	−0.02	−0.04	−0.04	−0.01	−0.02
	Total	−3.69	−0.14	−15.18	−10.57	−0.70	−18.07	−0.77	−4.69	−11.49	−13.01	−3.16	−11.64	−2.71	−0.87	−3.23
	Employment: formal	−0.43	−0.13	−4.04	−1.02	−0.25	−1.12	−0.45	−0.36	−3.80	−3.19	−0.39	−1.32	−0.49	−0.08	−0.50
	Employment: informal	−6.71	−0.15	−22.19	−13.30	−0.97	−23.12	−0.86	−5.54	−14.84	−18.70	−4.47	−15.15	−4.04	−1.12	−4.71

(continued)

Table 10.4 (continued)

	R1	R3	R6	R8	R11	R13	R15	R17	R19	R20	R21	R23	R24	–	Colombia
	Antioquia	Bogotá D.C	Caldas	Cauca	Cundina-marca	Huila	Magda-lena	Nariño	Quindio	Risaralda	Santander	Tolima	Valle del Cauca	Others	
Employment: low skills	−10.49	−0.14	−38.05	−15.20	−2.10	−35.95	−0.80	−6.65	−30.71	−33.55	−7.83	−24.88	−14.71	−2.08	−7.84
Employment: medium skills	−4.87	−0.15	−18.20	−12.57	−0.78	−21.79	−0.85	−5.43	−13.22	−15.43	−3.93	−13.87	−2.84	−0.98	−4.02
Employment: high skills	−0.51	−0.12	−2.34	−1.29	−0.25	−1.36	−0.39	−0.88	−2.56	−2.22	−0.74	−0.96	−0.69	−0.17	−0.48

(−33.55%), over 1/3 of the low-skilled work would cease if coffee was not produced and processed. We can observe similar results for the workers with medium and high qualifications, the latter feeling the most negligible impact, given its reduced participation in the production and processing of coffee.

Interestingly, Antioquia is not among the most relatively affected despite being one of the leading producer regions of both S2 and S14. This is because the coffee-related sectors represent only 1.69% of its gross production. Its main economic activities are related to services, mainly as a result of the location of the city of Medellín, the second largest economic center of Colombia. As a comparison, in the relatively most affected regions, the share of S2 and S14 together is around 10% in Caldas, 9% in Risaralda, 6% in Hulia, and 5% in Cauca.

Together, the results of gross output, value added, and employment highlight the social and economic importance of coffee production for some regions of Colombia. The more dependent a region is on the coffee-growing and coffee-processing activities, the more they would be harmed if the production of this good stops. In the same way, those would be other regions that would benefit more from policies that improved the cultivation productivity and increased the value added of coffee products.

10.4.2 What is the Domestic Value-Added Content of Colombian Coffee Exports?

Based on the method described in Sect. 10.3, we evaluated the domestic value-added content of the Colombian exports of coffee. Table 10.5 shows the aggregated results. The value added of exports represents 85.8% of the total value of gross coffee exports, with 70.1% associated with goods and 15.7% with services. The processing of coffee within the country is still small, so its contributions to the value added in goods and services occur mainly at the early stages of production. This also explains the low value-added concerning services. The low value-added content of Colombian coffee facilitates the re-export by some of its importers after undergoing some type of processing.[2]

The geographic distribution of the value added present in goods and services arising from coffee exports can be seen in Fig. 10.13. Considering the value added associated with coffee exports related to goods, the main producer regions have the largest participation in the value added: Antioquia, Caldas, Tolima, Huila, and Cauca.

Spatial patterns about services value added to coffee exports show that the regions of Antioquia, Bogotá D.C, and Valle del Cauca are the ones that most contribute to adding value to local chains related to services. Note that Bogota D.C is a region neither produces or processes coffee but provides significant value added to coffee exports through the provision of services, especially financial and insurance activities.

---

[2] Further details on Colombian role in coffee foreign trade, particularly exports, are provided in Chap. 13.

Table 10.5 Value added (VA) in Colombian coffee exports compared to gross coffee exports

	Billions of COPs	% of gross exports
Value added in coffee exports	5772	85.8
VA in goods	4713	70.1
VA in services	1059	15.7
Gross exports of coffee	6725	100

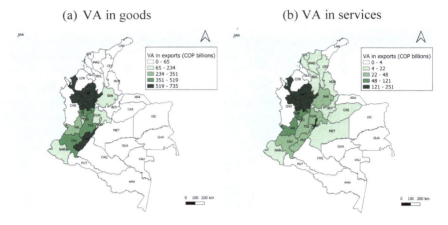

Fig. 10.13 Value added in exports (goods and services) by region (COP billions)

10.5 Final Considerations

Coffee is one of Colombia's most traditional exports, and it stands out in the international market. Coffee is also part of Colombian history and culture. It is difficult not to remember Colombia when we talk about coffee, one of the most consumed beverages in the world. Because of this historical value, the chapter provides an evaluation of the importance of the coffee-related sectors to the Colombian economy, employing the hypothetical extraction method to estimate the direct and indirect contributions of growing and processing activities.

While the total effects were modest, the country's GDP would be reduced by 1.38%, and the total value added would decrease by 1.04% if Colombia no longer produced coffee; the spatial concentration of growing and processing activities provides important sources of employment and income to households who would likely have few other opportunities. Concerning the labor market, without coffee-growing and processing sectors, Colombia would lose 3.23% of jobs. The workers who would be most impacted are those in an informal working relationship (−4.71%) and low skilled (−7.84%) in the departments of Caldas, Huila, Risaralda, and Quindío.

Another impact would be felt on foreign exchange inflow, as the coffee exporting sector is the fifth major source of external resources. Other economic activities could be affected, especially those that supply goods and services to coffee growing: agriculture, commerce, chemical, and land transport.

The analysis of the local value added content of exports shows that the participation of the services in the value added of exported coffee is much lower than the goods participation. This is because the processing of coffee is still very limited in the country, and it occurs at the first stages of the productive structure. Most of the value added in goods are in the main coffee producer regions. Bogotá D.C is among the regions with the highest value added in services even though no coffee is grown or processed in the region.

Currently, one of FNC's primary goals is to increase the value added of Colombian coffee products. This chapter shows how the Colombian economy can benefit from such a policy. First, by augmenting the level of processing of coffee, it can generate more jobs, income and support the livelihoods of thousands of workers and families who depend on coffee production. The increase in value added in coffee can also benefit several other sectors directly and indirectly, especially in coffee-producing regions. It may also highlight Colombia's participation in the international coffee market by exporting products with more value added.

Attention should be paid to the Chinese market; as noted earlier, the Chinese imports of Colombian coffee have risen dramatically in the last few years. If younger Chinese people continue to demand coffee, this source of demand could be an opportunity for Colombia to export products with a higher level of processing.

Another FNC initiative is to enhance the value added not only in the production system but in the provision of coffee and coffee-related services, such as in the coffee shops like Juan Valdez Café. This initiative can elevate the services share in the total value added of coffee and create more formal job opportunities, especially in large urban centers like Bogotá D.C.

References

Comtrade. UN Comtrade Database. Retrieved on February 10, 2021, from https://comtrade.un.org/
Dietzenbacher, van der Linden, E. J., & Steenge, A. E. (1993). The regional extraction method: EC input-output comparisons. *Economic Systems Research, 5*, 185–206.
FAOSTAT. Data. Retrieved on February 10, 2021, from http://www.fao.org/faostat/en/#data/QV
Federación Nacional de Cafeteros de Colombia (FNC). Home Page. Retrieved on January 10, 2021, from https://federaciondecafeteros.org/wp/federacion/estructura
Free World Map. (2022). *Colombia Physical Map*. Retrieved on August 25, 2022, from https://www.freeworldmaps.net/southamerica/colombia/map.html
Los, B., Timmer, M. P., & de Vries, G. J. (2016). Tracing value-added and double counting in gross exports: Comment. *American Economic Review, 106*(7), 1958–1966.
Ma, D. Slow brew: China's coffee revival and globalization. Retrieved on February 10, 2021, from https://macropolo.org/analysis/slow-brew-chinas-coffee-revival-and-globalization/
Machado, A. (2001). El café en Colombia a principios del siglo XX. *Desarrollo Económico y Social En Colombia Siglo, 20*, 77–97.

Miller, R. E., Blair, P. D. (2022). *Input-Output Analysis: Foundations and Extensions*, 3rd edn. Cambridge University Press.

Ocampo, J. A. (2015). *Café, industria y macroeconomía: ensayos de historia económica colombiana*. Fondo de Cultura Económica.

Palacios, M. (1979). *El café en Colombia, 1850–1970: una historia económica, social y política*. Bogotá: Presencial Ltda./Fedesarrollo. Retrieved on January 10, 2021, from https://babel.banrepcultural.org/digital/collection/p17054coll10/id/1013

Márcia Istake Ph.D. in Applied Economics from the University of São Paulo (USP) / Escola Superior de Agricultura Luiz de Queiroz (Esalq). She made a Post-doctorate at the Faculty of Economics, Administration and Accounting at the University of São Paulo (FEA/USP) at the University of São Paulo Regional and Urban Economics Lab (NEREUS). She is a full-time professor at the Department of Economics at the State University of Maringá (UEM) and Head of the Economics Department at the same institution.

Karina S. Sass Ph.D. in Economics from the University of São Paulo (USP). She is specialized in economic of climate change, impact evaluation and integrated methods of analysis.

Andrea Otero-Cortés Ph.D. in Economics from the University of North Carolina at Chapel Hill. Researcher, Center for Regional Economic Studies, Banco de la República, Colombia. Research fields: labor economics, development, and regional economics

Pedro Levy Sayon M.Sc. in Economics from the University of São Paulo (USP). Quantitative Methods Coordinator in a private consulting company in São Paulo, Brazil. His research interests include regional and urban economics, particularly infrastructure making use of econometric and input-output models.

Chapter 11
Urban Travelers Go to the Beach: Regional Effects of Domestic Tourism in Colombia

Eduardo Sanguinet, Luis Armando Galvis-Aponte, Inácio F. Araújo, and Eduardo A. Haddad

11.1 Introduction

Tourism has become an important source of development for regional economies. Recent evidence shows Colombia's tourism flows have increased mainly to the Caribbean coast departments (Bellón & González, 2014). This increase raises a debate about the efficiency of income transfer mechanisms, which allow the creation of regional development engines for growth. From the economic theory perspective, there is the possibility of distortions in the distributive effect, promoted by centralized income equalization policies between regions (see Chaps. 16 and 17) (Haddad et al., 2018).

Therefore, this chapter analyzes the potential of tourism to become an efficient mechanism for interregional income transfers in Colombia. In fact, the autonomous decision of agents to choose between spending in their region of origin, compared to spending in a tourist destination, can be understood as a mechanism to reduce externalities and market failures. Taking into account that fiscal redistribution policies could distort market mechanisms, consumer decisions to travel can be considered as an optimization outcome in which preferences and price signals play a crucial role without imposing distortions.

E. Sanguinet (✉)
Instituto de Economía Agraria, Universidad Austral de Chile, Valdivia, Los Ríos, Chile
e-mail: eduardo.sanguinet@uach.cl

L. A. Galvis-Aponte
Banco de la República, Cartagena, Colombia
e-mail: lgalviap@banrep.gov.co

I. F. Araújo · E. A. Haddad
University of São Paulo, São Paulo, Brazil
e-mail: inacio.araujo@usp.br

E. A. Haddad
e-mail: ehaddad@usp.br

In Colombia, domestic tourism flows follow a pattern of origin in core regions and destinations in the peripheries (DANE, 2018). One of the main tourist destinations is the Caribbean coast, which comprises eight out of the 33 administrative departments. This region presents lower socioeconomic indicators than the rest of the country (Galvis-Aponte, 2009). Our chapter argues that tourist expenditure acts as a source of local economic dynamics since it transfers resources from the richer origins to more disadvantaged destinations, making it relevant to assess the impact of travel expenditures on the tourism areas. Recently, the Colombian Ministry of Commerce, Industry, and Tourism (MinComercio) encouraged the so-called Orange Tourism—an instrument for promoting sustainable tourism—which generates cultural activities and economic and social development based on tourism management (PROCOLOMBIA, 2020). In this context, we argue that regional policy can be an essential instrument to attract tourist flows and generate positive effects for the local economy.

This chapter analyzes the regional impacts of Colombian tourists' consumption patterns, focusing on the Caribbean region, using an interregional input–output model. The interregional approach is appropriate to understand the interplay between regional inequalities and the tourism-induced effect for each origin–destination pair of urban travelers. The spillover effects depend on the structure of the sectoral and regional interdependence. Then, it is expected that the injection of resources will contribute to significant effects in the destination regions (Surugiu, 2009; Dwyer & Seetaram, 2012; Haddad et al., 2013). Following the international literature, we account for the net multipliers of gross production and employment (see Chap. 5 for specific definitions) to deal with regional measures (Haddad et al., 2013; Polo & Valle, 2012; Prasad & Kulshrestha, 2015).

There is little empirical evidence on the impacts of tourism in Colombian regions, with the majority adopting qualitative methods, such as Brida et al., (2011a, 2011b), Hernández-García (2013), and Bellón and González (2014). By addressing the systemic effects of interregional tourism flows across the regions, we generate evidence on the multiplier effects of domestic non-resident urban travelers on the Caribbean coast—national travelers' leading tourism destination. The economic assessment of the tourism effects captures the contribution to inclusive economic growth, especially through the potential for employment generation and income effects, both directly and indirectly. This study highlights the role of tourism in potentially reducing regional inequalities.

We have organized this chapter into six sections, including this introduction. The following section briefly discusses regional aspects of domestic tourism analysis applied to the Colombian case. The main channels of systemic effects of resource transfers from tourism are shown. Section 11.3 shows the empirical strategies applied to tourism studies in Latin America and worldwide. Next, in Sect. 11.4 we detail the method, data, and theoretical assumptions considered in our approach. We present the main findings of national and regional effects in Sect. 11.5, and the last section summarizes and concludes.

11.2 A Brief Approach to Tourism Analysis in Colombia

Tourism has been an industry that represents a substantial contribution to the growth of the Colombian economy. It has been documented that this sector can contribute more than a third of the total GDP growth (Brida et al., 2017). Evaluating solely the data from hotel networks, the one that receives most of the tourist potential´s effects, in 2013 this activity contributed about COP 8 billion to the economy and generated about 129 thousand direct jobs (Estrada-Jabela et al., 2016).

After the 2000s, the Colombian economy increased tourism's contribution to total economic activity (Rozo et al., 2014). According to MinComercio (2012), the number of international tourists in 2002 reached 1.1 million and by 2009, had grown to 2.5 million, representing a 127% increase in less than a decade. This context differed significantly from the 1990s when the tourism sector showed a contraction trend due to civil security and economic crises (López et al., 2004). During the 2000s, as pointed by Gardela and Aguayo (2003), Colombia's negative public image, the violence, and the economic slowdown made tourism output less competitive and more expensive than other countries. However, the economic scenario for tourism has changed considerably after the peace agreement signed in August 2016 and ratified in November of the same year between the Colombian government and the guerrillas of the Revolutionary Armed Forces of Colombia (FARC). In particular, World Bank data (2021) indicates an increase in the flow of international tourists in recent years, pointing out the potential opportunities for cash flows in regions with cultural and natural attractiveness.

Other indicators also show the dynamism of tourism in the Colombian economy. For example, between 2002 and 2009, the total inflow of foreign currency went from US$ 1.2 to US$ 2.6 billion. Likewise, average hotel occupancy rates have steadily increased, even while the supply of rooms is also increasing: 52.7% in 2010: 58.3% in 2011, 60.1% in 2012 (COTELCO, 2015). In 2018, Colombia received 4.3 million foreign visitors, with the USA, Venezuela, and Argentina the primary origins. Organization for Economic Co-operation and Development (OECD) data (2021) indicates that the tourism sector currently contributes about 2% of the Colombian GDP, also being a relevant activity for trade in services. Economically, the travel and tourism sector generated around of 2 million jobs direct and indirectly in Colombia in 2018, including 19% of new jobs, establishing itself as a relevant promoter of local entrepreneurship (DANE, 2018). In addition, domestic tourism shows a growth trend regarding the number of trips and interregional expenditures. In 2018, Colombia registered 23.3 million domestic trips, including both tourism and non-tourism-related travel flows, an increase of 4.0% compared to 2017. In 2019, more than 17 million domestic air passengers were recorded, representing an increase of 0.2% compared to the same period in 2018 (OECD, 2021). Interestingly, the tourism sector dynamics has a certain degree of heterogeneity in the national territory, which will become evident in the next section.

11.2.1 Geography of Domestic Tourism Expenditures in Colombia

Domestic travel has also gained greater economic relevance in recent years, becoming an important indicator of the country's level of well-being, employment, and income generation. The geography of domestic tourism flows follows a core-periphery pattern. The primary origin of urban travelers is the neighborhood of Colombia's capital, Bogotá D.C, as shown in Fig. 11.1. This region comprises large urban centers, which concentrate the country's highest levels of income and welfare.

In Colombia, the Caribbean coast is among the most favored tourist destinations, mainly due to the historic cities, the quality of the beaches, and the local gastronomic diversity. Specifically, the tourism flows occur toward four departments: Bolívar, Magdalena, Córdoba, and San Andrés. Some of the main cities of the country belong to this departments: Barranquilla, where the world-famous Barranquilla Carnival is celebrated; Santa Marta, known for its cultural diversity and rich ecosystems such as Tayrona National Park and the Sierra Nevada de Santa Marta; and Cartagena, known for the beauty of its colonial streets, its historic center, and its iconic Castillo de San Felipe de Barajas. The diversity of beaches with crystal clear waters is one of the leading local attractions, with imposing landscapes accompanying the Colombian musical and gastronomic culture. Accordingly, the Caribbean coast is a relevant destination for urban travelers, reinforcing the tourist industry potential that can generate effects on regional income and employment. It is expected, based on destination expenditures, an efficient effect of transfers from core areas to the periphery. Urban travelers from the Bogotá D.C region represent 57% of the total spending on interregional tourism in 2015.

However, there is still a set of characteristics that act so that tourism does not reach its full potential due to the lack of competitiveness. According to Such et al. (2009), several negative factors are persistent due to the lack of competitiveness. The latter includes factors related to insufficient infrastructure, limited training of employees, including relevant education programs, and awareness of opportunities in this sector, as well as problems centered on civil unrest. Further, there has been a lack of coordination in the private sector, with little promotion, discontinuity in tourism products, random application of tourism policies, public management deficiencies, and limited access to finance. For example, tourism in Cartagena, one of the most visited destinations, has been classified as a price elastic good which means that little competitiveness can have even more damaging effects for this sector (Galvis-Aponte & Aguilera-Díaz, 1999).

The uneven economic structure is formed by impoverished departments and others with a high socioeconomic level (Galvis-Aponte and Meisel-Roca, 2011). Caribbean departments have low social indicators and high levels of relative poverty. Figure 11.2a shows the regional distribution of the Basic Needs Index (BNI). The peripheral departments in Colombia's border have more significant needs in terms of socioeconomic conditions. In contrast, the central (core) areas show an opposite pattern, reinforcing the country's inequalities in development opportunities. The

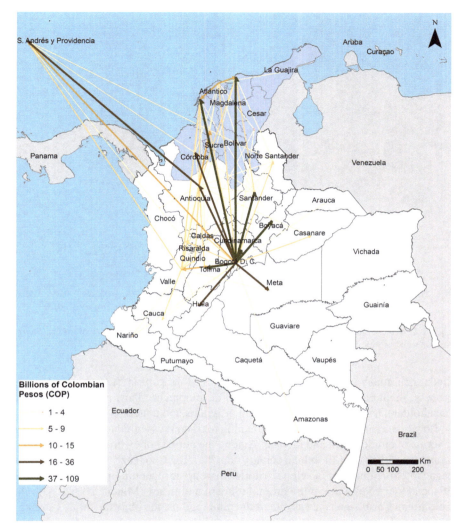

Fig. 11.1 Geography of domestic tourism expenditures (COP billions). *Source* Author's elaboration based on EGIT 2014–2015

concentration of economic activity, in terms of the GDP's departmental distribution, is seen in the large urban centers in and around Bogotá D.C, as shown in Fig. 11.2b.

The regional inequalities could be reduced by encouraging tourism as a local development strategy. The tourism's regional development in Colombia is planned on core departments. The central government's strategy is based on planning, market studies, product design, promotion and marketing, service provision (quality), and investment attraction (Sánchez & Hurtado, 2010). This strategy successfully raised regional awareness of the need to ensure an adequate basis for tourism development.

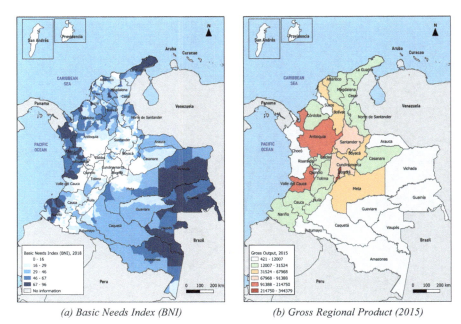

(a) Basic Needs Index (BNI)   *(b) Gross Regional Product (2015)*

Fig. 11.2 a Regional inequalities in Colombia. **b** Regional inequalities in Colombia. *Source* Author's elaboration based on DANE data

Since then, many of the departments have moved forward in the tourism planning process, including tourism in their overall development plans, involving different stakeholders, and designing promotional programs and materials.

Local governments' role in strengthening tourism is essential to guarantee effects in terms of employment and income. Among the public policy initiatives to promote tourist activity in the Colombian countryside, the "Turismo, Paz y Convivencia" plan began in 2014, aiming to develop territories for tourism, encouraging the construction of social synergies and culture around tourism and peace (Mincit, 2021). With the Colombian Caribbean coast as one of the pilot regions, the objective of this strategy is to generate more extensive value chains and improve the quality of life of the host communities through responsible and sustainable practices based on sustainability. According to Zúñiga and Castillo (2012), the problem is that there are still significant obstacles at the national level, such as deficient infrastructure, security, medical assistance, and inadequate regulatory structures for tourism. In addition, Castro (2011) points out the lack of fiscal order in management and waste which does not allow well-developed local strategies and policies to support the industry's consolidation. The following section discusses the potential economic effect of domestic tourist travel.

11.2.2 Systemic Effects of Tourism: Potential for Interregional Transfers

At the local level, economic activities around the tourism sector depend on an external demand factor. Different intersectoral mechanisms influence the generation of products and employment regionally. Indirect contributions to the tourism sector can be regarded as opportunities to spread systematical effects locally (Onder & Ayse, 2008). Domestic tourism is financed from national income, consisting of household consumption and government spending. The net effects of transfers presuppose a reduction in spending on other items in the consumption basket, implying a substitution effect or reduction of savings (Haddad et al., 2013). The substitution can be spatial as well, preferencing a Colombian destination for a foreign one.

The increase in society's welfare occurs in three situations of alternative expenditures decision-making by households (Oliveira Santos, 2012). The first is related to the demand for locally produced goods (imports substitution effect noted earlier), increasing income circulation at the local level. The second is associated with inefficient market distortions—in our case, assuming that these distortions in tourism-related sectors are less than those in other sectors. The third channel is related to positive externalities resulting from the social and regional redistribution of income and the appreciation of local culture.

Net benefits for the departments become an alternative mechanism to centralized income transfers. The autonomous decision of households to transfer income from origin to the destinations is a channel that allows the generation of systematical effects depending on the consumption basket.[1] As seen in Chap. 7, industry interdependencies associated with the core-periphery pattern allow household consumption to be an efficient channel for reducing interregional income gaps. In input–output studies, it is essential to consider that the results are dependent on regional and sectoral output multipliers. There are various multipliers related to output, income, government revenue, employment, and imports derived from structural interdependences. The spatial distribution of these multiplier effects (i.e., their distribution across regional and national economies) depends on structural, locational, and cultural factors. The magnitude of the multipliers can be decisive on the potential economic benefits resulting from tourist inflows in the peripheral regions of Colombia, as shown in Fig. 11.3.

Although there are differences in the magnitude of impacts, interregional input–output multipliers become relevant analytical tools for assessing tourism benefits as a channel for generating income and employment at the regional level. The differences in multipliers between the Colombian departments reveal how shocks in tourism spending can propagate throughout the whole economy. The tourism industry is

---

[1] Other studies are critical of the impacts of tourism on social development on a national and local scale. James (2009, p. 267), for example, argues that, for the Colombian Caribbean islands, "the economic benefits of tourism can be illusory for the population that needs them most and this activity is not realizing its full potential to mitigate unemployment, poverty, and inequality found in the region".

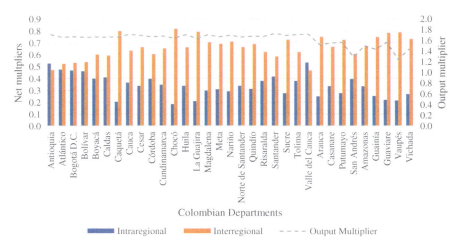

Fig. 11.3 Regional multipliers in Colombia, 2015. *Source* Interregional input–output table for Colombia, 2015. *Note* The figure shows the net intra and interregional multipliers, and the output is the average value for each Colombian department

labor intensive; hence, the supporters have been impressed by its potential to create employment and local income (Prasad & Kulshrestha, 2015). Since tourism is directly connected with various industries—such as accommodation, transport, entertainment, travel agents, management, finance, and health (Onder & Ayse, 2008)—the interregional and intraregional travels can generate direct and indirect effects on gross output, value added, and employment (Fig. 11.4).

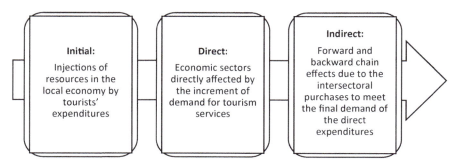

Fig. 11.4 Channels effects of tourism expenditures. *Source* Authors based on Prasad and Kulshrestha (2015)

11 Urban Travelers Go to the Beach: Regional Effects of Domestic Tourism ... 305

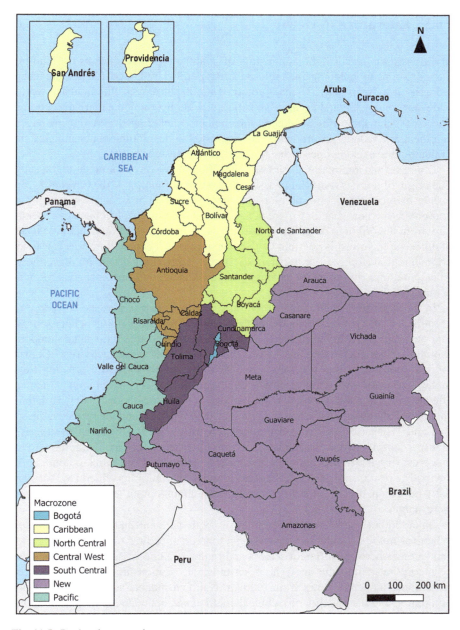

Fig. 11.5 Regional aggregation

11.3 Literature Review

In the last two decades, the application of quantitative techniques to the study of the tourism phenomenon gained relevance. As pointed by Dwyer (2012), the recent increase in tourism activities has promoted the expansion of this industry worldwide, generating demand for more specific studies concerning the tourism economic effects. At the same time, industry stakeholders, including destination managers and local and federal governments, are interested in developing better policies and evaluating the existing ones through quantitative research results.

Domestic and international tourism have different effects on the economic system. The origin of tourists is crucial to assess the source of funding. If the traveler is from his/her own country (domestic tourism), there is a foregone effect in the origin, as households are now spending more in the destination. This displacement of expenditure, from the origin to destination, justifies using input–output models for analyses of domestic travels. It is possible to calculate how much expenditure was lost in the original region (foregone or transferred). In turn, international tourism presupposes an external injection of travel expenses, often considered as an exogenous resource or shock to the economic system.

In the international literature, there has been a strong preference for adopting econometric or input–output modeling to understand the role of tourism. For example, Sun and Zhang (2015) used panel data to measure and test the spatial–temporal evolutionary characteristics and factors that affect the total productivity of China's tourism industry factors from 2001 to 2009. The results showed a growing trend in the total factor productivity, and technological progress is the dominant element affecting such trends. According to the authors, this provides evidence of the relationship between tourism, the levels of economic development, and the service industry. Sun and Wong (2014) assessed the structure cost stability by using the tourism industry capacity and accommodation industry data from Taiwan. The authors focus on comparing the results between econometric estimation and input–output coefficients. The results indicated that the income and profit multipliers fluctuated substantially but compensated for each other, while the input–output technical coefficients were stable.

Input–output models can be applied to both national and regional domains. When assuming a production technology, tourism spending for purchasing goods and services between different sectors and regions can be studied. Also, space can be incorporated into the analysis, describing the relationship between industrial sectors and monetary flows from tourism. National models assume the existence of a region and the equality of technical coefficients, not adequately measuring the effects at the local level. In turn, interregional models make it possible to assess the interdependence between industries and regions.

For analyses applied to tourism, the input–output models are consolidated in the international literature (Polo & Valle, 2012). Some studies have evaluated the relationship between foreign origin and the domestic economy. Salleh et al. (2012) studied the expenditure patterns of tourists from the Middle East countries and analyzed their impact on the Malaysian economy. The authors find that sectors that provide more services to tourists have benefited from a more significant impact than other sectors. Prasad and Kulshrestha (2015) analyzed the role of the tourism industry in generating employment in India. The input–output method was used to derive the employment multiplier and estimate the employment generated in the tourism sector due to an additional unit of foreign tourist spending. The results revealed that the expenditure of foreign tourists has a positive impact on the tourism sector, increasing the generation of jobs, directly and indirectly.

Regional approaches are also relevant. Li et al. (2016) examined the role of tourism development in reducing regional income inequality in China. The authors adopted a spatial–temporal autoregressive (econometric strategy) model to capture spatial and temporal dependence and spatial heterogeneity. The empirical results indicate that tourism development contributes significantly to the reduction of regional inequality, with domestic tourism making a more outstanding contribution than international tourism.

There is little empirical evidence on the systemic regional impacts of tourism in Latin American countries, with the majority adopting qualitative methods (Bellón & González, 2014; Brida, Riaño & Aguirre, 2011a, 2011b; Hernández-García, 2013). An exception is a study applied to Brazil by Haddad et al., (2013). Applying an input–output model, the authors analyzed the consumption patterns of tourists from different domestic origins and domestic destinations in Brazil regarding spending and composition. The results suggest that the total net multiplier effects of domestic tourism at the national level led to a zero-sum game, but the regional distributional effects are significant and asymmetric. Thus, domestic tourism could be evaluated as an important channel to re-allocate resources in a way that reduces inequality between Brazil regions.

The tourism effects in Colombia have been studied using qualitative and quantitative perspectives. For example, Brida et al., (2011a, 2011b) analyze how the local population of Cartagena (department of Bolívar) perceives the impacts of cruise tourism and the factors that affect the relationship between impacts and perceptions. With a qualitative focus, the authors revealed a positive social recognition of the economic impacts of tourism. Hernández-García (2013) explored the contribution of informal settlements to the tourism strategy and the brand of Medellín, characterized by that of "social urbanism". The results demonstrate informal settlements have a role in marking the city and promoting tourism in these areas. Furthermore, "social urbanism" helps build an image of a more authentic and distinguishable city from other cities in Colombia and Latin America.

Bellón and González (2014) discuss the relationship between tourism and development in Colombia from 1996 to 2012. The main conclusions point out that planning is fundamental to tourism policies' success. In turn, Benavides (2015) addresses the main elements of the tourism policy in Colombia over the last decade. The policy with the democratic security plan introduced a more substantial presence of security institutions, which intended to generate a favorable environment for investment and tourism. Certainly, the receptive tourism policy in Colombia aims to improve the competitiveness indicators based on the regional opportunity advantages.

Finally, the competitiveness of the tourism sector in Colombia depends mainly on natural and cultural resources that result in varying spatial advantages (Caldas, 2019). Again, the support for these claims is based on descriptive studies that do not use quantitative analysis. Therefore, we offer an alternative methodological proposal, using an interregional input–output (IRIO) model, which will facilitate the analysis of the short-term impacts of domestic tourism in all regions of the country.

11.4 Data and Methodology

The domestic tourism effects on the Colombian economy are made by demand shocks in the input–output model. There will be two stages: (i) construction of the domestic tourism spending matrix and (ii) short-term simulations and calculation of the coefficients of variation of the gross output and employment. Our study uses an interregional input–output model for Colombia, with 54 sectors and 33 departments calibrated for the base year 2015.[2] In the regional structure of the model, the Bogotá D.C is going to be treated as a specific region instead of a department.

Let us call X a matrix ($n.s \times n.s$) of gross national production broken down into n regions ($n \in \{1, \ldots, R\}$) and s sectors ($s \in \{s_1, \ldots, s_s\}$) of the Colombian economy. The technical coefficient matrix A ($n.s \times n.s$) includes the intermediate use required for production, and F ($d_f \times n.s$) is the final demand, with d_f components. As a result, we have the standard input–output system $X = BF$, where $B = (I - A)^{-1}$ is the Leontief inverse. The whole matrix notation is as follows:

$$X = \begin{bmatrix} x^1 \\ \vdots \\ x^R \end{bmatrix} A = \begin{bmatrix} a^{11} & \ldots & a^{1R} \\ \vdots & \ddots & \vdots \\ a^{R1} & \ldots & a^{RR} \end{bmatrix} F = \begin{bmatrix} f^1 \\ \vdots \\ f^R \end{bmatrix} B = \begin{bmatrix} b^{11} & \ldots & b^{1R} \\ \vdots & \ddots & \vdots \\ b^{R1} & \ldots & b^{RR} \end{bmatrix} \quad (11.1)$$

An origin–destination matrix v ($n.s \times n$) with interregional expenditures on tourism was built. Such data originates from The Internal Tourism Expenditure Survey (EGIT)[3] 2014–2015, elaborated by the MinComercio and the DANE. The different household consumption alternatives were represented by the breakdown of the final demand matrix, including the interregional tourism spending matrix, v. In specific:

---

[2] Chapter 5 of this book presents the interregional input–output (IRIO) model for Colombia.

[3] Between August 2014 and July 2015, the Internal Tourism Expenditure Survey was carried out in the 24 main cities and metropolitan areas of the country, with an increase in the coverage of 11 cities compared to the previous measurement, which reflects an increase in sample size to 39,825 households. In our analysis, we account expenditures by the populational weight of the survey. The Guainía department is not considered in the EGIT sample design.

Table 11.1 Tourism industry classification

Industry code	Industry description[a]
S38	Wholesale and commission or contract trade; retail trade (including retail fuel trade); trade-in motor vehicles and motorcycles, their parts, parts, and accessories
S40	Ground transportation and pipeline transportation
S45	Accommodation and food services
S53	Artistic, entertainment, and recreation activities and other service activities

Note [a] Sector classification of the interregional input–output model for Colombia

$$F = \begin{bmatrix} v^{11} & \cdots & v^{1R} \\ \vdots & \ddots & \vdots \\ v^{R1} & \cdots & v^{RR} \end{bmatrix} + \begin{bmatrix} c^1 \\ \vdots \\ c^R \end{bmatrix} + \begin{bmatrix} e^1 \\ \vdots \\ e^R \end{bmatrix} = \begin{bmatrix} f^1 \\ \vdots \\ f^R \end{bmatrix} \quad (11.2)$$

where $v^{\cdot R}$ represent the households' expenditures from their origins (.) on destination R, c^R are the other household expenditures in R, and e^R are the other expenditures of final demand. With the latter, it is possible to obtain the total output in each destination region R, according to the interregional input–output structure given by (11.3):

$$x^1 = B^{11}(v^{11} + \cdots + v^{R1} + c^1 + e^1) + \cdots + B^{1R}(v^{1R} + \cdots + v^{RR} + c^R + e^R)$$
$$\cdots$$
$$x^R = B^{R1}(v^{11} + \cdots + v^{R1} + c^1 + e^1) + \cdots + B^{RR}(v^{1R} + \cdots + v^{RR} + c^R + e^R)$$
$$(11.3)$$

EGIT classifies tourism expenditures in ten groups of economic activities, which have been associated with four industries of the input–output matrix as given in Table 11.1.

The final demand shocks of the destination regions (Fig. 11.5) were constructed from the origin–destination structure given by v. Following Haddad et al. (2013), we capture domestic tourism contribution to inclusive economic growth in terms of socioeconomic characteristics of employment (jobs) and income generation, both directly and indirectly. As Baster (1980) proposed, in an application for Scotland, Polo and Valle (2008) for the Balearic Islands, we employ just one vector for non-residents, interregional, and intraregional demands for each Colombian macro-region.

As in Haddad et al. (2013), two possible funding schemes for tourism expenditures are assumed, given the households' budget constraints. The justification for this is related to the allocation of resources in a national system. Other types of consumption are excluded, whether in the present or the future (intertemporal consumption assumption). The first source of resources implies reductions in personal savings, in which only the systematical effects of $v^{\cdot R}$ are considered, which provide the upper limit for the multiplier effects of expenditure in the short term in this modeling context. The alternative is given from the simultaneous equivalent reductions of monetary value in consumption in the respective regions of origin, representing a substitution effect induced in the consumption basket of travelers according to the consumption patterns of families provided in c^R. Sun and Wong (2014) demonstrate that the regional input–output model to estimate short-term tourism demand must consider the pattern of substitution in terms of household income. Furthermore, it was considered that consumer preferences are substituting tourism spending. In this regard, travelers replace their purchases in the region of origin with spending in the destination region. This provides a framework for interregional consumption transfers by households within the regional economic model.

According to the financing schemes, the net effects of transfers through domestic tourism expenditures must consider the consumption diverted from the travelers' origin. The net effect is given by

$$NE^R = TE^R - HE^R \tag{11.5}$$

where NE^R is the net effect, TE^R is the total effect, and HE^R is the hypothetical foregone home consumption effect. TE is the typical input–output effect on regional output, which can be expressed by $\Delta x^R = B \Delta f^{\cdot R}$ (Δf represents a change in final demand), considering the whole economy. The measure of HE^R considers the hypothetical amount spent by the region of origin and is given by

$$HE^{\cdot R} = \left[\frac{HH^{\cdot R}}{\left(x^R - HHTAX^R\right)} \odot v^{\cdot R} \right] \tag{11.6}$$

where **HE** is a matrix (sector-region x region). $HH^{\cdot R}$ is the household demand in the region of destination R for goods produced in the region of origin r, $HHTAX^R$ is the total taxes paid by .R households and x^R is the total household demand, and $v^{\cdot R}$ is the v-th amount of tourism' expenditure on destination R for goods produced in the region of origin r. The decomposition of the final demand allowed us to consider the impact of expenditures on Colombia's entire economic structure. Finally, impacting final demand, tourism expenditure generates effects on demand for regional production. It is important to note that results depend on the structure of industries and regional interdependences. As will be shown in the next section, it is expected to generate systemic effects in the destination regions.

11.4.1 Expenditure Patterns

The tourism expenditure pattern of interregional transfers is given in Table 11.2. Data was provided by DANE's EGIT (EGIT, 2015) and included relevant information on how much Colombian families spend on the destination departments when traveling for tourism purposes. Expenditure on interregional consumption by Colombian travelers reveals unilateral transfers from origin to destination. Interestingly, the expenditure spatial pattern reveals that the macro-region of Bogotá D.C is where most of the spending on tourism originates. The Caribbean coast region is the most representative destination, followed by South Central and Central West regions. The inequalities are reinforced according to intraregional consumption. Caribbean residents spend relatively little on tourism compared to other central regions. In the Caribbean, spending of travelers from Bogotá D.C represents 53% of total domestic expenditure.

When we look at intraregional travel patterns—between departments in the same macro-region—spending in the Caribbean and Central West is the most prominent. Brida et al., (2011a, 2011b) argue that the department of Bolívar, which is part of the Caribbean coast zone, has a single main tourist attraction, the city of Cartagena. In this case, our results follow Toro et al. (2015). They argue that "sun and beach destinations" (such as Cartagena, Santa Marta, and San Andrés) are the most visited or desired due to the potential travel demand. Coastal cities tend to be preferred for families to rest at certain times of the year. However, large urban centers, such as Bogotá D.C and Medellín, are also important domestic travel destinations due to their national and international economic position. The authors also point out that the "Coffee Belt" (Caldas, Risaralda, and Quindío) is an important destination for domestic travelers.

Geography plays a vital role in tourism expenditures across different destinations, as shown in Fig. 11.6 that describes the composition of travel spending. The largest share of spending by domestic tourists in Colombia is for accommodation and food services (S45), retail trade (S38), and transport services (S40), representing 46.51%, 20.69%, and 20.60%, respectively. It is interesting to note the different patterns of consumption between departments. The largest expenditures occur in Antioquia (Central West), Bogotá D.C, Bolívar (Caribbean), Boyacá (North Central), Cundinamarca (South Central), Magdalena (Caribbean), Santander (Central North), Tolima (Central South), Valle del Cauca (Pacific), and San Andrés (Caribbean).

11.5 Results

This section uses the consumption of goods and services by the urban travelers' expenditures and links them to tourism industries, as described in Table 11.1. The composition of spending is calculated using the matrix v (presented in the previous section), from which we can identify the money transfers between the seven Colombian macro-regions. The shocks to tourism demand in each destination region R depend on the regional distribution of tourism expenditures.

Table 11.2 Expenditures on tourism by origin–destination (COP billions)

		Destination							
		Pacific	Caribbean	Bogotá D.C	Central West	North Central	South Central	New	Total
Origin	Pacific	25.59	16.66	8.50	11.13	4.43	2.00	2.56	70.87
	Caribbean	1.39	39.29	6.37	6.03	2.07	0.52	0.88	56.55
	Bogotá D.C	16.92	139.95	0.13	31.19	62.51	147.50	25.89	424.09
	Central West	11.99	48.01	14.85	50.81	4.06	5.39	1.84	136.95
	North Central	0.75	15.26	7.71	3.25	18.02	0.39	0.56	45.94
	South Central	0.66	1.88	2.42	1.88	1.12	2.73	0.64	11.33
	New	0.35	2.03	2.61	0.80	0.76	1.11	2.14	9.80
	Total	57.65	263.08	42.59	105.09	92.97	159.64	34.51	755.53

Source Author's elaboration based on the EGIT (2014–2015), the MinComercio and the DANE

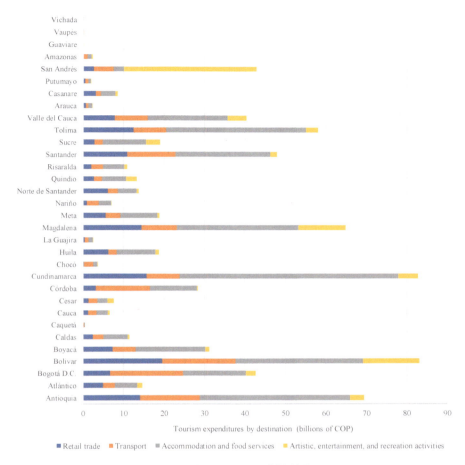

Fig. 11.6 Composition of expenditures by destination (COP billions)

11.5.1 National Effects

In this section, we present the analysis of short-term shocks resulting from the expenditures of urban travelers. The impacts of these expenditures on the regional and national economy can be seen when analyzing Table 11.5. In particular, the expenditure of each origin–destination pair is pre-multiplied by the national Leontief matrix B. This strategy allows us to measure the impact of the transfer of expenses at the destination and their contribution to national output. It represents a classic positive effect of the final demand shock. The impact of v on gross national production is 1,267.94 billion Colombian pesos (COP). There is evidence of positive systemic effects, with the core-periphery pattern being an essential driver of income redistribution from tourism flows. Specifically, 56.34% of the total effects are related to the expenses of tourists from Bogotá D.C. Regarding destinations, the South Central and Caribbean regions are responsible for most of the total national impact.

These results indicate that domestic tourism can be a relevant channel for increasing production and income in the Caribbean region. However, there is a transfer effect that must be evaluated. The positive impacts for the Caribbean may represent relative losses for the origin regions of the travelers. Therefore, it is important to consider the substitution effects of household consumption patterns. Urban travelers substitute consumption in their residence regions for consumption in tourism destinations, as we can see in Table 11.4.

The reallocation of households' expenses from their regions to tourist destinations represents a relative loss lower than the gains (Tables 11.3 and 11.4). The main macro-region affected is Bogotá D.C, followed by Central West. We can see that the relative losses are less than the gains in the Caribbean. This reveals the population's socioeconomic pattern concerning travels since more trips are within the region and fewer trips are made to other regions.[4] It is worth considering that the data used is associated with domestic travelers and expenses associated with the household's destination (EGIT, 2015). On the other hand, the results in Tables 11.3, 11.4 and 11.5 demonstrate that the Caribbean region can be considered a relevant destination for domestic tourism flows and further regional economic gains. It is interesting to pay attention to the consumption potential that the regions have. The macro-regions of Central West and Pacific are, after Bogotá D.C, the main "losers" in transferring household consumption based on tourism. The hypothetical foregone home consumption reveals a national effect of $-1,104.88$ billion COP. The net effects reveal a process of income redistribution and replacement of consumption patterns associated with domestic tourism. This result is given in Table 11.5, revealing a potential consumption related to regional development patterns.

The reallocation of household expenses from their origin to the tourist destination generated COP$163.06 billion, accounting the total net effect, representing about 21% of total domestic tourism expenditures in the same period. Similar evidence was found by Haddad et al. (2013) in Brazil. However, the net effect was about 3.3% of the total spent. Despite the differences in regional economic structure and country size, our results show a positive effect of redistribution based on interregional consumption patterns. Interestingly, the amount spent in the Caribbean (COP 52.36 billion) represents 32.1% of the total net effect (COP 163.03 billion). These results are explained by the assumption of present and future consumption (savings effect). Specifically, it is related to the foregone expenditure in the origin region compared to expenditure on the destination's areas.

It should be noted that the net national effect has a zero-sum game. Therefore, assuming that budget constraints imply financing tourism spending through consumption reductions in the region of origin, the positive effects are partially offset by the substitution effects. In this way, the composition of alternative financing allocations and the effects of associated import spillovers contribute to the result

---

[4] If shorter distances indicate less travel costs.

Table 11.3 Impacts on Colombian gross output (COP billions)

		Destination							Total
		Pacific	Caribbean	Bogotá D.C	Central West	North Central	South Central	New	
Origin	Pacific	43.23	26.72	14.39	18.62	7.26	3.38	4.17	117.77
	Caribbean	2.37	66.28	10.76	10.20	3.47	0.88	1.40	95.36
	Bogotá D.C	28.70	233.78	0.22	53.18	105.60	250.62	42.36	714.46
	Central West	20.40	78.50	25.13	85.84	6.86	8.86	3.04	228.63
	North Central	1.26	25.20	12.93	5.45	30.21	0.66	0.91	76.62
	South Central	1.10	3.08	4.07	3.17	1.84	4.59	1.06	18.91
	New	0.60	3.34	4.34	1.33	1.27	1.86	3.45	16.19
Total		97.66	436.90	71.84	177.79	156.51	270.85	56.39	1,267.94

Table 11.4 Total effects of foregone home consumption on national output (COP billions)

		Destination							Total
		Pacific	Caribbean	Bogotá D.C	Central West	North Central	South Central	New	
Origin	Pacific	−37.48	−24.37	−12.45	−16.3	−6.48	−2.93	−3.75	−103.76
	Caribbean	−2.03	−57.36	−9.31	−8.81	−3.01	−0.76	−1.28	−82.56
	Bogotá D.C	−24.74	−204.65	−0.19	−45.6	−91.42	−215.68	−37.85	−620.13
	Central West	−17.54	−70.08	−21.75	−74.26	−5.92	−7.88	−2.7	−200.13
	North Central	−1.1	−22.39	−11.34	−4.78	−26.48	−0.57	−0.82	−67.48
	South Central	−0.96	−2.75	−3.55	−2.76	−1.64	−4.01	−0.94	−16.61
	New	−0.51	−2.94	−3.79	−1.16	−1.1	−1.61	−3.1	−14.21
	Total	−84.36	−384.54	−62.38	−153.67	−136.05	−233.44	−50.44	−1,104.88

Table 11.5 Net effects on national output (COP billions)

		Destination							Total
		Pacific	Caribbean	Bogotá D.C	Central West	North Central	South Central	New	
Origin	Pacific	5.75	2.35	1.94	2.32	0.78	0.45	0.42	14.01
	Caribbean	0.34	8.92	1.45	1.39	0.46	0.12	0.12	12.80
	Bogotá D.C	3.96	29.13	0.03	7.58	14.18	34.94	4.51	94.33
	Central West	2.86	8.42	3.38	11.58	0.94	0.98	0.34	28.50
	North Central	0.16	2.81	1.59	0.67	3.73	0.09	0.09	9.14
	South Central	0.14	0.33	0.52	0.41	0.20	0.58	0.12	2.30
	New	0.09	0.40	0.55	0.17	0.17	0.25	0.35	1.98
	Total	13.30	52.36	9.46	24.12	20.46	37.41	5.95	163.06

found. Nevertheless, the national result reveals a potential for regional development in Colombia. Access to markets associated with the tourism sector can induce changes in households' consumption patterns, generating positive effects in greater value-added and intersector linkages. Due to this fact, public and private actions that allow potential tourists to boost consumption and generate superior welfare gains in these regions may increase the positive effect of consumption-based income redistribution. The following subsection decomposes these total net effects on production from domestic travels according to the primary origin (Bogotá D.C) and destination (Caribbean region).

This result is explained by offsetting the income generated in the economy and the expenses incurred by households: When spending is not made in the region of origin, it is allocated to the destination region. However, at the regional level, this assumption is likely relevant to understanding the potential impact of income transfers by household agents, which can generate direct and indirect effects on the local economies of travel destinations.

11.5.2 Regional Effects: Output and Employment

Table 11.6 shows the net results of interregional tourism spending for Bogotá D.C's output. As noted earlier, this region is the primary source in terms of spending on domestic travel. There is the potential to be negatively affected by families' decision to consume in tourist' destinations. It is relevant to analyze the signals' pattern, which details the net effect of the origin–destination pairs. The total net effect is negative, showing two critical facts. The first indicates indirect substitution effects due to residents' refusal to spend at the origin to generate demand in the tourist destination. The second represents an apparent redistribution effect from the richer (which spend more on tourism) to the most impoverished regions. We note that spending by Bogotá D.C residents in the Caribbean macro-region represents the largest share of Bogotá D.C's total negative effect, demonstrating the potential gain in output generated in the Caribbean departments. Besides, the impact of interregional demand influences Bogotá D.C's output. According to the interregional system, these results are based on Bogotá D.C's intermediate offer with all Colombian sectors and regions.

Domestic tourism's capacity to generate regional output gains in the Caribbean can be seen in Table 11.7. The net effect (the sum of regional results) is positive, indicating the impact of the transfer from other regions where tourists live. The impact of COP 212.2 billion represents about 81% of the total tourists' expenditures in the macro-region (as shown in the last row of Table 11.2), revealing a relevant effect for Caribbean local activities. It is interesting to note that even Caribbean travelers have positive effects in the region, demonstrating the potential for intraregional travel.

The exercises developed in this chapter allow us to capture domestic tourism's contribution to inclusive economic growth in terms of socioeconomic characteristics of employment (jobs) and income generation, both direct and indirectly. Economic activities related to the tourism industry are labor intensive, reinforcing the potential

Table 11.6 Regional effects of Bogotá D.C's output (COP billions)

		Destination							Total
		Pacific	Caribbean	Bogotá D.C	Central West	North Central	South Central	New	
Origin	Pacific	−1.55	−0.25	10.44	−0.54	−0.10	0.01	−0.05	7.96
	Caribbean	−0.08	−2.11	7.79	−0.47	−0.05	−	−0.03	5.05
	Bogotá D.C	−12.91	−104.23	0.06	−23.57	−44.04	−95.30	−18.39	−298.38
	Central West	−1.09	−0.74	17.75	−4.26	−0.17	−0.16	−0.09	11.24
	North Central	−0.11	−1.50	8.88	−0.46	−1.96	−0.03	−0.05	4.77
	South Central	−0.15	−0.31	2.60	−0.39	−0.18	−0.42	−0.10	1.05
	New	−0.08	−0.38	2.84	−0.18	−0.14	−0.13	−0.35	1.58
	Total	−15.97	−109.52	50.36	−29.87	−46.64	−96.03	−19.06	−266.73

Table 11.7 Regional effects of Caribbean's output (COP billions)

		Destination							Total
		Pacific	Caribbean	Bogotá D.C	Central West	North Central	South Central	New	
Origin	Pacific	−0.63	14.49	−0.15	−0.25	−0.04	−0.04	−0.04	13.34
	Caribbean	−1.29	16.25	−5.76	−5.28	−1.88	−0.45	−0.81	0.78
	Bogotá D.C	−0.68	166.8	−0.01	−1.04	−1.91	−7.69	−1.09	154.38
	Central West	−0.59	33.82	−0.62	−2.31	−0.13	−0.33	−0.08	29.76
	North Central	−0.07	13.93	−0.61	−0.24	−1.18	−0.03	−0.03	11.77
	South Central	−0.02	1.25	−0.06	−0.05	−0.03	−0.1	−0.02	0.97
	New	−0.02	1.67	−0.16	−0.04	−0.03	−0.07	−0.12	1.23
	Total	−3.30	248.21	−7.37	−9.21	−5.20	−8.71	−2.19	212.23

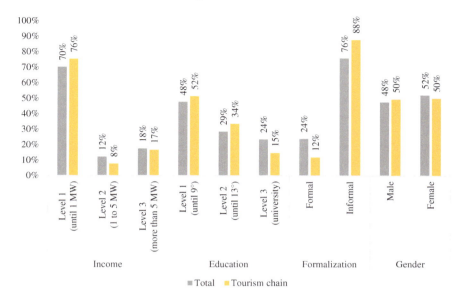

Fig. 11.7 Effects on the Caribbean labor market (share)

for positive regional economic activity. Figure 11.7 shows employment multipliers compared to the local labor market (workers' income, education, formalization, and gender).

This result indicates that employment is strongly associated with the occupational profile at the regional level, which tends to be reinforced by the increased demand for goods and services directly and indirectly. The impact on job creation is heterogeneous in terms of socioeconomics aspects. There is a larger effect on the employment of lower levels of wages, education, and informal workers. The generation of jobs for employed persons with higher education is lower than for lowest levels. This pattern highlights the level of education of the local tourism labor market in the Colombian Caribbean region (Estrada-Jabela et al., 2016).

11.6 Final Considerations

This chapter analyzed the role of domestic tourism as a mechanism for transferring and generating regional effects on the level of employment and income in Colombia. It was argued that tourism could be considered an efficient interregional convergence mechanism by reallocating monetary resources at the subnational level. The autonomous decision of household consumption to demand goods and services in tourism destinations reveals a problem of optimizing preferences, reducing distortions and negative externalities.

The input–output technique results indicate that interregional expenditures generate positive effects at national and regional levels, even considering the effects of substitution and import leaks. Our empirical approach made it possible to avoid overestimating regional effects by recognizing the interconnections between regions and industries within the economic system. The multipliers of national and regional output and employment revealed the redistributive potential from the core to the peripheral regions, which have geographical potentials that favor the tourism sector's activity. When observing the interregional flow pattern, the output and employment effects are strongly associated with tourists' origin and consumption patterns. The net effects of the expenditure's transfers in tourism-related domestic travels are generally positive, indicating that even interregional travel is to some extent offset by intraregional travel. Tourists from the Caribbean induce positive intraregional effects, as do travelers in the Central West and North Central macro-regions. In the metropolitan region of Bogotá D.C, however, this intraregional pattern is distinct, with trips to other regions having more significant positive effects.

The implications for regional tourism policy are important. Income disparities between Colombian regions that have persisted for many decades may find a contribution for their reduction through domestic tourism. The Caribbean departments have the ability to exploit local assets associated with the characteristics of the tourism goods and services that they can provide. The analysis of national effects reveals that, given the budget-constraint assumptions, the consumption-based multipliers play a zero-sum game. Although restrictive, this assumption provides an essential insight into the net effect of tourism consumption transfers within a country. Considering all the income households can spend at the national level, the effect tends to be zero: If it was not spent in the origin region, the expenditure was allocated to the destination. However, within the interregional system, the direct and indirect effects of transfers provide results that indicate potential multiplier effects that can support the development of peripheral areas.

Finally, the study reveals the potential for spreading regional development through incentives that increase travel and spending on the Caribbean coast when looking at the regional effects. Regional economic activity is positively affected in terms of output and employment. There is a clear space for public and private actions that strengthen the region's capacity to create local assets around the tourism sector. This would make it possible to attract more tourists and build a local innovation base that enhances investments and effects at the regional level.

References

Baster, J. (1980). Input-output analysis of tourism benefits. Lessons from Scotland. *International Journal of Tourism Management, 1*(2), 99–108.

Bellón, E. R., & González, L. G. (2014). *Tourism in Colombia: Growth versus development* (pp. 211–226). A Theoretical and Practical Study. Bringley, England Emerald Group Publishing Limited.

Benavides, G. F. (2015). Las políticas públicas del turismo receptivo colombiano. *Suma De Negocios, 6*(13), 66–73.

Brida, J. G., Monterubbianesi, P. D., & Zapata-Aguirre, S. (2011a). Impactos del turismo sobre el crecimiento económico y el desarrollo. El caso de los principales destinos turísticos de Colombia. *Revista De Turismo y Patrimonio Cultural, 9*(2), 291–303.

Brida, J. G., Riaño, E., & Aguirre, S. Z. (2011b). Residents' attitudes and perceptions towards cruise tourism development: A case study of Cartagena de Indias (Colombia). *Tourism and Hospitality Research, 11*(3), 181–196.

Brida, J. G., Rodríguez-Brindis, M. A., Mejía-Alzate, M. L., & Zapata-Aguirre, S. (2017). La contribución directa del turismo al crecimiento económico de Colombia: Análisis por ramas características del sector utilizando la Cuenta Satélite de Turismo-CST. *Revista De Estudios Regionales, 109*, 121–138.

Caldas Moreno, J. A. (2019). *Análisis de la competitividad de Colombia en el sector turístico en el periodo 2011–2018*, Tesis de grado, Fundación Universidad de América. Disponible en: http://repository.uamerica.edu.co/bitstream/20.500.11839/7673/1/533008-2019-III-NIIE.pdf

Castro, L. F. (2011). *Desafío de la competitividad turística en colombia para lograr ser de clase mundial*. Tesis de Postgrado. Universidad Militar Nueva Granada, Bogotá. https://repository.unimilitar.edu.co/handle/10654/17350

COTELCO. Asociación Hotelera y Turística de Colombia. (2015). *Informe de Indicadores Hoteleros 2015*. Disponible en: https://www.cotelco.org/estadisticas

Departamento Administrativo Nacional de Estadísticas. (2018). DANE. Disponible en: https://www.dane.gov.co/index.php/estadisticas-por-tema/servicios/turismo/encuesta-de-gasto-interno-en-turismo-egit

Dwyer, L., Gill, A., & Seetaram, N. (2012). *Handbook of research methods in tourism: Quantitative and qualitative approaches*, Cheltenham, Edward Elgar. https://doi.org/10.4337/9781781001295

Estrada-Jabela, A. M., Polo, L. E., Pérez-Valbuena, G. J., Hahn-de-Castro, L. W. (2016). Caracterización del mercado laboral en el sector hotelero de Cartagena y las principales áreas metropolitanas. *Documentos de Trabajo Sobre Economía Regional y Urbana*, No. 242, Cartagena, Banco de la República.

Galvis-Aponte, L. A. (2009). Geografía económica del Caribe continental. *Documentos de Trabajo Sobre Economía Regional y Urbana*, No. 119, Cartagena, Banco de la República.

Galvis-Aponte, L. A., Aguilera-Díaz, M. M. (1999). Determinantes de la demanda por turismo hacia Cartagena, 1987–1998. *Documentos de Trabajo Sobre Economía Regional y Urbana*, No. 9, Cartagena, Banco de la República,.

Galvis-Aponte, L. A., Meisel-Roca, A. (2011). Persistencia de las desigualdades en Colombia: un análisis espacial. In Bonilla-Mejía, L. (Ed.), *Dimensión regional de las desigualdades en Colombia*. Bogotá, Banco de la República.

Haddad, E. A., Galvis-Aponte, L.A., Araújo, I. F., & Vale, V. (2018). Impact assessment of scenarios of interregional transfers in Colombia. *Documento de Trabajo sobre Economía Regional y Urbana*, No. 272, Catagena, Banco de la República.

Haddad, E. A., Porsse, A. A., & Rabahy, W. (2013). Domestic tourism and regional inequality in Brazil. *Tourism Economics, 19*(1), 173–186.

Hernández-García, J. (2013). Slum tourism, city branding and social urbanism: The case of Medellin, Colombia. *Journal of Place Management and Development, 6*(1), 43–51.

James, J. (2009). El papel del estado en la construcción del desarrollo sostenible: El caso del turismo en el caribe insular. *Cuadernos De Economía, 28*, 265281.

Li, H., Chen, J. L., Li, G., & Goh, C. (2016). Tourism and regional income inequality: Evidence from China. *Annals of Tourism Research, 58*, 81–99.

López, M., Anato, M., & Rivas, B. (2004). Impacto de los acontecimientos mundiales en el turismo. *Casos De Estudio. Economía, 19–20*, 135–165.

Lv, Z. (2019). Deepening or lessening? The effects of tourism on regional inequality. *Tourism Management, 72*, 23–26.

Ministerio de Comercio, Industria y Turismo. (2021, January 20). *Turismo y Paz*. https://www.mincit.gov.co/minturismo/analisis-sectorial-y-promocion/turismo-y-paz

OECD. (2021, January 20). *OECD Tourism Trends ads Policies—Colombia*. https://doi.org/10.1787/6b47b985-en

Oliveira-Santos, G. E. (2012). *Economia do turismo*. São Paulo, Brazil, Aleph.

Onder, K., & Ayse, D. (2008). Effects of tourism sector on the employment in Turkey: An econometric application. In *Proceedings book first international conference on management and economics (ICME'08), current issues in emerging economies in global perspective* (pp. 365–337). Albania, University of Tirana.

Polo, C., & Valle, E. (2008). An assessment of the impact of tourism in the Balearic Islands. *Tourism Economics, 14*(3), 615–630.

Polo, C., & Valle, E. (2012). 12 Input-output and SAM models. In L. Dwyer, A. Gill, & N. Seetaram (Eds.), *Handbook of research methods in tourism: Quantitative and qualitative approaches* (pp. 227–245). Edward Elgar.

Prasad, N., & Kulshrestha, M. (2015). Employment generation in the tourism industry: An input-output analysis. *The Indian Journal of Labour Economics, 58*(4), 563–575.

PROCOLOMBIA. (2020). *Exportaciones no tradicionales, el turismo internacional y la inversión extranjera en Colombia*. Available at: http://procolombia.co

Salleh, N. H. M., Othman, R., Hasim, M. S., & Jaafar, A. H. (2012). The pattern and the impact of middle eastern tourist spending on Malaysia's economy. *Jurnal Ekonomi Malaysia, 46*(1), 53–63.

Sánchez, C. I., & Jaramillo-Hurtado, M. E. (2010). Policies for enhancing sustainability and competitiveness in tourism in Colombia. *Worldwide Hospitality and Tourism Themes, 2*(2), 153–162. https://doi.org/10.1108/17554211011037840

Such-Devesa, M. J., Zapata-Aguirre, S., Risso, W. A., Brida, J. G., & Pereyra, J. S. (2009). Turismo y Crecimiento Economico: Un Analisis Empirico de Colombia (Tourism and Economic Growth: An Empirical Analysis for the Case of Colombia). *Estudios y Perspectivas En Turismo, 18*(1), 21–35.

Sun, J., Zhang, J., Zhang, J., Ma, J., & Zhang, Y. (2015). Total factor productivity assessment of tourism industry: Evidence from China. *Asia Pacific Journal of Tourism Research, 20*(3), 280–294.

Sun, Y. Y., & Wong, K. F. (2014). Stability of input-output coefficients by capacity utilization for short-term tourism demand fluctuation. *Tourism Economics, 20*(3), 509–526.

Surugiu, C. (2009). The economic impact of tourism. An input-output analysis. *Revista Romana De Economie, 28*(2), 142–161.

Toro, G., Galán, M., Pico, L., Rozo, E., & Suescún, H. (2015). La Planificación Turística Desde El Enfoque De La Competitividad: Caso Colombia (Tourism Planning from the Approach to Competitiveness: Colombia Case Study). *Turismo y Sociedad, 16*, 131–185.

World Bank. (2021, January 20). *International tourism—Colombia*. https://data.worldbank.org/indicator/ST.INT.ARVL?end=2019&locations=CO&start=1995&view=chart

Zuñiga, A., & Castillo, M. (2012). Turismo en Colombia: resultados del sector (2007–2010). *Magazine Empresarial, 8*(15), 67–73.

Eduardo Sanguinet, Pontifical Catholic University of Rio Grande do Sul and Catholic University of North. Professor of Economics, Austral University of Chile, Chile. Research field: regional economics, agricultural and climate change policies, structural analysis, and labor market.

Luis Armando Galvis-Aponte Ph.D. in Geography, University of Illinois. Senior researcher, Center for Regional Economic Studies, Banco de la República, Colombia. Research fields: econometric methods, economic development, and regional.

Inácio F. Araújo, Doctor in Economics, Federal University of Juiz de Fora. Post-doctoral researcher, University of São Paulo, Brazil. Research fields: regional economics, input-output methods, and international trade.

Eduardo A. Haddad, Full Professor at the Department of Economics at the University of São Paulo, Brazil, where he directs the Regional and Urban Economics Lab (NEREUS). Affiliate Professor at the Faculty of Governance, Economic and Social Sciences of the Mohammed VI University and Senior Fellow at the Policy Center for the New South, Rabat, Morocco. President of the Regional Science Association International, RSAI (2021–2022).

Chapter 12
Regional Differences in the Economic Impact of Lockdown Measures to Prevent the Spread of COVID-19: A Case Study for Colombia

Jaime Bonet, Diana Ricciulli, Gerson Javier Pérez-Valbuena, Eduardo A. Haddad, Inácio F. Araújo, and Fernando S. Perobelli

12.1 Introduction

In order to prevent the spread of COVID-19, the Colombian government has been adopting several sanitary measures. After declaring the pandemic a national sanitary emergency on March 12, 2020,[1] the Ministry of Health and Social Protection (MinSalud) ordered mandatory preventive isolation of people over 70.[2] Subsequently, on March 22, the President announced the compulsory confinement of the whole population between March 25 and April 13.[3] The latter excluded essential economic sectors such as health, production of basic necessities, financial and banking services,

---

[1] Resolution 385 March 12, 2020.
[2] Resolution 464 March 18, 2020.
[3] Decree 454 March 22, 2020.

This research was previously published in the journal *Cuadernos de Economía*, Vol. 40, n. 85 (2021), pp. 977–998. https://doi.org/10.15446/cuad.econ.v40n85.90803.

J. Bonet (✉) · D. Ricciulli · G. J. Pérez-Valbuena
Banco de la República, Cartagena, Colombia
e-mail: jbonetmo@banrep.gov.co

G. J. Pérez-Valbuena
e-mail: gperezva@banrep.gov.co

E. A. Haddad · I. F. Araújo
University of São Paulo, São Paulo, Brazil
e-mail: ehaddad@usp.br

I. F. Araújo
e-mail: inacio.araujo@usp.br

F. S. Perobelli
Federal University of Juiz de Fora, Juiz de Fora, Brazil

assistance and care of children and older adults, pharmaceutical production, cleaning, disinfection and personal care products, public services, and telecommunications.

At the end of April, the confinement was extended to May 11, including exemptions for specific sectors as long as they met certain sanitary protocols.[4] For example, construction and several basic manufacturing activities were reactivated. Then, on May 6, the national government extended the confinement period again until May 25,[5] authorizing at the same time the reopening of COVID-19 free municipalities as long as they met proper biosecurity protocols.

An increasing number of studies have estimated the economic costs of confinement measures all over the world. The World Bank (2020) foresaw a profound fall in the growth of the Colombian GDP of around 2%, while the OECD (2020) estimated an initial impact of the paralysis of 23% of the GDP. The Center for Economic Development Studies (CEDE) (2020) showed that about nine million people's income depended on activities vulnerable to isolation measures and estimated that their closure would have cost at least 10% of the GDP per month. Moreover, Mejía (2020) found that in a scenario where isolation measures reduced between 37 and 49% of sectoral operations, the economic cost would range between COP$ 48 and COP$ 65 Trillion (4.5–6.1% of the GDP) per month.

Bonet et al. (2020) took a closer look at the regional impact of lockdown measures, finding that the confinement of 60% of total workers would be equivalent to approximately 13.3 million workers in isolation, from which approximately 70% were informal. Following the latter scenario of confinement, the authors also found that economic losses amounted to COP$59 Trillion or 6.1% of the national GDP. As expected, these effects were not homogeneous across regions and depended, among other factors, on the degree of exposition of the local economies to the isolation measures. For instance, the authors found that the most vulnerable departments were Antioquia, Boyacá, San Andrés, Santander, and Valle del Cauca, highly dependent on services activities affected by the confinement.

Since understanding these regional differences is critical for adopting public policies, we aim to compute and analyze the main regional heterogeneities observed in the economic impact of lockdown measures. To do so, we extend the multisectoral and multiregional input–output model described in Chap. 5, allowing us to partially extract workers from the different sectors of the economy and compute economic losses at the regional level.

Our results show differences over three dimensions: the labor market, the local economies, and sectoral impacts. Regarding the former, we find that peripheral regions (Amazonía, Caribe, Pacific, and Eastern plains and Orinoquía) accounted for a higher number of informal workers in isolation than inner regions (Coffee area and Antioquia, and Central). These economic losses range from 5.4% of the GDP in the Amazonía region to 6.3% in the Coffee area and Antioquia. Moreover, while the most significant losses in the Coffee area and Antioquia, Central, Caribe, and

---

[4] Decree 593 April 24, 2020.
[5] Decree 636 May, 2020.

Pacific regions are concentrated in service activities, in Amazonía, Eastern plains, and Orinoquía, the most affected sectors belong to agriculture and mining.

This chapter is organized as follows. Section 12.2 shows the amended input–output methodology used to compute the regional economic impact of the lockdown measures. Section 12.3 briefly characterizes the regional economies and their labor markets. Section 12.4 presents the results of the sectoral and regional economic impact resulting from the lockdown measures. The last section concludes.

12.2 Data and Methodology[6]

Following Haddad et al. (2019) and Bonet et al. (2020), we use an input–output flow table considering 54 sectors, where we split up the workers into q age groups and identify payments to wage earners for each group (Fig. 12.1).

where:

z_{ij}, with $i, j = 1, \ldots, n$ is the interindustry sales of sector i to sector j.

t_i and m_i ($i = 1, \ldots, n, c, i, g, e$) are the indirect taxes payments and imports, respectively.

l_{ij} and L_{ij} ($i = 1, \ldots, q$ and $j = 1, \ldots, n$) are the payments by sector for labor services and the total number of workers, respectively.

n_j ($j = 1, \ldots, n$) are the payments by sector for all other value-added items.

c_i, i_i, g_i, and e_i ($i = 1, \ldots, n$) are the components of final demand, f_i for household purchases, investment purchases, government purchases, and exports, respectively.

x_i ($i = 1, \ldots, n$) is the total sectoral output.

We assume that lockdown measures restrict part of the labor force, both age and sector-specific in the case of the COVID-19 pandemic.[7] We define $q \times n$ factors, $F_{q,n}, 0 < F_{q,n} < 1$, defining the share of non-restricted workers in each group and each sector. Therefore, we set the factor to unity in sectors without restrictions and zero for those with reasons to believe their economic activities are entirely restricted.

The next step is to apply each factor $F_{q,n}$ to its corresponding element in both matrices, the employment and the labor payments. In the former, we define the number of workers facing lockdowns, while in the latter, we compute, for each sector, the contribution of those workers to the total labor income. With the aggregate income associated with both restricted and non-restricted workers, we use its share in total labor payments by sector together with the sectoral labor payment coefficients, $\sum_i^q l_{ij}/x_j$. Then, we define a new set of penalty factors specific for each sector, F_n,

---

[6] Based on Haddad et al. (2020).
[7] In our multiregional modeling framework, control measures can also be region-specific.

		Processing sectors			Final demand				Total output
		1	...	54					
Processing sectors	1	$z_{(1,1)}$	...	$z_{(1,54)}$	c_1	i_1	g_1	e_1	x_1
	...	...	...	...	...	...	...	...	...
	54	$z_{(54,1)}$	...	$z_{(54,54)}$	c_{54}	i_{54}	g_{54}	e_{54}	x_{54}
Imports		t_1	...	t_{54}	t_c	t_i	t_g	t_e	t
Indirect taxes		m_1	...	m_{54}	m_c	m_i	m_g	m_e	m
Labor payments	1	$l_{(1,1)}$	...	$l_{(1,54)}$					l_1
	...	...	...	...					...
	q	$l_{(q,1)}$	...	$l_{(q,54)}$					l_q
Other payments		n_1	...	n_{54}					n
Outlays		x_1	...	x_n	c	i	g	e	
Employment	1	$L_{(1,1)}$	...	$L_{(1,54)}$					L_1
	...	...	...	...					...
	q	$L_{(q,1)}$	...	$L_{(q,54)}$					L_q

Fig. 12.1 Input–output flows

$0 < F_n < 1$, which identifies the share of the output in each sector connected with non-restricted workers.

This strategy allows carrying out different scenarios is based on goals for compliance with the measures. For example, if we would like to investigate a case that is both consistent with the set of pre-defined factors, $F_{q,n}$, and a desirable level of compliance, α,[8] we can find an adjustment weight (ω) to be applied across all $F_{q,n}$:

$$\omega F_{q,n} \Rightarrow \frac{\sum_i^q \sum_j^n L_{ij}^{\text{restricted}}}{\sum_i^q \sum_j^n L_{ij}} = \alpha \qquad (12.1)$$

After computing the factors, F_n, we use all the information to partially extract particular sectoral flows in the input–output flow, considering both demand and supply reductions.

---

[8] The α parameter corresponds to the percentage of occupied people in the whole economy whom are heeding isolation measures.

For the interindustry demand, we consider that $\forall z_{ij}, i, j = 1, \ldots, n$ for which we calculate a corresponding restricted flow, $\overline{z_{ij}}$:

$$\overline{z_{ij}} = \begin{cases} F_i z_{ij}, \text{ si } F_i < F_j \\ \\ F_j z_{ij}, \text{ si } F_i > F_j \end{cases} \quad (12.2)$$

One of the advantages of this approach is that, apart from the supply-side restrictions (those associated to F_i), it is also possible to include demand-side restrictions. For each final demand user, a demand-side factor, F_u, $u = c, i, g, e$, can also be defined. Each F_u is specified as follows: F_c is computed according to changes in foregone earnings by isolated workers. On the other hand, we assume that informal workers affected by the isolation face a total income loss, while formal workers face only a partial loss, according to a parameter δ, $0 < \delta < 1$. Accordingly, we also assume that changes in labor income are transferred to household demand changes.[9]

Considering that investment decisions taking place and government expenditures are unaffected (from the demand-side) in the short run, F_i and F_g are set to unity. This procedure allows us to use government reactions for simulating policy scenarios and computing alternative values for F_g. On the other hand, F_e is set to 0.75.[10] Also, in the median economy, exports would decline by 25%.

Then, we apply a rule with each component of the final demand (f_{iu}), where $\forall f_{iu}$, $u = i, g, e$ we compute the restricted flow $\overline{f_{iu}}$:

$$\overline{f_{iu}} = \begin{cases} F_i f_{iu}, \text{ si } F_i < F_u \\ \\ F_u f_{iu}, \text{ si } F_i > F_u \end{cases} \quad (12.3)$$

When considering household demand, we can apply the supply and demand constraints: $\forall f_{iu}, u = c$ the restricted flow, $\overline{f_{iu}}$, is computed such as $\overline{f_{iu}} = F_i F_u f_{iu}$. Based on the original and modified sectoral flows, we have now two matrices and two vectors: interindustry flows matrices $\mathbf{Z}$ and $\overline{\mathbf{Z}}$, and the final demand vectors, $\mathbf{f}$ and $\overline{\mathbf{f}}$, from which we can also derive the corresponding matrices of technical coefficients, $\mathbf{A}$ and $\overline{\mathbf{A}}$, for a given vector of sectoral output x.

The next step is to apply the extraction method (the extraction of particular sectors from the input–output matrix) to find the changes in output when some sectors are removed from the economy and the relative importance of a sector in this economy.[11] Haddad et al. (2020) developed a variant of the extraction method in the sense that they do not fully extract sectors, but only part of them according to the combined information given by $\overline{\mathbf{Z}}$ and $\overline{\mathbf{f}}$.

---

[9] Haddad et al. (2020) mention that government transfers to specific groups of workers, as a measure to attenuate the effects of the crisis, would also affect F_c.

[10] This assumption is based on the OECD (2020) projections for short-term declines in GDP for many.

[11] The extraction method was first proposed by Dietzenbacher et al. (1993).

With the complete sector flows, the output is given by $\mathbf{x} = (\mathbf{I} - \mathbf{A})^{-1}\mathbf{f}$. If $\overline{\mathbf{A}}$ corresponds to the restricted intersectoral trade flows and $\overline{\mathbf{f}}$ the corresponding final demand, the lockdown-related output of the economy is given by $\overline{\mathbf{x}} = (\mathbf{I} - \overline{\mathbf{A}})^{-1}\overline{\mathbf{f}}$. Consequently, the result of the partial extraction is given by $T = i'\mathbf{x} - i'\overline{\mathbf{x}}$, with T being a measure of the annual loss in the economy. Also, as always, pre-multiplying the vector of gross output ($\mathbf{x}$ or $\overline{\mathbf{x}}$) by the matrix ($\hat{\mathbf{v}}$), whose main diagonal is the variables' coefficients, we can translate sectoral gross output outcomes into other variables' outcomes. Daily foregone losses can be computed by dividing T or $\hat{\mathbf{v}}T$ by the weekdays.

12.3 A First View of the Pre-lockdown Regional Economies

In order to understand the potential effects of lockdown measures, it is critical to identify the main economic activities and the composition of the labor force in each region.[12] To do so, we use the sectoral composition of economic activities and the labor market information reported by the DANE in 2015. Despite variations in the aggregated data, the sectoral composition of employment and production of regional economies has remained relatively stable over the last few years.

Figures 12.2 and 12.3 present the regional economic structure and the sectoral distribution of employment, aggregated by the major branches of economic activity.[13] Regarding economic structure, services stand out as the activities with the highest participation in value-added in all regions. In most cases, its participation is close to 70%, only for Eastern plains and Orinoquía, these activities represent a lower proportion of 45% of total added value.

The distribution of the remaining sectors follows a similar pattern for the Coffee area and Antioquia, Central, Pacific, and Caribe regions. Manufacturing represents between 8.4 and 13.4% of total production in these territories, and agriculture between 7.2 and 12.7%. Mining is the only sector with significant variation across these regions, with contributions that range between 1.1% in the Coffee area and Antioquia and 10.6% in the Caribe. The case of Amazonía in particular has a manufacturing sector with low participation (1.7%). Regarding Eastern plains and Orinoquía, the lower participation of services (45%) is compensated with higher mining and agriculture contributions that amount to 36% and 17% of total value-added.

Figure 12.3 shows the sectoral distribution of workers for the six regions and the national aggregate. At first glance and compared with the distribution of economic activity, the regions Coffee area and Antioquia, Central, Caribe, and Pacific have a

---

[12] In this chapter, we divide the country in six regions: (1) Caribbean: San Andrés, La Guajira, Magdalena, Cesar, Atlántico, Bolívar, Sucre and Córdoba; (2) Coffee area and Antioquia: Antioquia, Caldas, Quindío and Risaralda; (3) Central: Bogotá, Boyacá, Cundinamarca, Huila, Norte de Santander, Santander and Tolima; (4) Pacific: Chocó, Valle del Cauca, Cauca and Nariño; (5) Eastern plains and Orinoquia: Arauca, Casanare, Vichada and Meta; and (6) Amazonia: Amazonas, Caquetá, Guainía, Guaviare, Putumayo and Vaupés.

[13] See sectoral classification in the Appendix Table 12.8.

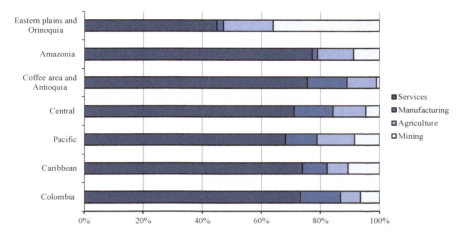

Fig. 12.2 Regional economic structure: participation of the main economic branches in the total value-added. *Source* Authors' elaboration based on DANE

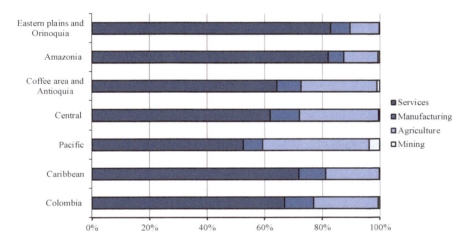

Fig. 12.3 Occupational structure by region: participation in the total labor force. *Source* Authors' elaboration based on GEIH

services sector with lower participation in employment than it has on value-added. Conversely, the remaining regions have higher participation of services in labor than in economic production. This pattern is particularly evident for the region Eastern plains and Orinoquía, where services contribute 45% of the total value-added, and workers in this sector represent 83% of the total in the region.

A second pattern, common to all regions, is related to mining and agriculture activities. While the former has high participation in value-added and low employment, agriculture contributes more to workers than economic production.

These results support the hypothesis of significant regional disparities, both inter- and intra-regional, previously documented in the literature (Bonet & Meisel, 2001; Galvis & Meisel, 2010). In order to analyze intra-regional differences, Tables 12.1 and 12.2 give, for each department, the share of each sector on total value-added and the number of workers, respectively.

Starting with the Caribe region, San Andrés stands out as a department where nearly all the value-added (97.2%) and workforce (93%) are related to the services sector. This island is highly dependent on tourism-related activities such as accommodation and food services. Although lower than San Andrés, the rest of the departments in the region also have a high contribution of services to value-added and employment. Also, agriculture and livestock employ an important proportion of labor in this region.

Regarding the Pacific, we can identify two departments that are distant from the general pattern observed in this region. For Chocó, services have low participation in value-added compared to its neighbors (56.1% compared with the regional average of 72.1%). Mining has the second-highest participation in value-added in this department, 26.3%, compared with a regional average of 2.5%. In terms of employment, mining has the highest contribution, 12.9%, in contrast with 2.5% for its neighbors. Furthermore, Valle del Cauca, the wealthiest department in the region and one of the richest in the country, has a services sector with high participation of workers relative to the one observed in its neighbors (75.8% compared with a regional average of 44.7%).

Bogotá D.C, the capital city, in the Central region, has a high participation of services in its total value-added (89.2%). A similar pattern is observed for employment in this sector with a participation of 83.9%, well above the regional average of 58.3%. It is worth mentioning that the capital city does not have the highest participation in manufacturing activities (10.6%); the first place is occupied by Cundinamarca (24.8%). Nevertheless, Bogotá D.C occupies the first place in employment contribution of the manufacturing sector (15.4%).

We do not observe significant differences in the sectoral composition of value-added for the region Coffee area and Antioquia. Services activities have similar participation in the four departments, and most of them coincide in that the second most important sector is manufacturing. The only difference is observed in Quindío, where the second most important sector is agriculture and livestock activities that accounts for 15.5% of total value-added.

In the Amazonía region, two departments differ in the observed regional pattern: Putumayo for its economic structure and Caquetá for its occupational composition. In the former case, services contribute 52.9% to total value-added, while for the other five departments, this sector contributes an average of 82%. In Putumayo, the second most important economic activity is mining (40.6%), driven by oil extraction, while for the rest of the departments in the region, agriculture and livestock are the main activities. Caquetá stands out in the region for having the lowest workforce participation in services activities (51.9%) in comparison with its neighbors (88.1%).

Finally, in the Eastern plains and Orinoquía region, Vichada stands out with a services sector with relatively high participation in the total value-added (65.3%).

Table 12.1 Departments' economic structure: participation of the main economic branches in the total value-added

Region	Department	Agriculture (%)	Mining (%)	Manufacture (%)	Services (%)
Caribbean	Atlántico	1.0	0.3	18.6	80.1
	Bolívar	4.8	2.7	17.1	75.4
	Cesar	8.9	35.5	4.0	51.6
	Córdoba	12.0	1.6	10.5	75.9
	La Guajira	3.9	43.5	0.6	51.9
	Magdalena	15.8	0.4	4.7	79.2
	Sucre	9.5	0.7	10.0	79.8
	San Andrés	1.3	0.1	1.4	97.2
Pacific	Chocó	16.8	26.3	0.9	56.1
	Valle del Cauca	6.2	0.2	19.5	74.1
	Nariño	15.2	4.2	3.1	77.5
	Cauca	12.7	2.9	19.8	64.6
Central	Bogotá D.C	0.0	0.2	10.6	89.2
	Boyacá	10.4	10.2	14.4	65.0
	Cundinamarca	14.6	1.1	24.8	59.5
	Huila	16.2	7.8	3.7	72.3
	Norte de Santander	10.2	3.3	7.3	79.2
	Santander	8.9	5.6	19.6	66.0
	Tolima	16.9	4.5	11.7	66.9
Coffee area and Antioquia	Antioquia	5.9	2.3	18.9	72.9
	Caldas	11.1	1.2	14.2	73.5
	Quindío	15.5	0.4	5.6	78.4
	Risaralda	7.3	0.4	14.9	77.4
Amazonia	Amazonas	17.0	0.2	2.0	80.9
	Caquetá	14.4	0.5	3.1	82.0
	Guainía	8.4	11.1	2.5	78.0
	Guaviare	19.7	0.5	1.8	78.0
	Putumayo	5.7	40.6	0.9	52.9
	Vaupés	7.4	0.4	0.2	92.0
Eastern plains and Oronoquia	Arauca	16.9	38.5	3.0	41.6
	Casanare	9.5	49.4	2.3	38.8
	Vichada	33.5	0.4	0.8	65.3
	Meta	8.0	55.5	2.2	34.4

(continued)

Table 12.1 (continued)

Region	Department	Agriculture (%)	Mining (%)	Manufacture (%)	Services (%)
Total (Colombia)		6.6	6.5	13.7	73.2

Source Authors' elaboration based on DANE
Authors' elaboration based on GEIH

The second characteristic of this department is that, while the second most important economic activity in Arauca, Casanare, and Meta is mining (38.5%, 49.4%, and 55.5%, respectively), in Vichada, agriculture is the most important sector. In terms of employment, Meta stands out for having a services sector with the lowest participation (67.9%) and higher participation in agriculture (25.2%). The rest of the departments have employment concentrated in the services sector.

These intra- and inter-regional economic and labor market views reveal important differences in structure that will allow us to better understand the regional and sectoral circumstances for a period before the COVID-19 pandemic and, thus, understand the consequences derived from the preventive isolation measures shown in the next section.

12.4 Results

Following the approach described in Sect. 10.2, we now present the results of the regional economic impact of isolation measures adopted to prevent the spread of the COVID-19 pandemic. In particular, we build from the aggregated economic effects found in Bonet et al. (2020) following a scenario where 60% of the total workers are in isolation. We present the disaggregation of economic losses by regions, departments, and economic sectors. The first sub-section shows the adjustment factors defined by Bonet et al. (2020) to capture the degree of exposition of each sector to isolation measures. The second sub-section presents the regional disaggregation of workers in isolation, and the final sub-section shows the regional and sectoral economic impacts.

12.4.1 Adjustment Factor F

For the input–output approach to be applied, we need to define a set of adjustment factors that tell us to what extent the confinement measures are restraining each economic sector's operation. Following Bonet et al. (2020), and based on the list of economic activities excluded from preventive isolation, Table 12.3 gives the F factor defined for each sector. Consistent with Mejía (2020) and CEDE (2020), we observe that sectors with the highest restrictions are those related to non-essential

Table 12.2 Occupational structure by departments: participation in the total labor force

Region	Department	Agriculture (%)	Mining (%)	Manufacture (%)	Services (%)
Caribbean	Atlántico	5.0	0.0	11.6	83.4
	Bolívar	23.4	0.5	7.0	69.1
	Cesar	23.4	0.2	7.3	69.1
	Córdoba	25.9	0.8	10.6	62.7
	La Guajira	21.1	0.2	18.6	60.1
	Magdalena	21.4	0.0	7.5	71.1
	Sucre	24.9	0.2	8.8	66.0
	San Andrés	3.4	0.0	3.6	92.9
Pacific	Chocó	41.1	12.9	3.5	42.5
	Valle del Cauca	12.7	0.5	11.1	75.8
	Nariño	47.7	0.3	7.4	44.6
	Cauca	45.5	2.0	5.5	47.1
Central	Bogotá D.C	0.7	0.0	15.4	83.9
	Boyacá	36.5	1.6	11.1	50.8
	Cundinamarca	27.7	0.1	8.2	64.0
	Huila	39.1	0.2	6.2	54.5
	Norte de Santander	26.5	0.3	9.4	63.8
	Santander	26.3	0.2	12.9	60.6
	Tolima	36.5	0.3	7.3	55.9
Coffee area and Antioquia	Antioquia	18.8	2.0	11.9	67.3
	Caldas	31.6	2.1	6.6	59.7
	Quindío	28.8	0.2	5.7	65.2
	Risaralda	26.0	0.2	9.2	64.6
Amazonia	Amazonas	6.4	0.1	7.5	86.0
	Caquetá	42.9	0.0	5.1	51.9
	Guainía	9.5	1.8	6.6	82.1
	Guaviare	6.7	0.5	6.0	86.8
	Putumayo	3.5	0.8	5.7	90.0
	Vaupés	2.0	1.1	1.1	95.8
Eastern plains and Oronoquia	Arauca	6.1	0.3	4.8	88.8
	Casanare	3.2	0.1	7.2	89.5
	Vichada	6.4	0.1	8.3	85.2
	Meta	25.2	0.2	6.6	67.9
Total (Colombia)		22.3	0.7	10.3	66.8

activities, such as arts, entertainment, and recreation, with an F factor of 0.1, while essential activities such as health and public administration face no restrictions and consequently have an F factor equal to 1.0. In particular, an F factor between 0 and 1 is defined for each sector depending on the exposition of each sector to isolation measures adopted by the government.

12.4.2 Workers in Isolation

Following the ordering defined by the F factor, we extract a group of workers uniformly across all regions until reaching 60% of them in isolation.[14] We include all workers over 70 years old irrespective of the sector they work in among the group in isolation. Figure 12.4 shows the proportion of workers in isolation across regions and differentiating between formal and informal employment. The percentage of workers in isolation ranges between 57.8% in Amazonía and 61% in the Caribe region. San Andres stands out with 64.6% (Table 12.1) of total employees in isolation in the latter.

It is also important to highlight the differences in the distribution of formal and informal workers. Even though 70.1% of confined workers at the national level are informal,[15] peripheral regions (Caribe, Pacific, and Amazonía) show higher participation of informal workers than in the inner regions. Although having the lowest percentage of workers in isolation, Amazonía shows the highest share of informal workers (87.7%), followed by the Caribe and Pacific regions with 81.7% and 76.3%, respectively. This proportion is lower than the ones observed in the Central and Coffee area and Antioquia regions, where informal workers represent 65.2% and 60.1%, respectively. This is consistent with a predominant informal economy in peripheral regions and reveals the greater socioeconomic vulnerability of isolated populations in these territories.

12.4.3 Economic Impact

Following the isolation of 60% of total workers, Bonet et al. (2020) found monthly economic losses that amounted to COP$59 trillion, representing 6.1% of the national GDP. As expected, the regional distribution of these losses is not homogeneous across the territory and depends on each region's share of the total national production. Similarly, sectors with the highest losses in each region contribute the most to local economic production. Nevertheless, when considering each sector's loss relative to

---

[14] Appendix Table 12.9 shows, by department, the percentage of workers in isolation under this particular scenario.

[15] Informality in this case is computed as the percentage of workers there do not make pension payments.

Table 12.3 Adjusting factors F

Id	Sector	Factor	Id	Sector	Factor
S1	Agriculture	0.900	S28	Manufacture of electrical equipment	0.500
S2	Coffee growing	0.900	S29	Manufacture of machinery and equipment n.e.c	0.500
S3	Livestock and hunting	0.900	S30	Manufacture of motor vehicles, trailers and semi-trailers	0.500
S4	Forestry and logging	0.500	S31	Manufacture of furniture	0.500
S5	Fishing and aquaculture	0.900	S32	Other manufacturing	0.500
S6	Mining of coal and lignite	0.500	S33	Electricity	1.000
S7	Extraction of crude petroleum and natural gas	0.900	S34	Gas, steam and air conditioning supply	1.000
S8	Mining of metal ores	0.500	S35	Water collection, treatment and supply	1.000
S9	Other mining and quarrying	0.500	S36	Sewerage; waste collection, treatment and disposal activities	1.000
S10	Processing and preserving of meat	0.900	S37	Construction	0.250
S11	Processing of vegetable and animal oils and fats	0.900	S38	Wholesale and retail trade	0.500
S12	Processing of dairy products	0.900	S39	Repair of motor vehicles and motorcycles	0.500
S13	Processing of grain mill products, starches and starch products	0.900	S40	Land transport and transport via pipelines	0.500
S14	Processing of coffee products	0.900	S41	Water transport	0.500
S15	Processing of sugar	0.900	S42	Air transport	0.500
S16	Processing of cocoa, chocolate and sugar confectionery	0.900	S43	Warehousing and support activities for transportation	0.500
S17	Processing and preserving of fruit and vegetables	0.900	S44	Postal and courier activities	0.500
S18	Manufacture of beverages; manufacture of tobacco products	0.900	S45	Accommodation and food service activities	0.100
S19	Manufacture of textiles; manufacture of wearing apparel	0.500	S46	Information and communication	1.000
S20	Manufacture of leather and related products	0.500	S47	Financial and insurance activities	1.000

(continued)

Table 12.3 (continued)

Id	Sector	Factor	Id	Sector	Factor
S21	Manufacture of wood and of products of wood and cork	0.500	S48	Real estate activities	0.250
S22	Manufacture of paper and paper products	0.500	S49	Professional, scientific and technical activities	0.250
S23	Manufacture of coke and refined petroleum products	0.900	S50	Public administration and defence; compulsory social security	1.000
S24	Manufacture of chemicals and pharmaceuticals	0.900	S51	Education	0.750
S25	Manufacture of rubber and plastics products	0.900	S52	Human health and social work activities	1.000
S26	Manufacture of other non-metallic mineral products	0.500	S53	Arts, entertainment and recreation; other service activities	0.100
S27	Manufacture of basic metals	0.500	S54	Activities of households as employers	0.100

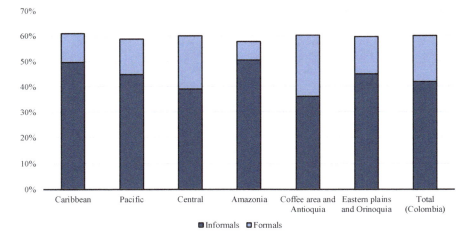

Fig. 12.4 Formal and informal workers in isolation by region: percentage of total workers

its contribution to the local GDP, the most vulnerable activities appear to be those with the most substantial restrictions in terms of isolation measures or those sectors that were highly dependent on restricted sectors. This section presents a detailed regional and sectoral description of the economic impact of lockdown measures in Colombia, assuming a scenario where 60% of total workers are in isolation.

First of all, the regional distribution of the aggregated economic impact reveals a high concentration of losses in the Central region with a share of 45.7% of total economic losses (Fig. 12.5). The latter is followed by the Coffee area and Antioquia region (18.9%), Caribe (14.6%), Pacific (13.9%), Eastern plains, and Orinoquía (5.8%), and Amazonía (1%). As mentioned before, this result is closely related to each region's share of the national value-added.

Incorporating in the analysis the regional differences in economic production, Fig. 12.6 shows regional losses as a proportion of local GDP. The Coffee area and Antioquia regions rank first with a total loss of 6.32% of their GDP, higher than the national aggregate loss of 6.1%. At the other end is Amazonía, with a total loss of 5.4% of its GDP.

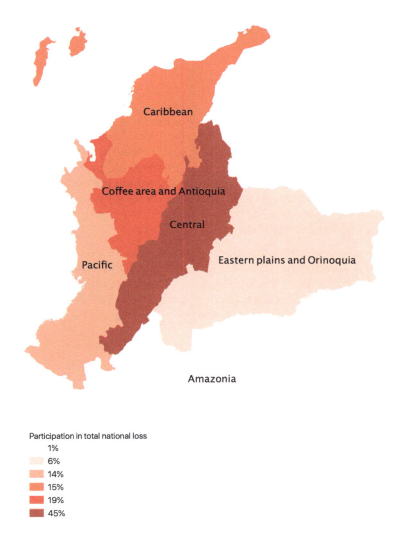

Fig. 12.5 Regional participation in the national economic loss

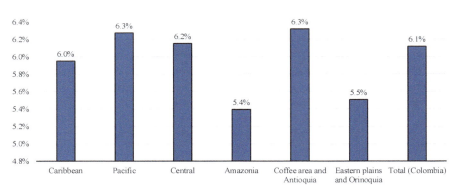

Fig. 12.6 Regional economic losses (% of the GDP)

The relative economic impact of each region is determined by its percentage of workers in isolation and the labor income they represent. Following the model's assumption that workers' remuneration is proportional to their participation in total value-added, the latter indicates workers' contribution to sectoral economic production. While in the Coffee area and Antioquia, the percentage of workers in isolation is 60.3%, and their labor income represents 53.1% of the total, in Amazonía, these percentages represent 57.8% and 40.3%, respectively. Results follow the same pattern when considering individual departments and their corresponding sectors. To support this argument, we present the disaggregated results for two regions: the Coffee area and Antioquia (ranking first) and Amazonía (ranking last).

The Coffee area and Antioquia region In this region, the department with the highest loss (as a percentage of the local GDP) is Antioquia with 6.4%, while on the other side is Caldas with a 6.1% loss (Fig. 12.7). Consistent with these results, the percentage of labor income restricted in Antioquia is 54%, the highest in the whole region, while in Caldas, the income of workers in isolation represents 49% of the total income (Appendix Table 12.10).

It is worth mentioning the case of Antioquia and its role as an input supplier to all the regions of the country. Notwithstanding Colombia's relatively low regional interdependence (Bonet, 2006), Antioquia ranks third in forward linkages after Bogotá D.C and Santander (Hahn, 2016; Chap. 7). This means that its production plays a considerable role in the operation of multiple economic sectors across the country, and therefore, it can be affected by lower demand in other territories. In particular, the most affected sectors in Antioquia are administrative and professional services that represent 12.2% of total losses, followed by real estate activities (11.4%), wholesale and retail trade (9.9%), construction (9.5%), and accommodation and food services (4.4%) (Table 12.4). Apart from being highly affected by confinement measures, these activities make an important contribution to the total economic production of this department, 39.8% as a whole. Regarding the rest of the departments in the region, Caldas and Risaralda follow a similar sectoral distribution of economic losses.

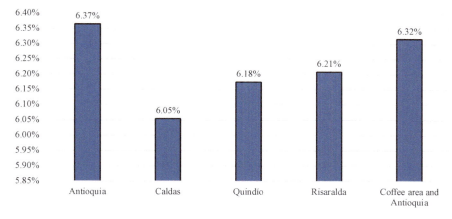

Fig. 12.7 Economic loss—coffee area and antioquia region (% of the local GDP)

At the same time, Quindío shows an important contribution of agriculture to total losses, consistent with its participation in this territory's value-added.

Following these results, a vulnerability index is computed to compare each sector's participation in the total loss and each sector's participation in the department's total value-added. In particular, this index is constructed as the quotient of these two indicators, which is then rescaled between 0 and 1 indicate low and high vulnerability, respectively. This index is given in Table 12.5 for each department's top five sectors in the Coffee area and Antioquia region.

These results show that the most vulnerable sectors in the region are: other mining and quarrying, manufacture of other non-metallic mineral products, mining of metal ores, arts, entertainment and recreation, activities of households as employers, and accommodation and food services. These activities are the ones that face the highest isolation restrictions in the region. For instance, the first three noted sectors have a percentage of workers in isolation of approximately 71%, while for the last two, this percentage reaches 94% (Appendix Table 12.11). While showing lower isolation restrictions, the economic losses of the first three sectors are exacerbated by their productive linkages with other restricted activities, especially from their role as input supplies to other sectors such as construction.

Amazonia region

The second case study is the region ranking last in economic losses. Figure 12.8 shows the economic losses of each department of the Amazonia region. Results show losses range between 5.5% (Putumayo) and 5.0% of GDP (Guainía). Consistent with these low relative losses, the percentage of workers in isolation in this region is between 46.8% (Vaupés) and 58.6% (Caquetá) (Appendix Table 12.9).

Regarding sectoral losses, crude oil and natural gas extraction stands out in Putumayo, where it represents 41.8% of the total economic impact, almost double that of any other loss observed in the region (Table 12.6). Other sectors showing high relative

Table 12.4 Sectors with the highest loss shares: departments belonging to the coffee area and antioquia

Department	Sector	Participation in the total loss (%)
Antioquia	Professional, scientific and technical activities	12.2
	Real estate	11.4
	Wholesale and retail trade	9.9
	Construction	9.5
	Accommodation and food services	4.4
Caldas	Professional, scientific and technical activities	11.1
	Real estate	9.3
	Construction	8.3
	Accommodation and food services	8.1
	Wholesale and retail trade	7.2
Quindio	Real estate	13.7
	Construction	13.4
	Wholesale and retail trade	10.2
	Accommodation and food services	8.7
	Agriculture	7.7
Risaralda	Professional, scientific and technical activities	12.6
	Construction	9.8
	Real estate	9.2
	Accommodation and food services	8.2
	Wholesale and retail trade	7.6

importance in regional losses are accommodation and food services, construction, and wholesale and retail trade.

In terms of vulnerability, the extraction of other mining and quarrying activities appears highly vulnerable across all departments in the region (Table 12.7). The only exception is Guainía, where manufacturing of other non-metallic mineral products ranks first as the most vulnerable sector. Consistent with previous results, other vulnerable activities are accommodation and food services and arts, entertainment, and recreation.

Although the highest vulnerability is related to primary sector activities such as mining, there is also an important impact on more labor-intensive activities in the Amazonia region. Table 12.12 in the Appendix gives the percentage of workers in isolation for these sectors. In particular, approximately 94% of total workers in activities related to accommodation and food services, arts, entertainment and recreation, and activities of household as employers are in isolation. Moreover, construction,

12 Regional Differences in the Economic Impact of Lockdown Measures ...   345

Table 12.5 Sectors with the highest vulnerability. departments belonging to the coffee area and antioquia

Department	Sector	Index
Antioquia	Manufacture of other non-metallic mineral products	1.000
	Arts, entertainment and recreation	1.000
	Other mining and quarrying	1.000
	Accommodation and food services	0.998
	Activities of households as employers	0.997
Caldas	Other mining and quarrying	1.000
	Arts, entertainment and recreation	0.983
	Accommodation and food services	0.981
	Activities of households as employers	0.981
	Extracción de minerales metalíferos	0.979
Quindio	Other mining and quarrying	1.000
	Manufacture of other non-metallic mineral products	0.991
	Arts, entertainment and recreation	0.982
	Activities of households as employers	0.981
	Accommodation and food services	0.980
Risaralda	Other mining and quarrying	1.000
	Manufacture of other non-metallic mineral products	0.987
	Arts, entertainment and recreation	0.984
	Activities of households as employers	0.982
	Accommodation and food services	0.981

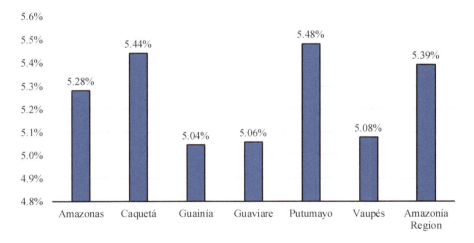

Fig. 12.8 Economic loss—Amazonia region (% of the local GDP)

Table 12.6 Sectors with the highest loss shares: departments belonging to the Amazonia region

Department	Sector	Participation in the total loss (%)
Amazonas	Wholesale and retail trade	19.7
	Fishing and aquaculture	15.8
	Accommodation and food service activities	14.1
	Education	9.7
	Air transport	8.0
Caquetá	Construction	20.6
	Accommodation and food service activities	14.2
	Real estate activities	10.5
	Livestock and hunting	10.4
	Wholesale and retail trade	7.2
Guainía	Construction	24.8
	Accommodation and food service activities	14.0
	Mining of metal ores	13.4
	Education	12.9
	Wholesale and retail trade	6.3
Guaviare	Agriculture	20.9
	Construction	20.8
	Accommodation and food service activities	12.6
	Wholesale and retail trade	10.7
	Education	8.7
Putumayo	Extraction of crude petroleum and natural gas	41.8
	Accommodation and food service activities	12.0
	Construction	8.6
	Education	6.8
	Real estate activities	5.9
Vaupés	Accommodation and food service activities	20.1
	Education	19.9
	Construction	19.4
	Wholesale and retail trade	9.5
	Air transport	6.9

real estate, and professional, scientific, and technical activities have approximately 85% of their total workers in isolation.

12 Regional Differences in the Economic Impact of Lockdown Measures ...

Table 12.7 Sectors with the highest vulnerability. Departments belonging to the Amazonia region

Department	Sector	Index
Amazonas	Other mining and quarrying	1.000
	Manufacture of other non-metallic mineral products	0.991
	Accommodation and food service activities	0.979
	Arts, entertainment and recreation	0.978
	Activities of households as employers	0.975
Caquetá	Other mining and quarrying	1.000
	Manufacture of other non-metallic mineral products	0.992
	Arts, entertainment and recreation	0.977
	Activities of households as employers	0.977
	Accommodation and food service activities	0.977
Guainía	Manufacture of other non-metallic mineral products	1.000
	Accommodation and food service activities	0.982
	Arts, entertainment and recreation	0.980
	Manufacture of wood and of products of wood and cork	0.976
	Manufacture of basic metals	0.958
Guaviare	Other mining and quarrying	1.000
	Manufacture of other non-metallic mineral products	0.993
	Accommodation and food service activities	0.977
	Activities of households as employers	0.976
	Arts, entertainment and recreation	0.976
Putumayo	Other mining and quarrying	1.000
	Manufacture of other non-metallic mineral products	0.995
	Arts, entertainment and recreation	0.982
	Accommodation and food service activities	0.981
	Mining of metal ores	0.978
Vaupés	Other mining and quarrying	1.000
	Accommodation and food service activities	0.977
	Arts, entertainment and recreation	0.975
	Activities of households as employers	0.975
	Postal and courier activities	0.941

12.5 Final Considerations

Results in this chapter are consistent with previous literature that document regional economic disparities in Colombia (Bonet & Meisel, 2001; Galvis & Meisel, 2011; Galvis et al., 2017) and highlight the importance of adopting public policies that include consideration of the spatial-sectoral-linkage dimension. This approach is of particular interest in circumstances where regions face different social and economic consequences depending mainly on their economic structure, the degree of the informality of their labor force, and the productive linkages of their sectors. For example, peripheral regions such as the Caribe, Pacific, and Amazonía have a higher percentage of workers in informality than the inner regions, implying a higher vulnerability of workers in isolation that may increase regional disparities.

In this chapter, we find intra- and inter-regional disparities in the economic impact of lockdown measures. Regarding the labor market, we find that while the peripheral regions of Amazonía, Caribe, Pacific, Eastern plains, and Orinoquía have the participation of informal workers in the group of employees in isolation of between 76.3% and 81.7%, in the inner regions of Coffee area and Antioquia and the Central regions, this percentage is 60.1% and 65.2%, respectively. This makes clear the higher vulnerability of isolated workers from peripheral regions that could stop receiving income due to the lockdown measures.

The second source of regional disparities is in the distribution of economic losses. Although economic losses are concentrated in the wealthiest economies (Bogotá D.C, Antioquia, Valle del Cauca, and Santander), relative to their GDP, losses fluctuate between 5.4% in Amazonía and 6.3% in the Coffee area and Antioquia. Moreover, the departments of San Andrés, Antioquia, Valle del Cauca, and Santander stand out with losses of around 6.4% of their GDP, while Meta and Putumayo receive the lowest impacts of 5.6% and 5.5%, respectively.

Regarding sectoral economic impacts, in the Coffee area and Antioquia, Central, Caribe, and Pacific, the highest losses are in services, administrative, professional and technical activities, construction, real estate, wholesale and retail trade, and food and accommodation services are the most affected. On the other hand, primary activities such as mining and agriculture suffer the highest losses in Amazonía and Easter plains, and Orinoquía regions.

It is worth mentioning the case of some departments that follow particular patterns: (1) Chocó, a department where the mining of metal ores accounts for 35.1% of the loss; (2) Cesar and La Guajira, two departments of the Caribe region with high participation of coal and lignite extraction on the total loss, 33.7% and 43%, respectively; (3) San Andrés, where 37.2% of its total loss is in the accommodation and food services sectors; (4) Arauca, Casanare and Putumayo with significant impacts in the extraction of crude oil and natural gas, with participation between 31% and 41.8% of the total loss; and (5) Guaviare and Vichada where losses in agriculture represent 20.9% and 21.5% of the total loss, respectively.

Finally, the economic sectors showing the highest vulnerability to lockdown measures are the same across all regions. These are accommodation and food services, activities of households as employers, arts, entertainment and recreation, manufacture of other non-metallic mineral products, and the extraction of mining and quarrying. All these sectors have in common a high percentage of workers in isolation. Another dimension that needs to be explored is the rebound or resilience status of each sector and region; as has been clear in many countries, the removal of COVID-19 restrictions (lockdowns) does not necessarily result in an immediate rebound. Supply chains take time to rebuild, workers may, in the interim, have explored other occupations or industry sectors. However, the additional dimension that dominates discussion in Colombia is the high share of informal workers in the labor force. This share varies by sector and region and adds a dimension that is missing in the recovery patterns observed in more developed economies.

Appendix

See Tables 12.8, 12.9, 12.10, 12.11 and 12.12.

Table 12.8 Sectoral classification by economic activity

Id	Sector	Economic activity
S1	Agriculture	Agriculture and livestock
S2	Coffee growing	
S3	Livestock and hunting	
S4	Forestry and logging	
S5	Fishing and aquaculture	
S6	Mining of coal and lignite	Mining
S7	Extraction of crude petroleum and natural gas	
S8	Mining of metal ores	
S9	Other mining and quarrying	
S10	Processing and preserving of meat	Manufacture
S11	Processing of vegetable and animal oils and fats	
S12	Processing of dairy products	
S13	Processing of grain mill products, starches and starch products	
S14	Processing of coffee products	
S15	Processing of sugar	
S16	Processing of cocoa, chocolate and sugar confectionery	
S17	Processing and preserving of fruit and vegetables	
S18	Manufacture of beverages; Manufacture of tobacco products	
S19	Manufacture of textiles; Manufacture of wearing apparel	
S20	Manufacture of leather and related products	
S21	Manufacture of wood and of products of wood and cork	
S22	Manufacture of paper and paper products	
S23	Manufacture of coke and refined petroleum products	
S24	Manufacture of chemicals and pharmaceuticals	
S25	Manufacture of rubber and plastics products	
S26	Manufacture of other non-metallic mineral products	
S27	Manufacture of basic metals	

(continued)

Table 12.8 (continued)

Id	Sector	Economic activity
S28	Manufacture of electrical equipment	
S29	Manufacture of machinery and equipment n.e.c	
S30	Manufacture of motor vehicles, trailers and semi-trailers	
S31	Manufacture of furniture	
S32	Other manufacturing	
S33	Electricity	Services
S34	Gas, steam and air conditioning supply	
S35	Water collection, treatment and supply	
S36	Sewerage; Waste collection, treatment and disposal activities	
S37	Construction	
S38	Wholesale and retail trade	
S39	Repair of motor vehicles and motorcycles	
S40	Land transport and transport via pipelines	
S41	Water transport	
S42	Air transport	
S43	Warehousing and support activities for transportation	
S44	Postal and courier activities	
S45	Accommodation and food service activities	
S46	Information and communication	
S47	Financial and insurance activities	
S48	Real estate activities	
S49	Professional, scientific and technical activities	
S50	Public administration and defence; compulsory social security	
S51	Education	
S52	Human health and social work activities	
S53	Arts, entertainment and recreation; Other service activities	
S54	Activities of households as employers	

Source Authors' calculations

Table 12.9 Workers in isolation by region: percentage of total workers

		Workers in isolation (%)
Caribbean	Atlántico	61.9
	Bolívar	60.7
	Cesar	60.4
	Córdoba	61.4

(continued)

Table 12.9 (continued)

		Workers in isolation (%)
	La Guajira	61.3
	Magdalena	60.7
	Sucre	58.6
	San Andrés	64.6
Pacific	Chocó	58.2
	Valle del Cauca	60.2
	Nariño	56.5
	Cauca	57.3
Central	Bogotá	61.5
	Boyacá	58.7
	Cundinamarca	58.7
	Huila	56.1
	Norte de Santander	59.2
	Santander	59.8
	Tolima	58.5
Coffee area and Antioquia	Antioquia	60.4
	Caldas	59.3
	Quindío	60.1
	Risaralda	60.6
Amazonia	Amazonas	54.8
	Caquetá	58.6
	Guainía	48.2
	Guaviare	56.3
	Putumayo	56.0
	Vaupés	46.8
Eastern plains and Orinoquia	Arauca	59.7
	Casanare	60.9
	Vichada	53.8
	Meta	59.5

Source Authors' calculations

Table 12.10 Income of workers in isolation by regions: percentage of the total income by department

		Income of workers in isolation (%)
Caribbean	Atlántico	51.3
	Bolívar	50.7
	Cesar	51.4

(continued)

Table 12.10 (continued)

		Income of workers in isolation (%)
	Córdoba	45.7
	La Guajira	48.9
	Magdalena	45.3
	Sucre	41.3
	San Andrés	58.2
Pacific	Chocó	50.5
	Valle del Cauca	41.2
	Nariño	44.9
	Cauca	52.4
Central	Bogotá	48.3
	Boyacá	51.8
	Cundinamarca	52.2
	Huila	48.0
	Norte de Santander	46.2
	Santander	54.1
	Tolima	48.3
Coffee area and Antioquia	Antioquia	54.0
	Caldas	49.0
	Quindío	49.2
	Risaralda	52.1
Amazonia	Amazonas	39.5
	Caquetá	42.2
	Guainía	41.2
	Guaviare	37.7
	Putumayo	36.1
	Vaupés	41.7
Eastern plains and Orinoquia	Arauca	48.5
	Casanare	44.7
	Vichada	50.8
	Meta	38.2

Source Authors' calculations

Table 12.11 Percentage of workers in isolation by department and region: coffee area and antioquia

	Antioquia (%)	Caldas (%)	Quindío (%)	Risaralda (%)
Agriculture	50.2	49	50	51
Coffee growing	50.6	51	53	51
Livestock and hunting	49.6	50	50	48

(continued)

Table 12.11 (continued)

	Antioquia (%)	Caldas (%)	Quindío (%)	Risaralda (%)
Forestry and logging	71.2	71	71	71
Fishing and aquaculture	48.1	56	52	48
Mining of coal and lignite	71.2			
Extraction of crude petroleum and natural gas	48.1			
Mining of metal ores	71.2	71	71	71
Other mining and quarrying	71.6	72	71	71
Processing and preserving of meat	48.1	48	48	48
Processing of vegetable and animal oils and fats	48.1	48	48	48
Processing of dairy products	49.0	48	48	48
Processing of grain mill products, starches and starch products	48.9	49	48	49
Processing of coffee products	48.1	48	52	48
Processing of sugar			48	48
Processing of cocoa, chocolate and sugar confectionery	48.1	49	48	48
Processing and preserving of fruit and vegetables	48.1	49	49	48
Manufacture of beverages; Manufacture of tobacco products	48.1	48	50	48
Manufacture of textiles; Manufacture of wearing apparel	71.6	74	72	71
Manufacture of leather and related products	72.5	72	71	73
Manufacture of wood and of products of wood and cork	71.2	71	72	73
Manufacture of paper and paper products	71.7	72	71	72
Manufacture of coke and refined petroleum products	48.1			
Manufacture of chemicals and pharmaceuticals	48.1	48	50	50
Manufacture of rubber and plastics products	48.4	48	53	48
Manufacture of other non-metallic mineral products	71.2	71	71	72
Manufacture of basic metals	71.6	72	72	72
Manufacture of electrical equipment	71.3	71	71	71
Manufacture of machinery and equipment n.e.c	71.2	71	73	71

(continued)

Table 12.11 (continued)

	Antioquia (%)	Caldas (%)	Quindío (%)	Risaralda (%)
Manufacture of motor vehicles, trailers and semi-trailers	71.2	71	71	71
Manufacture of furniture	71.7	72	71	72
Other manufacturing	73.2	72	73	72
Electricity	0.0	0	0	0
Gas, steam and air conditioning supply	0.0	0	0	0
Water collection, treatment and supply	0.0	0	0	0
Sewerage; Waste collection, treatment and disposal activities	15.0	10	0	10
Construction	85.7	86	86	86
Wholesale and retail trade	72.0	72	72	72
Repair of motor vehicles and motorcycles	72.9	74	72	73
Land transport and transport via pipelines	71.3	71	72	71
Water transport	71.2			
Air transport	71.2	71	71	71
Warehousing and support activities for transportation	71.6	71	72	74
Postal and courier activities	71.4	72	73	71
Accommodation and food service activities	94.3	94	94	94
Information and communication	0.7	3	5	1
Financial and insurance activities	0.2	1	0	1
Real estate activities	85.8	86	86	86
Professional, scientific and technical activities	85.7	86	86	86
Public administration and defence; compulsory social security	0.0	0	0	0
Education	57.0	57	57	57
Human health and social work activities	1.2	2	3	2
Arts, entertainment and recreation; Other service activities	94.2	94	94	94
Activities of households as employers	94.3	94	94	94

Source Authors' calculations

Table 12.12 Percentage of workers in isolation by department and sector: Amazonia region

	Amazonas	Caquetá	Guainía	Guaviare	Putumayo	Vaupés
Agriculture	54.2	50	50	50	51	48
Coffee growing		53			51	
Livestock and hunting	48.1	51	48	49	48	
Forestry and logging	71.2	74	71	71	71	71
Fishing and aquaculture	48.1	51	48		48	
Mining of coal and lignite						
Extraction of crude petroleum and natural gas					48	
Mining of metal ores			71		71	
Other mining and quarrying	71.6	71		71	75	71
Processing and preserving of meat	48.1	48	48	48	48	
Processing of vegetable and animal oils and fats						
Processing of dairy products	48.1	48	48	48	48	
Processing of grain mill products, starches and starch products	48.1	48	48	48	53	48
Processing of coffee products		48				
Processing of sugar		66				
Processing of cocoa, chocolate and sugar confectionery		48		48	48	
Processing and preserving of fruit and vegetables	48.1	48	48	48		48
Manufacture of beverages; Manufacture of tobacco products	48.1	48	74	48	48	56
Manufacture of textiles; Manufacture of wearing apparel	71.2	72	71	75	73	
Manufacture of leather and related products	71.2	72		71		
Manufacture of wood and of products of wood and cork		71	71	71	71	
Manufacture of paper and paper products	71.2	72		71	73	
Manufacture of coke and refined petroleum products						

(continued)

Table 12.12 (continued)

	Amazonas	Caquetá	Guainía	Guaviare	Putumayo	Vaupés
Manufacture of chemicals and pharmaceuticals	48.1	48		48	48	
Manufacture of rubber and plastics products		48				
Manufacture of other non-metallic mineral products	71.2	71	71	71	71	
Manufacture of basic metals	72.7	72	71	71	73	
Manufacture of electrical equipment		72			71	
Manufacture of machinery and equipment n.e.c	72.0	71	72	72	71	
Manufacture of motor vehicles, trailers and semi-trailers	71.2	76	71	71		
Manufacture of furniture	72.6	72	71	71	71	
Other manufacturing	71.2	72	71	71	71	
Electricity	0.0	0	0	0	0	0
Gas, steam and air conditioning supply		0		0	0	
Water collection, treatment and supply	0.0	1		0	0	
Sewerage; Waste collection, treatment and disposal activities	0.0	0		33	0	
Construction	85.7	86	86	86	86	86
Wholesale and retail trade	71.7	72	72	72	72	72
Repair of motor vehicles and motorcycles		72		72	72	
Land transport and transport via pipelines		71		72	72	
Water transport	71.2	71		71	71	
Air transport	71.2	71	71	71	71	71
Warehousing and support activities for transportation	71.2	72	71		71	
Postal and courier activities	71.7	71	71	72	71	71
Accommodation and food service activities	94.3	94	94	94	94	94
Information and communication	1.9	0	0	4	0	0

(continued)

Table 12.12 (continued)

	Amazonas	Caquetá	Guainía	Guaviare	Putumayo	Vaupés
Financial and insurance activities	0.0	0	0	0	0	0
Real estate activities	85.6	86	94	87	86	86
Professional, scientific and technical activities	85.9	86	86	86	86	86
Public administration and defence; compulsory social security	0.0	0	0	0	0	0
Education	57.0	57	57	57	57	57
Human health and social work activities	1.4	1	1	2	1	1
Arts, entertainment and recreation; Other service activities	94.2	94	94	94	94	94
Activities of households as employers	94.3	94		94	94	94

Source Authors' calculations

References

Bonet, J., & Meisel, A. (2001). La convergencia regional en Colombia: una visión de largo plazo, 1926–1995. In A. Meisel (Ed.), *Regiones, ciudades y crecimiento económico en Colombia*, Cartagena, Colección de Economía Regional, Banco de la República.

Bonet, J. (2006). Cambio estructural regional en Colombia: una aproximación con matrices insumo-producto. *Revista De Coyuntura Económica, Volumen XXXVI, No, 1*, 147–176.

Bonet-Moron, J. A., Ricciulli-Marin, D., Pérez-Valbuena, G. J., Galvis-Aponte, L. A., Haddad, E. A., Araújo, I. F., & Perobelli, F. S. (2020). Regional economic impact of COVID-19 in Colombia: An input-output approach. *Regional Science Policy and Practice, 12*, 1123–1150.

CEDE. (2020). La vulnerabilidad del empleo a la emergencia de COVID-19. *Nota Macroeconómica* No.11. Bogotá, Universidad de Los Andes—Facultad de Economía.

Dietzenbacher, van der Linden, E. J., & Steenge, A.E. (1993). The regional extraction method: EC input-output comparisons. *Economic Systems Research, 5*, 185–206.

Galvis, L., & Meisel, A. (2010). Persistencia de las desigualdades regionales en Colombia: Un análisis especial. *Documentos de trabajos sobre economía regional y urbana* (DTSERU), No. 120, Cartagena, Banco de la Republica de Colombia, Centro de Estudios Económicos Regionales (CEER).

Galvis, L., Galvis, W., & Hahn, L. (2017). Una revisión de los estudios de convergencia regional en Colombia. *Documentos de trabajos sobre economía regional y urbana* (DTSERU), No. 264, Cartagena, Banco de la Republica de Colombia, Centro de Estudios Económicos Regionales (CEER).

Haddad, E. A., Araújo, I. F., & Galvis, L. A. (2019). Matriz Insumo-Producto Interregional de Colombia, 2015. *Nota Técnica, TD NEREUS* 10-2019, The University of São Paulo Regional and Urban Economics Lab (NEREUS).

Haddad, E. A., Perobelli, F. S., & Araújo, I. F. (2020). Input-output analysis of COVID-19: Methodology for assessing the impacts of lockdown measures. *TD NEREUS* 01-2020, The University of São Paulo Regional and Urban Economics Lab (NEREUS).

Hahn, L. (2016). Encadenamientos regionales en Colombia 2004–2012. *Documentos de Trabajo Sobre Economía Regional y Urbana*, 234. Cartagena, Banco de la República.

Mejía, L. F. (2020). COVID-19: costos económicos en salud y en medidas de contención para Colombia. *Nota Editorial*, Fedesarrollo. Bogotá, 7 de abril 2020.

OECD. (2020). *Evaluating the initial impact of COVID-19 containment measures on economic activity*. OECD Economics Department.

World Bank. (2020). La Economía en los Tiempos del COVID-19. LAC Semiannual Report. Washington, D.C. April 2020. Descargado de https://openknowledge.worldbank.org/handle/10986/33555

Jaime Bonet is an economist from the Universidad de Los Andes in Bogotá with a master's degree in economics and a Ph. D. in regional planning from the University of Illinois at Urbana-Champaign. His research areas include regional and urban economics, local public finance, local economic development, and regional development history in Colombia.

Diana Ricciulli Ph.D. Student (Econ.), University of British Columbia. Professional researcher, Center for Regional Economic Studies, Banco de la República, Colombia. Research fields: political economy, economic history, and economic development.

Gerson Javier Pérez-Valbuena Ph.D. in economics, University of Essex (United Kingdom). Senior Researcher at the Center for Regional Economic Studies (CEER) at the Banco de la República, Colombia. He has published several articles and book chapters on topics related to regional and urban economics and subnational public finances.

Eduardo A. Haddad, Full Professor at the Department of Economics at the University of São Paulo, Brazil, where he directs the Regional and Urban Economics Lab (NEREUS). Affiliate Professor at the Faculty of Governance, Economic and Social Sciences of the Mohammed VI University and Senior Fellow at the Policy Center for the New South, Rabat, Morocco. President of the Regional Science Association International, RSAI (2021–2022).

Inácio F. Araújo Doctor in Economics, Federal University of Juiz de Fora. Pos-doctoral researcher, University of São Paulo, Brazil. Research fields: regional economics, input-output methods, and international trade.

Fernando S. Perobelli Doctor in Economics, University of Sao Paulo, Full Professor at Department of Economics at the Federal University of Juiz de Fora. He has published several articles in academic journals on topics such as energy, environment, regional economics, and sectorial analysis.

Part IV
Structural Development Issues

Chapter 13
Boiling Hot! Economy-Wide Impacts of Climate Change on Colombian Coffee Yields

Pedro Levy Sayon, Andrea Otero-Cortés, Federico Ceballos-Sierra, and Eduardo A. Haddad

13.1 Climate Change and Global Warming

The term climate change refers to a physical phenomenon in which there are globally long-lasting shifts in temperature, precipitation, cloudiness, among other atmospheric conditions, regarding their historical averages. Such variations might be caused by many different reasons, such as internal Earth processes, external forces (e.g., solar activity), or, more recently, human intervention. Contrary to popular belief, climate change distinguishes itself from global warming because the latter only encompasses temperature: the long-term heating of Earth's surface observed since the Industrial Revolution. In other words, although employed as such, the terms are not interchangeable.

On this note, one of the key objectives of the Goddard Institute for Space Studies (GISS)[1] is studying climate change in the twenty-first century and predicting long-term shifts in the average weather patterns resulting from this phenomenon. There is

---

P. L. Sayon (✉) · E. A. Haddad
University of São Paulo, São Paulo, Brazil
e-mail: pedro.sayon@alumni.usp.br

E. A. Haddad
e-mail: ehaddad@usp.br

A. Otero-Cortés
Banco de la República, Cartagena, Colombia
e-mail: aoteroco@banrep.gov.co

F. Ceballos-Sierra
International Center for Tropical Agriculture, Cali, Colombia
e-mail: fc3@illinois.edu

[1] A laboratory in the Earth Sciences Division of the Goddard Space Flight Center from the North American Space Agency (NASA) affiliated with the Columbia University Earth.

© The Author(s), under exclusive license to Springer Nature Switzerland AG 2023
E. A. Haddad et al. (eds.), *The Colombian Economy and Its Regional Structural Challenges*, Advances in Spatial Science, https://doi.org/10.1007/978-3-031-22653-3_13

Fig. 13.1 Global land–ocean temperature index. *Source* NASA, 2022

scientific consensus[2] that these changes observed in Earth's climate since early twentieth century are primarily driven by human activities, notably fossil fuel burning, which increases heat-trapping greenhouse gas levels in the atmosphere, raising the planet average surface temperature.

In fact, as seen in Fig. 13.1, there is a sharp detachment of temperatures from the baseline average starting just before 1980, marking the beginning of human-induced global warming. Not coincidentally, greenhouse gases emulate almost the same pattern, starting a couple of decades prior because there is a strong lagged component correlating emissions and temperature. Figure 13.2 is a graph demonstrating the previous statement.

While carbon dioxide (CO_2) is not the only greenhouse gas (GHG), it accounts for over 80%, making it an excellent proxy for measuring emissions. Before the Industrial Revolution, the concentration of pollutants was insignificant. The amount of CO_2 released annually remained relatively low before the mid-twentieth century. In 1950, the world emitted over 6 billion tons of this gas—about the same as the USA, or half of Chinese annual emissions in 2020. By 1990, it almost quadrupled, with approximately 23 billion tons. Since then, it has continued to proliferate, totaling in 2020 roughly 35 billion tons. While growth has slowed over the last few years, forecasts based on current climate policies suggest that total emissions have yet to reach their peak (Ritchie et al., 2020).

---

[2] Cook et al. (2016) and Myers et al. (2021).

Fig. 13.2 World annual CO_2 emissions. *Source* Our World in Data, 2022

In that context, it is relevant to inquire about the magnitude of the impact of human activity on climate and, reciprocally, the consequences of such new weather conditions on the economy. Many studies correlate global warming and productivity, particularly in industries involved in extracting raw materials, such as farming, logging, hunting, fishing, and mining. Furthermore, many developing countries have highly specialized primary-based economies, meaning that those sectors tend to make up more significant portions of the country's GDP. Among such cases, a few examples in Latin America come to mind: Chilean copper, Paraguayan soybeans, and—the case of interest for this chapter—Colombian coffee.

This chapter is organized as follows. Section 13.2 provides a literature review on the Colombian coffee industry since the nineteenth century. Section 13.3 explains the mechanisms through which a changing climate affects coffee productivity, especially how its magnitude relates to the Colombian case. Section 13.4 presents the computable general equilibrium (CGE) shock, as well as its results and interpretations. And, finally, Sect. 13.5 resumes the discussion of previous sections and concludes.

13.2 Colombian Coffee Industry Brief History

13.2.1 Early History (1830–1958)

Firstly, to evaluate how the changing climate might affect Colombian coffee yields, it is necessary to understand the nuances of Colombian economic history, especially regarding the coffee industry, which is entailed in this subsection. It should also be noted that it draws heavily on the work of Ocampo (2015). The most famous story about the origins of coffee in America indicates that the French first brought the seeds to their colonies in Guyana and the Antilles in the late seventeenth century. From this starting point, coffee-growing spread throughout the continent in the first half of the eighteenth century. It finally reached Colombia around the middle of this era when the Jesuit Order introduced the crop on its farms in the Eastern Plains (Orinoquía), the Cauca's Valley, and other smaller regions.

Nonetheless, coffee-growing remained a minor activity for over a century in Colombia and worldwide. In European countries, its consumption was restricted in the eighteenth century to the aristocracy, who could bear the high costs of an exotic drink. In 1790, for example, the total world trade in beans was 1.2 million 60 kg bags of unripe coffee, a tiny fraction of what it is today. Only in the late-nineteenth century, in the wake of the Industrial Revolution with the slow popularization of its consumption in Europe and the United States, did the growth of the coffee industry accelerate.

In Colombia, its first commercial experience came out as a subproduct of the pinnacle of coffee growing in the Venezuelan Andes after its independence. The first crops of relevant scale were produced in the Cúcuta region in the 1830s. From there, coffee growing spread first to Pamplona and Ocaña, in Norte de Santander, and later to Santander, Cundinamarca, and western Colombia.

It is not easy to know the actual magnitude of Colombian exports during the first years since much of what was registered in Cúcuta customs was Venezuelan coffee re-exported. Although there are higher estimates, it would not seem an exaggeration to affirm that the total production of coffee in Colombia in 1860 was between 30,000 and 40,000 bags. Registered exports, including Venezuelan coffee, had reached 55,000 bags by then. However, coffee was still a marginal item within Colombian foreign trade.

From then, coffee production experienced three other booms in the nineteenth century, which significantly displaced the coffee frontier to the country's interior. The first of these expansions took place in the 1860s. Exports rose to around 100,000 bags during this period, but production remained concentrated in Norte de Santander. When the Office of Statistics made the first attempt in 1874 to estimate the country's coffee production reliably, it amounted to about 110,000 bags, out of which 95,000 came from that region.

The second boom took place during the 1870s. This expansion made it possible to increase grain exports from 100,000 to 220,000 bags approximately and turn coffee into one of the crucial products of Colombian foreign trade. By the end of that decade, it already represented more than 20% of Colombia's external sales. This growth generated yet another and more significant shift in the production frontier. While Norte de Santander continued to increase its harvests until it yielded 120,000 bags in these years, most of the new production was concentrated in Santander and Cundinamarca, which by the middle of the following decade were producing 60,000 and 40,000 bags, respectively.

In the first case, expansion started at the beginning of the decade around the city of Bucaramanga, consolidating its economic dominance over this region at the expense of the historical centers to the south of this department. In Cundinamarca, on the other hand, the extension of plantations began a little later. In both regions, it was interrupted by the fall in international prices in the early 1880s and the civil war.

Shortly after political order was restored during the Regeneration, the third and most important coffee boom of the nineteenth century began. The country's production expanded considerably in the 1890s, reaching around 600,000 bags when the Thousand Days' War broke out. By then, it already represented about half of the Colombian exports. This expansion coincided with the best international prices of the second half of this era. In fact, in the early 1890s, coffee prices were 40% higher in real terms than in the 1870s and almost three times higher than in the mid-nineteenth century.

Other factors undoubtedly played a role in this process. As a reflection of the general crisis that Colombia's foreign trade experienced in the early 1880s, the depreciation of silver in the international market, and the subsequent introduction of paper money, the peso experienced a substantial real devaluation. During the initial stage of this process, coffee production costs tended to fall in terms of gold (the international monetary unit), thus promoting plantings. No less important was the landowners' access to credit granted by foreign business houses in conditions that were attractive for that time: 6% annual interest (with 1.5 or 2 additional percentage points of commissions), two years of term, and subsequent payment in coffee.

In regional terms, the expansion of the 1890s was the most diversified of the nineteenth century. The expansion axis was west of Cundinamarca (and the surrounding areas of Tolima), which increased its yields from 40,000 to 230,000 bags during these years. Outside this region, production began to expand on an appreciable scale in Antioquia, which by the end of this era was amounting to about 90,000 bags. Santander doubled its harvests until it reached around 120,000 bags. Norte de Santander and Cauca's Valley also participated, albeit on a more modest scale in the peak.

In western Cundinamarca, the expansion followed three different lines. The first of them followed the route from Bogotá D.C to Honda; the second, the province of Tequendama, accompanied by Bogotá River on its descent to the Magdalena River; and the third, the Sumapaz region, followed by the downslope route toward Girardot. Coffee development began in the first of these lines during the 1870s, from where it headed for Tequendama and, to a lesser extent, toward Sumapaz in the late nineteenth century. In Antioquia, coffee had begun to develop also in the 1870s in the vicinity of Medellín. However, by the end of this era, the expansion was concentrated in southeast Antioquia, especially in the Fredonia district. In Cauca's Valley, on the other hand, most of the development then had its epicenter in a geographic depression, in the vicinity of Cali and Palmira.

The first decade of the twentieth century did not seem particularly likely to result in a significant coffee expansion, as both prices and productivity remained low. Despite the enormous efforts made by the Government of São Paulo in Brazil to restrict planting and defend coffee prices, these were fruitless, and the prices have remained at extremely low levels since 1899. Furthermore, coffee farms had low productivity and were still being affected by the most remarkable civil conflict in Colombian history, thus rendering them incapable of yielding any development.

However, despite the unfavorable elements, the coffee industry took on an unexpected positive turn in the national economy starting at the second decade of the twentieth century. By the late 1920s, production had more than quintupled, surpassing over 3 million bags. The crop became Colombian main export commodity, and the country itself became one of the largest producers worldwide (second only to Brazil) and the first in soft coffees. At the turn of the twentieth century, 3.5% of all coffee in the world was being harvested in Colombia. By the end of the 1920 decade, on the other hand, this share had risen to 10%, and it would only continue to grow in the coming years.

This sudden growth implied a radical change in the agricultural frontier and the means of production. Increased production was concentrated in Antioquian colonization areas in Old Caldas: south of Antioquia, and north of both Tolima, and Cauca's Valley. This region had been populated since the early years of independence, and by the beginning of the twentieth century, it had acquired an important volume of inhabitants. The settlers initially developed slash-and-burn agriculture like that practiced in other country regions, but with additional commercial activities (e.g., pig fattening, saddlery). Coffee did not play an important part in this process, even in the late settlement regions (Quindío), since its long gestation period did not adapt to the requirements of the colonization process—coffee plants usually start to produce flowers three to four years after planted, rendering this activity not only uninteresting but also unfeasible in early years of subsisting economies.

Nonetheless, in the early twentieth century, the crop expanded rapidly in small and medium-sized properties that had developed in this region surrounding the Magdalena River thanks to a long struggle for land against the owners of unproductive farms from the settlers, the latter having had the support of the commercial elites of Medellín and, later, Manizales. Still, this scattering of peasant units did not prevent landowners from maintaining an appreciable concentration of property in the colonization areas. According to estimates from Palacios (2009), only 20% of land awards in Antioquia and Caldas between 1823 and 1931 (about 250,000 hectares) favored settlers of small and medium-sized owners (less than 50 hectares), although this pattern would later be reversed.

The advance of coffee in this region during the first three decades of the twentieth century was incredible. Antioquia and Caldas went from producing 90,000 bags in 1900 (around 15% of national yields) to 384,000 in 1913 (36%) and 1,622,000 in 1932 (47%). Production from Tolima and Cauca's Valley was about 110,000 bags in 1913 (10% of the total), but it was represented mainly by harvests from farms located on the west side of the first and on the south of the latter. In 1932, outputs from those departments were 802,000 bags (around 23% of national yields) and were concentrated in the central mountain range. In addition, the coffee industry started to spread to new regions of the country, especially Cauca, Nariño, Huila, Boyacá, and Magdalena. The traditional producing zones in Norte de Santander, Santander, and Cundinamarca concentrated 82% of national production by the end of the eighteenth century (500,000 bags). However, although in absolute terms those yields had increased until 1932 (820,000), relatively their share had declined to 24%.

If the coffee plantation system was the axis of expansion in the nineteenth century, the new production in the twentieth century came mainly from small- and medium-sized units. These estates were already dominant in 1923, when coffee farms of less than 12 hectares (about 20,000 coffee trees with the typical average densities of that time) controlled 56.4% of national production. These types of properties were managed mainly by their owners, thus indicating their character as small and medium-sized peasant units. Larger farms (units with more than 35 hectares of mature coffee containing up to 50,000 coffee trees) only represented then 23.5% of production. In 1932, this "popularization" process of coffee production had been intensified even more: small- and medium-sized units represented of 59.5% of production, whereas the plantation system was reduced to only 18.2%.

Furthermore, the great bonanza that the coffee economy experienced before the Great Depression (1929–1939) was not abruptly interrupted. On the contrary, it kept growing in later decades. In the early 1960s, harvests amounted to 7.8 million 60 kg bags of unripe coffee, about three times what it was in the second half of the 1920s, although it became less dynamic. Production and exports experienced a sharp increase throughout the first decades of the twentieth century (between 6 and 8% annually), only for harvests to stabilize at lower 5% growth rates in the 1930s. However, this started to slow even further in the 1940s, until it reached less than 2% in both the 1950s and the 1960s.

These trends were reflected in the national portion of world bean production and as well as in foreign trade. In the early 1930s, for example, Colombia controlled 10% of world coffee production and was responsible for 12.4% of international coffee exports. Those shares would keep growing until they both peaked at around 20% during the Second World War. With loss of dynamism, production and exports started to decline in the postwar period, only to stabilize in the 1960s in 13% and 12%, respectively.

During the coffee year 1955–1956, the Economic Commission for Latin America (ECLAC) and the Food and Agriculture Organization of the United Nations (FAO) carried out one of the most complete diagnoses of the Colombian coffee economy. For that year, these entities estimated that there were 1,156,000 people on coffee farms, equivalent to 9.1% of the country population. Between 1951 and 1955, coffee production had generated 13.1% of national income and a little more than a third of agricultural income. The comparison between the participation in national income and the proportion of population working in farms indicates that *per capita* income in coffee activities was higher than the country average, even if complementary agricultural activities carried out in the same production units are excluded.

By then, production was already dominated by small- and medium-sized estates. These types of production units were often managed by their owner, thus indicating their character as peasant units. Sharecropping had an important presence, particularly on medium-sized farms. The largest were usually managed by a hired manager. In total, it was estimated that 56% of the planted area was managed by its owner, 21% by sharecroppers and 23% by administrators.

Still, the coffee industry was starting to show clear signs of obsolescence, especially in large properties. In addition, even from a technical standpoint, the activity was already outdated, as Colombian coffee was almost an exclusive product of primary factors land and labor. This indicated the absence of not only large-scale capital investment, but also of modern agronomic practices. As at the beginning of the twentieth century, crop care was reduced to weeding, cleaning and pruning.

The highest yield of labor in cultivation work was obtained on farms under administration and the highest yield per hectare on land under sharecropping contracts. This and the lower productivity of small farms openly distort the idea that great advantages of peasant units were of a technological nature. On the contrary, these fell on medium-sized farms in either administration or sharecropping. The great dynamism of peasant units must thus be sought in another type of economic advantage: their ability to reduce to a minimum monetary cost associated with coffee production and to rely more intensively on family labor, given that the latter did not have possibilities of alternative commercial revenue.

13.2.2 The Present Era (2015)

More than half a century later, not much has changed in terms of coffee spatial distribution and average property size. In other words, much of production is still concentrated in those areas of early colonization surrounding the Magdalena River, within the Andean Mountain range, where those incipient peasant units had scattered throughout the nineteenth and early twentieth centuries. This also means that most of production is in small- and medium-sized properties, linked to family farming and sharecropping, respectively. Moreover, the historical development of Colombian coffee industry created a path dependence that dampened innovation in these traditional growing areas. And, although technology certainly did evolve, it was not enough to promote any revolution regarding capital intensity or diversification of species of any kind, as will be further detailed below.

In terms notoriety, on the other hand, Colombian coffee production has become a ubiquitous phenomenon, whose product is widely renowned for its quality, delicious taste and is consumed worldwide. Colombian coffee consecrated itself as the country primary crop, establishing Colombia as a major player in this commodity foreign trade. And, despite coffee farming accounting for less than 1% of national GDP, it plays a vital role in employment, as over half a million families benefit directly from it, potentially many more indirectly. Given its popularity and socioeconomic importance, researchers have inquired what could happen to Colombian coffee in a climate-changing setting.

Remembering the general production structure presented in Chap. 10, the first relevant characteristic of coffee supply chain is its division between two industries: growing (or harvesting) and processing—given the sector aggregation of the economy in the Colombian interregional input–output system (IIOS) from 2015. They are intimately interlinked and generate important backward and forward linkages to many other sectors.

By first considering coffee growing, its intermediate demands are dominated by basic chemical substances (e.g., fertilizers), agriculture (e.g., coffee seeds), electrical equipment, land transportation (e.g., tractors and trucks), and financial activities. Those five industries account for almost 90% of the total necessary inputs for coffee harvesting and are almost entirely provided domestically, except for the chemicals, where around half are imported. However, this intermediate consumption corresponds to only a third of total expenditure from coffee growing. In contrast, the other two-thirds are split almost equally between labor and capital, albeit the latter here comprises both land use associated costs and spendings dedicated to light machinery, and thus, coffee harvesting might be considered a labor-intensive activity. Finally, none of its output are exported, which means that all production is absorbed by the local market, a large share by coffee processing, which will be further detailed in the next paragraph.

Coffee processing, contrastingly, has over 80% of its intermediate demand supplied by coffee growing. In order of relevance, the others are coffee processing itself, wholesale and retail trade, financial activities, and plastic products (e.g., packaging). Adding the four latter to the former generates over 95% of the necessary inputs. Except for financial activities, where almost three-quarters are imported (likely foreign banks investing in the crop's production), most inputs are provided domestically once more. However, in contrast to coffee harvesting, intermediate demand here plays a major role, concentrating more than 90% of total expenditure, followed by capital with 7% and labor with no more than 1%, making processed coffee, a capital-intensive product.

Finally, another important distinction is that not all the production is destined for the local market. In fact, it is quite the opposite: processed coffee is an important export for the country, whose relevance will be illustrated shortly.[3] From Table 13.1, Colombian five most exported commodities in 2015 were, in order: petroleum, coal, chemical substances, basic metallurgical products, and coffee. While the latter is only the fifth in terms of the total value, it is the first among agricultural products and accounts for over 700,000 tons of exported volume.

---

[3] Further details regarding internal production and dynamics of Colombian coffee industry, as well as input–output exercises and value-added analysis are thoroughly covered in Chaps. 9 and 10.

Table 13.1 Colombian exports in 2015

Code	Commodity	Value (COP billions)	Share (%)
S7	Extracción de petróleo crudo y gas natural y actividades de apoyo para actividades de explotación	37.598	32
S6	Extracción de carbón de piedra y lignito	11.713	10
S24	Fabricación de sustancias químicas básicas	8.678	7
S27	Fabricación de productos metalúrgicos básicos	8.342	7
S14	Elaboración de productos de café	6.725	6
S1	Agricultura y actividades de servicios conexas	6.575	6
S23	Coquización, fabricación de productos de la refinación del petróleo y actividades de mezcla de combustibles	5.770	5
S45	Alojamiento y servicios de comida	4.850	4
S42	Transporte aéreo	4.146	3
S19	Preparación, hilatura, tejeduría y acabado de productos textiles	2.187	2
S49	Actividades profesionales, científicas y técnicas; Actividades de servicios administrativos y de apoyo	2.172	2
S25	Fabricación de productos de caucho y de plástico	1.779	1
S28	Fabricación de aparatos y equipo eléctrico; fabricación de productos informáticos, electrónicos y ópticos	1.733	1
S30	Fabricación de vehículos automotores, remolques y semirremolques	1.492	1
S22	Fabricación de papel, cartón y productos de papel y de cartón; actividades de impresión	1.463	1
S46	Información y comunicaciones	1.352	1
S26	Fabricación de otros productos minerales no metálicos	1.162	1
S29	Fabricación de maquinaria y equipo n.c.p	1.072	1
S15	Elaboración de azúcar y elaboración de panela	1.027	1
S11	Elaboración de aceites y grasas de origen vegetal y animal	962	1

Source Interregional Input–Output System for Colombia, 2015 (Chapter 5 of this book)

Additionally, The Atlas of Economic Complexity (TAEC)[4] provided Figs. 13.3 and 13.4, which display the destination countries of that commodity and the relative importance of Colombian coffee in terms of total exported value in 2015, respectively. Figure 13.3 shows that Colombian coffee is primarily consumed in the United States, Canada, and Japan, followed by Western Europe, Australia, Russia, and China, which means that most of its importers are developed countries whose per capita income is enough for their denizens to acquire a prime quality product such as this. Besides,

---

[4] Data visualization tool built at the Harvard Kennedy School of Government powered by Harvard Growth Lab that allows users to explore global trade flows across markets and track these dynamics over time.

China became an important player in international coffee market, as its imports rose by 586% from 2001 to 2009, albeit Colombian coffee exports to China rose only by 5,838% in the same period (United Nations, 2022).

Figure 13.4 displays Colombia as the third-largest coffee exporter worldwide, second only to Brazil and Vietnam, although the latter only produces robusta beans (Coffea canephora). Furthermore, while Brazilian coffee is the same as Colombian—arabica beans (Coffea arabica)—the former's quality is significantly reduced given its production structure. Also, it is noteworthy that countries that rank among the largest exporters are not necessarily the largest producers. Germany, Switzerland,

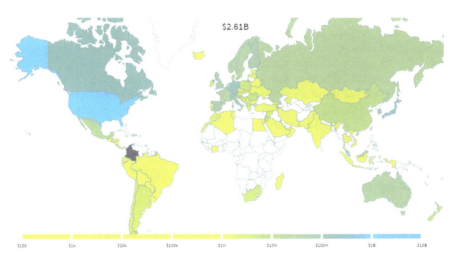

Fig. 13.3 Absolute destination of Colombian coffee in USD. *Source* The Atlas of Economic Complexity, 2021

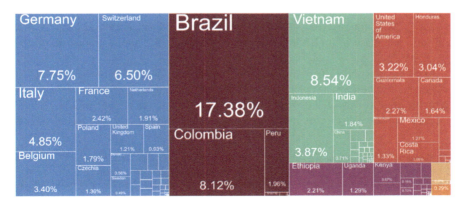

Fig. 13.4 Relative origin of coffee exports in 2015. *Source* The Atlas of Economic Complexity, 2021

Italy and the United States account for more than 20% of world exports and do not have a significant production of coffee, but rather add some value to imported *in natura* coffee and reexport them.

13.3 Underlying Harvesting Mechanisms

There are many ways in which climate affects coffee productivity. The Climate Institute[5] published a report evaluating the possible effects of climate change on coffee farming (Watts, 2016). According to it, the so-called Bean Belt, which is concentrated mainly on the tropical zone, is comprised of 70 coffee-producing countries, responsible for employing directly 25 million coffee farmers (mostly smallholders), housing 125 million families whose livelihoods are reliant on coffee and exporting approximately U$ 20 billion worth of coffee. Also, in Watts (2016), it is estimated that by 2050 half of the present farming land worldwide will be rendered unsuitable for the crop, and that by 2100 wild coffee species will become extinct.

This Section draws also on the work of Bunn et al. (2015), which further explains the underlying mechanisms of coffee harvesting and describes the channels along which climate change might affect coffee yields. According to it, there are fundamentally three elements responsible for shifting coffee productivity in a changing climate scenario: the rising temperature damages the beans, the more frequent droughts lower the crop growth, and the advancing pests, particularly the coffee berry borer (*Hypothenemus hampei*, henceforth CBB), stress the plant, reducing productivity.

Moreover, by exploring the Representative Concentration Pathways (RCP)[6] 2.6, 6.0, and 8.5, Bunn et al. (2015) simulate the reduction of coffee farming land for arabica beans by 2050. Respectively, those scenarios yield 58%, 49%, and 43% of loss, meaning that even if emissions were to be diminished drastically, inertial effects of climate change will still imply in depletion of over 40% of suitable land for this crop. The future climate data was generated by downscaling a general circulation model (GCM).[7] Finally, these results were then analyzed for latitude, altitude, region, and land-use classes in all three scenarios to hypothesize future impact on global coffee production.

As was stated before, Colombian coffee is composed mainly (if not exclusively) of arabica beans, which is a species that will likely experience a significant reduction in farmable area worldwide, regardless of scenario. Nonetheless, Bunn et al. (2015) do not focus specifically on Colombia, whose coffee suitability is shown to undergo both

---

[5] Organization whose primary goal is to conduct scientific research on climate change and inform the public of its key findings in order to provide decision-makers with adequate information on how to counter the coming hindrances of such phenomenon and aid them by prescribing policies to avoid those hardships.

[6] GHG concentration trajectories adopted by the Intergovernmental Panel on Climate Change (IPCC).

[7] Climate model composed of a mathematical algorithm simulating the general circulation of planetary atmosphere or ocean.

negative and positive effects from climate change, depending on region and altitude (which are very strongly tied to Colombian topology). Hence, these simulations only answer partially what might happen to Colombian coffee.

With a more focused approach, Ceballos-Sierra and Dall'Erba (2021) developed a multi-step model to forecast total coffee yields in each of the Colombian 1123 municipalities. The simulation uses two different inputs: precipitation and temperature. Water comes in the first step of the model, in which its absorption by the plant is calculated. After that, the output of the previous step determines the production of photosynthate using a measurement called Leaf Area Index (LAI). This, in turn, is what causes the coffee to flourish. Then, the temperature influences growth, the dynamics of production, and the life cycle of the coffee borer beetle. When all five sub-models have been wholly integrated, they yield coffee productivity, measured in kilograms by hectare (Fig. 13.5).

Previous forecasts have estimated an increase between 4 and 24% in coffee yields at the national level. However, with over 500 municipalities producing this crop, Ceballos-Sierra and Dall'Erba (2021) model predicts the expected outputs individually, resulting in a high degree of spatial heterogeneity. As previously mentioned, altitude plays a significant role in coffee suitability, and Colombia is a vast country, but more so when it comes to topology, having peaks as high as the Andean Mountain range and valleys as low as sea level. In terms of the model, this means that traditional growing areas near Magdalena River are expected to experience a decrease in productivity, whereas higher neighboring regions might see their coffee yields rise.

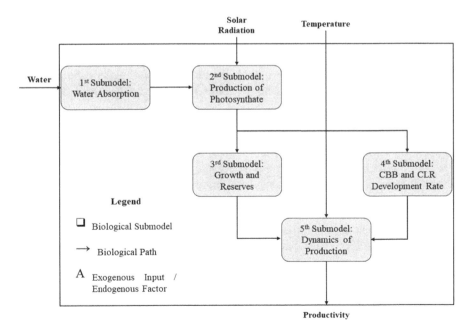

Fig. 13.5 Proposed model for coffee productivity. *Source* Ceballos-Sierra and Dall'Erba (2021)

Interestingly and contrary to worldwide estimates, Colombian coffee might benefit from a changing climate scenario.

Finally, for the CGE simulation, Ceballos-Sierra and Dall'Erba (2021) outputs were aggregated to a departmental level, and these results were transformed into a percent variation of productivity relative to a baseline scenario observed by the Colombian IIOS in 2015. The shock itself, its results and interpretations will be further detailed in the coming Sect. 13.4.

13.4 Climate Shock: Results and Analysis

In Ceballos-Sierra and Dall'Erba (2021) estimates, out of the 32 departments and the capital district in Colombia, only 18 of them are affected. It varies from a decrease of almost 23% to an increase of a little over 21%, and it affects only coffee harvesting (remembering, from Sect. 13.2, there are two coffee-related industries in Colombia—growing and processing). This happens mainly because, due to mechanisms mentioned above through which temperature and humidity affect crops output, only the primary-based industry is directly influenced in a climate change scenario. Moreover, it should also be noted that computations are all simulated with a long-term closure (both capital and labor are endogenous variables in the model), given that climate change is, by its very nature, a long-run phenomenon. Table 13.2 and Fig. 13.6 illustrate the inputs of the model discriminated by region and the role of topology in its composition, respectively.

There is a clear overlay between the country elevation and the climate shock. Due to Colombian unique topology, higher regions tend to have colder temperatures, even when close to the Equator. This means that departments whose elevations are closer to the sea level are already suitable for coffee but will experience a drop in productivity. In contrast, the Andean Mountain range might see its lands become farmable for coffee.

Given the CGE structure, negative values should be interpreted as increasing productivity and vice versa. For instance, as the simulation will occur in all input augmenting technical change, a positive shock value observed in Table 13.2 means that coffee growing will require more inputs to produce the same output level (the reverse logic applies to negative values). For more information on the equations used to specify the model, see Chap. 6.

The scheme in Fig. 13.7 provides a clear picture of how each macroeconomic variable influences the output in the new equilibrium. It provides both variations relative to themselves in the baseline scenario and how much they contribute, in absolute, to the total percentage change in the GDP. Also, the top half represents the income approach computations, while the bottom covers expenditure. The first relevant information here is that this shock induces a 0.212% increase in national income. Interestingly, less than 10% of this variation is due to the shock in all input augmenting technical change. More than 80% comes from capital, and around 11% comes from taxes on the income side. On the other hand, almost 85% of the total growth in the

Table 13.2 Productivity shock by department

Code	Department	Shock
R13	Huila	−21.38
R23	Tolima	−16.28
R11	Cundinamarca	−10.37
R1	Antioquia	−7.98
R17	Nariño	−5.92
R8	Cauca	−5.70
R19	Quindío	−1.91
R6	Caldas	−0.94
R20	Risaralda	−0.54
R7	Caquetá	−0.03
R12	Chocó	0.29
R26	Casanare	0.83
R16	Meta	4.27
R9	Cesar	4.36
R24	Valle del Cauca	6.16
R5	Boyacá	15.28
R18	Norte de Santander	15.86
R21	Santander	22.73

Source Ceballos-Sierra and Dall'Erba (2021)

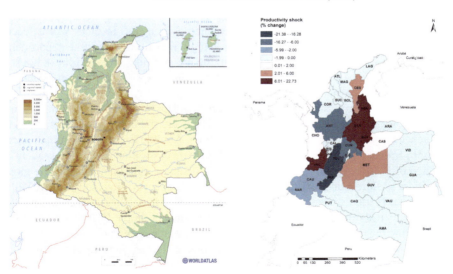

Fig. 13.6 Topology and productivity shock. *Source* World Atlas, 2021

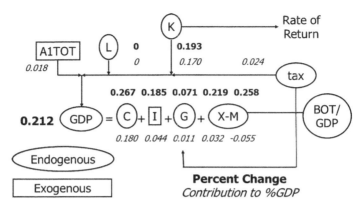

Fig. 13.7 Macroeconomic results. *Source* CEER model

GDP is captured by an increase of 0.267% in household consumption when looking from the expenditure side. The rest comes from investment (21%), exports (15%), government spending (5%), and imports influence this change negatively (− 26%) as it also rises in absolute terms.

Figure 13.8 illustrates the decomposition of total impact on production among the different departments affected by the initial input, which is a very different number from that observed in the productivity shock in Table 13.2. As mentioned previously, the latter makes up only a small portion of GDP change. Therefore, what is shown above is the aggregate effect in each of those regions after the algorithm finished iteration and the economy reaches convergence once again. In other words, each value accounts for the change in coffee growing yields in its respective department and the difference in labor and capital from the income side, or variations in household consumption, investments, government spending, exports, and imports from the expenditure approach.

The most relevant region in terms of impact is Huila, whose contribution alone accounts for almost 45% of GDP increase. These are the other departments which influence the product variation positively: Tolima, Antioquia, Cauca, Cundinamarca, Nariño, Caldas, Quindío, and Risaralda. Together, those nine departments yield a change of 0.271% in national income. On the decrease side, Santander is the most significant, with around two-thirds of total negative impact on GDP, followed by Valle del Cauca, Norte de Santander, Cesar, Boyacá, and Meta. These six accumulate a negative contribution of 0.059%. The total (net) impact on the GDP is obtained by subtracting the latter from the former. While other regions generate no relevant effect on GDP, that does not mean they do not experience changes in GRP distribution.

In that regard, Huila and Tolima are the departments whose GRP has increased the most, emulating the most significant productivity gains with the initial shock. They are followed by Cundinamarca, a region whose contribution to national income in the simulation, counterintuitively, is second to Antioquia and Cauca (besides the already mentioned previous regions). This happens, nevertheless, due to the share of those

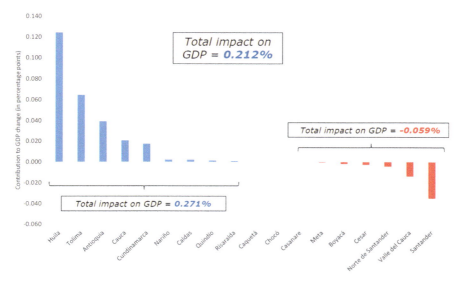

Fig. 13.8 Contribution to GDP change by origin of shock. *Source* CEER model

departments output in the economy. In other words, even though Cundinamarca's growth relative to itself was higher than Antioquia and Cauca, their share in national GDP is larger, which means that a smaller percentual variation still yields higher absolute effects in Colombia. To further enforce this argument, the fourth and fifth biggest GRP percentage changes are Vichada and Sucre, respectively, which do not even appear in Fig. 13.8, given the small contribution they pose to income in this scenario (Fig. 13.9).

On the reduction side, Santander occupies the bottom of the list, replicating the pattern observed in Table 13.2 and in Fig. 13.8. It is followed by Caldas, Quindío, Norte de Santander, and Cesar, out of which only the latter two play a relevant role in reducing Colombian GDP. The others do not significantly impact the national income for the same reason described previously: Their economies are relatively small compared to other departments. Another detail worth mentioning is that no other region displayed a percentage change in GRP greater than one in the module except for the top two. This means that despite spatial heterogeneity in production changes, the overall results tend to be minor, consistent with the CGE model structure, as the shock occurs only in coffee farming. Finally, it should be noted that the geographical results also overlap the country topology, as shown in Fig. 13.6.

Figure 13.10 focuses on sectoral results, exploring interindustry linkages in the Colombian economy. As expected, most affected industries are coffee-related, namely growing and processing. However, what comes as a surprise is that despite the initial productivity shock having happened only in the first of these, the latter presented a higher percentage change in activity level in the new equilibrium. It achieved a 4.5% growth rate, whereas the farming branch stayed a little below 4%.

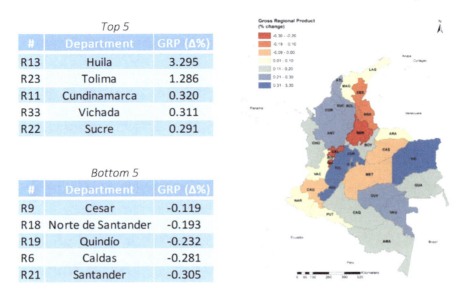

Fig. 13.9 Gross regional product percentage change. *Source* CEER model

This happens due to its supply chain in Colombia and the strong connection between those activities (see Chap. 10).

Most of the output from coffee-growing goes to processing, meaning that it does not benefit from increased productivity in other sectors and hence increased demands

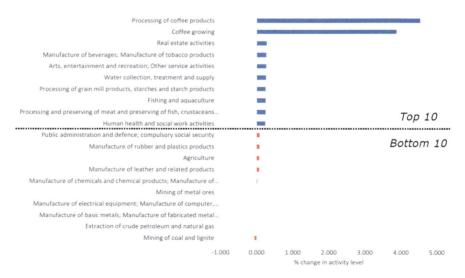

Fig. 13.10 Impact on activity level by sector. *Source* CEER model

for unripe beans. At the same time, the other industry provides its products to different consumers and is more integrated into the national economy. Furthermore, about one-third of total harvesting expenses are allocated for labor, which means that a minor necessity of inputs in this activity induces income effects on salaries. Ironically, this result does not affect the sector that originated it first. Only a very small share of its sales comes from final demand.

Beyond the top two sectors, the most affected industries are real estate, beverages and tobacco, entertainment, water supply, mill products, fishing, processing, preserving meat, and human health and social work activities. Interestingly, all eight displayed an increased activity level no higher than 0.5% each. In other words, after coffee-related sectors benefit from the shock, the impact is relatively homogenously distributed many other activities. It can be explained by the same mechanisms responsible for growth in the previous two: increased demands for their products and cheaper inputs now available.

Another curious observation is that even in the ten least affected industries, five of them still yielded positive results, with four showing no relevant signs of changes in activity level and one lone sector presenting itself in a pronounced decline relative to the initial equilibrium—mining of coal and lignite. When comparing sectoral and regional results, there is a clear difference: The former is much more heterogeneous, not only in magnitude but also in direction, as many departments showed a decrease in GRP.

Finally, Fig. 13.11 focuses on primary factor mobility. Labor behavior, portrayed on the left side, also reflects Colombian topology, as if workers are migrating from lower departments to mountainous regions in search of new jobs now provided by a growing coffee industry. From the right side, capital stock also matches this phenomenon, but more departments receive investment, particularly those in the Amazonía.

13.5 Final Remarks

Colombian coffee has a fascinating history, as it was brought to America by the French. However, its first commercial experience in the country came out half a century later, almost accidentally due to one neighbor successful enterprise. From then, the industry experienced a series of transformations in the coming couple of centuries as the nation was molding itself politically and economically into what it is known today as contemporary Colombia. At the same time, the second half of the twentieth century, along with the last couple of decades, has seen the emergence of a worldwide debate regarding the contribution of human activity to a natural phenomenon called climate change. Throughout these years, the scientific community has established a clear causation relationship between those two and started posing difficult questions to leaders and policymakers around the world, whose answers would define actions that could prevent some of the coming hindrances imposed by such new weather conditions, thus diminishing the loss of humankind

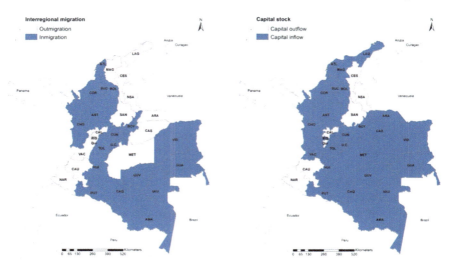

Fig. 13.11 Impacts of primary factor mobility. *Source* CEER model

life quality on Earth. This chapter tried to answer one of those inquiries, particularly those regarding the crop prospects responsible for one of the world's most popular drinks: Colombian coffee.

The chosen methodology was a CGE model whose parameters were calibrated using the Colombian national IIOS from 2015. The inputs for the climate shock were provided by Ceballos-Sierra and Dall'Erba (2021), in which the long-run scenario was simulated using a multi-step model encompassing the many stages of development of the plant. Intriguingly, even with heterogeneity among different regions, the productivity variation in coffee-growing is overall positive in Colombia due to the country's particular topology. However, it is safe to express that this last characteristic, elevation, played a significant role: as the temperatures become warmer, lower regions will become unsuitable for harvesting, whereas the Andean Mountain range will potentially experience a sharp increase in yields. It is also important to note that despite macroeconomic results being relatively small, consistent with the given inputs, they are heterogenous among different departments, replicating the pattern from the previous statement. The sectoral results were more homogenous, and coffee-related industries (growing and processing) were most positively affected by the shock, which is expected given the production structure of this commodity.

It is important not to interpret the results as implying a positive impact of climate change for Colombia. Even if working in a general equilibrium framework, i.e., accounting for all markets equilibria simultaneously and not only the coffee industry, but the inputs also reflect a situation in which the latter is the only effectively affected by future climate characteristics. At the same time, everything else will remain unaltered, which is a strong assumption. While this does not necessarily invalidate the results encountered, it does certainly raise questions in the sense of what would happen to other sectors in this setting, not only as an indirect result of coffee productivity increase but also as a direct consequence of those new weather patterns, thus rendering this exercise as an option for future analysis of the same nature.

As for the next steps per se, this work could also be subject to the development itself by accomplishing a few additional exercises. The first example that comes to mind is introducing a more detailed analysis regarding the difference between production quantity and quality. Various scenarios only compare the difference in total crop yields in the entirety of this research and the simulation that powers the climate shock. However, they do not consider that these outputs are not automatically the same. For instance, even if coffee farming moves to higher elevations in the Andean Mountain range, those newly planted beans do not necessarily reflect the same quality as those harvested closer to sea level, resulting in a substantial difference in the resulting coffee flavor. This effect will reflect the commodity's price, which is also a measurement of productivity used in the CGE structure.

Moreover, the model does not consider any uncertainty, rendering the shock a deterministic exercise. By integrating a stochastic module into the simulation, given by the standard deviations of the multi-step prediction process, results come out not as one single outcome anymore, but as a broad set of different possible scenarios, with various probabilities of occurrence for each of them, which makes them all more credible as randomness occupies a vital place. Finally, this CGE framework also makes room for incorporating land as a primary factor, enriching the analysis that has already been carried out. However, this last suggestion strongly relies on data availability for calibration.

References

Bunn, C., Läderach, P., Rivera, O. O., & Kirschke, D. (2015). A bitter cup: Climate change profile of global production of Arabica and Robusta coffee. *Climatic Change*, 89–101.

Ceballos-Sierra, F., & Dall'Erba, S. (2021). The effect of climate variability on Colombian coffee productivity: A dynamic panel approach. *Agricultural Systems, 190*, 103–126.

Clarke, R. J., & Macrae, R. (Eds.). (2012). *Coffee: Technology* (vol. 2). Elsevier Applied Science.

Cook, J., Oreskes, N., Doran, P., Anderegg, W., Verheggen, B., Maibach, E., & Rice, K. (2016). Consensus on consensus: A synthesis of consensus estimates on human-caused global warming. *Environmental Research Letters, 11*(4), 048002.

Lynas, M., Houlton, B., & Perry, S. (2021). Greater than 99% consensus on human caused climate change in the peer-reviewed scientific literature. *Environmental Research Letters, 16*(11), 114005.

Myers, K., Doran, P., Cook, J., Kotcher, J., & Myers, T. (2021). Consensus revisited: Quantifying scientific agreement on climate change and climate expertise among Earth scientists 10 years later. *Environmental Research Letters, 16*(10), 104030.

Ocampo, J. A. (2015). Una breve historia cafetera de Colombia, 1830–1958. In J. A. Ocampo (Ed.). *Café, industria y macroeconomía: Ensayos de historia económica colombiana* (Primeira edición ed., pp. 59–106). FCE, Banco de la República.

Palacios, M. (2009). *El café en Colombia, 1850-1970. Una historia económica, social y política* (Cuarta edición ed.). El Colegio de México

Ritchie, H., Roser, M., & Rosado, P. (2020). *CO_2 and Greenhouse Gas Emissions. Retrieved from Our World in Data.* Available at: https://ourworldindata.org/co2-and-other-greenhouse-gas-emissions

United Nations. (2022). *UN Comtrade.* Retrieved from UN Comtrade Database. Available at: https://comtrade.un.org/

Watts, C. (2016). *A Brewing Storm: The Climate Change Risks to Coffee.* The Climate Institute.

Pedro Levy Sayon M.Sc. in Economics from the University of São Paulo (USP). Quantitative Methods Coordinator in a private consulting company in São Paulo, Brazil. His research interests include regional and urban economics, particularly infrastructure making use of econometric and input-output models.

Andrea Otero-Cortés Ph.D. (Econ), University of North Carolina at Chapel Hill. Researcher, Center for Regional Economic Studies, Banco de la República, Colombia. Research fields: labor economics, development, and regional economics.

Federico Ceballos-Sierra Ph.D. in Agricultural and Consumer Economics (ACE) from the University of Illinois at Urbana-Champaign. Postdoctoral Fellow at the International Center of Tropical Agriculture. He has published articles on climate change and technology diffusion in journals such as Agricultural Systems and the Journal of Agricultural Education and Extension.

Eduardo A. Haddad Full Professor at the Department of Economics at the University of São Paulo, Brazil, where he directs the Regional and Urban Economics Lab (NEREUS). Affiliate Professor at the Faculty of Governance, Economic and Social Sciences of the Mohammed VI University and Senior Fellow at the Policy Center for the New South, Rabat, Morocco. President of the Regional Science Association International, RSAI (2021-2022).

Chapter 14
The Geography of Manufacturing Productivity Shocks in Colombia

Gerson Javier Pérez-Valbuena, Carlos Eduardo Campos, Ademir Rocha, and Eduardo A. Haddad

14.1 Introduction

An economy's output is a positive function of physical and human capital given the technology. Constant returns to scale and competitive factor market assumptions make it possible to calculate the growth rate of output implied by the growth of production factors. Consequently, deviations between the observed and implicit output growth rate can be explained by technological changes, institutional aspects (laws, bureaucratic aspects), mistakes in economic modeling (modeling hypothesis), and other factors. This difference, commonly called the Solow residue, characterizes the total factor productivity (TFP).

Thus, the TFP is the change in output level that cannot be explained by changes in the quantity of production factors. It is a residual of random shocks, management effort and reorganization, quality of inputs, process innovations, increases in workers' knowledge, and knowledge embodied in intermediate inputs (Paz, 2014). Moreover, the TFP contains the growth contributions of new technology and more efficient markets and institutions, and its very nature indicates that one cannot easily specify an underlying TFP production process (Evenson, 1997).

G. J. Pérez-Valbuena
Banco de la República, Cartagena, Colombia
e-mail: gperezva@banrep.gov.co

C. E. Campos
Federal University of São Carlos, São Carlos, Brazil
e-mail: cespnl@outlook.com

A. Rocha (✉) · E. A. Haddad
University of São Paulo, São Paulo, Brazil
e-mail: ademir.rocha@usp.br

E. A. Haddad
e-mail: ehaddad@usp.br

© The Author(s), under exclusive license to Springer Nature Switzerland AG 2023
E. A. Haddad et al. (eds.), *The Colombian Economy and Its Regional Structural Challenges*, Advances in Spatial Science, https://doi.org/10.1007/978-3-031-22653-3_14

In the macroeconomic literature, the effect of TFP on the rate of output growth (or other economic variables) gains importance in the Real Business Cycle (RBC) theory (King & Rebelo, 1999; Long & Plosser, 1983; Prescott, 1982, 1986). In this case, using dynamic general equilibrium models, economic fluctuations can be interpreted as an equilibrium outcome resulting from the economy's response to exogenous shocks, especially on the supply side.

In a regional economy, productivity changes can be decomposed into the MAR (Marshall-Arrow-Romer) and Jacobs effects. The MAR effect occurs when the increase in productivity within a firm causes productivity spillovers in other firms in the same sector (intra-industry spillovers). Thus, the concentration of an industry in a region can help in the knowledge spillovers between firms. Meanwhile, the Jacobs' effect analyzes how a productivity shock in one sector is transmitted to other sectors (inter-industry spillovers). In this idea, Jacobs' theory indicates that industries located in diversified industrial areas have more significant benefits (Arrow, 1962; Glaeser et al., 1992; Jacobs, 1969; Marshall, 1920; Romer, 1986, 1990). Thus, it is possible to perceive the relationship between productivity shock and productive interdependence.

According to Caliendo et al. (2018), fluctuations in aggregate economic activity may come from a wide variety of aggregate and disaggregated events. These events can reflect underlying changes that are sectoral or specific to a sector and a region. The heterogeneity of these potential changes implies that an economy's sectoral and regional composition is fundamental to the determination of their aggregate impact. This chapter quantifies, through a detailed CGE model of the Colombian economy, described in Chap. 6, the impacts of changes in the TFP on its manufacturing sectors.

This chapter presents a set of analyses around TFP changes in the Colombian manufacturing sector. Section 14.2 provides a review of the relevant literature, while Sect. 14.3 studies how productivity shocks in the manufacturing sector, classified by technological intensity, spread across Colombian sectors and regions. In this case, we observe the effects of the shock on economic variables in the long run. Section 14.4 performs analyses of the regional competition-complementarity and equity-efficiency. We compute Colombia's GDP growth and regional inequality from the productivity shock in the manufacturing sector. Finally, in Sect. 14.5, we carry out an analysis of the identification of key sectors in the Colombian economy. We would like to see which manufacturing sectors are in this group. For this, an analysis is made focusing on the supply side. So, we look at the impact of productivity shocks on real GDP. Section 14.5 concludes.

14.2 Literature Review

CGE models are widely used to assess the impacts of TFP changes on the economy. CGE models consider the economy as a system of interdependent markets, in which the numerical values of equilibrium of all variables must be determined simultaneously. Any exogenous disturbance (e.g., TFP change) can be measured through the set of endogenous variables in the economy (Haddad, 1999).

Hanson and Rose (1997) analyzed the impact of non-neutral technological change on US income distribution using simulation techniques within a CGE modeling framework. They found that labor-augmenting technological change increases income inequality. They also found that capital-augmenting technological change combined with labor-augmenting technological change leads to greater income inequality, but to a lesser extent.

Lee and Roland-Holst (2001) used a dynamic CGE model to investigate how increased productivity in Japan can induce economic benefits in East Asian countries. The results showed that Japanese real GDP growth, resulting from a shock in the TFP, is not sufficient to generate growth of partner countries. On the other hand, when considering externalities in the form of productivity spillovers from Japan, partner economies may experience more substantial induced growth.

Using a static CGE model for Japan, Doi et al. (2001) analyzed the impact of the efficiency improvement (increased total factor productivity) in the port sector on the Japanese economy. The technological efficiency in the ports reduced the cost of shipping transportation, and the forward and backward linkages of imports and exports introduced some positive gains in the national GDP.

Haddad and Hewings (2001) assessed the long-term economic impacts of productivity changes in the transportation sector. They used an interregional CGE model calibrated for Brazil; the results indicated a positive impact on output. However, the effects are regionally different, a finding that seems to have occurred when subnational impacts are considered.

Ianchovichina et al. (2001) analyzed the global effects of a slowdown in TFP on agriculture and forest resources using a dynamic multi-regional CGE model with land-use details. The slowdown in agricultural TFP could lead to higher crop prices in all regions of the world. Still, higher rates of conversion of forest areas into agricultural areas are expected in this scenario.

A multi-regional dynamic CGE model of the Australian economy was used in Giesecke (2002) to identify the causes of the divergent growth performance between two Australian regional economies (Tasmania and the rest of Australia). Technological change (related to productivity) caused economic activity to expand strongly in both regions. However, the mainland experienced more rapid growth in real output than that experienced by Tasmania.

Das et al. (2005) developed a multi-regional CGE model for the USA, analyzing technological policy shifts (that induce TFP improvement) in the forest sector. Productivity improvements in all regions would promote output growth and increase trade everywhere for forest products.

At a very small spatial scale, Cutler & Davies (2010) used a CGE model for Fort Collins, Colorado, USA, to examine how changes in labor, capital, and total productivity affect economic activity in the region. Productivity change in four sectors was evaluated: manufacturing, computer manufacturing, retailing, and high services. Increasing total productivity led to beneficial impacts on the economy. This result is more relevant than changes in labor and capital productivity. In addition, the high services sector, which consists of medical, legal, business services, engineering services, and biotech, resulted in the most significant increase in real household income. Burnett et al. (2012) examined the effects of four alternative economic growth variables to understand how each factor uniquely impacts an economy: exports, sectors that produce output for local consumption, TFP, and population. For this, they used a CGE model calibrated for Fort Collins, Colorado, USA. Among the factors, TFP change in specific sectors resulted in a more significant increase in employment, total tax revenue, real household income, and migration. In this case, an increase in TFP resulted in two mechanisms that stimulate economic growth. First, prices drop causing the city's price index to decrease, which leads to positive effects on real income and consumption for all households. Secondly, the increase in TFP leads to increased demand for factors. The greater flow of households and capital allows economic value creation through knowledge spillovers.

Berhane (2013) examined the effect of productivity improvement in the manufacturing sector on the macroeconomy, sectoral output, factor and household income, and welfare of households in Ethiopia. For this, a recursive dynamic CGE model was calibrated. Three policy simulations of high, medium, and low TFP growth rates were simulated on agro-processing, non-agro-processing, and overall manufacturing activities. An increase in TFP led to growth in real GDP, sectoral output, and households' welfare.

Using a dynamic CGE model, Mabugu & Chitiga Mabugu (2014) assessed trade policy reforms (trade liberalization/tariff reduction) on growth, poverty, and welfare in South Africa. TFP effects were assumed to be induced by trade liberalization. It is possible to see a positive effect on economic growth and gains in welfare and poverty reduction in the long run. The mining sector was the biggest beneficiary of the reform in sectoral terms.

From this brief review of a sample of the literature, the economic and social gains arising from productivity changes depend on the stimulated sector. A rational way to allocate economic resources and pursue increased productivity is through the identification of the sectors that bring the most significant payoffs (called key sectors). It is crucial to have a systemic view of the economy in this process. De Miguel et al. (2014) proposed a supply-side key sector analysis approach. Using a CGE model calibrated for regions in Spain, they studied the impact of productivity gains on consumer welfare (real disposable income and equivalent variation). Thus, the sectors that bring the most benefits in terms of welfare are identified as key sectors. In this case, the private services and trade sectors were the most relevant.

The effects resulting from changes in productivity, in regional terms, are not unidirectional and depend on the country's regional heterogeneity (or on the analyzed socio-geographic unit). Greater productive efficiency in a region can generate output growth and reduce inequality. However, in other situations, it can promote growth with inequality. These two paths are described by Richardson's (1973) competitive-complementary (generative) theory of regional growth. On the competitive side, regions compete for a predetermined level of growth. Thus, the relationship between regions can be seen as a zero-sum game, in which economically more prepared regions will gain at the expense of other regions' losses. In this case, the policy will aim to maximize national growth and allocate it in the best way among regions. This approach leads to the equity-efficiency dilemma. On the complementary (generative) side, national growth is seen as a result of what happens in the regions. Thus, improvements in one region generate benefits for the entire system. Consequently, the objective function of policy is to maximize regional growth (Marquez & Hewings, 2003; Nazara et al., 2001; Sonis & Hewings, 2000).

From the literature review, we realized that (i) the CGE models are robust and widely used tools for evaluating the impact of TFP changes on the economy and (ii) the simulation results are closely related to the economic structure of the analyzed place. With this in mind, we proceeded with an assessment of the long-run economic impacts from TFP changes in the Colombian manufacturing sector.

14.3 Geography of Colombian Manufacturing Activity

Colombia is known as a country of heterogeneous regions. The Andes Mountains that cross the country from south to north give rise to diverse regional characteristics of natural resources, climatic and edaphic conditions, road network availability, customs, and culture that shape its economic activities. It is important to note that historically Colombia's population distribution has been predominantly concentrated near the mountain ranges (Pérez & Meisel, 2020).

Regional disparities in Colombia and their evolution have been the object of increasing analysis since the 1990s. In general, these studies suggest that Colombia has experienced regional polarization processes (Bonet & Roca, 2009; Cárdenas et al., 1993; Galvis & Hahn, 2016; Gómez, 2006; León & Benavides, 2015; Martínez, 2006; Royuela & García, 2015; Vásquez & Bara, 2009). Barón et al. (2004) analyzed some international case studies on the implementation of regional policies and proposed actions that take advantage of the heterogeneous characteristics of the regions to reduce regional disparities that persist in Colombia.

According to De Marchi et al. (2018), some developing countries have shown fast catch-up trajectories due to integration with global value chains (GVCs), configuring an opportunity for developing countries to take advantage of external know-how and innovation. However, Bogotá D.C (capital city of Colombia) and its surrounding municipalities are examples of a significant regional economic polarization that exacerbates the structural challenges that affect the Colombian economy and hinder the country's full potential insertion into GVCs. This chapter aims to analyze the regional economic dynamics in Colombia, identify the potential trade-offs between equity and efficiency, and point to potential economic policies to enhance the TFP of manufacturing sectors.

As in most Latin American economies, Colombia has undergone an accelerated structural reform based on liberalization policies during the 1990s. The most important facts of the reform process have to do with trade liberalization, labor reforms, and a new role for the State (Birchenall, 2001). Furthermore, according to Ramírez et al.

(2014), the Constitution enacted in 1991 conceived a "decentralization model" with the rearrangement of the State and the relationships between levels of government aiming at social equity. The objectives of decentralization, as stated in the Constitution, were to improve the access of the population to social and public services, with an emphasis on education, health, water supply, and sanitation, to target resources toward the poorest population to take them out of poverty and to diminish territorial inequalities (Bonet & Galvis, 2016, 2020).

Using information from the interregional input–output system, Fig. 14.1a shows that the majority of Colombian GDP is concentrated in Bogotá D.C (25.31% of total Colombian GDP), Antioquia (14.36%), Valle del Cauca (9.36%), Cundinamarca (5.90%), and Santander (5.83%). In turn, the manufacturing sector (see description in Table 14.1) represents 13.62% of the Colombian GDP, the second most relevant activity for the country, behind only the services sector.

Although government policies have attempted to promote greater regional equity, it can be seen from Fig. 14.1b that the manufacturing sector was concentrated in some of the Colombian departments, mainly in what is called "the golden triangle": the capital city Bogotá D.C and Cundinamarca (representing 19.72% and 10.70% of the Colombian manufacturing GDP, respectively), Antioquia (19.89%), and Valle del Cauca (13.76%).

Figure 14.1c shows the shares of manufacturing GDP classified into low, medium, and medium/high technological intensities by Colombia´s departments (see technological classification in the second column of Table 14.1). This classification of industries by tech intensity is a widely applied method for grouping industries for policy-relevant analysis (UNIDO, 2010). The results show interesting patterns. Bolívar, Santander, Norte de Santander, and Boyacá have a manufacturing sector mainly classified as medium–high technological intensity. The department of Bolívar has 87.63% of its manufacturing GDP classified as medium–high technology. In this case, the main economic activities are refined petroleum and chemicals and pharmaceuticals. The Santander and Norte Santander departments have 72.65 and 67.10% of their manufacturing GDP classified as medium–high technological intensity. The main sectors are manufacturing other non-metallic mineral products, refined petroleum and chemicals, and pharmaceuticals. Finally, Boyacá has 55.92% of its manufacturing GDP classified as medium technological intensity. In this case, the most relevant sectors are manufacturing basic metals and other non-metallic mineral products.

It is worth mentioning that in Colombia, from different dimensions and perspectives faces a core-periphery pattern, where internal departments or regions are the ones with the best conditions (high GDP, low poverty levels, low informality), while those in the periphery are in the worst condition (Bonet & Galvis, 2016). In terms of technological intensity, results also suggest a core-periphery pattern, since peripheral regions show the lowest levels of tech intensity: Caquetá, Cesar, Chocó, La Guajira, Magdalena, Arauca, Casanare, Putumayo, San Andrés, Amazonas, Guainía, Guaviare, Vaupés, and Vichada.

Fig. 14.1 Regional distribution of manufacturing GDP in Colombia, 2015. Note: Regions list abbreviation—Amazonas (AMA), Antioquia (ANT), Arauca (ARA), Atlántico (ATL), Bogotá D.C (D.C), Bolívar (BOL), Boyacá (BOY), Caldas (CAL), Caquetá (CAQ), Casanare (CAS), Cauca (CAU), Cesar (CES), Córdoba (COR), Cundinamarca (CUN), Chocó (CHO), Guainía (GUA), Guaviare (GUV), Huila (HUI), La Guajira (LAG), Magdalena (MAG), Meta (MET), Nariño (NAR), Norte de Santander (NSA), Putumayo (PUT), Quindío (QUI), Risaralda (RIS), San Andrés, Providencia y Santa Catalina (SAP), Santander (SAN), Sucre (SUC), Tolima (TOL), Valle del Cauca (VAC),Vaupés (VAU), and Vichada (VID)

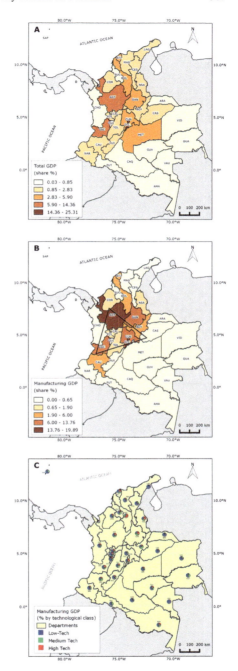

Table 14.1 Manufacturing sectors, by technological classification

Sector ID	Technological classification	Sector description (CIIU Rev. 4 A.C)
S10	Low	Processing and preserving of meat and preserving of fish, crustaceans, and mollusks
S11	Low	Processing of vegetable and animal oils and fats
S12	Low	Processing of dairy products
S13	Low	Processing of grain mill products, starches, and starch products
S14	Low	Processing of coffee products
S15	Low	Processing of sugar
S16	Low	Processing of cocoa, chocolate, and sugar confectionery
S17	Low	Processing and preserving of fruit and vegetables
S18	Low	Manufacture of beverages; manufacture of tobacco products
S19	Low	Manufacture of textiles; manufacture of wearing apparel
S20	Low	Manufacture of leather and related products
S21	Low	Manufacture of wood and products of wood and cork, except furniture; manufacture of articles of straw and plaiting materials
S22	Low	Manufacture of paper and paper products; printing and reproduction of recorded media
S23	High	Manufacture of coke and refined petroleum products
S24	High	Manufacture of chemicals and chemical products; manufacture of pharmaceuticals, medicinal chemicals, and botanical products
S25	Medium	Manufacture of rubber and plastics products
S26	Medium	Manufacture of other non-metallic mineral products
S27	Medium	Manufacture of basic metals; manufacture of fabricated metal products, except machinery and equipment
S28	High	Manufacture of electrical equipment; manufacture of computer, electronic and optical products
S29	High	Manufacture of machinery and equipment n.e.c.; repair and installation of machinery and equipment
S30	High	Manufacture of motor vehicles, trailers, and semi-trailers; manufacture of other transport equipment
S31	Low	Manufacture of furniture
S32	Medium	Other manufacturing

Note: The classification of manufacturing sectors by tech intensity is based on UNIDO (2010)

14.4 Data and Methodology[1]

To analyze the effects of TFP change in the manufacturing sector on the Colombian economy, first, we want to understand how productivity shocks in the manufacturing sector spread across Colombian sectors and regions through the country's linkages structure. Secondly, we perform competition-complementarity and equity-efficiency analyses of Colombian regions from the exogenous productivity shock. Thirdly, using productivity shocks, we identify the key sectors of the Colombian economy on the supply side.

We use Johansen's linearization approach to estimate the system's implicit elasticities from the productivity shocks (see Chap. 6). In this way, if $\mathbf{V}$ is a solution vector of a system of equations in the Johansen-type general equilibrium models class, we can rewrite the system so that $\mathbf{F}(\mathbf{V}) = 0$, where $\mathbf{F}$ represents a functional vector with the equations of the model. Therefore, if we differentiate the system, it is possible to represent it as $\mathbf{A}(\mathbf{V})\mathbf{v}$—where $\mathbf{A}$ is the matrix of the partial derivatives and $\mathbf{v}$ represents the vector of changes of $\mathbf{V}$. A further transformation of the system allows us to evaluate the (implicit) elasticities of the endogenous variables to (1%) shocks given in the exogenous variables (see Dixon & Parmenter, 1996). In other words, to calculate the set of implicit TFP elasticities in the context of the CEER model, we will define shocks of 1% to TFP in each manufacturing sector in each Colombian department.

Equation (14.1) presented below formalizes the procedure:

$$\varepsilon_{i,j} = \frac{\partial y_{i,j}}{\partial \text{TFP}_{i,j}} \cdot \frac{\text{TFP}_{i,j}}{y_{i,j}}$$
$$= \frac{\partial y_{i,j}}{y_{i,j}} \cdot \frac{\partial \text{TFP}_{i,j}}{\text{TFP}_{i,j}} \Rightarrow \varepsilon_{i,j} \cong \frac{\Delta\% \text{ of } y_{i,j}}{\Delta\% \text{ of TFP}_{i,j}} \tag{14.1}$$

where $\varepsilon_{i,j}$, $y_{i,j}$, and $\text{TFP}_{i,j}$ represent the TFP elasticity of sector i in region j, the output of sector i in region j, and the TFP of sector i in region j, respectively.

In summary, mapping the sectoral/regional TFP elasticities in manufacturing sectors will allow us to identify some of the weak and strong sectors and linkages in the Colombian economy from a different perspective so that policymakers may generate better policies or improve those already in place.

---

[1] The methodology described in this section refers to the procedure for calculating the elasticities of total factor productivity (TFP). The framework for the CEER model and its database can be found in Part II.

14.5 Results

14.5.1 Economic Effects of Productivity Changes

This section will assess how changes in the manufacturing sector's TFP can affect the Colombian economy. In the simulations, we initiate a shock of 1% in the exogenous variable related to the productivity of primary inputs of the manufacturing sectors of the CEER model.

This increase in productivity runs through two main channels, namely the cost channel and the technical change channel. In the former, the increase in productivity reduces the price of composite goods, which leads to changes in real income and demand from economic agents (firms, investors, and households). Consequently, this will affect factor demand (labor and capital) and sector output. In the latter, the increase in productivity reduces the need for production factors, leading to a drop in their prices. This impacts the agents' real income and the consequent change in the economy's output.

The productivity shock in manufacturing sectors generated a 0.078% increase in the Colombian GDP in the long run. This change was due to the export component that changed by 0.459% and government spending that increased by 0.024%, driven by increases in tax collection.

Relating the simulation results with the modeling shock channels, it is possible to affirm that an increase in productivity in the manufacturing sector can reduce the price of composite goods in the Colombian economy, making them more competitive in the foreign market. This could be a growth vector for Colombia's long-run output.

14.5.2 Regional Equity-Efficiency Trade-Off

The purpose of this section is to identify the possible long-run trade-off between equity and efficiency present in the Colombian economy from the simulation results of the TFP shock in the manufacturing sector classified by technological intensity. To simplify our analysis, we have aggregated Colombian departments into macro-regions: Bogotá D.C, Caribe, Central-Norte, Central-Occidental, Central-Sur, Nuevos, and Pacífico. For more details, see Table 14.2. Some manufacturing sectors promote GDP growth and contribute to reducing inequality. On the other hand, others only promote GDP growth at the expense of greater inequality. Figure 14.2 indicates, in the long run, that the increase in productivity of low and medium–high technology manufacturing sectors in Bogotá D.C raised the GDP but increased inequality in Colombia, which reiterates the existence of the regional polarization process described by Bonet & Roca (2009). Furthermore, these results corroborate Hauknes (2009), since medium–high and low-medium tech industries, identified as specialized-supplier industries, were essential for the production, transmission, and application of technology and consequently for economic growth.

14 The Geography of Manufacturing Productivity Shocks in Colombia

Table 14.2 Colombian macro-regions aggregation

ID	Macro-regions	Departments
BOG	Bogotá D.C	Bogotá D.C
CAR	Caribe	Atlántico, Bolívar, Cesar, Córdoba, La Guajira, Magdalena, and Sucre
CN	Central-Norte	Boyacá, Norte de Santander, and Santander
CO	Central-Occidental	Antioquia, Caldas, Quindío, and Risaralda
CS	Central-Sur	Cundinamarca, Huila, and Tolima
NUE	Nuevos	Amazonas, Arauca, Caquetá, Casanare, Guainía, Guaviare, Meta, Putumayo, Vaupés, and Vichada
PAC	Pacífico	Cauca, Chocó, Nariño, and Valle del Cauca

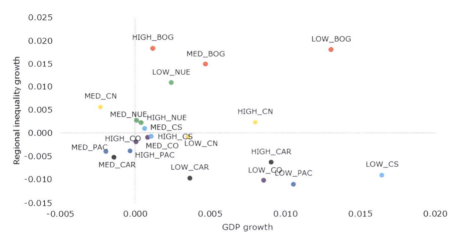

Fig. 14.2 Regional equity versus efficiency in Colombian regions: long run (%). Note: Regions list abbreviation—Bogotá D.C (BOG), Caribe (CAR), Central-Norte (CN), Central-Occidental (CO), Central-Sur (CS), Nuevos (NUE), and Pacífico (PAC)

Besides, the TFP increase of low-tech manufacturing in Caribe, Central-Sur, Central-Occidental, and Pacífico regions tends to promote a considerable reduction in inequality and a significant rise in the country's GDP. It shows the potential impact of productivity shifts (e.g., technological change, solving bureaucratic problems) in regions outside the core to reduce regional disparities in Colombia.

14.5.3 Regional Competition Versus Complementarity

It is also important to understand the trade-off between competition and complementarity in Colombia as a guide for implementing regional economic policies.

		Productivity shock in manufacturing (origin)						
		Bogotá D.C	Caribe	Central Norte	Central Occidental	Central Sur	Nuevos	Pacífico
Effect on Gross Regional Product	Bogotá D.C	+	-	-	-	+	+	-
	Caribe	-	+	-	-	-	+	-
	Central Norte	-	-	+	-	-	+	-
	Central Occidental	-	-	-	+	-	-	-
	Central Sur	+	-	-	-	+	-	-
	Nuevos	+	+	+	+	+	+	+
	Pacífico	-	-	-	-	-	+	+

Fig. 14.3 Regional competition versus complementarity: long-run simulation

According to Nazara et al. (2001), since regional interaction can take diverse forms, a simple classification involves the possibility of a region engaging in a competition or complementarity mode with another.

To perform a regional competition-complementarity analysis, we simulate TFP shocks in the manufacturing sector located in the Colombian macro-regions and observe the effects on the long-run output value of the other regions. Figure 14.3 summarizes the results. The (+) sign indicates a positive economic spillover representing regional complementarity. The opposite (-) indicates a competitive relationship between regions. It is generally possible to verify a competitive relationship between Colombian regions, except in the Nuevos region. In other words, the increase in the productivity of the manufacturing sectors in a region tends to reduce the output of other regions.

This result corroborates Bonet (2003), who found evidence that Colombia has a high level of competition between their regions. The results are consistent with the observed income polarization process and reinforce the idea that policymakers should consider competitive regional relations before proposing any economic policy.

14.5.4 Supply-Side Key Sector Analysis

Our subsequent analysis seeks to identify the manufacturing sectors in which productivity gains induce more significant economic improvements for Colombia (real GDP growth). In this case, we use an idea of a key sector driven by the supply side based on De Miguel et al. (2014). Highlighting the most relevant sectors can help in the strategic use of resources to invest in technology or encourage innovation, for example.

In practice, we simulate productivity shocks (1% change in TFP) across all sectors present in the CEER model using a long-run closure. We observe which sectors induce a more significant systemic response from this exogenous shock. In this exercise, it is particularly advantageous to use the CGE approach as it is possible to follow the entire path of the exogenous shock and how it affects different economic agents (producers, consumers, etc.) and regions. We consider those that are impacted above the average in terms of real GDP as key supply-side sectors.

Table 14.3 shows the sectors identified as a key sector-supply side for Colombia. In the group of manufacturing sectors, the processing of dairy products, the processing of grain mill products, beverages and tobacco products, and petroleum refining products stand out. In other words, when there is a productivity incentive, the mentioned sectors generate above-average economic benefits.

It differs from the traditional Rasmussen-Hirschman (R-H) analysis that classifies key sectors from the demand side. In this case, key sectors demand and are demanded above average (backward and forward linkages). Applying the R-H approach to the Colombian economy, we found that the processing of grain mill products, paper products, petroleum refining products, and chemicals stands out (see Table 14.3).[2]

Thus, considering supply and demand, the processing of grain mill products and the petroleum refining sector are common to both demand and supply sides. Assuming that economic policies must be efficient, generating more significant benefits given the incentives, the results presented in this section can be a guideline for Colombian policymakers.

14.6 Final Considerations

This chapter analyzed the economic effects arising from changes in productivity in the Colombian manufacturing sector. We found that the geography of the Colombian manufacturing sector reveals significant concentration in the "golden triangle" composed of the regions of Bogotá D.C and Cundinamarca, Antioquia, and Valle del Cauca. These regions account for about 64% of Colombia's manufacturing GDP. Also, increases in TFP manufacturing led to a 0.078% increase in Colombian real GDP. In addition, the TFP changes in low technological manufacturing can increase GDP and reduce inequality between Colombian regions. This pattern is not seen for TFP-enhancing policies in the medium–high technological intensity sectors. Furthermore, productivity increases in manufacturing sectors in one region result in reductions in the product of other regions. Thus, changes in TFP do not lead to generalized benefits. Finally, the key sector analysis, considering the supply and demand side, highlights the processing of grain mill products and the petroleum refining sector.

Some general lessons can be elaborated from our analyses. They serve directly the Colombian reality but also provide insights for developing economies such as Latin American countries. Since economic activities such as the manufacturing sector are usually concentrated in a particular region, mapping them can help identify potentials and challenges. Specifically, productivity changes involve several regional discussions; economic impacts, competition-complementarity, equity-efficiency, and identification of key sectors are examples of this. For our case, productivity changes, especially in the manufacturing sector, do not have a homogeneous effect. The spatial organization of economic activities, productive interdependence, and technological level are essential determinants of results. The information presented in this chapter

---

[2] For more details on R-H indices, see Chapter 10.

Table 14.3 Key sectors in the manufacturing group

Sector ID	Sector description (CIIU Rev. 4 A.C)	Supply side	Demand side
S10	Processing and preserving of meat and preserving of fish, crustaceans, and mollusks		
S11	Processing of vegetable and animal oils and fats		
S12	Processing of dairy products	X	
S13	Processing of grain mill products, starches, and starch products	X	X
S14	Processing of coffee products		
S15	Processing of sugar		
S16	Processing of cocoa, chocolate, and sugar confectionery		
S17	Processing and preserving of fruit and vegetables		
S18	Manufacture of beverages; manufacture of tobacco products	X	
S19	Manufacture of textiles; manufacture of wearing apparel		
S20	Manufacture of leather and related products		
S21	Manufacture of wood and products of wood and cork, except furniture; manufacture of articles of straw and plaiting materials		
S22	Manufacture of paper and paper products; printing and reproduction of recorded media		X
S23	Manufacture of coke and refined petroleum products	X	X
S24	Manufacture of chemicals and chemical products; manufacture of pharmaceuticals, medicinal chemicals, and botanical products		X
S25	Manufacture of rubber and plastics products		
S26	Manufacture of other non-metallic mineral products		
S27	Manufacture of basic metals; manufacture of fabricated metal products, except machinery and equipment		
S28	Manufacture of electrical equipment; manufacture of computer, electronic and optical products		
S29	Manufacture of machinery and equipment n.e.c.; repair and installation of machinery and equipment		
S30	Manufacture of motor vehicles, trailers, and semi-trailers; manufacture of other transport equipment		
S31	Manufacture of furniture		
S32	Other manufacturing		

can help with more rational action by policymakers, especially those linked to the topics of regional impacts from changes in productivity (e.g., technology, R&D investments, institutional changes, etc.) and national insertion in global value chains.

References

Arrow, K. (1962). The economic implications of learning by doing. *Review of Economic Studies, 29*(3), 157–173.
Barón, J. D., Valbuena, G. J. P., & Rowland, P. (2004). A regional economic policy for Colombia. *Revista De Economía Del Rosario, 7*(2), 49–87.
Berhane, B. (2013). The effect of improved productivity of the manufacturing industries on the Ethiopian economy: A Computable General Equilibrium (CGE) analysis. *Ethiopian Journal of Economics, 22*(1), 1–24.
Birchenall, J. A. (2001). Income distribution, human capital, and economic growth in Colombia. *Journal of Development Economics, 66*(1), 271–287.
Bonet, J. (2003). Colombian Regions: Competitive or Complementary? *Revista De Economia Del Rosario, 6*, 1.
Bonet, J., & Galvis, L. A. (2016). *Sistemas de transferencias subnacionales: Lecciones para una reforma en Colombia*. Banco de la República-Colombia.
Bonet, J., & Roca, A. M. (2009). Regional economic disparities in Colombia. *Investigaciones Regionales Journal of Regional Research, 14*, 61–80.
Bonet, J., Pérez, G. J., & Monteiro, J. (2020) Las finanzas públicas territoriales en Colombia: dos décadas de cambios. In J. Bonet, & G. Valbuena (Eds.) *20 años de estudios sobre el Caribe colombiano*, pp. 225–275. Banco de la República.
Burnett, P., Cutler, H., & Davies, S. (2012). Understanding the unique impacts of economic growth variables. *Journal of Regional Science, 52*(3), 451–468.
Caliendo, L., Parro, F., Rossi-Hansberg, E., & Sarte, P. D. (2018). The impact of regional and sectoral productivity changes on the U.S. economy. *The Review of Economic Studies, 85*(4), 2042–2096.
Cárdenas, M., Pontón, A., & Trujillo, J. P. (1993). Convergencia y migraciones interdepartamentales en Colombia: 1950–1983. *Coyuntura Económica, 23*(1), 111–137.
Cutler, H., & Davies, S. (2010). The economic consequences of productivity changes: A computable general equilibrium (CGE) analysis. *Regional Studies, 44*(10), 1415–1426.
Das, G. G., Alavalapati, J. R., Carter, D. R., & Tsigas, M. E. (2005). Regional impacts of environmental regulations and technical change in the U.S. forestry sector: A multi-regional CGE analysis. *Forest Policy and Economics, 7*(1), 25–38.
De Marchi, V., Giuliani, E., & Rabellotti, R. (2018). Do global value chains offer developing countries learning and innovation opportunities? *The European Journal of Development Research, 30*(3), 389–407.
De Miguel, F. J., Llop, M., & Manresa, A. (2014). Sectoral productivity gains in two regional economies: Key sectors from a supply-side perspective. *The Annals of Regional Science, 53*(3), 731–744.
Dixon, P. B., & Parmenter, B. R. (1996). Computable general equilibrium modelling for policy analysis and forecasting. In H. Amman, D. Kendrick, & J. Rust (Eds.), *Handbook of Computational Economics, vol. 1* (pp. 3–85). North Holland.
Doi, M., Tiwari, P., & Itoh, H. (2001). A computable general equilibrium analysis of efficiency improvements at Japanese ports. *Review of Urban and Regional Development Studies, 13*(3), 187–206.
Evenson, R. E. (1997). Industrial productivity growth linkages between OECD countries, 1970–90. *Economic Systems Research, 9*(2), 221–230.

Galvis, L. A., & Hahn, L. (2016). Crecimiento municipal en Colombia: El papel de las externalidades espaciales, el capital humano y el capital físico. *Sociedad y Economía, 31*, 149–174.

Giesecke, J. (2002). Explaining regional economic performance: A historical application of a dynamic multi-regional CGE model. *Papers in Regional Science, 81*, 247–278.

Glaeser, E. L., Kallal, H. D., Scheinkman, J. A., & Shleifer, A. (1992). Growth in cities. *Journal of Political Economy, 100*(6), 1126–1152.

Gómez, C. (2006). Convergencia regional en Colombia: un enfoque en los arreglos monetarios y en el sector exportador. *Ensayos Sobre Economía Regional, 45*.

Haddad, E. A. (1999). *Regional inequality and structural changes: Lessons from the Brazilian experience*. Ashgate.

Haddad, E. A., & Hewings, G. J. D. (2001). *Transportation costs and regional development: An interregional CGE analysis* (pp. 83–101). Baden-Baden, Nomos Verlag.

Hanson, K., & Rose, A. (1997). Factor productivity and income inequality: A general equilibrium analysis. *Applied Economics, 29*, 1061–1071.

Hauknes, J., & Knell, M. (2009). Embodied knowledge and sectoral linkages: An input-output approach to the interaction of high-and low-tech industries. *Research Policy, 38*(3), 459–469.

Ianchovichina, E., Darwin, R., & Shoemaker, R. (2001). Resource use and technological progress in agriculture: A dynamic general equilibrium analysis. *Ecological Economics, 38*(2), 275–291.

Jacobs, J. (1969). *The Economy of Cities*. Vintage.

King, R. G., & Rebelo, S. T. (1999). Resuscitating real business cycles. In J. Taylor & M. Woodford (Eds.), *Handbook of Macroeconomics, vol. 1* (pp. 927–1007). North Holland.

Kydland, F. E., & Prescott, E. C. (1982). Time to build and aggregate fluctuations. *Econometrica: Journal of the Econometric Society, 50*(6), 1345–1370.

Lee, H., & Roland-Holst, D. (2001). *Trade and Transmission of Endogenous Growth Effects: Japanese Economic Reform as an Externality for East Asian Economies*. Mimeo. https://www.gtap.agecon.purdue.edu/resources/res_display.asp?RecordID=719

León, G., & Benavides, H. (2015). Inversión pública en Colombia y sus efectos sobre el crecimiento y la convergência departamental. *Revista Dimensión Empresarial, 13*(1), 57–72.

Long, J. B., Jr., & Plosser, C. I. (1983). Real business cycles. *Journal of Political Economy, 91*(1), 39–69.

Mabugu, R., & Chitiga Mabugu, M. (2014). Can trade liberalization in South Africa reduce poverty and inequality while boosting economic growth? Macro–micro reflections. *Development Southern Africa, 31*(2), 257–274.

Marquez, M. A., & Hewings, G. J. D. (2003). Geographical competition between regional economies: The case of Spain. *The Annals of Regional Science, 37*(4), 559.

Marshall, A. (1920). *Principles of Economics*. Macmillan.

Martínez, A. (2006). Determinantes del PIB per cápita de los departamentos colombianos 1975–2003. *Archivos De Economía, 318*, 1–28.

Nazara, S., Sonis, M., & Hewings, G. J. D. (2001). Interregional competition and complementarity in Indonesia. In *Discussion Paper* REAL 01-T-2, Urbana, Illinois, The Regional Economics Applications Laboratory.

Paz, L. S. (2014). Inter-industry productivity spillovers: An analysis using the 1989–1998 Brazilian trade liberalization. *The Journal of Development Studies, 50*(9), 1261–1274.

Pérez, G. J., & Meisel, A. (2020). City Size Distribution in Colombia and Its Regions, 1835–2005. In J. Poot & M. Roskruge (Eds.), *Population Change and Impacts in Asia and the Pacific, vol 30* (pp. 49–75). Springer.

Prescott, E. C. (1986). Theory ahead of business-cycle measurement. *Carnegie-Rochester Conference Series on Public Policy, 25*, 11–44.

Ramírez, J. M., Díaz, Y., & Bedoya, J. G. (2014). Decentralization in Colombia: Searching for social equity in a bumpy economic geography. In *Working Paper 62*. Fedesarrollo.

Richardson, H. W. (1973). *Regional Growth Theory*. Wiley.

Romer, P. M. (1986). Increasing returns and long-run growth. *Journal of Political Economy, 94*, 1002–1037.

Romer, P. M. (1990). Endogenous technological change. *Journal of Political Economy, 98*, 71–102.

Royuela, V., & García, G. A. (2015). Economic and social convergence in Colombia. *Regional Studies, 49*(2), 219–239.

Sonis, M., & Hewings, G. J. (2000). Regional competition and complementarity: Comparative advantages/disadvantages and increasing/diminishing returns in discrete relative spatial dynamics. In P. W. J. Batey & P. Friedrich (Eds.), *Regional Competition* (pp. 139–158). Springer, Berlin.

UNIDO. (2010). *Industrial Statistics: Guidelines and Methodology*. Vienna, Austria. https://www.unido.org/sites/default/files/2012-07/Industrial%20Statistics%20-%20Guidelines%20and%20Methdology_0.pdf

Vásquez, L. F., & Bara, J. L. R. (2009). Convergencia económica regional: El caso de los Departamentos colombianos. *Ecos De Economia, 13*(28), 167–197.

Gerson Javier Pérez-Valbuena Ph.D. (Econ.), University of Essex (UnitedKingdom). Senior Researcher at Centro de Estudios Económicos Regionales (CEER) – Banco de la República, Colombia. He has published several articles and book chapters on topics related to regional and urban economics and subnational public finances.

Carlos Eduardo Campos Ph.D. candidate (Econ.), Federal University of Viçosa. MSc. (Econ.), Federal University of São Carlos. Researcher at the Department of Rural Economics at the Federal University of Viçosa, Brazil. His research interests include energy and regional economics. He has previous experience with econometric methods, input-output models, and computable general equilibrium models.

Ademir Rocha Ph.D. (Econ.), University of São Paulo. Lecturer and Researcher at the Department of Economics at the University of São Paulo, Brazil. He has experience in the field of economic modeling and has published articles on regional and urban economics and climate change economics.

Eduardo A. Haddad Full Professor at the Department of Economics at the University of São Paulo, Brazil, where he directs the Regional and Urban Economics Lab (NEREUS). Affiliate Professor at the Faculty of Governance, Economic and Social Sciences of the Mohammed VI University and Senior Fellow at the Policy Center for the New South, Rabat, Morocco. President of the Regional Science Association International, RSAI (2021-2022).

Chapter 15
The Interplay of Services Productivity and the Competitiveness of Colombian Exports

Inácio F. Araújo, Eduardo A. Haddad, Maria Aparecida S. Oliveira, and Diana Ricciulli

15.1 Introduction

Services are increasingly important worldwide, as their share in global GDP reached 65.0% in 2018, and in Colombia, 57.8%. Services also present a large and increasing share of value-added in global and regional value chains, with an overall contribution to the value of manufacturing exports. Therefore, a substantial service value is incorporated into the exports of goods (Haddad & Araujo, 2021). In this chapter, we will focus on service value-added in exports from Colombia, a country that shows a historical dependence on natural resource-intensive exports. We situate our analysis in the collapse phase of the boom or "super-cycle" of commodity prices that has generated significant macroeconomic challenges in the country in recent years. Moreover, we add to the discussion the within-country geography of trade-in value-added since the locational preferences help understand how the spatial patterns of natural resource-intensive activities differ dramatically from that for services.[1]

We use interregional input–output analysis to measure the services value-added embodied in the Colombian exports. Our main results show that when local value

---
[1] For an analysis of the activities spatial patterns in Colombia, see Chap. 7.

I. F. Araújo (✉) · E. A. Haddad
University of São Paulo, São Paulo, Brazil
e-mail: inacio.araujo@usp.br

E. A. Haddad
e-mail: ehaddad@usp.br

M. A. S. Oliveira
Federal University of São Carlos, São Carlos, Brazil
e-mail: aparecidaoliveira@ufscar.br

D. Ricciulli
Banco de la República, Cartagena, Colombia
e-mail: driccima@banrep.gov.co

© The Author(s), under exclusive license to Springer Nature Switzerland AG 2023
E. A. Haddad et al. (eds.), *The Colombian Economy and Its Regional Structural Challenges*, Advances in Spatial Science, https://doi.org/10.1007/978-3-031-22653-3_15

chains (within-country) of exports are considered, especially in natural resource-rich commodities, *servicification*[2] has potential asymmetric locational impacts, benefiting larger urban agglomerations in the more developed regions and reinforcing regional inequality. Services are traded directly and indirectly embodied in the sales of goods (Chun et al., 2021; Pattnayak & Chadha, 2022). While the geography of natural resources may act as a driver to reduce regional inequality, interregional and intersectoral linkages are likely to act in the opposite direction. Thus, analyzing (local) services embodied in export goods provides one of the main sources of regional inequality in natural resource-rich Latin American countries, such as Colombia.

In summary, the internal geography of services value-added in exports *vis-à-vis* the location patterns of natural resources in Colombia may add another source of tension to current trade negotiations in Colombia. To the extent that there will be mismatches between the sequencing, cadence, and intensity of policies promoting a greater insertion of Colombia and other Latin American countries into regional and global value chains may lead to a novel form of the geography of discontents in the region (Haddad & Araujo, 2021). To increase and sustain its competitiveness in global value chains, Colombia requires policies, capabilities, and infrastructure to promote intermediate services.

The chapter adds another layer of analytical material by simulating TFP changes in Knowledge-Intensive Business Services (KIBS). Overall, the competitiveness of firms in open economies is increasingly determined by access to high-quality and low-cost services. In an analysis of the Mexican economy, Haddad et al. (2022) show that changes in services productivity have potential effects on increasing the export competitiveness of goods. Thus, we use the CEER model to assess the effects of changes in KIBS productivity on the competitiveness of Colombian exports.

Also, evidence shows that increases in export competitiveness can also be achieved from service productivity shocks (Hoekman & Shepherd, 2017; Kordalska & Olczyk, 2021). Previous studies also show a relationship between KIBS and the manufacturing industry, such as Ciriaci et al. (2015), Antonioli et al. (2020), Di Berardino and Onesti (2020), Kong et al. (2021), and Herrero and Rial (2022). Productivity shocks in services can propagate throughout the economy due to the inter-industry and interregional interdependence of production chains, which can be identified through input–output linkages, as demonstrated by Hanel (2000), Keller (2002), Hauknes and Knell (2009), Foster et al. (2012), and Gonçalves et al. (2017).

Our results from the CEER model show that the effects of the TFP growth of KIBS on exports are more relevant for the mining industry, medium–high technology manufacturing industries, and business sectors in Colombia. Factor income effects are more substantial in the long run, generating stronger impacts on domestic absorption *vis-à-vis* foreign exports. In contrast, the effects of the exports are less relevant due to the relatively small share of KIBS sales for exports (direct effect) and to export sectors with relatively inelastic export demand (indirect effect).

---

[2] Refers to the utilization of services in manufacturing production.

Table 15.1 Participation of the sectors in gross exports and the value-added in exports

Sectors	Gross exports (COP billions)	Share in gross exports (%)	Value-added in exports (COP billions)	Share in value-added in exports (%)
Non-services	103,683	87.0	66,218	67.8
Services	15,314	13.0	31,429	32.2
KIBS	*3753*	*3.0*	*10,803*	*11.1*
Other services	*11,561*	*10.0*	*20,626*	*21.1*
Total	118,997	100.0	97,647	100.0

Source Based on IIOM-COL, 2015

The chapter is organized into four sections in addition to this introduction. Section 15.2 shows the contribution of services, and specifically KIBS, to Colombian exports. Section 15.3 describes the simulation of TFP changes in KIBS using the CEER model and describes the main shock transmission mechanisms. Section 15.4 presents the CEER model outcomes. Finally, the last section concludes the chapter.

15.2 Do Service Sectors Matter to Exports?

Services have small direct participation in gross exports in Colombia. However, according to Haddad and Araújo (2021), "there is substantial value-added of services incorporated in goods exports". We replicated Haddad and Araújo (2021) to measure the importance of KIBS value-added embodied in Colombian exports. We used the Interregional Input–Output Matrix for Colombia (IIOM-COL) for 2015 and the same method applied by Haddad and Araújo (2021) to measure the value-added embodied in exports. Table 15.1 shows the share of the sectors in gross exports and the value-added in exports. Services account for 13% of gross exports, and 32% of the value-added incorporated into exports—about a third of this value (11%) comes from KIBS.[3] This result shows the importance of KIBS in the domestic (within-country) supply chain of Colombian exports.

Although KIBS account for only 3% of Colombia's gross exports, 11% of the value-added in exports comes from the KIBS sectors. An important portion of this value, 6.8%, is incorporated in exports of goods, compared to 1.1% in exports of services (except KIBS) and 3.1% in exports of KIBS (Table 15.2). The integration between manufacturing and business services can improve the strategies for the countries to achieve a more upstream position in the global chain value. Kordalska and Olczyk (2021) found that the Baltic countries and the Czech Republic improved

---

[3] KIBS are identified in the sectoral classification of the Interregional Input–Output Matrix and the CEER model by the services: information and communications (sector 46), financial insurance activities (sector 47), and professional, scientific, and technical activities (sector 49). Chapter 5 presents the complete sectoral classification.

Table 15.2 Trade-in value-added: Colombia, 2015

Value-added embodied in exports	COP billions	%
Exports of goods		
VA in goods	64,937	66.5
VA in service sectors (except KIBS)	12,943	13.3
VA in KIBS	6669	6.8
Total VA	**84,550**	**86.6**
Exports of services (except KIBS)		
VA in goods	1211	1.2
VA in service sectors (except KIBS)	7400	7.6
VA in KIBS	1069	1.1
Total VA	**9680**	**9.9**
Exports of KIBS		
VA in goods	69	0.1
VA in service sectors (except KIBS)	288	0.3
VA in KIBS	3060	3.1
Total VA	**3417**	**3.5**
Total exports		
VA in goods	66,218	67.8
VA in service sectors (except KIBS)	20,631	21.1
VA in KIBS	10,798	11.1
Total VA	**97,647**	**100.0**

Source Based on IIOM-COL

their positions and participation in global value chains through the vertical integration of KIBS into manufacturing sectors.

Table 15.3 presents the share of the value-added embodied in the Colombian exports distributed by nine groups of sectors. The content of value-added from KIBS corresponds to 7.9% of exports of goods, 11.1% of exports of services (except KIBS), and 89.5% of exports of KIBS.

Bogotá D.C (25%), Antioquia (14%), and Valle del Cauca (10%) concentrate half of the Colombian GDP (DANE, 2021). The service sectors follow the pattern of spatial concentration of income. GDP from service sectors is distributed among these three departments at 28%, 14%, and 10%, respectively. GDP from the KIBS sectors in these three departments is even more concentrated—40%, 17%, and 11%, respectively. KIBS sectors tend to be highly spatially concentrated in core metropolitan regions (Strambach, 2001). The geographical proximity of research and innovation centers where human capital is more abundant, particularly in large and capital cities, explains this pattern (Cuadrado-Roura, 2013).

Gross exports are also spatially concentrated in Colombia. However, the spatial pattern of exports reveals a dichotomous profile of specialization in Colombian regions. According to the IIOM-COL for 2015, Meta (17.4%), Antioquia (13.4%),

Table 15.3 Sectoral distribution of services value-added in total exports: Colombia, 2015

	Classification	Value-added embodied in exports (in COP billions)			Value-added embodied in exports (in %)		
		Non-services	Services (except KIBS)	KIBS	Non-services	Services (except KIBS)	KIBS
1	Agriculture	10,530.7	371.5	5.5	12.5	3.8	0.2
2	Mining	36,012.5	155.8	9.3	42.6	1.6	0.3
3	Manufacturing	18,394.2	683.7	54.2	21.8	7.1	1.6
4	Business services	3474.9	3429.7	134.7	4.1	35.4	3.9
5	Construction services	260.2	74.9	11.8	0.3	0.8	0.3
6	Distribution services	2709.7	735.2	49.8	3.2	7.6	1.5
7	Transport services	6189.8	2790.9	61.6	7.3	28.8	1.8
8	KIBS	6669.4	1073.3	3059.9	7.9	11.1	89.5
9	Other services	308.3	364.8	30.3	0.4	3.8	0.9
	Total	84,549.9	9679.8	3417.1	100.0	100.0	100.0

Source Based on IIOM-COL

and Casanare (10%) account for around 40% of exports of goods, mainly concentrated in natural resource-intensive commodities, while Bogotá D.C (31.2%), Antioquia (12.6%), and Valle del Cauca (8.7%) account for 52.5% of service exports. The latter regions concentrate 37.1%, 16.5%, and 11.3%, respectively, of KIBS exports in Colombia.

More sophisticated service exports tend to benefit the larger urban agglomerations in the more developed regions, reinforcing regional inequality (Haddad & Araujo, 2021). KIBS also tend to be located in larger urban centers, affecting their regional competitiveness (Ferreira et al., 2016). Figure 15.1 shows the spatial distribution of value-added embodied in Colombian exports. Meta (19.5%), Antioquia (12.2%), and Casanare (9.3%) account for 41% of the value-added incorporated in exports. Meanwhile, Bogotá D.C (34.1%), Antioquia (18.1%), and Valle del Cauca (11.9%) concentrate 64.1% of the value-added incorporated in KIBS exports (see Table 15.6 in Appendix).

This section analyzed the characteristics of the domestic supply chains of Colombian exports using data from value-added embedded in exports. We have seen that KIBS are key to the production chain. Roson and Sartori (2016) show that relatively small sectoral productivity shocks could propagate through the input–output trade relationships and lead to sizable macroeconomic variability. Therefore, given the importance of KIBS value-added embodied in exports, the remainder of the chapter

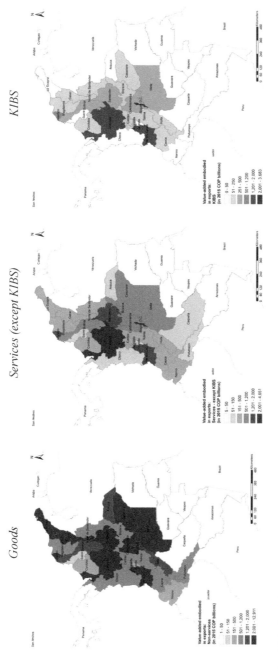

Fig. 15.1 Spatial patterns of value-added embodied in exports of goods, services, and KIBS: Colombia (in 2015 COP billions). *Note* Table 15.6, in the appendix, presents the regional values used to draw the maps. *Source* Based on IIOM-COL

explores the effects of changes in the productivity of KIBS on Colombian export competitiveness.

15.3 Data and Methodology

We use the CEER model described in Chapter 6 to analyze the impact of the productivity increase of KIBS on the competitiveness of Colombian exports.

In the CEER model, Eq. 15.1 specifies firms' primary factors use. It is derived under the assumption that industries choose their primary factor inputs to minimize costs subject to obtaining sufficient primary factor inputs to satisfy their technological requirements (nested Leontief/CES specification). The CEER model includes technical change variables to allow for factor-specific productivity shocks.

$$x^{(1j)r}_{(g+1,s)} - a^{(1j)r}_{(g+1,s)} = \alpha^{(1j)r}_{(g+1,s)} x^{(1j)r}_{(g+1,\cdot)}$$
$$- \sigma 3^{(1j)r}_{(g+1)} \left(p^{(1j)r}_{(g+1,s)} + a^{(1j)r}_{(g+1,s)} - \sum_{l \in F} \left(\frac{V(g+1,l,(1j),r)}{V(g+1,\cdot,(1j),r)} \right) \left(p^{(1j)r}_{(g+1,l)} + a^{(1j)r}_{(g+1,l)} \right) \right)$$

$$j \in H; \; s \in F; \; r \in S^* \tag{15.1}$$

where $x^{(1j)r}_{(g+1,s)}$ is the demand by sector j in region r for each primary factor; $a^{(1j)r}_{(g+1,s)}$ is the exogenous sector-specific variable of (saving) technical change for primary factor s in region r; $p^{(1j)r}_{(g+1,s)}$ is the price paid by sector j in region r for primary factor s; $\sigma 3^{(1j)r}_{(g+1)}$ is a parameter measuring the sector-specific elasticity of substitution among different primary factors; and $V(g+1,l,(1j),r)$ is an input–output flow coefficient that measures purchasers' value of factor l used by sector j in region r.

The $a^{(1j)r}_{(g+1,s)}$ is the exogenous sector-specific variable of (saving) technical change for primary factor s in region r. We simulate a change in the productivity of the primary factor ($a^{(1j)r}_{(g+1,s)}$) equivalent to a 1% productivity gain in all regions (r) and factors (s) for the KIBS ($j = 46, 47,$ and 49). The transmission mechanisms between the productivity gain and the competitiveness of exports occur through variations in relative prices by the cost change and technical change (Fig. 15.2).

In the cost change channel, the productivity increase of the primary factors used in the KIBS reduces prices in the economy. As a result, there is an increase (decrease) in the real income of firms, investors, and families. It makes the firms more (less) competitive, provides potentially higher (lower) returns on investments, and makes households richer (poorer). This would increase (decrease) domestic and foreign demand for Colombian products, which would increase (decrease) the production of the companies. Therefore, there would be an increase (decrease) in the demand for primary factors, raising (reducing) prices. Through the technical change channel, the TPF growth of the KIBS leads to a reduction in the labor and capital requirements

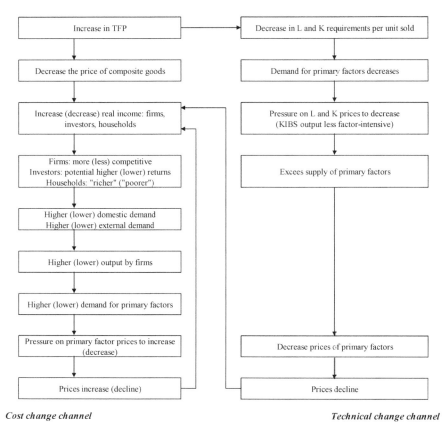

Fig. 15.2 Causal relations underlying the simulations results

for each unit produced, reducing demand for these primary factors of production, which leads to a reduction in their prices.

If the effect of the price reduction observed in the technical change channel overcomes the effect of the price change in the cost change channel, there will be an overall price reduction in the economy. Competitiveness gains in exports occur through a reduction in the price of exports.

We use the long-run closure of the CEER model, which allows us to simulate KIBS productivity gains. In the long run, the technological level is exogenous, and the factors might move between sectors and regions. The model assumes that productivity gains influence the economy over a more extended adjustment period. The rate-of-return differentials across sectors, regions, and productivity differentials, in the long run, stimulate the movement of capital in the CEER model.

15.4 Results

This section presents the CEER model outcomes for simulating the productivity increase of the KIBS sectors. Table 15.4 shows the macroeconomic results and their breakdown (subtotal) for the KIBS sectors (information and communication; financial insurance activities; professional, scientific, and technical activities).

Productivity shocks in KIBS propagate across the entire Colombian economy due to inter-industry and interregional linkages along supply chains. GDP growth

Table 15.4 Macroeconomics results (%)

	Total	Subtotal		
		Information and communication	Financial insurance activities	Professional, scientific, and technical activities
Aggregate primary factor payments	0.179	− 0.051	0.018	0.212
Aggregate payments to capital	0.133	− 0.058	0.014	0.177
Aggregate payments to labor	0.236	− 0.057	0.047	0.245
Real GDP from the expenditure side	0.266	0.022	0.075	0.169
Aggregate real investment expenditure	0.208	− 0.013	0.054	0.166
Real household consumption	0.329	0.018	0.104	0.206
Aggregate real government demands	0.147	0.008	− 0.023	0.162
Export volume	0.060	0.030	0.020	0.010
Import volume	0.171	− 0.035	0.038	0.168
Average real wage	0.363	0.024	0.116	0.223
Consumer price index	− 0.088	− 0.075	− 0.056	0.043
Exports price index	− 0.104	− 0.049	− 0.034	− 0.021
Government price index	− 0.087	− 0.082	− 0.010	0.004

of 0.266% is mainly driven by domestic components of final demand. Professional, scientific, and technical activities make the most significant contribution to GDP growth. This sector has strong forward linkages in the Colombian input–output system; as a result, shocks in this sector can generate strong effects on the domestic supply chain. The average real wage grew 0.363%, and the consumer, exports, and government price indices declined after the shock.

15.4.1 Regional Impacts

Figure 15.3 shows the impact of the TPF growth in KIBS sectors on the GRP by the Colombian department. Although the production of the KIBS sectors is strongly spatially concentrated in Colombia, the impacts of increasing the productivity of KIBS sectors are spatially uneven.

Figure 15.4 shows the correlation between the GRP growth and the GRP at the baseline. The departments with the highest GRP growth are those with the lowest GRP at the baseline. However, Fig. 15.4 shows two patterns of impacts on GRP. The departments specialized in the production of mineral-intensive commodities (Meta, Casanare, Cesar, La Guajira, Arauca, and Putumayo) have the smallest impact on GDP growth. On the other hand, the departments where the main urban centers and the manufacturing industry are located (Bogotá D.C, Antioquia, Cundinamarca, Valle del Cauca, Santander, Bolívar, and Atlántico) show distinct patterns of GDP growth.

The sectoral composition of the departmental supply chain determines the impacts on GRP. Departments with a lower content of non-service value-added embodied in their production chain present higher GDP growth (Fig. 15.5).

Propagation of the KIBS productivity gains over other sectors is more substantial for those activities with greater inter-industry interdependence with the KIBS sectors. The interdependence with KIBS occurs mainly with the other service sectors in the Colombian input–output system. This pattern reflects the low-technology intensity of the Colombian manufacturing industry, which is poorly integrated with the complex and technology-intensive service sectors.

Productivity shocks propagate with a lower intensity along supply chains due to the weak integration of KIBS into manufacturing and other service sectors in the Colombian economy. Figures 15.10 and 15.11, in the appendix, show an international comparison of KIBS value-added embodied in the non-service and services final demand, respectively. Vertical integration of KIBS into non-services sectors in Colombia (4%) ranks 34th in the ranking formed by 38 OECD countries (Appendix-Fig. 15.10). Colombia also has the lowest share of KIBS value-added embodied in the non-services final demand among a selected group of Latin American countries (Argentina, Brazil, Chile, Costa Rica, and Peru). Although the integration of KIBS into other service sectors is stronger than with manufacturing sectors, KIBS value-added embodied in the service final demand is small (Appendix-Fig. 15.11).

15 The Interplay of Services Productivity and the Competitiveness ...   411

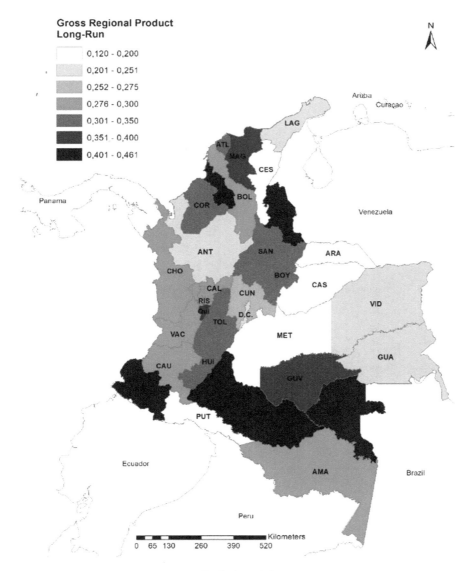

Fig. 15.3 GRP changes by departments (in % change): long run

Ciriaci and Palma (2016) show that KIBS vertical integration into the final demand of manufacturing has increased over time in the largest European economies.

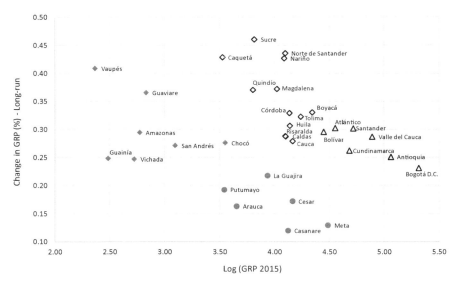

Fig. 15.4 Correlation between the GRP change and GRP in baseline

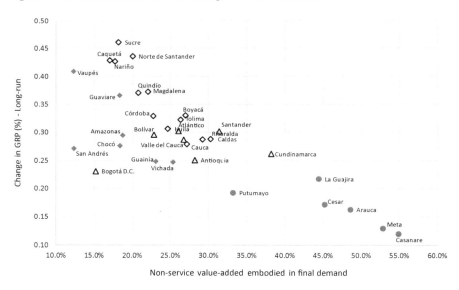

Fig. 15.5 Correlation between the GRP change and non-service value-added embodied in final demand (Based on IIOM-COL, 2015). *Note* Non-services sectors—agriculture, mining, and manufacturing

15.4.2 Interregional Linkages and the Propagation of KIBS Productivity Shocks

KIBS value chain is spatially concentrated in urban areas of the wealthiest departments (Bogotá D.C, Antioquia, and Valle del Cauca). Thereby, service has potential asymmetric locational impacts. We test the hypothesis of asymmetric locational impacts by repeating our 1% KIBS productivity gain simulation exercise, applying individual shocks in each department. Figure 15.6 shows the results of the 33 simulations on GRP and GDP. TFP growth of KIBS located in Bogotá D.C impacts all other departments strongly and promotes the most significant increase in the national GDP (0.12%)—although the net effect on Bogotá D.C of a simultaneous shock across all departments is only 0.23%.

The Colombian departments, except for Bogotá D.C, Antioquia, and Valle del Cauca, have weak interregional linkages. Therefore, KIBS productivity gains mainly impact local production chains and provide little propagation through interregional trade relationships. These local effects are reinforced by the characteristic of the Colombian input–output system, in which KIBS vertical integration into the supply chain is weak and occurs essentially with the service sectors, mainly sold in the departmental internal markets.

15.4.3 Impacts on Foreign Exports

The productivity gain in the KIBS sectors has the potential to increase Colombian exports by 0.06%, and about half of this increase (0.03%) is driven by the information and communication sector (Table 15.5).[4] Goods exports increased by 0.04%, and services exports increased by 0.17%. Our results are in line with the findings of Arnold et al. (2016). They show that India's policy reforms in services (banking, telecommunications, and insurance) allowed firms to access better, newer, and more diverse business services. These changes in the service sectors have positive effects on the productivity of manufacturing firms providing greater foreign and domestic competition. Muller and Zenker (2001), Rubalcaba and Kox (2007), and Cusumano et al. (2015) also present evidence that business services and KIBS sectors play a fundamental supporting role in the production and competitiveness of manufacturing enterprises.

Mining and quarrying (S9), the manufacture of basic metals (S27), and trade (S38) present the most significant export growth (Fig. 15.7). The highest growth in exports in manufacturing is from the medium and medium–high technology sectors, such as paper and paper products (S22), refined petroleum products (S23), chemical products (S24), non-metallic mineral products (S26), metal products (S27), and the manufacture of motor vehicles (S30). These manufacturing sectors can benefit from

---

[4] Chapter 9 provides a detailed analysis of the profile of foreign exports by the Colombian department.

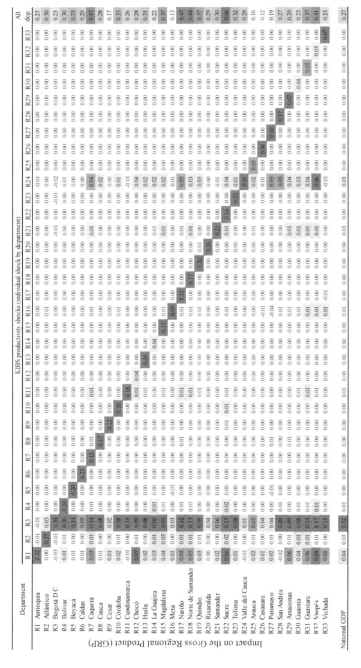

Fig. 15.6 Impact of the KIBS productivity shocks by the department on GDP and GRP. *Note* R1–R33 columns show the impacts of KIBS productivity gains with individual shocks in each department. The last column shows the results of a single simultaneous productivity shock across all departments

Table 15.5 Export volume results by sectors

Sector	Total	Subtotal		
		Information and communication	Financial insurance activities	Professional, scientific, and technical activities
Goods	0.044	0.022	0.021	0.001
Services	0.174	0.087	0.014	0.073
KIBS	*0.685*	*0.271*	*0.037*	*0.377*
Other services	*0.009*	*0.028*	*0.007*	*− 0.026*
Total	0.060	0.030	0.020	0.010

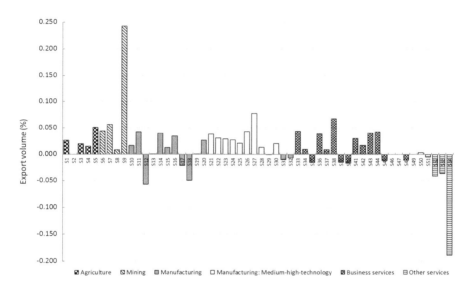

Fig. 15.7 Change in export volume by sector (%). *Note* The names of the sectors are available in Appendix 2 of Chapter 5. The growth rates in KIBS exports are not represented in this figure: 0.72% in information and communication (S46), 0.68% in financial insurance activities (S47), and 0.67% in professional, scientific, and technical activities (S49)

higher productivity in KIBS, and since they have an upstream position in the production chain, they can drive gains across the economy. Effects on the exports are less relevant due to the relatively small share of KIBS sales for exports (direct effect) and to export sectors with relatively inelastic export demand (indirect effect).

The service sectors with the highest export growth are trade (S38), storage and complementary activities in transport (S43), and post office (S44). When KIBS productivity increases, exports from some sectors fall. This reduction may be assigned to the relative price change that modifies the terms-of-trade of interregional flows with impacts on foreign exports.

15.4.4 Sensitivity Analysis

We focus on the sensitivity of a particular parameter, the price elasticity of export demand, which is central to our evaluation of the impacts of the shock of KIBS productivity on the competitiveness of Colombian exports. The price elasticity of export demand of the CEER model is estimated through a time series database with the specification of changes in prices and quantities of Colombian exports.[5] The results of the CEER model depend on the confidence in the estimate of this parameter. We, therefore, perform a formal sensitivity analysis of the main results regarding uncertainty in this parameter.

Figure 15.8 shows the variation of the CEER model outcome after an increase (decrease) in the parameter of the price elasticity of exports of all commodities concerning the values of this parameter at baseline. The parameter sensitivity results are presented for the variables: export volume (*natexpvol*), foreign-currency value of exports (*natexport*), exports price index (*natxi4*), and real GDP from the expenditure side (*natgdpreal*). Lower price elasticity of exports implies lower export volume growth and higher GDP growth. Our results are consistent with Hertel et al. (2007), who showed that small price elasticity of export demand generates large terms-of-trade effects by reducing the responsiveness of export demand.

We also assess the sensitivity of the real GDP components from the expenditure side to changes in the price elasticity of exports. Figure 15.9 shows that lower GDP growth associated with higher price elasticities and demand for exports is related to lower growth in real household consumption (*natcr*) and aggregate real investment expenditure (*natir*).

15.5 Conclusions

KIBS value-added embodied in Colombian exports has a spatially concentrated pattern. This concentration occurs in urban areas with a high population and supply of skilled labor, i.e., Bogotá D.C, Antioquia, and Valle del Cauca. Therefore, *servicification* has potential asymmetric locational impacts, benefiting areas with agglomeration economies. The results of our simulations based on the CEER model show that the

---

[5] Chapter 6, Sect. 6.4, presents the estimation of the price elasticity of export demand for each commodity of the CGE model for Colombia.

15 The Interplay of Services Productivity and the Competitiveness ... 417

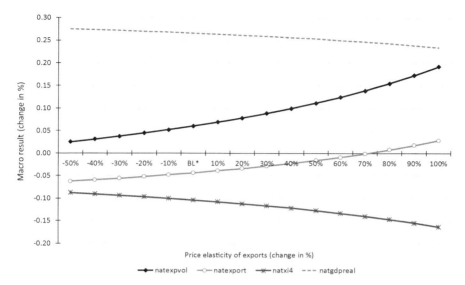

Fig. 15.8 Sensitivity of the main results to changes in the price elasticity of export demand. *Note* *BL: Baseline. Export volume (*natexpvol*), foreign-currency value of exports (*natexport*), exports price index (*natxi4*), and real GDP from the expenditure side (*natgdpreal*)

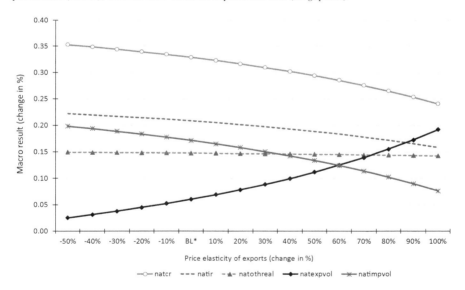

Fig. 15.9 Sensitivity of the real GDP components from the expenditure side to changes in the price elasticity of export demand. *Note* * BL: Baseline. Real household consumption (*natcr*), aggregate real investment expenditure (*natir*), aggregate real government demand (*natothreal*), export volume (*natexpvol*), and import volume (*natimpvol*)

productivity shocks in the KIBS sectors can propagate through inter-industry linkages and generate a potential competitiveness gain for Colombian exports. However, these effects are weakened due to the KIBS' low vertical integration with tradable sectors in the Colombian economy. We assess the sensitivity of the CEER model outcome regarding the uncertainty under the price elasticity of export demand, a key parameter in our analysis, showing its importance to the model's results.

Appendix

See Table 15.6, Figs. 15.10 and 15.11

Table 15.6 Spatial patterns of non-services and services value-added embodied in exports of goods and services: Colombia, 2015

Region		Value-added embodied in exports (in 2015 COP billions)			Value-added embodied in exports (in %)		
		Non-services	Services (except KIBS)	KIBS	Non-services	Services (except KIBS)	KIBS
R1	Antioquia	8097.38	2803.17	1955.09	12.23	13.59	18.10
R2	Atlántico	2220.15	1399.37	570.74	3.35	6.78	5.28
R3	Bogotá D.C	3917.72	4650.62	3682.83	5.92	22.55	34.09
R4	Bolívar	1652.65	907.69	343.10	2.50	4.40	3.18
R5	Boyacá	1111.76	694.96	165.91	1.68	3.37	1.54
R6	Caldas	809.38	318.75	160.75	1.22	1.55	1.49
R7	Caquetá	29.70	50.64	11.37	0.04	0.25	0.11
R8	Cauca	1113.14	226.85	146.61	1.68	1.10	1.36
R9	Cesar	5009.75	444.01	172.00	7.57	2.15	1.59
R10	Córdoba	311.25	213.62	114.54	0.47	1.04	1.06
R11	Cundinamarca	3074.37	851.73	385.38	4.64	4.13	3.57
R12	Chocó	579.03	62.47	5.83	0.87	0.30	0.05
R13	Huila	1464.31	473.36	113.88	2.21	2.29	1.05
R14	La Guajira	3550.91	311.72	25.68	5.36	1.51	0.24

(continued)

Table 15.6 (continued)

Region		Value-added embodied in exports (in 2015 COP billions)			Value-added embodied in exports (in %)		
		Non-services	Services (except KIBS)	KIBS	Non-services	Services (except KIBS)	KIBS
R15	Magdalena	882.90	298.32	63.75	1.33	1.45	0.59
R16	Meta	12,911.23	1104.58	435.36	19.50	5.36	4.03
R17	Nariño	470.75	173.69	49.41	0.71	0.84	0.46
R18	Norte de Santander	549.92	274.46	66.67	0.83	1.33	0.62
R19	Quindío	218.69	124.83	42.64	0.33	0.61	0.39
R20	Risaralda	640.11	332.74	181.76	0.97	1.61	1.68
R21	Santander	4060.62	1228.11	470.56	6.13	5.95	4.36
R22	Sucre	121.54	136.63	25.53	0.18	0.66	0.24
R23	Tolima	1034.53	331.16	132.77	1.56	1.61	1.23
R24	Valle del Cauca	3631.43	1920.25	1286.51	5.48	9.31	11.91
R25	Arauca	1672.03	111.83	23.91	2.53	0.54	0.22
R26	Casanare	6134.83	910.53	135.53	9.26	4.41	1.25
R27	Putumayo	894.76	84.87	21.84	1.35	0.41	0.20
R28	San Andrés	0.87	125.66	9.65	0.00	0.61	0.09
R29	Amazonas	2.28	28.73	1.18	0.00	0.14	0.01
R30	Guainía	32.65	6.36	0.34	0.05	0.03	0.00
R31	Guaviare	9.23	11.10	0.84	0.01	0.05	0.01
R32	Vaupés	0.68	8.57	0.13	0.00	0.04	0.00
R33	Vichada	6.97	5.25	0.56	0.01	0.03	0.01
	Colombia	**66,217.52**	**20,626.65**	**10,802.66**	**100.00**	**100.00**	**100.00**

Source Authors' preparation from the Interregional Input–Output Matrix for Colombia (IIOM-COL), 2015

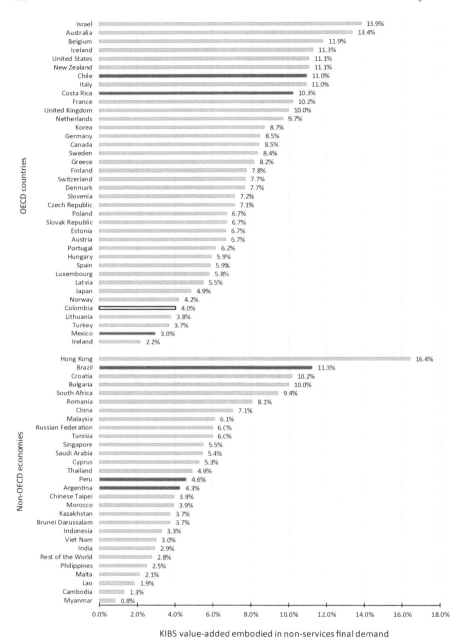

Fig. 15.10 Domestic KIBS value-added embodied in non-services final demand. *Note* KIBS: Telecommunications (D61), IT and other information services (D62T63), financial and insurance activities (D64T66), and professional, scientific, and technical activities (D69T75). Non-services sectors: agriculture, mining, and manufacturing. *Source* Authors' own from the 2021 edition of OECD Inter-Country Input–Output (ICIO) Tables for 2018

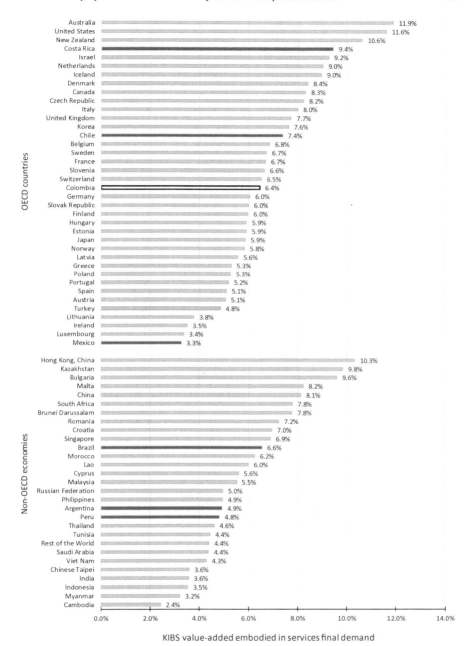

Fig. 15.11 Domestic KIBS value-added embodied in services final demand. *Note* KIBS: Telecommunications (D61), IT and other information services (D62T63), financial and insurance activities (D64T66), and professional, scientific, and technical activities (D69T75). *Source* Authors' own from the 2021 edition of OECD Inter-Country Input–Output (ICIO) Tables for 2018

References

Antonioli, D., Di Berardino, C., & Onesti, G. (2020). Specialization and KIBS in the Euro area: A vertically integrated sector perspective. *International Review of Applied Economics, 34*(2), 267–290.

Arnold, J. M., Javorcik, B., Lipscomb, M., & Mattoo, A. (2016). Services reform and manufacturing performance: Evidence from India. *The Economic Journal, 126*(590), 1–39.

Chun, H., Hur, J., & Son, N. S. (2021). Global value chains and servicification of manufacturing: Evidence from firm-level data. *Japan and the World Economy, 58*, 101074.

Ciriaci, D., Montresor, S., & Palma, D. (2015). Do KIBS make manufacturing more innovative? An empirical investigation of four European countries. *Technological Forecasting and Social Change, 95*, 135–151.

Ciriaci, D., & Palma, D. (2016). Structural change and blurred sectoral boundaries: Assessing the extent to which knowledge-intensive business services satisfy manufacturing final demand in Western countries. *Economic Systems Research, 28*(1), 55–77.

Cuadrado-Roura, J. R. (2013). The Location of Services Industries. In J. R. Cuadrado-Roura (Ed.), *Services Industries and Regions: Growth, Location and Regional Effects* (pp. 253–284). Spring-Verlag.

Cusumano, M. A., Kahl, S. J., & Suarez, F. F. (2015). Services, industry evolution, and the competitive strategies of product firms. *Strategic Management Journal, 36*(4), 559–575.

DANE (2021). *Cuentas Nacionales Departamentales, 2015.* Producto Interno Bruto - PIB a precios constantes. Cuadro 2: Producto Interno Bruto por departamento, series encadenadas de volumen con año de referencia 2015, 2005–2020pr. Departamento Administrativo Nacional de Estadística, Bogotá, D.C. Actualizado el 25 de junio de 2021.

Di Berardino, C., & Onesti, G. (2020). The two-way integration between manufacturing and services. *The Service Industries Journal, 40*(5–6), 337–357.

Ferreira, J. J. M., Raposo, M. L., Fernandes, C. I., & Dejardin, M. (2016). *Knowledge intensive business services and regional competitiveness.* Routledge.

Foster, N., Poschl, J., & Stehrer, R. (2012). Manufacturing productivity: Effects of service sector innovations and institutions. *WIIW Working Paper*, 89. City, country.

Gonçalves, E., Perobelli, F. S., & de Araújo, I. F. (2017). Estimating intersectoral technology spillovers for Brazil. *The Journal of Technology Transfer, 42*(6), 1377–1406.

Haddad, E. A., & Araújo, I. F. (2021). The internal geography of services value-added in exports: A Latin American perspective. *Papers in Regional Science, 100*(3), 713–744.

Haddad, E. A., Araújo, I. F. Ibarrarán, M. E., & Elizondo, A. (2022). Assessing the impacts of Knowledge-Intensive-Business-Services (KIBS) productivity on the competitiveness of Mexican exports: A spatial general equilibrium approach. 61st ERSA Congress, Pécs, Hungary.

Hanel, P. (2000). R&D, interindustry and international technology spillovers and the total factor productivity growth of manufacturing industries in Canada, 1974–1989. *Economic Systems Research, 12*(3), 345–361.

Hauknes, J., & Knell, M. (2009). Embodied knowledge and sectoral linkages: An input-output approach to the interaction of high-and low-tech industries. *Research Policy, 38*(3), 459–469.

Herrero, D., & Rial, A. (2022). "Productive linkages in a segmented economy: the role of services in the export performance of German manufacturing. *Economic Systems Research*, 1–28.

Hertel, T., Hummels, D., Ivanic, M., & Keeney, R. (2007). How confident can we be of CGE-based assessments of free trade agreements? *Economic Modelling, 24*(4), 611–635.

Hoekman, B., & Shepherd, B. (2017). Services productivity, trade policy and manufacturing exports. *The World Economy, 40*(3), 499–516.

Keller, W. (2002). Trade and the transmission of technology. *Journal of Economic Growth, 7*(1), 5–24.

Kong, Q., Shen, C., Sun, W., & Shao, W. (2021). KIBS import technological complexity and manufacturing value chain upgrading from a financial constraint perspective. *Finance Research Letters, 41*, 101843.

Kordalska, A., & Olczyk, M. (2021). Linkages between services and manufacturing as a new channel for GVC development: Evidence from CEE countries. *Structural Change and Economic Dynamics, 58*, 125–137.

Muller, E., & Zenker, A. (2001). Business services as actors of knowledge transformation: The role of KIBS in regional and national innovation systems. *Research Policy, 30*(9), 1501–1516.

Pattnayak, S. S., & Chadha, A. (2022). Servicification and manufacturing exports: Evidence from India. *Economic Modelling, 108*, 105756.

Roson, R., & Sartori, M. (2016). Input-output linkages and the propagation of domestic productivity shocks: Assessing alternative theories with stochastic simulation. *Economic Systems Research, 28*(1), 38–54.

Rubalcaba, L., & Kox, H. (2007). *Business services in European economic growth*. Palgrave Macmillan.

Strambach, S. (2001). Innovation processes and the role of Knowledge-Intensive Business Services (KIBS). In K. Koschatzky, M. Kulicke, & A. Zenker (Eds.), *Innovation, networks: Concepts and challenges in the European perspective* (pp. 53–68). Physica.

Inácio F. Araújo Doctor in Economics, Federal University of Juiz de Fora. Post-doctoral researcher, University of São Paulo, Brazil. Research fields: regional economics and input-output methods.

Eduardo A. Haddad Full Professor at the Department of Economics at the University of São Paulo, Brazil, where he directs the Regional and Urban Economics Lab (NEREUS). Affiliate Professor at the Faculty of Governance, Economic and Social Sciences of the Mohammed VI University and Senior Fellow at the Policy Center for the New South, Rabat, Morocco. President of the Regional Science Association International, RSAI (2021-2022).

Maria Aparecida S. Oliveira Doctor in Applied Economics, Federal University of Viçosa. Associate Professor at the Department of Economics, Federal University of São Carlos. Research fields: economic structural change and sectorial linkages.

Diana Ricciulli Ph.D. Student (Econ.), University of British Columbia. Professional researcher, Center for Regional Economic Studies, Banco de la República, Colombia. Research fields: political economy, economic history, and economic development.

Chapter 16
Impact Assessment of Interregional Transfers Scenarios in the Colombian Economy

Luis Armando Galvis-Aponte, Inácio F. Araújo, Vinícius A. Vale, and Eduardo A. Haddad

16.1 Introduction

Persistent poverty, economic decay, and lack of opportunities are the main problems of less developed regions (Rodríguez-Pose, 2018). Difficulties lagged regions face in generating revenues have led central governments to implement several interregional transfer schemes as policy initiatives to combat regional inequalities. Thus, fiscal equalization policies have been used to redistribute tax revenues from areas with the highest financial capacity to more impoverished regions, allowing a more equitable distribution of public services (Bacarreza et al., 2016).

Fiscal equalization strategies have been used in different countries, including developed and developing economies: Germany (Baskaran et al., 2017; Buettner, 2009; Henkel et al., 2018; Jüßen, 2006), Italy (Siano & D'Uva, 2017), Norway (Borge et al., 2014), Spain (Salinas & Solé-Ollé, 2018), USA (Austin et al., 2018; Kline & Moretti, 2014), Canada (Albouy, 2012), Australia (Groenewold & Hagger, 2007; Groenewold et al., 2003), Japan (Otsuka et al., 2010), OECD countries (Kyriacou et al., 2015 and 2017), China (Chen & Groenewold, 2011, 2013), Brazil (Haddad et al., 2013), and Nigeria (Maystadt & Salihu, 2018), and Indonesia (Resosudarmo et al., 1999).

L. A. Galvis-Aponte
Banco de la República, Cartagena, Colombia
e-mail: lgalviap@banrep.gov.co

I. F. Araújo · E. A. Haddad
University of São Paulo, São Paulo, Brazil
e-mail: inacio.araujo@usp.br

E. A. Haddad
e-mail: ehaddad@usp.br

V. A. Vale (✉)
Federal University of Paraná, Curitiba, Brazil
e-mail: viniciusvale@ufpr.br

Interregional transfers are widely used to boost regional development. However, few empirical studies have tested for the presence of spatial interactions induced by fiscal decentralization (Siano & D'Uva, 2017). The literature has mainly focused on the local impact of interregional transfers. This study intends to shed light on this knowledge gap by analyzing spatial interactions induced by fiscal decentralization policies and their respective impacts on regional growth. More specifically, our interest lies in the economic effects of different scenarios of the current interregional transfer scheme in Colombia embedded in a spatial general equilibrium framework.

Colombia presents strong regional disparities in terms of per capita income, social services, and infrastructure (Rueda, 2004). This heterogeneity affects own-source revenue capacity and public services provision in the regions. Interregional transfers during the 2000s accounted for 52% to 58% of the Colombian central government spending (Bird, 2012). The transfers from the Central National Government (CNG) seek to alleviate the lack of own-source revenues in peripheral regions. Despite the relevance of policies to reduce regional inequalities in Colombia (see Bonet, 2006; Bird, 2012; Bonet & Ayala-Gracía, 2015; Ter-Minassian, 2016), there is not enough evidence on their broader economic implications.

Colombian redistributive policies face several problems. A central concern regards the criteria used to allocate resources: they involve not only efficiency or equity concerns. There are various interests associated with lobbying groups (Rueda, 2004). There is an extensive discussion on the efficiency of decentralization of public spending (Bonet, 2006; Bonet & Ayala-García, 2015; Lozano & Julio, 2016; World Bank, 2009). Nevertheless, given that transfers are an important mechanism to reduce regional economic disparities in Colombia, an active policy based on the decentralization of public expenditure may be an important part of the CNG actions.

The central hypothesis behind our study is that the productive regional structure can partially neutralize the redistributive effects of interregional transfers, given the intense polarization observed in the Colombian economy (Haddad et al., 2009). Our analysis seeks to address two main issues: (i) is an increase in interregional transfers to lagged regions required to reduce regional economic inequality in Colombia; and (ii) what economic effects would alternative criteria generate. Most of the existing literature focuses on different experiences in developed countries—such as the USA and European countries—which may differ significantly from the experiences of developing countries (Chauvin et al., 2017; Glaeser & Henderson, 2017). This chapter contributes to a better understanding of the effectiveness of policies to reduce regional disparities in a developing country characterized by substantial regional inequality in a polarized economic setting.

We adopt the CGE model described in Chap. 6. We consider the following alternative redistribution criteria: (i) the share of each department in the national population; (ii) the number of poor people; and (iii) horizontal fiscal equity gaps. The results show that increases in transfers to lagged regions may compromise growth in the more prosperous regions of Colombia, reducing overall economic growth. This result may suggest that territorial interventions focused on lagged areas may not be the best strategy for overall efficiency if not appropriately designed.

The remainder of this chapter is structured as follows. Section 16.2 motivates the impact of interregional transfers on regional inequality in Colombia. Section 16.3 presents the model used in our simulations. Section 16.4 designs the simulation experiments, presenting and discussing results in Sect. 16.5. A final section concludes and discusses the broad implications for regional policy.

16.2 Regional Inequalities and Subnational Transfers

Several countries use intergovernmental transfers to poorer regions as a policy instrument to alleviate interregional inequalities. Fiscal decentralization can potentially allow public-good levels to adjust and suit local demands (Borge et al., 2014), which can help reduce long-term disparities between regions (Jüßen, 2006). However, these transfers not always positively affect national economic growth (Ania & Wagener, 2016).

The implementation of Canadian equalization policies appears neither efficient nor equitable (Albouy, 2012). German intergovernmental transfers to poor regions did not foster economic growth. Transfers may perpetuate underdevelopment if, for instance, recipients use them to subsidize declining industries (Baskaran et al., 2017). Furthermore, intergovernmental transfers may be harmful to economic growth in German regions due to the diversion of activity away from core cities to remote areas with lower productivity (Henkel et al., 2018).

Rodríguez-Pose and Ezcurra (2009, 2010) suggest a negative association between fiscal decentralization and economic growth. However, their result is highly contingent on the initial level of local development and the policy preferences of subnational governments. On the one hand, decentralization in high-income countries has been linked to reducing regional inequality. On the other hand, in low and medium-income countries, fiscal decentralization has been associated with a significant rise in regional disparities since the positive effects of political decentralization have been unable to compensate for economic drawbacks.

In countries with poor governance of subnational governments, greater decentralization is likely to widen income differences between the regions. As a result, poor institutional environments may undermine the best strategy to promote economic growth and facilitate lagging areas (Barca et al., 2012). In this perspective, countries endowed with good quality institutions can harness the benefits of fiscal decentralization to promote regional development (Bacarreza et al., 2016; Kyriacou et al., 2015, 2017).

Traditional supply-led development intervention can also fail (Rodríguez-Pose, 2018). This strategy may stimulate assisted economies to become increasingly dependent on transfers and welfare from the central governments. As a result, subsidizing poor or unproductive places is likely a suboptimal transference mechanism for the poor (Kline & Moretti, 2014). This has led to place-based policies for regional development (Barca et al., 2012; Partridge et al., 2015), which could allegedly overcome the "false" trade-off between efficiency and equity (Rodríguez-Pose, 2018). Place-based policies may not mean large-scale transfers but place-based tailoring of federal policies to local needs; federal politics based on one-size-fits-all interventions are woefully inappropriate for diverse regional economies (Austin et al., 2018).[1] For this reason, academics have defended distributional policies that are place-based and that address all dimensions of regional development—not solely economic components (Iammarino et al., 2017).

16.2.1 Colombian Institutional Details

Regional disparities in Colombia are persistent (Galvis-Aponte & Meisel, 2010). The department of Bogotá D.C exerts a marked economic polarization in the production of the other Colombian departments. The average per capita income in Bogotá D.C, between 1975 and 2000, is higher than twice the national average and more than eight times the per capita income of Chocó, the poorest department (Bonet & Meisel, 2008). Furthermore, Colombia has experienced a process of polarization in per capita departmental production (Royuela & García, 2015; Vásquez & Bara, 2009), which increased during the 1990s (Barón, 2003). Some economic policies established in the 1990s have strengthened agglomeration forces around the main Colombian departments—Bogotá D.C, Antioquia, and Valle del Cauca. Moreover, those policies have not presented the expected positive impacts on reducing disparities among the departments (Vásquez & Bara, 2009). The spatial dynamics have led to a greater concentration of the population (26.4%) and economic activity (37.0%) in the major cities and capitals of the three departments above—Bogotá D.C, Medellín, and Cali (Royuela & García, 2015).

CNG has used fiscal decentralization and interregional transfers to reduce regional disparities. The political process of decentralization in Colombia began in the 1980s. Specifically, with the Law 78 of 1986, decentralization was complemented by granting more resources to mayors and governors. Such resources would come from the taxes collected by the CNG in each tier, which would return to them in the form of territorial transfers (Bonet et al., 2016).

In 2001, Law 715 created the General Participation System (SGP), which modified how resources are assigned to local authorities. In addition to the specific destination (earmarked) portion to be spent on health and education, a general-purpose item was included that could be spent on projects of water and basic sanitation, recreation, culture, and sports, and finally, a fraction that would be of discretional use. Also, there would also be transfers for the following items: the indigenous reserves (resguardos), the school nutrition programs, the National Pension Fund of the Territorial Entities (FONPET), and the riverside municipalities of the Magdalena River.

---

[1] Although there is an argument that place-based policies are distortionary and only slow the economic adjustments, Partridge et al. (2015) suggest the potential efficacy of place-based policy.

Most of the transfers are earmarked and can only be used to foster specific sectors, such as education, health, and water and sanitation. There has been a recent discussion regarding how resources are distributed among the subnational units. Zapata and Concha (2016) show that the CNG employs around 42 criteria to define the share of the resources that go to each municipality or department. The authors conclude that only 14 of these criteria would be enough for achieving better results regarding the administration, use of resources, and incentives for local administrators to improve tax revenue collection.

Similarly, Bonet et al. (2016) showed that the law regulating the transfers is inconsistent with the many functions assigned to the subnational units. Effectively, there is a vast number of tasks carried out by municipalities and departments using the same resources. Galvis-Aponte (2016) also showed that resource usage is inefficient by municipalities. Using the primary receivers of resources, the author demonstrated that municipalities could improve coverage and quality of health and education services with fewer resources.

Previous studies have tried to analyze the effectiveness of the Colombian fiscal transfer policy on regional disparities reduction. Bonet (2006) identified an increase in regional income disparities in Colombia due to fiscal decentralization. Bonet and Meisel (2008) found that decentralization policies had not positively impacted long-run regional inequality trends. During the period of decentralization policy strengthening (1975–2000), income concentration increased in Bogotá D.C. However, Royuela and García (2015) suggest that transfers through regional remittances had a crucial role in the process of regional convergence of real household disposable income, despite regional per capita GRP having remained concentrated. Lozano and Julio (2016) identified positive effects of fiscal decentralization on regional economic growth.

16.3 Specification of the CEER Model

We use the CEER model described in Chap. 6: a fully operational spatial CGE model for Colombia (Haddad et al., 2009). The model uses an approach similar to Peter et al. (1996), Haddad (1999), and Haddad and Hewings (2005) to incorporate interregional economic structure. We use an absorption matrix published by Haddad et al. (2018) as the basis to calibrate the CGE model, together with a set of elasticities borrowed from the econometric literature applied to Colombia. This database captures economy-wide effects through an intricate plot of input–output relations.

The CEER model qualifies as a Johansen-type model in that the solutions are obtained by solving the system of linearized equations, following the Australian tradition. A typical result shows the percentage change in the set of endogenous variables after a policy is carried out, compared to their values in the absence of such a policy in a given environment. Interregional linkages play an essential role in the functioning mechanisms of the model. These linkages are driven by trade relations (commodity flows) and factor mobility (capital and labor migration). Interregional trade flows are incorporated; interregional input–output relations are required to calibrate the model, and interregional trade elasticities play a crucial role (see Haddad, 2009).

In the model, governments consume mainly public goods provided by the public administration sectors. Equation (16.1), which is the critical equation for the design of our simulations, shows the movement of government consumption concerning movements in real tax revenue for regional governments[2]:

$$x_{(is)}^{(5)r} = \text{taxrev}^r + f_{(is)}^{(5)r} + f^{(5)r} + f^{(5)}$$
$$i \in G;\ s = 1b, 2;\ r, b \in S^* \tag{16.1}$$

where $x_{(is)}^{(5)r}$ is the regional governments demand in region r for good i from region s; $f_{(is)}^{(5)r}$ is a commodity and source-specific shift term for regional government expenditure in region r, $f^{(5)r}$ is the shift term for regional government expenditure in region r, and $f^{(5)}$ is an overall shift term for regional government expenditure. Finally, taxrev^r is the percentage change in real revenue from indirect taxes in region r so that government demand moves proportionally to endogenous changes in regional and national tax bases.

We define changes in regional output, which will be the focus of our analysis, as weighted averages of changes in regional aggregates, according to Eq. (16.2):

$$GRP^r grp^r = C^r x_{(\bullet\bullet)}^{(3)r} + INV^r z^{(2\bullet)r} + GOV^{(5)r} x_{(\bullet\bullet)}^{(5)r} + GOV^{(6)r} x_{(\bullet\bullet)}^{(6)r}$$
$$+ \left(FEXP^r x_{(\bullet\bullet)}^{(4)r} - FIMP^r x_{(\bullet 2)}^{(\bullet)r} \right) +$$
$$\left(DEXP^r x_{(\bullet,1r))}^{(\bullet)s} - DIMP^r x_{(\bullet(1s))}^{(\bullet)r} \right)$$
$$r \in S^*;\ s \in S^*\ \text{for}\ s \neq r \tag{16.2}$$

where grp^r is the percentage change in real GRP in region r; and the coefficients GRP^r, INV^r, $GOV^{(5)r}$, $GOV^{(6)r}$, $FEXP^r$, $FIMP^r$, $DEXP^r$, and $DIMP^r$ represent, respectively, the following aggregates in region r: investment, local government spending, central government spending, foreign exports, foreign imports, domestic exports, and domestic imports. National output, GDP, is, thus, the sum of GRP^r across all r regions. Note that regional domestic trade balances cancel out.

---

[2] We present the full specification of the CEER core in Chap. 6. In what follows, we use the same notation used there.

16.3.1 Modeling the Fiscal Transfer Scenarios

What if existing transfers-SGP-were redistributed according to different criteria, such as regional population, regional poverty, or regional fiscal gaps? Let us first define the scenarios of interregional transfers in the context of our model specification. We depart from the benchmark values for the coefficient $V(\bullet, \bullet, (5), r)$, which refers to the total expenditure of regional governments, $GOV^{(5)r}$ in Eq. (16.2). We assume that transfers from the central government are used to finance part of regional government spending in region r and, as such, isolate intergovernmental transfers from $GOV^{(5)r}$ for each r. Also, for each region r information on expenditure and transfers -SGP- of municipalities and departments, obtained from a panel built by the CEDE and the Ministry of Finance, were aggregated for each department, and their respective shares in total regional government expenditure were calculated. These shares were then applied to regional government expenditure in the CEER model ($GOV^{(5)r}$) to estimate total regional transfers.

We have reallocated the estimated transfers for each department according to different parameters for the three scenarios discussed below. With this information, we can calculate the size of the "shock" by imposing region-specific changes in $f^{(5)r}$ (Eq. 16.1), the shift term for government expenditure in region r, that are proportional to changes in $GOV^{(5)r}$ (Eq. 16.2), according to each redistribution scheme.

In order to evaluate the impact of interregional transfers in Colombia, our simulations are carried out under the two standard closures: short-run and long-run. The simulations with the CEER model capture the effects in a comparative-static framework. The distinction between short-run and long-run closures lies in the treatment of capital stocks and labor mobility—that is, in the short-run capital and labor are not mobile.

16.4 Fiscal Scenarios

In the current distribution of subnational transfers, Bogotá D.C, Valle del Cauca, and Antioquia receive the highest share (Fig. 16.1b).[3] As these are the country's leading economies, the CNG transfers concentrate in the more prosperous areas. In relative terms, however, Fig. 16.1c suggests that interregional government transfers provide an explicit strategy of geographic targeting to reduce spatial disparities in Colombia, transferring resources from the main industrial regions (Bogotá D.C, Antioquia, and Valle del Cauca) and the oil-producing departments (Meta, Casanare, Santander and Arauca) to the rest of the country. Whether they achieve the goal of classical regional policies, namely reducing regional disparities through direct income transfers to poorer departments, remains to be tested.

In what follows, we propose different stylized scenarios in which the prevalent regional gaps may be potentially reduced through a change in transfer criteria. When

---
[3] The estimated benchmark shares are available in Table 16.5 in Appendix.

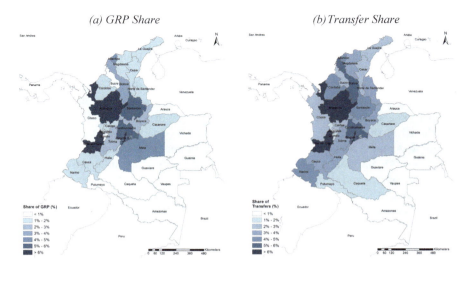

Fig. 16.1 Benchmark shares. *Source* author elaboration using data from Budget Execution Reports of the National Planning Department of Colombia

defining the scenarios, we consider previous literature on this topic. Zapata and Concha (2016) studied the current distribution of transfers among the municipalities in Colombia. They showed that some criteria may increase incentives for local authorities to improve socio-economic indicators, while others reduce such incentives due to fiscal laziness. Population size is among the criteria that incentivize mayors to improve coverage of basic services, while poverty is among the criteria that induce fiscal laziness.

The first scenario considers the population share in each department. In this case, transfers are proportional to the size of the population of each administrative unit. This means that the most populous departments such as Antioquia, Valle del Cauca, and Atlántico, together with Bogotá D.C, have the highest share in transfer redistribution. Since these departments are the leading economies in the country (in terms of regional product), with a higher potential to exploit agglomeration economies in the main urban areas, this scenario follows a redistributive criterion that is more closely related to efficiency. In these scenarios, the poorer departments would experience a reduction in transfers, such as Chocó, Sucre, Amazonas, and Vichada (Table 16.6 in Appendix).

We also simulate two alternative scenarios using redistributive criteria that target regional disparities. In this case, the definition of shares is more closely related to the equity criteria. The first "equity" scenario considers the share of impoverished people in each administrative unit (department). Note that this is not based on poverty rates. In this case, departments with the highest number of poor inhabitants receive the highest number of transfers. This intermediate scenario goes beyond population share, taking into account each department's needs to redistribute resources to the neediest population. When using the extreme poverty criterion, the primary recipients of the shock in the redistribution of transfers are the departments of La Guajira, Cauca, Córdoba, Chocó, and Huila. Hence, from an equity perspective, La Guajira (the poorest department on the Caribe coast) and Chocó (the poorest in the Pacífico) are among the most benefited departments based on this redistribution criterion (Table 16.7 in Appendix).

The last scenario is built using a measure of the fiscal gap in terms of horizontal equity. The calculations were made using the measure of horizontal fiscal disparity proposed by Bonet and Ayala-García (2017). Shares are calculated as follows. First, the authors obtain the per capita spending needs in a given administrative unit, according to spending groups (water, education, health, housing, etc.). Once they have the per capita values, total expenditure is calculated using the population for each municipality. Next, the authors use data envelopment analysis (DEA) to calculate the potential revenues for each municipality. Comparing potential revenues with the spending needs corresponds to the fiscal gap. The results of Bonet & Ayala-García show that the poorest municipalities are the ones with the most prominent fiscal gaps. We employ a measure of the share of the needs to propose the second equity scenario for CNG transfer redistribution. In this case, the more privileged regions are the New Departments; the departments of Vaupés, Guainía, Amazonas, and Guaviare, from the Amazonía region, are among the most significant receivers (Table 16.8 in Appendix).

To apply the shocks to the spatial CGE model, we calculated the proportion of the original amount in $GOV^{(5)r}$ represented by the new amount to be redistributed. The detailed calculations for the shock representation in each scenario are described in Appendix.

16.5 Simulation Results

This section presents the simulation results of the three scenarios described in Sect. 16.4: population, fiscal gap, and extreme poverty. The first and second parts focus on the effects on gross regional product (GRP) associated with each scenario. The third part considers scenarios in which productivity gains accompany the changes in transfer redistribution.

16.5.1 Effects of Governmental Transfer Redistribution

Simulations based on the three transfer redistribution scenarios in Colombia point to an overall slight increase in national GDP in the short-run (Table 16.1).[4] However, only the scenario based on population (Scenario 1) foresees an overall growth in the long-run. This means that if the redistributive scenario is based on more transfers assigned progressively with extreme poverty rates (Scenario 2) or fiscal gap (Scenario 3), the Colombian economy would face a potential decrease in long-run GDP.

The results for the three scenarios also allow us to evaluate the impact of transfer redistribution on regional inequality. In the short-run, Colombian departments that would receive more transfers based on the three redistribution scenarios received a positive impact on their GRPs. Nevertheless, some departments that would foresee increases in transfers, in the long-run, showed a reduction in their GRP in scenarios 2 and 3. To evaluate the spatial distribution of potential winners and losers, we map each department's results in the short-run (Fig. 16.2) and the long-run (Fig. 16.3).

16.5.2 Spillover Effects on Regional Growth

The analysis of transfer impacts on long-run GRP, depicted in Table 16.2, is of distinct interest in our study: there is a direct association between regional growth and the net increase in transfers. Some regions benefiting from net gains in interregional transfers would experience reduced GRP in the long-run. In addition, some regions in scenario 1, even with a loss in transfers, have shown a positive change in GRP in the long-run (Cesar, Magdalena, and Norte de Santander).[5] The explanation for these results may lie in the role played by interregional linkages. These spatial interactions are not intuitive and are seldom taken into account in the analysis of fiscal decentralization.

Regional interdependence has two main transmission mechanisms that may assist in understanding the long-run results: (i) productive regional structure, and (ii) interregional factor mobility in the CEER model. Interregional factor mobility allows us to

---

[4] Considerations on short-run and long-run differ in the way the equilibrating mechanisms are set through the closures of the model, discussed in Chap. 6.

[5] Cesar shows the same patter in short-run.

disaggregate the simulation results into (a) direct effects of government transfers; and (b) interregional spillover effects (Table 16.3). We confirm that a net increase in transfers would have a positive direct effect on GRP. Nonetheless, the transfer outcome may also be associated with a negative spillover effect, which, in some cases, may be greater than the direct effect on GRP. This is the first mechanism through which the redistribution of transfers may impact regional growth: interregional trade linkages. Regions that receive more resources face substantially more pressure on local prices, which, in turn, reduces the relative competitiveness of locally produced goods. As a result, trade diversion occurs, increasing imports (trade deficit) in non-self-sufficient regions (generally specialized in non-tradable products). Therefore, the increase in transfers to these regions does not induce growth due to more substantial import penetration.

Table 16.1 Effects on gross regional product (in percentage change)

Code	Department	Scenario 1 (population)		Scenario 2 (extreme poverty)		Scenario 3 (fiscal gap)	
		Short-run	Long-run	Short-run	Long-run	Short-run	Long-run
D1	Antioquia	**0.6449**	**2.0252**	**0.3688**	− 0.4457	**0.1857**	− 1.8000
D2	Atlantico	**0.7242**	**2.1221**	**1.0402**	**1.4113**	**0.7028**	− 0.4780
D3	Bogota, DC	− 0.2559	− 0.1635	− 1.2648	− 5.2744	− 1.8365	− 7.9064
D4	Bolivar	**0.1203**	**0.7351**	**1.1322**	**1.0320**	**0.6458**	− 1.2459
D5	Boyaca	− 0.3451	− 0.4008	− 0.2468	− 3.2512	− 0.2541	− 4.9841
D6	Caldas	**0.5225**	**1.8073**	**0.7636**	− 0.0541	**0.4261**	− 2.2648
D7	Caqueta	− 7.7867	− 15.5334	− 5.7479	− 14.8901	**6.9011**	**9.4883**
D8	Cauca	− 0.3010	− 0.2643	**2.8032**	**3.9388**	**2.3189**	**1.7586**
D9	Cesar	**0.0234**	**0.1468**	**1.1030**	**1.5681**	**1.5266**	**1.8348**
D10	Cordoba	**0.1828**	**1.0119**	**4.2359**	**7.2064**	**3.2297**	**3.1916**
D11	Cundinamarca	**0.3012**	**0.7735**	− 0.4395	− 4.3380	− 0.9227	− 7.1831
D12	Choco	− 5.5183	− 6.5645	**0.8977**	− 0.0879	**5.7274**	**4.5308**
D13	Huila	**0.4182**	**1.3428**	**1.5906**	**1.4137**	**1.4150**	− 0.3838
D14	La Guajira	**1.0406**	**1.5721**	**4.2324**	**5.5783**	**5.4817**	**6.9091**
D15	Magdalena	− 0.2892	**0.1607**	**2.1227**	**2.7447**	**2.2995**	**1.5006**
D16	Meta	− 0.0762	− 0.0797	− 0.2023	− 0.1767	**0.5249**	**0.6795**
D17	Narino	− 0.7255	− 1.0218	**2.8676**	**4.3085**	**3.5808**	**4.0562**
D18	Norte de Santander	− 0.1588	**0.3461**	**0.8492**	− 0.4448	**1.5096**	− 0.4514
D19	Quindio	**0.3126**	**1.6731**	**0.9527**	− 0.0411	**0.1438**	− 4.2429
D20	Risaralda	**0.6235**	**2.1509**	**0.2867**	− 1.1549	**0.2905**	− 2.7193
D21	Santander	**0.2884**	**1.1234**	− 0.2088	− 1.9730	-0.2338	− 3.1002
D22	Sucre	− 2.9651	− 5.6717	**0.4324**	− 0.8982	**2.0239**	**0.5061**
D23	Tolima	− 0.9712	− 1.8523	− 0.0678	− 2.6108	− 0.7840	− 5.9356

(continued)

Table 16.1 (continued)

D24	Valle del Cauca	**0.1739**	**0.7811**	− 0.1386	− 1.8897	− 0.6479	− 4.3409
D25	Arauca	− 1.4311	− 1.8563	− 1.8084	− 2.9932	**0.2375**	− 0.6979
D26	Cas anare	**0.0600**	**0.0178**	− 0.1423	− 0.0184	**0.3859**	**0.6066**
D27	Putumayo	-2.5234	− 3.7052	− 3.1824	− 5.8796	**1.8855**	**1.1046**
D28	Archipielago de San Andres	**0.3251**	**0.7569**	− 0.3844	− 3.8211	− 2.0296	− 7.4812
D29	Amazonas	− 4.1575	− 6.3885	− 5.3902	− 11.4575	**20.7316**	**30.3659**
D30	Guainia	− 3.8497	− 5.9280	− 4.9083	− 9.6643	**39.9020**	**63.7194**
D31	Guaviare	− 7.8254	− 14.6410	− 9.1523	− 20.4731	**26.2331**	**47.1988**
D32	Vaupes	**2.1402**	**4.7429**	**0.0334**	− 2.7343	**64.2845**	**117.4976**
D33	Vichada	− 7.5748	− 13.4592	− 8.7659	− 19.6994	**72.9265**	**129.3798**
COLOMBIA		**0.0043**	**0.0043**	**0.0003**	− 0.0177	**0.0004**	− 0.0315

The second transmission mechanism is related to migration, i.e., the mobility of the factors of production. In the long-run, given that markets are in equilibrium and the unemployment rate remains at benchmark value, regions that tend to increase their output attract more population. In the long-run, the free mobility of production factors allows for changes in the distribution of capital stock and labor, affecting the factors' marginal rate of returns. Groenewold and Hagger (2007), Chen and Groenewold (2011, 2013), Henkel et al. (2018), Rodríguez-Pose (2018), and Austin et al. (2018) have shown that the effects of interregional transfers on regional disparities are sensitive to the hypotheses of perfect labor mobility. Therefore, changes in the distribution of fiscal transfers in an environment allowing for labor mobility across regions can drive migration from less productive to more productive regions, affecting production and regional growth.

16.5.3 Effects on Regional Inequality

Do gains in equity follow from the aggregate outcomes? To answer this question, we have calculated, for each scenario, the long-run locational Gini index (Fig. 16.4). Compared to the benchmark, we observe a reduction in output concentration among the Colombian regions in Scenarios 2 (extreme poverty) and 3 (fiscal gap). It is worth mentioning that this change in output concentration—and the consequent reduction in regional disparities—occurs only partly due to the higher growth of the more impoverished regions (see Table 16.1). Output concentration change is also related to a decrease in GRP in more prosperous regions. Therefore, while having positive effects in terms of equity, the result of this redistributive policy may undermine national growth in the long-run.

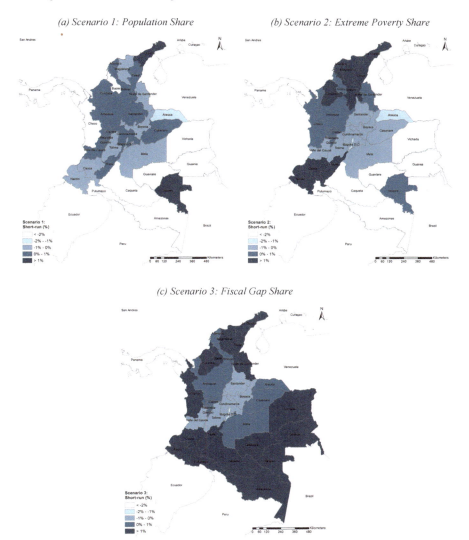

Fig. 16.2 Effects on gross regional product: short-run

These results suggest a trade-off between encouraging economic activity in peripheral regions and limiting the growth of other regions. When we look at national welfare, measured in terms of the equivalent variation and income concentration in relation to our benchmark specification, we find that this trade-off may not be compensated by an increase in national welfare (Table 16.4).

Conversely, in the counterfactual scenario based on extreme poverty, the income concentration decreased by -0.812%, and national welfare decreased by -0.034%.

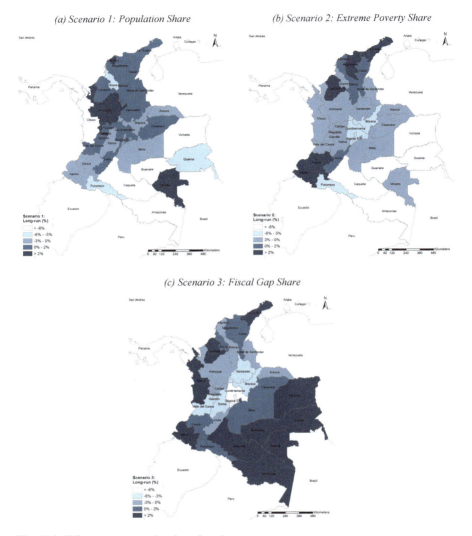

Fig. 16.3 Effects on gross regional product: long-run

When transfers are redistributed based on the fiscal gap, the income concentration decreases by −2.100%, and welfare decreases by −0.052%.

On the other hand, in the counterfactual scenario based on population, the national GDP would increase by 0.004%, welfare would increase by 0.010%, and income concentration in relation to our benchmark specification would increase by 0.406%.

Our results are in part similar to Royuela and García (2015) and Lozano and Julio (2016), in which positive effects of fiscal decentralization on reducing regional

16 Impact Assessment of Interregional Transfers Scenarios …

Table 16.2 Effect on gross regional product: long-run

Code	Department	Scenario 1		Scenario 2		Scenario 3	
		Transfer Redistribution based on population (shock f5gen)	Percentage change of Gross Regional Product (long-run)	Transfer redistribution based on poverty (shock f5gen)	Percentage change of Gross Regional Product (long-run)	Transfer redistribution based on fiscal gap (shock f5gen)	Percentage change of Gross Regional Product (long-run)
D1	Antioquia	14.44	2.03	7.03	− 0.45	1.69	− 1.80
D2	Atlantico	13.09	2.12	14.67	1.41	8.53	− 0.48
D3	Bogota, D.C	− 4.94	− 0.16	− 20.46	− 5.27	− 29.00	− 7.91
D4	Bolivar	0.96	0.74	16.47	1.03	8.59	− 1.25
D5	Boyaca	− 7.98	− 0.40	− 3.75	− 3.25	− 2.52	− 4.98
D6	Caldas	7.92	1.81	12.33	− 0.05	7.18	− 2.26
D7	Caqueta	− 77.11	− 15.53	− 60.10	− 14.89	64.25	9.49
D8	Cauca	− 4.87	− 0.26	43.72	3.94	36.82	1.76
D9	Cesar	**− 0.63**	**0.15**	18.49	1.57	26.48	1.83
D10	Cordoba	1.16	1.01	33.14	7.21	25.37	3.19
D11	Cundinamarca	9.68	0.77	− 3.82	− 4.34	− 12.98	− 7.18
D12	Choco	− 45.06	− 6.56	7.27	− 0.09	46.86	4.53
D13	Huila	8.12	1.34	30.02	1.41	26.99	− 0.38
D14	La Guajira	15.82	1.57	66.97	5.58	87.74	6.91
D15	Magdalena	**− 4.60**	**0.16**	21.19	2.74	24.24	1.50
D16	Meta	− 3.58	− 0.08	− 6.92	− 0.18	17.84	0.68
D17	Narino	− 6.43	− 1.02	24.42	4.31	31.01	4.06

(continued)

Table 16.2 (continued)

D18	Norte de Santander	**−2.40**	0.35	9.52	−0.44	*17.54*	*−0.45*
D19	Quindio	4.35	1.67	*15.44*	*−0.04*	2.96	*−4.24*
D20	Risaralda	10.06	2.15	*3.63*	*−1.15*	4.70	*−2.72*
D21	Santander	8.28	1.12	−7.59	−1.97	−8.28	*−3.10*
D22	Sucre	−21.48	−5.67	*0.73*	*−0.90*	13.07	0.51
D23	Tolima	−16.01	−1.85	−1.07	−2.61	−11.50	−5.94
D24	Valle del Cauca	3.79	0.78	−4.69	−1.89	−15.99	−4.34
D25	Arauca	−39.76	−1.86	−49.49	−2.99	*5.77*	*−0.70*
D26	Cas anare	1.68	0.02	−3.84	−0.02	15.03	0.61
D27	Putumayo	−22.24	−3.71	−27.84	−5.88	17.29	1.10
D28	Archipielago de San Andres	10.08	0.76	−0.90	−3.82	47.53	−7.48
D29	Amazonas	−35.01	−6.39	−42.91	−11.46	172.87	30.37
D30	Guainia	−24.27	−5.93	−30.66	−9.66	242.27	63.72
D31	Guaviare	−76.80	−14.64	−89.03	−20.47	246.96	47.20
D32	Vaupes	9.81	4.74	*2.26*	*−2.73*	309.67	117.50
D33	Vichada	−45.59	−13.46	−51.63	−19.70	442.27	129.38

Note In the emphasis bold are the departments that lost transfer but have shown a positive percentage change in GRP (long-run). In the emphasis italics are those that have gained in transfers but have shown a negative percentage change in GRP (long-run)

Table 16.3 Direct and spillovers effect on gross regional product (in percentage change)

Code	Department	Scenario 1 (population)		Scenario 2 (extreme poverty)		Scenario 3 (fiscal gap)	
		Direct effect	Spillover effect	Direct effect	Spillover effect	Direct effect	Spillover effect
D1	Antioquia	0.81	1.22	*0.39*	*− 0.84*	*0.10*	*− 1.90*
D2	Atlantico	1.43	0.69	1.60	− 0.19	*0.93*	*− 1.41*
D3	Bogota, DC	− 0.01	− 0.15	− 0.05	− 5.23	− 0.07	− 7.84
D4	Bolivar	0.10	0.63	1.70	− 0.67	*0.88*	*− 2.13*
D5	Boyaca	− 0.74	0.34	− 0.34	− 2.91	− 0.23	− 4.75
D6	Caldas	1.01	0.80	*1.57*	*− 1.63*	*0.92*	*− 3.18*
D7	Caqueta	− 15.78	0.24	− 12.30	− 2.59	13.17	− 3.68
D8	Cauca	− 0.58	0.31	5.17	− 1.23	4.35	− 2.59
D9	Cesar	**− 0.05**	**0.20**	1.63	− 0.06	2.33	− 0.49
D10	Cordoba	0.29	0.73	7.91	− 0.71	6.07	− 2.88
D11	Cundinamarca	0.48	0.30	− 0.19	− 4.15	-0.64	− 6.54
D12	Choco	− 7.11	0.55	*1.15*	*− 1.24*	7.41	− 2.88
D13	Huila	0.93	0.42	3.43	− 2.02	*3.09*	*− 3.47*
D14	La Guajira	1.36	0.21	5.78	− 0.20	7.57	− 0.66
D15	Magdalena	**− 0.78**	**0.94**	3.61	− 0.86	4.12	− 2.62
D16	Meta	− 0.15	0.07	− 0.29	0.12	0.76	− 0.08
D17	Narino	− 1.49	0.47	5.68	− 1.37	7.21	− 3.16
D18	Norte de Santander	**− 0.46**	**0.81**	*1.83*	*− 2.28*	*3.38*	*− 3.83*
D19	Quindio	0.62	1.05	*2.22*	*− 2.26*	*0.43*	*− 4.68*
D20	Ris aralda	1.29	0.86	*0.46*	*− 1.61*	*0.60*	*− 3.32*
D21	Santander	0.49	0.63	− 0.45	− 1.52	− 0.49	− 2.61
D22	Sucre	− 6.31	0.64	*0.21*	*− 1.10*	3.85	− 3.34
D23	Tolima	− 2.14	0.29	− 0.15	− 2.46	− 1.54	− 4.40
D24	Valle del Cauca	0.29	0.50	− 0.35	− 1.54	− 1.20	− 3.14
D25	Arauca	− 2.10	0.24	− 2.61	− 0.38	*0.31*	*− 1.00*
D26	Casanare	0.06	-0.04	− 0.14	0.12	0.54	0.06
D27	Putumayo	− 3.87	0.16	− 4.84	− 1.04	3.02	− 1.91
D28	Archipielago de San Andres	0.61	0.15	− 0.05	− 3.77	− 2.87	− 4.61
D29	Amazonas	− 6.94	0.55	− 8.50	− 2.96	34.43	− 4.06
D30	Guainia	− 6.56	0.64	− 8.29	− 1.37	65.97	− 2.25
D31	Guaviare	− 15.85	1.21	− 18.36	-2.11	51.31	− 4.11
D32	Vaupes	3.88	0.87	*0.91*	*− 3.64*	123.85	− 6.35

(continued)

Table 16.3 (continued)

Code	Department	Scenario 1 (population)		Scenario 2 (extreme poverty)		Scenario 3 (fiscal gap)	
		Direct effect	Spillover effect	Direct effect	Spillover effect	Direct effect	Spillover effect
D33	Vichada	− 13.78	0.32	− 15.59	− 4.11	135.82	− 6.44

Note In the emphasis bold are the departments that lost transfer but have shown a positive percentage change in GRP (long-run). In the emphasis italics are those that have gained in transfers but have shown a negative percentage change in GRP (long-run). See Table 16.2

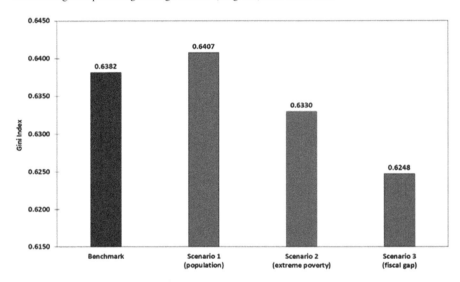

Fig. 16.4 Locational Gini index under alternative scenarios

Table 16.4 Long-run effects under alternative scenarios (in percentage change)

Scenario	National GDP	Locational Gini Index	Relative equivalent variation
Scenario 1 (population)	0.004	0.406	0.010
Scenario 2 (extreme poverty)	− 0.018	− 0.812	− 0.034
Scenario 3 (fiscal gap)	− 0.032	− 2.100	− 0.052

Note Equivalent variation is measured by the ratio of the equivalent variation to pre-shock regional household disposable income

disparities in Colombia were found. The results of Scenario 1 (population) are consistent with findings in Bonet (2006) and Bonet and Meisel (2008). These studies find that the current distribution of interregional government transfers and the distribution based on population shares in our scenario are not strong enough to reduce regional inequalities and income concentration in Bogotá D.C.

16.5.4 Effects of Government Transfer Redistribution Accompanied by Productivity Gains

Departments in Colombia have earmarked resources, and most are allocated to payroll in education and health services or to cover health expenditure in the subsidized health system. They are primarily allocated as current expenditure rather than capital expenditure in the form of investment or infrastructure (Bird, 2012; Bonet & Ayala-García, 2015). Therefore, the long-run trend in the increase in income disparities may result from the absence of adequate incentives to promote the efficient use of these resources by regional governments (Bonet, 2006). Efficient resource usage could promote productivity gains in regions benefitted by the transfers from the CNG.

We consider scenarios where productivity gains accompany the transfer redistribution from this perspective. In other words, we assume counterfactual scenarios where a net increase in transfers is accompanied by a hypothetical allocation of the additional resources to improve long-run total factor productivity (TFP),[6] enhancing investment. In these new counterfactual scenarios, we assume the same changes in regional government transfers as the previous simulations; however, we also assume a uniform increase in productivity in the use of primary production factors across the regions that increase their received resources through government transfers. The productivity for the remaining regions is maintained constant. The objective is to capture productivity gain associated with the scenarios of transfer change, which can prevent losses in national growth associated with a given redistribution scenario.

Figure 16.5 shows the potential growth in the Colombian GDP in the long-run for the three scenarios of transfer reallocation after a threshold gain in productivity across regions with increased net transfers. In Scenario 1 (based on population shares), there is a potential GDP growth associated with all values of regional productivity. In Scenario 2 (based on extreme poverty shares), regional productivity should grow at least 0.04% to compensate for the loss in resources that the most prominent regional economies undergo. Finally, in Scenario 3 (based on a fiscal gap), the threshold beyond which regional productivity offsets the loss in regional output is 0.06%.

---

[6] We make the simulation by imposing regional-specific changes in $a_{(g+1,s)}^{(1j)r}$, the shift term for the productivity of the primary factors of production in region r, in Eq. (6.8) in Chap. 6.

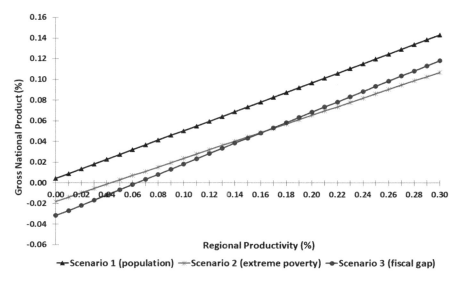

Fig. 16.5 Threshold for regional TFP growth that offsets national GDP loss

16.6 Final Considerations

Colombia is one of the most unequal countries in Latin America. In order to reduce regional disparities, decentralization policies have introduced mechanisms to redistribute revenues from the CNG to its departments. However, regional inequalities persist. This study has analyzed the effects of alternative transfer scenarios for regional allocation in Colombia. We simulated three counterfactual scenarios in which redistributive policies are redesigned and assessed their potential effects on regional growth and inequalities. The simulations conducted in this work contribute to analyzing the impact on regional growth related to some of the broad objectives that central governments pursue when allocating transfers to subnational governments.

Our results provide quantitative answers that may help policymakers better understand how fiscal transfers affect the national economic activity in the Colombian interregional system. The proposed scenarios suggest that fiscal transfers significantly increase GRP in areas that benefit from net increases in resources, reducing regional disparities. We observe a reduction in output concentration among the Colombian regions in Scenarios 2 (extreme poverty) and 3 (fiscal gap) in terms of equity gains. However, the productive regional structure and factor mobility can neutralize the redistributive effects of subnational transfers.

Despite improved regional cohesion, the more redistributive scenarios may hamper overall growth. Although there may be a short-run improvement in GRP growth rates, long-run effects related to productive regional structure and factor mobility may lead to an overall loss in country-wide growth. The CNG needs to consider these two aspects in reassessing transfer criteria. In order to compensate for the potential overall GDP loss, the redistribution scenario based on the fiscal gap is the one that requires a more modest rate of growth in TFP, simultaneously achieving better regional equity outcomes.

Appendix—Scenario and Detailed Shocks

Table 16.5 describes the estimated benchmark shares, while Fig. 16.6 shows its spatial distributions. Concerning population share, Fig. 16.6a, we can highlight the importance of departments such as Valle, Cundinamarca, Antioquia, Santander (along the Andean Mountains), Bolívar, Atlántico (in the Caribbean coast), and Bogotá. In terms of extreme poverty shares, departments in the Caribbean and the Pacific end up with higher weight in the distribution (Fig. 16.6b). In Fig. 16.6c, Córdoba, Antioquia, Valle, and Nariño are the departments that receive the highest shares of transfers based on the fiscal gap.

Tables 16.6, 16.7 and 16.8 show the current share of distributed resources and the proposed scenarios following the population, extreme poverty, and horizontal fiscal gap criteria. For example, Table 16.6, column (A), shows the current amount of regional expenditures for each Colombian Department; column (B) shows how much of those expenditures come from CNG transfers. If we take the total amount of SGP and redistribute it based on the population share, we obtain column (C). This means that Antioquia would receive 3766.56 million COP instead of 2438.30 million COP. In such a case, a net transfer redistribution of 1328.26 million COP is shown in column (D).

To apply the shock to the spatial CGE model, we have calculated the proportion of the original amount in $GOV^{(5)r}$ that represents the new amount to be redistributed - column (D) over column (A), in the last column of Table 16.6. The numbers in this column represent the change in transfer value per department. For instance, on top of the current regional government expenditures, Antioquia would receive 14.44% more transfers if we redistribute the SGP resources based on population shares. Analogously, we may read Tables 16.7 and 16.8, based on extreme poverty and horizontal fiscal gap, respectively.

Table 16.5 Benchmark shares

Code	Department	% Transfer	% Pop	% Poverty	% Fiscal Gap
D1	Antioquia	8.647	13.357	10.941	9.198
D2	Atlántico	3.492	5.095	5.289	4.538
D3	Bogotá, D.C.	19.593	16.254	5.770	0.000
D4	Bolívar	4.254	4.348	5.880	5.102
D5	Boyacá	3.186	2.729	2.971	3.042
D6	Caldas	1.801	2.109	2.280	2.080
D7	Caquetá	2.268	0.986	1.269	3.336
D8	Cauca	3.142	2.882	5.470	5.102
D9	Cesar	2.159	2.129	3.049	3.434
D10	Córdoba	3.398	3.505	6.457	5.740
D11	Cundinamarca	4.360	5.491	3.915	2.845
D12	Chocó	2.010	1.042	2.166	3.017
D13	Huila	2.042	2.387	3.317	3.189
D14	La Guajira	1.422	1.877	3.351	3.949
D15	Magdalena	2.909	2.627	4.204	4.391
D16	Meta	2.150	1.947	1.756	3.164
D17	Nariño	4.025	3.608	5.607	6.034
D18	Norte de Santander	2.969	2.835	3.501	3.949
D19	Quindío	1.105	1.193	1.418	1.165
D20	Risaralda	1.599	2.009	1.747	1.791
D21	Santander	3.529	4.360	2.768	2.698
D22	Sucre	2.761	1.775	2.794	3.360
D23	Tolima	3.939	2.997	3.876	3.262
D24	Valle del Cauca	8.841	9.605	7.894	5.617
D25	Arauca	0.969	0.544	0.441	1.030
D26	Casanare	0.683	0.725	0.587	1.060
D27	Putumayo	1.257	0.715	0.579	1.678
D28	Archipiélago de San Andrés	0.132	0.160	0.130	0.000
D29	Amazonas	0.292	0.158	0.128	0.952
D30	Guainía	0.146	0.085	0.069	0.760
D31	Guaviare	0.502	0.228	0.185	1.381
D32	Vaupés	0.068	0.091	0.074	0.780
D33	Vichada	0.350	0.144	0.116	2.355

Source Author elaboration

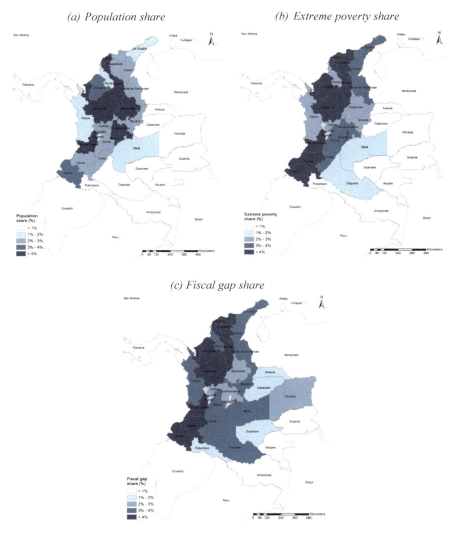

Fig. 16.6 Simulated department transfer shares from the central government. *Source* Author elaboration

Table 16.6 Scenario 1: Subnational transfers based on population, 2012 (Billions COP)

Code	Department	BAS5	Transfers to be redistributed	Transfer redistribution based on population share	Net transfer redistribution based on population share	*Shock (f5gen)*
		(A)	(B)	(C)	(C) - (B) = (D)	*(D)/(A)*100*
D1	Antioquia	9198.72	2438.30	3766.56	1328.26	*14.44*
D2	Atlantico	3454.84	984.82	1436.90	452.08	*13.09*
D3	Bogota, D.C	19,050.58	5525.26	4583.54	− 941.72	*− 4.94*
D4	Bolivar	2784.60	1199.59	1226.24	26.65	*0.96*
D5	Boyaca	1616.43	898.49	769.52	− 128.97	*− 7.98*
D6	Caldas	1095.66	507.88	594.61	86.73	*7.92*
D7	Caqueta	468.71	639.59	278.18	− 361.41	*− 77.11*
D8	Cauca	1501.36	885.93	812.81	− 73.11	*− 4.87*
D9	Cesar	1357.74	608.89	600.29	− 8.61	*− 0.63*
D10	Cordoba	2603.47	958.15	988.37	30.22	*1.16*
D11	Cundinamarca	3292.28	1229.62	1548.33	318.72	*9.68*
D12	Choco	605.82	566.90	293.94	− 272.96	*− 45.06*
D13	Huila	1198.02	575.82	673.15	97.33	*8.12*
D14	La Guajira	812.35	400.87	529.42	128.55	*15.82*
D15	Magdalena	1723.92	820.23	740.91	− 79.32	*− 4.60*
D16	Meta	1603.08	606.28	548.96	− 57.32	*− 3.58*
D17	Narino	1827.39	1135.00	1017.52	− 117.48	*− 6.43*
D18	Norte de Santander	1575.49	837.35	799.57	− 37.78	*− 2.40*
D19	Quindio	571.61	311.64	336.49	24.85	*4.35*
D20	Risaralda	1149.67	450.87	566.58	115.71	*10.06*
D21	Santander	2827.71	995.15	1229.39	234.24	*8.28*
D22	Sucre	1294.20	778.48	500.52	− 277.97	*− 21.48*
D23	Tolima	1659.60	1,110.84	845.13	− 265.70	*− 16.01*
D24	Valle del Cauca	5684.44	2,493.09	2,708.69	215.61	*3.79*
D25	Arauca	300.90	273.15	153.50	− 119.64	*− 39.76*
D26	Casanare	706.40	192.68	204.55	11.87	*1.68*
D27	Putumayo	686.48	354.41	201.74	− 152.67	*− 22.24*

(continued)

Table 16.6 (continued)

D28	Archipielago de San Andres	78.33	37.23	45.13	7.89	*10.08*
D29	Amazonas	107.64	82.30	44.62	− 37.69	*− 35.01*
D30	Guainia	71.46	41.30	23.96	− 17.35	*− 24.27*
D31	Guaviare	100.39	141.51	64.40	− 77.10	*− 76.80*
D32	Vaupes	64.80	19.31	25.66	6.35	*9.81*
D33	Vichada	127.81	98.78	40.51	−58.27	*− 45.59*
	Total	**71,201.89**	**28,199.71**	**28,199.71**	**0.00**	

Note In the CEER model, BAS5 is the total expenditures of regional governments, $GOV^{(5)r}$; and *f5gen* is in the shift term for government expenditures in region r, $f^{(5)r}$.

Table 16.7 Scenario 2: Subnational transfers based on extreme poverty, 2012 (Billions COP)

Code	Department	BAS5	Transfers to be redistributed	Transfer redistribution based on extreme poverty share	Net transfer redistribution based on extreme poverty share	*Shock (f5gen)*
		(A)	(B)	(C)	(C) - (B) = (D)	*(D)/(A)*100*
D1	Antioquia	9198.72	2438.30	3085.29	646.99	*7.03*
D2	Atlantico	3454.84	984.82	1491.47	506.66	*14.67*
D3	Bogota, D.C	19,050.58	5525.26	1627.15	−3898.12	*− 20.46*
D4	Bolivar	2784.60	1199.59	1658.17	458.58	*16.47*
D5	Boyaca	1616.43	898.49	837.94	−60.56	*− 3.75*
D6	Caldas	1095.66	507.88	643.00	135.11	*12.33*
D7	Caqueta	468.71	639.59	357.89	−281.70	*− 60.10*
D8	Cauca	1501.36	885.93	1542.38	656.46	*43.72*
D9	Cesar	1357.74	608.89	859.90	251.00	*18.49*
D10	Cordoba	2603.47	958.15	1820.85	862.70	*33.14*
D11	Cundinamarca	3292.28	1229.62	1104.01	−125.61	*− 3.82*
D12	Choco	605.82	566.90	610.95	44.05	*7.27*
D13	Huila	1,198.02	575.82	935.42	359.60	*30.02*
D14	La Guajira	812.35	400.87	944.91	544.04	*66.97*
D15	Magdalena	1723.92	820.23	1185.56	365.33	*21.19*
D16	Meta	1603.08	606.28	495.30	−110.97	*− 6.92*
D17	Narino	1827.39	1135.00	1581.16	446.16	*24.42*

(continued)

Table 16.7 (continued)

D18	Norte de Santander	1575.49	837.35	987.31	149.96	9.52
D19	Quindio	571.61	311.64	399.88	88.23	15.44
D20	Risaralda	1149.67	450.87	492.63	41.75	3.63
D21	Santander	2827.71	995.15	780.48	− 214.67	− 7.59
D22	Sucre	1294.20	778.48	787.98	9.49	0.73
D23	Tolima	1659.60	1110.84	1093.11	− 17.72	− 1.07
D24	Valle del Cauca	5684.44	2493.09	2226.20	− 266.88	− 4.69
D25	Arauca	300.90	273.15	124.24	− 148.91	− 49.49
D26	Casanare	706.40	192.68	165.55	− 27.12	− 3.84
D27	Putumayo	686.48	354.41	163.28	− 191.13	− 27.84
D28	Archipielago de San Andres	78.33	37.23	36.52	− 0.71	− 0.90
D29	Amazonas	107.64	82.30	36.11	− 46.19	− 42.91
D30	Guainia	71.46	41.30	19.39	− 21.91	− 30.66
D31	Guaviare	100.39	141.51	52.13	− 89.38	− 89.03
D32	Vaupes	64.80	19.31	20.77	1.46	2.26
D33	Vichada	127.81	98.78	32.79	-65.99	− 51.63
	Total	71,201.89	28,199.71	28,199.71	0.00	

Note In the CEER model, BAS5 is the total expenditures of regional governments, $GOV^{(5)r}$; and *f5gen* is in the shift term for government expenditures in region r, $f^{(5)r}$.

Table 16.8 Scenario 3: Subnational transfers based on horizontal fiscal gap, 2012 (Billions COP)

Code	Department	BAS5	Transfers to be redistributed	Transfer redistribution based on fiscal gap share	Net transfer redistribution based on fiscal gap share	Shock (f5gen)
		(A)	(B)	(C)	(C) − (B) = (D)	(D)/(A)*100
D1	Antioquia	9198.72	2438.30	2593.92	155.62	1.69
D2	Atlantico	3454.84	984.82	1279.67	294.85	8.53
D3	Bogota, D.C	19,050.58	5525.26	0.00	− 5525.26	− 29.00
D4	Bolivar	2784.60	1199.59	1438.76	239.17	8.59
D5	Boyaca	1616.43	898.49	857.72	− 40.77	− 2.52
D6	Caldas	1095.66	507.88	586.57	78.69	7.18

(continued)

16 Impact Assessment of Interregional Transfers Scenarios … 451

Table 16.8 (continued)

D7	Caqueta	468.71	639.59	940.73	301.14	*64.25*
D8	Cauca	1501.36	885.93	1438.76	552.83	*36.82*
D9	Cesar	1357.74	608.89	968.40	359.50	*26.48*
D10	Cordoba	2603.47	958.15	1618.61	660.46	*25.37*
D11	Cundinamarca	3292.28	1229.62	802.39	− 427.23	*− 12.98*
D12	Choco	605.82	566.90	850.81	283.91	*46.86*
D13	Huila	1198.02	575.82	899.23	323.40	*26.99*
D14	La Guajira	812.35	400.87	1113.66	712.79	*87.74*
D15	Magdalena	1723.92	820.23	1238.16	417.94	*24.24*
D16	Meta	1603.08	606.28	892.31	286.03	*17.84*
D17	Narino	1827.39	1135.00	1701.61	566.61	*31.01*
D18	Norte de Santander	1575.49	837.35	1113.66	276.30	*17.54*
D19	Quindio	571.61	311.64	328.56	16.92	*2.96*
D20	Risaralda	1149.67	450.87	504.95	54.08	*4.70*
D21	Santander	2827.71	995.15	760.88	− 234.27	*− 8.28*
D22	Sucre	1294.20	778.48	947.65	169.16	*13.07*
D23	Tolima	1659.60	1110.84	919.98	− 190.86	*− 11.50*
D24	Valle del Cauca	5684.44	2493.09	1,584.02	− 909.06	*− 15.99*
D25	Arauca	300.90	273.15	290.52	17.37	*5.77*
D26	Casanare	706.40	192.68	298.82	106.14	*15.03*
D27	Putumayo	686.48	354.41	473.13	118.72	*17.29*
D28	Archipielago de San Andres	78.33	37.23	0.00	− 37.23	*− 47.53*
D29	Amazonas	107.64	82.30	268.38	186.08	*172.87*
D30	Guainia	71.46	41.30	214.43	173.13	*242.27*
D31	Guaviare	100.39	141.51	389.43	247.93	*246.96*
D32	Vaupes	64.80	19.31	219.96	200.66	*309.67*
D33	Vichada	127.81	98.78	664.04	565.26	*442.27*
	Total	71,201.89	28,199.71	28,199.71	0.00	

Note In the CEER model, BAS5 is the total expenditures of regional governments, $GOV^{(5)r}$; and f5gen is in the shift term for government expenditures in region r, $f^{(5)r}$.

References

Albouy, D. (2012). Evaluating the efficiency and equity of federal fiscal equalization. *Journal of Public Economics, 96*(9–10), 824–839.

Ania, A. B., & Wagener, A. (2016). Decentralized redistribution in a laboratory federation. *Journal of Urban Economics, 93*, 49–59.

Austin, B., Glaeser, E., & Summers, L. (2018). Saving the Heartland: Place-Based Policies in 21st Century America. *Brookings Papers on Economic Activity.* https://www.brookings.edu/wp-content/uploads/2018/03/AustinEtAl_Text.pdf

Bacarreza, G. C., Vazquez, J. M., & Yedgenov, B. (2016). Reexamining the determinants of fiscal decentralization: What is the role of geography? *Journal of Economic Geography, 17*(6), 1209–1249.

Barca, F., McCann, P., & Rodríguez-Pose, A. (2012). The case for regional development intervention: Place-based versus place-neutral approaches. *Journal of Regional Science, 52*(1), 134–152.

Barón, J. (2003) ¿Qué Sucedió con las Disparidades Económicas Regionales en Colombia Entre 1980 y 2000? *Documentos de Trabajo Sobre Economía Regional,* 38, Cartagena, Banco de la República.

Baskaran, T., Feld, L. P., & Necker, S. (2017). Depressing dependence? Transfers and economic growth in the German states, 1975–2005. *Regional Studies, 51*(12), 1815–1825.

Bird, R. M. (2012). Fiscal Decentralization in Colombia. *Working Paper* 12–23, Atlanta, USA, International Center for Public Policy.

Bonet, J. A. (2006). Fiscal decentralization and regional income disparities: Evidence from the Colombian experience. *The Annals of Regional Science, 40*(3), 661–676.

Bonet, J. A., & Ayala–García, J. (2015). Transferencias intergubernamentales y disparidades fiscales horizontales en Colombia. *Documentos de trabajo sobre economía regional,* 231 Banco de la República—Sucursal Cartagena.

Bonet, J. A., & Ayala–García, J. (2017). The Territorial Fiscal Gap in Colombia. *Documentos de trabajo sobre economía regional,* 251 Banco de la República—Sucursal Cartagena.

Bonet, J., & Meisel, A. (2008). Regional economic disparities in Colombia. *Investigaciones Regionales, 14*, 61–80.

Bonet, J., Pérez, G. J., & Ayala-García, J. (2016). Contexto histórico y evolución del SGP en Colombia. In: J. Bonet & L. A. Galvis-Aponte (Eds.), *Sistemas de transferencias subnacionales: lecciones para una reforma en Colombia.* Bogotá: Banco de la República, pp. 83–128

Borge, L. E., Brueckner, J. K., & Rattsø, J. (2014). Partial fiscal decentralization and demand responsiveness of the local public sector: Theory and evidence from Norway. *Journal of Urban Economics, 80*, 153–163.

Buettner, T. (2009). The contribution of equalization transfers to fiscal adjustment: Empirical results for German municipalities and a US-German comparison. *Journal of Comparative Economics, 37*(3), 417–431.

Chauvin, J. P., Glaeser, E., Ma, Y., & Tobio, K. (2017). What is different about urbanization in rich and poor countries? Cities in Brazil, China, India and the United States. *Journal of Urban Economics, 98*, 17–49.

Chen, A., & Groenewold, N. (2011). Regional equality and national development in China: Is there a trade-off? *Growth and Change, 42*(4), 628–669.

Chen, A., & Groenewold, N. (2013). The national and regional effects of fiscal decentralisation in China. *The Annals of Regional Science, 51*(3), 731–760.

Galvis-Aponte, L. A., & Meisel, A. (2010). Persistencia de las desigualdades regionales en Colombia: Un análisis especial. *Documentos de trabajo sobre economía regional 120,* Cartagena, Banco de la República.

Galvis-Aponte, L.A. (2016). Eficiencia en el uso de los recursos del SGP: los casos de la salud y la educación. In: J. Bonet & L. A. Galvis-Aponte (Eds.), *Sistemas de transferencias subnacionales: lecciones para una reforma en Colombia.* Bogotá: Banco de la República, pp. 163–191

Glaeser, E., & Henderson, J. V. (2017). Urban economics for the developing World: An introduction. *Journal of Urban Economics, 98*, 1–5.

Groenewold, N., & Hagger, A. J. (2007). The effects of fiscal equalisation in a model with endogenous regional governments: An analysis in a two-region numerical model. *The Annals of Regional Science, 41*(2), 353–374.

Groenewold, N., Hagger, A. J., & Madden, J. R. (2003). Interregional transfers: A political economy CGE approach. *Papers in Regional Science, 82*(4), 535–554.

Haddad, E. A. (1999). *Regional inequality and structural changes: Lessons from the Brazilian economy*. Ashgate.

Haddad, E. A., & Hewings, G. J. D. (2005). Market imperfections in a spatial economy: Some experimental results. *The Quarterly Review of Economics and Finance, 45*(2–3), 476–496.

Haddad, E. A., Bonet, J., Hewings, G. J. D., & Perobelli, F. S. (2009). Spatial aspects of trade liberalization in Colombia: A general equilibrium approach. *Papers in Regional Science, 88*(4), 699–732.

Haddad, E. A., Luque, C. A., Lima, G. T., Sakurai, S. N., & Costa, S. M. (2013). Impact Assessment of Interregional Government Transfers: Lessons from the Brazil Experience. In: Roura, J. C. & Aroca, P. (Eds.), *Regional Problems and Policies in Latin America*. Springer: Berlin, Heidelberg, pp. 475–493.

Haddad, E., Faria, W., Galvis-Aponte, L. A., & Hahn, L. W. (2018). Matriz insumo-producto interregional para Colombia. *Revista De Economía Del Caribe, 21*, 1–24.

Haddad, E. A. (2009). Interregional Computable General Equilibrium Models. In M. Sonis & G. J. D. Hewings (Eds.), *Tool Kits in Regional Science: Theory, Models, and Estimation* (pp. 119–154). Springer.

Henkel, M., Seidel, T., & Suedekum, J. (2018). Fiscal transfers in the spatial economy. CESifo Working Paper, 7012, city country, institution.

Iammarino, S., A. Rodríguez-Pose, and M. Storper. (2017). Why regional development matters for Europe's economic future. *Working Paper* WP 07/2017. Brussels, European Commission, Directorate-General for Regional and Urban Policy.

Jüßen, F. (2006). Interregional Risk Sharing and Fiscal Redistribution in Unified Germany. *Papers in Regional Science, 85*(2), 235–255.

Kline, P., & Moretti, E. (2014). People, places, and public policy: Some simple welfare economics of local economic development programs. *Annual Review of Economics, 6*(1), 629–662.

Kyriacou, A. P., Muinelo-Gallo, L., & Roca-Sagalés, O. (2015). Fiscal decentralization and regional disparities: The importance of good governance. *Papers in Regional Science, 94*(1), 89–107.

Kyriacou, A. P., Muinelo-Gallo, L., & Roca-Sagalés, O. (2017). Regional inequalities, fiscal decentralization and government quality. *Regional Studies, 51*(6), 945–957.

Lozano, I., & Julio, J. M. (2016). Fiscal decentralization and economic growth in Colombia: Evidence from regional-level panel data. *Cepal Review, 119*, 65–82.

Maystadt, J. F., & Salihu, M. K. (2018). National or political cake? The political economy of intergovernmental transfers in Nigeria. *Journal of Economic Geography*, 1–24.

Otsuka, A., Goto, M., & Sueyoshi, T. (2010). Industrial agglomeration effects in Japan: Productive efficiency, market access, and public fiscal transfer. *Papers in Regional Science, 89*(4), 819–840.

Partridge, M. D., Rickman, D. S., Olfert, M. R., & Tan, Y. (2015). When spatial equilibrium fails: Is place-based policy second best? *Regional Studies, 49*(8), 1303–1325.

Peter, M. W., Horridge, M., Meagher, G. A., Naqvi, F., Parmenter, B. R. (1996). The theoretical structure of Monash-MRF. *Working Paper* OP-85, Clayton, Victoria, Monash University, IMPACT Project.

Rodríguez-Pose, A. (2018). The Revenge of the Places that Don't Matter (and what to do About it). *Cambridge Journal of Regions, Economy and Society, 11*(1), 189–209.

Rodríguez-Pose, A., & Ezcurra, R. (2009). Does decentralization matter for regional disparities? A cross-country analysis. *Journal of Economic Geography, 10*(5), 619–644.

Rodríguez-Pose, A., & Ezcurra, R. (2010). Is fiscal decentralization harmful for economic growth? Evidence from the OECD countries. *Journal of Economic Geography, 11*(4), 619–643.

Resosudarmo, B. P., Wuryanto, L. E., Hewings, G. J. D., & Saunders, L. (1999). Decentralization and income distribution in the interregional Indonesian economy. In G. J. D. Hewings, M. Sonis, M. Madden, & Y. Kimura (Eds.), *Understanding and Interpreting Economic Structure* (pp. 298–315). Advances in Spatial Sciences, Springer-Verlag, Heidelberg.

Royuela, V., & García, G. A. (2015). Economic and Social Convergence in Colombia. *Regional Studies, 49*(2), 219–239.

Rueda, L. (2004). Gasto público y convergencia regional en Colombia. *Revista Ensayos Sobre Política Económica, 45,* 222–268.

Salinas, P., & Solé-Ollé, A. (2018). Partial fiscal decentralization reforms and educational outcomes: A difference-in-differences analysis for Spain. *Journal of Urban Economics, 107,* 31–46.

Siano, R., & D'Uva, M. (2017). Fiscal decentralization and spillover effects of local government public spending: The case of Italy. *Regional Studies, 51*(10), 1507–1517.

Ter-Minassian, T. (2016). Teoría y práctica internacional en las transferencias intergubernamentales. In: J. Bonet & L. A. Galvis-Aponte (Eds.), *Sistemas de transferencias subnacionales: lecciones para una reforma en Colombia.* Bogotá: Banco de la República, pp. 21–35

Vásquez, L., & Bara, J. (2009). Convergencia económica regional: El caso de los departamentos Colombianos. *Ecos De Economía, 28,* 167–197.

World Bank. (2009). *Colombia decentralization: Options and incentives for efficiency.* Report N. 39832–CO. Washington, DC.

Zapata, J.G., & Concha, T. (2016). Una reflexión para mejorar la eficiencia en la asignación de las transferencias intergubernamentales en Colombia. In: J. Bonet & L. A. Galvis-Aponte (Eds.), *Sistemas de transferencias subnacionales: lecciones para una reforma en Colombia.* Bogotá: Banco de la República, pp. 131–159

Luis Armando Galvis-Aponte Ph.D. (Geog.), University of Illinois. Senior researcher, Center for Regional Economic Studies, Banco de la República, Colombia. Research fields: econometric methods, economic development, and regional economics.

Inácio F. Araújo Doctor in Economics, Federal University of Juiz de Fora. Pos-doctoral researcher, University of São Paulo, Brazil. Research fields: regional economics and input–output methods.

Vinicius A. Vale Ph.D. in Economics. Professor of Economics at Federal University of Parana and Researcher at the Center for Studies in Urban and Regional Development (NEDUR). His research interests focus on regional economics, international economics, and environmental economics, with emphasis on computable general equilibrium and input-output models.

Eduardo A. Haddad Full Professor at the Department of Economics at the University of São Paulo, Brazil, where he directs the Regional and Urban Economics Lab (NEREUS). Affiliate Professor at the Faculty of Governance, Economic and Social Sciences of the Mohammed VI University and Senior Fellow at the Policy Center for the New South, Rabat, Morocco. President of the Regional Science Association International, RSAI (2021-2022).

Chapter 17
Royalties and Regional Disparities

Jaime Bonet, Gerson Javier Pérez-Valbuena, and Eduardo A. Haddad

17.1 Introduction

The extraction of non-renewable natural resources has the potential to generate income to finance government activities. Rent capturing through taxation may enhance the public sector's ability to harness natural resources' potential to sustain a broad-based development. Colombia, an important oil and coal producer and exporter in Latin America, is pursuing success in this endeavor. The country's strategy, associated with the Sistema General de Regalías (SGR), is grounded on asset formation through domestic investment, focusing on the long-term intergenerational transfer of wealth and upfront expenditures to generate short-run growth effects, with a strong focus on social and regional equity.

There are different fiscal tools available to raise mining-based government revenue. Because royalties are generally payable irrespective of a project's profitability (Otto et al., 2006), they tend to be a preferable fiscal tool to secure income from natural resources operations (Lilford, 2017). Royalties reflect payments made in reference to the amount and value of the mineral produced (sales revenue). The most common form of royalties, called *ad valorem*, collects revenues based on a percentage of the value of the resource extracted. This percentage is usually applied to the gross value of production without accounting for production costs.

In this context, the Colombian royalties scheme is assessed in this chapter. The regional allocation of the royalties' revenue to funding regional development projects

---

J. Bonet (✉) · G. J. Pérez-Valbuena
Banco de la República, Cartagena, Colombia
e-mail: jbonetmo@banrep.gov.co

G. J. Pérez-Valbuena
e-mail: gperezva@banrep.gov.co

E. A. Haddad
University of São Paulo, São Paulo, Brazil
e-mail: ehaddad@usp.br

is simulated. Whether there is a fair regional distribution of the rents from mining activities in Colombia remains a disputable debate. We rely on simulations with the CEER model for the Colombian economy for this appraisal.

Imposing royalties on mining operations may bring substantial costs to the economy (Ergas et al., 2010; Dobra and Dobra, 2013; Postali, 2015), including resource sterilization and its consequences (Lilford, 2017). There are potential losses for the industry, which face additional costs to its operations. Nonetheless, if recycled into the economy to finance public expenditures, royalties' revenues may provide upfront benefits to the government.

This chapter aims to calculate the general equilibrium effects of the royalty payments by the mining activities in Colombia, disentangling these effects. The strategy is to hypothetically remove the existing royalty payments from the Colombian economy and assess their economy-wide impacts. The main contribution of this chapter is that, to the best of the authors' knowledge, it is the first time that the effects of a royalties' reform in Colombia are analyzed in a general equilibrium setup.

In what follows, Sect. 17.2 presents the main characteristics of the SGR. Section 17.3 discusses some of the critical characteristics of the case study. Section 17.4 introduces the additional features of the model described in Chapter 6 relevant to this assessment, while Sect. 17.5 summarizes the main simulation results associated with the use of royalties as a fiscal tool in Colombia. Section 17.6 concludes.

17.2 The *Sistema General De Regalías* (SGR)

In Colombia, a high production of non-renewable natural resources, hydrocarbons, oil and gas, represent 60.5% and 13%, respectively, of the total production, and mining with the remaining 26.5%, with coal accounting for the dominant share, 83%. The Constitution of 1991 established that the revenues (royalties) from the exploitation of natural resources were allocated to the territories where the exploitation was taking place and those territories through which the transportation was carried out. This sharing design implied a significant concentration of recipients since only a few departments and municipalities were entitled to receive royalties. For example, this spatial concentration is apparent for oil production since it only involves less than 100 out of 1100 municipalities and half of the departments (Bonet et al., 2020). One characteristic of this royalty sharing scheme is that it did not consider poverty or population size as criteria to allocate the resources. Another is that the royalties were conditioned to be invested in particular sectors (education, nutrition, health, and sanitation). The legislation established that 80% of the resources were distributed within the producer territories (direct royalties), and the remaining 20% to non-producing territories (indirect royalties) conditional on the presentation and approval of investment projects by the National Royalties Commission (Law 141 of 1994 and Law 756 of 2002).

Poor results in development and inequality reduction (Benavides et al., 2000; Gaviria et al., 2002; Sánchez et al., 2005) led to significant changes in the royalty allocation system. The Legislative Act 05 of 2011 (later regulated by the Law 1530 of 2012) resulted in a more equitable system, SGR. This scheme introduced several modifications to amend some of the drawbacks mentioned above. The first significant transformation was that, from 2012 onwards, every territory would participate in the sharing scheme irrespective of its status as a producer or non-producer. However, producing regions would still be able to receive an additional share in the form of direct royalties. A second change was that, under the SGR, for the departments and municipalities to have access to the royalties, they would have to go through the steps of presenting their investment plans for approval.[1]

Another innovation brought by the new SGR is the introduction of a series of funds aimed at different targets depending on their purposes: Science, Technology and Innovation (FCTeI); Savings and Stabilization (FAE); Regional Development (FDR); and Regional Compensation (FCR). Also, a previously created fund, Pension Savings of the Territorial Entities (FONPET), is a recipient of part of the royalties. Regarding the distribution of the resources, FAE, FCTeI, and FONPET receive 50% of the SGR, while the remaining 50% was allocated between the FCR, the FDR, and the direct royalty payments.

The new SGR also conceived a new mechanism for the approval of the projects put forward for consideration by departments and municipalities. The new evaluation and decision-making bodies are the Administration and Decision Boards (OCAD), whose composition, according to the Decree 1075 of 2012, depends on the government level to which the investment project belongs. OCADs include two national government delegates, the corresponding governor, and 10% of the mayors in that jurisdiction for projects submitted by departments. For projects submitted by municipalities, OCADs include one delegate of the national government and the corresponding mayor and governor of that jurisdiction. In the case of regional projects, OCADs are made up of four ministers, the director of the DNP, all the governors of that region, two mayors per department, and one mayor representing the capital cities. The national OCAD is reserved only for the analysis and approval of science and technology projects related to the FCTeI fund. As expected, the procedures required to make the royalties fully accessible to departments and municipalities create a temporal mismatch between the extraction of natural resources, the allocation of resources as royalties, and the actual availability to finance investment projects.

Additional reforms to the royalty scheme were introduced between 2017 and 2020. In 2017, a new fund was created focusing on financing projects related to the peace treaty implementation in Colombia (Legislative Act 04/2017). According to this legislation, this fund would receive 7% of the SGR and 70% of the financial returns generated by the SGR during the next twenty years, during which FONPET would receive be 7% of the SGR, instead of the previously established 10%. Then, in

---

[1] These investment projects presented by departments and municipalities have to satisfy two conditions: (i) the project must be part of the corresponding development plan and (ii) the project's main purpose must intend the improvement of the population's well-being.

2019, a new reform came out with the purpose of the redistribution of the SGR, where: 20% was destined for territories exploiting and transporting natural resources; 15% for the poorest departments and municipalities; 35% for regional investment based on three criteria: poverty, population, and unemployment; 1% for projects related to the environment protection and reforestation; 10% for science, technology, and innovation projects; 2% for the administration and supervision of the system; and 1% for the operating expenses. The remaining SGR resources will be allocated to the pension liabilities and savings for investment stabilization (Legislative Act 05/2019 and Law 2056/2020).

17.3 Case Study

The mining sector in the CEER model includes four different activities, fully integrated into the model. The activities are mining of coal and lignite (S6), extraction of crude petroleum and natural gas (S7), mining of metal ores (S8), and other mining and quarrying (S9). Their geographical distribution is not homogenous across the country. S6 production is mainly concentrated in two departments, Cesar (52.8%) and La Guajira (37.8%), while S7 production is essentially located in Meta (49.7%) and Casanare (19.1%). These latter two activities (S6 and S7) not only represent more than 95% of the total mining output in the country but also are located in departments with small population numbers (the four represent 7% of the total national population although they cover 15% of the total national area). Another aspect to consider is the so-called resource curse, which has been extensively analyzed in the literature. For the case of Colombia, the most recent works are Bonet et al. (2020) and Ayala & Dall'Erba (2021).

Under a resource curse scenario, a country or region that is highly dependent on natural resources does not show significant improvement in socioeconomic indicators, such as poverty reduction or positive well-being changes, due to the windfall coming from the royalties. On the one hand, Bonet et al. (2020) found positive effects on subnational investments in both departments and municipalities, where the 2012 reform has a lot to do with these positive outcomes. Ayala & Dall'Erba (2021) showed evidence that royalties from natural resource exploitation have negatively affected health care and education provision efficiency. Despite there being evidence in favor or against the resource curse hypothesis, depending on the sector or the dimension analyzed, what is true is that some of the significant natural resources producers have some of the highest monetary poverty figures (La Guajira 53.3% and Cesar 42.3%, compared with the national average of 27.8%).

In 2015, mining activities were responsible for 5.8% of the national value-added and 42% of total exports. S7 was its primary output (69.5% of total mining output), followed by S6 (18.5%), S8 (7.5%), and S9 (4.5%). Most of the coal and petroleum output was exported to other countries (92.6% and 60.8%, respectively), while the output of the other two mining activities was mainly directed to supply local value chains. In case of the extraction of crude petroleum and natural gas, there are important domestic forward linkages with the oil refinery sector since 34% of its output is used as an intermediate input to local sectors.

From a backward-linkage cost perspective, intermediate consumption of domestic inputs was responsible for 37.9% of total costs of mining activities, varying from 25.9% in the coal sector to 41.0% in the petroleum and natural gas sector. Overall, payments to value-added components by the four mining activities averaged 56.9% of total payments, above the national average of 50.1%. It is noteworthy that the value-added generated by the mining sectors was very capital-intensive. While the national ratio of capital to labor payments reached 1.58, the figures for S6 to S9 were 3.21, 5.82, 9.80, and 8.71 (Table 17.1 and Fig. 17.1).

In 2015, the central government raised COP 6384 billion in royalty revenue. Royalties on different mining products were aggregated within the four different mining activities of the model. The implicit *ad valorem* tax, calculated based on the number of collected royalties as a percentage of the output value of the resource extracted, ranged from 11.08% to coal, 7.6% to petroleum and natural gas, 4.76% to metal ores, and only 0.61% to other mining activities. To estimate the royalty revenue generated in each department, we applied those rates to the respective regional sectoral output (Table 17.2).

There is a temporal mismatch between the collection of the royalty revenue and its actual use to finance regional development projects, as discussed in Sect. 17.2. The lack of agility by some regional governments to allocate the available funds brings about fiscal inefficiency concerns that may postpone the implementation of investment projects aimed to foster regional growth and welfare. Table 17.3 presents our estimates of the regional allocation of the royalty resources raised in 2015, considering the amount spent by regional governments within two years (2016–2017) and the remaining available resources that were "not used". Our identification strategy considered the budgetary execution of the royalty resources in 2016–2017, calculating the annual average to define the regional allocation of the 2015 royalty revenue (Columns B and C in Table 17.3). Considering the estimated regional government expenditures in the benchmark year (Column A),[2] we computed a measurement of royalty dependency for each department in Column D. Our measure of fiscal dependency, in Column E, compares the average annual number of resources spent in the following two years to the amount that was made available in the benchmark year. Finally, Columns F and G present the amount of royalty revenue used by regional governments and the amount that remained to be used. Thus, according to our estimates, in 2015, from the total amount of royalty revenue raised by the central government and made available to Colombian regional governments, 62% was spent, while the remaining 38% did not enter the economic system as income injections (foregone royalties expenditures).

---

[2] See Chap. 16.

Table 17.1 Mining sector in Colombia: aggregate linkages structure, 2015

	S6		S7		S8		S9		Total	
	COP bi	%	COP bi	%	COP bi	%	COP bi	%	COP bi	%
Intermediate consumption	906	7.2	21,028	34.0	5235	95.6	3328	88.5	30,495	36.4
Investment demand	28	0.2	3103	5.0	1	0.0	−51	−1.3	3081	3.7
Household demand	6	0.1	122	0.2	79	1.4	7	0.2	215	0.3
Regional government demand	0	0.0	1	0.0	1	0.0	2	0.1	4	0.0
Central government demand	0	0.0	1	0.0	1	0.0	2	0.0	3	0.0
Foreing exports	11,713	92.6	37,598	60.8	162	3.0	474	12.6	49,947	59.6
Statistical discrepancies	0	0.0	0	0.0	0	0.0	0	0.0	0	0.0
Total demand	**12,653**	**100.0**	**61,853**	**100.0**	**5478**	**100.0**	**3,762**	**100.0**	**83,746**	**100.0**
Intermediate consumption	3271	25.9	25,347	41.0	1729	31.6	1414	37.6	31,761	37.9
Imports	427	3.4	2793	4.5	107	1.9	128	3.4	3454	4.1
Taxes and subsidies	122	1.0	668	1.1	51	0.9	63	1.7	904	1.1
Value added	8833	69.8	33,046	53.4	3592	65.6	2156	57.3	47,627	56.9
Gross output	**12,653**	**100.0**	**61,853**	**100.0**	**5,478**	**100.0**	**3,762**	**100.0**	**83,746**	**100.0**
K/L ratio	3.21		5.82		9.80		8.71		1.58[a]	
Export elasticity	−0.420		−0.478		−0.040		−1.658		−0.692[a]	

S6 - Mining of coal and lignite; S7—Extraction of crude petroleum and natural gas; S8 - Mining of metal ores; S9 - Other mining and quarrying
[a]National total
Note Numbers in bold correspond to the sum of values across the corresponding rows

17 Royalties and Regional Disparities

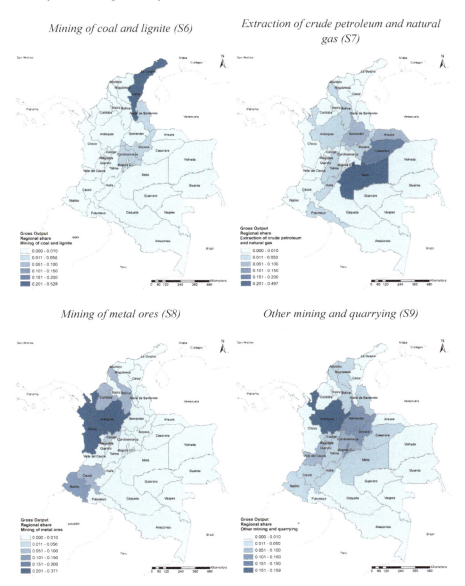

Fig. 17.1 Regional distribution of the mining output, 2015

17.4 Modeling the Royalties Revenues and Expenditures

We use the CEER model to evaluate the impacts of the royalties imposed on the mining sector. We model royalties' payments as an *ad valorem* production tax on the total cost of production in the mining industries. Output price (adjusted for production

Table 17.2 Regional and sectoral distribution of royalties revenues, 2015 (COP billions)

Code	Department	S6	S7	S8	S9	Total	%
D1	Antioquia	2.04	105.35	96.68	3.64	207.73	3.25
D2	Atlántico	0.00	0.00	0.00	1.02	1.02	0.02
D3	Bogotá, D.C.	0.00	0.00	0.00	3.42	3.42	0.05
D4	Bolívar	0.00	54.60	14.03	1.06	69.69	1.09
D5	Boyacá	40.00	231.07	0.72	2.35	274.14	4.29
D6	Caldas	0.00	0.00	8.21	0.30	8.51	0.13
D7	Caquetá	0.00	0.00	0.00	0.17	0.17	0.00
D8	Cauca	0.19	5.25	21.94	0.55	27.93	0.44
D9	Cesar	741.09	42.55	0.00	0.20	783.83	12.28
D10	Córdoba	0.03	0.00	14.20	0.06	14.29	0.22
D11	Cundinamarca	48.46	2.32	0.00	1.77	52.56	0.82
D12	Chocó	0.00	0.00	65.83	0.05	65.88	1.03
D13	Huila	0.00	135.62	0.28	0.61	136.51	2.14
D14	La Guajira	530.63	41.06	0.00	0.09	571.78	8.96
D15	Magdalena	0.00	1.96	0.00	0.27	2.22	0.03
D16	Meta	0.00	2332.83	0.00	0.50	2333.33	36.55
D17	Nariño	0.00	1.63	31.31	0.46	33.40	0.52
D18	Norte de Santander	36.85	19.14	0.00	0.30	56.29	0.88
D19	Quindío	0.00	0.00	0.34	0.24	0.57	0.01
D20	Risaralda	0.00	0.00	0.83	0.35	1.18	0.02
D21	Santander	2.70	295.15	0.28	2.87	300.99	4.71
D22	Sucre	0.00	4.50	0.00	0.11	4.62	0.07
D23	Tolima	0.00	91.19	0.84	0.71	92.74	1.45
D24	Valle del Cauca	0.47	0.00	2.53	1.30	4.30	0.07
D25	Arauca	0.00	241.09	0.00	0.08	241.17	3.78
D26	Casanare	0.00	898.97	0.00	0.30	899.26	14.09
D27	Putumayo	0.00	193.80	0.09	0.01	193.90	3.04
D28	Archipiélago de San Andrés	0.00	0.00	0.00	0.01	0.01	0.00
D29	Amazonas	0.00	0.00	0.00	0.01	0.01	0.00
D30	Guainía	0.00	0.00	2.40	0.00	2.40	0.04
D31	Guaviare	0.00	0.00	0.00	0.03	0.03	0.00
D32	Vaupés	0.00	0.00	0.00	0.01	0.01	0.00
D33	Vichada	0.00	0.00	0.00	0.02	0.02	0.00
	Total	1,402.45	4,698.09	260.54	22.87	6,383.95	100.00

taxes) of sector j, in region r, PX_j^r, is given by the weighted average of value-added prices and the cost of intermediate inputs:

$$PX_j^r\left(1 - \text{prodtax}_j^r\right) = X_j^{r-1}\left\{PV_j^r V_j^r + \sum_i a_{ij}^{rs} PC_i^s X_j^r\right\} \quad (17.1)$$

where prodtax_j^r is the rate of production tax on sector j in region r.

We define the scenario for interregional transfers of royalty revenue in the context of our model specification, similar to the strategy developed in Chap. 16. We assume that the central government transfers its annual royalty revenue to finance different components of regional government spending in region r, according to the information provided in Table 15.3. With this information, we can calculate the size of the "shock" by imposing region-specific changes in $f^{(5)r}$ (Eq. 1 in Chap. 16), the shift term for government expenditure in region r that are proportional to changes in $GOV^{(5)r}$ (Eq. 2 in Chapter 16), according to the combined values presented in Columns F and A. By using the values in Column F to define the amount of royalty

17 Royalties and Regional Disparities

Table 17.3 Subnational royalties transfers-based 2015–2016 expenditure structure (COP billions)

Code	Department	BAS5 (in COP billions)	Regional Allocation Structure (%)	Royalties Allocation (in COP billions)	Royalties Dependency (%)	Fiscal Efficiency*	Royalties Expenditures (in COP billions)	Foregone Royalties Expenditure (in COP billions)
		(A)	(B)	(C)	(C)/(A) = (D)	(E)	(F)	(G)
D1	Antioquia	9198.72	6.08	388.04	4.22	0.497	192.9	195.2
D2	Atlantico	3454.84	2.50	159.44	4.61	0.460	73.3	86.2
D3	Bogota, D.C.	19,050.58	1.86	118.58	0.62	0.200	23.7	94.9
D4	Bolivar	2784.60	4.92	313.91	11.27	0.584	183.2	130.7
D5	Boyaca	1616.43	3.66	233.85	14.47	0.631	147.5	86.4
D6	Caldas	1095.66	1.47	94.03	8.58	0.380	35.7	58.3
D7	Caqueta	468.71	1.87	119.54	25.50	0.248	29.7	89.9
D8	Cauca	1501.36	3.82	244.16	16.26	0.362	88.3	155.8
D9	Cesar	1357.74	5.35	341.23	25.13	0.696	237.4	103.9
D10	Cordoba	2603.47	5.85	373.61	14.35	0.508	189.7	183.9
D11	Cundinamarca	3292.28	3.19	203.54	6.18	0.362	73.7	129.8
D12	Choco	605.82	2.96	188.93	31.19	0.352	66.5	122.4
D13	Huila	1198.02	3.76	239.95	20.03	0.694	166.6	73.3
D14	La Guajira	812.35	5.48	349.84	43.07	0.733	256.5	93.4
D15	Magdalena	1723.92	3.75	239.12	13.87	0.686	164.1	75.1
D16	Meta	1603.08	7.70	491.68	30.67	1.000	491.7	0.0
D17	Narino	1827.39	4.41	281.39	15.40	0.302	85.0	196.4

(continued)

Table 17.3 (continued)

Code	Department	BAS5 (in COP billions)	Regional Allocation Structure (%)	Royalties Allocation (in COP billions)	Royalties Dependency (%)	Fiscal Efficiency*	Royalties Expenditures (in COP billions)	Foregone Royalties Expenditure (in COP billions)
		(A)	(B)	(C)	(C)/(A) = (D)	(E)	(F)	(G)
D18	Norte de Santander	1575.49	2.96	189.12	12.00	0.811	153.3	35.8
D19	Quindio	571.61	0.88	56.45	9.88	0.075	4.3	52.2
D20	Risaralda	1,149.67	1.24	79.43	6.91	0.459	36.5	42.9
D21	Santander	2,827.71	3.60	229.71	8.12	1.000	229.7	0.0
D22	Sucre	1,294.20	3.80	242.33	18.72	0.490	118.7	123.6
D23	Tolima	1,659.60	2.75	175.60	10.58	0.792	139.1	36.5
D24	Valle del Cauca	5,684.43	3.19	203.78	3.58	0.226	46.0	157.8
D25	Arauca	300.90	2.14	136.84	45.48	1.000	136.8	0.0
D26	Casanare	706.40	4.26	271.69	38.46	1.000	271.7	0.0
D27	Putumayo	686.48	2.04	130.29	18.98	0.904	117.8	12.5
D28	Archipielago de San Andres	78.33	0.72	45.68	58.32	0.871	39.8	5.9
D29	Amazonas	107.64	0.73	46.71	43.39	1.000	46.7	0.0
D30	Guainia	71.46	0.62	39.76	55.63	0.622	24.7	15.0
D31	Guaviare	100.39	0.91	57.78	57.56	0.781	45.1	12.6
D32	Vaupes	64.80	0.62	39.51	60.98	0.151	6.0	33.6
D33	Vichada	127.81	0.92	58.42	45.71	0.626	36.6	21.8

(continued)

Table 17.3 (continued)

Code	Department	BAS5 (in COP billions)	Regional Allocation Structure (%)	Royalties Allocation (in COP billions)	Royalties Dependency (%)	Fiscal Efficiency*	Royalties Expenditures (in COP billions)	Foregone Royalties Expenditure (in COP billions)
		(A)	(B)	(C)	(C)/(A) = (D)	(E)	(F)	(G)
	Total	71,201.89	100.00	6383.95	8.97	0.620	3,958.23	2,425.72

[a]Share of 2015–2016 average execution to the 2015 allocation of regional royalty (C)

Asterisk denotes participation of the average royalties spent between 2016 and 2017 in the total royalties allocation of 2015.

Note BAS5 is the total expenditures of regional governments

expenditures in each department, we consider our measure of fiscal efficiency as only part of the revenue will enter the system.

Thus, a production tax on the mining sector will increase its production costs, increasing the price of mining output and mining-related products. This *cost change channel* is one of the two main channels to achieve the model's results. The second is the *government demand channel* which operates when we allow royalty revenues to enter into the system to finance government expenditures (Fig. 17.2).

17.5 Results

What if existing royalties levied on mining production were hypothetically removed from the Colombian economy? We run the CEER model under three variants of a short-run macro-adjustment closure to measure its impacts and disentangle the effects of different channels.

Closure 1 focuses on the cost change channel on the potential economic losses due to the taxation and royalty impositions. This setting is a standard short-run closure in the Australian suite of CGE models (Horridge et al., 2000). On the supply side, we make the capital stock, technology, and the real wage exogenous. With the real wage given, the model can determine aggregate employment. With employment, technology, and capital determined, the model can determine aggregate output (GDP). Aggregate household consumption, investment, and other demands (and inventories) are fixed on the demand side. With GDP determined from the supply side and domestic absorption (household consumption, investment, government consumption, and inventories) given, the trade balance must act as an endogenous "swing" variable to satisfy the GDP identity. If the GDP increases/decreases relative to domestic absorption due to our shock, the trade balance must move toward surplus/deficit. We then make Closure 1 more flexible by allowing government consumption to move with tax revenue in Closure 2, which focuses on the upfront benefits through taxes and royalties payable to the central government and transferred to regional governments. In Closure 3, we also allow household consumption to move with factor income.

Table 17.4 presents the simulation results comparing the three adjustment scenarios. Results for Closure 1 show that, due to eliminating royalty payments by the mining sectors, the GDP would increase by 0.074% relative to domestic absorption. Thus, the trade balance would move toward surplus. Compared to Closure 2, in which royalty revenue goes through the economy as regional government expenditures, the GDP would have a decrease of 1.047%. This difference is mainly due to the inelastic nature of the demand and the supply curves for mining products. Not allowing real factor income to affect household consumption in Closure 3 further harms GDP results (-1.570%).

We also calculated the impacts of the royalties' payments on sectoral output and departments' real GRP. Figure 17.3 highlights those sectors that achieved the top and bottom performance, while the first three columns of Table 17.5 present the regional results for the effects of removing royalties in Colombia.

17 Royalties and Regional Disparities

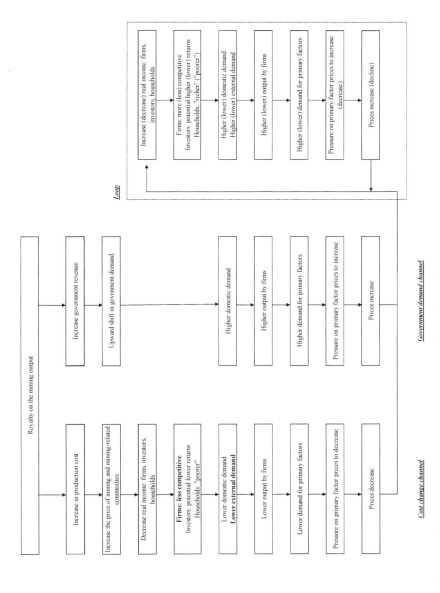

Fig. 17.2 Causal relations underlying the system of equations of the CEER model

Table 17.4 Macroeconomic impacts of a hypothetical withdrawal of royalties payments by the mining sectors (in percentage change)

	Closure 1	Closure 2	Closure 3	Efficiency cost
Aggregate payments to capital	1.266	−3.206	−14.605	2.978
Aggregate payments to labor	0.275	−5.898	−16.831	3.140
Aggregate capital stock, rental weights	0.000	0.000	0.000	0.000
Aggregate employment, wage bill weights	0.203	−2.827	−3.671	0.628
Real GDP from expenditure side	0.074	−1.047	−1.570	0.275
Aggregate real investment expendiutre	0.000	0.000	0.000	0.000
Real household consumption	0.000	0.000	−3.359	0.674
Aggregate real regional government demands	0.000	−14.257	−14.336	3.167
Aggregate real central government demands	0.000	−6.891	−6.481	−0.439
Export volume index	0.546	1.575	4.617	−0.767
Import volume index, CIF weights	0.034	−1.973	−7.947	1.500
National average utility	0.000	0.000	−5.928	1.058
%-point change in economy-wide unemployment rate	−0.164	2.706	3.619	−0.799
Average real wage	0.000	0.000	0.000	0.000
Real devaluation	−1.183	−2.819	−7.611	1.210
Consumer price index	0.072	−3.071	−13.165	2.512
Exports price index, local currency	−1.183	−2.819	−7.611	1.210
Regional govenment price index	0.075	−5.273	−15.268	2.814
Central government price index	0.075	−5.140	−15.142	2.839

From Table 17.5, we calculated the Locational Gini Index (Fig. 17.4). Compared to the benchmark, we observe a slight reduction in the Gini in Closure 1, while in Closures 2 and 3, the Locational Gini increases suggesting an increase in output concentration among the Colombian regions when we remove the effects of the use of royalty revenue in financing regional government expenditures. In other words, while the cost change channel does not impose any significant change in the Gini, the government demand channel, reinforced by household income effects, tends to reduce regional inequality through distributional impacts. It is worth mentioning that this change in output concentration—and the consequent reduction in regional disparities—occurs due to the higher growth of the more impoverished regions (see Table 17.5).

These results are evident for La Guajira, Cesar, Meta, Casanare, Putumayo, and Arauca, all of which belong to peripheral regions. These results consistently show

17 Royalties and Regional Disparities

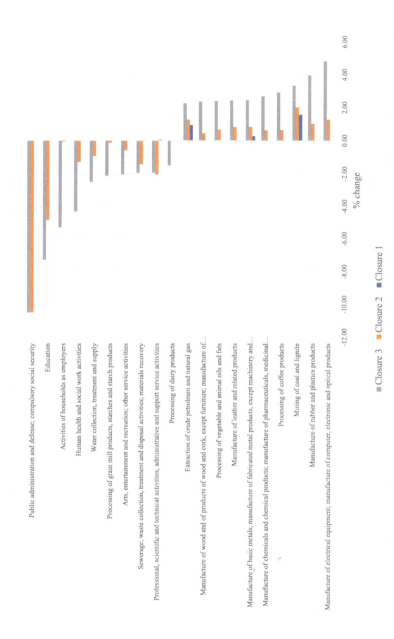

Fig. 17.3 Impacts on sectoral activity of a hypothetical withdrawal of royalties payments by the mining sectors (in percentage change)

Table 17.5 Effect on gross regional product (in percentage change)

Code	Department	Closure 1	Closure 2	Closure 3	Efficiency cost
D1	Antioquia	0.024	−0.444	−0.679	0.146
D2	Atlantico	0.019	−0.558	−1.045	0.241
D3	Bogota, D.C.	0.014	−0.599	−1.133	0.170
D4	Bolivar	0.051	−0.915	−1.358	**0.345**
D5	Boyaca	**0.107**	**−1.069**	−1.478	0.244
D6	Caldas	0.014	−0.617	1.040	**0.363**
D7	Caqueta	0.006	**−1.410**	**−2.835**	**2.221**
D8	Cauca	0.016	−0.948	−1.244	**0.700**
D9	Cesar	**0.537**	**−3.574**	**−4.528**	**0.344**
D10	Cordoba	0.013	**−1.262**	**−2.434**	**1.044**
D11	Cundinamarca	0.021	−0.366	−0.685	0.195
D12	Choco	0.065	**−3.246**	**−4.910**	**2.477**
D13	Huila	**0.078**	**−1.393**	**−2.076**	**0.375**
D14	La Guajira	**0.631**	**−3.967**	**−5.888**	**0.587**
D15	Magdalena	0.011	**−1.324**	**−2.409**	**0.518**
D16	Meta	**0.516**	**−3.531**	**−3.822**	−0.125
D17	Narino	0.015	**−1.087**	**−2.133**	**1.316**
D18	Norte de Santander	0.051	**−1.301**	**−2.425**	0.268
D19	Quindio	0.009	−0.540	−1.131	**0.630**
D20	Risaralda	0.011	−0.602	−1.067	**0.290**
D21	Santander	0.068	−0.595	−0.774	0.002
D22	Sucre	0.017	**−1.501**	**−2.915**	**1.507**
D23	Tolima	0.046	−1.015	**−1.600**	0.186
D24	Valle del Cauca	0.015	−0.461	−0.727	0.201
D25	Arauca	**0.368**	**−5.038**	**−5.376**	−0.052
D26	Casanare	**0.480**	**−4.250**	**−4.358**	−0.095
D27	Putumayo	**0.382**	**−14.848**	**−16.089**	0.227
D28	Archipielago de San Andres	0.008	**−2.359**	**−3.396**	**0.421**
D29	Amazonas	0.005	**−5.385**	**−6.848**	0.146
D30	Guainia	0.020	**−6.479**	**−8.655**	**3.533**
D31	Guaviare	0.004	**−4.804**	**−6.944**	**1.420**
D32	Vaupes	0.002	**−2.500**	**−4.379**	**10.980**
D33	Vichada	0.001	**−4.872**	**−6.210**	**2.877**
	TOTAL	0.074	−1.047	−1.570	0.275

Note Values in bold refer to those cases where the effects where higher (positive or negative)

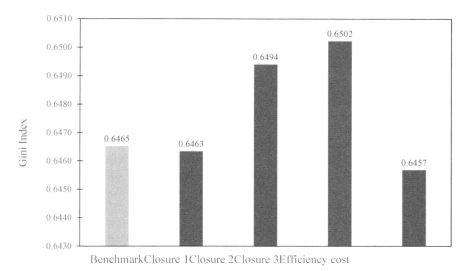

Fig. 17.4 Locational gini index under alternative closures

how implementing redistributive policies (the SGR 2012 reform sought more equally redistributed resource revenues) can make a difference in favor of economically challenged regions. Another interesting result is that the highest reduction of the GRP occurs through the government demand channel in which royalty revenue goes through the economy as regional government expenditures (between Closures 1 and 2). These results have also revealed the presence of clear and well-defined regional heterogeneities in the effects of royalties in the Colombian economy. The highest losses over more restrictive scenarios fall onto the peripheral and most disadvantaged regions with no apparent exceptions. These results are of significant relevance for future resource revenue reforms since it sheds light on the redistributive potential of a windfall from the exploitation of non-renewable natural resources. Therefore, while having positive effects in terms of equity, the result of this redistributive policy does not seem to undermine national growth in the short run.

17.6 Final Considerations

The more inelastic the demand or the supply of a taxed item, the lower the excess burden of the tax because of the smaller reduction in quantity sold as a result of the tax. Mining output in Colombia is mainly exported and faces low export demand elasticity (Table 17.1). Moreover, given its high K/L ratio, short-run responses are restricted under fixed capital stock environments. Thus, taxing mining output may raise government revenue with a low excess burden, at least in the short term.

Good governance of natural resources indicates that governments should direct a substantial part of tax revenue raised from the mining sector into asset formation through domestic investment programs, focusing on the long-term intergenerational transfer of wealth (Collier & Venables, 2011). In the Colombian case, potential short-run upfront growth effects, as shown in our simulations, may tempt governments to deviate from the long-run focus of the current fiscal regime. As mentioned in Sect. 17.2, after the 2012 royalties reform, Colombia faced a series of modifications to previous regulations where the participation of producing territories increased. This reform has resulted in royalties returning to the scenarios where few territories receive higher participation relative to the benchmark 2012's reform. The results in this chapter are of the utmost importance since every single distributional change in resource revenues will significantly impact socioeconomic indicators.

One final comment refers to the cost of "fiscal inefficiency", defined in our context as the timely mismatch between royalty payments to the government and their allocation for actual use, which may postpone the potential short-run benefits of recycling the resources into the system. The results presented in the last column of Tables 17.4 and 17.5 refer to the simulation of imposing contemporaneous full recycling of the available royalties' resources into the economy. The short-run impacts reveal a potential impact of increasing national GDP in comparison to the benchmark value (0.275%), welfare (0.675% increase in real household consumption and 1.058% in average national utility), further reducing regional inequality (lower Locational Gini—Fig. 17.4). *Again, this assumes that the royalty revenues earn no income while they are "parked" awaiting approval for distribution.*

References

Ayala, J., & Dall'Erba, S. (2021). The natural resource curse: Evidence from the Colombian municipalities. *Papers in Regional Science*, 100(2), 581-602. https://doi.org/10.1111/pirs.12577

Benavides, J., Carrasquilla, J., Zapata, G., & Velasco, A. (2000). Impacto de las regalías en la inversión de las entidades territoriales. Bogotá, Fedesarrollo. http://hdl.handle.net/11445/1562.

Bonet, J., Pérez, G. J., & Marín-Llanes, L. (2020). Oil shocks and subnational public investment: The role of institutions in regional resource curse. *Energy Economics, 92*, 105002. https://doi.org/10.1016/j.eneco.2020.105002

Collier, P., & Venables, A. J. (2011). Key decisions for resource management: Principles and practice. In P. Collier & A. J. Venables (Eds.), *Plundered nations?* (pp. 1–26). Palgrave Macmillan.

Dobra, J., & Dobra, M. (2013). State mineral production taxes and mining law reform. *Resources Policy, 38*(2), 162–168.

Ergas, H., Harrison, M., & Pincus, J. (2010). Some economics of mining taxation. *Economic Papers, 29*(4), 369–383. https://doi.org/10.1111/j.1759-3441.2010.00090.x

Gaviria, A., Zapata, J., & González, A. (2002). Petróleo y región: El caso del Casanare. Cuadernos de Fedesarrollo, 8, Bogotá, Fedesarrollo. http://hdl.handle.net/11445/1905

Horridge, M., Parmenter, B., & Pearson, K. (2000). *ORANI-G: A general equilibrium model of the Australian economy*. City, country Centre of Policy Studies. https://doi.org/10.1016/j.resourpol.2012.10.005

Lilford, E. V. (2017). Quantitative impacts of royalties on mineral projects. *Resources Policy, 53*, 369–377. https://doi.org/10.1016/j.resourpol.2017.08.002

Otto, J., Andrews, C., Cawood, F., Doggett, M., Guj, P., Stermole, F., Stermole, J., & Titon, J. (2006). *Mining royalties: a global study of their impact on investors, government, and civil society*. D.C., The World Bank.

Postali, F. A. S. (2015). Tax effort and oil royalties in the Brazilian municipalities. *Economia, 16*(3), 395–405. https://doi.org/10.1016/j.econ.2015.08.001

Sánchez, F., Mejía, C., Herrera, F. (2005). Impacto de las regalías del carbón en los municipios del Cesar 1997–2003. Bogotá, Cuadernos PNUD, Investigaciones sobre desarrollo regional. https://censat.org/es/publicaciones/impacto-de-las-regalias-del-carbon-en-los-municipios-del-cesar-1997-2003

Jaime Bonet is an economist from the Universidad de Los Andes in Bogotá with a master's degree in economics and a Ph.D. in regional planning from the University of Illinois at Urbana-Champaign. He is the Director of the Center for Regional Economic Studies (CEER) at the Banco de la República, Colombia. His research areas include regional and urban economics, local public finance, local economic development, and regional development history in Colombia.

Gerson Javier Pérez-Valbuena Ph.D. in economics, University of Essex (United Kingdom). Senior Researcher at the Center for Regional Economic Studies (CEER) at the Banco de la República, Colombia. He has published several articles and book chapters on topics related to regional and urban economics and subnational public finances.

Eduardo A. Haddad Full Professor at the Department of Economics at the University of São Paulo, Brazil, where he directs the Regional and Urban Economics Lab (NEREUS). Affiliate Professor at the Faculty of Governance, Economic and Social Sciences of the Mohammed VI University and Senior Fellow at the Policy Center for the New South, Rabat, Morocco. President of the Regional Science Association International, RSAI (2021–2022)

Printed by Printforce, the Netherlands